Nicolás Kanellos is founding publisher of the noted Hispanic literary journal *The Americas Review* (formerly *Revista Chicano-Riqueña*) and of the nation's oldest and most esteemed Hispanic publishing house, Arte Público Press. He has been professor of Hispanic literature at the University of Houston since 1980. In 1994 Dr. Kanellos was appointed by President Bill Clinton to the National Council for the Humanities.

His work *The Hispanic-American Almanac* won a 1993 RASD Award from the Reference and Adult Services Division of the American Library Association. Among his other books are *Biographical Dictionary of Hispanic Literature of the United States* (1989) and *Mexican American Theater: Legacy and Reality* (1987). Dr. Kanellos is the director of a major national research program, Recovering the Hispanic Literary Heritage of the United States, whose objective is to identify, preserve, study, and make accessible tens of thousands of literary documents of those regions that have become the United States from the colonial period to 1960.

Recognized for his scholarly achievements, Dr. Kanellos is the recipient of a 1990 American Book Award, a 1989 award from the Texas Association of Chicanos in Higher Education, the 1988 Hispanic Heritage Award for Literature presented by the White House, as well as various fellowships and other recognitions. His monograph, *A History of Hispanic Theater in the United States: Origins to 1940* (1990), received three book awards, including that of the Southwest Council on Latin American Studies.

Luis Valdez is considered the father of Chicano theater. He has distinguished himself as an actor, director, playwright, and filmmaker. As the founding director of El Teatro Campesino, a theater of farmworkers in California, he inspired young Chicano activists across the country to use theater as a means of organizing students, communities, and labor unions. In 1978 Valdez broke into mainstream theater with the production of his play *Zoot Suit*. In 1986 his play *I Don't Have to Show You No Stinking Badges* enjoyed a successful run at the Los Angeles Theater Center. Valdez added a major Hollywood production to his credits with the writing and directing of the 1987 hit movie *La Bamba*. Valdez's plays, essays, and poems have been widely anthologized.

The Hispanic Almanac

FROM COLUMBUS
TO
CORPORATE AMERICA

For my mother and father, Inés and Charlie, with all my love.

Para mis padres Inés y Charlie con todo cariño.

N.K.

The Hispanic Almanac

FROM COLUMBUS TO CORPORATE AMERICA

Nicolás Kanellos

Foreword by
Luis Valdez

DETROIT • LONDON • WASHINGTON, D.C.

The Hispanic Almanac:
From Columbus to Corporate America

Published by Visible Ink Press™
a division of Gale Research Inc.
835 Penobscot Building
Detroit, MI 48226-4094

Visible Ink Press is a trademark of Gale Research Inc.

Most Visible Ink Press books are available at special quantity discounts when purchased in bulk by corporations, organizations, or groups. Customized printings, special imprints, messages, and excerpts can be produced to meet your needs. For more information, contact Special Markets Manager, Gale Research Inc., 835 Penobscot Bldg., Detroit, MI 48226.

ISBN 0-7876-0030-X

CONTENTS

**Foreword by
Luis Valdez
xi**

**Introduction
xv**

**Advisors
xix**

**Contributors
xxi**

◆ Hispanic Identity in the United States Today ◆ Language ◆ Religion ◆ Hispanic Diversity ◆ Origins of Hispanics in the United States ◆ Immigration Patterns ◆ Central and South Americans and Other Hispanics ◆ The Family ◆ Hispanic Women's Issues ◆ Hispanic Children and Youth ◆ The Future of the Hispanic People

**Transitions
3**

◆ Spanish Legacy ◆ The Indigenous Caribbean Populations ◆ The Indigenous Mexican Population ◆ The Spaniards in the Valley of Mexico ◆ Movement to the North ◆ Anglo Encroachment into the Mexican North ◆ Mexicans Under U.S. Rule ◆ Africa and the Making of Society in Cuba and Puerto Rico ◆ Independence of Cuba and Puerto Rico ◆ Early Mexican Immigration to the United States ◆ The Mexican Revolution and Immigration to the United States ◆ The "Mexico Lindo" Generation ◆ Depression, Repatriation, and Acculturation ◆ World War II and the Mexican-American Generation ◆ From Chicanos to Hispanics ◆ Migration to the United States from Puerto Rico ◆ Early Settlement of Puerto Ricans in the United States ◆ Post–World War II Puerto Ricans in the United States ◆ The Revolution of Fidel Castro and Cuban Immigration

**History
49**

◆ Facts and Figures About Hispanic Business ◆ Prominent Hispanics in Business

**Business
129**

Labor
155
◆ Hispanics in Organized Labor ◆ Immigration and Migration ◆ Hispanic Employment in Industry ◆ Federal Employment Programs and Laws ◆ Youth Employment ◆ Women's Employment ◆ Income, Poverty, and Unemployment

Politics
189
◆ Hispanics in the Political Process ◆ Hispanic Voting and the Voting Rights Act of 1965 ◆ Hispanics in Congress ◆ Hispanic Members of the 103d U.S. Congress ◆ Selected Hispanic Members of Congress, 1822–1992 ◆ Hispanics in the Executive Branch ◆ Selected Prominent Hispanic Federal Officials ◆ Prominent Hispanic Politicians in State Government ◆ Prominent Hispanic Metropolitan Leaders ◆ Hispanic Judges in Federal Courts ◆ Hispanic Judges in State Courts ◆ Hispanics in the Public Interest ◆ Selected Prominent Hispanic Attorneys and Law Professors

Media
255
◆ Treatment of Hispanics in General Market Media ◆ General Market Newspapers ◆ General Market Television ◆ Advertising ◆ Hispanic-Oriented Print Media ◆ Hispanic-Oriented Newspapers ◆ Hispanic-Oriented Magazines and Periodicals ◆ Hispanic-Oriented Electronic Media ◆ Selected Hispanics in Media

Art
301
◆ The Sources of Hispanic Art ◆ New Spaniards and Mexicans: 1599 to 1848 ◆ Hispanic Art from 1848 to 1920 ◆ Traditional Arts from 1920 to the Present ◆ Hispanic Artists: 1920s through the 1950s ◆ Hispanic Artists: 1960s and 1970s ◆ Hispanic Artists: 1970s to the Present ◆ Chicano Murals

Literature
373
◆ The Nineteenth Century ◆ The Early Twentieth Century ◆ World War II to the Present ◆ Outstanding Hispanic Literary Figures

Theater
443
◆ Hispanic Theater in the United States: Origins to 1940 ◆ Post–World War II to the Present ◆ Outstanding Figures in Hispanic Theater

Film
497
◆ Depiction of Minority Groups in Early American Film ◆ Conglomeration of the Film Industry and the Production Code ◆ First Decades: The Bandido, Buffoon, Dark Lady, Caballero, and Gangster ◆ Hispanics in

Film during the 1930s and the Era of Social Consciousness ◆ Decline of the Production Code, Emergence of the Civil Rights Movement, and New Developments in Film: 1960s and 1970s ◆ Hollywood Films Since 1980 ◆ The Emergence of Hispanic Films ◆ Hispanics in Film: Future Directions ◆ Outstanding Hispanics in the Film Industry

Music 561

◆ Hispanic Musical Cultural Expression ◆ The Corrido and Canción-Corrido ◆ Música Norteña ◆ The Mexican-American Orquesta ◆ Salsa ◆ Latin Jazz/Rock ◆ Música Tropical ◆ The Contemporary Music Scene ◆ Prominent Hispanic Classical Musicians

Sports 603

◆ Hispanics and Sport ◆ Baseball ◆ Rodeo ◆ Other Sports ◆ Hispanic Athletes

Index 633

Photography Credits 643

FOREWORD

Human civilization in the Western Hemisphere has been evolving for at least ten thousand years without interruption. How then to begin to describe the process of evolution that has resulted in that great hurricane called America? Through the centuries humanity has evolved through the cultural and racial fusion of the generations, people on people, nation on nation, in a vortex of historical confrontation, war, restless peace, and finally acceptance and fusion. Tragically, the glue that binds the human tribes together begins with bloodshed but inevitably, triumphantly, it also ends with blood, as forbidden lover inescapably finds forbidden lover to procreate the offspring of an unthinkable love.

Racism and miscegenation have danced hand in hand across the continents for millennia, giving rise to generation upon generation of bewildered children forced to purchase their humanity with tokens of genetic identity. Notions of superior race and culture have repeatedly animated human beings to undertake war and conquest in the name of God, religion, economics, and politics. Yet the tale of human progress remains the same. Civilizations come and go, but the genetic distillation of the human race goes on and on. It is as if the winds themselves have conspired on the Planet Earth to blow all the peoples of humankind into an eventual cultural and racial chrysalis. A place called America.

The term Hispanic seems to refer to an aspect of this place, yet it embraces something of its essence as well. Centuries of confrontation and interaction on the Iberian peninsula had already profoundly deepened the human mixture called the Spanish people when Columbus landed in the New World in 1492. This fusion of Iberian, Celtic-Gaelic, Moorish, and Jewish peoples was destined to blend with the native peoples of the Americas, Asia, and Africa to create the so-called Hispanic, which is why the term itself seems slightly inadequate to the task of describing its own complexity.

The point is that the term Hispanic refers to the entire process of the Americas, and not just to another wave of immigrants. Without Hispanics there is no America; without America, there are no Hispanics. It is as simple and complex as that. How do you extricate the essence of the word from its continental significance? Even Filipinos, who were the first Asian Hispanics, became so through contact with the Spanish galleons sailing across the Pacific from Acapulco.

The entire thrust of Hispanic-American history has served the Manifest Destiny of the hemisphere: to bring the races and cultures of the world together under a common sky, while defending human rights even as it struggles to define them. Human equality was pronounced and embraced by exponents of American democracy throughout the hemisphere, by Benito Juárez and José Martí no less than by Thomas Jefferson and Abraham Lincoln, but its roots can also be found deep in the land, in the indigenous pre-Columbian ideals of Deganawida and Quetzalcoatl in the Confederacies of the Iroquois and Mayapan.

Puerto Rican, Cuban, Mexican, or any of the other Hispanic manifestations of our American identity can only serve to illustrate the rich diversity of our continental origins. Our roots in America run deep indeed, but it is our future that binds our children and grandchildren together as continental Americans. Americans, naturally, by virtue of our birth, presence, and citizenship in the United States, but Americans, ultimately, because of our hemispheric roots. This *Hispanic Almanac* is thus more than it seems. Witness herein the birth of the hemispheric American. For we are all Yankees.

Ironically, as indigenous linguistic influences would have it, the term Yankee has a pre-Columbian origin, stemming from a combination of two words: Yan (Yankuik), meaning "new," and Ki, meaning "man." Seen through the eyes of the Iroquois, Algonquin, Arawak, Taino, Yaqui, Aztec, Maya, Inca, or any of the indigenous peoples of the very ancient New World, the Europeans were all Yankees or "new men." But it is the children and grandchildren and great grandchildren of the mix, the blend, the fusion of the humanity of the Americas that are truly new.

What else does all our history promise and portend but the certainty of human contact and interaction? To fear its consequences is to deny the inevitable. Beyond Hispanic, beyond Anglo, beyond white, black, yellow, and red, it is our common destiny to someday become hemispheric Americans, one and all. Therein lies our hope, our equality, and our future.

Luis Valdez

INTRODUCTION

The Hispanic Almanac: From Columbus to Corporate America is the first widely available information source to cover a broad range of important aspects of Hispanic life and culture. Hispanics comprise people of the United States whose ancestors—or who themselves—originated in Spain, the Spanish-speaking countries of South and Central America, Mexico, Puerto Rico, Cuba, or the Dominican Republic. At once among the oldest and newest immigrants in the American mosaic, Hispanics share a rich culture marked by diversity. In all its multiplicity, this culture continues to profoundly influence the collective American experience.

With a Hispanic population of more than 22 million, the United States is the fifth-largest Spanish-speaking country in the world. The number of Hispanics in this country has grown by 53 percent in the last decade. It is projected that by the year 2000, almost 33 million Hispanics—constituting the nation's largest ethnic group—will be living in the United States.

The majority of Hispanics are working-class citizens. Even those Hispanics in the professional class share working-class backgrounds. Most are *mestizos*—the product of mixed races and cultures—for the Spanish, American Indian, and African heritages have blended in every aspect of life to produce today's Hispanic peoples. The Spanish culture, which introduced and reinforced a common language and religion for these peoples for centuries, still serves as a unifying factor for Hispanics today, regardless of whether or not an individual speaks Spanish in daily life. While the Spanish spoken by Puerto Ricans, Mexican Americans, and Cuban Americans is somewhat different, they share the experience of being bilingual. These central factors—social class, ethnicity, linguistic-cultural background—unify the people; similar factors unify the information presented in *The Hispanic Almanac,* which also strives to respect the tremendous diversity in racial, ethnic, geographic, and historical backgrounds among Hispanics today.

Each of the twelve chapters in *The Hispanic Almanac* tells part of the story and reveals the impact of Puerto Ricans, Mexican Americans, Cuban Americans, and other Hispanics. Biographical profiles in many chapters highlight Hispanics who have excelled in their fields of endeavor. Information throughout the book on individuals and various subjects can be found through the index. More than 200 illustrations—including photographs, drawings, tables, and figures—punctuate the discussion in each chapter.

The Hispanic Almanac: From Columbus to Corporate America is a paperback abridgment of a massive library reference, *The Hispanic-American Almanac,* which was the product of a national team of outstanding scholars who invested their time, energy, and genius to create the first comprehensive treatment of Hispanics. In their labors for the *Almanac,* as well as in their day-to-day work, these scholars have been actively engaged in the difficult task of working with original documentary sources, oral interviews, and field work to create a written record of Hispanic life where none before existed. The contributors, and the *Hispanic Almanac,* are dedicated to filling an informational void that has existed for too long relating to the history and culture of Hispanics. I am gratified that this fine work now finds a wider readership through this edition.

Acknowledgments

My most sincere thanks to all the contributors to this volume, for indulging me in my obsession and for producing such wonderfully researched and written chapters, despite the pressure I exerted on you for making deadlines and supplying illustrations and other materials.

My deepest appreciation and thanks to my assistant, Hilda Hinojosa, who helped organize, type, and maintain oral and written communications with the contributing scholars and with my editors. This book was made possible with her able, efficient, and enthusiastic support.

This edition was shaped for Visible Ink Press by Julie Winklepleck. Mark C. Howell designed the pages and Art Chartow the cover. Continuous typesetting was supplied by Marco DiVita at the Graphix Group. Thanks also to Fatima Sulaiman for research on Hispanics in politics; Charles Ramírez-Berg, Patricia Constantakis-Valdéz, Chon Noriega, Diana Ríos, and Kenton Wilkinson for collaboration on the Media chapter; Margaret Chamberlain for photo management; Michele Lonoconous for text permissions; and Gina Misiroglu, Iris Cloyd and Sharon Remington for proofreading and processing.

Nicolás Kanellos

ADVISORS

Dr. Edna Acosta-Belén

Director, Center for Caribbean and Latin American Studies, University of Albany

Dr. Rodolfo Cortina

Director, Bibliographic Database, Recovering the U.S. Hispanic Literary Heritage Project, and Professor of Spanish, Florida International University

Dr. Rodolfo de la Garza

Professor of Political Science, The University of Texas at Austin

Dr. Ricardo Fernández

President, Lehman College, City University of New York

Dr. Arturo Madrid

Director, the Tomás Rivera Center, Claremont, California

Dr. Michael Olivas

Associate Dean of Law and Director of the Institute for Higher Education Law and Governance, University of Houston

CONTRIBUTORS

Roberto Alvarez
Department of Anthropology, Arizona State University

Ramiro Burr
San Antonio Express-News and *Billboard*

Gilbert Paul Carrasco
School of Law, Villanova University

José Fernández
Department of Foreign Languages, University of Central Florida

María González
English Department, University of Houston

Gary Keller
Bilingual Review Press, Arizona State University

John Lipski
Department of Modern Languages, University of New Mexico

Thomas M. Leonard
Department of History, Philosophy & Religious Studies, University of North Florida

Tatcho Mindiola

Mexican American Studies Program, University of Houston

Silvia Novo Pena

Department of English and Foreign Languages, Texas Southern University

Manuel Peña

Foreign Languages, California State University, Fresno

Jacinto Quirarte

College of Fine and Applied Arts, University of Texas, San Antonio

Arturo Rosales

Department of History, Arizona State University

Guadalupe San Miguel

History Department, University of Houston

Federico Subervi

Department of Radio-Television-Film, University of Texas, Austin

Dennis Valdez

Chicano Studies Program, University of Minnesota

Jude Valdez

College of Business, University of Texas, San Antonio

The
Hispanic
Almanac

From Columbus to Corporate America

Transitions

In the last twenty-five years Hispanics have received a great deal of atten-tion and have become part of the national consciousness. There are several reasons for this, the foremost being the rapid increase in the size of the His-panic population. As can be seen from the statistics presented in this chap-ter, Hispanics are increasing at a much higher rate than the total popula-tion and are expected to become the nation's largest minority group sometime early in the next century.

A second reason for the increased attention is immigration to the United States, especially undocumented migration from Mexico. The size of the immigrant population and its effects on society have been intensely de-bated. The political turmoil in Central America, especially in El Salvador, has added to the debate as Central Americans have migrated to the United States to escape the crises in their countries.

The bilingual-bicultural movement has also focused attention on Hispanic demands that society's institutions, especially those devoted to education, develop programs in Spanish as well as in English to meet their needs and reflect their culture. These programs are controversial among many non-Hispanics.

A fourth reason for the expanded awareness of Hispanics is the economic and political power that Hispanics have gained as their numbers have grown. The sheer size of the Hispanic population makes it an important economic group in areas where Hispanics are concentrated. Hispanics are also an important voting bloc and now elect members of their own to political positions in states such as Florida, California, Texas, New Mexico, and New York. In other states Hispanics play an important role in electing non-Hispanics to office.

These issues, among others, are pushing many Hispanic concerns to the forefront, and for many observers of American society portend a national minority group whose economic, political, and social influence can only continue to increase.

HISPANIC IDENTITY IN THE UNITED STATES TODAY ♦ ♦ ♦ ♦ ♦ ♦

Today an uneasy ethnic solidarity exists among Hispanics. At the political level there is much rhetoric that attempts to bring them all under one rubric, and, indeed, the term "Hispanic" has been fostered as an agent of this process. While Cubans are conservative on issues dealing with Cuba and communism, they share the same ideology with Mexican Americans and Puerto Ricans when it comes to cultural maintenance and resistance to what many consider debasing American values. Another bond is language, an issue that has been forced into the political arena by the "English only" movement. All Hispanics resent the onus placed on them because they speak Spanish, a language that is despised in many quarters of the Anglo-American community.

Spanish-speaking communities in the United States are, in approximate descending order of size, of the following origins: Mexican, Puerto Rican, Cuban, and Central American. In the latter category, Nicaraguans and Salvadorans are the most numerous. The Dominican population of New York City is rapidly growing; Dominican Spanish is quite similar to that of Puerto Rico, although members of each group are aware of differences. Large numbers of Colombians are found in Miami, New York City, and elsewhere, but they come from many dialectic zones of Colombia and do not exercise a strong centralizing influence on any variety of U.S. Spanish. Finally, several small but close-knit Spanish-speaking groups' use of Spanish does not fall under the four large categories previously mentioned. These include Sephardic (Judeo-) Spanish-speakers in New York, Miami, and other urban areas, the Isleños of southeastern Louisiana, descendants of Canary Island settlers who arrived at the end of the eighteenth century, and the pre-Castro Cuban Spanish communities of Key West and Tampa, which have been overshadowed by more recent Cuban immigration.

Language

Cubans, Puerto Ricans, and Dominicans can instantly identify their own forms of Spanish, but outsiders note more similarities than differences among the varieties of Spanish that originate in the Caribbean. Pronunciation is the single most important unifying factor, since Caribbeans are known for "swallowing" the final consonants, which are clearly heard, for example, in the Spanish of Mexico and parts of Central America. This slurring over final sounds also contributes to the impression that Caribbean Spanish is spoken faster than other varieties.

Even during the colonial period, striking differences in the Spanish spoken in different regions of Central America could be observed, in fashions that do not always correspond to what might be supposed by looking at a map. For instance, Costa Rica, the southernmost Central American nation, shares more similarities with Guatemala, at the far north, than with neighboring Nicaragua. Honduran and Salvadoran Spanish blend together smoothly, but the contrast with Guatemalan Spanish is striking, and Nicaraguan Spanish is also rather different. Costa Rican Spanish bears no resemblance to neighboring Panamanian Spanish to the south, which is not surprising in view of the fact that Panama was formerly a province of Colombia, administered from Bogotá and largely populated from Colombia's coastal provinces, where even today speech is very similar to that of

A bilingual shopping district in El Paso, Texas.

Panama. Guatemalan Spanish, on the other hand, is similar to the Spanish of Mexico's Yucatán region, largely due to the common Mayan heritage.

The pronunciation of Nicaraguan Spanish is in many ways similar to Cuban and Puerto Rican Spanish. To the casual listener, Salvadoran Spanish is closer to Mexican Spanish than to any of the Caribbean varieties, an impression that is confirmed by history. Salvadoran and Mexican Spanish share a large quantity of vocabulary items derived from Native American languages, principally Nahuatl and to a much lesser extent Mayan.

Mexican varieties of Spanish share more similarities with Central American speech, particularly Salvadoran, than with any Caribbean dialects. The same Native American language families had a strong influence on Mexican Spanish, and the patterns of colonial administration resulted in similar profiles in central Mexico and the highland capitals of Central America. "Mexican" Spanish existed in what is now U.S. territory several centuries before the nations of Mexico and the United States came into being. More Mexican Spanish was incorporated through U.S. territorial expansion (the Texas revolution and the Mexican-American War), and still more Mexican varieties are the result of twentieth-century immigration. Each stage of Mexican Spanish presence in the United States has its own peculiarities, although the similarities outweigh the differences.

The majority of Hispanics born or raised in the United States speak English, as a home language or a strong second language. Arrivals from Spanish-speaking countries also learn English, to a greater or lesser extent depending on such factors as age upon arrival, previous study of English, urgency of using English in the workplace or in the home environment, children in school who bring English into the home, and economic conditions that provide opportunities for acquiring English. As happens with speakers of other languages, Spanish-speakers who learn English during adolescence or later frequently retain an "accent," regardless of the level of fluency eventually attained. Even in bilingual communities where most residents learned English in childhood, a slight "Hispanic" flavor is often found in English.

Traditionally, Hispanic English has been seen in a negative light, as a way of speaking that needs to be corrected. More recently, linguists have studied Hispanic English as it is actually used, without preconceived notions, and have discovered that it also has a role in maintaining community solidarity. The shift from Spanish to English is affecting all Hispanic groups in the United States, and maintaining an ethnically marked form of English is sometimes a semiconscious way of resisting total assimilation to the American "melting pot." Research has demonstrated that some speakers deliberately switch varieties of English depending on whether they are inside the ethnic neighborhood or in an Anglo-American setting. Community activists and grass roots political campaigners often find it more effective to use ethnic varieties of English, which arouse a more favorable response from their audience. Among educators and community leaders, debate is ongoing as to the desirability of Hispanic English. Some feel that it is an impediment to economic and social advancement, while others insist that it is the attitudes of society that must be changed first. This controversy shows no signs of being resolved in the near future.

Except for recent arrivals, or in a few isolated rural areas, the majority of Hispanics in the United States speak English. A gradual but definite shift from Spanish to English occurs in most Hispanic communities, the same course followed by every other immigrant language brought to the United States, and the speed with which this language shift takes place is increasing.

Bilingual aisles in the Tianguis market in Montebello, California.

It is frequently asked whether or not a uniquely "U.S." variety of Spanish exists. It seems, after considering the full panorama of Spanish-language usage in the United States, that the answer in general is no. Spanish in the United States continues to be divided mainly according to the country of ancestral origin: Mexican, Puerto Rican, Cuban, and so forth. Even in cities where more than one large Hispanic group is found, a single language variety usually prevails. Despite dictionaries that claim to describe such dialects, it is almost impossible to justify the existence of "American" varieties of Spanish: "Mexican American," "Puerto Rican American,"

"Cuban American," and so forth. What is found in the United States is greater use of English, and shifting of some Spanish words to match equivalent English terms. This does not make for separate dialects of Spanish, especially since the use of English elements is not consistent from speaker to speaker. In fact, the claim of a special U.S. Spanish is often a by-product of negative attitudes toward Spanish-speakers in the United States, as held by Spanish-speakers from other nations as well as by many Americans.

The nonexistence of a unique U.S. Spanish dialect is not a negative result. Spanish use in the United States is expanding rather than shrinking, and this expansion involves styles and ranges of language in addition to the number of speakers. U.S. Spanish is, more than ever, closely tied both to the international Spanish-speaking community and to American society and culture. What is uniquely U.S. Spanish is the complex pattern of bilingual language usage, which finds its highest form of expression in bilingual literature. By being able to communicate bilingually, U.S. Spanish-speakers command an extraordinarily rich language repertoire, which is at once part of Latin American and U.S. society and also uniquely Hispanic.

Religion

Hispanics are an eminently religious people. Throughout the centuries, regardless of the accessibility of priests or places of worship, or the availability of religious instruction, they have maintained their faith through the nuturing of their families and villages. Often misunderstood and chastised as ignorant, retrograde, or pagan, they have clung to the symbols of a deep spirituality received from their elders. Religious expression is apparent in the exchanges of everyday life—in the readiness with which Hispanics add the expressions *gracias a Dios* (thanks be to God) or *Si Dios quiere* (God willing) and the ever-present invocations to God, the Virgin, and the saints. That the manner of religious expression for U.S. Hispanics is fundamentally Christian and Catholic is natural; Catholicism is still the religion of choice of Hispanics everywhere. The most recent surveys reveal that 75 percent of U.S. Hispanics consider themselves Catholic, 19 percent Protestant, and 5 percent "other" (Jewish, Jehovah's Witnesses, Mormon, to name a few).

An instrument of evangelization, most widely utilized in the Spanish territories now encompassed by the United States, was the mission, a temporary institution established and run by priests who resided among or in proximity to native populations. The missionary usually came right on the heels of the conquistador and built his rudimentary chapel and convent at a reasonable distance from the military garrison, once the area was somewhat pacified. Instead of force, it was the missionary's works of mercy and his teachings that often brought about the evangelization of the natives. The vulnerability of the unarmed, nonthreatening padre was often his greatest strength. Missionaries could succeed where the conquistadors failed. Such was the case in the Sonora region of northern Mexico (southern Arizona today) and in the peninsula of Baja California, where the hostility of the natives prevented the soldiers from making inroads. After several failed attempts, the Mexican viceroy entrusted the Jesuits with this conquest, which they performed successfully with no other weapon than the cross.

The mission, in most cases, served as a center for religious instruction and a beachhead from which the padre could set out to scout for other promising mission sites, where another beachhead in the evangelization process could be established. Missions, therefore, as was the case in Florida and the Southwest, tended to stretch out over a territory much like the links of a chain. This arrangement, in turn, facilitated the logistics of supplying and defending them. The Texas and California missions established by the Franciscan friars were rather ambitious institutions. Some were villages unto themselves. The Indians learned Christian doctrine and a variety of skills—farming, animal husbandry, weaving, metalwork, leather craft, carpentry, and masonry—aimed at bringing about economic self-sufficiency to populations that once depended on collecting, hunting, or fishing for their sustenance. These missions became very wealthy, supplying not merely their own residents but the garrisons and townships in the immediate area.

The assertion that missions and missionaries served the purposes of the empire cannot be denied. The missions contributed to the pacification of the Indians, and in so doing facilitated the process of colonization. They fostered the development of townships in their immediate vicinity. Furthermore, by Christianizing and Hispanicizing the Indians, the missionaries transformed entire populations into loyal subjects of the Spanish kings and obedient followers of the Roman Church.

The missions were secularized during the first part of the nineteenth century, either for political reasons or because their original aims had been achieved. By this time and because in most cases their residents had fused with the people of the surrounding townships and farms, missions became the nuclei for modern-day parishes. It is not uncommon for the descendants of the first Indian neophytes baptized within mission walls to still flock to the same old church buildings generation after generation.

One of the services offered by the church, which served to both Cristianize and Hispanicize the native and mestizo populations, was formal education. In townships and missions, the clergy was expected to establish schools, both for boys and girls, to teach the children to read and write and learn the catechism. The curriculum sometimes included Indian languages.

By the time of the Treaty of Guadalupe Hidalgo in 1848, the mission system had disappeared, but the faith was kept alive by the people. Secular priests belonging to the northern dioceses of Mexico ministered to the needs of the faithful as well as they could, considering the vast distances

Impact of The Anglo Conquest on Religion

An annual mass to Our Lady of Guadalupe.

The role that the missions played in the development of California cannot be overexaggerated. The development of a population from the fusion of the Hispanic mestizo settlers that came from Mexico and the native populations, the founding of townships and villages, and the emergence of a prosperous agricultural and cattle industry are primarily owed to the missions.

they had to travel and the sparseness of their numbers. In distant villages and ranches, months and years would pass without a visit from a priest. In northern New Mexico, the Brotherhood of the Penitentes (*Fraternidad Piadosa de Nuestro Padre Jesús Nazareno*—the Pious Fraternity of Our Father Jesús the Nazarene) filled in the spiritual vacuum. These penitential organizations, which, according to some historians, have their roots in the Third Order of St. Francis, a lay arm of the Franciscans, practiced scourging and a rigorous piety centered on the sufferings of Christ. In the absence of clergy, they organized liturgies for the different feasts in the church calendar and taught religion to the young.

Although originally Rome had intended for the bishops of northern Mexico to continue administering the affairs of the church in what had now become the southwestern frontier of the United States, the North American bishops protested, voicing the displeasure of their government and probably their own jealousy. Political expediency forced the Vatican to bow before the pressures of the new rulers and appoint foreign bishops to each newly erected diocese or vicariate. The effects of this decision are still felt today. Texas, which fell under the diocese of Coahuila, was made a missionary vicariate under Rome in 1841. In 1847 the diocese of Galveston (now Galveston-Houston) was erected by the Vatican. It encompassed the entire state and its first bishop was Jean Marie Odin, a native of Lyon, France. The spiritual needs of the thousands of European Catholic immigrants that poured into Texas became the primary concern of the local church. Neglect of the Hispanic faithful became the norm.

The fate of the church in Texas was repeated in New Mexico, Arizona, Colorado, and California. Vicariates and dioceses were erected in all conquered territories, and with rare exceptions non-Hispanic bishops were appointed to head them. The new bishops and vicars, in turn, brought in almost exclusively European priests and congregations of religious men and women. The disdain that the newcomers felt toward the native population was reflected in the myth that its clergy were worthless and lazy. Underlying this assumption was the fear of the authorities that Hispanic priests were by virtue of their place in the community natural leaders who could induce their flocks to rebellion. To be Catholic you first had to be American, you had to pray in English, you had to give up your traditional religious practices.

Although the original attitude of the English-speaking conquerors of the Mexican Southwest was that Hispanics would eventually disappear, migrations from Mexico, Cuba, and Puerto Rico in the latter part of the nineteenth century and the early years of the twentieth mandated a new approach on the part of the Church. The Church now saw itself as an instrument in the process of integrating Hispanics into the mainstream. For this purpose, national parishes were established for Hispanics, an approach utilized with other ethnic groups, such as the Polish, the Italians, and the Germans. Contrary to other nationalities, however, native Hispanic priests who could supply leadership and role models for their own people were seldom available. One of the salient reasons for this absence was the failure by church authorities to promote vocations among Hispanics, who, because of prevalent social and economic conditions, could seldom meet the educational standards required by seminaries and novitiates. The gap was filled by Spanish-speaking priests of other national origins.

Although in the 1950s and 1960s the number of Hispanic priests and nuns increased, they were often not allowed to work with their own people. Archbishop Patrick Flores, the highest-ranking Hispanic in the U.S. Catholic Church today, likes to recall how as a young priest assigned to a predominantly Hispanic parish in Houston, he was forbidden by his pastor the use of Spanish except in the confessional.

The first Hispanic to be ordained bishop was Patrick Flores, the son of poor migrant workers. Born Patricio Fernández Flores on July 26, 1929, in Ganado, Texas, the seventh of nine children, Flores received his early education in Ganado and Pearland, Texas and graduated from Kirwin High School in Galveston. He then attended St. Mary's Seminary in La Porte, Texas, and St. Mary's Seminary in Houston. He was ordained a Catholic priest on May 26, 1956, and served in a variety of functions in the diocese of Galveston-Houston, including as director of the Bishop's Committee for the Spanish-Speaking, until March 18, 1970, when Pope Paul VI appointed him to serve as auxiliary to the Archbishop of San Antonio. On May 5, 1970, he was consecrated as bishop. Bishop Flores was the first Mexican American elevated to the hierarchy of the Catholic church in the United States. On May 29, 1978, Bishop Flores was installed as the bishop of the diocese of El Paso, where he served until he was installed as the archbishop of San Antonio on October 13, 1979. Bishop Flores has received many honors and has pioneered programs in the church and in government on behalf of the civil rights of Hispanics and immigrants. In 1983, he was one of four bishops elected to represent the United States at the synod of bishops in Rome. In 1986, he was awarded the Medal of Freedom (Ellis Island Medal of Honor) in honor of the Statue of Liberty's one hundreth birthday.

*A family at mass,
Houston, Texas.*

**Protestantism
and Hispanics**

Latin America was missionary territory for the nineteenth-century U.S. Protestant churches. As the Latin American nations gained their independence from Catholic Spain, Protestant England's traditional foe, English-speaking missionaries, aware of the anticlericalism present in the independence movements south of the border, decided that the time had come for the spiritual conquest of the region. Proselytism of Hispanics born in the United States was now a goal of the Protestant ministers who traveled south to the lands newly conquered from Mexico. Those who converted were valuable as Spanish-speaking leaders who could be sent to the promising mission fields of Mexico.

In 1898, after the end of the Spanish-American War, Protestant missionaries descended upon Cuba and Puerto Rico, where they achieved a modicum of success. Some were born in Cuba or Puerto Rico and had converted as exiles in the United States. Catholicism was seen by many as the faith of the old oppressive order and Protestantism as a more enlightened faith.

Conversion, however, implied relinquishing traditional values. For Hispanics to become Protestant entailed a surrender of their identity similar to that expected of Hispanic Catholics in the United States. Becoming Protestant required Americanization, partly because Catholicism was so ingrained in Hispanic culture. When these Cuban and Puerto Rican Protestants migrated to the United States, they had a sense of alienation from both the Anglos and their own compatriots.

The seeds planted during the first part of the twentieth century began to root and by the 1930s a Spanish-speaking Protestant clergy was emerging. For Methodists and Presbyterians, a big stumbling block was the integration of Hispanics into national conferences of their respective churches. Hispanics, wishing to preserve their cultural and linguistic identities, often fear being absorbed by the non-Hispanic majority in the conferences. One of the most successful of the mainstream Hispanic churches has been the Rio Grande Conference, which includes Hispanic Methodists in Texas and New Mexico. Its roots date back to the early 1930s when Francisco Ramos and Alfredo Náñez, the first Hispanic to receive his B.D. degree from Southern Methodist University, were selected as presiding elders of the Texas American Conference. In 1939 it became the Rio Grande Conference, a powerful group of churches that has chosen, in spite all pressures, to remain independent. Under similar historical circumstances, the Latin American Conference of southern California opted to merge with the Anglo conferences, a move that has resulted in declining membership. The less structured nature of the Southern Baptists and the Pentecostals, whereby each congregation retains partial or total autonomy, has contributed to their increasing Hispanic membership, the only mainstream churches to experience such growth.

Pentecostalism, a brand of evangelical Christianity that is sweeping Central and South America, is growing in leaps and bounds among U.S. Hispanics. Its popularity seems to rest in the small-community atmosphere of the individual churches, which allows Hispanics a feeling of belonging. More particularly, because Pentecotalism does not dismantle for Hispanics the building blocks of their religious expression, Hispanic converts to Pentecostalism find in their new church room to express their religiosity. Although Pentecostalism disallows Catholic traditions such as processions and other external religious manifestations, it provides the convert with a highly emotional form of worship. The place that the saints and the Virgin occupied as protectors, intercessors, and healers of suffering humanity is now replaced with the healing powers of the Holy Spirit. Catholic clerical authority finds its counterpart in the authority that those who have received the baptism of the Holy Spirit acquire. Interestingly enough, the charismatic renewal movement in the Roman Catholic Church, which like the Pentecostals stresses the worship of the third person of the Trinity (God the Holy Spirit), is most popular among Hispanics.

Popular Religiosity

Hispanics who live in the territories occupied by the United States in the nineteenth century and those who migrated from Mexico and the other Spanish-American countries have succeeded in preserving the religious traditions of their forefathers. Perhaps because of the almost universal scarcity of priests in the Spanish-speaking Americas, the family and the home have

An East Los Angeles shop offering charms, candles, herbs, and perfumed oils to Hispanics seeking supernatural solutions to a variety of problems.

always been at the center of Hispanic religiosity. This religiosity is not necessarily derived from the teachings of childhood catechisms nor the homilies of parish priests. It is formed by assimilating and adapting the private religious practices that individuals observe within their extended family, which includes not only relatives, but friends and neighbors as well.

The religious instruction of the children, rosaries, novenas, *promesas* or *mandas* (the practice of making sacrificial offerings for some specific purpose), and the wearing of scapulars and medals occur or are promoted in the home usually at the behest of the grandmother or some other elderly female figure. For Hispanics, religion is often the concern of the women, who must look out for the spiritual well-being and even the salvation of their menfolk. In this context, it should be noted that in some cultures, particularly among Hispanics of Mexican origin, the *quinceañera* (fifteenth birthday) celebration, which marks the coming of age of the young girls, involves a mass or prayer service with a sermon that usually reminds the young woman of her future responsibilities as a Christian wife and mother.

The special meaning of the Virgin for Hispanics cannot be stressed enough. For the males she is the understanding mother who forgives and intercedes for her errant sons; for the women she sympathizes with the earthly travails of a mother, sister, or daughter.

Within the Hispanic household it is not unusual to find a place that functions as an altar. In creating the altar, the Hispanic woman tries to gather within the confines of her private domain symbols of the spiritual forces on which she depends for assistance in fulfilling her primary responsibility as caretaker of a family. The home altar might be nothing more than a religious picture before which candles are lit in a wordless form of prayer; it can be a statuette of a saint, Christ, or the Virgin on a table or a television set accompanied by a vase filled with flowers; or it can be elaborate, attempting to approximate an altar within a church, with a profusion of religious images, hand-embroidered cloths, candles, incense, holy water, and other objects of Roman Catholic worship.

Evolving Pan-Hispanicism

Variety entertainment programs, soap operas, and talk shows that air nationally on Spanish-language television networks and radio stations are many times crafted to bring a balanced appeal to the variegated Spanish-speaking peoples taking their turn at the American opportunity structure. A plethora of slick-cover magazines have appeared in the last ten years aimed at all the Hispanic groups. Some use English, others Spanish, or they contain bilingual renditions. This process alone, perhaps unwittingly, is bound to evolve a pan-Hispanicism unique to the United States.

In large cities such as Los Angeles, Chicago, Houston, and Miami, Hispanics of all kinds are thrown together and many times common ties re-

The development of a rubric "hispanidad" has been facilitated by three Spanish-language television networks and hundreds of radio stations that indirectly pound the message of ethnic bonding into millions of Hispanic homes.

sult in an affinity and some mingling. In Chicago, Mexicans and Puerto Ricans, who have lived together since the 1940s, have merged into political coalitions, and interethnic marriages have produced thousands of Mexican-Puerto Rican offspring. The melding of Salvadorans, Puerto Ricans, Mexicans, and Spaniards in San Francisco has also been transpiring for a long time, and there, during the heady 1960s movements, a strong Latino consciousness emerged in such barrios as the Mission District. In Houston (as in other areas), entrepreneurs have tapped the Hispanic market, creating a chain of enormous food stores called Fiesta that cater to the tastes of every imaginable Hispanic group.

Another possible scenario is that differences will make for a separate evolution in the respective communities. As each Hispanic group evolves in the United States, with separate identities, they may become ensconced and comfortable in their own elaborated ethnicity. Indeed, this is true of the older and larger Hispanic groupings, who see themselves as Mexican Americans, Cuban Americans, and mainland Puerto Ricans. Hispanos in northern New Mexico, who are for all intents and purposes Mexican Americans, at times even remain insular from this group. So what can be expected from them when it comes to identifying with a larger national denomination?

Furthermore, interethnic prejudices still persist at the community level between Hispanics. For example, at times Latin Americans or Spaniards living in the United States distance themselves from Mexican Americans or Puerto Ricans so that they will not be mistaken for them by non-Hispanics who hold prejudices against those groups. They may buy into Anglo-American prejudices and unwarranted stereotypes against certain groups in an unconscious effort to ingratiate themselves with the mainstream population. This is true even if back home they might have never dreamed of having these misgivings toward fellow Latins.

Another common source of inter-Hispanic antipathy is based on class origin. If the majority of one group is working class, as is the case with Mexicans, Puerto Ricans, and Central Americans, middle-class immigrants who come from South America often find it difficult to relate to what they consider a lower-class culture. They also demonstrate this orientation, of course, toward the working class back in their homelands. That phenomenon is also borne out among some upper-class Mexicans in the United States who look with disdain at compatriots who come from the *clases populares.*

Puerto Rican domino players in New York City.

There is even opposition to amalgamation among some Hispanic intellectuals who see the whole trend toward Hispanicization as a tool of consumerism. Obviously, it would be easier to aim at a large market rather than at disparate groups. There is also a residue of resentment within some in the Hispanic community toward Cuban exiles because of that group's persistent support of a conservative foreign policy toward Latin America. But the ultimate fear is that a bland, malleable ethnic group will emerge.

The process is going to find its own level. Despite the destructive prejudices that exist between Hispanic groups or the well-intended admonitions of intellectuals, common roots exist between Hispanics regardless of national or class origin. These will eventually make crucial links that no one can foresee. Rather than resist, Hispanics would be better off trying to shape this irresistible force into a positive ideal of kinship and humanity so that they can take their rightful place in the American mosaic, and even become a remarkably potent political power.

HISPANIC DIVERSITY ♦ ♦ ♦ ♦ ♦ ♦ ♦ ♦ ♦ ♦ ♦ ♦ ♦ ♦ ♦ ♦ ♦ ♦ ♦

In 1991 Hispanics numbered approximately 22 million people and composed approximately 9 percent of the total U.S. population of 249 million. If the number of undocumented Hispanic immigrants could be accurately counted, the growth rate and size of the Hispanic population would be greater. At the current rate of growth (which exceeds that of non-Hispanics), Hispanics will double in size by the year 2020 and will number approximately 43 million people. Yet the Hispanic population is not a homogeneous group. It shares a common culture, but beyond this, the groups that make up the Hispanic population differ significantly in many important ways. The three major groups are Mexican Americans, Puerto Ricans, and Cubans. Other Hispanic peoples are from the Domican Republic, Central and South America, and of various other Latin American descent. There are major historical, cultural, and demographic differences between these groups.

To understand the problems facing many Hispanics, how the problems arose, and why they still exist today, we must examine the Hispanic-American experience in history. Unique milestones have shaped the collective experience of Hispanics and have influenced American attitudes and decisions throughout the past. Unlike any other ethnic group in the United States, Hispanics are the only people to become citizens by conquest, with the exception of certain Native Americans.

◆ ◆ ◆ ◆ ◆ ◆ ◆ ORIGINS OF HISPANICS IN THE UNITED STATES

The history of Mexicans, Puerto Ricans, and Cubans is radically different. The Spaniards conquered the Indians of Mexico, and by mating with them, produced the *mestizo* or Mexican people. Mexicans, therefore, have a strong Indian as well as Spanish heritage.

The islands of Cuba and Puerto Rico were also conquered by the Spaniards. Both islands were originally populated with the Arawak and Carib Indians, whom the Spaniards forced into slavery to work in the mines and fields in Puerto Rico and the sugarcane fields in Cuba. The Spaniards began importing slaves from Africa to Cuba and Puerto Rico, and eventually the African slaves outnumbered and began to marry into the Indian population. Thus, Cubans and Puerto Ricans not only have an Indian and Spanish heritage but a strong African ancestry as well.

The Hispanic experience is unique in U.S. history. Hispanics are at once the oldest and the newest immigrants to the United States. In a nation of immigrants from all over the world, Hispanic immigrants have endured a long history of obstacles.

From the landing of Christopher Columbus in 1492 until the early nineteenth century, the entire Spanish-speaking world was controlled by Spain. The Spanish settled in North America long before the American Revolution, with the earliest settlement established at Saint Augustine, Florida, in 1563. Spanish settlers then began immigrating to the Southwest and founded El Paso, Texas, in 1598 and Santa Fe, New Mexico, in 1609. By 1760 there were an estimated 20,000 settlers in New Mexico and 2,500 in Texas. In 1769 the mission at San Diego, California, was established and the colonization of California began.

Mexican Americans

In 1810 in Mexico, Father Miguel Hidalgo y Castilla led the revolt against Spain, and Mexico gained its independence in 1821. Soon after Mexico became independent, Anglo-American settlers began to move into the Mexican territories of the present-day U.S. Southwest, especially Texas. In 1836 the Anglo settlers declared the Republic of Texas independent of Mexico. In 1846 the United States invaded Mexico under the banner of Manifest Destiny. The treaty of Guadalupe Hidalgo ended the Mexican War that same year. Under the treaty, half the land area of Mexico, including Texas, California, most of Arizona and New Mexico, and parts of Colorado, Utah, and Nevada, was ceded to the United States. The treaty gave Mexican nationals one year to choose U.S. or Mexican citizenship. Seventy-five thousand Hispanic people chose to remain in the United States and become citizens by conquest. James Gadsden was later sent to Mexico to complete the U.S. acquisition of the Southwest and negotiated the purchase of an additional 45,532 square miles, which became parts of Arizona and New Mexico. As more Anglos settled in the newly acquired lands, the new Hispanic Americans gradually became a minority population in the Southwest. The 1848 gold rush lured a flood of Anglo settlers to California, which became a state in 1850. Settlement in Arizona and New Mexico occurred at a slower pace, and they both became states in 1912.

The Treaty of Guadalupe Hidalgo guaranteed the property rights of the new Hispanic-American landowners by reaffirming land grants that had been made by Spain and Mexico prior to 1846. However, the treaty did not explicitly protect the language or cultural rights of these new U.S. citizens. Over the next fifty years, most Southwestern states enacted language laws inhibiting Hispanic participation in voting, judicial processes, and education. More devastating, the Reclamation Act of 1902 dispossessed many of these same Hispanic Americans of their land. Only in New Mexico were the civil rights of the descendants of the original Spanish-speaking settlers protected.

Such conditions of discrimination discouraged immigration to the United States for most of the late nineteenth century, even though the United States had no immigration statutes relating to the admission of foreign nationals until 1875. In fact, entering the country without a visa was not a punishable offense until 1929. However, in the 1890s there was a demand for low-wage laborers to construct American railroads, and Mexican immigration was encouraged, especially after 1882, when Congress passed the Chinese Exclusion Act of 1882, which virtually ended immigration from China to the United States.

Twentieth Century Population Movements

By 1910 conditions in Mexico deteriorated under the considerable political repression of the dictatorship of President Porfirio Díaz, who ruled Mexico for thirty-four years, from 1876 to 1910. Dispossession of property, widespread poverty, and runaway inflation forced many Mexicans to join forces in revolt. After the Mexican Revolution began in 1910, hundreds of thousands of people fled north from Mexico and settled in the Southwest. Between 1910 and 1930 about 10 percent of the entire population of Mexico immigrated to the United States, including 685,000 legal immigrants. They were welcomed during this period because of the labor needs of the expanding U.S. economy. Special rules were developed in 1917, during World War I, to permit "temporary" Mexican farm workers, railroad laborers, and miners to enter the United States to work. By the late 1920s as much as 80 percent of the farm workers in southern California were of Mexican descent.

The Great Depression of the 1930s brought rapid change to Mexican immigration. From 1929 to 1934, more than 400,000 persons were "repatriated" to Mexico without any formal deportation proceedings. Thousands of U.S. citizens were illegally deported because they were of Mexican descent.

During World War II, the United States again needed workers and immigration was encouraged. In 1942 an arrangement was made with the Mexican government to supply temporary workers, known as "braceros," for American agriculture. Formalized by legislation in 1951, the Bracero Program brought an annual average of 350,000 Mexican workers to the United States until its end in 1964.

Mexican Americans again faced economic difficulties and discrimination because of competition for jobs during the late 1950s. This led to Operation Wetback, in which 3.8 million persons of Mexican descent were deported between 1954 and 1958. Only a small fraction of that amount were allowed deportation hearings prior to being deported. Thousands more legitimate U.S. citizens of Mexican descent were also arrested and detained.

In 1965 the United States enacted a law placing a cap on immigration from the Western Hemisphere for the first time, which became effective in 1968. Immediate family members of U.S. citizens were not subject to the cap and could legally immigrate. Legal immigration from Mexico averaged about 60,000 persons per year from 1971 to 1980. A substantial number of undocumented persons entered the United States from Mexico during those years, and that number has increased dramatically since. Estimates of the number of undocumented immigrants in the United States often range from 3 to 5 million people. In the early 1980s programs to apprehend undocumented immigrants were again implemented, and once more there were reports of violations of civil rights of U.S. citizens and lawful permanent residents of Mexican descent.

Mexican Americans are only a part of the entire Hispanic population. Many other Spanish-speaking peoples became U.S. citizens under different circumstances. For example, Florida, Puerto Rico, and Cuba were possessions of Spain until the nineteenth century.

Caribbean Experiences

Cubans deplaning Pan Am in Miami, 1967.

Florida was claimed for Spain after its discovery by Juan Ponce de Leon in 1513. Saint Augustine in Florida was the earliest settlement established in North America, founded in 1563. It remained a possession of Spain until 1819. After Andrew Jackson led a U.S. military force into Florida, capturing two Spanish forts, Spain sold Florida to the United States for $5 million under the Onís Treaty.

Puerto Ricans, like the first Mexican Americans, became U.S. citizens through conquest. In 1898, following the brief Spanish-American War,

Puerto Rico became a possession of the U.S. through the Treaty of Paris. Many Puerto Ricans assumed that annexation meant that all Puerto Ricans were U.S. citizens, thus entitling them to all the rights and privileges of citizenship. However, that was not the case. Many Puerto Ricans were denied the right to vote, and many were prevented from moving to the U.S. mainland.

Nearly twenty years later, the Jones Act of 1917 finally resolved this problem, making all Puerto Ricans U.S. citizens. Since then, Puerto Ricans have had the unrestricted right to travel between the island and the mainland. By the early 1920s, there were significant Puerto Rican communities in U.S. cities, most notably New York.

Cuba also became a U.S. possession in 1898 through the Treaty of Paris, which ended 387 years of Spanish rule. However, Cuba was a possession only for a brief time and became independent in 1902. In the late nineteenth century, a small number of Cubans migrated to the United States, mainly to Florida and New York. By 1930 only about 20,000 Cubans lived in the United States, and by 1950 only about 35,000.

The vast majority of Cuban Americans immigrated to the United States after 1959, when Fidel Castro took power in Cuba. Between 1959 and 1962, 25,000 Cubans were "paroled" to the United States using a special immigration rule. The immigration laws did not provide for special refugee status without proof of physical persecution until 1965. In 1966 a program was initiated to airlift Cubans to the United States, but it was halted by Castro in 1973. Over 250,000 Cubans were airlifted to the United States during that period.

About 10 percent of Cuba's population immigrated to the United States between 1966 and 1973.

Throughout the remainder of the 1970s, many Cubans immigrated to the United States by routes through other Latin American countries. In 1980 a "boatlift" of Cubans from Mariel Harbor was permitted by Castro, and about 130,000 refugees arrived in the United States. Controversy surrounded this boatlift because a small percentage of the refugees were from Cuban prisons and institutions for the mentally ill.

Today about 1 million Cuban Americans live in the United States, with the majority residing in Florida, although there are increasing numbers in California, Illinois, Massachusetts, New York, and New Jersey. While many early Cuban refugees expected to return to Cuba, the continuation of the Communist regime under Castro has led many to conclude that they will not be able to go back. They have become naturalized citizens at a much higher rate than any other Hispanic immigrant group.

IMMIGRATION PATTERNS ♦ ♦ ♦ ♦ ♦ ♦ ♦ ♦ ♦ ♦ ♦ ♦ ♦ ♦ ♦ ♦ ♦ ♦

People frequently refer to "Central America" as though it were a single entity. Indeed, the countries that form modern Central America (with the exception of Belize) did enjoy a fleeting moment of unity: following independence from Spain in the early 1820s, the Central American republics formed the ill-fated Central American Union, an attempt to federate five tiny nations into a significant regional power. After several unsuccessful trial alliances, the union was definitively dissolved in 1854, and the Central American republics have gone their own way ever since.

At different times in U.S. history, waves of immigrants have arrived from other Latin American countries, such as Nicaragua, Colombia, the Dominican Republic, Guatemala, Honduras, and El Salvador, as well as many others. More than half of these immigrants have come to the United States since 1970. Often they have entered the United States through Mexico. Some have entered legally under established immigration quotas; others have come as students or tourists and stayed in this country after their temporary legal status expired. Many immigrants from the Caribbean and Central and South America have come through circuitous and difficult routes to escape civil war, poverty, and repression.

More recent Central American immigration can be traced largely to economic and political conditions in the source countries, especially during the past two decades. During the 1960s, the establishment of the Central American Common Market led to economic growth and improved conditions in the region. In 1969, however, the border war between Honduras and El Salvador led to the collapse of the common market and the rapid decline of economic conditions in Central America.

Since 1979 political upheaval and civil wars in Nicaragua, El Salvador, and Guatemala have contributed to large migrations of refugees to the United States. The number of Central and South Americans in the United States in 1950 was about 57,000. Estimates in 1985 ranged from 1.4 million to 1.7 million, but these figures may be low because of difficulties in accurately counting large numbers of undocumented emigrants from Central and South America.

Immigration patterns to the United States are different for Mexican Americans, Cubans, and Puerto Ricans. The primary factor that pulls Mexican immigrants to the United States today is the demand for cheap labor. Constant migration from Mexico means that within the Mexican-American community there is always a large number of Mexican immigrants.

As a result of the two immigration movements the number of Cubans in the United States increased rapidly. In 1959 there were only 30,000 Cubans in the United States, and in 1991 there were 1.1 million. Cubans have become a major economic, political, and cultural force in Florida, especially in Miami, which has the largest concentration of Cubans in the United States.

The pattern of migration from Puerto Rico to the United States is different from that of either Mexico or Cuba. Puerto Rico became a possession of the United States in 1898, and Puerto Ricans were granted United States citizenship in 1917. Thus, Puerto Ricans who migrate to the United States are not considered immigrants in the same sense as Mexicans and Cubans. Today there are approximately 2.4 million Puerto Ricans living in the United States and 3.5 million living on the island of Puerto Rico.

Americans have always taken pride in their immigrant heritage but ironically have feared new immigration at the same time. Since the United States declared its independence from Great Britain in 1776, protectionism has had its place in the population's subconscious. In later years it was often used as justification for restricting immigration.

In 1965, a major revision of immigration law resulted when Congress amended the Immigration and Nationality Act of 1952, which maintained a restrictive limit on immigration from particular countries. The national

The Development of U.S. Immigration Law

A group of Hispanics have just been issued their temporary residence cards, 1991.

origin quota system was abolished. A complex seven-category preference system for granting visas was created in its place. The 1965 amendments gave preference to family reunification. Spouses, parents, and children of U.S. citizens were given preference in awarding visas and were not bound by a quota. The amendments maintained limits on immigration through the seven-category preference system, providing for immigration from each country of no more than 20,000 immigrants per year. Race or national origin was no longer a consideration. More important, the 1965 amendments imposed a quota ceiling on immigration from countries in the Western Hemisphere as well. This marked the first time in U.S. history that such a numerical restriction was placed on immigration from these countries.

Amendments to the law passed in 1978 removed the ceilings for each hemisphere and established a worldwide competition for 290,000 visas granted each year. Every country in the world was subject to the seven-category preference system and to the 20,000-per-year limit. The 1965 and 1978 amendments led to a dramatic shift in immigration. No longer were Europeans, formerly favored by law, the largest group of immigrants. They now represented only 13 percent of the total. Asians benefited most, representing 21 percent of the total number of immigrants entering the United States per year. Immigration from Latin American countries and the Caribbean remained at about 40 percent of the total.

The Immigration Act of 1990 continues to permit immigration of immediate relatives of U.S. citizens without numerical limitation but sets a "pierceable" overall cap on worldwide immigration of 700,000 for fiscal years 1992 through 1994, and of 675,000 for fiscal year 1995. The seven-category preference system has been replaced by one based on family relationships, employment, and diversity. The per-country limit is 25,000.

The 1970s and early 1980s brought a different kind of immigration problem to the attention of the American public. The rise in politically motivated violence in Central America spurred a massive increase in undocumented immigration to the United States. The flight of "boat people" from Indochina following the Vietnam War created an enormous refugee settlement challenge for the United States. In a six-month period alone in 1980, some 125,000 Cubans arrived in Florida in an uncontrolled sea migration to the United States. At about the same time, over 10,000 Haitians fled the repressive regime of dictator Jean Claude Duvalier and sailed to the United States in overcrowded fishing boats.

Guatemalan children wait for their farmworker parents to return from the fields.

These immigrants, or more appropriately, refugees, created a problem for U.S. immigration authorities. They were not eligible to enter the United States under established quotas without visas, nor could many of them meet the requirements to enter the United States under an exemption to the quota system as "refugees." Previous U.S. law provided for the admission of persons fleeing persecution or having a well-founded fear of persecution from Middle Eastern or Communist-dominated countries. This was advantageous to the Cubans fleeing Fidel Castro and the Vietnamese fleeing the Communist regime in Vietnam but was no help to the thousands of Central Americans who were fleeing political violence. The Refugee Act of 1980 removed the ideological definition of refugee as one who flees from a Communist regime, thus allowing thousands to enter the United States as refugees who otherwise would have been excluded.

Geographic Concentration

The majority of Hispanics are concentrated in the five southwestern states of California, Colorado, New Mexico, Arizona, and Texas. Approximately 63 percent of the total U.S. Hispanic population reside in these five states. Four states outside the Southwest account for 26 percent of the Hispanic population: New York, Florida, Illinois, and New Jersey. Puerto Ricans are the largest group in New York and New Jersey, and Cubans are the largest in Florida. Puerto Ricans and Mexican Americans are the largest groups in Illinois.

The ten states with the largest increase in the number of Hispanics are California, Texas, New York, Florida, Illinois, New Jersey, Arizona, New Mexico, Colorado, and Massachusetts, in that order. The increase in the size of California's Hispanic population is particularly noteworthy. It increased dramatically, from approximately 4.5 million in 1980 to 7.6 million in 1990, or by 69 percent. This rate of increase exceeded the national Hispanic increase of 53 percent. The size of California's Hispanic population is in fact larger than the total population of all but nine states.

Birthrates

Mexican Americans have the highest birthrate of the three groups, followed by Puerto Ricans and then Cubans. Mexican-American women between the ages of 35 and 44, for example, have given birth, on the average, to 3.6 children. The average for Puerto Rican women in the same age group is 3.2 children, and for Cuban women, 2.0 children. The Cuban average is even lower than the 2.6 average of the total U.S. population.

When reviewing the statistics of this diverse culture, it helps to understand the new phase of the labor history of Hispanics that began around the turn of the twentieth century, when employers in the Southwest, and soon afterward in the Midwest, began to recruit workers from the Mexican border. Their efforts set in motion a movement that has shaped migration patterns from Mexico throughout the twentieth century. Using labor contractors and other recruiters, they brought in workers from Mexico to perform largely unskilled, low-paying tasks. This planned labor migration quickly stimulated another pattern of individual migration that took on an independent character of its own and outpaced the rate of migration by labor recruitment. During the early twentieth century, a majority of Hispanic workers in the United States were Mexican immigrants and their children. In sheer numbers, the new arrivals soon overwhelmed the older Mexican-descent residents in most parts of the Southwest and Midwest, except New Mexico.

Occupation and Education

Mexico offered U.S. employers a reservoir of workers because of its high level of unemployment and very low incomes. The wage differential between Mexico and the United States throughout the century has always been very sharp. At present, an unskilled wage worker in the United States can earn approximately ten times as much as in Mexico, although the differences are largely offset by much higher prices for food, rent, and other living expenses in the United States.

In the early twentieth century, Mexicans were recruited largely for agricultural, railroad maintenance, and mining enterprises. Smaller numbers found employment in domestic and other service occupations, and in manufacturing. Mexican immigrant families often worked as a single unit in cotton, sugar beet, and fruit and vegetable planting, cultivation, and harvesting operations, especially in the Southwest. In other occupations, including mining, manufacturing, and most service occupations, adult workers were the rule, as child labor laws were harder to evade, restricting the employment of children.

As a result of the patterns of labor recruitment that evolved in the early twentieth century, cities and towns on and near the Mexican border, and eventually throughout the Southwest and in many Midwestern settings, developed large labor pools of Mexican workers who were available to perform unskilled, low-paying jobs throughout the year. Characteristically, the Mexican workers found employment largely in seasonal tasks and experienced high rates of unemployment and frequent changes in employers. Although many of them brought skills from Mexico, few of the tasks they performed in the United States required high levels of training or English-language proficiency to perform.

Education and Skill Levels

A major feature of this later labor migration has been the inclusion of people from a much wider range of countries in Latin America, and with a greater diversity of working backgrounds. Whereas Mexicans and Puerto Ricans continue to migrate for the most part as unskilled, semiskilled, or skilled workers, immigrants from other parts of the Caribbean and Central and South America have a wide range of backgrounds, including business and professional. This is particularly true of Cubans, the third most numerous Hispanic group in the United States. Their major wave of immigration occurred following the victory of the Cuban Revolution in 1959, and it included many prominent professionals and businesspeople. Later waves of Cuban immigrants were not as prosperous. The Mariel boatlift included many individuals from very poor, unskilled backgrounds, and with a lack of adequate job training. Many of them have had great difficulty becoming incorporated into the work regimen of the United States.

Cuban Americans are primarily a middle-class population with relatively high levels of education, occupational status, and income. Mexican Americans are primarily a working-class population holding blue-collar occupations and have low levels of education and income. Generally, Puerto Ricans rank in between Cubans and Mexican Americans, but are closer to Mexican Americans than Cubans in terms of their educational attainment, occupational status, and income.

The high educational level of Cubans is seen in the number of Cuban high school and college graduates: 61 percent have a high school education and approximately 19 percent have a college education. Among Puerto Ricans, 58 percent have a high school education and 10 percent have completed college. Among Mexican Americans, 44 percent have completed high school and only 6 percent are college graduates.

The high level of education among Cubans reflects the middle-class status of the Cubans who migrated to the United States in the early 1960s. Later generations of Cubans are continuing to achieve high levels of education as well. Among Cubans ages 25 to 34, for example, approximately 78 percent are high school graduates and 20.4 percent have a college education.

Mexican-American males are in the labor force in a larger proportion than either Cuban or Puerto Rican males; 80 percent of all Mexican-American males over age sixteen are participating in the nation's work force, in comparison with 73 percent of the Cuban and 66 percent of the Puerto Rican males. What Mexican American, Puerto Rican, and Cuban males have in common is being concentrated in the skilled and semiskilled occupations. Approximately 50 percent of all Mexican-American males and 43 percent of all Cuban and Puerto Rican males hold skilled and semiskilled occupations. Where the groups differ is in managerial and professional and technical sales and administrative support occupations. Cubans hold more of these types of occupations than either Puerto Ricans or Mexican Americans.

There are more Cuban females in the labor force than either Puerto Rican or Mexican-American females. Approximately 55 percent of all Cuban females over age sixteen are in the civilian labor force, compared with 42 percent of Puerto Rican females and 51 percent of Mexican-American females.

The female occupational distribution resembles that of the males in that Cuban females have a higher occupational status than Puerto Rican and

Mexican-American females. One significant difference is the higher proportion of Mexican-American females in service occupations. Approximately 27 percent of the Mexican-American females hold service occupations, compared with 16 percent of Puerto Rican and Cubans females.

♦ ♦ CENTRAL AND SOUTH AMERICANS AND OTHER HISPANICS

In addition to Mexican Americans, Puerto Ricans, and Cubans, the Hispanic population consists of Dominican Americans, Central and South Americans, and people who are classified by the U.S. Census Bureau as "other Hispanic origins." This latter category includes those whose origins are in Spain and those identifying themselves generally as Hispanic, Spanish, Spanish American, Hispano, Latino, and so on. Central and South Americans make up 13.8 percent of the total Hispanic population, and those of "other Hispanic origins" make up 7.6 percent.

Generally, Central and South Americans and "other" Hispanics tend to have characteristics that resemble the Cubans rather than the Mexican-American or Puerto Rican populations. The median age of Central and South Americans and "other" Hispanics is 27.9 and 31.0 years, respectively. Both groups tend to be highly educated. Approximately 15.1 percent of Central and South Americans and 16.2 percent of "other" Hispanics have four or more years of college.

Both groups also have a relatively high occupational status, with 12.7 percent of males and 14.5 percent of females of the Central and South American groups holding managerial and professional occupations; the respective figures for "other" Hispanics is 20.5 percent for males and 19.8 percent for females. At the lower end of the occupational hierarchy, Central and South Americans and "other" Hispanics tend to mirror the situation of Cubans, Mexican Americans, and Puerto Ricans in that there is a relatively large number of males concentrated in the operators, fabricators, and laborers category and a large number of females concentrated in the service occupations.

THE FAMILY ♦

The family is considered the single most important institution in the social organization of Hispanics. It is through the family and its activities that all people relate to significant others in their lives and it is through the family that people communicate with the larger society. The family incorporates the idea of *la familia* (the greater family), which includes in addition to the immediate nuclear household, relatives that are traced on both the female and male sides. These include parents, grandparents, brothers and sisters, cousins, and to a certain extent any blood relatives that can be identified through the hierarchy of family surnames. This broad-ranging concept has important consequences for actual social and cultural behavior. It places individuals as well as nuclear families into a recognizable network of social relations within which mutual support and reciprocity occur.

Important supportive institutions of la familia include the extended family, *parentesco* (the concept of familism), *compadrazgo* (godparenthood), *confianza* (trust), and family ideology. Among Hispanics, family ideology sets the ideal and standards to which individuals aim; it is the guiding light to which all look and attempt to shape their behavior for themselves as well as for the perception others have of them. It holds all individuals together and all individuals should put family before their own concerns. It is the means of social and cultural existence. Family ideology also defines the ideal roles and behaviors of family members. The ideal family is a patriarchy that revolves around a strong male figure who is ultimately responsible for the well-being of all individuals "under his roof." The concept of "machismo" is embedded in this ideal, in which men are viewed as virile, aggressive, and answerable only to themselves. In real life, however, this is rarely realized. Degrees of male authoritarianism vary both within and across groups, but for the most part women are strong contributors to decision making and are often the internal authority figures in the family. In both subtle and direct ways, women not only contribute to decision making but often have the authority in the family. This is contrary to the stereotype in which the woman is viewed as subservient and deferent to "her man" and that child rearing and household chores should be her main concern. In fact, one of the greatest of changes in the Hispanic family in the United States is in the woman's role. A very high percentage of households are headed by women, especially among Puerto Ricans in New York. However, family ideology continues to be verbally expressed as a value and cultural norm, often in contradiction to actual family behavior.

A child's birthday party,
New York City.

Children should be subservient and show respect to all elders, *respeto* (respect) being a concept held by all individuals. In a variety of studies in education, Hispanic children, especially those of new migrants, do behave in a "culturally prescribed manner" that is congruent with family ideology. However, as in all other aspects of family ideology among Hispanics, children's roles have experienced drastic changes. Education in the American system and exposure to people outside the immediate family and network of relatives has affected children in many ways. Children often become the social brokers between their parents and the outside world. They are the best speakers of English and know society's cultural nuances more thoroughly than parents.

Hispanic groups in the United States do not generally live in an extended family household. The reality is that Hispanics tend to favor the nuclear family and a separate household. The extended family living in single households is generally a transitory stage in family and household development. It is seen primarily during the migrant stages of first arrival when newcomers need support and help in adjusting and finding their way in a new environment. The reality of the extended Hispanic family is that it transcends geographical barriers and has functioning units in both the country of origin as well as in the United States. It is in this sense that the institution of the family has taken on a hybrid form through the strategic expression of migrants adapting to a new environment.

Hispanics have used the extended family in conjunction with other kinship institutions that form part of the greater familia and family ideology. As in the family in general, the Catholic religion has had a very strong influence in familia institutions. Religious rites of baptism and marriage take on special meaning that have evolved into sociocultural expressions important among Hispanics in the United States. Compadrazgo (godparenthood), marriage, and parentesco (kinship sentiment) are primary institutions that need to be understood in relation to the family. These are multidimensional elements that together help maintain la familia. Compadrazgo is formed usually through the baptism of a child, with parents choosing *padrinos* (godparents) from close friends or relatives. Compadrazgo is the extension of kinship to nonrelatives and the strengthening of responsibilities between kin. Padrinos also sponsor the child in baptism and confirmation ceremonies. They are also chosen to be best man and bridesmaid at weddings. *Compadres* (co-parents) ideally have special responsibilities toward the godchild and in the past have been expected to take the parental role if parents were to pass away, except in the case of marriage sponsorship. This special parental relationship is maintained throughout life. In addition, although not recognized in much of the literature, the *ahijado/a* (godchild) has a special responsibility towards the padrino. This is manifested in varying degrees, but can be seen when the padrino is elderly; ahijados may pay special attention almost as if the padrino/a were a grandparent.

Confianza (trust) is of particular importance to both the institutions of compadrazgo and parentesco among Hispanics in the United States, and is the basis of the relationships between individuals in many spheres of social activity. It is evident in business relations among entrepreneurs who work on the basis of trust, and among friendships in which trust is fundamental. But confianza goes beyond relationships between individuals and forms the underlying base of reciprocity of all types. Confianza is the primary factor that builds relationships and forms the basis for trust in the institutions of parentesco and compadrazgo. In a sense, the combined expression and practice of compadrazgo and parentesco produce the continued trust that is expressed as confianza. To have confianza with an in-

The José Carmona family
of Kansas City.

dividual is not just to regard that person with trust, but to regard the relationship with special sentiment, respect, and intimacy. Confianza developed in friendship can, for example, lead to a relationship of compadrazgo and to expressing parentesco to individuals who are not kin, as for example an individual who is from a home region and is a friend or compadre of kin.

The institution of marriage varies tremendously among Hispanics in the United States, and like the family in general has been adapted to a number of different socioeconomic conditions. The value of a religious wedding is not, nor has it ever been, the sole means for recognizing unions between men and women. Among Dominicans, for example, marital unions consist of *matrimonio por la iglesia* (church wedding), *matrimonio por ley* (civil marriage), and *unión libre* (free union). Church weddings carry higher prestige and are more prevalent among persons of higher socioeconomic status, but free unions allow for early cohabitation in the migrant settlement. Marriage, however, has been an institution that strengthens extended family ties and incorporates individuals and their kin into network alliances under parentesco. Marriage, in addition to its important function of uniting conjugal pairs in critical household formation and procreation of children, is an institution used in the primary adaptive processes to the United States. Marriage among Hispanics continues to be within their own group (endogamous), that is, Mexicans marrying Mexicans, Puerto Ricans marrying Puerto Ricans, and so on. Some intermarriage happens between groups, but this is infrequent, and there is a growing rate of intermarriage with Anglo-Americans, especially among second-generation Hispanics. This is especially true of Mexican Americans.

HISPANIC WOMEN'S ISSUES ✦ ✦ ✦ ✦ ✦ ✦ ✦ ✦ ✦ ✦ ✦ ✦ ✦ ✦ ✦ ✦ ✦ ✦ ✦

**Traditional
Attitudes
Regarding Hispanic
Female Roles**

The traditional cultural stereotype of the Hispanic female is based on a dualistic perspective of the sexes and a strong belief in appropriate roles for each gender. Traditional attitudes regarding female roles are also informed by the assumption that "natural" gender roles exist, and any deviation is deemed inappropriate. Hence, females and males are strongly encouraged to accept the prescribed gender roles. These include submissive behavior for females and aggressive behavior for males. The wife is expected to accept the husband's role as absolute authority. The woman is characterized as self-sacrificing to the needs of others and confined to the home. She is to be nurturing to husband and children. A woman's primary function is to bear and raise her husband's children. Training for these roles begins early. In childhood, girls are expected to help with the housework and care for the other children. Boys are given more freedom than girls and expected to learn what roles each will assume as adults.

The most traditional role of the female is to be wife and mother. Her domain becomes the home, the private realm, and not the public realm. The male is expected to take on the responsibilities for providing for the family and engaging in the public realm. He is the ultimate authority in the family. Among the roles of children, a daughter must always be responsive to the males in the family. A female is the responsibility first of her father and then her husband. Self-autonomy and independence are considered inappropriate for a female and are labeled selfish. The quality of selflessness is the highest, most treasured quality in a female. It is the female who is traditionally allowed to be emotional. The male is expected to remain a stoic individual and is commonly discouraged from expressing his emotions. Traditionally, it is the female who is expected to uphold and defend the moral code of the community. She is expected to follow the strictly defined code more vehemently than the male. This is also true for religion. Religious rituals and beliefs are the responsibility of the female. She is the spiritual and moral leader of the family.

Officially, Hispanic communities are patriarchal, and yet slowly women have gained power in the public realm, subverting traditional gender roles. For example, Puerto Rico is considered a male-centered society, yet San Juan had a female mayor, Felisa Rincón de Gautier. During the Mexican Revolution of 1910, women played an important role and became national heroes. The first acknowledged Mexican poet was Sor Juana Inés de la Cruz, a woman. Traditional gender attitudes, which informed women of the importance of passive, nurturing behavior, did not stop women from seeking power in and outside the family.

Although the Hispanic communities have a strong investment in traditional gender roles and attitudes toward them, throughout history stereotypes of Hispanic women as passive and subservient family members have been somewhat inaccurate.

Hispanics and Women's Liberation

The American women's movement and heightened consciousness about forms of oppression has politicized some Hispanic women who have become active in women's organizations. Nevertheless, the contact between Hispanic women and feminists has been limited. Few Hispanic women become members of feminist organizations. The reasons for the limited participation include racism within those organizations and the sense by Hispanics that an underlying assumption of feminism is an attempt to destroy the concept of family.

The women's movement is seen by the Hispanic community as destructive to the common good of the family. The movement also carries assumptions about the importance of independence and self-autonomy, a direct challenge to traditional Hispanic attitudes concerning the importance of relationships to family and community. As critics of the women's movement some Hispanic women, such as Margarita Melville in *Twice a Minority: Mexican American Women* and Marta Cotera in her writing, argue that the feminist movement is alienating to Hispanic women because of its devaluation of traditional values. What has emerged from Hispanic women's experience with feminism is an acknowledgment by Hispanic feminists of pride in their traditional heritage but with a realistic attitude toward its limitations, as well as an acknowledgment of the limitations of feminism. For example, African-American women first discussed feminism's ignorance of cultural differences, creating the space for development of Hispanic feminism.

Hispanic women who have become interested in the women's movement have often found themselves accused of "selling out" their culture— vendidas.

Hispanic feminism is different from mainstream feminism because it tries to accommodate cultural traditions and spiritual issues. Concerns that Hispanic feminism attempts to address include economic and educational needs and child care, as well as how those issues are affected in the context of Hispanic cultural traditions. While the women's movement has focused attention on issues concerning gender inequality, traditional gender roles were already in the process of being challenged and questioned. The women's movement provided the example and the language with which Hispanic women could challenge traditional attitudes toward women's roles.

One of the realities that comes with change is the accompanying high level of stress. Tension and discomfort within families increase with change. Marital strife seems to be a product of the renegotiation of gender roles. Children are also given confused signals as to appropriate and inappropriate behavior. Feminism has created more questions than answers.

While economic necessity sent Hispanic women into the work force originally, women now have more options as to their roles in society. They may opt for a traditional role or a nontraditional one, or a combination of the two, spending a certain period of their time in traditional roles and then moving on to the work force.

One of the most important attributes of Hispanic women is their diversity. To consider them all alike is to take away from their identity and simplify their complex world. So when we discuss Hispanic women, we must also keep in mind what diversity means within that group.

Hispanic women make up approximately 4.5 percent of the U.S. population. Within that group are several subgroups, including Mexican-Americans, Puerto Ricans, Cubans, Dominicans, and natives of the specific regions of Central and South America. Each subgroup can trace specific cultural traditions to their region of origin. For example, the Caribbean influence on Puerto Rican and Cuban women in the United States is different from the Mexican influence on Mexican-American women.

Class status levels among Hispanic women are as varied as in the mainstream society: working class, middle class, upper class, white collar, blue collar. Depending on the individual, her values may represent her class more than her culture.

Another important difference among Hispanic women is educational level. A large proportion have had no formal education. Then there are those who have had formal education but have not completed high school; this is a large segment of the population, reflecting the less than 50 percent high school graduation rate among Hispanics. The attitudes and values expressed by these women are influenced by their education.

Education

Fewer than half of Hispanics graduate from high school, and in certain communities the dropout rate is almost 75 percent. Also, most Hispanic parents of adolescents do not possess a college degree. In five states with some of the highest concentrations of Hispanics, only 7 percent of Hispanics hold college degrees. There are very few educated role models for adolescent girls. The pattern these girls see consistently is that of a woman who has quit school. Among Hispanic women, who are becoming single heads of household in ever-increasing numbers, few even have high school degrees. In addition, of those who do graduate from high school, fewer than half enroll in college. And the majority of those who do attempt higher education enter two-year colleges. For Hispanic girls, low aspirations are the norm conveyed to them. The pattern that emerges is that of an undereducated, underskilled population of women who are fast becoming single parents. However, as mentioned earlier, Hispanic women are beginning to recognize the necessity for education in order to find employment opportunities and are beginning to return to school.

The differences that define Hispanic women can be understood as the same differences that define all individuals: cultural traditions, language, class, education, religious affiliation and race. The diversity that exists in the general population also exists in the subgroups of Hispanics.

Employment has become one of the most important issues Hispanic women face. Now that many of the traditional roles for women have been challenged, they face the stresses of seeking and keeping employment. In 1981, among Hispanic women over age twenty, approximately 50 percent were employed. That number has consistently grown, and Hispanic women are more likely to be employed in service industries or clerical work than in other areas. Hispanic women are also more likely to earn a great deal less than most of the population. The U.S. Bureau of the Census (1985) reports that Hispanic men earn approximately 75 percent of what the Anglo male population earns. Anglo women earn approximately 72 percent of what Anglo men earn. And Hispanic women earn 62 percent of what the Anglo males earn. Another pattern emerges: Hispanic women are consistently underemployed and underpaid. These employment patterns show the status of Hispanic women in the economic realm. They are some of the lowest paid workers in the country.

Employment

Single Heads of Household and Child Care

Hispanic women are becoming single heads of household in ever-increasing numbers. As women assume the roles of traditional heads of household, child care becomes a necessary issue. Faced with the limited availability of affordable child care, Hispanic women may find themselves unable to afford to work. They stay at home to care for their children and find themselves unable to meet monetary needs. Unable to find affordable child care, they turn to the state for assistance.

One response of many Hispanics to the shortage of affordable child care is to turn to the extended family. Many Hispanic children are cared for by their grandmothers or aunts. The ability to turn to members of the family is one of the strengths of Hispanic culture. The closeness of Hispanic families allows a woman to turn to her mother or sister or some family member in times of need. For many Hispanic women this closeness is a double-edged sword. Along with the closeness comes a sense of not having any privacy, as well as feeling suffocated by the abundance of nurturing. Common among Hispanic women is an inability to acknowledge individuality. These women only know themselves in relation to their parents, their children, their husband. Once they decide to assert their individuality, they find themselves faced with emotional stress.

For many Hispanic women, issues of survival for themselves and their children continue to be the most immediate concern. Undereducated, underemployed, and with a very high reproductive rate compared with other groups in the nation, these women face the harsh issue of day-to-day survival.

Health Issues

Health issues of Hispanic women have only recently begun to be explored by the medical establishment. Already documented, however, are several common ailments. For example, evidence indicates that Hispanic women, because of their traditional cultural diet, are at high risk for diabetes.

Another issue is the ability to pay for health services. Many Hispanic women are underinsured or have no health insurance. Many hold jobs like housekeeping and farm work that provide very limited or no health benefits. As with the rest of the population, the inability to receive affordable health care is quickly reaching crisis levels.

There exists a truly invisible Hispanic woman—the illegal alien. Without immigration papers, usually with no formal education and no skills in English, the Hispanic woman who is not a citizen or legal alien in the United States is silenced and invisible. Estimates vary as to the number of illegal aliens. They continue to be the most exploited members of the Hispanic community.

Many of these women work in the fields as migrant workers. Farmers are able to pay substandard wages and not fear government reprisal because these workers hold no legal rights in the United States and hence will not report them. These women also work in service industries, as unskilled laborers and as housekeepers. Because of their illegal status and limited English, an underground community exists in the midst of U.S. society.

Illegal Aliens

A cultural and personal concern for Hispanic women is religion. While most Hispanic women are Catholic, many are beginning to question much of the traditional attitudes the church has about women. As Catholic dogma is very clear as to the status of women—subservience to man and God—women are beginning to test the limits of dogma. Admittedly, few Hispanic women actively voice their opposition to the dictates of the Catholic church; a more quiet revolution is actually occurring. For example, the Catholic church does not condone artificial forms of birth control, yet more and more Hispanic women are seeking birth control.

Religion

Traditionally, the woman's position in the Catholic church has been to serve the needs of the community. Women have not been allowed to participate in the Mass except as members of the congregation. If a woman wanted a more active role in the church, she became a nun and lived in a world separate from all males and laypersons. The leadership and power within the church was reserved only for priests. However, in the past thirty years the church has encouraged a more active role for women. Clearly, a change has occurred in the status of women within the traditional ceremony, allowing both male and female laypersons to participate in the Mass. In its own ranks, the church still continues the practice of limiting and designating certain duties to either the priest or the nun. The most exalted positions within the Catholic church—priest, bishop, cardinal, pope—continue to be reserved only for men. The leadership of the church continues to remain the domain of men.

Politics   In the political realm, Hispanic women continue to be underrepresented, if not ignored. No research has been done on the voting patterns of Hispanic women. What is now becoming more readily available is the voting patterns for Hispanic communities. Whether or not Hispanic women differ from Hispanic men in their political participation is unclear.

Politically, Hispanic women are just beginning to make an impact, symbolized by three Hispanic women currently serving in Congress. Hispanic women politicians are active at the city and county level, and the pattern suggests that as they continue to gain more experience in politics at the local levels they will move on to the state and national political arenas.

Hispanic women have many diverse concerns, as do all women. The fear, however, is that Hispanic women will continue to be invisible politically. This may change with continued growth in the community, the recognition of Hispanic women by politicians, businesses, and researchers, and the demands that Hispanic women themselves will make. The tradition of subservience, silence, and passivity will need to be changed if Hispanic women are to make a greater impact on the general society.

HISPANIC CHILDREN AND YOUTH ♦ ♦ ♦ ♦ ♦ ♦ ♦ ♦ ♦ ♦ ♦ ♦ ♦ ♦ ♦

Early in the next century Hispanic children will constitute the majority of the school enrollment in the nation's most populous states: California, New York, Texas, and Florida. They are already approaching or have surpassed those figures in such urban centers as Los Angeles, Houston, and New York City. With "white flight" to the suburbs and the rapid growth of private schools in the United States, more racial segregation in the nation's schools may exist today than before the momentous *Brown v. Board of Education* decision in 1954. Hispanic and African-American youths are not only racially isolated in schools, they are the segment of society most adversely directly affected by social policy and trends that have turned the inner cities into havens for unemployment, drug culture, and rampant crime. With dropout rates as high as 80 percent in some urban school districts and their parents already making up the ranks of the working poor, Hispanic youth is destined to an underclass life of unemployment, marginalization, and internment by the criminal justice system.

An underperforming economy at the close of the century, coupled with increased immigration from Latin America, has created considerable anti-immigrant sentiment in the states traditionally most welcoming of entrants to the lower end of the labor pool: California, Florida, New York, and Texas. Politicians and nativists have created a bandwagon of complaints and protests decrying the high costs of absorbing immigrants, supposedly with welfare, education, and the criminal justice system ranking highest. And high among proposals by politicians is the withholding of public education to children of undocumented immigrants. This follows

Guadalupe Aztlan school children, Houston, Texas.

upon years of onslaught against the use of foreign languages, and Spanish in particular, by the "English Only" movement.

The microcosm of Hispanic at-risk youth is a segment of the society with among the highest rates of teen pregnancy and affliction with AIDS, both because of intravenous drug use and high levels of prostitution. Unless youths in general in the United States are attended to in a better and more humane manner, Hispanic youth in particular will continue to be endangered and also represent a considerable danger to society as a whole.

THE FUTURE OF THE HISPANIC PEOPLE ✦ ✦ ✦ ✦ ✦ ✦ ✦ ✦ ✦ ✦ ✦ ✦

Clearly, Hispanics represent the fastest growing population in the United States. They have always constituted an important, although unrecognized, resource for the country, providing from the early days of the Republic the human and technological resources that would eventually make the Southwest, in particular, a richly endowed contributor to the national economy and the national identity. Whereas Hispanics were political expatriates and welcomed immigrants in the early states of the Republic, by the turn of this century they were Americans by conquest of the northern half of Mexico and of Puerto Rico and Cuba. During the twentieth century they have been economic and political refugees to the United States in direct proportion to the growth of this country's political and economic imperialism. The cumulative effect of this three-centuries-long relationship will result in the twenty-first century in Hispanics becoming omnipresent in every sector of U.S. society as this diverse group becomes the largest minority in the United States and ascends to economic and political power.

But the group will have to bear the brunt of developing solutions to its internal organization—particularly the limits placed upon the role of women in its families and in the workplace, and the racism and tension within and among Hispanics themselves. External issues also require creative answers: prejudice against and segregation of Hispanics in education, unemployment and underemployment, crime and drug use, poor health services, the ravages of diseases such as AIDS, and the reappearance of illnesses once thought eradicated in the United States, such as tuberculosis and bubonic plague.

What is sure to attend the Hispanicization of the United States in the twenty-first century is a new definition of political and economic borders as well as of linguistic and cultural borders. The approval of the North American Free Trade Aggreement places the United States, Canada, and Mexico well on the road to an integration of the three largest economies of the hemisphere, leading to a unified workforce, a common currency, and tricultural-trilingual (English, Spanish, and French) commerce.

The growth of Spanish-language print and electronic media, not only in the United States but throughout the hemisphere, will reinforce and preserve the language and cultural identity of Hispanics into the far-off future. Currently three Spanish-language television networks broadcast the same programs and sentiments by satellite the length of the hemisphere, far outstripping the reach of English-language television. And those three networks are headquartered in the United States! Where the airwaves and cables go, so will print culture, as well as other forms of material and expressive culture. The next century is sure to solidify and further integrate not only Hispanism in the United States but among the Spanish-American republics, as well, who are also ready to integrate their economies with an eye towards total hemispheric economic integration into the future. From this hemispheric perspective, the role of Hispanics and Hispanic culture in the United States becomes central to developing potential for becoming the central hub for negotiations in all spheres of life of the Hispanophone, Anglophone, and Francophone Americas.

With the end of the Cold War and the attendant resolution of regional conflicts, particularly in Central America, and the return of governments to democratic rather than autocratic rule in the Southern Cone, some of the traditional barriers to isolationism and discord among the Spanish American republics may have met sufficient terminus to prepare the Southern Hemisphere for economic integration. But both Mexico and the countries of the Southern Hemisphere have to share the benefits of economic advancement more equitably in their societies, with particular attention to the long-marginalized and exploited indigenous populations, as illustrated by the stength of powerful guerrilla movements, such as the Shining Path in Peru and the Zapatista Liberation Army in Chiapas, Mexico. The United States interpretation of stability in Latin America can no longer be the support of dictators and oligarchies, nor can United States industry continue to encourage degradation of the environment and undermine the organization of labor by relocating to Latin America industries that inordinately exploit human and natural resources. These larger issues all determine the destiny of Hispanics in the United States, which

Economic, Political, and Cultural Integration

has always been conditioned by the dynamics of international trade and politics.

It is not surprising, then, that the future of Hispanics depends on many factors that are regional, national, and international in scope. Hispanism is an international identity. It is bilingual, bicultural, multinational, multiracial. How Hispanics interact on national and international levels will help to define the prosperity or bankruptcy of hemispheric life in the next century.

History

This chapter presents an historical overview of the major Hispanic groups that have made their home in the United States, focusing on peoples from Mexico, Puerto Rico, and Cuba. While each group is unique unto itself, several factors deeply rooted in the formation of their national and cultural identity bind them together. Foremost among these are their link to Spain and the geographical proximity the nations share within the Caribbean and the Gulf of Mexico.

SPANISH LEGACY ♦

The Spanish spoken in the two Caribbean islands and in Mexico had its roots in Spain, because it is from there that the main thrust of colonization took place. The Castilian language spoken in Spain can be traced to a long evolution that began with the earliest human inhabitants of the Iberian Peninsula more than fifty thousand years ago.

Mexicans, Cubans, and Puerto Ricans share many things in common. The main language spoken by the groups is Spanish, most are Roman Catholic, and much of their folklore is similar.

The presence of Paleolithic man (game hunters and cave dwellers) in the Iberian Peninsula is known because of archaeological evidence left by the culture, the most famous being cave drawings of the animals on which the dwellers depended for food. More advanced cultures are known as Iberian but not much is known about these early agricultural and village people except that they migrated to the peninsula from Africa several thousand years before the birth of Christ.

A few centuries later, about 1000 B.C., a wave of Celtic warriors, hunters, and part-time keepers of livestock converged on the peninsula from somewhere in present-day Hungary near the Danube River. They mixed with the Iberians and established a unique Iberian-Celtic culture. These Gaelic-speaking nomads eventually settled in almost every part of Europe. The strongest cultural vestiges with which most Americans are familiar are those of Scotland, Wales, and Ireland. In Spain and France, cultural manifestations from the Celtic period are also evident, although not as salient as in the British Isles. There is, for example, in northwest Spain a province known as Galicia, where Gaelic characteristics have lingered to the present time. There, such Gaelic modes as the bagpipe and the kilt are used in ceremonies.

Gaelic culture in the rest of Spain, however, was overwhelmed by a series of invasions and colonization efforts, which shortly before the birth of Christ greatly transformed the linguistic, racial, and economic systems of the peninsula. The first interlopers having significant influence in the evolution of the peninsula were the Greeks and the Phoenicians, who arrived about the same time as the Celts. Both groups went to Iberia to mine tin and establish a series of trading outposts. They were not prodigious colonizers, and Iberian-Celtic culture remained strong, although over time the more advanced cultural expression of the Greeks and Phoenicians became diffused among the earlier settlers. The Iberian-Celts developed sculpture and other artistic motifs that significantly took on the characteristics of Greek classical realism, and they borrowed technological innovations, such as transportation vehicles and mining techniques.

Later in the second century B.C. Carthage, a civilization centered along a large portion of the North African coast that was greatly influenced by Greek achievements, challenged the expansion of the Roman Empire in Europe and Africa. The Carthaginians were not successful in the Iberian Peninsula, however. They were able to wrest authority over the region away from the Greeks, but in 133 B.C., the Romans defeated the Carthaginian army at Numantia. This was just one of the many Roman victories that ensured the expansion of Rome into most of Europe, including the Iberian Peninsula.

The Roman colonization of Iberia was classic in every sense of the word. Unlike previous invaders, such as the Greeks, Phoenicians, and Carthaginians, they settled in, families and all, subordinated and enslaved the natives, and set up a plantation system based on slave labor. They remained in the peninsula until their empire began to crumble about A.D. 400.

From the Latin-speaking Romans, Iberia acquired some of its most significant linguistic, cultural, political, and economic institutions, in turn giving Spain and Latin America many of their present-day characteristics.

Castilian, the language we now call Spanish, became the dominant language everywhere in the Iberian Peninsula except Portugal. The kingdom of Castile managed to conquer and dominate every other region of Iberia except Portugal. It was the Romans who distinguished between the western and eastern parts of the peninsula, giving the name "Hispania" to the east and "Lusitania" to the west. The word "Spain" came from "Hispania," and although Portugal did not retain "Lusitania" as a place-name, any term associated with that country or its language is still prefixed by "Luso-," just as "Hispanic" refers to Spain or its heritage.

The political system introduced by the Romans had a profound effect on the evolution of government structures at all levels in Spain, and by extension, in its colonies in Spanish America. Perhaps the most enduring feature of this legacy is the careful attention given to the formation of city political culture. The Romans called this process *civitas.* Anyone who travels in almost any town in Latin America can see a faithful replication of the town square, or *plaza,* with its main Catholic church engulfed in a carefully drawn complex of government buildings dominated by the municipal or state center. The Romans also thought that it was the responsibility of government to build a bathhouse, an amphitheater, and a coliseum near the town center, regardless of the size of the town. This tradition, of course, was followed in Latin America, where one can find similar institutions, even in small villages, if only in modest proportions. In the United States, such a civic impulse is certainly present, but not to the same degree as in Latin America. Many U.S. towns and cities took their shape in response to purely economic exigencies, and then some planning, or virtually none at all, followed.

The legal and judicial system in Latin America is quite different from the common law tradition familiar to people living in England and its former colonies. The Latin American judicial system, drawn from the Napoleonic Code, does not have juries. Rather, judges make the final decisions on all cases brought before the courts.

Apart from their language and governmental legacies, the Romans were influential in other areas as well. For example, the large farms and ranches found in Latin America, typical of the landholding system in Spain and Portugal, came from the Roman plantation system known as *latifundia*. Finally, Christianity, especially Catholicism, was one of Rome's most enduring legacies. In Iberia, the religion became Rome's greatest cultural and historical hallmark, to be spread even further one thousand years later when Spain embarked on its own powerful empire.

Other ethnic groups followed the Romans into Spain, leaving a continuing heritage that also is part of the Hispanic tradition throughout Latin America and in the United States. The most aggressive of these were Germanic tribes that had been migrating from Asia Minor, slowly penetrating every region where Rome held sway. Some Germanic tribes had been within the empire long enough to serve in Roman legions as mercenaries, and many others were romanized by them. When the Roman Empire fell, some of these Germanic tribes began to carve out their own fiefdoms along with other groups in the empire. But outside tribes, more barbaric and less inclined to Roman ways, poured into the former Roman realms, pillaging and carving out their own regional baronies. Vandals, Berbers, and Visigoths moved into the Iberian Peninsula but were eventually romanized. As Roman political influence declined, the Germanic clans, already having relinquished many aspects of their language, began to speak one of the variations of Latin evolving in the peninsula, and they embraced Christianity. The latter process was of such intensity that, as the Germanic tribes mixed with the inhabitants of Spain, who by then were an admixture of all the groups that had previously lived in Iberia, they all came to call themselves Christians as a means of identifying themselves ethnically.

The era known as the Dark Ages was named because the brilliance of Rome and all the achievements associated with the empire faded.

Iberia was now lapsing into the Dark Ages. This was the beginning of feudalism, an era in which hundreds of small baronies, carved out of the vastness of the Roman Empire, resorted to raiding each other for territor-

ial aggrandizement. The economic system that had held the empire together evaporated, leaving in its place a factional economic and political
system. Technologically, the Germanic tribes were underdeveloped, and
they depended a great deal on raising livestock. From the empire of Rome
they managed to salvage some rudimentary metallurgical and other techniques of production. Because a great part of their lives were spent raiding
and pillaging, the tribes introduced to Iberia a warrior cult, which was
perhaps the most important cultural ingredient of their society. Along
with this came the rigid code of conduct that usually accompanied such
societies. Adherence to Christianity, once they entered into former Roman
realms, added a religious fervor to the military code. This impulse found
its expression throughout Christian Europe in the Crusades against the
Muslim peoples and in Iberia in a phenomenon known as the Reconquest.

Perhaps Iberia would have remained under the solid sway of feudalism, as
did the rest of Europe, if it had not been for the invasion of Arabic-speak-
ing Muslims from North Africa in the beginning of the eighth century.
More commonly known as the Moors, these latest newcomers to the
peninsula remained for eight hundred years and, next to the Romans, had
the greatest influence on the culture of the Iberians. The invasion was
spurred by the rise of an Islamic expansion impulse in North Africa that
quickly engulfed the Persian Gulf all the way to India and north into
southern Europe. This expansion was inspired by a religious fervor left
after the life of Mohammed, the founder of Islam, who was born in Mecca
in the seventh century A.D.

The first Moors crossed the Strait of Gilbraltar in A.D. 711, and they
brought to the peninsula such an advanced culture that its merits could
not help but influence the moribund feudal structure left in the wake of
Rome's decline. The Muslims left few stones unturned in their quest for
technological and philosophical knowledge, borrowing and improving on
much of what was known to the world at the time. From the Far East they
acquired advanced metallurgical skills, including the making of steel, and
medicinal knowledge. In the civilizations of the West, Muslims stemmed
the decline of Greek and Roman philosophical, agricultural, and architectural systems.

The Moors pushed the Christians all the way to the northern reaches of
Iberia, but many Christians remained behind Moorish lines, where they
were tolerated and allowed to maintain and evolve their Christian and
Castilian cultures. Along with the Moors came thousands of Jews, who

Years of survival in the desert engendered among the Arabs thorough knowledge of how to preserve and manage water resources. This ability, which they put to good use in much of the semiarid peninsula, was a useful inheritance for the Spaniards who settled in similar terrain in the Americas.

were also tolerated in Islamic domains, and many of whom served as merchants, teachers, and medical practitioners in such great Muslim cities as Sevilla, Granada, and Cordoba.

The surge that pushed the Christians north lasted until the eleventh century, when the Moorish caliphate of Cordoba began to disintegrate into smaller, less-effective kingdoms. The Christian Castilians then embarked on a protracted effort to regain the lands they had lost to the Moors in the previous three hundred years. This Reconquest was attempted piecemeal fashion, since Castilians could not mount unified efforts, because both their economic and political systems were feudal.

The Reconquest lasted until 1492, when King Boabdil was ousted from Granada, the last Moorish stronghold, by the forces of the Castilian queen Isabella and her Aragonese husband, Ferdinand. The marriage of these two monarchs from neighboring Iberian kingdoms in 1469 unified the two largest kingdoms on the peninsula and eventually led to the entire unification of Spain. However, the whole peninsula was not to be consolidated in this fashion because the Portuguese, in the western portion of Iberia, had managed by themselves to defeat and eject the Arab caliphs at the beginning of the fifteenth century, before Castile did.

Before the Catholic Kings, as Ferdinand and Isabella came to be known, could effectively accomplish this unity, however, the power of the feudal lords acquired by partition of former Moorish caliphates had to be curbed. Ferdinand and Isabella accomplished this by several means. First, they embarked on establishing political institutions that challenged the local rule of the nobility. Then, they linked the long struggle of the Reconquest to their own process of consolidation, thus appropriating the nascent nationalism evoked by that struggle to unify the disparate baronies of the peninsula.

In 1492, the Catholic Kings expelled the Moors and the Jews from Spain. In 1493, they acquired from Pope Alexander VI, who himself had been born in Spain, the papal patronage. This was a concession of major proportions, because it gave the Spanish monarchs complete dominion over the operations of the Catholic church in Spain. As one can imagine, this was a vehicle of great advantage for the consolidation efforts envisioned by the two monarchs.

The long initial struggle to fend off and finally push out the Moors engendered in the Germanic Castilians an even more resilient warrior culture that by 1492 was, no doubt, the most salient expression of their society. Values such as valor, honor, audacity, and tenacity were highly prized. But the Castilians inherited many other positive characteristics from the many groups that had invaded and inhabited Iberia. Little was lost from such exposure, so when Columbus sailed and encountered the New World in 1492, Spain was truly a compendium of its multiethnic past. This complexity of cultures became the Hispanic stamp imprinted on its colonies in the New World.

Columbus's fateful voyage certainly changed the course of history. It opened a vast new region for exploration and exploitation for the Europeans.

♦ ♦ ♦ ♦ ♦ ♦ ♦ ♦ **THE INDIGENOUS CARIBBEAN POPULATIONS**

In Mexico, some twenty-five million Indians lived in the confines of what are now the central regions of the country. Their civilization was quite advanced, and in spite of major efforts by the Spaniards to eradicate indigenous culture, much has remained to this day. But in the Caribbean, the Indians were fewer in numbers, and they were not as developed as those on the Mexican and South American mainland. Tragically, cultural and racial genocide took a greater toll in the Caribbean. The indigenous populations there were greatly reduced almost from the outset of the colonization process because of diseases, brought over by Spaniards, to which the Indians had no immunities. Nonetheless, the inhabitants of Cuba and Puerto Rico have retained many vestiges of indigenous society. The largest non-Hispanic influence in the Caribbean came from Africa. Thousands of slaves were brought over first to work the mines, then to work the large sugar plantations that served the Spaniards as the mainstay of the island economies. Today the vestiges of this important heritage are seen in much of Caribbean culture and, of course, in the racial makeup of Caribbean peoples.

The indigenous groups in the Caribbean were mainly Carib and Arawak, who lived in seminomadic villages throughout the Greater and Lesser Antilles (which make up the bulk of the Caribbean islands), and as far south as the coasts of what are today Venezuela and the Guineas. The Carib were considered by the Spaniards to be fiercer than the Arawak, but both groups hunted, fished, and gathered wild plants such as the manioc root for food.

Their way of life had evolved very little in thousands of years. Since the traditional methods of obtaining food had always yielded results, few incentives existed for innovation. Their lives revolved around villages that they were prone to abandon when economic need dictated. Politically, they depended on a council of elders for guidance. Religious beliefs were linked to the hunting-gathering economy, and they relied primarily on shamans for observance of rituals. Village homes required very little to build. Those using palm leaves and wood ribbing were among the most sophisticated. Some lived in dugouts that were called *barbacoas*.

When the Spaniards moved on to the Central American mainland, they remembered the word barbacoas *and applied it to the cooking of meat in pits, a common form of preparation in central Mexico. Hence, the word "barbecue" has stuck to this day.*

Before the Spanish Conquest, the Taino Indians, an Arawakan group that dominated the islands of Cuba and Puerto Rico, had a highly developed social and political system. In the twelfth century, they had displaced, throughout the Antilles, the less developed Ciboney, who lived in cavelike dwellings and who foraged and fished to survive. Taino-Arawak settlement was based on fishing and extensive planting of corn, squash, and chile, the same foodstuffs cultivated on the Mexican mainland. Because of extensive dependence on fishing, the Taino had an extraordinary maritime ability and moved from island to island setting up villages whose populations numbered in the hundreds. But shortly before the Spanish occupation of the Greater Antilles, warlike Carib Indians swept into the Caribbean and drove many of the Arawak out and captured their women. As a result, to the Spaniards, Arawak became known as a language of females. Like the Arawak, the Carib were excellent sailors who crossed much of the Caribbean in huge canoes that were fitted with woven cloth sails and carried as many as fifty people.

The simple lifestyle of these island people was drastically altered after the arrival of Columbus and the Spaniards. The first island settled by the Europeans was Hispaniola, which is the present-day Dominican Republic. Columbus naively ordered his translator to enter into negotiations with the Great Mogul of India, insisting, as he did until his death in 1506, that he had found a direct route to India by sailing west from Spain. As quickly deduced by everyone, except Columbus it seems, what the great discoverer had encountered was a gigantic landmass that blocked direct passage to the real India; even so, the name "Indies" stuck. The name "America" was adopted in northern Europe because of the writings of Amerigo Vespucci, the Italian cartographer who explored the newly found lands. The Spaniards, however, always referred to the New World as Las Indias.

The fate of these "Indians," so called because of the colossal miscalculation made by Columbus, was tragic beyond almost any other experience of indigenous peoples in the Americas. From their rude conquest Columbus and his settlers envisioned rewards that the natives were ill-prepared to deliver. Columbus, a Genoese from a seafaring merchant tradition, insisting that he was in Asia, expected to trade with the simple Carib and Arawak. The trouble was that the Caribbean natives had no surplus after they took care of their needs, and even if they had, their fare was of little use to Columbus in setting up trading posts.

Most of the Spanish settlers accompanying Columbus were steeped in the tradition of the Reconquest, and they counted on a subjugated population to do their bidding. They expected to establish feudal baronies. Columbus opposed such a tradition, but he capitulated nonetheless and gave his men *encomiendas*. Developed in feudal Spain, the encomienda was booty given to a Spanish conqueror of a Moorish caliphate. The award was usually the land that had belonged to the caliph, and according to Christian standards of the time, the prize was befitting a hero who had defeated the despised "infidels," as the Moorish Muslims were known. But just as the natives were unable to fit into Columbus's trade scheme, they were just as unsuited to provide labor or tribute, for that would have required them to have lived in a more sophisticated society.

The Spanish attempt to establish feudal baronies resulted in a debacle for all parties involved. But it was worse for the Indians, who were either worked to death in gold mines that yielded little gold or were forced to feed the demanding Spaniards. The result was mass starvation. The final blow in this endless chain of mistreatment was the introduction of European diseases, such as smallpox and measles, against which the natives had no immunities. This inadvertent intrusion was the most tragic of the European offerings. Numbering over one million in the Caribbean islands before Columbus's voyage, the Indians were eventually decimated. Indian lineage however, was not extinguished altogether. Numerous offspring resulted from the Spanish ravishing of Indian women, creating a small but formidable mestizo population, which continued the Indian genes in the islands.

The Conquest of Cuba

When Columbus and his Spanish sailors first arrived on the island that was named Cuba on October 27, 1492, they disregarded the Indian tribes that lived by subsistence agriculture and fishing. Columbus's attention was fixed on Hispaniola, where the first permanent Spanish colony had been established. It was not until 1508 that the island was systematically charted by Sebastián de Ocampo, who circumnavigated the island gathering information about the coastlines and harbors that would prove useful for the eventual occupation.

The first Spanish political system was not established in Cuba, however, until many years after Columbus's encounter with the natives of the Caribbean. Diego Velásquez de Cuéllar was commissioned governor of Cuba in 1511 after he had led an expedition that defeated the Arawak-Taino Indians. Velásquez, who first arrived in the New World at Hispaniola with Columbus's second voyage in 1493, was by then a veteran colonist with many years of experience in dealing with Caribbean natives. In the conquest, which was conducted in typical Spanish fashion, hundreds of men, women, and children were slaughtered. Many fled to the mountains or to other islands, such as Puerto Rico, only to be caught up with again in later expeditions.

Spared the encomienda for some nineteen years after the first arrival of Europeans in the Caribbean, Cuban Indians were finally subjected to the abhorrent institution after 1511. Columbus, who had expected trade, not feudal conquest, gave this prerogative to his men in Hispaniola, setting the precedent for the next sixty years of Spanish conquest. Giving this grant was against Columbus's better judgment, but he found that he had no choice because it seemed like the only way to reward the Spaniards who demanded some kind of prize for their participation in the momentous expedition.

Velásquez had no such scruples, and the parceling out of human beings proceeded in hasty fashion. Velásquez himself became a virtual feudal lord of Cuba, and by 1515 he founded what became Cuba's two largest cities, Santiago and Havana. His power was such that he directed the explorations of the Mexican Gulf Coast by Francisco Hernández de Córdoba and his nephew Juan de Grijalva. These expeditions betrayed the existence of civilizations in the interior of Mexico, prodding Velásquez to put his brother-in-law, Hernán Cortés, in charge of the expedition that resulted in the conquest of Mexico. Velásquez remained governor of Cuba until the 1520s, and, like that of other Spanish conquerors, his rule left an indelible stamp on the formation of Cuban society.

The initial Cuban economy, based on raising livestock and placer mining of gold, was propped up with labor provided by the ubiquitous encomienda. Because of the demand for pork, cattle hides, and gold in the other Spanish colonies, especially after the conquest of Mexico, Cuba provided tremendous opportunity for the first settlers.

Unfortunately, European disease and the forced labor in the mines took a grim toll and many Indians became ill and died, or were virtually worked to death. The amount of gold on the island was limited. Soon the supply was exhausted, frustrating the Spaniards to such a point that they made the Indians work harder so that decreasing sources could yield the same previous results. Indiscriminate livestock raising was also destructive to the Indian way of life. Huge, untended herds trampled the fragile crops, reducing the harvest on which the Indians depended as their main source of food. Ironically, the Spanish-based economy in Cuba declined very quickly because of competition from livestock raisers in Mexico and in other new colonies.

Velásquez had gotten rich in Hispaniola by engaging in the subjugation of whatever peoples he found. He repeated his endeavor in Cuba and prospered there as well.

Then, when silver was discovered in the Zacatecas province of Mexico and Potosí in Peru, a rush to these areas depopulated Cuba when many fickle Spaniards left to find riches elsewhere. They clamored to leave for newly conquered Mexico and Peru, even though the Crown futilely imposed harsh sanctions to those that deserted their encomiendas. The near-abandonment of the initial economy was so disastrous for the Indians that it makes their unwilling sacrifice even more tragic. The surviving indigenous groups must have wished that more of the exploitative Spaniards had left and never returned. But the Cuban economy revived. Because of the ideal position of the island, it became an entrepôt for silver coming from New Spain (roughly the area of present-day Mexico) and Peru and for European goods destined for the rich colonial markets.

Havana's fine harbor allowed the city to achieve dominance by the mid-sixteenth century, even though it did not become the capital of Cuba until 1607. The British and French, anxious to capture the booty offered by incoming ships, subjected the city to numerous attacks. Fortifications made the city safer, and it soon became the most important naval and commercial center for the Spanish colonies in the Caribbean. Ships with gold and silver from Mexico and South America were formed into fleets at Havana in the 1550s so that the Spanish navy could protect them from pirates during the journey back to Spain. By the eighteenth century, Havana was the New World's greatest port.

**The Conquest of
Puerto Rico**

Unlike Cuba, the island of Puerto Rico was not seen by Europeans until Columbus's second voyage to the New World in 1493. The Taino Indians living on the island called it Borinquen, but Columbus renamed it San Juan Bautista, even though he did not attempt to settle the island, concentrating instead on Hispaniola. As in Cuba, the Taino also received a few years of respite from the Spanish mistreatment. But sixteen years later, Ponce de León and a crew of fifty followers subdued the thirty thousand or so inhabitants of the island, and it was renamed Puerto Rico. The Spaniards overwhelmed the large population of Taino Indians by using terror tactics as they approached each village. Reducing the Indians' ability to resist Spanish incursions throughout the Caribbean was lack of cohesion and the poor communication among the scattered villages. If they had offered organized resistance, even in the face of superior weapons, horses, and other advantages held by the Spaniards, it would have been impossible for the Spaniards to succeed.

Puerto Rico means "rich port," and it was for the Spanish conquerers.

Following the pattern established in the Caribbean, in Puerto Rico the Spaniards immediately set out to raise livestock and other foodstuffs for the expanding colonial market. But sugarcane was also planted after the conquest, and the natives were pressed into the encomienda to tend to these crops. Harsh treatment and lack of experience with systematic labor rendered the Indians almost useless for work on sugar plantations, however. Besides, by the 1580s, diseases had all but wiped out the Indians of Puerto Rico. The flourishing of sugar production would have to await the coming of large numbers of African slaves.

THE INDIGENOUS MEXICAN POPULATION ♦ ♦ ♦ ♦ ♦ ♦ ♦ ♦ ♦ ♦

In Mexico the greatest cultural influence, along with the Spanish language, was its momentous indigenous history. In 1518, Hernán Cortés set out from Cuba to explore the mainland of Mexico in order to confirm reports of the existence of large, native civilizations in the interior. As the Spaniards were to discover, the reports were indeed true beyond their wildest dreams. It is theorized that civilization in southern Mexico, or Mesoamerica as the area is known archaeologically, had its beginning in the vast migrations across the Bering Strait more than fifty thousand years ago. The first humans to cross into the North American continent entered in waves before the strait was inundated by the melting polar caps in

10,000 B.C. Their livelihood depended on hunting the giant mastodons and other big game and gathering wild plants.

Social organization was limited, since they were mobile and traveled in small bands following the trail of animals. At best, they had a leader who ruled by consent of the other hunters and who had proved his worth in both hunting and defending his group from marauders. They lived in caves and rude shelters as they traversed the countryside in their pursuits. Their religious beliefs were simple. Like other Paleolithic big-game hunters from Europe, Africa, and Asia, they worshiped the very game on which they depended for food. Hence, drawings of mastodons and tapirs have been found on the bone artifacts they used as tools, leaving archaeologists to surmise that this was a form of worship.

Hunting and gathering, which provided a healthy, plentiful diet (Paleolithic man was bigger than present descendants), might have continued, but a significant climatic change about 7200 B.C. forever altered the course of human history in Mesoamerica. The area became more arid, creating the desert conditions we know today. The lush green land on which large animals depended for food disappeared. Humans had to turn to other sources of food and entered a stage designated the Archaic period. The former hunters became scroungers, depending on wild plants for their sustenance and to a lesser degree on smaller animals for protein. During this long period, which lasted until 2500 B.C., the gatherers became more and more adept at food acquisition and storage, but they also discovered that they could cultivate some of the plants for which they previously scrounged.

This discovery was the first major step toward civilization. Slowly, the inhabitants of Mesoamerica began to plant and irrigate the seeds of wild plants, such as maize, squash, beans, and amaranth. In the process, they also domesticated some of the wild animals they hunted. Unlike in the rest of the world, wild cattle and horses had not survived the decline of big game. Only the bison in the northern part of the continent lived on. Domestic animals included only turkeys and small dogs. Not surprisingly, the course of development for the Indians of the Americas did not include beasts of burden except for the Indians themselves.

Still, once domestication of both plants and animals pervaded Mesoamerica, in an era called the Formative period, 2500 B.C. to A.D. 250, material progress proceeded at an astonishing rate. First, villages appeared throughout the region as new techniques of cultivation resulted in flourishing plots of crops. Terracing, the plowing of platforms on hills, and *chinampas* (man-made islands on bodies of water), greatly increased the ability to produce. The resulting surpluses released many workers from agricultural work and made possible the emergence of specialists, such as potters, toolmakers, and even entertainers, such as musicians, acrobats and dancers.

At the end of the Formative period, religious leaders demanded the construction of huge temples and other religious institutions, which started to assume such dominance that the Mesoamerican world revolved entirely around metaphysical arrangements. A pantheon of deities was inspired by the need to pay homage to the elements essential to agriculture. Thus, the most important gods were those that symbolized the sun, the mother earth, and, of course, water.

In addition the simple metaphysical exigencies related to hunting and gathering gave way to a dramatic sophistication in religious practices, a process hastened by the ability to specialize. Farmers increasingly needed more precise prediction of the weather so that planting and harvesting could be planned accordingly. Shaman priests provided this valuable knowledge as they studied the heavens and acquired the astronomical skills necessary to forecast weather changes. Farmers looked to their religious leaders more and more for guidance, leading to a dependence that put the priests with their metaphysical teachings in leadership roles. Such control gave priests political power, which they exercised to their advantage. They demanded tribute and labor from the commoners and leaders alike, until the priesthood and the leadership converged into a theocracy.

About A.D. 250, throughout the Americas pre-colombian civilization reached its apogee and human development entered into the era known as the Classical period. Large urban centers with specialized production techniques entered into trade arrangements with other cities. During the Formative period, between 1200 B.C. and 400 B.C., a high civilization (which in most of Mesoamerica did not appear until the Classical period) had emerged in selected regions of Mesoamerica. A society known today as the Olmec built large cities with ceremonial centers and advanced architecture, pottery, and art. But most important, the Olmec developed a knowledge of astronomy and math that allowed them to invent a calendar system almost as accurate as ours today. Such development was limited to La Venta and San Lorenzo on the Gulf of Mexico, while the rest of Mesoamerica continued in the village mode even after the decline of these great centers.

In the classical era, many communities, especially those of the Maya and Zapotec, whose centers were close to the old Olmec centers, probably were influenced by the older, declined civilization. The Zapotec, in fact, occupied Monte Albán, a city with marked Olmecan characteristics, while the Maya built centers like Chichén Itza in Yucatán and El Tajín in Vera

Cruz. The Maya excelled in math and astronomy, a definite inheritance from the Olmec, and they produced the most delicate pieces of art in all the Americas.

The newer methods (terracing and chinampas) of cultivation were more beneficial to the societies of the hilly and lake-filled Valley of Mexico. There Teotihuacán, the most impressive center in the Classical period, was built twenty-five miles northeast of the what is now Mexico City. The city had over 200,000 inhabitants, huge pyramids, and a large market where the most advanced pottery and obsidian wares were traded.

Throughout Mesoamerica, thriving agricultural communities existed, dedicated to cultivating maize, the ears of which were about ten times larger than during its initial planting in the Archaic period. Maize was indispensable, but an array of other crops were also important in the diet of Mesoamericans. Unfortunately, in the tenth century A.D., one by one the Classical centers in both the highlands and the tropical lowlands declined. Archaeological evidence points to several causes. In the Mayan lowlands, reliance on slash-and-burn agriculture probably led to the exhaustion of the soil. The method works as long as there is plentiful new land to be brought under cultivation. Also, another climate change (bringing even drier weather) prompted nomadic outsiders from the north, known as Chichimecas, to migrate to Mesoamerica looking for water. It is believed that these newcomers pillaged and sacked the cities of Mesoamerica one by one. The Classical period thus came to an end, and although the barbaric newcomers replaced and imitated the old civilizations, they never surpassed them in philosophical or technical achievement. Because of the warlike orientation of the new cities, the era has been called the Militaristic period. This was the state of society when the Spaniards arrived in the early fifteenth century.

The Toltec were the first of the former Chichimeca group of tribes to have approached the degree of development of their predecessors. Their most impressive city was Tula, about sixty miles northwest of the present-day Mexican capital. The center, known for its giant monoliths, which resemble sentries on guard, remained the most important city in the Valley of Mexico until it too fell to other marauding Chichimeca. The Toltec also occupied the city of Monte Albán, which had served the Zapotec before them. According to myth, it is to there that Quetzalcoatl, the god known as the plumed serpent, was banished and expected to return in the future. As with Tula, the Toltec also abandoned Monte Albán, probably for the same reasons.

One of the last Chichimeca tribes to enter the central valley was the Aztec, who just a few years prior had left their mythical homeland of Aztlán in search of a new home, as Huitzilopochtli, their god of the sun, had mandated. According to legend, they would know where to settle once they encountered an eagle devouring a serpent on top of *nopal* (prickly pear cactus) in the middle of a lake. They wandered south looking for the sign and finally saw it in the middle of Lake Texcoco, where they built Tenochtitlán.

This legend has a basis in truth. The Aztec arrived in the Valley of Mexico about the thirteenth century and were such a nuisance, since they continued the Chichimeca life-style of pillaging, that they were banished by Atzcapotzalco leaders to an island in the center of the lake, which they fortified and used as a base of operation. From there they imitated other city-states and built their own magnificent city, which surpassed all the others in size and beauty, while they defeated and dominated the other communities in the lake region. They went through several stages and emperors until the Spaniards conquered them in 1521.

The Conquest of Mexico

If there were any doubts among the Spaniards about the existence of an advanced civilization in the interior of Mexico, they were put to rest almost as soon as Cortés landed on the Gulf Coast at a bay he named Veracruz. The reports received from the natives first encountered on the Mexican mainland were too compelling for any misgivings. After scuttling some of his ships so that the four hundred Spaniards that accompanied him could not return, Cortés set out to find the source of this civilization. Cortés, an audacious conquistador from Estremadura in southern Spain, had inherited that warrior mentality so deeply ingrained in that part of the Iberian Peninsula. In the time-honored tradition of the Reconquest, Cortés wanted to subjugate the civilization of Mexico and establish himself as its feudal lord.

After declaring the landing site a town (Veracruz), the conquistadores set out for the city of Tenochtitlán, which was considered a populous center of great wealth and power. Along the way he and his men encountered resistance in Cholula, but through the intelligence and language-interpreting services offered him by an Indian maiden given to him by Indians in Tabasco, he was able to defeat the Cholulans and continue on to Tenochtitlán. On the way he picked up Indian allies from the city of Tlaxcala. This Indian group became a ready ally because the Aztec were their hated enemy. Various Aztec leaders had attempted to dominate them and force them to pay tribute, as they had done with other cities in the valley for years. But the Tlaxcalans resisted fiercely. Moctezuma, the Aztec emperor who ruled the great city of Tenochtitlán, had spies who had kept him informed of the progress of the approaching Spaniards ever since they had landed on the coast. But he did not know what to make of them. Paradoxically, he was at a loss as to how to deal with the intruders. The Aztec emperor actually thought that Cortés was the long-lost god Quetzalcoatl, and that the rest of the Spaniards were immortal. By the time the Europeans arrived at the city, Moctezuma was paralyzed with indecision and Cortés seized the opportunity to sequester the vacillating king in his palace. The Spaniards set up house inside the walls of the city, as did the thousands of Tlaxcalan allies. On July 1, 1520, the Spaniards were forced out, just a year after they had come into the city. The Spaniards called this *La noche triste* (The Sad Night). Moctezuma was stoned to death by his own people during this debacle.

Cortés was not a man to give up very easily and so he retreated to the town of Coyoacán, where he set up headquarters to plan the defeat of the city. He quickly built brigantines and armed them with cannons. Cortés laid siege to the city, not allowing supplies to go in. In time he attacked the starving Aztecs and the neighboring Tlatelolcans, who were also decimated by European diseases.

The seige finally forced a surrender and Cortés had the city of Tenochtitlán razed. The beginning of Spanish Mexico commenced with the building of a European city on top of the old Aztec capital. However, the old conqueror was eventually stripped of his power, banished back to Spain, and replaced by professional viceroys who ostensibly represented the needs of the Crown. The Spaniards then ruled Mexico until 1821, a full three hundred years after the conquest, indelibly stamping their Hispanic mark on Mexican society. Still, what is considered Indian remained in many ways.

◆ ◆ ◆ ◆ ◆ ◆ ◆ ◆ ◆ THE SPANIARDS IN THE VALLEY OF MEXICO

After Cortés razed Tenochtitlán, he set out to build a Spanish city, ironically rescuing from the rubble the very same building materials used by the Aztec. His conquistadors then continued to explore and bring under

Spanish rule other indigenous communities. Pedro de Alvarado ventured south to the Yucatán Peninsula and Guatemala, while Cortés's enemy and rival, Nuño de Guzmán, brutally subjugated the vast realm of the Tarascans to the west. Cortés dispensed encomiendas left and right as a way of rewarding his men, but he reserved for himself the largest encomienda of all, practically all of Oaxaca. In 1529, he was authorized to use the title El Marqués del Valle de Oaxaca.

In the initial years of the conquest, the encomienda remained, as in the Caribbean, the main prize sought by conquistadors. Many of the onerous aspects of the institution had been somewhat mitigated with the Laws of Burgos. Promulgated by the Crown in 1512, the regulations were in response to the extremely harsh treatment that desperate colonists in the Caribbean imposed on natives through the deplorable encomienda. Now Spaniards had to abide by regulations that forbade overworking the Indians and that required the *encomendero* (the recipient of an encomienda) to provide for the spiritual welfare of the Indians. This usually consisted of supporting a prelate and building a church within the jurisdiction of the encomienda grant. In New Spain, as the vast territory claimed by Spain on the North American continent came to be called, the encomienda became for the Indians an acculturation vehicle to Spanish ways.

The most important Spanish acquisition for the Indians, usually through the encomienda, was Catholicism. Spanish friars in the beginning of the colonization process exhibited a great amount of zeal, imbued as they were with an inordinate amount of idealism, which characterized the Catholic church during this period of internal reform. They traveled far and wide, proselytizing and winning over hundreds of thousands to the Christian faith. The converts were so numerous, however, that they could not really assimilate Catholicism completely and the tendency was to combine, syncretically, pre-Colombian beliefs with the new teachings.

By 1540, another major phenomenon began to drastically change the social and racial character of central Mexico. From the moment they set foot on Mexican soil, the conquistadors violated the women of the conquered tribes and took them as concubines, with only a few marrying among the Indians. The consequence was a large progeny of children who were half Spaniard and half Indian. This new racial ensemble came to be known as mestizo, and after a few generations, the possible variations of mixture became so profuse that over one hundred categories existed by the end of colonial rule in 1821.

In 1504, Queen Isabella died, and twelve years later King Ferdinand succumbed as well. Succeeding them was their heir, Charles V, who was born to their daughter Juana la Loca and her Hapsburg husband Prince Phillip of Austria. It fell to the young king to wrest that realm away from Cortés and his encomenderos, a process begun almost as soon as the value of the conquest was realized. In 1524, Charles established the Council of the Indies, designed to oversee the administration of the colonies of the New World. An *audiencia* (a court of judges and administrators) was appointed in 1527 as a major step in asserting royal control. It was presided over by Nuño de Guzmán, who set out to destroy the power of Cortés, his old rival. But the rapacious Guzmán seemed to be a worse threat than the feudalistic Cortés, and the whole audiencia slate was replaced a year later by a president and judges more loyal to the Crown. To supervise and establish the Catholic faith, Juan de Zumárraga was named archbishop of New Spain in 1527.

The most ambitious move in the effort to consolidate royal power in New Spain was the appointment of Antonio de Mendoza, an extremely capable administrator who served the Crown well as viceroy for many years. In 1542, the New Laws were promulgated, a stroke designed to end the feudal encomienda, ensuring the predominance of Hapsburg control over the area. Mendoza found that he could not effectively implement the restrictive measures without provoking insurrection from the armed encomenderos, and so he opted for allowing the controversial institution to die out on its own. Encomiendas were only good as long as there were Indians to parcel out, but because of the horrible epidemics caused by European diseases, the indigenous population was decimated within a century.

In the meantime, the Spanish zeal for exploration and conquest led to incursions north of the Caribbean islands and Mexico into many regions of what is today the United States. Juan Ponce de León had sailed and landed on the shores of Florida in 1513, exploring most of the coastal regions and some of the interior. Continuing their maritime adventures, the Spanish explorers in the 1520s cruised along the northern shore of the Gulf of Mexico, seeing Alabama, Mississippi, and Texas and also sailing up the Atlantic coast to the Carolinas. Between 1539 and 1541, a large, well-equipped group of explorers led by Hernando de Soto journeyed into the interior of North America looking for mineral wealth, through present-day Florida, Georgia, South Carolina, Alabama, Mississippi, Arkansas, Louisiana, and Texas.

At the same time that de Soto was in the midst of his exploration, Francisco Vásquez de Coronado prepared for a momentous trek that took him

Neither Isabella nor Ferdinand lived to see the conquest of the great Aztec Empire by conquistadors who were intent on making their prize a personal and feudal domain.

and another large group of Spaniards north to present-day Arizona, New Mexico, Texas, and Oklahoma. In 1541, he set out from Mexico City in search of the Seven Cities of Cíbola, a mythical region rumored to rival Tenochtitlán in wealth and splendor. To supply Coronado's party, Hernando de Alarcón sailed up the Gulf of California and took his three ships against the current of the Colorado River, reaching present-day Yuma, Arizona.

MOVEMENT TO THE NORTH ✦ ✦ ✦ ✦ ✦ ✦ ✦ ✦ ✦ ✦ ✦ ✦ ✦ ✦ ✦ ✦ ✦ ✦

In transcendental terms, Coronado's feat has great historical significance. But at the time, his explorations were considered a disappointment because of the failure to find the fabled cities of Cíbola and Quivera. Dispelling the myths of greater glory and riches in the far north dampened enthusiasm for any further forays so far from the viceroyalty of Mexico City. In addition, the discovery of silver in the immediate north, soon after Coronado returned empty-handed, ensured that the Spaniards would concentrate all their efforts closer to their home base, and the expansion and real settlement northward commenced in earnest.

In 1546, Captain Juan de Tolosa, leading a small expedition of soldiers and missionaries into El Gran Chichimeca, as the wild region north of Querétaro was known, discovered a rich vein of silver in a mountain known as La Bufa. The strike was located in what is now the city of Zacatecas, some three hundred miles north of Mexico City. It was the first of a series of finds in a fanlike pattern spreading from Zacatecas into Guanajuato, Querétaro, and San Luis Potosí. In the last half of the sixteenth century, Spanish officials in Madrid, far from central Mexico, concentrated all their efforts on spurring mining activity both in New Spain and in Peru, where even greater silver deposits were uncovered.

The area known as the Central Corridor was named for its location on a plateau escarpment between two large mountain ranges, the Sierra Madre Occidental to the west and the Sierra Madre Oriental to the east.

But before the rich minerals could be adequately exploited, the Central Corridor had to be made safe from hostile Indian tribes. Although sparsely settled by the nomadic Chichimecas, the natives resisted the unwelcome intrusion of large numbers of Spaniards and mestizo workers, precipitating fifty years of Indian warfare. By the end of the sixteenth century, the nomads were brought under control through a combination of extensive military and religious proselytizing campaigns. As the mining regions were carved out from Chichimeca territory, thousands of mestizos, sedentary Indians from the former Aztec Empire, and Spaniards migrated to the *reales* (mining camps), settling permanently. The mining economy and the arid desert environment of El Gran Chichimeca engendered unique social conditions where a new Mexican ethnic identity was forged. Here the population was not as linked to either the large, sedentary Indian civilization and culture of the central highlands or the cities that were large centers of administration, commerce, and Spanish culture, such as Mexico City and Puebla.

While the inhabitants of the mining frontier drew on Spain and the more settled Indian areas for cultural continuity, the exigencies of the new environment generated an even more vibrant source of identity and culture. The process was carried north as the mining frontier moved in that direction in the seventeenth and eighteenth centuries. By 1800, the Spaniards had reaped $2.25 billion worth of silver from the vast array of rich mines. In the Spanish system, all wealth belonged to the Crown and the miner was granted a *real* (a royal concession giving him or her the right to exploit the mine). The Crown received one-fifth of all the take, or the royal fifth; however, these concessions would remain in the miner's family, ensuring a continuation of *patria potestad* (the original authorization) usually under a patriarch.

Within a few years the grantees of the reales turned to wage labor, and hundreds of thousands of mestizos, who were born in the decades immediately after the conquest in the highlands, poor Whites, and acculturated Indians poured into the Central Corridor to work not only in mining but also on the haciendas, which specialized in raising livestock and agriculture for consumption in the reales. Thus, the hacienda became an indispensable corollary to mining, and within a few decades both of these activities determined the social arrangements of the region. The economy, based on wage labor, created a proletariat that was able to work in a more diverse opportunity structure than in the central highlands.

Smaller mining operators followed missionaries north to the frontier. A persistent pattern emerged in which the missionaries tamed the Indians so that the Hispanic miner could follow, once they were "softened" to European ways. The missionaries provided the service unwittingly, but they served that purpose nonetheless. Parral, at the northern end of the corridor in Chihuahua, and Alamos, in Sonora, were thus settled by Spanish-Mexicans. By the mid-1600s, the mines had played out, so then miners in the frontier were forced to settle down and turn to agriculture and the operation of smaller-scale mining known as *gambusino*.

For today's Mexican Americans, the social and cultural transformation of the Central Corridor is particularly important, because the Hispanic culture that emerged in northern New Spain (today's American Southwest) during the colonial period is an extension and reflection of the mining society in this region. In addition, Mexican immigrants who in the early twentieth century swelled existing Hispanic communities throughout the United States came from this region as well, reinforcing the unique Mexicanness that had already been established in the Southwest.

The reasons for settling the extreme northern frontier of New Spain were not as related to mining as they were in the case of the Central Corridor. Nonetheless, the process of colonization was a slow but sustained extension of the northward movement that started with the founding of the Zacatecas mines. By the time Mexico acquired its independence from Spain in 1821, permanent colonies existed in coastal California, southern Arizona, south Texas, and most of New Mexico and southern Colorado. The imprint of evolving Mexican culture so evident in the Central Corridor was also stamped on today's Southwest. It contained a mestizo-*criollo* (pure-blooded Spanish descendant) racial mixture with a strong reliance on raising livestock, subsistence agriculture, and mining. Leaders of most colonizing expeditions were persons born in Spain, but the rank-and-file soldiers, artisans, and workers in general were of mixed blood (mestizos) or criollos born in New Spain.

The first foray out of the Central Corridor, after Coronado's unsuccessful trek, was in the 1590s into Pueblo Indian territory in northern New Mexico. Fifty years earlier, Coronado had written of these sedentary Indians who lived in large agricultural settlements containing multistory houses with well-ordered political and religious systems. His attempts to buffet them into encomiendas provoked fierce resistance, and as a result he and his party were forced to abandon New Mexico. This failure contributed to the overall disillusionment with exploration. Nonetheless, the possibility of exploiting the labor of the Pueblos and saving their souls, modest as this potential might have been, remained a lure after Coronado. The attraction glowed even more forty years later when Antonio de Espejo reported in 1583 the possibility of silver deposits in New Mexico.

Spurred by Espejo's report, Juan de Oñate, the grandson of a Zacatecas mining pioneer from Spain, was granted a charter to explore into present-day New Mexico as early as 1595. In 1598 he and his group set out along the Central Corridor from the more civilized Zacatecas to the uncertainty of the north. Oñate's party, made up of Spaniards, criollos and mestizos, also contained Tlaxcalan Indians, who had remained loyal to the Spaniards, after helping Hernán Cortés defeat the Aztec in 1521. They served in menial positions as carriers, servants, and laborers. After reaching the Rio Grande, the explorers and missionaries then traveled along the river valley, established a minor post in present-day El Paso, and continued on up through upper Rio Grande valley into Pueblo Indian territory.

Oñate was ordered to return in 1608, but Franciscan missionaries and settlers remained attracted to the communities of sedentary Indians. Santa Fe was founded in 1610, followed by other settlements. The clerics wanted to convert the Indians, and the civilians hoped to put them into encomiendas and demand gold as tribute. The efforts to enslave the Indians backfired, however. In 1680, a Pueblo Indian named Popé led a rebellion that forced the Spaniards and Christianized Indians out of northern New Mexico southward toward El Paso, and they founded Ysleta just north of El Paso. The latter community is said to have housed the *genízaros* (acculturated Indians made up of Comanche captive-slaves), Christianized Pueblos, and the faithful Tlaxcalans. Sixteen years later, many of those settlers who had fled returned to northern New Mexico and reestablished a Hispanic presence, but with a new respect for the Pueblos.

The Pueblo uprising also turned the interest of Spaniards toward Texas. But the story of the exploration of Texas has to be told within the context of the colonization of the large province of Coahuila, of which Texas was an extension. The first newcomers were prospectors searching for precious metals, and indeed some silver mines were opened in Monclova, Coahuila, such as the Santa Rosa. But the diggings were sparse and most of the attention was soon turned to agriculture and livestock. Motivated by the need to provide foodstuffs and livestock to the rich mining regions to the south, in 1689 the first royal *mercedes* (land grants) were granted to Spaniards in the fertile valleys of Monclova, just south of the present border.

Like Oñate, the Spaniards in the northeast also brought Tlaxcalan Indians to provide labor for their haciendas. Many of these enterprising natives established themselves as artisans in Saltillo and acquired a reputation as excellent weavers and silversmiths. Many of the modern inhabitants of Coahuila and immigrants to Texas from this area are descendants of the Tlaxcalans. Saltillo acquired great importance because it served as an entrepót between the livestock-raising areas to the north and the silver and mercantile communities to the south. In the eighteenth century, a new dynasty of Spanish kings, the Bourbons, initiated reforms that led to a revitalization of the silver industry. As a consequence, by 1767 Saltillo had become a prosperous commercial hub with a population of over two thousand, and as new settlers arrived to colonize the northeast, they filtered through this beautiful colonial city.

Large, sprawling haciendas with huge herds of cattle and sheep characterized the economy and societal life of the northeast by 1800. The biggest landholding belonged to the Sánchez-Navarro family. It was sixteen million acres in size. This latifundia was so immense that it took in almost half of the province, and its mainstay was sheep raising. Peonage was the lot of many of the lower classes, as that was the only method by which *hacendados* (landowners) could deter their workers from going off to work in mines. But hindering the effectiveness of the haciendas were constant depredations by the Comanche, who had learned that raiding the livestock regions was more prosperous than hunting the buffalo. This provoked the Spanish government to establish buffer zones across the Rio Grande, or the Rio Bravo, as it is known in Mexico.

At the turn of the eighteenth century, a persistent priest named Francisco Hidalgo, from his base of San Juan Bautista, a settlement on the Rio Grande about 150 miles west of Laredo, zealously set out to work among the Indians north of the river. Initially his requests for support were ignored by Spanish officials, so he sought help from the French, which prompted the Spaniards to act, because they recognized the threat France would pose if her colonists made inroads with the natives. Domingo Ramón in 1717 was sent to colonize along the Nueces River and to build missions. In 1718, the San Antonio de Béjar and de Valero churches were built where the city of San Antonio is located today. The chapel in the de Béjar mission was called El Alamo. The efforts to colonize Texas remained very difficult because of the nomadic, warlike character of the tribes. Therefore, instead of spreading the gospel, the Spaniards spent most of their time pacifying the resistant natives.

The French remained a threat, however. To thwart Spanish efforts to colonize and settle Texas, the French supplied the Indians with firearms and gunpowder. Nonetheless, colonization remained a priority on the Spanish colonial agenda. In 1760 after the Seven Years' War (also known as the French and Indian War), which united France and Spain against Britain,

France ceded claims to all lands west of the Mississippi in order not to give them to the victorious British. Overnight, New Spain's territory expanded dramatically. Then, in the American Revolution of 1776, the Spaniards, because of their alliance with France, were able to obtain lands all the way to Florida. Basically all of that territory had few Hispanic settlers, however. In Texas, most of the Hispanic settlers lived in clusters of villages along the lower Rio Grande Valley. By 1749, 8,993 Hispanics and 3,413 Indians lived in what came to be known as Nuevo Santander. Laredo was on the north bank of the river and Meier, Camargo, and Reynosa were on the south bank.

Also during this same period, colonists were pushing north and establishing ranches in the Nueces River Valley. The Crown encouraged the settlement of this region in order to create a buffer zone against all intruders, such as the Comanche and the French. By 1835, 3 million head of livestock, cattle, and sheep roamed the region between the Nueces River and the Rio Grande, and about five thousand persons inhabited the region. Most border people did not inhabit the towns, however. Instead, they lived on ranches as tight-knit family groups and clans on land granted by the Spanish Crown. Having to withstand the depredations of the Comanche promoted even tighter cohesion and class cooperation than was true on the larger haciendas farther south in the interior of Mexico.

The biggest town in the vast Nuevo Santander province, Reynosa, was larger than Philadelphia in 1776.

Arizona was the next area of the northernmost frontier to be explored and settled. The region was part of the province of Sonora, but it acquired a distinct geographical name, Pimería Alta, because of the numerous Pima Indians that inhabited southern Arizona and northern Sonora. Its settlement, then, was simply an extension of the colonization of Sonora. The first Europeans in Sonora were Jesuit missionaries who in 1591 introduced a new religion, European crops, and livestock to Yaqui and Mayo in southern Sonora. The natives were more receptive to the latter offerings than to the former, but they were receptive, nonetheless. When the first Hispanic colonists arrived some fifty years later, they found wheat and other European crops abundantly planted by Indians on mission lands.

Pedro de Perea, a miner from Zacatecas, was allowed the first *entrada* (Spanish Crown colonization sanction) into Sonora in 1640 and he arrived with forty soldiers in 1641. Because of problems with local leaders in Sinaloa and Jesuit missionaries in Sonora, he went to New Mexico, where he recruited twelve families and five Franciscan priests. The local Jesuits objected to the viceroy in Mexico City, and eventually the Francis-

These communities became the focus for the Hispanicization of the Indians, and the Mexicans here evolved a unique cultural system known today in Mexico as sonorense *(sonoran). It is characterized by an intrepid spirit that was shaped by the necessity of learning to survive in the most challenging environment of the Spanish Empire.*

cans went back, but the families stayed. Then a series of silver discoveries led to more settlement along the Sonoran River valleys by colonists who came directly from Zacatecas, Durango, and Sinaloa.

By the 1680s, most settlers dedicated their efforts to mining, but many others raised crops and livestock to supply the mines. Farmers and miners lived in the same towns, which usually contained a store for goods not available locally. The Hispanics introduced tools, livestock, and crops never before seen in Sonora.

Intense dependence on mining made the Sonoran communities very unstable, because when production of the local mine played out, the community dispersed. Also, mercury, which was indispensable to the amalgamation of silver, was a monopoly of the Spanish Crown. In the seventeenth century, prices were hiked up so high that it was impossible to operate the mines profitably. As happened elsewhere in New Spain when mining opportunity waned at the end of the century, more and more Mexican settlers engaged in subsistence agriculture rather than mining. But also, as elsewhere in New Spain, the eighteenth-century Bourbon reforms precipitated in Sonora a growing and booming economy. More Hispanics came in from the other provinces of New Spain and from Spain itself. Consequently, the indigenous population declined in proportion. In 1765, only 30 percent of the population was considered Hispanic, while by 1800 that figure had changed to 66 percent.

In the Santa Cruz Valley, Pimas and Tohono O'odom (known as Pápagos by Spaniards) predominated in the northern half near Tucson, and Hispanic settlers occupied the southern part. The missionaries, however, preceded the settlers, pacifying the Indians and making the area safer for colonization. This impetus surged the line of Hispanic settlement even farther north in Sonora to Pimería Alta (northern Sonora and southern Arizona), theretofore the domain of Jesuit missions. In 1691, Father Eusebio Kino, an untiring Jesuit missionary, made the first inroads into Arizona and established a mission in 1700 at San Xavier del Bac, near present-day Tucson, and in 1702 founded another mission some thirty miles south in Tumacácori. In 1706, a presidio was established next to that complex, in Tubac, complementing the mission in much the same way as the haciendas did the reales.

By the 1730s, Hispanic settlers were in what is now the Santa Cruz Valley of the Sonoran Desert, mining silver at Arizonac just south of the present-day border. The name "Arizonac" was Pima for "land of few springs" and is how the state of Arizona derived its name. To deal with disturbances like the uprisings instigated by the Pima in the 1750s or the incursion by the Apache in the 1730s, the Hispanics built presidios and Mexican settlers manned these military garrisons, extending their influence even farther north. Basically, the same pattern of missions and presidio life as in the earlier settlements was established along the Altar and Santa Cruz valley of Pimería Alta in the eighteenth century. Ironically, the farther north Hispanics moved, the more they relied on wheat rather than maize as a staple. This was even true among the Indians. The Tohono O'odom, for example, had taken to making what we know today as "Indian fried bread" and wheat flour tortillas.

Because Jesuit influence in the Spanish Empire had become so pervasive, in 1767 the Bourbons expelled them from the realm, and the Hispanic communities throughout Sonora were forced to undergo significant alterations. After the expulsion, the mission system declined despite the Franciscans replacing the Jesuit order. Former mission farms were put to livestock raising, and because foodstuffs from the missions were scarce, the Hispanics had to engage in more extended agricultural activity. As a result, Mexican settlements proliferated in the river valleys of the Sonoran Desert. Small villages existed everywhere, and the new arrivals assumed the way of life forged by the earlier settlers. Between the 1790s and 1820s, the Apache threat subsided because of successful military tactics and negotiations on the part of local leaders, and Hispanic settlements began to thrive in Pimería Alta. At one point as many as one thousand Hispanics lived in the Santa Cruz Valley. But with the independence of Mexico, the Spanish Crown abandoned its fortifications and the Apache lost no time in taking advantage of the opportunity. Overrunning Pimería Alta, they forced Hispanic settlers to the southern part of the desert.

As in Arizona, the establishment of colonies in California was an extension of the Spanish drive into northwestern New Spain. In 1769, José de Gálvez, an aggressive representative of the Bourbons in New Spain, gave orders to settle Alta California from Baja California, and the same year a tired expedition led by the Franciscan Fray Junípero Serra founded the San Diego mission. A year later another mission was built in Monterey. During this period of flux, Juan Bautista de Anza, the Sonoran-born son of a Spanish official who himself became an officer, and Pedro de Garcés, a Spanish Franciscan missionary, founded the first overland route to California in 1774.

For the Franciscans, converting numerous California Indians became the main incentive in the drive northward. The first exploration of Juan Bautista de Anza resulted in the reinforcement of a mission along the beautiful Pacific coast in Monterey and the additional building of a presidio. Two years later, de Anza lead another expedition and founded San Francisco, where the presidio is still a landmark.

In a few years, familiar religious and military institutions, the mission and the presidio, dotted the California coastline all the way from San Diego to San Francisco. Soldiers of various racial mixtures, missionaries, and Indians made up the demographic profile of the coast. The soldiers were encouraged to go as settlers and to take their families, as was the tradition in other frontier regions of New Spain. Those who did not have mates found suitable partners among the Indian women, to the chagrin of the missionaries, who considered the mestizo soldiers a bad influence on the Indian communities. As time went by, many of the soldiers became landowners, especially after 1831, when mission property was confiscated by the now independent Mexican government. Some of these former soldiers acquired thousands of acres, laying the foundation for some of the old California families.

ANGLO ENCROACHMENT INTO THE MEXICAN NORTH ♦ ♦ ♦ ♦

While the thirteen colonies had been under the colonial tutelage of England, they had enjoyed more freedom than the colonists in the Spanish realms.

While Spain attempted to hold off encroachment into the northern regions of New Spain by other European imperialists, a series of events took place that changed the relationship between the Hispanic and Anglo areas of North America. In 1776, Anglo-Americans declared their independence from England, and thirty-four years later Hispanics proclaimed their independence from Spain. In both areas new nations were formed. The thirteen former British colonies came to be known as the United States of America in 1781, and the newly independent people of New Spain named their nation the Republic of Mexico.

Both areas had immense problems as they experimented with new forms of government and attempted to get their economies afloat. Mexico, however, had the most difficult time. Anglo-Americans had a preexisting political structure and economy, which allowed them to make a relatively smoother transition into independent status. Spain ruled and controlled the domains with an iron hand and had imposed a rigid economic and social caste system on its colonial subjects, which allowed the Catholic church to have inordinate influence on their everyday lives. As a consequence, the Mexicans were not as well prepared for the democratic ideals to which they aspired in the 1824 constitution. The result was years of confusion and interminable internal strife, which greatly weakened the economy and made the new nation vulnerable to outside powers.

The area of greatest weakness was in the far northern frontier. As has been indicated, Spain had difficulty in peopling its vast territory in New Spain. This condition made the area even more vulnerable to outside powers. To augment its forces in the interior of New Spain, which were busy squelching the independence movement that had started on September 16, 1810, with the insurrection of Father Miguel Hidalgo y Costilla, the Spaniards withdrew their troops from the frontier presidios. This further weakened the lines of defense in the north, inviting incursions from the newly independent but aggressive North Americans.

The danger of Yankee encroachment was apparent to the Spaniards much earlier. In 1803, a powerful France under Napoleon Bonaparte acquired from Spain the Louisiana Territory, which she had ceded during the Seven Years' War in the previous century. Napoleon, who was vying for dominance in Europe and needed revenue quickly, sold the vast territory to the United States, and then the borders of the expanding infant nation connected directly with New Spain.

Anglo-Americans lost no time in determining what the new acquisition meant for the fledgling country. To the consternation of Spain, President Thomas Jefferson funded the historical expedition of Lewis and Clark in 1804. Spain was obviously worried that the exploration was a prelude to the settlement of the territory by Anglos. Then in 1806, Zebulon Pike, an army officer searching for the headwaters of the Red River in Arkansas, entered Spanish territory in Colorado, built a fort, and raised the colors of the United States. Spanish officials found and destroyed the fortification and arrested Pike and his men. Taken to Santa Fe and then to Chihuahua City farther south, Pike saw more of New Spain than most anybody else who was not a Spanish subject. In the memoirs of his adventure, Pike recognized the potential for trade with Mexico. This piqued the interest of many of his fellow Anglo-Americans.

A series of other events demonstrated that Anglo-Americans were anxious to fulfill what they considered their Manifest Destiny to settle areas even beyond their sovereign realm. In 1820, Stephen Long led a revolt, ostensibly as part of the independence movement against the Spanish, but obviously he was acting as a filibusterer for his countrymen. Spain finally entered into deliberations with Moses Austin, a Catholic from Missouri, to settle Anglo-Catholic families in Texas. The rationale for this seemingly paradoxical policy was to people the region between the more populated portions of New Spain and the United States with persons who owed a loyalty to Spain, even if they were not Hispanic. Initially, the Austin colony was made up of three hundred families in east Texas who were given generous empresario land grants. The stipulation was that they had to be Catholic, become subjects of the Crown, and abide by Spanish law. Moses died during the process and so the contract was concluded with Stephen, his son. These negotiations were concluded in 1821, right before Mexico acquired its independence under the leadership of Augustine Iturbide, a former Spanish officer who wanted to lead the newly independent nation down the path of monarchy. But Mexico honored the agreements that were established by Spain.

Iturbide was overthrown in 1823 and a more liberal constitutional government was established in 1824. The new constitution called for a president, a congress, nineteen states with their own legislatures, and four territories. That same year, Erasmo Seguín, a delegate to the national congress from Texas, persuaded a willing congress to pass a colonization act designed to bring even more Anglo settlers to Texas. Between 1824 and 1830, thousands of Anglo families entered east Texas, acquiring hundreds of thousands of free acres and also buying land much cheaper than they could have in the United States. By 1830, Texas had eighteen thousand Anglo inhabitants and their African slaves, who numbered over two thousand.

Anglo-Americans found it difficult to live under Mexican rule from the outset. They had an aversion to the Spanish language and the Mexican laws and legal system (in particular, the nonexistence of juries). In 1824, Texas was joined with Coahuila into a gigantic state, with most of the population residing in the Coahuila portion of the entity. Anglo-Texans rankled at the remoteness of the seat of government in faraway Saltillo in Coahuila, and exacerbating this sentiment was the inability of the Mexican government to provide adequate protection from the marauding Comanche. Anglos also feared the threat to the institution of slavery on which they were so dependent. Indeed, in 1829 the Mexican government abolished slavery during the liberal administration of Vicente Guerrero, the second president under the constitution. The uproar in Texas was so intense that Guerrero decided not to enforce the law. Nonetheless, slave-holders in Texas knew that their days were numbered.

Perhaps the most vexing development for Texans was the Immigration Law of 1830. In 1827, Manuel Mier y Terán, a military officer charged with assessing the general conditions in Texas, concluded that Anglos posed a threat to the sovereignty of Mexico. Then in 1830, a coup d'état by Guerrero's vice president, Anastasio Bustamante, installed a conserva-tive government that was intent on closing off the borders of Mexico to outsiders. The result was the law that forbade any new immigration into Texas, an act that greatly concerned Anglos, who wanted to expand the economy and their culture by emigration from the United States.

All in all, the sentiment for independence from Mexico was on the increase in Texas. In 1832, General Antonio López de Santa Anna ousted Busta-mante and was elected president the following year. But he allowed his lib-eral vice president, Valentín Gómez Farías, to institute some anticlerical re-forms against the Catholic church. This provoked powerful Mexican conservatives to act decisively. Somehow, General Santa Anna was per-suaded in 1835 to oust his own vice president and to dissolve congress and institute a more closed system than even Bustamante had attempted a few years earlier. One of the first steps taken by Santa Anna under his central-ized conservative constitution of *Las Siete Leyes* (The Seven Laws) was to dismantle the state legislatures and dismiss the governors and replace them with military officials. In Texas, Mexican troops were sent to enforce re-strictive customs along the Gulf Coast, leading to a skirmish with Anglos, who did not want their trade with the United States disrupted.

To the disgruntled Texans, all seemed lost. The rumblings for indepen-dence increased. Late in 1835, Santa Anna sent General Martín Perfecto de Cos to San Antonio to administer the new federal laws, but he was re-pelled by Anglo-Texans and Mexican Texans who were determined to re-sist. The Anglos fortified themselves in the mission of El Alamo and awaited the inevitable retribution. Santa Anna decided then to take mat-ters into his own hands and, mustering a large force, descended on San Antonio. Mexican-Texan scouts warned of the impending attack, but Anglo defenders under Colonel Travis did not believe the first messages. When it was obvious that the threat was real, the Anglos prepared for bat-tle. Instead of attacking immediately, the Mexican army laid siege to the fortified mission, which lasted two weeks. Santa Anna ordered a *degüello* attack, which means taking no prisoners, and all the vastly outnumbered defenders were killed, even after they surrendered.

The long Kentucky rifles of the defenders of the Alamo had a much longer range than Santa Anna's artillery and muskets. With their superior weaponry, Travis and his men, who included such legendary heroes as Davey Crockett and Jim Bowie, took many Mexican lives before succumbing.

After the massive defeat at the Alamo, the Texas army, led by General Sam Houston, fled eastward with Santa Anna's troops in hot pursuit. At Goliad, a town east of San Antonio, the Mexicans decisively defeated the Texans, and, as at the Alamo, they took no prisoners. These defeats served to galvanize Texan resistance, and eventually Santa Anna committed a military blunder that led to the defeat of his army and his capture at San Jacinto, located near present-day Houston. The Texans declared their independence and wrested from a reluctant Santa Anna terms of surrender that included Texas's independence. Mexican officials never accepted the agreement reached with Santa Anna, but Texas remained independent, nonetheless, until 1845, when it was annexed to the United States.

The Texas rebellion caused hard feelings between Mexico and the United States, and the rift eventually grew to proportions of war in 1846. In 1836 Mexico had charged the United States with backing the rebels, an allegation denied vehemently by U.S. officials. That the United States immediately recognized the Texas republic was proof enough for the Mexicans, however, and they warned that annexation of Texas by the United States would mean war. Another cause of discord between the two uneasy neighbors was two million dollars in damage done to Anglo-American properties in Mexico as a consequence of revolutionary violence in Mexico.

Then in February 1845, the United States voted for the annexation of Texas, and Mexico broke off relations but stopped short of declaring war. Apparently, Mexico at this point was about to recognize Texas's independence and did not want any border problems. Still, the issue that eventually brought the two nations into warfare was the matter of the boundary. When Texans declared their independence in 1836, they claimed the lower Rio Grande as their southern border. The Mexicans insisted that the Nueces River, a few hundred miles to the north, was the border. With the annexation, the United States accepted the Texas version of the boundary dispute.

It was no secret that many Anglo-Americans wanted to fulfill their Manifest Destiny of expanding their country all the way to the Pacific coast. At the very moment of annexation, U.S. officials under President James K. Polk continued trying to buy vast areas of Mexico's northernmost territories, including California. In the fall of 1845, the American president sent John Slidell to Mexico with an offer of 25 million dollars for California, but Mexican officials refused to even see him. General Zachary Taylor was then sent across the Nueces River to set up a blockade of the Rio Grande at its mouth on Port Isabel, and Mexicans retaliated by attacking the U.S. troops on April 25, 1845. Casualties ensued. President Polk immediately went to Congress and obtained a declaration of war against Mexico.

Two years of war followed. That it took so long was somewhat surprising, considering Mexico's weak political situation. From the time that Texas was annexed until the war ended in 1847, six different presidents attempted to make foreign policy, quite often at odds with each other. Nonetheless, the Mexican will to resist was underestimated, and it was difficult for an inexperienced U.S. Army to fight on foreign soil. The U.S. invasion took place from four different directions. Troops under General Taylor crossed north across the Rio Grande, while General Stephen Watts Kearny took an army overland to New Mexico and then to California. There he encountered considerable resistance from the Californios (Mexican Californians) at the Battle of San Pascual before reaching Los Angeles. California was also assaulted by sea by Commodore John C. Fremont. But the most decisive drive was by General Winfield Scott, who bombarded Vera Cruz and then proceeded with the most sizable force all the way to Mexico City, with the Mexicans offering the greatest resistance at Churubusco (part of present-day Mexico City).

Not all Americans supported the war. Newspapers carried reports that General Scott had admitted that his men had committed horrible atrocities. By September, his troops occupied Mexico City. General Santa Anna had been president since December of 1846, but his attempts to fend off the American invasion were hopeless and in November he resigned in disgrace. The Mexicans refused to come to the bargaining table until they were thoroughly routed. Finally, in February 1848, they signed the Treaty of Guadalupe Hidalgo, which brought the war officially to an end.

The treaty provided fifteen million dollars for the vast territories of New Mexico, Arizona, and California and parts of Nevada, Utah, and Colorado. The provisions of the treaty most important to an understanding of the history of Mexican Americans had to do with the Mexicans who remained in the territory acquired by the United States. They had a year to retreat into Mexico's shrunken border or they automatically would become citizens of the United States. They would then acquire all the rights of citizens. In addition, the treaty assured southwest Mexicans that their property would be protected and they would have the right to maintain religious and cultural integrity. These provisions, which the Mexican negotiators at the town of Guadalupe Hidalgo had insisted on, seemed protective of the former Mexican citizens, but these stipulations were only as good as the ability and desire to uphold the promises.

MEXICANS UNDER U.S. RULE ✦ ✦ ✦ ✦ ✦ ✦ ✦ ✦ ✦ ✦ ✦ ✦ ✦ ✦ ✦ ✦ ✦

The territorial acquisition delineated in the Treaty of Guadalupe Hidalgo did not include southern Arizona and southern New Mexico. That region, which included the area from present-day Yuma along the Gila River (twenty-five miles south of Phoenix) all the way to the Mesilla Valley, where Las Cruces, New Mexico, is located, was sold to the United States by General Santa Anna the year that he returned to power in 1853. Ironically, hundreds of Mexicans who in 1848 had moved south into the Mesilla Valley or the Santa Cruz Valley in southern Arizona found themselves in the United States again. The provisions in the Gadsden Treaty regarding Mexicans in the newly annexed territory were similar to those in the Treaty of Guadalupe Hidalgo. Few Mexicans had any faith that any of the provisions protecting Mexicans would be honored, and many were embittered because they felt betrayed by Mexico. But the Mexican government did attempt to attract Mexicans from the southwestern United States into what became the northernmost Mexican region in the present-day border states. Of the 80,000 or so Mexicans living in the ceded territories, only a few thousand took up the offer.

The Supreme Court ruled in 1855 that the Treaty of Guadalupe Hidalgo did not apply to Texas, but Mexicans in Texas were supposedly protected under the 1836 constitution of the Republic of Texas, which was modified to become a state constitution in 1845.

The promise that the remaining Mexicans would receive all the rights accrued to U.S. citizens did not really materialize. New Mexico, with the largest number of Hispanics, perhaps 60,000, was able to achieve some political self-determination for its citizens. But there and everywhere else in what was now the southwestern United States, the newly minted U.S. citizens were systematically discriminated against. Except in New Mexico, Anglo immigration overwhelmed Mexicans in the newly acquired territories almost from the beginning. In Texas, for example, the population increased from 30,000 in 1836 to 140,000 in 1846. While there was migration from Mexico, this rapid increase in population was mainly due to the influx of Anglos from the United States. Mexicans were outnumbered six to one.

The 1836 Texas constitution stipulated that all residents living in Texas at the time of the rebellion would acquire all the rights of citizens of the new republic, but if they had been disloyal, these rights were forfeited. Numerically superior Anglos, embittered with Mexicans during the rebellion, retaliated by mistreating or forcing Mexicans off their property. Many Mexicans simply crossed the border and went to Mexico. In 1857, Anglo businessmen attempted to run off Mexican teamsters, who had dominated the transport of goods in south Texas since the colonial period, by hiring thugs to strong-arm the carters off the trails. The attempt was not wholly successful, but it demonstrated the increasing antipathy toward Mexicans and a continuing violation of the guarantees offered by the Treaty of Guadalupe Hidalgo.

When Texas joined the union in 1845, only one Mexican Texan was a delegate to the convention that framed the new state constitution. And in the convention itself, there were many who felt that Mexicans should not be allowed to vote. But in the end, they were not denied suffrage. In spite of this victory, Mexican Texans were intimidated into not voting, and the result was that few politicians were Mexicans. After Texas became a state, few Mexicans participated in politics. In 1850, of the sixty-four members in the state legislature, none were born in Texas or Mexico. Whenever Mexicans did vote, their power was diminished because they were dominated by political bosses who were able to buy in mass the votes of Mexicans. In addition, there were White-only primaries from which Mexicans were barred, and since the Democratic party dominated in Texas, the elections were really decided in these primaries. Poll taxes, that is, taxes levied for voting, also served to deter from voting those with few economic resources; this included most Mexicans.

In California, while Mexican and Anglos did not have the same legacy of conflict that characterized race relations in Texas, many of the newcomers were from the U.S. South, where prejudice against racial minorities was the rule. Political participation of Californios was also minimal in the state, although in the beginning their integration was more evident than in Texas. For example, out of forty-eight delegates, eight Mexican Californians were selected to participate in the state constitutional convention of 1849 when California joined the Union.

The constitutional convention was the last major political event in which Mexicans participated. The gold rush of 1849 attracted thousands of Anglos, which resulted in an even more imbalanced ratio of Mexicans to Anglos. In 1850, Mexicans were 15 percent of the population, but twenty years later that figure dropped to only 4 percent. Political and economic influence declined first in the north, the area that attracted the majority of

One of the most onerous laws was the Foreign Miners tax of 1850, which levied a charge for anyone who was not a U.S. citizen. While some miners were French, Australian, or Irish, most "foreigners" were Mexicans or South Americans, who possessed superior mining skills. There can be no doubt that the tax was designed to eliminate this competition from the gold diggings.

Anglos, because of the goldfields. The lack of political influence led to legislation contrary to Californio interests. For example, in 1851 the six southern counties where most Mexicans resided were taxed five times the rate of other local entities. In 1855, so-called greaser laws were passed that prohibited bearbaiting, bullfights and cockfights, clearly aimed at prohibiting the customs of the Californios. Vagrancy laws were passed, also aimed at Mexicans, because when a community wanted to force Mexicans out, these laws were applied selectively.

In New Mexico, Mexicans participated more fully in both the economy and in politics than in any other region. A major reason for this was that Hispanic New Mexicans remained a numerical majority until the turn of the century. Anglos came to quickly dominate the southeastern part of the state, but New Mexican Hispanics maintained control in the north around Santa Fe and Albuquerque. From 1850 to 1911, Hispanics dominated most key political slots and controlled the territorial legislature until the 1890s. Ironically, one reason it took so long for the New Mexican territory to become a state was a reluctance among Anglo politicians in Washington, D.C., to allow a new state dominated by Mexicans.

In Arizona, which was part of the New Mexican territory until 1863, Mexicans maintained some political power in the area that was purchased under the Gadsden Treaty in 1853. This was especially true in and around Tucson, which became the territorial capital after Arizona separated from New Mexico. Political and economic cooperation was more evident between Anglos and Mexicans in this area because economic activity depended greatly on trade through the state of Sonora. With the coming of the railroads in the 1880s, however, the relationship between both groups became more strained as a new influx of Anglos who did not need to cooperate with Mexicans overwhelmed the older Anglo population. Politically, this demographic shift translated into lack of political power. The territorial seat was removed to Prescott, away from Mexicans, and eventually to Phoenix when Arizona became a state. Mexicans in southern Arizona retained a modicum of political power, and the few Hispanic legislators in Arizona until the 1950s all came from that section.

Lack of protection for Mexicans in the Southwest was most obvious in the violation of property rights. While the Treaty of Guadalupe Hidalgo was vague regarding property, it did constitute the most definite commitment in the document. As more Anglos entered the Southwest and the area became more economically developed, land values rose and the thirst for land became more apparent. The system of keeping records of property claims differed between Mexico and the United States. As a consequence, proof of title became an immediate burden for Mexicans throughout the newly acquired territories.

To address the issue of property ownership, Congress passed the California Land Act of 1851 to facilitate legalization of land belonging to Californios prior to the takeover. Instead of helping the Californios resolve their property problems quickly, however, official procedures sometimes took years, forcing the ranchers to turn over huge tracts of land to the very lawyers who were adjudicating their cases. Then in 1862, the Homestead Act was passed in Congress, allowing squatters in the West to settle and claim vacant lands. In California, thousands converged on lands claimed by Mexicans, creating legal entanglements that were many times settled in favor of the squatters. Many of the homesteaders were front men for speculators who took these free lands and held them for future use or sale.

In the New Mexico territory, an even slower system, the surveyor of general claims office, was established in 1854. It took that office fifty years to settle just a few claims, and in the meantime many Mexicans in New Mexico were also defrauded of their land in grabs similar to those in California. During the 1890s, for example, as the Santa Fe Railroad was built from Kansas through the northern part of the territory, land speculators known as the Santa Fe Ring concocted ruses that divested hundreds of Hispanic landowners of their farms and ranches.

All in all, New Mexicans did not suffer the same degree of land usurpation as in other parts of the Southwest, but the acreage held by Hispanics prior to the Mexican-American War declined considerably. In the final analysis, while the Treaty of Guadalupe Hidalgo did not precisely define the rights of Mexicans, it is clear that most of the guarantees were not upheld and Mexicans in the Southwest declined considerably, economically and politically, during their experience with Anglo domination. But by the 1890s, considerable immigration from Mexico resulted in the swelling of Mexican communities throughout the Southwest, changing the character of Mexican life in the United States.

AFRICA AND THE MAKING OF SOCIETY IN CUBA
AND PUERTO RICO ♦

While New Spain evolved a society made up primarily of an Indian-Spanish race mixture, Africans and Europeans commingled with the few Indian survivors to form the Spanish Caribbean community. Sugarcane transformed the Caribbean region into a lucrative source of wealth for the Spaniards. But because the natives were too few, another adequate source of labor was found in Africa. The slave trade had been started by the Portuguese in the fifteenth century, but it did not become profitable until the great plantation system developed in such American regions as Brazil, the British colonies in North America, and, of course, the Caribbean islands.

The source of slaves in Africa was the western coast between the Senegal River to the north and Angola to the south. Africans were captured and sold to European traders, usually Portuguese, by slave hunters who many times were also Africans. Varying forms of slavery already existed among these ethnic groups where workers toiled in large-scale agricultural systems. Slaves were sought in this area, rather than in other African areas, because the people there already had some experience with systematic work demands.

The slaving expeditions in West Africa brought untold anguish to the Black Africans who were affected by the raids. Families were broken up as the young males (the most sought after) were torn from their homes. That was only the beginning of the suffering, however. In preparation for the odious voyage, captured Africans were first housed in overcrowded slave castles called *barranconas,* where thousands perished. In the trip across the Atlantic, thousands more died in the crowded hulls of the slave ships making their way either to the Caribbean islands or Brazil, where these human beings were auctioned off and sold like cattle in huge markets.

In the Caribbean islands, this human chattel was sent to work the hundreds of plantations developed by colonists from the major European imperial powers. Not all slaves wound up on the plantation fields, however, as they were also sold to artisans as helpers or to the huge households of rich merchants within the plantations themselves. Although males were preferred as slaves, hundreds of thousands of females also entered the market. Women worked just as hard, and it was not lost on slave owners that by coupling slaves of the opposite sex, even by promoting a family structure based on the new conditions encountered in the Caribbean, they could ensure that the offspring of the slaves would be born into slavery. This perpetuated a valuable commodity within their own domain.

In Cuba and Puerto Rico, under Spanish rule until the end of the nineteenth century, slavery was legal until late into the nineteenth century. But the growth of slavery everywhere in the Caribbean New World was intimately linked to the fortunes of sugarcane production. However, a large-scale sugar plantation system did not emerge in either Cuba or Puerto Rico until the end of the eighteenth century. Up to that point, independent peasant farmers, squatters that relied little on African slaves, and peons on large haciendas predominated. The development of slavery was slow as a consequence. Between 1550 and 1650, the slave population only increased from 1,000 to 5,000.

But that does not mean that life was in any way promising for slaves. Whenever they could, *cimarrones* (runaway slaves) ran away to Orient province, creating scores of fortified communities called *palenques*. Indicative of the discontent of the Africans in Cuba was the persistence of the feared slave rebellions. For example, 300 rebelled on one plantation in 1727, killing practically all of the Whites, and one year later all the copper mines were closed off in Santiago because of uprisings in that province.

In the late eighteenth century, the African population began to rise rapidly. Following thirty years of warfare between the European imperial powers, the British occupied Cuba in 1763, ushering in an intensive period of economic development; thus, sugarcane production expanded dramatically. From the time the first African slave stepped foot on Cuba to 1770, 60,000 were introduced to the island. Then between 1770 and 1790 there was a striking increase in slave traffic. At least 50,000 Africans arrived in those years alone. At the end of the century, a unique opportunity arose for investors in Cuban sugar production—the collapse of the Haitian sugar industry after rebels had ravaged that country in the 1790s—leading to an even larger number of slaves on the island. During this time, 30,000 French émigrés and their slaves entered Cuba from Santo Domingo during a time of rising prosperity in sugar and coffee.

The slave population continued to grow into the early nineteenth century, and by 1827, African slaves accounted for about 40 percent of the Cuban population, which was over 700,000. By midcentury, the percentage of

In Cuba before the nineteenth century, free Africans were more proportionally numerous than anywhere else in the Western Hemisphere, because the sugar economy was never as ensconced there as in other colonies, such as those of the British. These freedmen engaged in all kinds of trades and activities, creating a class of African-Cubans that enjoyed a status of independence not as attainable to Blacks in the British colonies. The ramifications of this more relaxed relationship, at least as it existed before the nineteenth century, is crucial to the persistence of African culture in Cuba.

African-born slaves expanded to about 70 percent of the slave population and, for the first time, Blacks outnumbered Whites. In the 1850s, the combination of free Afro-Cubans and slaves made the Black population over 56 percent. According to one study, 550,000 slaves were imported into Cuba between 1812 and 1865 in spite of the worldwide ban on the slave trade that was instituted by the British in the 1820s.

A remarkable expansion in Cuban sugar production accounted for the growth of slave traffic in the nineteenth century. While many slaves toiled on coffee *fincas* or haciendas or tobacco *vegas,* most worked on sugar *ingenios.* The percentage of Blacks, which throughout the colonial period had been among the smallest in the Caribbean, was now larger than anywhere else. Quite predictably, during the nineteenth century, slave rebellions became more common. In these, Whites were often killed, and retribution was quick and brutal. Suppression of the uprisings was often consummated by the indiscriminate execution of slaves, regardless of their involvement. Rebellions increased because of the larger number of newly arrived slaves from Africa with immediate memories of their lost freedom; they were resentful and less accepting of their lot.

Independence sentiment was retarded in Cuba because of this reliance on slavery by Whites. Lacking was the diversity of dissatisfied classes that characterized other colonies in New Spain whose independence struggles started early in the nineteenth century. Island society reflected the dichotomy of the Black and White races more than ever. The Haitian example, where the independence movement was unleashed by the pent-up emotions of slaves, struck a familiar chord of fear among the White planter class.

But the world was changing as industrialization and technological innovation required new markets and the use of more diverse amounts of raw materials. Cuba could not remain out of step for long in its use of outmoded methods in the production of sugar. In the second half of the nineteenth century, some Cuban and Spanish capitalists realized that Cuba's success in the impending order required diversified production and the use of wage labor that was cheaper and more efficient than slavery. As a consequence, the sugar industry was modernized, made more competitive, and expanded. Foreign capital from the United States was largely responsible for the innovations, and the colonial economy passed increasingly into the hands of North Americans.

To meet the wage-labor demands, 125,000 Chinese were brought to Cuba between 1840 and 1870 to work as cane cutters, to build railroads in rural areas, and to serve as domestics in the cities. Also, the influx of European immigrants, primarily from Spain, increased during that period. Newly arrived Spaniards became concentrated in the retail trades and operated small general stores called *bodegas*. In the 1880s, slavery was abolished by Spain in a gradual program that took eight years. The influx of new people in this period made Cuba more heterogeneous, leading to the social diversity that is so apparent today. Immigration to the United States before the revolution of 1959 was more reflective of this racial variety. But as Cubans fled communism in recent years, the outflow came more from the descendants of European emigrants.

In the nineteenth century the slave traffic did increase, but it was not as important in establishing a rural culture as was the case in Cuba. In many regions of Puerto Rico, a large class of rural poor Whites and persons with a mixed European, African, and Indian heritage dominated. Their way of life was strictly preindustrial. Country folk eked out a living as peasants, tenants on subsistence farms, or craftsmen in the towns and villages. This group came to be known as *jíbaros* (a South American word for "highlander" or "rustic") and remain to this day an identifiable group in both Puerto Rico and on the U.S. mainland.

As happened in Cuba in the first half of the 1800s, the importation of slaves increased because of an expansion in sugar plantations. At the same time, however, foreign investment and immigration grew, and the mixed classes who comprised the rural peasants and working people were marginalized by an empowered planter class and a large-scale export agricultural system. But the influx of slaves during the nineteenth century was larger than ever and African culture achieved a greater voice at the folk level, albeit mixing with a still strong jíbaro expression.

In Puerto Rico there has not been an upheaval such as the Mexican Revolution of 1910 or the Cuban Revolution of 1959 that would have provoked large-scale immigration of the middle and upper classes to the United States. As a consequence, the character of Puerto Rican society in the United States is more reflective of Puerto Rico's diversity. Unlike the case of Cubans in Florida, in New York and other cities where Puerto Ricans have gone in large numbers, the fine blend of jíbaro/mestizo, African, and European cultures is evenly dispersed. In Mexican-American society, on the other hand, the impact of the upper classes has been greatly miti-

In Puerto Rico, although African slaves were brought over almost immediately after the settlement of the island by Spaniards, they never quite acquired the numerical importance that they had in Cuba. In fact, the proportion of slaves in Puerto Rico never exceeded 14 percent. In 1775, for example, out of a total Puerto Rican population of 70,250, only 6,467 were slaves. As a result, one hundred years later when slavery was abolished, the transition to wage labor was easier than in Cuba.

gated by their wholesale return to Mexico after the revolution in the 1920s and during the Great Depression. Moreover, since the 1940s, the amplified immigrant stream that continues to arrive to this day is largely working class.

INDEPENDENCE OF CUBA AND PUERTO RICO ✦ ✦ ✦ ✦ ✦ ✦ ✦ ✦ ✦

As is the case with Mexico, independence from Spain and the eventual subordination of the island economies to U.S. interests provide the foundation for understanding migration from Cuba and Puerto Rico. Along with the Philippines, Cuba and Puerto Rico remained the only major Spanish colonies that did not secede during the massive struggles that wracked the entire Spanish Empire in the early nineteenth century. In the second half of the century, both these Caribbean holdings experienced conspiracies and rebellions, although efforts to finally obtain independence were not successful until 1898. In Cuba, a nationalist movement was vitalized in the latter part of the century as Spain's treatment of the colony became increasingly arbitrary. A crosscut of the Cuban classes became more and more resentful as the inept and corrupt colonial government imposed heavier taxes and, through censorship, restricted their freedom.

But much of the sentiment for liberty came from the sizable class of middle-class farmers and merchants who opposed slavery and desired to be free of the Spanish colonial tie. On the first issue, Madrid waffled, and although total freedom was eventually granted to the slaves, it came very slowly. In October 1868, a group of Cuban rebels led by Carlos Manuel de Céspedes, a Black general, took advantage of revolutionary fomentation in Spain itself and declared independence at Yara in the eastern portion of the island. This region had few slaves and was a hotbed of emancipation activity.

A provincial government headed by de Céspedes was established in Orient province, where Yara is located, and from there the movement obtained widespread support. The bloody Ten Years' War ensued, in which Spanish attempts to evict the rebels from the eastern half of Cuba were unsuccessful. Guerrilla tactics used by the rebels stymied the efforts of Spanish troops, but neither side could really win a clear victory. The war came to an end when both rebels and Spaniards signed the Pact of El

Zajón in 1878. The document promised amnesty for the insurgents and home rule; it also provided freedom for the slaves that fought on the side of the rebels.

Eventually, slavery was abolished, but Spain's failure to provide political reform provoked the Cubans to reconsider independence. In 1895, the poet and patriot José Martí opened the final battle for independence. Much of the planning for this insurrection was done in New York, where Martí had obtained Yankee support. But looming darkly behind the whole liberation cause were North American economic and political interests. Because of its proximity, Cuba had strategic value for the United States, but as long as it was under Spain, many Americans thought that it would not fall into the wrong hands. In the nineteenth century, Americans tried to buy the island from Spain on several occasions. In 1869, taking advantage of the chaos of the Ten Years War, the United States offered $100 million for the island but was rejected. So it was not surprising, when independence seemed more likely at the end of the nineteenth century, that U.S. officials pressed to influence the unfolding process.

Before the Civil War, Southerners wanted to annex Cuba in order to expand the territory under slavery, but antislavery interests in the United States thwarted any such plans.

The trajectory toward independence in Puerto Rico was not as conspicuous as in Cuba, but a strong sentiment for freedom emerged, nonetheless. Puerto Rican nationalism was influenced by the same conditions that provoked the feeling in Cuba. While the planter classes expressed a wish for political autonomy from the mother country, they also wanted to maintain an economy based on slavery and peonage. Equivocal and confused about their desires, the criollo elites vacillated and were reluctant to assume the lead toward acquiring independence.

The nationalist movement was directed more by activists from the urban middle class and small farmers. This was especially true after 1850, when the Madrid government assumed a more mercantilistic stance. But in spite of high-tariff barriers that were designed to force Puerto Ricans to pay more for American-made goods, so that Spanish merchandise would be cheaper, Spain's hold over the Spanish Caribbean steadily declined as it lost control over the sugar trade to the Americans. By 1870, 68 percent of Puerto Rican sugar products were marketed in the United States and only 1 percent were sent to Spain. Exerting its imperial power, Madrid, by the time of independence, managed to regain 35 percent of the market and continued to provide the Caribbean colonies with some finished products. Still, U.S. merchants were buying 61 percent of all Puerto Rican exports, while providing the lion's share of all industrial machinery necessary for processing sugar cane. Eventually, it became evident to the Puerto Ricans, as it did to the Cubans, that the link to the mother country was both intrusive and unnecessary.

The earliest indication of a strong united Puerto Rican nationalism goes back to 1867. On April 27, a mutiny among Spanish troops stationed on the island provoked the colonial governor, who was uneasy over the possibility of freedom movements, to not only execute the mutineers but also round up and exile known sympathizers of independence. Among these was Ramón Emeterio Betances, who fled to New York, where he joined other like-minded Puerto Ricans and Cubans. On September 23, 1868, this group declared an abortive insurrection known as El Grito de Lares. Members of the *criollo* middle class and free Afro-Cubans who lived in the coffee-growing region of Lares were the main supporters of the effort. The poorly planned attempt was doomed from the outset, and Spain easily defeated the insurrectionists.

But the movement did not die with the failure of the Lares revolt. As in Cuba, Puerto Ricans remained dissatisfied with the mother country's feeble attempts to redress their accumulating grievances. Later in the century, such patriots as the intellectual José Julián Acosta and the young and untiring newspaper editor Luis Muñoz-Rivera were responsible for forcing major concessions from Spain. A covenant was signed in 1897 that granted to both Cuba and Puerto Rico autonomy and home rule.

But much of the movement for complete independence was already set in motion, and these gestures from Spain were too little, too late. Increasingly, a vital core of Puerto Rican conspirators joined their Cuban co-colonialists in a movement for freedom. But every leap toward freedom from Spain threw the revolutionaries into the American sphere of influence. When José Martí initiated the final battles for independence in 1895 in Cuba, much of his preparation was done in the United States. Martí had started his proindependence party, the Cuban Revolutionary Party (PRC) in Tampa, Florida. Many of the patriots, such as Tomás Estrada Palma, the first president of independent Cuba, acquired U.S. citizenship while in exile and then returned to the island to join the insurgency. Tragically, the valiant efforts of these patriots involved them with the United States to such a degree that the final price was costly. In the end, Cuba and Puerto Rico traded one master for another.

American support quickly turned into outright confiscation of the Cuban and Puerto Rican rebel cause. President William McKinley, reflecting an

American longing for a maritime empire, seized the opportunity given him by the *Maine* and declared war against Spain on April 28. Five months later Spain capitulated and signed the Treaty of Paris, transferring Cuba, Puerto Rico, and the Philippines to the United States. President McKinley quickly achieved the overseas realm that he wanted.

Cuba, unlike Puerto Rico, was allowed to become independent and promulgate a constitution, but hopes for true Cuban sovereignty were quickly dashed when Cuban politicians were pressured into including the Platt Amendment in their founding document. The provision allowed the United States to intervene militarily in Cuban affairs. The two neighboring Caribbean islands had much in common but had evolved separate cultural and ethnic identities. Overnight, both began an intimate, albeit antagonistic, relationship with the United States. Out of such closeness, migration to the mainland ensued.

When the American battleship the USS Maine *blew up mysteriously in Havana Harbor in April 1898, "yellow press" newspapers in the United States clamored for war against Spain.*

♦ ♦ ♦ EARLY MEXICAN IMMIGRATION TO THE UNITED STATES

Mexican immigration to the U.S. by the beginning of the twentieth century can roughly be placed in three categories. The first is migrants who were left outside the borders of a shrinking Mexico after 1836, 1848, and 1853 and the natives who, although not really migrants, were considered foreigners in their native land. The second category consists of migrants who continued entering and leaving the U.S. Southwest in a preestablished pattern that preceded the takeover. The third and most important group, in terms of the bigger picture of immigration, are Mexicans who arrived in response to the dramatically expanding need for laborers after the 1880s.

Three significant events occurred in Anglo-Mexican relations that set the stage for this immigration pattern. The Texas Rebellion (1836), the Mexican War (1848), and the Gadsden Purchase (1853) severed immense territorial lands from Mexico and the eighty thousand or so Mexicans that were living on them. These Spanish-speaking settlers were dispersed in sparsely settled areas throughout the lost territories. In less than forty years, they had been subjects of Spain and citizens of Mexico and were now entering a new phase. The inhabitants were descendants of the Spanish-Mexican settlers who had migrated from the interior of Mexico and in many areas had pushed aside or conquered the indigenous groups that occupied the land before them. Now they found themselves conquered and colonized, separated from their political and cultural roots by an invisible and, for a time, unpatrolled boundary line.

When the United States took over these territories, it acquired a Mexican population that was for all intents and purposes a continuation of Mexico's northern frontier. The inhabitants during the Mexican period had migrated freely back and forth across what was later to become a border. Movement made by parents, grandparents, brothers, uncles, and kin of all types meant that an extensive network of family ties existed in the region that was now politically divided. In southern Arizona, for example, thousands of Mexicans had abandoned their lands for Sonora during the independence period in the early nineteenth century, mostly because of a menacing increase in Indian depredations.

In spite of the changed political status, migration within the border region continued during the early occupation period, and immigrants were, for the most part, oblivious to the geopolitical distinctions that national governments made so carefully. Various factors stimulated this migration. In some cases economic inducements, such as the discovery of gold in California, provoked a massive outpouring of miners from Sonora and other parts of Mexico. They arrived before the influx of the Anglo forty-niners, and mining techniques introduced by these northern Mexican miners prevailed in the numerous mining centers of California during the heyday of the gold rush. After 1836, thousands of peons fled the large haciendas of northeast Mexico, seeking their freedom in south Texas; the border was much closer now.

In general, before 1870 there were only minimal economic inducements to Mexican immigration to the United States. Anglos who came after 1836 and 1848 interacted within the native Mexican economy through raising stock and some mining. Markets for southwestern products did expand during the early years of the Anglo takeover, as population growth throughout the territories demanded more foodstuffs. Mexicans in Texas, New Mexico, and California, however, had been trading with American interests in the East before the Texas rebellion and the Mexican border campaign. With the changeover to American rule, trade patterns were little changed, except that markets in the East for cattle hides, tallow, wool, and other stock-raising products widened and diversified. Furthermore, in New Mexico and Arizona a flourishing trade developed as the U.S. Army increased its efforts to subdue and destroy the nomadic Indian tribes. Provisions for troops and Indian reservations were channeled through private merchant houses in Santa Fe, Albuquerque, and Tucson.

Trade with Mexico, which before the nineteenth century had been the main source of external activity in all of the Southwest, continued after 1848, and many Mexicans entered the Southwest as transport workers or to act as agents for merchant houses in Monterrey. During the American Civil War, when southern ports were blocked off by the Union Navy, cotton was transported through Texas to such Mexican ports as Tampico in order to ship the product to European markets. Moreover, Arizona ports of entry to Mexico served California exporters and importers as a gateway to the Mexican ports of Guaymas and Mazatlan for shipping to the United States east around the Cape of Good Hope and over the Isthmus of Panama.

Initially, the labor needs of this slowly expanding economy were met by the resident population. Some immigration from Mexico, Europe, and the eastern United States provided the rest. Except for some cotton in Texas and gold and silver mining in other southwestern areas, there was little requirement for intensive labor use. After 1880, because of the railroad, dramatic changes in the southwestern economy stimulated Mexican immigration tremendously. Radical economic transformations that occurred not only in the Southwest but in Mexico as well dictated this later trend. By 1900, a railroad network integrated Texas, New Mexico, Arizona, and California with northern Mexico and parts of central and southern Mexico. The economic impact of the railroads soon drew Mexicans into the United States in a movement that dwarfed the influx of previous years. After the 1880s, then, the strong ties that previous *norteño* (northern) immigrants had to the Southwest and its native peoples diminished as railroads induced the migration of Mexicans whose roots were farther and farther from the border.

In northern Mexico, similar railroad building took place during the same years. The new railroads were financed by American interests, and, as in the American Southwest, the northern Mexican economy became linked to the crucial markets of the U.S. industrial basin in the Midwest and the Northeast. In northern Mexico, an economic transformation resulted, and adjacent areas along both sides of the U.S.-Mexican border supported similar agriculture and mining interests that depended completely on the same railroad network to market their products.

The Southwest was still sparsely populated during this period of rapid economic growth. Thousands of Anglos and Europeans had come in be-

During the two decades before 1900, 127,000 Mexicans entered the United States from Mexico, one and one-third times as many as the native Mexican population in 1848.

fore the railroad era, and even more came after trains revolutionized transportation. Initially, many were induced by the discovery of gold and silver, but more consistently they came as farmers, small-scale merchants, and clerks and to work in other middle-sector positions. Many of them were squatters who slowly drew away the lands of the old Mexican elites. But a great many were middle-class entrepreneurs and agents of eastern companies who during the railroad era forcibly acquired millions of acres that had once belonged to wealthy Mexicans. It was these entrepreneurs who were responsible for the huge agribusiness and mining development in the Southwest. In the process it was discovered that the resident Mexican population was not sufficient to meet the growing labor needs. The poorer classes of Anglos did not compete with Mexicans because of the low wages offered in agriculture or because of the menial type of labor involved. Besides, many of the poorer Anglos were involved in their own endeavors on small farms and ranches.

In California, Chinese labor continued to be used after the building of the transcontinental railways from northern California during the 1860s and the development of southern California after the 1870s. In the 1880s, the first Chinese exclusion acts were passed by Congress in response to nativist pressures, but surreptitious entry continued into the twentieth century. In other parts of the Southwest, a dependence on Mexican labor remained the only alternative. Since railroad building in most of Mexico had resulted from the same thrust that built the lines in the Southwest, workers from Mexico were used in the construction, and the same reserves were utilized within both political zones. European laborers were also used in the West, but only a small number filtered southwest of industrialized cities like Chicago and Kansas City.

In New Mexico, which contained the largest native population of Mexicans after the 1848 takeover, many of the old elites made the transition into the new economic and political structure, which was increasingly dominated by Anglos.

Once Mexican immigrants were in the United States, they could, in many ways, identify with the Southwest, which at the turn of the century was still very Mexican. Nevertheless, the Mexican was an immigrant in every sense of the word. Unable to speak or understand English, the dominant language, they were subject to immigration laws and regulations and forced to adapt to a foreign pattern of racism and discrimination. The native Mexican American, while faced with similar problems, was able after lengthy exposure to the gringo to make the adaptations necessary for survival and to participate more within the system.

Among the immigrants themselves, adaptation and the difficulty of life in the United States varied. Much depended on their economic conditions when crossing the border, the ability to transport families, the type of labor they performed, the distance between origins in Mexico and ultimate destination in the United States, and the type of community they lived in once in the United States. Before the Mexican Revolution of 1910, because practically all immigrants came from the lower classes, poverty was an endemic problem. The only commodity that such immigrants could trade was their labor.

These newer immigrants tended to cluster around existing Mexican communities, and their cultures competed with and then mingled with the older norteño-Southwest societies. Distinctions were made among the Mexicans themselves, whenever the three groups were thrown together, and often a social order existed, with the central Mexican at the bottom.

Rapid economic expansion in the Southwest also meant that the settlement of Mexicans shifted beyond the original native Hispanic centers. Anglos and Mexicans were attracted to the numerous new communities that sprang up along the length of the railway lines in new agricultural sections and in the emerging mining districts. Here the Mexican *colonias* (colonies) were all new, made up of displaced Southwest natives and Mexican immigrants. Such communities were formed in cotton-based towns in Texas during the early 1900s, and the same was true of the countless communities in the sugarbeet-growing regions of Colorado and California and in the mines of Arizona and New Mexico.

By 1915, Mexicans could be found as far north as Chicago and Kansas City. Most were from west-central Mexico. Thus, when the United States demanded a greater amount of labor during World War I, it was the inhabitants of the cities and villages along the railroad lines in Mexico, who already had exposure to the American North, particularly those from the Bajío region of Mexico, who were recruited. During the fifteen years or so following the start of the Mexican Revolution in 1910, a massive outpouring from Mexico greatly changed the demographic profile of Mexicans in the United States.

THE MEXICAN REVOLUTION AND IMMIGRATION TO THE
UNITED STATES ♦

During the Mexican Revolution, large numbers of middle-class Mexicans joined the emigrant streams for the first time. They composed a group that was critical to the formation of Mexican expatriate culture in the United States.

The Mexican Revolution entailed a tremendous exodus of human beings fleeing political persecution, military impressment, depressed economic conditions, and simply the crossfire of violent events. The hard-fought struggles and their aftermath bred new social and economic conditions that drastically altered and disrupted Mexican society to the point that many, who would not have emigrated under their previous circumstances, flocked to the United States in large numbers.

After Francisco I. Madero issued the Plan de San Luis Potosí in 1910, eventually hardly any region of Mexico was left untouched by the struggle that followed; almost every citizen and foreigner in the republic was affected. All in all, Mexicans endured twenty years of bloodshed. Many were caught up in the struggle because they believed the revolution was for the best. Others did not want the revolution, because it was not in their interest. The majority simply did not understand it or could not relate to its limited goals. Many of the disaffected, finding their Mexico torn asunder, left.

Most refugees were from the lower and middle classes, but families like the Creels and the Terrazas of Chihuahua, and other wealthy *norteños,* lived comfortably while in the United States, accompanied by their liquid assets, which were deposited in American banks along the border. It was not until 1915 that the flight of large numbers of refugees assumed massive proportions in the Bajío (west-central Mexico) and its environs, during a time when not only the direct destruction of the battles, but also the economic side effects of war, served to expel people from Mexico. During the struggles in Mexico, World War I spurred growth in every sector of the U.S. economy, owing primarily to the nation's position as a supplier to warring factions in Europe. Labor requirements had never been so great, yet disruption in trans-Atlantic transportation during the war and utilization of potential European emigrants in opposing armies were beginning to hinder the influx of workers from traditional European sources. When the United States became directly involved, American laborers were drafted, and a vacuum was created in industry, agriculture, mining, and transportation. These sectors looked south of the border to meet demands for expanding labor requirements during a time when Mexico was experiencing one of its worst economic crises.

Obtaining easy access to Mexican labor during this time of duress in Mexico and labor scarcity in the Southwest proved to be more difficult than had been the case in previous years, however. In February, Congress, in response to nativist pressures, enacted the Immigration Act of 1917, imposing a literacy requirement and an eight-dollar head tax on all individual immigrants. The act was passed before the United States entered the war, apparently without considering the manpower shortages that the wartime economy could create. The bill was designed to curb an "undesirable" influx from southern and eastern Europe, an immigrant group characterized by immigration officials as being two-thirds illiterate. Nevertheless, the act ultimately inhibited immigration to the United States from Mexico. Some of the Mexican states, such as Michoacán, a source of large numbers of emigrants, had illiteracy rates as high as 85 percent. In addition, the eight-dollar head tax was prohibitive for most migrants, many of whom arrived at the border destitute. Legal immigration of Mexicans suffered a temporary setback that year.

Surreptitious entry continued, but initially the interests that needed Mexican labor wanted legal, free, and easy access to this valuable reserve to the south. As the summer harvests approached, agriculturists and related interest groups became desperate, and they pressured Congress to waiver implementation of immigration laws in the case of Mexicans. During June, Congress complied, but the waiver was applicable only to agricultural workers, and there was so much red tape involved in meeting waiver requirements that eventually both the employers and Mexican workers preferred illegal entry. In essence, the general requirement of the 1917 act stimulated clandestine immigration. Unauthorized immigration intensified in later years after another act, in 1924, required that Mexicans add a ten-dollar visa fee to the already existing head tax, thus increasing the total that every immigrant paid to eighteen dollars. A lucrative trade emerged after 1917 in smuggling illegal aliens across the Rio Grande. It consisted mainly of ferrying large groups of Mexican laborers on rafts to the U.S. side.

If the 1917 act proved to be an obstacle to legal entry, agriculturalists and other interest groups were more frustrated by what seemed a worse threat to their steady supply of labor. In May 1917, the Selective Service Act became law. While Mexican citizens were not eligible for the draft in the United States, unless they applied for their first naturalization papers, they were obliged to register with the local draft board, a requirement that Mexicans were loathe to comply with for fear of being drafted. Besides, during this era, first-generation Mexican Americans were indistinguishable from many Mexican-born citizens. Consequently, nationals from Mexico were mistakenly drafted anyway.

The conscription problem was eventually resolved and Mexican immigration resumed a normal flow. Mexicans by 1915 were also beginning to enter California in larger numbers. Asian labor had been heavily relied on in the past, but the southern California agricultural sector had expanded tremendously since 1915, and Chinese workers no longer sufficed. Secretary of Labor William Wilson suggested in June 1917 that the waiver be extended to nonagricultural sectors, such as transportation. The years of rapid economic expansion brought about by U.S. involvement in World War I resulted in Mexican migration to geographic regions that they previously never worked in, in such sectors as oil fields, munitions factories, meat-packing plants, and steel mills. Hundreds of colonias expanded or were established anew in cities such as Los Angeles, Kansas City, Chicago, Phoenix, and Houston.

Ironically, few Mexican immigrants of this era settled where traditional southwestern Hispanic culture was strong, such as in northern New Mexico and southern Colorado. Mexicans migrated to work, and work was more plentiful in areas where there were fewer Hispanics, in new agricultural towns, or in industrial cities that were built by Anglos, such as Chicago or Houston.

A lamentable side effect of the struggle was an increase in anti-Mexican prejudice. Americans resented and feared the revolution, which many times was brought to their doorstep at the border. The revolutionary Pancho Villa and his followers, for example, raided into American territory to obtain supplies, and on some occasions Americans were killed in these incursions. In 1914, President Woodrow Wilson ordered the invasion of Vera Cruz in an effort to depose Victoriano Huerta, a general who assassinated President Francisco Madero, the founder of the revolutionary movement, and took over Mexico. To get support from the American people for the invasion, however, Mexicans were cast as undisciplined and violent. By the 1920s, Anglo-American opinion of Mexicans was lower than before the revolution, and these emotions were taken out on Mexicans living in the United States. Americans failed to see that brutality is part of any war, not just a trait manifested by Mexicans during this era. Indeed, strong parallels exist between the behavior of soldiers, both Union and Confederate, during the American Civil War.

THE "MEXICO LINDO" GENERATION ♦ ♦ ♦ ♦ ♦ ♦ ♦ ♦ ♦ ♦ ♦ ♦ ♦ ♦

In the 1920s, economic expansion continued, owing to commercial agriculture and large-scale mining activity. But in addition, the United States was experiencing an all-time-high economic expansion in manufacturing. Increasingly, Mexican labor was used in cities. At the same time, immigration increased to floodtide proportions, coming from farther south in central Mexico, including Jalisco, Guanajuato, Michoacán, and San Luis Potosí. With the new infusion of immigrants from areas so remote from the Southwest, Mexicans found few familiar surroundings in agricultural or mining towns and in cities like Houston, Dallas, and Chicago. Also in this period, the vast majority of persons living in the United States who were considered of Mexican origin were either born in Mexico or the children of immigrants; the original Mexican residents of the United States were considered "Americans."

During the Mexican Revolution, a sizable portion of the Mexican urban middle classes and elites, who were the critical core in Mexico imbued with nationalistic feelings, immigrated to the United States. They were the most important source of nationalism, in addition to being the carriers of *indigenismo* (pride in the Indian heritage of Mexico) and other forms of patriotism.

Obviously, the maintenance of Mexican culture and the Spanish language was seen as the most necessary nationalist statement. The names given to their mutual aid societies, such as La Sociedad Benito Juárez, México Bello, Sociedad Cuauhtemoc, to name a few, demonstrate the close allegiance to Mexico. During this time the self-identifier was Mexicano/a in Spanish and Mexican in English.

Finding work, setting up homes, building churches, and coping with a hostile reception from Anglos dominated the lives of Mexicans in the colonias. Segregation, police brutality, and general rejection drove home the need to coalesce and embrace unity. The badge of inferiority imposed by the Anglo provoked the immigrants to dispel negative stigma by forcefully demonstrating that Mexicans engaged in positive cultural activities. They believed that Mexican artistic and cultural contributions were as good or better than those in Anglo America.

Another strong component of immigrant identity was a form of indigenismo, or the proud recognition of Mexico's pre-Columbian Indian ancestry. This ideology was deeply rooted in Mexican history and given profound expression by Mexican intellectuals and writers in the colonial period and throughout most of the nineteenth century. Understandably,

---

The majority of the Mexicans entering the United States between 1910 and 1930 were seeking work and intended to return home. Indeed, many did. But even those who remained harbored a dream of someday going back. Another characteristic of this emerging identity was an exaggerated loyalty to Mexico, coupled with a dutiful celebration of the Mexican patriotic holidays (fiestas patrias). The formation of this "México Lindo" (Pretty Mexico) identity became a full-fledged phenomenon in the nation's immigrant colonias.

the sentiment was carried to the colonias in the United States by immigrant leaders who deliberately maintained and projected this image. In this respect, reverence to Our Lady of Guadalupe, the Virgin Mother, who is considered to be an Indian, and the homage paid to Benito Juárez, also an Indian, is part of this tradition. Every major colonia in the United States had an organization named after Juárez and a Catholic church named Our Lady of Guadalupe. Religion served to provide more than a spiritual focus. It served to give a sense of purpose to the community, because it was the immigrants themselves who built and maintained the churches.

But in this early era the immigrants had to contend with intense police brutality, segregation, abuse in the workplace, and general rejection from the mainstream community. In the early part of the century *El Congreso Mexicanista* (The Mexican Congress) was held in Texas in order to implement a strategic plan to stem the tide of legal abuses and violence against Mexicans. The meeting was attended by representatives from Mexican communities across Texas, and although the lack of political power limited its success, the effort demonstrated that Mexicans were willing to defend themselves. It also served as model for later political mobilization. In later years, many other organizations also strived to end abuses against Mexicans in the justice system, such as the *Asamblea Mexicana,* organized in Houston in 1925. Perhaps the most distressing abuse was the disproportionate execution of Mexicans in prisons throughout the United States; Mexicans spent much of their collective energy attempting to save condemned men. In many parts of the United States, Mexicans formed organizations, usually called *La Liga Protectora Mexicana* (The Mexican Protective League), that served to protect the legal rights of Mexicans. On several occasions, Mexican consuls met with the state governor or the board of pardons and paroles, usually accompanied by members of Mexican organizations that had collected petitions with thousands of signatures pressing for clemency.

In 1921, a depression caused severe destitution among Mexicans who suddenly found themselves unemployed. The Mexican government, working through its consulate service, formed *comisiones honoríficas* (honorary commissions) to protect the rights of hundreds of thousands Mexicans who found themselves stranded in many communities and unable to return home after prices for mining and agricultural products had collapsed. Thousands were repatriated with money provided by the Mexican government, but those that remained found themselves destitute until the economy recovered.

A Mexican worker being fingerprinted for deportation.

Recovery from the 1921 crisis was quick, and economic expansion throughout the 1920s went beyond the boom conditions precipitated by World War I. Mexicans were again in demand, and during this decade their influx dwarfed previous entries. Resistance to Mexican immigration was intense, however. The larger their numbers became in the United States, the more nativists thought Mexicans were a threat to cultural and racial integrity. But employers would not countenance any restriction of a valuable labor supply. Indeed, when the National Origins Quota Act was passed in 1924 to curtail immigration, lobbyists representing agricultural and mining interests managed to persuade Congress not to include the Western Hemisphere. This ensured that the Mexican labor source would be protected. Nativists, such as Representative John C. Box of Texas, wanted to stop immigration from Mexico completely, but in the spirit of the prosperous decade, the desires of the powerful employers who needed Mexican labor were not overcome.

During this period, a product of the heavy inflow was the appearance of many new colonias with familiar México Lindo institutions. The leadership promoted cohesion and unity more successfully when practically everyone was newly arrived, was segregated from the rest of the society, and was working and bringing in some money. They expected their stay in the United States to be temporary, although most stayed until their death. As the American-born children of those who remained grew older, slowly the elders' influence waned as younger family members began to adopt American ways and identify with the United States as their permanent home.

DEPRESSION, REPATRIATION, AND ACCULTURATION ♦ ♦ ♦ ♦ ♦

The Great Depression altered the lives of everyone, and it also dramatically changed the evolution of the Mexican colonias. Mexicans who had been so desirable as workers in the previous decade became unwanted throughout the United States in the 1930s. From throughout the U.S., thousands of Mexicans left, many times pressured by community authorities. But those that resisted repatriation were more rooted and, in most cases, had families with growing children. Indeed, during the decade, a generation grew up that had no memories of Mexico. Their only home had been the barrios in their immigrant communities.

A cultural shift became apparent in the early 1930s. The dominant immigrant posture of the 1920s gave way to "Mexican American" adaptation, which was characterized by assimilation of U.S. values and a less faithful adherence to Mexican culture. By the mid-1930s it was apparent that a fusion of cultures was evolving. Cultural expression of Mexican Americans in this period was obviously influenced by Anglo society. Immigrant symbolism did not disappear in the 1930s, but the reinforcing influence from Mexico declined with the Depression-related hiatus in immigration. Ostensibly pure Mexican traditions were barely kept alive by the aging immigrants, who also were losing their influence over younger Mexican Americans born in the United States.

The México Lindo source of identity, then, however virulent it seemed in the initial colonia-building stage, did not survive the massive repatriation of Mexicans that had been provoked by the Great Depression. Repatriation, especially from the large cities, was massive and highly organized. This was especially true in Los Angeles and industrial cities in the Mid-

Men waiting in line at the relief office during the Depression.

west, but thousands left from more rural communities as well. For those remaining in the United States, Americanization was seized upon by the new leadership through organizations such as the Latin American Club in cities like Phoenix and Houston and the Mexican American Political Club in East Chicago. These groups, of course, were intent on achieving political clout. Even the word "Mexican" seemed to be abandoned in this period, as the term "Latin American" attests. Besides, the leaders of these organizations were no longer immigrants who intended to return to Mexico. They consisted of a new and younger generation that was either born in

The League of United Latin American Citizens (LULAC), initially very strong in Texas, eventually spread to other parts of the United States.

the United States or very young upon arriving. Overall in the decade, significant alterations took place for the second-generation Mexican Americans that had been born or raised in the United States. Increasingly more graduated from high school, and their expectations from the larger society were more extensive. The depression of the 1930s subsided because of wartime spending, and by the end of the decade, thousands of young Mexican Americans had grown up in this country exposed to the greater Anglo society through such New Deal agencies as the Civilian Conservation Corps and National Youth Administration, both designed to enroll young people and keep them off the streets during this era of massive unemployment.

WORLD WAR II AND THE MEXICAN-AMERICAN GENERATION ♦

When the United States declared war in 1941, Mexican Americans responded to the war effort enthusiastically. In spite of continuing discrimination, patriotism among Mexican Americans was intense, as they felt like part of the United States. Unlike their parents, they had no direct ties to Mexico. Thousands joined their White and Black counterparts in all branches of the armed forces. Most Mexican women stayed behind, but many moved to California and other industrial areas in the boom years of the war and worked in places where Mexicans had never been allowed. The League of United Latin American Citizens (LULAC) spread throughout the United States in the 1940s, and thousands of Mexicans not serving in the military engaged in many "homefront" efforts, such as bond drives. After the war, Mexican Americans strove to achieve political power by making good use of their war record. Many Mexican-American war veterans were motivated by the continued discrimination that greeted them after the war. In 1947, the American G.I. Forum was organized by Mexican-American veterans in response to the denial of a funeral home in Three Rivers, Texas, to bury a Mexican American killed in the Pacific. The organization went on to become a leading advocate for civil rights. In addition, many American Legion posts for Mexican Americans were founded by these same veterans.

Immigration to the United States greatly decreased during the Great Depression, during which time a generation of Mexican Americans was greatly influenced by Anglo culture. Because few new immigrants came, much cultural reinforcement from Mexico was lost. When the war ended,

Mexican-American GIs came back by the thousands to their barrios in cities and small towns alike. Many young people who had postponed wedding plans during the years of strife now married and had babies. These Mexican-American soldiers came back more assertive, ready to take their place in a society that, by any reckoning, they had fought to preserve. After the war, hundreds of young married Mexican-American couples moved to the growing suburbs and were further acculturated.

Mexican culture in the United States did not subside in spite of acculturation, however. The Bracero Program was instrumental in reviving immigration to the United States during the war years, reinstating the crucial link to Mexico. The program, in which U.S. labor agents actually went to Mexico and recruited thousands of workers, was prompted by the wartime need for labor. The experienced *braceros* (manual laborers) inspired many others to immigrate on their own. Many of these contract laborers worked primarily in agricultural communities and in railroad camps until the program ended in 1965; however, some of them stayed, or returned after they were delivered back to Mexico. Ever since then, the renewal of immigration has continued unabated.

But in spite of the resurgence of Mexican immigration and the persistence of Mexican cultural modes, Mexican Americans could not help but become Americanized in the milieu of the 1950s and 1960s, when more and more acquired educations in Anglo systems, lived in integrated suburbs, and were subjected to Anglo-American mass media, especially when television came into its own. It is difficult to measure just how pervasive Americanization was at that time, however. Certainly, the culture of Mexican Americans, fused as it was with general society in the United States, was more acceptable. But prejudice and rejection persisted. Nonetheless, Mexican Americans, more integrated into society, were more effective than ever in their efforts to break down obstacles to economic and social mobility. For example, in the 1950s and early 1960s segregation was abolished in Texas, Arizona, and many other communities, largely through the efforts of LULAC and the Alianza Hispano Americana (Hispanic American Alliance), another civil rights organization in the Southwest.

The Mexican movie industry, which came into its own in the 1940s, by the 1950s dominated the Spanish-speaking market on a worldwide basis and also ensured that Mexican culture entered with a new vigor into Mexican-American communities. It was logical that Mexican movies found a large market in the United States, where so many of Mexico's people were living and where no other medium equaled it as a vibrant exponent of Mexican culture. Only the record industry had as pervasive a Mexicanizing impact on Mexican-American culture.

FROM CHICANOS TO HISPANICS ◆ ◆ ◆ ◆ ◆ ◆ ◆ ◆ ◆ ◆ ◆ ◆ ◆ ◆ ◆ ◆ ◆ ◆

The late 1960s and early 1970s was a time of intellectual foment and rebellion in the United States. Caught up in the mood, young Mexican Americans throughout the country sought a new identity while struggling for the same civil rights objectives of previous generations. This struggle became known as the Chicano movement. The word "Chicano" was elevated from its pejorative usage in the 1920s to denote lower-class Mexican immigrants and from its slang usage of the 1940s and 1950s to substitute for Mexicano. It now symbolized the realization of a newfound and unique identity. Proudly, Chicanos proclaimed an Indo-Hispanic heritage, and accused older Mexican Americans of pathologically denying their racial and ethnic reality because of an inferiority complex.

The concept of Aztlán, the mythical place of origin of the Aztec, became the Chicano movement name for the Southwest.

In the movement, an attempt was made to use some of the same symbols of their immigrant grandfathers, but with a few added touches. Tapping several intellectual traditions, movement leaders attempted to define true ethnic character. Allusions were made to factual and mythical pasts used so often by *indigenistas* (indigenists). In addition, participants in the movement differed from the previous Mexican-American generation in that they did not care whether they were accepted and they rejected assimilation. Many of the images they construed reflected their alienation as they blended pachuco cultural modes, *pinto* (ex-convict) savvy, pre-Columbian motifs, and myth with a burning conviction that Chicanos were deliberately subordinated by a racist American society. Chicano student organizations sprang up throughout the nation, as did barrio groups such as the Brown Berets. Thousands of young Chicanos pledged their loyalty and time to such groups as the United Farmworkers Organizing Committee, which, under César Chávez, had been a great inspiration for Chicanos throughout the nation. An offshoot of both impulses, the farm worker and the student movement, was La Raza Unida party in Texas, an organization formed in 1968 to obtain control of community governments where Chicanos were in the majority.

In the 1980s, the term "Hispanic," which has considerable longevity, took a special generic meaning referring to any person living in the United States who is of Spanish ancestry. In the Mexican-American community, the term has been eagerly accepted, and only vestiges remain of the virulent nationalism of Chicano movement days evoked to forge an identity. The United Farmworkers Organization and La Raza Unida party, the latter still existing in various communities, are direct heirs of the movement, but they do not seem to have prospered in recent years. Use of the term Hispanic represents a rejection by the Mexican American leadership of both cultural nationalism and radical postures.

In essence, the "Hispanic Generation" is the latest synthesis of radicalism and nationalism. Those Chicanos that identify with Hispanic are more nationalistic than the GI generation, while rivaling Chicano movement activists in their fervor for civil rights. They also accept a nonwhite racial identity, paying lip service to the concept of Aztlán. But the new upbeat, sophisticated, "professional" image that the term conjures is alluring to the new generation.

Today, immigration from Mexico and Latin America continues unabated, a condition that has to be taken into account as we trace the continuing development of Mexican communities throughout the United States. Since the 1960s, a massive influx of Hispanic immigrants has reinforced Hispanic culture in the United States. All in all, the culture and identity of Mexican Americans will continue to change, reflecting both inevitable generational fusion with Anglo society and the continuing influence of immigrants, not only from Mexico, but from throughout Latin America.

The fiestas patrias celebrations have continued down to this date. Unlike those in the 1920s organized by the México Lindo leaders, the historical reasons for celebration do not figure in a very precise fashion. For example, during the Cinco de Mayo celebration, very little is said about the 1862 Battle of Puebla. Instead, the day seems to have been converted into a celebration of the Hispanic presence in the United States.

♦ ♦ ♦ ♦ ♦ ♦ ♦ ♦ ♦ ♦ ♦ ♦ ♦ **MIGRATION TO THE UNITED STATES FROM PUERTO RICO**

Most of the two million Puerto Ricans who have trekked to the U.S. mainland in this century are World War II- or postwar-era entries. And unlike the immigrant experience of Mexicans, or Cubans before 1959, the vast majority of Puerto Ricans entered with little or no red tape. After 1920, the passage of the Jones Act granted Puerto Ricans citizenship, even if they were born on the island. Migration out of Puerto Rico was a defined trend quite a few years before the Spanish-American War, however, establishing a pattern that would be repeated and accelerated in the twentieth century.

The first migrant wave was stimulated by escalating economic relations between Puerto Rico and the United States. Exchange between both areas actually began in the eighteenth century but did not achieve large proportions until the second half of the nineteenth century. Still a colony of

Spain, however, the island was subjected to the mother country's mercantilistic hold, thus trade was clandestine. For Puerto Rican planters and Yankee merchants, the exchange of sugar and molasses produced on the island for American goods that were cheaper than those from Spain was mutually satisfying. The chain of smuggling activity that led to the first Anglo incursions into Texas and California was, significantly, part of this very same process. The economic contact with North Americans eventually resulted in the divestment of Texas, New Mexico, and California from Mexico. A similar fate was in store for Puerto Rico and Cuba.

In the early nineteenth century the economic relationship was sufficiently mature for Cuban and Puerto Rican traders to found a benevolent society in New York to serve merchants and their families from both island colonies. But economic ties were not the only attraction in the United States for Puerto Ricans and Cubas. Many also found in the northern colossus a haven for plotting against Spain. From the time of El Grito de Lares, an insurrection in 1868, to the time Puerto Rican exiles formed part of the Cuban Revolutionary party's governing board at the end of the century, hundreds traveled to the mainland. Staying for years, some sent for families and found employment to sustain themselves. While most of the first exiles were from the criollo middle classes, eventually skilled artisans and laborers, all dissatisfied with Spain's rule, joined their compatriots in New York.

Large-scale immigration, however, is linked more to structural changes in the Puerto Rican economy during the course of the latter nineteenth century than any other condition. The freeing of slaves in the 1870s and the rise of coffee as a significant competitor of sugar created new land-tenure systems and more fluid labor conditions. As in Mexico during the regime of Porfirio Díaz, such radical changes disrupted the fabric of rural life, forcing Puerto Ricans into day agricultural labor or into the urban centers like San Juan. The population also increased dramatically in the course of the nineteenth century, from 583,000 in 1860 to 1 million in 1900. Meanwhile the labor market was not developing at the same rate. As a consequence, many of the unemployed decided to cast their lot with contractors who sought agricultural workers in other regions of the Caribbean. Eventually others found their way to the United States.

But hastening the process of migration to the United States was the acquisition of Puerto Rico after the Spanish-American War. In May 1898, Spanish fortifications in San Juan were bombarded by the U.S. Navy while U.S.

Army troops invaded the rest of the island to ferret out the Spaniards. Cheering crowds, longing for their independence, enthusiastically welcomed the U.S. forces entering Ponce under General Nelson Miles. Little did they know that soon they would trade the sovereignty of Spain for the tutelage of the United States. Quickly, a military government was established for Puerto Rico under General Guy V. Henry. But the transition was negotiated not with Spain, but with Puerto Ricans led by Luis Muñoz-Rivera. Muñoz had assumed the leadership of the home-rule government granted by the Spanish Crown just before the occupation by the United States, and now he had to deal with another foreign interloper.

A quasi republic under U.S. dominance was established by the Foraker Act in 1900. It created a lower house with thirty-five members, but the highest-ranking officials had to be appointed by the president of the United States. In essence, there would have been more self-direction under the autonomy agreement reached with Spain right before the American takeover. Muñoz-Rivera continued to serve his people as a politician, however, as an organizer of the Federalist party and as commissioner to the United States Congress from the protectorate. To the dismay of Puerto Ricans, this position did not carry very much power.

In spite of the victory of the Jones Act, Puerto Rico was quickly deluged by American economic interests. Absentee landlords built large, modern sugar plantations that wiped out even more preindustrial subsistence farming than was the case during the last years of the Spanish period. Even coffee production, in which thousands of workers had been employed, declined as the capital-intensive sugar plantations and refineries covered much of the island. In the towns and cities, artisans such as independent shoemakers, carpenters, and other craftsmen found their livelihoods abolished by manufactured commodities produced in the United States.

To be sure, as a result of the American intervention, schools, hospitals, and public projects were built. This development, designed to improve life on the island, also paved the way for the new American investors and hastened the end of a way of life on which most Puerto Ricans depended for survival. Additionally, jobs that employed many women in tobacco factories and domestic service all declined. As the twentieth century progressed, island workers were marginalized and reduced to part-time miscellaneous work, which in Puerto Rico is known as *chiripeo*. Unemployment and underemployment created even greater pressure to leave Puerto Rico.

In 1917 the Jones Act, a proviso more to the liking of Puerto Ricans, was enacted. Skillful diplomacy by island politicians resulted in the passage of this congressional bill that created two Puerto Rican houses of legislature whose representatives were more properly elected by the people. More important, in terms of how it would affect future immigration, the act conceded U.S. citizenship to Puerto Ricans.

In the early part of the century, Hawaii's sugar industry was in need of ex-perienced workers, and a few thousand Puerto Ricans were recruited. First they were shipped to New Orleans by ship, then by train to San Francisco, and then by water again for the last leg of the journey. Small colonias emerged in both San Francisco and New Orleans because some workers decided not to make the full trip and remained at these debarka-tion points. Most of the island people migrated to the eastern seaboard of the United States, however. In 1910, according to census figures, 1,513 Puerto Ricans were living on the mainland, two thirds in New York. Like Mexicans, their fellow Hispanics in the Southwest, Puerto Ricans contin-ued to arrive during World War I and the prosperous 1920s when jobs were plentiful.

U.S. immigration policy also influenced the pattern of migration from Puerto Rico. Two national origin quota acts designed to curtail immigra-tion from eastern and southern Europe and Asia were passed in 1921 and 1924. With fewer workers coming in from these areas, a labor shortage ensued. The Western Hemisphere was not included in the quota policy, however, and so employers turned there for labor. Mexico became a major source of workers, as did Puerto Rico. It was easier for recruiters to target Puerto Ricans because they could travel freely to the mainland as citizens. By 1930, there were approximately fifty-three thousand living in various North American communities, although most were in New York City. There, they concentrated in Brooklyn, the Bronx, and East Harlem. As their numbers increased in later years, these barrios remained the core areas of first arrival.

EARLY SETTLEMENT OF PUERTO RICANS IN THE UNITED STATES ♦

The establishment of Puerto Rican colonias was similar to that of the Mex-ican immigrant colonias, characterized earlier as the México Lindo phase of the Mexican-American experience. As Puerto Ricans first arrived on the mainland, they looked back to their island origins for identity. Although Puerto Rico, unlike Mexico, was not an independent nation, the vital na-tionalism pervading the island during the rise of independent sentiment was tapped by newcomers to the United States looking for a source of eth-nic consciousness. In the quest for roots during the Puerto Rican struggle for independence from Spain, the pre-Hispanic name of the island, Borinquen, was revived. Immigrants, in their new environment, used Borinquen *querido* (beloved Borinquen) to refer to a homeland to which they felt closer once they had left it. When the United States took over the island, love and identification with their roots increased even more, and many Puerto Ricans felt the U.S. occupation was as a continuation of the colonial experience.

The Spanish language, perpetuated through a barrage of newspapers, music, and theater, also solidified Borinquen kindredness and allowed Puerto Ricans to identify with other Hispanics in New York, such as Cubans and Spaniards.

The Catholic religion also served as a cohesive ingredient. As it did for Mexicans in Mexico, Catholicism in Puerto Rico took a unique shape according to the exigencies of local island society. On the mainland, the particular features of Puerto Rican worship served as an additional focus, bringing the islanders together in a common ceremony. Still, it was mainly in New York where Catholic churches existed that catered primarily to Puerto Ricans, albeit other Spanish-speakers also attended. Significantly, language affinity was perpetuated in these religious institutions as well.

Formal multipurpose organizations and clubs were probably the most important vehicle for cohesion, and they also served to make Puerto Rican settlement more visible in the city. The most common associations were the *hermandades* (brotherhoods). These societies, which could be traced to emancipation groups in the nineteenth century, provided mutual aid and intensified ethnic nationalism. Attending to primordial needs of the community, the brotherhoods appeared very quickly after the arrival of Puerto Ricans on the mainland. Additionally, merchant organizations and groups associated with labor unions also proliferated.

Political activity was also apparent during the initial building stages of the colonias. Associated with the desire for independence back home, such groups as the Club Borinquen had as their main agenda through such periodical organs as *El Porvenir* (The Future) and *La Revolución* (The Revolution), freedom from colonial rule. But because throughout most of this century Puerto Ricans were citizens before they set out from their homeland, they were able to participate much more than Mexican immigrants in American electoral politics. Usually associating with the Democratic

In the so-called Harlem Riots, in July 1926, Puerto Ricans were attacked by non-Hispanics as their numbers were becoming larger in Manhattan neighborhoods. As the Puerto Ricans united to defend themselves, symbols of the homeland common to all, regardless of regional origin, became a powerful bond.

party, but not always, they organized political groups and joined the ethnic machines prevalent in eastern cities as early as 1918. This of course was one year after the Jones Act granted Puerto Ricans citizenship. In the 1920s, *La Liga Puertorriquena* (The Puerto Rican League), an organization made up primarily of community associations, became an unabashed supporter of the Democratic party.

As was the case in the Mexican colonias in the United States, Puerto Rican businessmen perpetuated ethnic bonds by providing Caribbean food, barbershops, religious relics, and, very important, Latin records, and the phonographs to play them. Music and theater were two of the most important exponents of Puerto Rican solidarity, and by the 1930s such theaters as El Teatro Hispano in New York featured not only Spanish-language drama but also musical groups. Puerto Ricans pursued their penchant for music at the family level, as well. Practically every gathering, whether it was a baptism, wedding, or coming-out party, had the obligatory singing trio of two guitar players and a maraca player. The music itself intensified the link with the homeland and defined Puerto Ricans' experience as immigrants. Rafael Hernández, a trained composer and owner of a music store in New York, wrote numerous songs that embodied the spirit of this genre. Hernández's most famous piece is *"Lamento Borincano"* (Borinquen Lament). The song, like the Mexican *"Canción Mixteca"* (Mixteca Song), was a poignant but romantic reminder of the beauty and rural simplicity of the homeland.

As happened with Mexican immigrants during the Great Depression, there was a reverse migration. Between 1930 and 1934, probably 20 percent of the Puerto Ricans living in the United States went back to the island, although they were not coerced to the same degree as Mexicans to return home. Those who could hang on to their jobs, primarily in service sectors of New York and other eastern cities, became acculturated more to life in the United States. Moreover, the U.S. cities in which Puerto Ricans lived had a vital urban life that exerted a strong influence on growing families.

POST-WORLD WAR II PUERTO RICANS IN THE UNITED STATES

The most massive migration of Puerto Ricans, almost 2 million, occurred after World War II. While the wartime Bracero Program brought over

100,000 Mexicans to work in the labor-scarce economy of the war period, Puerto Ricans did not start immigrating in large numbers until the post-war boom era. They came in response to a classical push-pull phenomenon. Simply put, wages were higher and employment was more plentiful than on the island. Operation Boot Strap, a strategy designed to develop Puerto Rico economically, resulted in altering the employment structure, as had the modernization of the sugar industry earlier in the century. The project was the brainchild of the popular governor Luis Muñoz Marín, the son of nationalist patriot Luis Muñoz-Rivera. The plan emphasized investment, primarily American, in light industry and manufacturing. To a large degree, the process did provide more technical employment for some Puerto Ricans. But as investors turned away from sugar production, agricultural employment declined, and Operation Boot Strap did not adequately provide replacement jobs. Then in the 1960s, petrochemical plants and refineries, activities that required even less labor than light industry, pervaded much of the economy. The net result was inevitable: more migration.

New York Mayor Robert Wagner (left) shakes hands with Puerto Rican Governor Luis Muñoz Marín (right) as they share the reviewing platform with U.S. Attorney General Robert Kennedy during the annual Puerto Rican Day Parade in New York City.

As their numbers increased on the mainland, Puerto Ricans transcended their New York home, moving to textile mill towns in Rhode Island and Connecticut, factories in Chicago, and the steel mills of Pennsylvania, Ohio, and Indiana. The most remarkable feature of the new immigration was that it was airbound. The large volume of passengers leaving Puerto Rico soon drove the price of fares down and gave opportunity to new airlines, which pressed surplus World War II cargo planes into service. By 1947, over twenty airlines provided service between San Juan and Miami and San Juan and New York. In the 1950s, Puerto Ricans were also landing in New Jersey cities and paid, on average, forty dollars for a one-way ticket.

The newer arrivals, like their Mexican counterparts in Los Angeles and Chicago, crowded into large barrios in New York and other eastern cities. The cold weather in the Northeast was inhospitable and almost unbearable for the hundreds of thousands who had left their warm tropical island. Adaptation in this environment was very difficult, indeed. What is abundantly clear, and here there are some very close parallels to the Mexican-American experience during the postwar period, is that early Puerto Rican immigrants built a foundation of organizations and institutions that made life more bearable for later arrivals.

Many second-generation Puerto Ricans acquired some social mobility within the society to which their parents had migrated before the war, and in some cases these first-generation parents were already professionals upon arriving. Basically, however, prewar communities that cushioned the shock for the immigrants were strongly working-class in structure, very much like Mexican Americans. Unlike Mexican Americans, second-generation Puerto Ricans in the 1930s did not coalesce into organizations like the League of United Latin American Citizens, which was started in Texas in 1929 by frustrated Mexican Americans who found practically every avenue to opportunity in the United States blocked. Perhaps for Puerto Ricans in the United States before the 1950s, segregation was not as intense as it was for Mexicans in the Southwest, a problem that was particularly acute in Texas.

The second-largest concentration of Puerto Ricans outside the New York City area sprang up in the Chicago area. The birth of the Chicago colonias dates to World War II. Today, approximately 200,000 live in the city proper, and many thousands more in Gary and East Chicago, Indiana, and Milwaukee. One of the most important organizations in the early formation of the colonias was the *Caballeros de San Juan* (Knights of St. John).

Its main function was to provide leadership and religious values in the Puerto Rican community. Other groups known as hermandades emerged in the 1950s and 1960s and were similar to the ones formed in New York in the early 1900s. Religion continued to serve as a focal point of the community, and Puerto Ricans identified strongly with the folk level of worship, as did Mexican immigrants. In fact, they shared, in an amicable arrangement, Our Lady of Guadalupe churches in both South Chicago and in East Chicago with Mexicans.

As more and more Puerto Ricans committed to remaining on the mainland during the 1950s and 1960s, they encountered a great amount of rejection, but at the same time they demonstrated a growing concern for social and economic mobility. Their early employment pattern consisted of menial jobs in the service sector of the Chicago economy and in light factory work—in essence low-paying work. And because of housing discrimination, Puerto Ricans were relegated to low-rent but overcrowded housing. Exacerbating these grievances were inequities in the courts and a persistent pattern of police brutality in the barrio.

To face that challenge they resorted, as did Mexican Americans during this same period, to self-help and civil rights organizations. Like Mexican Americans, thousands of Puerto Ricans served in World War II and the Korean conflict. Because many of these soldiers left directly from the island, before they could speak English, the military became an educational experience. Upon being discharged, many opted to remain on the mainland, where economic opportunity seemed to beckon. But even for former soldiers, there were still many obstacles that had to be overcome to achieve any kind of equality.

The emergence of the Puerto Rican Forum in New York in the mid-1950s demonstrated a clear departure from the Borinquen querido organizations of the 1930s and 1940s that defined their identity in terms of political and cultural links to the island. The forum proposed an agenda to eliminate problems associated with urban poverty. In 1961, *Aspira* (Aspire) was founded to promote the education of youth by raising public and private sector funds. Clearly, both of these organizations were similar to the Mexican American organizations in the Southwest during the same period. Aspira, more than the Puerto Rican Forum, acquired a national following, serving Puerto Ricans wherever they lived in large numbers.

But when these organizations did not seem to alleviate the frustrations and despair that was common in many barrios, the politics of passion

In 1966, hundreds of Chicago Puerto Rican youths went on a rampage, breaking windows and burning down many of the businesses in their neighborhoods. Ostensibly, the riots were in response to an incident of police brutality, but the underlying causes were broader, linked to the urban blight that characterized their life in Chicago.

broke out. During this time, the rise of militant organizations that rejected the orientation of earlier groups emerged. As the Chicano and Black pride movements pervaded the consciousness of their respective communities, a similar voice was heard in the Puerto Rican barrios throughout the country. Foremost among the new militants were the Young Lords, a grass roots youth group that was similar to the Black Panthers in the Black community and the Brown Berets in the Chicano. They promoted Borinquen pride and put forth an agenda to change poverty-stricken neighborhoods. In both New York and Chicago, the Young Lords promoted neighborhood improvements using tactics such as sit-ins in service agencies and churches.

Today, Puerto Rican immigration is not as intensive as in past years, nor does it compare to the continuing and massive immigration from Mexico. But Puerto Ricans continue the movement back and forth, and such proximity keeps the fervor of their identity alive. Puerto Rico's status vis-á-vis the United States is still uncertain. In 1953, the island's capacity was upgraded from its protectorate status to commonwealth, a change that had the support of many Puerto Ricans. Today the island is divided, however, over the issue of what the island's relationship should be with the United States. Some would like to see Puerto Rico become a state, while others want independence. Independence, however unlikely, would eliminate the ability of Puerto Ricans to enter and leave the mainland freely. Probably for that reason alone, many who have families scattered on both the island and the mainland oppose such a status.

Puerto Ricans are, next to Mexican Americans, the largest Hispanic group in the United States and will continue to play an important role in the evolution of the rubric Hispanic ethnicity that emerged in the 1980s and is pervading the United States at the present time. Whatever the future brings in terms of the mainland-island political link, the millions of Puerto Ricans who came in the course of the last two centuries have already left their mark.

Early Cuban Immigration to the United States

Large-scale Cuban immigration to the United States occurred much more recently than that from either Puerto Rico or Mexico. In fact, over one million Cubans have entered the country since the Cuban Revolution of 1959. But like those of Puerto Ricans, Cuban communities in the United States can be traced back to the nineteenth century. From the outset, Florida, because of its proximity to the island and its Hispanic past, has been the destination of practically all Cubans. Each wave, starting with the first one in the 1860s, has many similar characteristics. A feature that distinguishes Cuban immigration from Mexican and Puerto Rican immigration is that Cubans have come in similar proportions from the middle class and the working class. As has been indicated, most immigrants from Mexico and Puerto Rico have been from the working class.

As early as the first major independence attempt, in 1868, Cubans left for Europe and the United States in sizable numbers. At least 100,000 had left by 1869, both as political refugees and in quest of better economic conditions. The wealthier émigrés fled to Europe to live in relative luxury, but middle-class merchants and professionals went to cities on the U.S. East Coast, such as New York. But the majority were workers who crossed the ninety miles or so to Florida. Cuban cigar manufacturers in Florida that had been operating in Key West since the 1830s eagerly welcomed the new arrivals for their factories. Key West was ideal for cigar-making because of its access to the tobacco plantations of Cuba. But more important, Cuban cigar-makers, such as the Spaniard Vicente Martínez Ybor, abandoned their Cuban operations and relocated to Florida, where they would not be as affected by Spanish mercantilistic policies. By the 1870s, Key West had become practically a Cuban town.

The Cuban community in the Florida town soon manifested strong ethnic solidarity, made even stronger by the affinity they felt for the Cubans fighting for independence back in their island home. Revolutionary clubs were formed to raise funds for the cause and to help such exiles as Carlos Manuel de Céspedes, who were organizing support in New York in the 1860s. A few years before he launched the 1895 independence bid, Jose Martí visited Key West often and considered the Florida town's Cuban community a key source of support for the cause of independence.

Once they established a base, Cubans became involved in local American politics. By 1875, there were over one thousand Cubans registered to vote in Monroe County, where Key West is located. The city's first mayor, who had the same given name as his father, was the son of Carlos Manuel de Céspedes, the hero of the Ten Years' War. In 1885, following labor problems in Key West, the manufacturer Martínez Ybor moved his operations to an area east of Tampa. The new development was named Ybor City, and soon other cigar manufactures located in the new complex. Countless cigar workers followed, and Tampa became the center of cigar-making in Florida. As in Key West, ethnic solidarity was bonded by the commitment

The third-largest group, influential beyond their numbers in the formation of "Hispanidad," as the poet Octavio Paz termed the identity of Hispanics in the United States, are the Cuban Americans.

to Cuban independence. Consequently, class differences were blurred as both wealthy owners and workers saw themselves supporting the same sacred cause. Other Cuban communities in Florida, smaller than the Key West and Tampa enclaves, also supported the independence movement, providing the exile aggregation with strong intraethnic links throughout the state. Racial differences between the White and Black Cubans tested the ability to bond, however. The tension became worse in Florida when Jim Crow laws separated the races and Cuban Blacks were forced to form their own institutions.

When Cuba was free of Spain, many exiles went back, but for many who had set roots in their respective émigré communities and who had children growing up in the United States, returning was difficult. Significantly, the Cuban presence in Florida during the last half of the nineteenth century was marked by many accomplishments. The first labor movements were Cuban, many businesses were operated and owned by Cubans, bilingual education received an impetus in the state, and, in cities like Key West and Tampa, Cubans were responsible for many improvements in city services and civic culture.

As Cuban political and economic influence increased in the nineteenth century, the Cubans played an increasingly more important role in U.S. policy toward the Spanish colonies in the Caribbean. But while helping the cause of independence, U.S. politicians also wanted to control a Cuba that one day would be free of Spanish dominance. Just as the struggle for Cuban independence had resulted in chaotic conditions leading to emigration, domination by Americans in the twentieth century fostered economic and political tensions that also provoked exile and emigration.

The Florida enclaves, established by earlier immigrants, served the Cubans who continued to arrive in Florida during the first fifty years of this century. Many left Cuba because of continued political turmoil on the island. In the 1920s, for example, a small number of young intellectuals moved to Miami to escape the repressive policies of Gerardo Machado and to plot against him. A dictator who ruled Cuba with the blessing of the United States, Machado was finally overthrown by a worker and student coalition in 1933. His demise was precipitated by the collapse of the U.S. economy, on which Cuba was completely dependent. He and his cronies, then, like countless others before them, also sought asylum in Florida. Since Cuba did not really achieve political peace after Machado's ouster, Miami, as well as other Florida communities, continued to be a refuge for Cubans who were not welcome in Cuba by the politicians in power.

◆ ◆ ◆ ◆ ◆ ◆ ◆ ◆ ◆ ◆ THE REVOLUTION OF FIDEL CASTRO AND CUBAN IMMIGRATION

It was for political reasons as well that the most dramatic exodus out of Cuba began after 1959. That year, Fidel Castro made his triumphant entry into Havana after he and his revolutionaries had defeated the brutal and repressive regime of Fulgencio Batista, a dictator who had been deeply involved in Cuban politics since the 1930s. Batista had become perhaps the most astute opportunist in the history of Cuba, and he returned Cuba to levels of corruption not seen since the Machado years. But at least in this period, he seemed content to allow democracy to take its course by allowing elections. Two irresolute and corrupt administrations followed Batista's in 1944 and 1948, dashing any hopes that these new leaders would bring political stability and honesty to the troubled island republic. Consequently, many Cubans became disillusioned with the promises of democracy. Then in 1952, Batista seized power again, this time as an arrogant dictator. Batista then took Cuba to new heights of repression and corruption.

For much of this time, Batista had the support of the United States. Ever since Cuba's independence, Americans had remained ever-vigilant about political events on the island. While policy toward Cuba followed the distinct requirements of the various U.S. administrations, both Republican and Democrat, the main course of foreign policy was to protect the extensive investments held by Americans in Cuba. The Platt Amendment allowed for intervention in Cuba whenever it seemed necessary to an American president. Indeed, before the 1920s, U.S. troops were sent three times to Cuba to intervene in internal affairs.

In the opinion of many Cubans, the United States had blatantly held Cuba as an economic and political colony. Even though the hated Platt Amendment was abrogated in 1934, it was apparent that Americans, during Batista's last rule in the 1950s, controlled most of the economy and much of the political process. By the time a young lawyer named Fidel Castro initiated guerrilla warfare against Batista, the former sergeant's feral methods of running his country began to alienate even the most cynical of American supporters. Thus, when Castro came to power in February 1959, his 26th of July Movement did not meet too much resistance from the United States, and at home he acquired a wide and popular following.

To Washington officials during the presidency of Dwight D. Eisenhower, Castro turned out to be more than what they bargained for, however. The

Batista was only an army sergeant when in 1935 he led a barracks revolt that overthrew a president installed by the military to replace the banished dictator Antonio Machado. Then the next year, Batista overthrew the government that he himself had helped come to power, and in 1940, after a series of machinations, he was elected the first president under a new constitution promulgated that same year.

young revolutionary exhibited an eclectic ideology, but it was clear that the new government was no longer going to permit American dominance, a stance which quickly alienated the Eisenhower administration. Another position, soon embraced by Castro, involved extensive land reform and radical restructuring of the economy. Very quickly, many of those affected, such as landowners and other members of the upper classes, turned against the revolution. Castro, to protect his fledgling movement, repressed those who resisted, and soon thousands of the disaffected left for the United States in a time-honored tradition established during the many previous shake-ups.

Increasingly, Castro adopted socialistic ideas and turned to the Cuban Communist party for support, but not before the Eisenhower administration broke off relations with his revolutionary government. Eventually, the Soviet Union pledged its support to Castro, while the American government initiated a plan to welcome refugees. Eisenhower's motives to allow disaffected Cubans to enter the United States unencumbered were largely political. The 1950s were characterized by a cold-war mentality in which the Soviet Union and the United States waged an intense propaganda campaign for world prominence and acceptance. The flight of refugees was correctly anticipated by American officials to be middle class and essential to Cuba's economic well-being. Thus, their escape would deprive Cuba of technical and professional skills, serve as a propaganda victory against communism, and, by extension, deliver a blow to the Soviet Union's world prestige. But the Eisenhower administration projected another role for the exiles. Considering the history of discontented Cubans using the United States as a mustering point for insurgency against governments on the island, American officials foresaw the potential for a repetition with the latest wave of arrivals.

With the election of John F. Kennedy to the presidency, relations between the two countries did not improve. President Eisenhower had encouraged Cuban refugees to prepare an invasion of Cuba to topple Castro, and in the cold-war atmosphere of the early 1960s, Kennedy subsumed this policy. In April 1961, Cuban exiles who were trained and armed by the United States but who did not receive direct military support in their invasion attempted a foray into Cuba that was doomed from the beginning. The failure of the infamous Bay of Pigs invasion embittered the thousands of Cubans who were in exile, but Castro's position at home was strengthened. To many observers throughout the world, especially in the Third World, the United States was clearly taking the side of the usurpers, who attempted to overthrow a legitimately based government.

With the Bay of Pigs fiasco behind him, Kennedy continued to welcome Cuban refugees and to provide more structured military training for Cubans, most of whom still desired another attempt at overthrowing Cuba's Communist government. But in 1962, Kennedy redeemed himself from the Bay of Pigs disgrace by backing down the Soviet Union on a Russian plan to establish missile bases in Cuba. After this, the more viable of the two courses inherited from the Eisenhower years was to expand the refugee program.

Increasingly, welcoming refugees became more important to the U.S. policy of destabilizing the Cuban revolutionary government than armed insurrection or outright invasion. Such a course deprived Cuba of the merchants, technicians, and professionals so necessary to the island's struggling economy. In the ten years after the disastrous Bay of Pigs invasion, almost 500,000 Cubans left the island. Because of the heavy influx, a special program was initiated to settle the refugees outside of Florida. Although the majority of the fleeing Cubans stayed in Florida, thousands more went to other regions of the United States, especially to California,

A legally immigrating Cuban woman is reunited with her granddaughter in Miami.

New York, and Chicago, areas that already had large populations of Hispanics. An elaborate project ensued that included numerous prerogatives
for incoming Cubans. Refugee emergency housing, English-language
training, federal educational funds for Cuban children, and medical care
became part of a package that facilitated the immigration process.

When Lyndon B. Johnson became president after Kennedy's assassination, he also vowed to embrace Cubans who wished to leave the island.
Cubans then qualified for immigration status under special immigration
provisions for refugees fleeing repressive governments. But Fidel Castro
himself announced as early as 1965 that Cubans could leave Cuba if they
had relatives in the United States. Castro stipulated, however, that Cubans
already in Florida had to come and get them at Camarioca Bay. Nautical
crafts of all types systematically left Miami to Camioraca, returning laden
with anxious Cubans eager to rejoin their families on the mainland. The
spectacle of the motley fleet of boats converging on Miami docks was dramatic, but the trip was also dangerous for the thousands of fleeing
Cubans. Many of the boats were not seaworthy and capsized. An airlift
was then organized with a great deal of publicity and fanfare. Thousands
more arrived in the United States before the flights ended in 1973.

Castro also tapped the refugee issue so that he could gain moral backing
from the rest of Latin America and from the millions of Cubans living on
the island who still supported him. He charged those who wanted to leave
the island with betrayal, branding the emigrants with the epithet *gusano*
(worm), which rhymes with *cubano* and is a derogatory name. In addition,
he constantly reminded the world that, while Americans welcomed
Cubans as displaced persons fleeing political persecution, they would not
allow the same considerations to Chileans, Haitians, and other Latin
Americans escaping repressive governments.

The final and most dramatic influx of Cubans came in the early 1980s. By
that time much of the hard antipathy that Cubans felt toward Castro had
become as much ritualistic as real. A generation had grown up in the
United States that did not have the same sentiments as their parents. In
addition, President Jimmy Carter, determined to depart from the cold-war
policies of his predecessors, made advances toward Castro, urging recon-
ciliation with the Cubans in the United States. Remarkably, moderate elements within that community responded and advocated harmonizing relations with the aging Castro. In 1977, a group of young Cuban exiles
called the Antonio Maceo Brigade traveled to Cuba to participate in ser-

vice work and to achieve a degree of rapprochement with the Cuban government. Back in Florida, many of the exiles branded these young envoys
as traitors, and a clear message was sent out to rest of the Cuban community that any sympathizers would have to face their wrath.

Nonetheless, Castro's overtures to the exiled Cubans escalated and they
were met with some positive response. His offer was the more attractive
because he promised to release political prisoners as well, most whom had
relatives in the United States. Cuban-American adherence to reconcilia-
tion with Castro and his government continued to provoke intense opposition from conservative members of the exile community, however. Indeed, some of the advocates of a dialogue with the Communist leader
were assassinated by armed paramilitary Cubans, but in spite of the opposition, relations between the exile community and Castro improved during the Carter years. They improved so much, in fact, that the earlier tact
of using the refugee issue for propaganda purposes was lost as the tension
abated between Castro and Cubans in the United States.

In April 1980, however, a dramatic incident received worldwide attention: a bus carrying a load of discontented Cubans crashed through the
gates of the Peruvian embassy in Havana and the passengers received political asylum from Peru. When it became apparent that what the gate-
crashers really wanted was to leave Cuba, Castro began to revise his policy of gradually allowing Cubans to leave. In a calculated move, the Castro
government announced that whoever wanted to leave Cuba should go to
the Peruvian embassy. Immediately, ten thousand people crowded in. The
Cuban government then processed and gave exit documents to those who
came forth. Cuban exiles who happened to be on the island at the time of
the embassy gate-crashing, upon their return to Miami, organized a flotilla
of forty-two boats. With Castro's blessing, they began the round-the-clock
evacuation of the "Havana Ten Thousand," and Carter, as did presidents
before him, decided to welcome the new influx of Cuban exiles.

Since the flotilla converged at Mariel Harbor to pick up passengers, which
totaled over 125,000 by the time the boat lifts ended at the end of 1980,
the refugees became known as the Marielitos. The explanation given by
Castro for this whole phenomenon was rather simplistic. He charged that
his policy of allowing exiles to visit the island had contaminated many erstwhile revolutionaries with the glitter of consumerism. It is probably true
that travelers from the United States to the island did tempt Cubans with
their abundance of consumer products, convincing many that life in a cap-

A shrimp fishing boat heavily loaded down with Cuban refugees sails for Key West during the boat lift.

italist society was easier than life in Cuba. Nonetheless, Castro had to accept that socialism was at this point experiencing many difficulties and not delivering on many of the promises made some twenty years earlier.

The new refugees differed significantly from the earlier waves of displaced Cubans. Few were from the middle and upper classes of pre-Castro Cuba, as were most exiles then living in the United States, and there were also some racial differences. The new arrivals were more reflective of the general racial composition of Cuba; many Blacks and mulattoes were in the Marielito ranks. Furthermore, in a crafty move, Castro deliberately cast out many political and social misfits during the boat-lift, an act that unfairly stigmatized the majority of 1980 émigrés, who were in the main normal, hardworking Cubans.

During the Marielito exit, Fidel Castro and President Carter became entangled in a now familiar struggle over which country would get more political capital from the refugee issue. Thousands of new arrivals crowded into processing centers, living in tent cities and even a football stadium in

Miami! Many of the refugees became frustrated over the delay in being able to leave the camps. For many the stay in these "temporary camps" stretched out into months, even years. The Castro government was quick to imply that the United States was not really that anxious to provide refuge to Cubans who were poor, uneducated, and racially not as White as the previous influx.

While these charges probably had some validity, the truth was more complex. Unlike previous émigrés, most of the Marielitos did not have families in Florida or elsewhere in the United States, and receiving a discharge from a camp required having an American sponsor. At first Cuban Americans and other Americans were anxious to provide this service, but as the excitement and newness of the boat-lift wore off, sponsors became harder to come by. The stigma suffered by Marielitos also led to difficulties once they were released. To be sure, a hard-core criminal element was dispersed among the new arrivals, but Marielitos were no different than the millions of immigrants who had preceded them to American shores in previous years. They sought to work and to find opportunities in their new environment. After all, that was the reason they had come.

As did Mexicans and Puerto Ricans, Cubans before the Castro era immigrated to the United States to work, to flee violence and repression, and, in general, to make a new life for themselves. Consequently, to survive, they forged fraternal organizations and looked to their homeland and culture to provide them with the necessary identity to build strong ethnic solidarity. In this respect Cuban Americans differ little from Mexican Americans and Puerto Ricans.

The vast, overwhelming majority, however, arrived in this country during the past thirty years. To be sure, fewer Cubans than Mexicans have immigrated to the United States in this same period, but the influx of the latter is part of a very long history of massive working-class immigration across the border. Cubans, because of the political conditions that provoked them to leave, were primarily from the more privileged classes. As a consequence, advantages of education, wealth, and racial acceptance allowed them to succeed in the United States at a faster pace than Mexicans and Puerto Ricans. In addition, because it was politically convenient, Cubans received an inordinate amount of assistance from U.S. administrations, from Eisenhower to Reagan, which helped their effort to settle and adapt. This has provoked invidious comparisons and charges that the cards were stacked in their favor. Much of this sentiment has some foundation in fact,

The Cuban community has now acquired such deep roots in the United States that the term "exile" for many is no longer applicable. The post-Castro refugees and their children, along with descendants of Cubans who came to the United States earlier in the century, are now just another ethnic group in this country. They are part of the larger aggregate of Hispanics in the United States.

Fidel Castro and
Patrick Flores

but it also has to be recognized that Cuban Americans have demonstrated a great amount of their own native initiative and drive, a fact that accounts for a large part of their success.

F. Arturo Rosales

*B*usiness

On January 1, 1994, the North American Free Trade Agreement between the United States, Mexico, and Canada went into effect. It has long been anticipated in the Hispanic community that NAFTA would greatly benefit many Hispanic-owned businesses for various reasons, including the advantage of Hispanics in knowing the Mexican culture, having the ability to conduct business in Spanish, and having a history of serving as cultural mediators for international business; the concentration of Hispanic companies in states that border geographically on Mexico; and the possibility of rendering services to larger U.S. corporations desiring to do business in Mexico. In the larger sphere, it is anticipated that Hispanics working in large U.S. corporations will become invaluable in the process of these companies setting up to do business in Mexico and with Mexican clients. Whether in operating their own businesses or serving as mediators for other firms, Hispanics in business have the opportunity, as never before, to be the planners, facilitators, and entrepreneurs of international trade. This trade will include not just Mexico but all of Spanish America as other countries in the hemisphere pursue integrating their economies with that of North America.

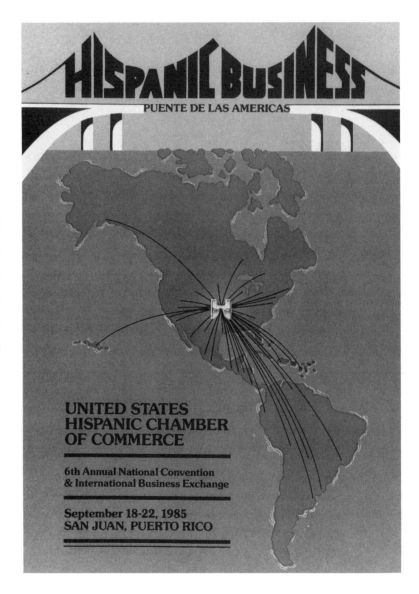

Poster for the 1985 United States Hispanic Chamber of Commerce convention showing that Hispanic business people are the bridge for commerce in the Americas.

FACTS AND FIGURES ABOUT HISPANIC BUSINESS ◆ ◆ ◆ ◆ ◆ ◆ ◆

Hispanic-owned businesses form a dynamic and complex sector of commerce in the United States. During the 1980s, Hispanic-owned businesses made impressive and important advances. In 1977, there were approximately 219,000 Hispanic-owned businesses, according to the U.S. Census Bureau. By 1982, slightly more than 248,000 Hispanic-owned businesses were thriving, a 13 percent increase. By 1987, 422,000 Hispanic-owned businesses were performing, an increase of 70 percent. By comparison, the number of nonminority businesses grew 18 percent from 1977 to 1982 and 14 percent from 1982 to 1987.

Caution needs to be exercised in interpreting Hispanic business growth over the three periods. The data collected in each of the census periods are not entirely compatible. Changes in survey methodology, for example, account for some of this incompatibility. However, there is no doubt that significant growth of Hispanic-owned businesses has occurred. Table 1 charts the growth of Hispanic-owned and nonminority-owned businesses for three census periods. (The U.S. Congress has authorized economic censuses to be taken at five-year intervals.)

TABLE 1
HISPANIC AND NONMINORITY BUSINESSES

YEAR	HISPANIC	NONMINORITY
1977	219,355	10,210,000
1982	248,141	12,059,950
1987	422,373	13,695,480

Sources: United States Bureau of the Census, 1980, 5; 1986, 4; 1991, 1.

Although 54 percent of all Hispanic businesses are owned by Mexican Americans, other ethnic groups within the U.S. Hispanic community have significant business interests. For example, 15 percent of all Hispanic businesses are owned by Cuban Americans, and 7 percent are owned by Puerto Ricans. Figure 1 provides information on business ownership by Hispanic origin.

Many Hispanic businesses have no employees and are staffed by a single individual who is typically the owner. Approximately 83,000 of the 422,000 Hispanic-owned companies have one or more employees. Nationally, these businesses employ close to 265,000 individuals, have an annual payroll of $3.2 billion, and have sales in excess of $17 billion.

While the number of Hispanic-owned businesses is growing, at present they make up only 3 percent of the total number of companies in the country. If all Hispanic-owned firms in the United States were merged into a single business, that "business" would have gross sales in excess of $24.7 billion. This new, merged Hispanic company would be equivalent in sales to Boeing, which ranks fifteenth on Fortune magazine's list of the five hundred largest U.S. companies.

TABLE 2
NUMBER OF BUSINESSES, SALES VOLUME, NUMBER OF EMPLOYEES, AND PAYROLL BY HISPANIC ORIGIN OF OWNERS

HISPANIC ORIGIN	ALL BUSINESSES		BUSINESSES WITH PAID EMPLOYEES			
	FIRMS	SALES (THOUSAND $)	FIRMS	EMPLOYEES	ANNUAL PAYROLL (THOUSAND $)	SALES (THOUSAND $)
Mexican	229,706	11,835,080	49,078	148,008	1,687,401	8,403,796
Puerto Rican	27,697	1,447,680	4,629	13,231	179,379	903,848
Cuban	61,470	5,481,974	10,768	47,266	638,459	4,227,065
Other Central or South American	66,356	3,202,238	10,793	27,386	343,039	2,031,768
European Spanish	24,755	2,054,537	5,299	21,196	293,976	1,628,133
Other Hispanic	12,389	710,091	2,341	7,759	101,088	534,822
Total	422,373	24,731,600	82,908	264,846	3,243,342	17,729,432

Source: United States Bureau of the Census, 1991, 12.

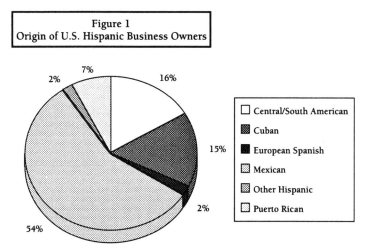

Figure 1
Origin of U.S. Hispanic Business Owners

2% 7% 16%

15%

2%

54%

- ☐ Central/South American
- ▨ Cuban
- ■ European Spanish
- ▨ Mexican
- ▨ Other Hispanic
- ☐ Puerto Rican

Table 2 includes a breakdown by Hispanic origin of the number of companies, sales generated, number of employees, and annual payroll.

The majority of Hispanic-owned companies are concentrated in services and retail trade. These two categories made up 60 percent of all Hispanic businesses and accounted for 55 percent of gross sales. Table 3 presents the number of companies and volume of sales for Hispanic businesses by industry category.

TABLE 3
HISPANIC BUSINESSES BY MAJOR INDUSTRY CATEGORY

INDUSTRY CATAGORY	NUMBER OF COMPANIES	SALES (MILLION $)
Agricultural services	16,365	694
Mining	829	29
Construction	55,516	3,438
Manufacturing	11,090	1,449
Transportation and public utilities	26,955	1,380
Wholesale trade	10,154	2,445
Retail trade	69,911	7,643
Finance, insurance, and real estate	22,106	864
Services	184,372	6,031
Industries not classified	25,075	758
Total	**422,373**	**24,731**

Source: United States Bureau of the Census, 1991.

TABLE 4

NUMBER AND SALES VOLUME OF HISPANIC BUSINESSES IN THE TEN LARGEST MSAs* vs. THOSE IN THE ENTIRE STATE

MSA	MSA		STATE	
	BUSINESSES	SALES (THOUSAND $)	BUSINESSES	SALES (THOUSAND $)
Los Angeles–Long Beach, CA	56,679	3,346,076	132,212	8,119,853
Miami-Hialeah, FL	47,725	3,771,247	64,413	4,949,151
New York, NY	23,014	1,239,513	28,254	1,555,801
Houston, TX	15,967	584,356	94,754	4,108,076
San Antonio, TX	15,241	657,174	94,754	4,108,076
San Diego, CA	10,373	559,444	132,212	8,119,853
Riverside–San Bernardino, CA	10,195	576,537	132,212	8,119,853
Anaheim–Santa Ana, CA	9,683	650,604	132,212	8,119,853
El Paso, TX	8,214	450,840	94,754	4,108,076
Chicago, IL	7,848	506,393	9,636	588,646

*MSA=Metropolitan Statistical Area.
Source: United States Bureau of the Census, 1991, 4.

Hispanic-owned businesses exist in virtually every state. However, 78 percent of Hispanic companies, with 80 percent of the gross sales, are concentrated in California, Texas, Florida, New York, and New Mexico. Most of the Hispanic businesses in these states are located in large urban areas. Table 4 shows the ten metropolitan statistical areas (MSAs) with the largest number of Hispanic companies and their sales. These ten MSAs account for close to 50 percent of the total number of Hispanic businesses in the United States and 50 percent of the gross sales. But the greatest concentration of the 100 Fastest Growing Hispanic Companies are located in California and Florida, according to an August 1993 study conducted by *Hispanic Business* magazine.

Hispanic-owned businesses for the most part are small businesses. Hispanic businesses with employees total 82,908. Fully 72 percent of these businesses had one to four employees in 1990. In addition, 17 percent had five to nine employees, and .2 percent had one hundred employees or more (see Table 5). In terms of sales generated by Hispanic businesses, 70 percent of them generated less than $25,000 in annual sales (see Table 6). This would lead one to conclude that there is a large proportion of Hispanic business owners with part-time operations. This conclusion is supported by evidence that 55 percent of all Hispanic business owners spend fewer than forty hours per week working with their businesses (see Table 4).

TABLE 5
NUMBER OF EMPLOYEES IN HISPANIC BUSINESSES

PERCENTAGE OF BUSINESSES	NUMBER OF EMPLOYEES
72	1-4
17	5-9
7	10-19
3	20-49
0.8	50-99
0.2	100+

Source: United States Bureau of the Census, 1991, 86.

However, a *Hispanic Business* magazine study in August 1993 compared the 100 Fastest Growing Hispanic Companies with the *Inc.* magazine 500 Fastest Growing Companies and found that Hispanic companies tend to employ more people. The average staff of the 100 Fastest Growing was 203, compared with 145 for the *Inc.* 500.

TABLE 6
SALES VOLUME OF HISPANIC BUSINESSES

PERCENTAGE OF BUSINESSES	SALES ($)
34	Less than 5,000
35	5,000-24,999
20	25,000-99,999
7	100,000-249,999
3	250,000-999,999
1	1,000,000 or more

Source: United States Bureau of the Census, 1987, 140.

Large-size Hispanic businesses are also growing. *Hispanic Business* monitors the 500 largest Hispanic companies in the nation; the latest list is reproduced in Table 7A (see p. 138). The list demonstrates the broad diversity of large Hispanic companies. Table 7B (see p. 140) lists the fastest-growing Hispanic companies, as compiled by *Hispanic Business*.

Hispanic business owners tend to be dynamic individuals who in some ways are very much like their nonminority counterparts and in other ways quite different. Hispanic business owners are likely to be younger than their nonminority counterparts. In Table 8 the owner's age for both groups is compared. In all, 80 percent of all Hispanic business owners are married, while a comparable 79 percent of nonminority business owners are married. The *Hispanic Business* study of the 100 Fastest Growing Hispanic firms also found that the companies were more likely to be owned by women (12 percent) than the non-Hispanic fastest growing companies.

Hispanic business owners have less formal education than their nonminority counterparts. Approximately 7 percent of all Hispanic business owners possess an undergraduate college degree, compared with 15 percent for nonminority business owners. On the other hand, 27 percent of all Hispanic business owners possess a high school diploma or equivalent, as opposed to 32 percent of their nonminority counterparts. In Table 9 the formal education of Hispanic business owners is compared with their nonminority counterparts.

Generally, a larger percentage of Hispanic business owners are first-time entrepreneurs compared with their nonminority counterparts. Approximately 15 percent of Hispanic business owners have previously owned a business, while 21 percent of their nonminority counterparts have. In addition, only 28 percent of Hispanic business owners have close relatives who own a business, while 40 percent of nonminority business owners do. Hispanic business owners as a group also possess less managerial experience than their nonminority counterparts; approximately 10 percent have ten or more year's experience as managers prior to establishing their business, while 21 percent of nonminority business owners possess such experience. Finally, 30 percent of Hispanic businesses were established prior to 1976, compared with 42 percent of nonminority businesses. These data confirm that Hispanic business owners as a group tend to have less business experience and tend to be more recent entrants into the world of business than their nonminority counterparts. Variations between Hispanic and nonminority business owners across several dimensions are shown in Table 10.

TABLE 8
HISPANIC AND NONMINORITY BUSINESS OWNERS BY AGE

	UNDER 25	25-34	35-44	45-54	55-64	OVER 65
Hispanic business owners	4%	22%	28%	24%	14%	4%
Nonminority business owners	3%	20%	25%	22%	18%	9%

*Source: United States Bureau of the Census, 1987, 10.
Note: 4 percent of Hispanic business owners and 3 percent of nonminority business owners did not report age.

TABLE 9
HISPANIC AND NONMINORITY BUSINESS OWNERS BY YEARS OF EDUCATION

	LESS THAN 9 YEARS	9-11 YEARS	HIGH SCHOOL DIPLOMA	1-3 YEARS OF COLLEGE	COLLEGE DEGREE	MORE THAN 5 YEARS OF COLLEGE
Hispanic business owners	19%	11%	27%	20%	7%	12%
Nonminority business owners	5%	8%	32%	20%	15%	18%

Source: United States Bureau of the Census, 1987, 18.
Note: 4 percent of Hispanic business owners and 2 percent of nonminority business owners did not report education.

TABLE 7A

THE THIRTY LARGEST HISPANIC BUSINESSES

RANK	COMPANY AND LOCATION	CHIEF EXECUTIVE	TYPE OF BUSINESS	NUMBER OF EMPLOYEES	YEAR STARTED	SALES ($ MILLIONS)
1	Goya Foods, Secaucus, NJ	Joseph A. Unanue	Hispanic Food Mfg./Mktg.	1,600	1936	453.00
2	Burt on Broadway Auto. Grp. Englewood, CO	Lloyd G. Chavez	Automotive Sales & Svc.	600	1939	422.76
3	Sedano's Supermarkets Miami, FL	Manuel A. Herren	Supermarket Chain	1,500	1962	224.56
4	Galeana's Van Dyke Dodge Inc. Warren, MI	Frank Galeana	Automotive Sales & Svc.	334	1977	186.30
5	Cal-State Lumber Sales Inc. San Diego, CA	Benjamin Acevedo	Wood Products Sales	98	1984	169.64
6	Ancira Enterprises Inc. San Antonio, TX	Ernesto Ancira Jr.	Automotive Sales & Svc.	300	1983	168.00
7	International Bancshares Corp. Laredo, TX	Dennis E. Nixon	Financial Svcs.	650	1979	160.70
8	Handy Andy Supermarkets San Antonio, TX	A. (Jimmy) Jimenez	Supermarket Chain	1,705	1983	148.00
9	Frank Parra Autoplex Irving, TX	Tim & Mike Parra	Automotive Sales & Svc.	284	1971	146.62
10	Normac Foods Inc. Oklahoma City, OK	John C. Lopez	Meat Products Mfg.	255	1970	142.77
11	Lloyd A. Wise Inc. Oakland, CA	A.A. Batarse Jr.	Automotive Sales & Svc.	291	1914	137.21
12	Infotec Development Inc. Santa Ana, CA	J. Fernando Niebla	Aerospace Engr./Systems Devel.	600	1978	126.03
13	CTA Inc. Rockville, MD	C.E. (Tom) Velez	Aerospace/Defense Systems	1,280	1979	115.94
14	Capital Bancorp Miami, FL	Abel Holtz	Financial Svcs.	632	1974	114.17
15	COLSA Corp. Huntsville, AL	Francisco J. Collazo	Engineering Svcs.	700	1980	112.00

TABLE 7A
THE THIRTY LARGEST HISPANIC BUSINESSES (CONT'D)

RANK	COMPANY AND LOCATION	CHIEF EXECUTIVE	TYPE OF BUSINESS	NUMBER OF EMPLOYEES	YEAR STARTED	SALES ($ MILLIONS)
16	**Troy Ford** Troy, MI	Irma B. Elder	Automotive Sales & Svc.	115	1967	111.09
17	**CareFlorida Inc.** Miami, FL	Paul L. Cejas	Health Care Svcs.	194	1986	110.60
18	**Gasteria Oil Corp.** Brooklyn, NY	Oscar Porcelli	Gasoline Stations	450	1972	108.00
19	**Eagle Brands Inc.** Miami, FL	Carlos M. de la Cruz Sr.	Beer Dist.	200	1984	97.95
20	**Precision Trading Corp.** Miami, FL	Israel Lapciuc	Consumer Electronics	35	1979	96.00
21	**Condal Distributors Inc.** Bronx, NY	Nelson Fernandez	Food Dist.	250	1968	95.00
22	**TELACU Industries|** City of Commerce, CA	David C. Lizarraga	Economic Devel./Financial Svcs.	600	1968	93.00
23	**Rosendin Electric Inc.** San Jose, CA	Raymond J. Rosendin	Electrical Contracting	650	1919	91.00
24	**Mexican Indust. in Michigan Inc.** Detroit, MI	Henry J. Aguirre	Automotive Trim Mfg.	800	1979	87.50
25	**Vincam Group Inc.** Miami FL	Carlos A. Saladrigas	Employee Leasing	6,500	1985	85.30
26	**Ruiz Food Products Inc.** Dinuba, CA	Frederick R. Ruiz	Mexican Food Mfg.	1,123	1964	83.26
27	**United Poultry/Belca Foodservice** Atlanta, GA	Alfredo Caceres	Foodservice Dist./Export	108	1976	78.22
28	**Pan American Hospital** Miami, FL	Carolina Calderin	Health Care Svcs.	600	1963	76.00
29	**H & H Meat Products Co. Inc.** dba H & H Foods, Mercedes, TX	Liborio E. Hinojosa	Meat Packing/Dist.	310	1947	68.79
30	**Advanced Sciences Inc.** Albuquerque, NM	Ed L. Romero	Environ. Engineering Svcs.	492	1977	66.59

Source: *Hispanic Business*, January 1994.

TABLE 7B

THE FASTEST GROWING HISPANIC-OWNED COMPANIES

Rank	Company and Location	Type of Business	Number of Employees	Year Started	Sales ($ Millions)	Compound Growth Rate 1988–1992
1	**Superior Tomato and Avocado Co. Inc.** San Antonio, TX	Fresh Vegetables & Fruit Dist.	175	1988	30.10	250.25
2	**Shadrock Petroleum Products Inc.** San Antonio, TX	Petroleum/Natural Gas Products Dist.	9	1946	41.67	243.31
3	**Research Management Consultants Inc.** Camarillo, CA	Environ. Engineering Svcs./Info. Syst.	188	1987	16.00	216.70
4	**Stature Construction Co.** Houston, TX	General Contracting	8	1987	11.45	178.87
5	**HJ Ford Associates Inc.** Arlington, VA	Systems Engineering/Integ.	105	1981	9.21	152.95
6	**PCI International** Lafayette, LA	Food Ingredien/Coconut Export	5	1981	4.54	134.44
7	**Trandes Corporation** Lanham, MD	Transport. Engr./Logistics/Mgmt.	180	1980	11.17	132.00
8	**O.I.V. Systems Inc.** San Antonio, TX	Computer Programming	76	1988	7.65	127.94
9	**Oasis Technology Inc.** Camarillo, CA	Computer Software/System Design	5	1979	4.78	124.52
10	**Cal-State Lumber Sales Inc.** San Diego, CA	Wood Products Sales	98	1984	169.64	121.88
11	**Compu-Centro USA Inc.** El Paso, TX	Computer Sales/Svc./Training/Net.	39	1986	8.03	118.85
12	**MVM Inc.** Falls Church, VA	Investigation/Security Svcs.	1,152	1979	24.45	117.43
13	**Compatible Micro Solutions Inc** dba CMS, El Paso, TX	Computer Sales/Syst. Integ.	23	1987	3.29	111.01
14	**HBLF** Jacksonville, FL	Translations/Typesetting/Printing	76	1986	2.72	105.36
15	**Certified Abatement Systems Inc.** Houston, TX	Asbestos & Lead Abatement	50	1987	5.00	101.03

TABLE 7B

THE FASTEST GROWING HISPANIC-OWNED COMPANIES (CONT'D)

RANK	COMPANY AND LOCATION	TYPE OF BUSINESS	NUMBER OF EMPLOYEES	YEAR STARTED	SALES ($ MILLIONS)	COMPOUND GROWTH RATE 1988–1992
16	**Perii Systems Inc.** Ho-Ho-Kus, NJ	Systems Engineering/Integ.	30	1987	2.18	99.66
17	**Scientech Inc.** Idaho Falls, ID	Environ. Safety/Waste Mgmt.	257	1983	20.43	89.64
18	**Sani Serv Inc.** Indianapolis, IN	Ice Cream/Yogurt Machine Mfg.	96	1977	28.00	88.88
19	**Maria Elena Toraño and Assos. (META)** Miami, FL	Mgmt. Consulting Svcs.	228	1980	15.45	88.84
20	**Operational Technologies Corp.** San Antonio, TX	Environ. Engineering Svcs.	156	1986	6.96	88.61
21	**Vincam Group Inc.** Miami, FL	Employee Leasing	6,500	1985	85.30	87.51
22	**Tru & Associates Inc.** Vista, CA	Petrol/Lubricant/Coal Prod. Dist.	3	1983	5.20	86.06
23	**Montoya & Sons Construction Co. Inc.** Schiller Park, IL	General Contracting	55	1986	10.31	84.28
24	**Shifa Services Inc.** Hackensack, NJ	Janitorial Svcs./Plant Maintenance	800	1980	13.80	84.15
25	**C.P.F. Corporation** Washington, DC	Janitorial/Painting Svcs.	417	1984	5.10	81.81
26	**Copier Depot Inc.** Miami FL	Copier Equipment and Sales	23	1972	3.80	80.25
27	**Film Roman** N. Hollywood, CA	TV/Theater Anim. Entertain. Dist.	210	1984	25.00	77.83
28	**Pinto Brothers Construction Inc.** Chicago, IL	General Contracting/Painting	100	1987	7.20	73.21
29	**JC's Mid America Building Services Inc.** Carol Stream, IL	Janitorial/Painting Svcs.	480	1979	10.40	71.58
30	**Comprehensive Technologies Internatl. Inc.** Chantilly, VA	Software Develop./Systems Integ.	490	1980	39.23	70.57

Source: *Hispanic Business*, January 1994.

Other interesting similarities and contrasts exist between the groups. Slightly over 76 percent of Hispanic business owners used $10,000 or less in capital to start or acquire their business, while 72 percent of nonminority business owners required $10,000 or less. Start-up capital requirements for Hispanic and nonminority businesses are illustrated in Table 11.

The sources of start-up capital for Hispanic and nonminority business owners are varied. The major portion for both groups has come from personal savings. However, 19 percent of nonminority business owners borrowed the capital from commercial banks, while 15 percent of Hispanic business owners did so. Approximately 8 percent of nonminority business owners obtained the capital from family and friends, compared with 13 percent of Hispanic business owners. Sources of start-up capital for Hispanic and nonminority business owners are illustrated in Figure 2.

TABLE 10
HISPANIC AND NONMINORITY BUSINESS OWNERS
ACROSS FOUR CHARACTERISTICS

	HISPANIC BUSINESS OWNERS (%)	NONMINORITY BUSINESS OWNERS (%)
College education	7	15
First-time entrepreneur	85	79
Management experience of 10 years or more	10	21
45 years of age or older	42	49

Source: United States Bureau of the Census, 1987, 10, 18, 37, 74.

TABLE 11
START-UP CAPITAL REQUIRED FOR HISPANIC AND NONMINORITY BUSINESS OWNERS

	NONE	$1 – 4,999	$5,000 – 9,999	$10,000 – 24,999	$25,000 – 49,999	$50,000 – 99,999	$100,000 – 249,000	$250,000 OR MORE
Hispanic Businesses	27%	37%	12%	11%	4%	2%	6%	4%
Nonminority Businesses	27%	34%	10%	11%	6%	3%	2%	6%

Source: United States Bureau of the Census, 1987, 82.
Note: 6 percent of Hispanic business owners and 6.4 percent of nonminority business owners did not respond.

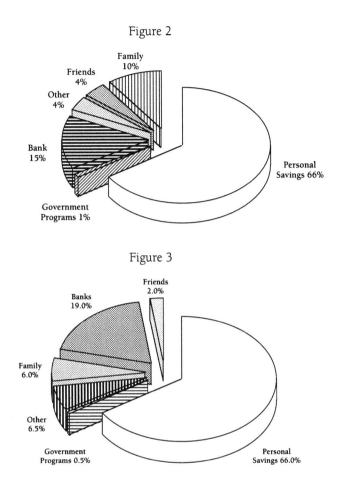

Figure 2

Figure 3

Some indication of business productivity can be obtained by examining net profit or loss of Hispanic businesses and comparing them to nonminority businesses. More than 4 percent of Hispanic-owned businesses generated net profits of $50,000 or more, Compared with 6 percent of for nonminority businesses. Approximately 14 percent of Hispanic businesses reported a loss, while 16 percent of nonminority businesses did. In terms of productivity when measured by profit or loss, it can be concluded that minority businesses are as productive as nonminority ones. Profit and loss for Hispanic and nonminority businesses are compared in Table 12.

The dominant form of Hispanic-owned businesses is the sole proprietorship; this is also the dominant form of all U.S. businesses. Sole proprietorship requires no legal documentation. Anyone who merely begins a business is automatically a sole proprietor unless he or she applies for in-

TABLE 12
PROFIT AND LOSS FOR HISPANIC AND NONMINORITY BUSINESSES

Profit

	Less than $5,000	$5,000 –9,999	$10,000 –19,999	$20,000 –24,999	$25,000 –29,999	$30,000 –49,999	$50,000 –74,999	$75,000 –99,999	$100,000 –249,000	$250,000 or more
Hispanic	26%	14%	12%	4%	2%	4%	2%	1%	1%	0.5%
Non-minority	27%	11%	11%	4%	3%	5%	2%	1%	2%	1%

Loss

	Less than $5,000	$5,000 –$9,999	$10,000 –24,999	$25,000 or more
Hispanic-Owned Businesses	11%	2%	1%	0.6%
Nonminority-Owned Businesses	12%	2%	1%	1%

Source: United States Bureau of the Census, 1987, 114.
Note: 18.9 percent of Hispanic businesses and 17 percent of nonminority businesses did not respond.

corporation. If two or more individuals join in a business venture, they are a partnership.

The majority of Hispanic companies—94 percent—are operated as proprietorships, according to the U.S. Bureau of the Census. This is comparable to nonminority owned businesses, 92 percent of which are proprietorships. Hispanic-owned corporations account for 2 percent of the total number of Hispanic companies, while 3 percent of nonminority firms are corporations. Approximately 4 percent of Hispanic businesses are partnerships, compared with 5 percent of nonminority businesses.

Hispanic-owned businesses differ significantly from their nonminority counterparts in at least one area. Hispanic businesses tend to hire other Hispanics or minorities. Approximately 67 percent of Hispanic businesses report that their work force consists of 75 to 100 percent minority employees. This is quite a contrast to the 14 percent of nonminority businesses that reported their work force consist of 75 to 100 percent minority employees. The percentage of minority employees in both Hispanic and nonminority businesses is summarized in Table 13.

TABLE 13
MINORITY EMPLOYEES IN HISPANIC AND NONMINORITY BUSINESSES

	NO MINORITY EMPLOYEES	1-9%	10-24%	25-49%	50-74%	75-100%
Hispanic Businesses	11	2	4	5	11	67
Nonminority Businesses	65	6	6	5	4	14

Source: United States Bureau of the Census, 1987, 130.

A very limited amount of information is available on the failure rate of Hispanic-owned businesses. Unfortunately, it is difficult to identify exactly when and if a business terminates. Business termination, of course, does not necessarily mean business failure. Some companies terminate voluntarily, without owner or creditor losses. Some research of Hispanic companies indicates that these businesses fail at a rate slightly higher than those of similar nonminority firms. However, more research needs to be undertaken to determine rates and causes of failures. There is some evidence that minority firms are burdened by higher debt structure, resulting in more problems, especially during recessions or tight money periods.

Hispanic-owned businesses make up a sector of the U.S. economy that will continue to increase in number and productivity. Business ownership will continue to be available career option for growing numbers of Hispanics.

PROMINENT HISPANICS IN BUSINESS ♦ ♦ ♦ ♦ ♦ ♦ ♦ ♦ ♦ ♦ ♦ ♦ ♦

Deborah Aguiar-Vélez (1955–)

Computers

Born on December 18, 1955, in New York City, Aguiar received a B.S. degree in chemical engineering from the University of Puerto Rico in 1977 and a certificate from the University of Virginia Entrepreneurial Executive Institute in 1989. In her early career, she was a systems analyst for Exxon and then worked in the small-business division of the New Jersey Department of Commerce. After that she founded and was president of her own business, Sistemas Corporation. Her honors include selection in 1990 as the Outstanding Women Entrepreneur Advocate by American Women in Economic Development and selection for Coca-Cola commercials as a Hispanic woman entrepreneurial role model. Aguiar has served on the boards of the Hispanic Women's Task Force, the Hispanic Leadership Opportunity Program, and the New Jersey Women's Business Advisory Council, which she chaired from 1987 to 1988.

Gabriel Eloy Aguirre (1935–)

Sanitation

Born on January 12, 1935, in Akron, Ohio, Aguirre worked for SaniServ in Indianapolis in the service and sales divisions from 1957 to 1977; in 1977, he became the owner of the company. For his outstanding success with the company, he was named the 1987 Minority Entrepreneur of the Year by the president of the United States. Aguirre has been very active in the community, serving on numerous boards and as president of school boards and police commissions. Since 1988, he has been a member of the board of the U.S. Senate Task Force on Hispanic Affairs.

Carlos José Arboleya (1929–)

Banking

Born on February 1, 1929, in Havana, Cuba, Arboleya is a graduate of the University of Havana who developed his early career in banking as the Havana manager of the First National City Bank of New York. After the Cuban Revolution of 1959, he immigrated to the United States and worked at a number of banks in Miami, moving up the ranks from clerk to bank administrator. By 1966, he was executive vice president of the Fidelity National Bank of South Miami; by 1973, the co-owner, president, and director of the Flagler Bank; and by 1977, president and CEO of the Barnett Banks of Miami. Since 1983, he has been vice chairman of the Barnett Bank of South Florida. Arboleya has remained active in the profession and the community, serving as vice president of the American Institute of Banking and on the boards of such organizations as the Inter-American Affairs Action Committee, the National Advisory Council for Economic Opportunity, the American Arbitration Association, and the Cuban American Foundation. Among his many honors are the American Academy of Achievement Gold Plate Award in 1974, the Horatio Alger Award of the American Schools and Colleges Association in 1976, and the American Red Cross Man of the Year Award in 1988.

Born on September 3, 1947, in Havana, Cuba, Cabañas received a B.S. degree in hotel and restaurant management from Florida International University in 1974 and went on to rise through the ranks at Sheraton, Doral, and Stouffer hotels until becoming the founding president and CEO of the Benchmark Hospitality Group in the Woodlands, Texas, in 1979. Benchmark properties include the Woodlands Executive Conference Center and resort, the Woodlands Country Club, the Exxon Conference Center, the Tournament Players Golf Course, and the San Luis Resort Hotel on Galveston Island. He has been a president of the International Association of Conference Centers, from which he received a Distinguished Service Award in 1988. Cabañas serves on the industry advisory committee for the Conrad Hilton School of Hotel and Restaurant Management of the University of Houston and is a past president of the International Association of Conference Centers.

Humberto Cabañas (1947–)

Hotel Management

Cuéllar is the chairman and CEO of the fifty-year-old restaurant chain founded by his family. Formerly known as El Chico Corporation, the Dallas-based chain is now Southwest Cafes and has, under Cuéllar's direction, expanded to various states under such local names as Cantina Laredo, Cuéllar's Cafe, Casa Rosa, and El Chico Restaurants. First becoming associated with the corporation in 1970, he served in various capacities, including manager of quality control, product research and development, and director of marketing research. In 1977, Campbell Taggart acquired the restaurant chain, and Cuéllar enrolled at North Texas State University and received an M.B.A. degree. After founding various restaurants of his own,

Gilbert Cuéllar, Jr.

Restaurant Chain Executive

he and his father were able to repurchase El Chico Corporation in 1982. In 1986, Cuéllar was named chairman of the corporation.

Roberto C. Goizueta (1931–)

Beverage Company Executive

Born on November 18, 1931, in Havana, Cuba, Goizueta received a B.S. degree in chemical engineering in 1953 from Yale University. He began at the Coca-Cola Company as an assistant vice president of research in 1964; by 1981, he had become the chairman of the board and CEO of Coca-Cola, one of the world's largest corporations. Goizueta has been active in service nationally and internationally. He is the founding director of the Points of Light Initiative and sits on the boards of the Ford Motor Company and Eastman Kodak, among others. Since 1980, he has been a trustee of Emory University. Among his many honors are being chosen a Gordon Grand Fellow of Yale University in 1984, the 1984 Herbert Hoover Humanitarian Award of the Boys Clubs of America, and the 1986 Ellis Island Medal of Honor.

Fredrick J. González (1949–)

Design Engineering Executive

Born on June 28, 1949, in Detroit, Michigan, González received a B.S. degree in engineering and an M.S. degree in architecture and urban planning from Princeton University in 1971 and 1972, respectively. After working for three years as an architect for Smith Hinchman Grylls Associates, in 1975 he and his father founded their own firm, González Design Engineering, in Madison Heights, Michigan, for which he has served as CEO since 1977, when his father died. In 1979, he also became the president of Semi-Kinetics, a printed circuit board assembly line in Laguna Hills, California. Since a 1968 automobile accident, González, who had been a high school football star, has been paralyzed from the waist down. Despite this and business barriers, González has become an outstanding businessman. Among his and his company's honors are being named by the White House as the National Minority Service Firm of the Year in 1975, selection as the 1989 Minority Businessman of the Year, and selection as the 1989 Minority Supplier of the Year by the National Minority Business Development Council. González participates on many boards, including the board of directors of the U.S. Hispanic Chamber of Commerce. González and his brother-partner, Gary, have been featured in full-page ads by General Motors as successful suppliers to the car company.

Frederick González

Born on May 19, 1940, in New York City, Lorenzo received a B.S. degree from Columbia University in 1961 and an M.B.A. degree from Harvard University in 1963. He began his career in air transportation as a financial analyst for Trans World Airlines from 1963 to 1965 and by 1966 had founded and become chairman of his own company, Lorenzo Carney and Company. From 1972 to 1980 he served as president and chairman of Texas International Airlines, which eventually became a major national and international holding company for Continental Airlines, for which he served as president from 1980 to 1985 and then as chairman and CEO from 1986 to 1990. After developing the company into the world's largest carrier through the purchase of various other carriers, Lorenzo was embattled by strikes, rising costs, and competition and the problems of deregulation, and he was eventually forced to resign.

Frank A. Lorenzo (1940–)

Former Airline Company Executive

Born on November 23, 1934, in New York City, Milán received a B.S. degree in accounting from Hunter College in 1957 and pursued additional courses towards the M.S. degree at the City College of New York. He rose

Ed Milán (1934–)

Controller

Frank Lorenzo

through the ranks as a career accountant in oil companies, serving in the United States, Canada, England, Peru, and Nicaragua. After serving in a number of vice presidential positions in the financial divisions of Tenneco Oil, one of the largest U.S. corporations, Milán was named vice president and controller in 1989. Milán serves on a number of advisory boards, including those of Arte Publico Press and the accounting programs for Texas Tech and Texas A&M Universities. Milán was also an outstanding college basketball player; and in 1957, he was selected Hunter College Athlete of the Year, and in 1991, he was inducted into the Hunter College Athletic Hall of Fame.

Robert Ortega, Jr.

(1947–)

Construction Company
Executive

Born on February 1, 1947, in El Paso, Texas, Ortega received B.S. and M.S. degrees in civil engineering from the University of Texas at El Paso in 1970 and 1980, respectively. He worked as an engineer in the U.S. Public Health Service, the U.S. Bureau of Reclamation, and the El Paso Housing Department before founding Construction Management Associates in 1983. In 1988, his company was rated the fifth-fastest-growing Hispanic company in the United States by *Hispanic Business* magazine. In 1989, the company was named the Outstanding Small Business for the City of El Paso by the Small Business Administration. In 1980, Ortega was named Young Engineer of the Year and, in 1989, Engineer of the Year by the Texas Society of Professional Engineers. He is a past president of the Texas Society of Civil Engineers and of the Associated Builders and Contractors.

Born on August 9, 1958, in New York City, John Rodríguez is cofounder and president of AD One, an advertising and public relations firm in Rochester, New York. Rodríguez completed his bachelor's degree at the Rochester Institute of Technology, where he majored in advertising and photography. He continues his education by attending classes at local universities and is currently working toward a master's degree in communications. As a young entrepreneur, he has built his company, AD One, into a successful firm that specializes in international sales promotion, recruitment, and the Hispanic market. AD One has successfully completed projects for many clients across the region, including Eastman Kodak Company, Bausch and Lomb, Preferred Care, The University of Rochester, the Girl Scouts, Rochester City School District, and Mobil Chemical.

John Rodríguez (1958–)

Advertising and Public Relations

Rodríguez has a strong sense of responsibility toward the community in which he lives and works. His commitment to his community and to Hispanic people is expressed in many ways. He brings issues to the surface by talking about them and then taking appropriate action. Rodríguez translates his thoughts into action in his involvement with the Rochester Hispanic Business Association and memberships with the Monroe County Human Relations Commission, the United Way of Greater Rochester, the Puerto Rican Youth Development and Resource Center, as well as many other organizations in the area. He is also quite active as a member of the Citizens' Advisory Committee to Vision 2000, a major project to revitalize downtown Rochester. Rodríguez has also ventured into politics. He served as campaign director for his sister-in-law, Nancy Padilla, the first Hispanic elected to the Rochester City Council. For Rodríguez, having individuals sensitive to the Hispanic community in key policy-making positions is critical.

Oscar Rodríguez was born and raised in San Antonio, Texas. He spent seventeen years as a very successful entrepreneur in Boston, Massachusetts. During his "exile" in Boston he obtained his master's of business administration degree at Harvard and then proceeded to start and sell three successful computer-oriented companies.

Oscar Rodríguez

Computers

In 1985, after a highly successful business career, Rodríguez returned to his native San Antonio and joined forces with Héctor Dávila to buy out a failing computer services company. The new company, Antares Development Corporation, assumed the computer support responsibility for sixty of San Antonio's most respected firms. By the end of 1988, Antares Development Corporation had become one of the premier suppliers of computer services in San Antonio.

During the downturn in the computer industry in the late 1980s, Antares reexamined its mission as well as the future of the computing industry. This analysis led to a whole new outlook for the company. Specifically, Antares identified three new technologies that it saw as the future of computing: networking, data base management systems, and UNIX operating systems. Antares, under the guidance of Oscar Rodríguez, put into place a corporate strategy that was aimed at building a respected institution.

By early 1990, Antares had retrained its staff in new technologies and was well on the way to developing a set of new products and services based on its new direction. In 1990, the company increased sales by 50 percent.

Oscar Rodríguez has defined the goals of his company through the year 2000. First, he wants to have 1000 corporate clients with whom Antares has an ongoing support relationship. A second goal for the firm is to earn the Malcolm Baldridge National Award for Quality in the service sector. There is every reason to believe that these goals will be accomplished.

Eduardo G. Santiago (1949–)

Controller

Born on September 26, 1949, in Ponce, Puerto Rico, Santiago received a B.S. degree in accounting from Baruch College in 1975 and an M.B.A. degree in finance from Pace University in 1979. He began his career as an accounting clerk for Guy Carpenter & Co. in 1969. He worked for American International Marine and for MacMillan until 1975, when he became the controller of Philip Morris International.

Lionel Sosa (1939–)

Advertising

Born on May 27, 1939, in San Antonio, Texas, Sosa became a graphic artist who developed a career in advertising, founding his own company, Sosart, in 1966. In 1974, he became a partner of Ed Yardang and Associates. In 1984, he founded Sosa and Associates, for which he serves as chairman and CEO. Sosa and Associates is the leading firm in handling national accounts targeted at Hispanic consumers. In 1990, *Adweek* magazine named Sosa and Associates the Agency of the Year and the Hottest Agency in the Southwest, with 1989 billings of $54.8 million. Sosa's clients include American Airlines, Anheuser-Busch, Burger King, Coca-Cola USA, Montgomery Ward, and Western Union. Among his many awards are the 1990 Entrepreneur of the Year, the 1989 Marketing Person of the Year Award, the 1989 Silver Award from the Public Relations Society of America, and the Gold ADDY from the American Advertising Foundation in 1988. Sosa is active in the community, participating on many local and national boards.

Born on April 14, 1931, the son of Catalina Yarza and Clifford Whitehill, Whitehill received a B.A. degree from Rice University in 1954, an LL.B. from the University of Texas, and an LL.M. from Harvard University in 1957 and 1958, respectively. He became a corporate attorney, working for various companies in Houston and New York until joining General Mills in Minneapolis as an attorney in 1962. He moved up the ranks to vice presidential positions. He attained his present position of senior vice president, general counsel and secretary in 1981. Among his honors is the 1988 Whitney North Seymour, Sr., Award from the American Arbitration Society. Among the many boards and directorates on which Whitehill serves are the National Hispanic Scholarship Fund and the United Nations Association of the USA, both of which he directs.

Clifford Lane Whitehill (1931–)

Corporate Attorney

Independently owned businesses are the foundation of economic activity in the United States. They embody the American dream of financial independence and self-determination. Even in the relatively mediocre economy of the past decade, Hispanic businesses have continued to grow and prosper. The impressive gains made by Hispanic-owned businesses in the past decade will most assuredly continue into the next decade as younger and better educated Hispanics are attracted to self-employment. Business ownership will become an increasingly attractive career option for growing numbers of Hispanics.

Jude Valdez and Nicolás Kanellos

*L*abor

Hispanics are the fastest growing major group in the labor force of the United States. Between 1980 and 1990 the number of Hispanics in the work force increased by 48 percent, representing 20 percent of U.S. employment growth. The employment of Hispanic women during this period increased by 56 percent, or more than two and one-half times the rate of other women.

Between 1980 and 1990 Hispanics increased from 6.1 million to 9.6 million persons in the U.S. work force. Their youth relative to other groups in the work force and continued high rates of immigration indicate that Hispanics will continue to increase their representation, to an estimated 14.2 million by the year 2000.

Although the numbers have increased rapidly, conditions of employment for Hispanics have deteriorated during the 1980s. Many worker protections and benefits have been lost, incomes have declined in absolute terms, and the gap between Hispanics and Anglos has widened sharply.

In 1991 the median weekly earnings of Hispanic men were $328, compared with $374 for Afro-American men and $509 for Anglo men. Hispanic wom-

en's weekly earnings were $293, compared with $323 for Afro-American women and $374 for Anglo women. This means that Anglo women and Afro-American men earned 74 percent, Afro-American women 62 percent, Hispanic men 66 percent, and Hispanic women 56 percent of that earned by Anglo men. By March 1991, unemployment among Hispanics had reached 9.9 percent, compared to 6.0 percent for Anglos.

HISPANICS IN ORGANIZED LABOR ✦ ✦ ✦ ✦ ✦ ✦ ✦ ✦ ✦ ✦ ✦ ✦ ✦ ✦ ✦

As a predominantly working people, Hispanics have long been involved in efforts to organize as workers. One of their earliest groups, the *Caballeros de Labor* (Knights of Labor), was active in the Southwest in the late nineteenth century. Modeled after the American organization by the same name, Knights of Labor, its major stronghold was in New Mexico. It was never formally chartered, and it was more interested in land loss to recently arriving Anglos than labor issues.

During the late nineteenth and early twentieth centuries, a much greater number of Hispanic workers organized their own *mutualistas*, or mutual aid societies. These organizations engaged in social activities and provided for basic needs of workers, including insurance and death benefits for members. Mutualistas functioned largely as self-help organizations and did not threaten employers, which helps explain their greater success than unions.

Apart from the mutualistas, labor organizing among Hispanics in the late nineteenth and early twentieth centuries was hindered by several factors. Hispanics were concentrated geographically in largely antiunion settings in the South and Southwest. They also faced hostility and discrimination because of societal attitudes, which often portrayed them as taking jobs away from Anglo workers. The major labor organization in the nation, the American Federation of Labor (AFL), tended to be craft-exclusive and structurally not interested in the participation of largely unskilled Hispanic workers. More important, the AFL itself could not resolve internally the nativism and racism pervasive in American society that often led it and its local unions to adopt exclusionary policies. These problems severely reduced Hispanic participation in organized labor and resulted in significant organizing efforts outside the mainstream labor federation.

In the early twentieth century, union organizing among Hispanic workers increased in many areas. The most notable efforts took place in agriculture, which was still the most significant single occupation for Hispanics. Most organizing took place under the auspices of independent Mexican unions, while in some cases independent interethnic unions or multiethnic organizations existed, often with support from the radical Industrial Workers of the World. Railroad and other urban workers joined together for brief periods under the leadership of independent or Socialist organizations and, occasionally, the AFL. Many miners formed union organizations with the support and encouragement of the Western Federation of Miners in the early years of the twentieth century.

Following a low point during the 1920s, labor organizing among Hispanic workers reached new peaks during the Great Depression. Independent organizations not affiliated with mainstream organized labor were most active and more typically composed of independent Mexican groups, Socialists, and members of the Communist party. In the later 1930s leaders in the newly formed Congress of Industrial Organizations (CIO) also exhibited interest in organizing unskilled workers, and the CIO participated in the famous pecan shellers' strike in San Antonio in 1938, involving mostly young Mexican and Mexican-American women. Organizers Emma Tennayuca and Manuela Solís Seger gained attention in Texas at that time and remained active in labor for many years afterward.

Organizing and strikes also occurred in the 1930s among mining, industrial, and agricultural workers throughout the country. Mexican farm workers in California were particularly active throughout the decade. Their efforts were highlighted by the Central Valley cotton strike of 1933, in which several groups of independent Mexican union organizers and radicals offered support. The AFL considered these activities a serious challenge to its dominance, and in many occupations it permitted the formation of local unions for the first time to attract Mexican workers into its fold.

The turbulence of the 1930s reflected a sharp increase in expressions of sympathy toward unionism and unions among Hispanic workers. Much

Mexican cotton workers.

of the support had been latent but untapped until that time. Immigrants from Mexico frequently had strong union sympathies because of their earlier experiences before they arrived in the United States. Yet, traditional unions made only partial inroads into the Hispanic working population during the decade, hindered by continued employment discrimination, the success of employer efforts to pit workers against each other, and divisions within organized labor.

World War II served as a partial brake to direct labor organizing among Hispanic workers. But progressive elements within organized labor remained active, particularly in the struggle to eliminate many of the statutory forms of employment discrimination that Hispanics and other workers continually faced. Their efforts contributed to the formation of the Fair Employment Practices Committee (FEPC) in 1941. The FEPC investigated discrimination throughout the country by private companies with government contracts. Over a third of its cases in the Southwest involved Mexicans. Despite the efforts of President Truman, the FEPC was terminated at the end of World War II.

Unionization among Hispanic workers increased rapidly in the 1940s and 1950s, as Hispanic workers and sympathizers within both the AFL and CIO struggled for reforms that permitted them equal access and fair treatment. In many local unions they formed their own caucuses to demand representation and changes in discriminatory procedures by the union hierarchy and to encourage the union to challenge discriminatory practices by employers. They demonstrated union loyalty, sympathy, and a class-consciousness reinforced by their work experiences and treatment in the workplace. During this period they participated in many notable strikes, including the "salt of the earth" strike by miners in Silver City, New Mexico, which was led by the International Mine, Mill and Smelter Workers Union between 1950 and 1953. The efforts of the National Farm Labor Union, later called the National Agricultural Workers Union, to organize in California during the 1940s and 1950s were also noteworthy. Union leader Ernesto Galarza demonstrated keen insight as a union leader, scholar, and role model for a later generation of Chicano activists.

Among Hispanics, a number of independent unions again began to form in both Puerto Rico and in the continental United States. The most notable was the National Farm Workers Association in California, led by César Chávez. It began as an independent organization in 1962 and became part of the AFL-CIO in 1966. It is now known as the United Farmworkers of America. During its numerous strikes and boycotts of table grapes, wines, and lettuce, it popularized many tactics, involving ethnic alliances, community organizing, and a focus on protecting the environment, which suggest alternative organizing strategies for organized labor in the future. Another creative venture, The East Los Angeles Community Union (TELACU), was formed in 1971 as the result of cooperative efforts between the United Auto Workers and community organizers in East Los Angeles to build a "community" union.

Union organizing activity in the United States peaked in the 1950s. From the early 1960s through the 1970s, the number of union members in the nation increased, though at a much slower rate than overall employment. The decrease in the rate of unionization during this period resulted from the reduction of jobs in highly unionized sectors, the growth of employment in traditionally nonunion occupations, the lack of vigilance of union leadership, increasingly sophisticated antiunion activities among employers, and unfriendly government policy that did not enforce protective labor legislation.

From the beginning of the Reagan presidency in 1981 until 1985, union membership fell rapidly while total employment rose. Between 1985 and

César Chávez, 1969.

1990 union membership declined more slowly, while total employment continued to rise. The decline in the 1980s is due to factors unfavorable to unions during the past generation, coupled with the most hostile federal government policy toward labor organizing and unions since the 1920s.

Unionization levels vary according to geography and occupation. Rates are highest in the Northeast and Midwest, and lowest in the South and Southwest, where Hispanic workers are most concentrated. In 1989 unionization in the public sector stood at 37 percent of workers, com-

Harvest time at Almadén's Paicines vineyards in the Gavilan Mountain area of San Benito County, California, 1965.

pared with 12 percent in private industry. It seems that private employers had a greater ability than the government to thwart worker organization despite the more rigid laws restricting labor organizing in the public sector. In the private arena, the more highly unionized sectors include transportation and public utilities at 32 percent, construction and manufacturing at 22 percent, and mining at 18 percent. In other major areas of private employment, union membership ranged from only 1 to 6 percent.

Union membership in 1991 was 16.1 percent of the working population over age fifteen, reflecting the continued decline over the past three decades. Unionization stood at 20 percent for men and 13 percent for women.

Approximately 1.3 million Hispanics are union members. Although many Hispanics serve as union officers, vice-presidents, and directors, the only Hispanic to become president of one of the eighty-eight unions in the AFL-CIO was César Chávez of the United Farm Workers. In 1973 the Labor Council of Latin American Advancement (LCLAA) formed to promote the interests of Hispanics within organized labor.

IMMIGRATION AND MIGRATION ✦ ✦ ✦ ✦ ✦ ✦ ✦ ✦ ✦ ✦ ✦ ✦ ✦ ✦ ✦ ✦

Immigration remains an important factor accounting for the expansion of the labor force in the United States. The rates of immigration in the 1980s approached the levels of the early 1900s. Legal immigration during the first decade of the century reached 8.8 million, while during the 1980s 7.3 million immigrants were granted permanent residence. The immigrants are overwhelmingly young and in search of employment, and Hispanic immigrants continue to account for more than 40 percent of the total.

Several formal and informal programs have been established to encourage immigration of workers to the United States. The best-known forms of organized labor recruitment have involved agricultural workers from Mexico and Puerto Rico. These include the mechanisms in the Bracero Program and Operation Bootstrap. Labor recruitment by the U.S. Farm Placement Service to encourage labor migration for temporary seasonal employment has also influenced permanent settlement patterns. The H-2 Program within the Immigration and Nationality Act of 1952, as amended by the Immigration Reform and Control Act of 1986 (IRCA), continues to guide immigration patterns to the United States.

Immigration from Mexico, Central and South America, and the Caribbean has been encouraged by labor recruiters and by informal networks that link individual families and communities in Latin America and the United States together.

Internal migration has also affected the population patterns of Hispanics within the United States. The most general patterns of migration include the dispersal of Mexicans from their historic concentrations in the Southwest to the Midwest, the Pacific Northwest, and recently to Florida and the East Coast; the spread of Puerto Ricans beyond New York to other areas of the country; and the relocation of Cubans to places other than Miami. Most of this migration has been through informal mechanisms, established at the level of individuals and families, and by word of mouth.

The major net flows of Hispanics within the United States are from the Northeast and Midwest to Florida, Texas, and California; from New York to neighboring states in the Northeast; and from California to neighboring states in the West. Cuban Americans are becoming increasingly concentrated at somewhat higher levels in Florida, while Central and South Americans are becoming more concentrated in California and New York. People of Mexican origin are tending to disperse from the Southwest, while Puerto Ricans are moving away from their center of concentration in New York City.

The total impact of migration and immigration in the 1970s and 1980s has been twofold. In absolute numbers, Hispanics have dispersed to a greater number of states and in wider areas within those states. In proportionate terms, they have concentrated at somewhat higher rates in the states already having large Hispanic populations. In 1970, 82 percent of the Hispanic population of the nation lived in nine states, with the proportion rising to 86 percent in 1990. The major recipients of Hispanic immigrants are California, Texas, and New York, and to a lesser degree Florida, Illinois, and New Jersey.

The Bracero Program

The Bracero Program, also referred to as the Mexican Farm Labor Supply Program or the Mexican Labor Agreement, began as a bilateral agreement between the governments of Mexico and the United States. It was given congressional sanction in 1943 as Public Law 45. Both governments considered it an important part of the Mexican contribution to the World War II effort.

The program was very popular among agricultural employers, who quickly organized and lobbied Congress to ensure its continuation beyond the end of the war. They were able to extend it temporarily several times, claiming a shortage of able and willing workers in the United States. At the peak of the program in the late 1950s, the United States admitted more than 400,000 contract workers each season, almost twice as many as the number entering the country during the entire wartime emergency from 1942 to 1947.

Mexican Bracero workers picking strawberries in the Salinas, California, area, 1963.

The term bracero *(from the Spanish* brazo, *meaning arm), generally applied to day laborers, is sometimes used to refer to any Mexican worker in the United States under legal auspices. It includes workers entering the country under the H-2 Program of the Immigration and Nationality Act of 1952 and the H-2A Program of the Immigration Reform and Control Act of 1986, as well as Mexican commuters often referred to as "green carders."*

The program was anathema to Mexican Americans and labor groups, who eventually gathered convincing evidence that, despite contract guarantees, braceros were not protected against abuses by employers and labor contractors, their working conditions were not adequate, and they frequently were not paid the wages guaranteed them by contract. The opposition also demonstrated the program had an adverse effect on wages and working conditions of domestic workers and stifled unionization efforts not only in agriculture, but also in southwestern industry. The struggle against the program in the 1950s focused largely on its adverse effects, seeking reforms requiring employer compliance with contract guarantees and permitting braceros joining unions. This effort, nevertheless, failed, convincing opposition later in the decade to conduct an all-out attack on the program. Ultimately a combined group of labor union representatives, Mexican-American groups, religious and civic organizations, and their allies gained the support of a more pro-labor Democratic administration and obtained Congressional termination of the "temporary" program in 1964.

Since 1964 employer groups in agriculture have initiated several efforts in Congress to pass new and modified versions of the Bracero Program by hiring temporary seasonal contract workers from Mexico. None of their efforts have succeeded. Termination of Public Law 78 was an important victory for Mexican-American and labor groups and helped pave the way for a flurry of labor organizing efforts in agriculture in the late 1960s.

The Maquiladoras

The abolition of the Bracero Program also demanded greater efforts by the Mexican government to relieve its own unemployment via industrialization. The most important element of its border industrialization program is the *maquiladora* (assembly plant) program, initiated in 1965. Mexico found industrialists and politicians in the United States very interested in the industrialization program. Mexico hoped that it could raise the standard of living in the northern border region, while both the U.S. and Mexican governments were concerned about the possible negative political and economic consequences of leaving hundreds of thousands of Mexican workers stranded on the border without employment when the Bracero Program was ended. Industrialists were eager to reap the benefits offered

Women working on an electronics plant assembly line.

by tax and tariff breaks and by the availability of unemployed and under-employed workers in Mexico.

The central feature of the plan established "twin plants" on both sides of the Mexico-U.S. border. It also set up a duty-free zone, which permits industrialists in the United States to ship unfinished goods to Mexico under bond for partial assembly or completion. The goods are then returned duty free to the "twin plant" on the U.S. side, to complete the manufacturing process. In the early years of the program, about two-thirds of the products involved in the program were electric and electronic goods. As the program expanded in the 1970s and 1980s, the range of products expanded rapidly. By the end of the 1980s, electric and electronic goods represented only about 35 percent of the total; textiles, clothing, and shoes, 18 percent; furniture, 10 percent; transportation equipment (including car motors), 9 percent; and a range of other goods, 28 percent.

The scale of production in the maquiladora industry also grew impressively. In 1966 it comprised 57 plants with about 4,000 workers. By 1979 it had about 540 plants hiring 120,000 workers, and by 1986 there were 844 plants employing 242,000 workers. By 1990 more than 1,000 plants were employing about 450,000 workers. It is estimated that by 1995 there will be at least 1,500 plants with more than 1 million workers engaged in the program.

The maquiladora program in its actual operation is not at all as it was initially conceived. Its original intent was to alleviate the unemployment of male workers stranded at the end of the Bracero Program. Yet, the work force in the maquiladoras from the beginning has been approximately 85 percent female, mostly teenage women with very high rates of turnover. The program does not offer steady employment or work to unemployed men.

Still yet another flaw in the original plan is that the "twin plant" concept never became operational. While the production phase was conducted in the Mexican plants, the "plants" on the U.S. side were essentially warehouses. Like their counterparts in Mexico, the operations in the United States offered low-wage, unskilled employment. The maquiladora program in effect, thus, became a runaway shop taking advantage of cheap Mexican labor and exemption from tariffs.

U.S. companies involved in maquiladora operations assert that the program enables them to produce in Mexico rather than transfer their operations to Asia. Yet, during the 1980s Japanese industrialists took advantage of the maquiladoras to send greater amounts of raw materials to Mexico to have them finished, then shipped duty free into the United States. This led to a storm of protest in the United States, because, as Representative Duncan Hunter complained, "The Japanese can essentially use the program simply as a conduit into American markets without conferring benefits on American businessmen." In their discussion of the maquiladora program, very few politicians have considered the adverse impact on the much larger group of workers in the United States continuously displaced by the program.

The North American Free Trade Agreement between Mexico and the United States expands even further the maquiladora concept in scale offering potentially greater tax abatements for U.S. businesspeople. It will increase the number of runaway shops already relocated from the South and Southwest across the border, where labor costs are lower, and worker and environmental protection very weak. Furthermore, in Mexico it is difficult for organized labor and environmental and public interest groups from the United States to challenge corporations that are rooted in the United States and produce almost exclusively for the domestic market. Although advocates of the Free Trade Agreement maintain that it will expand the size of markets in both Mexico and the United States, the sharp wage differential between Mexico and the United States makes it very difficult for Mexicans to afford to purchase the goods produced for export to the United States. In terms of worker protection, environmental damage, and the threat to the unity of Hispanic and Latin American workers on both sides of the border, the maquiladora program and the Free Trade Agreement pose even greater threats than the Bracero Program.

Migrant Farm Labor

A migrant worker is a person employed at a job temporarily or seasonally and who may or may not have a permanent residence in another community, state, or nation. It is a misconception to portray farm workers solely as migrants or Hispanics, or to portray all migrant workers as farm workers. Migrants comprise only a small portion of the total of the ethnically diverse farm labor force of the United States. Seasonal migrant workers are employed in a wide range of occupations, including mining, forestry, and fishing, in addition to agriculture, which is the best-known form of migrant labor in the United States.

Most people who work on farms are either families who own or rent them or residents of nearby farms and communities who travel to work and re-

In the late nineteenth and early twentieth centuries, the size of the migrant labor force expanded rapidly owing to the introduction of large-scale commercial agriculture that was linked to the industrialization and urbanization of the nation's population. Millions of people left the farms and joined immigrants in the cities, augmenting the demand for foods they could not produce themselves.

turn home at the end of the workday. Migrant farm workers are concentrated in the harvest operations of fruit and vegetable crops in several locations throughout the United States. At other times of the year, they seek employment in agricultural or other occupations, often where they are permanently settled.

The number of migrant agricultural laborers has declined sharply since the late 1930s, when about 4 million people worked each season. Because of the problems of keeping track of them, it is very difficult to make an accurate estimate of their numbers. It is likely that about 1 million people were employed as migrant farm workers in the United States annually during the 1980s.

Agricultural migrants at the turn of the century frequently were foreign immigrants who worked on farms temporarily while saving money to buy farms or seeking more permanent employment in nearby cities. On the West Coast, a large portion of the migrant farm workers at the end of the nineteenth and early twentieth centuries were Asians, while in other parts of the country most were Europeans and their children. With the expansion of the sugar beet, vegetable, and cotton industries in the early twentieth century, Mexican migrant workers increasingly took over seasonal farm labor, frequently returning to the Mexican border or nearby cities at the end of work in a crop or at the end of the season.

With the onset of the Great Depression, many Mexican migrant workers were displaced by southern laborers, who dominated the migrant agricultural labor force in the 1930s and 1940s. In the 1950s and 1960s Afro-American workers continued as the most numerous migrants along the eastern seaboard states, while Mexican and Mexican-American workers soon dominated the migrant paths between Texas and the Great Lakes, the Rocky Mountain region, and the area from California to the Pacific Northwest. Some observers noted very rough patterns of movement referred to as "migrant streams" that went northward from Florida, Texas, and Southern California each season in the 1940s and 1950s; but these became increasingly blurred over time.

In spite of more sophisticated government programs on behalf of farm workers and governmental efforts to coordinate the needs of workers with the demands of employers since the 1950s, the movement of migrant workers between jobs remains very haphazard. Migrant and seasonal farm

A woman picks fruit in a California orchard.

workers continue to experience long periods of unemployment, and are among the worst-paid and least-protected workers in the nation. They suffer high rates of illness, retain low levels of education, and they find few advocates within political circles. As outsiders to local communities, often separated by language and ethnic barriers, they seldom participate in decisions affecting the communities where they are employed.

In the 1960s and 1970s the migrant agricultural work force changed rapidly. With the rise of the Black Power and Chicano movements, the appearance of modest protective legislation, and the increasingly successful unionization efforts of farm workers, employers increasingly sought to recruit and hire foreign workers to replace the citizens. Along the East Coast, they recruited increasingly from the Caribbean, and supplemented with workers from Mexico and Central America. In other parts of the country, they recruited mostly from Mexico and Central America. In the 1980s and 1990s the vast majority of migrant farm workers in the United States have been foreign born. Many of them migrate seasonally from Mexico and the Caribbean to the United States through the H-2 Program, which became an important mechanism of labor recruitment following the termination of the Bracero Program. In recent decades, undocumented workers from Latin America have become the most important part of this labor force in many locations.

HISPANIC EMPLOYMENT IN INDUSTRY ✦ ✦ ✦ ✦ ✦ ✦ ✦ ✦ ✦ ✦ ✦

Service Industries

The employment profile of workers in the U.S. has changed sharply in recent decades. The major category of service is increasing, while that of manufacturing is declining. The service industries include a wide range of activities, from private household work, restaurant, hotel, and food services, and health and personal service occupations. Employment in service industries, which nearly doubled between 1970 and 1990, is high among females in most areas. The rate of Hispanic employment in service occupations is about double that of the non-Hispanic population for males, and about 40 percent higher for females.

In March 1989, 17.7 percent of employed Hispanic men worked in service industries, compared with 9 percent for non-Hispanic men. The rates were 24.1 percent for Hispanic women and 17.1 percent for non-Hispanic women.

Manufacturing and Basic Industries

Manufacturing and basic industries, traditionally the mainstay of the U.S. economy and historically the indicator of the leading economic nations in the world, are declining rapidly. Manufacturing occupations include precision production workers, craft and repair people, as well as operators, fabricators, and laborers. Both Hispanic males and females are highly overrepresented in this category, males by almost 25 percent and females at rates roughly double those of non-Hispanic females.

In 1989, about 47.9 percent of Hispanic males were employed in the broad category of manufacturing, compared with 39.8 percent of non-Hispanic males. Among females, 21.3 percent of Hispanics worked in manufacturing, compared with 10.5 percent of non-Hispanics.

◆ ◆ ◆ ◆ ◆ ◆ ◆ ◆ FEDERAL EMPLOYMENT PROGRAMS AND LAWS

Title VII and the Equal Employment Opportunity Commission

The Economic Opportunity Act (EOA) of 1964 was the centerpiece of President Lyndon B. Johnson's War on Poverty. The philosophy behind the War on Poverty espoused private initiative and local efforts had not resolved longstanding problems of discrimination and poverty during the postwar boom in the United States. Furthermore, the government believed efforts to improve conditions were consistently thwarted by private interests, often in conjunction with local and state governmental authorities, where low-income or poverty-stricken families, African Americans, and Hispanics were seldom represented. The federal government, thus, decided to initiate a program to provide training for workers to encourage recruitment, and to monitor hiring practices of public and private employers across the nation.

The EOA also created the Office of Economic Opportunity (OEO) to administer a number of programs on behalf of the nation's poor. These included the Job Corps, the Community Action Program (CAP), and the Volunteers in Service to America (VISTA).

The Job Corps is a job-training program whose goal seeks to help disadvantaged youths ages sixteen to twenty-one find employment. In 1990 the typical Job Corps enrollee was eighteen years old, 83.5 percent were high school dropouts, 75 percent were minorities, 75 percent had never had a prior full-time job, 67 percent were male, and almost 40 percent came from families on public assistance.

VISTA, conceived as a domestic equivalent to the Peace Corps, worked with the poor in urban and rural locations. CAP was the primary OEO program, in which local groups combined the efforts of local government, business, labor, civic, and religious organizations and the poor to mobilize local resources to alleviate poverty.

Title VII of the Civil Rights Act of 1964 comprised the most important statute of the War on Poverty addressing employment discrimination. It prohibits discrimination on the basis of gender, creed, race, or ethnic background, "to achieve equality of employment opportunities and remove barriers that have operated in the past." Discrimination is prohibited in advertising, recruitment, hiring, job classification, promotion, discharge, wages and salaries, and other terms and conditions of employment.

Title VII also established the Equal Employment Opportunity Commission (EEOC) as a monitoring device to prevent job discrimination. In effect, it renewed and expanded the Fair Employment Practices Committee, which had been dismantled at the end of World War II. The EEOC works in conjunction with state agencies in investigating charges of discrimination.

The issue of employment discrimination led to a great deal of litigation, and several of the important employment lawsuits directly involved Hispanics. *Espinoza v. Farah Manufacturing Company* (1973) held that Title VII does not protect discrimination against aliens. The Supreme Court also held, however, that Title VII prohibits practices that have "the purpose or effect of discriminating on the basis of national origin." In *Carino v. University of Oklahoma* (1984), the Court held that an employer cannot refuse to hire an individual "because the individual has the physical, cultural or linguistic characteristics of a particular national origin group," or discriminate "because of the individual's accent or manner of speaking."

In reaction to equal employment legislation and the increasing presence of Hispanics and other non-English-speaking people in the workplace, some states in the past several years have enacted so-called English-only amendments to their constitutions. Collectively they imposed English as the official language of their state.

Following the spirit of this legislation, many employers attempted to restrict the use of foreign languages by imposing "English-only" rules in the workplace. Such actions are prohibited under Title VII, which prohibits discrimination on the basis of national origin. EEOC policy provides that rules "which require employees to speak English only at all times are presumptively unlawful because they unduly burden individuals whose primary language is one other than English, and tends to create a hostile or discriminatory environment based on national origin."

Language rights have thus become an important employment issue challenging Hispanic workers in the 1990s, particularly where their numbers are high. Public and private employers commonly engage in hiring Hispanic employees because of their special skills as translators, but seldom grant them compensation or consider such skills as important factors in job promotion. In *Pérez et al. v. Federal Bureau of Investigation* (1988), Hispanic FBI agents offered their special skills to the FBI more than Anglo Spanish-speakers and non-Spanish-speakers, but did not receive compensation. The federal district court held that by being concentrated in interpreting tasks, the Hispanic agents were treated differently from and denied promotional opportunities offered to Euro-American agents.

As a result of positive legislation and court interpretations, conditions of employment for Hispanics registered significant improvements in several areas during the 1960s and much of the 1970s.

During the Nixon presidency, the first efforts to dismantle President Lyndon B. Johnson's War on Poverty began. The Nixon administration did not overtly attack the concept of equal opportunity, nor did it challenge the theories or actual programs already established to deal with the chronically unemployed. Rather, its desire for changes focused on attempts to realign political relationships involving federal, state, and local governments and community organizations.

The EEOC and CETA Under Presidents Nixon and Carter

Its remedies were part of its New Federalism program. The Great Society programs in the Office of Economic Opportunity (OEO) were centralized, with training programs and a strong oversight mechanism headed by the federal government. Local involvement was conceived largely through participation in the organizations where citizens were directly involved, especially through the Community Action Program (CAP). The New Federalism sought to reduce federal involvement and place the programs in the hands of state and local governments.

While in theory local control should be superior in meeting local needs, the creators of the New Federalism conceived the change in political terms. The political problem they perceived was that under the War on Poverty programs, a modest shift in local power occurred away from the old elites—particularly Anglo politicians—in the direction of the poor, particularly Hispanics and African Americans. They believed they could return power to the old elites by removing the presence of the federal government and eliminating the community organizations.

The poor were justifiably dubious of Nixon's argument that local officials were most responsive to those most in need, having recent memories of breaking down local barriers to education and employment, with the assistance of federal government intervention.

The Nixon administration placed all employment and training programs, previously in the OEO, into the new Comprehensive Employment and Training Administration (CETA), created in 1973. The major difference between the old and the new poverty efforts was that the earlier employment and training programs were clearly targeted to specific population groups and allocated as "categorical" grants, on the basis of national and local considerations. Under CETA, allocations were granted directly to local politicians in the form of "bloc" grants to state and local governments, which could then make decisions on the kinds of programs to establish. Another change was that the CETA plan reduced the power of the federal government's regulations, standards, and other monitoring mechanisms created to ensure the efficacy of the local programs. Furthermore, although the new plan intended to allow local people to determine needs locally, no affirmative action guidelines were established to ensure that the poor and, especially, women, African Americans, and Hispanics, the people for whom the programs were intended, would be represented in the decision-making process. This was particularly evident as CAP was severely weakened. The success of CETA rested on the goodwill of federal and local authorities. During the Nixon administration, many of the community leaders were removed and CETA programs were made increasingly the province of local politicians.

During the Carter administration, the federal government expressed an increased commitment to equal opportunity, and CETA was strengthened. It is no coincidence that at this time the economic well-being of Hispanics and other non-whites peaked and the gap with the white population narrowed.

Furthermore, CETA was considered a success by most of its Hispanic participants. In fiscal year 1978, 142,000 youths, or slightly more than one-tenth of those enrolled in CETA programs, were Hispanics. Overall, approximately 5 percent of the country's Anglo youth, 19 percent of African Americans, and 13 percent of Hispanic youth participated in CETA programs that year. Hispanic participation ranged from 23 percent of Puerto Ricans, 13 percent of Mexican Americans, and 7 percent of Cubans. Interviews conducted that year indicated that more than 87 percent were satisfied with the program, and more than 70 percent believed that it improved their job chances. Nevertheless, CETA and government training programs for the unemployed were being more strongly criticized than ever before by their nonparticipant detractors, who found their own opportunity when Ronald Reagan was elected president.

The Reagan administration philosophy led to a profound change in government policy on job training programs based on both political and economic thought. Politically, the Reagan administration adopted the position that although it must still provide a "safety net" to assist the needy, such assistance should be distinguished from support, and that support is not a federal government responsibility. It also carried the New Federalism concept much further politically and economically than President Nixon by reducing the amount of federal assistance for job creation and other social service programs.

The Job Training Partnership Act

The federal government also reduced its direct involvement by operating more in "partnership" with private business as well as state and local government bodies. The impact of government philosophy and policy is clearly evident in the Job Training Partnership Act (JTPA) of 1983, the central employment training program of the Reagan and Bush years. The JTPA, like its predecessor, CETA, delivers employment and training services to the economically disadvantaged in need. Compared with CETA, the JTPA depends much more on the private sector to deliver these services.

The new program departs sharply from earlier direct job creation strategies that were central to projects of the 1960s and the 1970s. Federally funded jobs created by the Public Service Employment, offering employment to both the cyclically and structurally unemployed, were eliminated under the JTPA. Part of the concept of less government support for the poor, it represented a 60 percent reduction in subsidies for youth employment. It severely reduced employment prospects for many disadvantaged youth whose first full-time employment had come from CETA and its predecessors.

Several structural problems in the Job Training Partnership Act specifically hinder Hispanic participation. A high proportion of Hispanics are needy, in part because of a nearly 50 percent high school dropout rate and because over one-fourth are not fully proficient in English. The JTPA penalizes these people more than any other among the poor by not including precisely those who are most disadvantaged and harder to place. In addition, the JTPA has income-based eligibility stipulations requiring that people must either be receiving food stamps or not have more than a specific level of income. Many Hispanics who are eligible for JTPA, however, are imbued with a work ethic that makes them unwilling to accept food stamps. Still others are not eligible because they are willing to accept jobs that place them in an income level slightly above the sharply increased level of eligibility requirements. Another problem is that the JTPA has increased requirements for documentation of eligibility beyond those of CETA—a policy that has been criticized as unduly burdensome. Furthermore, Mexican Americans, in particular, lack familiarity with government programs, and the means of informing them about JTPA programs are woefully lacking. Finally, Hispanics lack a presence in most JTPA policy-making forums, and thus lack consistent advocates to set policies.

The impact of Reagan job training policy, continued under the Bush administration, is further evident in the case of the Job Corps, created under the EEOC, and presently part of the JTPA. The Job Corps has residential and nonresidential centers where enrollees take intensive programs in education, vocational training, work experience, and counseling. It is popular in both parties of Congress, and the U.S. Department of Labor (USDL) has acknowledged its success. A 1985 USDL study determined that the Job Corps returns $1.38 to the U.S. Treasury in only three years for each $1.00 invested by the federal government. The funds come from continuing taxes paid by former Job Corps trainees once they begin employment and from reduced welfare payments. The Job Corps, serving the most disadvantaged, nonetheless, was among the programs cut most sharply by the JTPA.

The structural design of the incentives process created by the JTPA reveals severe difficulties in the program. Local JTPA offices are motivated by incentives based on the actual number of people hired by private employers. This has led to the process of "creaming" in client selection. Creaming selects the least-disadvantaged individuals because they are the easiest to place. The programs have targeted services primarily to in-school youth or high school graduates; thus, service to high school dropouts has declined sharply.

Furthermore, local employers are paid by JTPA funds to hire employees. This leads to widespread abuse, for it allows employers to receive government funds to "hire" individuals they would have otherwise hired without

JTPA "incentives" of several weeks' or months' pay. The JTPA has become a major government subsidy for private employers, not a training program for those most in need.

Originally New Federalism was designed to transfer power from the federal government to local agencies and employers. In effect, it has taken away power from the poor and from community organizations, remaining largely pushed out of the decision-making process. In the past, community organizations worked in conjunction with federal government administrators. Under the JTPA, however, funding is granted directly to governmental agencies and private proprietors as rewards for their support. Because the monitoring system is so lax and community participation dismantled, efforts to expose the JTPA have been long delayed. As a result, the JTPA has shortchanged the needs of Hispanics, African Americans, and others most in need of training, as well as society at large, while serving the narrow interests of employers in the private sector and their allies.

During the 1980s the Reagan and Bush administrations also launched an attack on civil rights legislation as it extended to the workplace. The new Supreme Court justices appointed by Presidents Reagan and Bush helped change the direction of court protection of employees. In effect, its rulings have relaxed the duties of employers and have made it much more difficult for women and non-Whites to convince the courts that violations of civil rights laws have taken place. The attack peaked in a series of 1989 Supreme Court decisions relating to employment law. In *Patterson v. McLean Credit Union*, the Supreme Court ruled that an individual could no longer sue for racial harassment at work under a 1966 civil rights statute: "A practice of racial harassment adopted after an employee was hired does not by itself violate that employee's rights under the statute." In effect, it permitted the employer to hound Ms. Patterson out of her job because of race.

Employment Rights

In *Wards Cove Packing Co. v. Antonio,* the Court ruled that a group of employees who were able to demonstrate that an Alaska cannery that hired Whites for well-paid and skilled jobs and minorities for low-paid, unskilled jobs, and even segregated employees by race in mess halls and dormitories, did not offer sufficient evidence of employment discrimination. It reversed twenty-eight years of well-established law in its holding by imposing a heavier burden on employees in proving its employer did not have legitimate business reasons for engaging in such practices.

During the same period, other Supreme Court cases severely limited the filing of discrimination charges, and further ruled that a civil rights statute could not be used to sue local governments for damages for acts of discrimination. These and other cases successfully narrowed the coverage of civil rights statutes, making it extremely difficult for women and minorities to prove discrimination.

The erosion of past civil rights legislation by the Supreme Court during the Reagan and Bush administrations resulted in efforts by representatives of civil rights, African American, and Hispanic organizations to initiate a push for a new Civil Rights Act in 1990 to return to previous standards. The legislation sought to redress the discriminatory impact of recent Supreme Court decisions that in sum eliminated much of the thrust of equal employment opportunity law established in the previous generation. Although the 1990 bill had overwhelming support in both houses of Congress, the Bush administration vetoed the legislation on the grounds that it promoted quotas. A series of compromises produced a watered-down Civil Rights Act in 1991.

Affirmative Action

Affirmative action, centering on the Civil Rights Act of 1964, was a central concept of the Great Society programs of the Johnson administration. It accepted the premise that the high levels of unemployment and ongoing discrimination that women and many non-White groups encountered were impediments to the vision of the Great Society. The federal government accepted the responsibility to devise "affirmative action" programs to remedy such discriminatory practices and their consequences.

The federal mandate was to encourage employers to voluntarily increase the presence of underrepresented minorities in the work force to levels commensurate with their presence in the local community. Compliance officers in the Equal Employment Opportunity Commission (EEOC) and the Department of Labor set goals, targets, and timetables for employers.

Affirmative action programs were immediately criticized by some conservative elements who argued that affirmative action favored minorities over more "qualified" Anglos. The struggle over affirmative action continued into the 1970s and 1980s, when opponents coined the term "reverse discrimination," by which they suggested that White males were victims of discrimination as a result of affirmative action on behalf of women, African Americans, Hispanics, and other underrepresented groups.

The attacks on affirmative action have had a profound impact on hiring policies in many sectors of private and public employment. They have contributed to the overall decline of the economic position of Hispanics and other ethnic minorities during the 1980s, both in absolute levels and in comparison with Anglo-Americans. It is most telling in top management positions in large corporations, where most surveys indicate that at least 95 percent of positions are still held by White males.

The federal government has failed not only to abide by its responsibility to serve as watchdog over affirmative action policies in the private sector but also to take affirmative steps itself. Although the Reagan administration could point to an increase in Hispanic representation in the federal work force from 4.3 percent to 4.8 percent between 1980 and 1988, the Hispanic population during that period increased from 6.4 percent to 8.1 percent. Thus, Hispanic underrepresentation in federal employment during the Reagan administration increased sharply, from 50 percent to 69 percent. The underrepresentation was most stark in the highest levels. At the top scale of government, senior executive service, Hispanics accounted for only 1 percent of the employees.

Affirmative action is designed to counter the effects of practices that exclude individuals from the workplace and other settings because of race, color, creed, gender, and national origin. It accepts the assumption that because of their background, many highly qualified people have been passed over in hiring and promotion practices and that steps should be taken to rectify exclusionary practices.

Immigration and Naturalization Service

The number of undocumented aliens cannot be precisely determined, and is the subject of intense debate. In the 1970s Immigration and Naturalization Service (INS) Commissioner Leonard Chapman, seeking to increase funding and expand the power of his organization, claimed that the U.S. harbored as many as 12 million undocumented workers. Other observers most commonly place the number in the range of 3.5 million to 5 million people.

Popular perceptions and the press portray almost all undocumented workers as Mexicans. This is further bolstered by the policies of the INS, whose enforcement efforts are concentrated along the land border between Mexico and the United States, rather than at seaports and airports, or along the United States' northern border. About 95 percent of INS apprehensions are Mexicans, yet it is likely that only about half of all undocumented workers in the United States are Hispanics, the remainder being mostly natives of Europe and Asia.

In addition to their numerical importance, undocumented workers have been at the center of several political battles. On several occasions in re-

The term "undocumented workers" refers to people who are in the United States without proper immigrant papers. It is intended to be descriptive and neutral, in contrast to the term "illegal," which has negative connotations and implies criminality. The presence of undocumented aliens in the United States violates civil statutes, not criminal laws. Some undocumented workers enter the country without legal authorization, while others enter under temporary permits but then extend their stay.

cent decades, a national hysteria among citizens developed over their presence, typically during periods of economic recession and depression. Debates intensified during those periods over whether the undocumented take jobs away from U.S. citizens.

Operation Wetback, which occurred during a time of recession in 1954, involved a concerted campaign by the federal government that successfully apprehended more than 1 million undocumented Mexican workers. The frenzy subsided when the government and private employers expanded the scale of the Bracero Program, reducing the demand of agricultural employers for undocumented workers.

Following abolition of the Bracero Program in the mid-1960s, the number of undocumented workers again began to increase, and a new hysteria appeared in public circles, accompanied by increased activity by the border patrol. By 1977 the INS was again apprehending more than 1 million undocumented workers each year.

The effect of undocumented workers on the economy has stirred a wide-ranging debate in the nation. One side of the argument is that they are a major drain on public services and that they displace U.S. citizens by accepting low-paying jobs. These arguments frequently are based on stereotypes and ethnic biases, and they seldom address the related issue of why employers are permitted to disregard protective labor statutes and immigration law.

An opposing position is that the undocumented pay taxes, and because they seldom use available social services, they make a very positive contribution to the nation's economy. Further, the jobs in which they are employed typically are those that others are unwilling to perform.

Undocumented workers retain most employment rights of citizens, including those of minimum wage, joining and participating in union activities, the right to sue over contracts, and other protection under federal labor law. They are also deemed "employees" within the meaning of the National Labor Relations Act, and are protected under its provisions. Legal cases have also recognized the right to worker's compensation and protection under the Fair Labor Standards Act. Yet, employers frequently use the INS to escape their responsibilities under these laws and report for deportation workers who attempt to organize unions or assert other employment rights.

Sensitive to the increased immigration that began in the 1960s and the economic uncertainty of the 1970s, the Ford administration appointed several task forces to address the issue of undocumented entry into the United States. It encouraged several congressional representatives to introduce new legislation to control immigration to the United States. After more than a decade of debate, Congress enacted the Immigration Reform and Control Act of 1986, popularly referred to as IRCA.

The Immigration Reform and Control Act of 1986

IRCA contains three major provisions. First, it establishes civil and criminal penalties, referred to as employer sanctions, on employers who fail to verify the documentation of employees hired since 1986 whether they are eligible to work. This marks the first time in the history of the United States that employers have been prohibited by law from hiring undocumented workers. Second, IRCA provided a one-time provision to legalize undocumented workers in the United States. The legalization process included a separate program to legalize seasonal agricultural workers (SAWs) in the United States. Third, the law specifically prohibits several forms of employment discrimination. In response to the concerns of Hispanic and civil rights groups that the employer sanctions would result in discrimination, the law mandated that the General Accounting Office (GAO) conduct in an ongoing investigation of the impact of IRCA for three years. IRCA specifically provides Congress with the statutory authority to repeal employer sanctions if the GAO's final report were to conclude that widespread discrimination existed. To facilitate the provisions of the law, Congress also strengthened the power and personnel of the INS.

The GAO made its final report on IRCA to Congress on March 29, 1990. It observed that the implementation and enforcement of employer verification and sanctions provisions were not carried out satisfactorily, that they had caused a widespread pattern of discrimination against members of minority groups, and that they caused unnecessary regulatory burdens on employers. Many employers were confused about the law and its application and initiated illegal discriminatory hiring practices against Hispanics, Asians, and other people who appeared "foreign." Even Anglo workers experienced discriminatory practices. The GAO concluded that a "widespread pattern" of discrimination existed based on national origin, practiced by 19 percent of the employers surveyed, that included not hiring foreign-appearing or foreign-sounding job applicants for fear of noncompliance with the law. In a "sting" operation involving pairs of Hispanic and Anglo "testers," it found that "Anglo testers received 52 percent more job offers than the Hispanic testers with whom they were paired."

The GAO investigation was narrow in its view of what constituted "widespread discrimination" and did not support repealing employer sanctions. Other agencies and civil rights activists documented cases of discrimination, such as employers' firing applicants for legalization along with undocumented workers, depriving them of seniority and other benefits, imposing English-only rules, withholding paychecks, failing to pay overtime, harassing them sexually, assaulting them physically, and violating other civil and constitutional rights. In effect, IRCA pushed undocumented workers into even less regulated and more exploitative jobs.

Employers have also suffered the impact of employer sanctions. Estimates of total costs to businesses to perform record-keeping required by employer sanctions vary from $182 million to $675 million per year. Furthermore, businesses are paying millions of additional dollars in fines and otherwise suffering financially because of loss of workers and INS intrusions into the workplace.

In meeting one of its original goals, preventing the entry of undocumented workers into the United States, IRCA appears to have been successful in its first two years. Since that time, the entry of undocumented workers has increased sharply. In the early 1990s it appears that the prohibitions of IRCA have not had a long-term impact on rates of undocumented entry into the country. They have proved to be a nuisance to employers and an additional burden to all workers—undocumented, legal residents, and citizens alike.

Thus, the GAO report and other evidence confirmed the fears of Hispanic groups before its enactment—that the law would intensify discrimination against Hispanics. On the basis of the GAO report and other evidence, employer sanctions are causing widespread discrimination. Hispanic activists are trying to convince Congress to comply with its own mandate and repeal employer sanctions.

YOUTH EMPLOYMENT ♦

The Hispanic work force is younger than other major work force groups, and in the future it will represent an even greater portion of the work force. Hispanics have lower levels of schooling than other groups. Among youths ages sixteen to twenty-one not attending college, more than two-fifths of employed Afro-Americans and Anglo-Americans are high school graduates, compared with less than one-third of Hispanics. Hispanic youths are more likely to work full time and year round than either Anglo- or Afro-American youths. As with other groups, Hispanic male youths are more likely to be employed than females.

Youths of all backgrounds tend to have much higher unemployment rates than older workers, and their rate of unemployment is more sensitive to business cycles. Anglo youths have the lowest unemployment level, while African Americans have the highest rate of unemployment, which tends to be less sensitive to changes in the economy than either the Anglo or Hispanic rates. Unemployment rates for Hispanics fluctuate between the two others. During upturns in the economy, the rate of unemployment declines more sharply for Hispanic youths, while during downturns, it rises much more rapidly than for either Anglo- or Afro-Americans.

In the third quarter of 1990 the median weekly earnings for full-time male workers ages sixteen to twenty-four were $283 for Anglos, $255 for African Americans, and $238 for Hispanics. Among female youths, the earnings were $250 for Anglos and $225 for Afro-Americans and Hispanics.

◆ ◆ ◆ ◆ ◆ ◆ ◆ ◆ ◆ ◆ ◆ ◆ ◆ ◆ ◆ ◆ ◆ ◆ **WOMEN'S EMPLOYMENT**

During the past decade, the number of Hispanic women in the work force increased more rapidly than any other major population group, and by the end of the decade their rate of participation nearly equaled those of women in other groups. The distinctiveness of Hispanic women in employment has been largely erased. Between 1978 and 1988, Hispanic female participation in the work force more than doubled, from 1.7 million to 3.6 million. In 1988, 56.6 percent of Hispanic women were in the work force, compared with 66.2 percent of Anglo women and 63.8 percent of African Americans. The lower rate for Hispanic women can be attributed largely to their younger age and higher number of children than Afro- and Anglo-American women.

In 1988 Hispanic women formed 6.5 percent of the civilian labor force. Of the total of 3.6 million Hispanic women workers, 58.5 percent were of Mexican origin, 10.4 percent were Puerto Rican, 6.6 percent were of Cuban origin, and the other 24.5 percent were of other Hispanic backgrounds. By ethnicity, 53.9 percent of women of Mexican origin, compared with 54.9 percent of Cuban origin and 41.4 percent of Puerto Rican origin were employed.

In March 1988, 41.1 percent of working Hispanic women were employed in technical, sales, and administrative support occupations, rates not much different from those of other women. At that same date, sharper differences existed in occupations of high and low pay and status. In the higher-status managerial and professional jobs, 15.7 percent of Hispanic women found employment, versus 25.3 percent of all women. Meanwhile, 16.6 percent of Hispanic women worked as lower-paid operators, fabricators, and laborers, compared with only 8.8 percent of all women. Very few Hispanic women may be found in extractive occupations, in mechanic and repairer jobs, or in most construction trades.

In the fourth quarter of 1990, the median weekly earnings of Hispanic women was $283, compared with $313 for Afro-American women and $361 for Anglo-American women. Because of sharp increases in the work force, Hispanic women in the 1990s are about as likely to be employed in wage labor as other women. But their incomes remain substantially below those of women in the other major groups.

INCOME, POVERTY, AND UNEMPLOYMENT ✦ ✦ ✦ ✦ ✦ ✦ ✦ ✦ ✦ ✦ ✦

In 1990 median family income for Anglo-American families was $36,915; for African Americans, $21,423; and for Hispanics, $23,431. Per capita income was $15,265 for Anglos, $9,017 for Afro-Americans, and $8,424 for Hispanics. Among Hispanics, family income was highest among Cuban and lowest among Mexican families.

As individual workers, the incomes of Hispanic men and women in the late 1980s and early 1990s were lower than either Anglo- or African Americans. Between 1982 and 1988 the income gap between Hispanic and non-Hispanic families increased as median family income for Hispanic families fell from 68 percent to 57 percent of non-Hispanic family incomes.

Between 1978 and 1988 the proportion of Hispanic children living in poverty rose more than 45 percent, and by 1990, 40 percent of Hispanic children were living in poverty. Between 1980 and 1990 the rate of poverty for all Anglo-Americans rose from 10.2 percent to 10.7 percent, after peaking at 12.1 percent in 1983; for African Americans it changed from 32.5 percent to 31.9 percent, after peaking at 35.7 percent in 1983; and for Hispanics it rose from 25.7 percent to 28.1 percent. During this same period, poverty rates for Anglo children under age eighteen rose from 13.4 percent to 15.1 percent; for African American children from 42.1 percent to 44.2 percent; and for Hispanic children from 33 percent to 39.7 percent. In 1987 70.1 percent of Hispanic female-headed households with children were living in poverty.

In 1988 the unemployment rate for Anglos was 4.7 percent, compared with 11.7 percent for African Americans, and 8.2 percent for Hispanics. By 1991 the rate for Anglos rose to 6.0 percent, for Afro-Americans to 12.4 percent, and for Hispanics to 9.9 percent.

Hispanics are three times as likely as non-Hispanic Whites to be poor. In 1990, 28.1 percent of Hispanics, versus 10.7 percent of Whites and 31.9 percent of Afro-Americans, lived below the poverty level. By 1991 the number of Hispanic families in poverty was 1.2 million. During the 1980s the number of poor Hispanic families increased by 30 percent, while the number of poor White families declined by 10.3 percent.

Dennis Valdez

♦ ♦ ♦ ♦ ♦ ♦ ♦ ♦ PROMINENT HISPANIC LABOR ORGANIZERS

**César Chávez
(1927–1993)**

Born in 1927 near Yuma, Arizona, to a family of migrant farm workers, César Chávez attended nearly thirty schools, eventually achieving a seventh grade education. During World War II he served in the navy, after which he returned to migrant farm labor. He eventually settled down in 1948 in the barrio of Sal Si Puedes (Get Out if You Can) in San Jose, California. It was in San Jose that he began working for the Community Ser-

vice Organization (CSO) as a community organizer. By 1958 he had become general director of the CSO in California and Arizona. In 1962, wishing to organize farm workers, he resigned the CSO directorship and moved to Delano, California, where he became head of the United Farmworkers Organizing Committee, which has become today the United Farm Workers, AFL-CIO. From 1965 on, Chávez and his fledgling union embarked on a number of history-making strikes and national boycotts of agricultural products that have become the most successful in the history of farm labor in the United States. Principally because of Chávez and his organization's efforts, the California legislature passed the California Labor Relations Act in 1975, which provides secret ballot union elections for farm workers. Owing to his efforts, as well, there have been many improvements in wage, health, and housing conditions for farm workers in California and Arizona. Chávez is remembered as a tireless and spiritual leader of farm workers everywhere, bringing to national attention their plight through media appearances and interviews, hunger strikes, and well-organized boycotts.

UFW march as part of boycott on non-union lettuce, table grapes, and wine.

Born on May 29, 1918, in El Paso, Texas, Bert Corona attended public schools in El Paso and college in California, where he graduated with a degree in law from the University of California, Los Angeles. Between 1936 and 1942 he was active in developing unions in the Southwest. He worked with the CIO in organizing cannery and warehouse workers. His union work eventually led to politics, where he became a pioneer in developing Mexican-American political organizations. In 1959 he was one of the principal founders of the Mexican American Political Organization; he was also a founder of the National Congress of Spanish-Speaking People. Corona was a pioneer in education for Mexican Americans, contributing to the development of the Mexican American Youth Conference and even serving as president of the Association of California School Administrators.

**Bert Corona
(1918–)**

Born in Tepic, Nayarit, Mexico, Ernesto Galarza immigrated to the United States as a refugee with his family during the Mexican Revolution. Galarza attended schools in Sacramento, California, where he was orphaned while

**Ernesto Galarza
(1905–)**

UFW leader Dolores Huerta (center) leads a rally along with Howard Wallace, president of the San Francisco chapter of the UFW.

in high school and thus had to support himself. Galarza went on to Occidental College and then received a master's degree from Stanford University in 1929. He later received a Ph.D. degree in education from Columbia University. Galarza then worked as a research assistant in education for the Pan American Union from 1936 to 1940, when he was promoted to chief of the Division of Labor and Social Information. In 1947 he became research director for the National Farm Labor Union, AFL, and moved to San Jose, California. During the next twelve years he dedicated his life to agricultural workers, serving as secretary-treasurer and vice president of the union. During the 1960s Galarza worked as a professor, researcher, and writer, writing various books on farm labor topics. In the 1970s he developed materials for bilingual education, including original books for children.

Dolores Fernández Huerta (1930–)

Born in Dawson, New Mexico, Dolores Fernández Huerta received her early education in Stockton, California. In 1955 she began work with Fred Ross and César Chávez, pioneer organizers of Mexican-American chapters of the Community Service Organization. She worked with Chávez in forming and administering the United Farm Workers Union. With years of experience in organizing migrant workers, striking, and negotiating contracts, Huerta eventually became the lobbyist for the UFW in Sacramento, California. She has gained an international reputation as an excellent speaker and politician.

*P*olitics

In the past thirty years, Hispanic Americans have become one of the largest and fastest-growing groups of elected officials in the United States. Congressman Bill Richardson states, "National candidates and both major political parties are undertaking major campaigns to woo Hispanic American support. We are recognized as the nation's fastest growing minority group and are being courted as such. This attention will only increase our political strength."

HISPANICS IN THE POLITICAL PROCESS ♦ ♦ ♦ ♦ ♦ ♦ ♦ ♦ ♦ ♦ ♦

Widespread political activity at the national level by Hispanic Americans has been intermittent since the first Hispanic was elected to Congress. Joseph Marion Hernández was elected to Congress representing Florida in 1822 as a member of the Whig party. No other Hispanic held national office for thirty years. A total of eleven Hispanics were elected to the U.S. Congress in the entire nineteenth century, all from New Mexico except for one from California and Congressman Hernández from Florida. From the turn of the century until the 1950s, a total of fifteen Hispanics served in Congress—five from New Mexico, two from Louisiana, and eight resident commissioners from Puerto Rico, which became a U.S. possession in 1898. Since the 1960s the number of Hispanic Americans elected to Congress has been steadily increasing. In 1994 twenty Hispanics are serving in the 103d U.S. Congress.

For a century the majority of Hispanic Americans holding political office at the local level was limited to southwestern states, southern Florida, and New York City. Since the 1960s growth in the population of Hispanics and favorable civil rights legislation have combined to create opportunity for Hispanic candidates to win public office in other areas of the country. Hispanic Americans have made the greatest inroads at the municipal level. Hispanics now hold elected office at the local level in thirty-five of the fifty states.

Harry P. Pachón, national director of the National Association of Latino Elected and Appointed Officials (NALEO), stated that in 1990 NALEO identified "4,004 Hispanic Americans holding publicly elected offices throughout the country." Pachón stated that "although this number is only a small fraction of the nation's 504,404 elected officials, less than one percent, the number of Hispanic elected officials for various states is quite large."

HISPANIC VOTING AND THE VOTING RIGHTS ACT OF 1965 ♦ ♦

The primary aim of the Voting Rights Act of 1965 was African-American enfranchisement in the South. Specifically, obstacles to registration and voting faced by African Americans were the major concern of those who framed the statute in the 1960s. Its potential as a tool for Hispanic Americans was not fully realized until the act was extended and amended in 1970.

The 1970 amendments to this landmark legislation added a provision that was designed to guard against inventive new barriers to political participation by requiring federal approval of all changes in voting procedure in certain jurisdictions, primarily southern states. Disgruntled officials in Mississippi and other southern states embarked on schemes to dilute African-American voter impact in elections by eliminating single-member districts and creating at-large voting.

The U.S. Supreme Court responded, in *Allen v. State Board of Elections,* by extending federal authority to object to proposed discriminatory alterations in voting districts, the introduction of at-large voting, and other such changes, in addition to reaffirming the original power to object to discriminatory innovations involving registration and voting.

Until 1980 (with the single exception of the 1930 census), the U.S. Census Bureau classified Hispanic Americans as "White," and many people argued that to extend coverage of the Voting Rights Act to a group who considered themselves White was unjustifiable. The Fifteenth Amendment rights secured by the statute protected against denial of the right to vote only on account of "race, color or previous condition of servitude." If Hispanic Americans were White, they were ineligible for the special protection of the Voting Rights Act.

During congressional hearings to extend the Voting Rights Act in 1975, J. Stanley Pottinger, assistant attorney general of the U.S. Justice Department's Civil Rights Division, saw the labeling problem as inconsequential and told Congress that the Justice Department's practice "has been to treat Indians, Puerto Ricans, and Mexican Americans as racial groups." His argument hardly settled the matter for everyone, but Congress agreed to amend the act to include "language minorities," which specifically included Spanish-speakers.

Vilma S. Martínez, then-president of the Mexican American Legal Defense and Educational Fund (MALDEF), testified before Congress in 1975 about voting districts in Texas where assistance to non-English-speaking voters was being denied. She testified further that Texas had been gerry-mandering voting districts to give unfair advantage to English-speaking residents. State action creating at-large voting, annexations to voting districts, and redistricting plans fragmented Hispanic voting strength. Additionally, majority vote requirements, numbered posts, and other confusing procedural rules diminished the likelihood that a Hispanic American would gain an elected office.

Congress acted decisively. The Voting Rights Act Amendments of 1975, which extended the provisions of the Voting Rights Act of 1965, made permanent the national ban on literacy tests. The amendments condemned any action by states, which was no longer limited to southern states, to realign voting districts to dilute the impact of minority voters who resided within the district. Any redistricting plan would have to be approved by the federal government.

In 1980 the U.S. Supreme Court, in *City of Mobile v. Bolden,* rejected a challenge to at-large elections in Mobile, Alabama, because the Court was not convinced that the city had acted with the purpose of discriminating against minority voters. The Court, in its sharply divided decision, found that the city had not violated the Voting Rights Act.

Congress reacted to the Supreme Court decision with the important Voting Rights Act Amendments of 1982. The amendments, under Section 2, prohibit any voting law or practice created by a state or political subdivision that "results" in denial of the right of any citizen of the United States to vote on account of race, color, or language-minority status. The amendments eliminated the need to prove that the state or political subdivision created a voting law with the "intention" of discriminating against minority voters.

In one of the first cases to be tried under Section 2 of the 1982 amendments, *Velásquez v. City of Abilene,* prominent judge Reynaldo G. Garza delivered the opinion of the U.S. Court of Appeals for the Fifth Circuit. Garza stated for the court that the intention of Congress was clear in cases of vote dilution, referring to the 1982 amendments. Garza stated that the city of Abilene's use of at-large voting, bloc voting, and other voting mechanisms resulted in vote dilution and had a discriminatory effect on Hispanic American voters in the city.

A year later the Fifth Circuit Court made a similar ruling in *Jones v. City of Lubbock*. The city of Lubbock, Texas, a medium-sized city with a diverse population, had a clear White majority. Under an at-large voting scheme, the majority uniformly elected an all-White city council. The court found that the voting method used by the city polarized voting between the White majority and minority voters, and the result was discrimination against minority voters.

In the last decade, holdouts of racially discriminatory electoral patterns have been coming under intense pressure from the courts to end discrimination against minority voters. The success in the courts has contributed to the growing numbers of Hispanic Americans holding elected offices across the United States. In 1991, for the first time in history, the city of Abilene had two Hispanics on its city council; the city of Lubbock had one Hispanic on its city council, as well as a Hispanic county commissioner.

✦ ✦ ✦ ✦ ✦ ✦ ✦ ✦ ✦ ✦ ✦ ✦ ✦ ✦ ✦ ✦ ✦ ✦ ✦ **HISPANICS IN CONGRESS**

The growing Hispanic population remains significantly underrepresented in the U.S. Congress today. Currently, Hispanics comprise just 4 percent of the House of Representatives, yet they comprise 9 percent of the United States's population. No Hispanics serve in the U.S. Senate. Hispanic-American voting levels have traditionally fallen well below the national average. In spite of favorable legislation, advocates actively seeking to increase Hispanic-American voter registration still cite poverty, inadequate education, language barriers, and alienage as critical obstacles that have discouraged voting. Despite these problems, Hispanic Americans have been going to the polls in increasing numbers.

The November 1992 elections brought eight new Hispanic representatives and two new Hispanic delegates to the House. These new members of the 103d Congress joined ten returning Hispanic incumbents. Many of the new members were elected following redistricting in their states. Hispanic representatives hail from the states of California, Florida, New Mexico, New York, Illinois, New Jersey, and Texas. The three nonvoting Hispanic members are the resident commissioner of Puerto Rico and the delegates from Guam and the Virgin Islands. Seventeen of the Hispanic members are Democrats, and several occupy powerful positions in the

Democratic hierarchy of the House. Congressman Henry B. González of Texas is the chairman of the powerful House Banking, Finance and Urban Affairs Committee and Congressman E. (Kika) de la Garza of Texas is the chairman of the House Agriculture Committee. Congressman Bill Richardson of New Mexico is now Chief Deputy Majority Whip; he is the first Hispanic in Congressional history to serve in a House leadership position. The Democratic Steering and Policy Committee, which makes Democratic committee assignments, now has three Hispanics: de la Garza, Richardson, and Congressman Ed Pastor of Arizona. Four Hispanic members are Republicans: Congresswoman Ileana Ros-Lehtinen of Florida, Congressman Lincoln Diaz-Balart of Florida, Congressman Henry Bonilla of Texas, and the nonvoting delegate, Ron de Lugo, from the Virgin Islands. No Hispanics yet serve in Republican leadership positions.

No Hispanic-American candidate has been elected to the U.S. Senate since 1970, when New Mexico Democrat Joseph Manuel Montoya won his second and last election. Senator Montoya served in the Senate from 1965 to 1977. The only other Hispanic American to be elected to the Senate was New Mexico Democrat Dennis Chávez, who served with great distinction from 1935 to 1962. Both Senators Chávez and Montoya served as members of the U.S. House of Representatives prior to being elected to the Senate.

Congressional Hispanic Caucus

The Congressional Hispanic Caucus, organized in December 1976, is a bipartisan group of members of Congress of Hispanic descent. The caucus is dedicated to voicing and advancing, through the legislative process, issues affecting Hispanic Americans in the United States and its territories.

Organized as a legislative service organization under the rules of Congress, the caucus is composed solely of members of the U.S. Congress. Under these rules, associate membership is offered to dues-paying members of Congress who are not of Hispanic descent. With its associate members, caucus membership represents twenty states, Puerto Rico, Guam, and the U.S. Virgin Islands.

Although every issue that affects the quality of life of all U.S. citizens is a Congressional Hispanic Caucus concern, national and international issues that have a particular impact on the Hispanic community are the focus. The caucus monitors legislative action as well as policies and practices of the executive and judicial branches of government that affect these issues.

♦ ♦ ♦ ♦ ♦ ♦ HISPANIC MEMBERS OF THE 103D U.S. CONGRESS

Xavier Becerra (1958–)

D-California

Xavier Becerra was born in Sacramento, California, on January 26, 1958. He received both his undergraduate and law degrees from Stanford University. Becerra was Deputy Attorney General of California from 1987 to 1990, and he served as an Assemblyman in the California State Legislature from 1990 to 1992. He was elected to the House of Representatives in 1992. In addition to being one of three freshman whips in the House, Becerra is a member of the Education and Labor Committee, the Judiciary Committee, and the Science, Space and Technology Committee.

Henry Bonilla (1954–)

R-Texas

Henry Bonilla was born in San Antonio, Texas, on January 2, 1954. He received a Bachelor of Journalism degree from the University of Texas at Austin in 1976. Most of Bonilla's professional career has been in television news. In 1989, he became executive producer for public affairs at KENS-TV in San Antonio, a position that involved heading up civic and community projects on behalf of the television station. Bonilla has been involved in numerous civic organizations and has been recognized for his service in the the community. Bonilla's victorious campaign in 1992 marks the first time an Hispanic Republican has been elected to Congress from Texas. He serves on the House Appropriations Committee, a position not held by a Republican freshman in more than twenty-five years. Bonilla represents the 23d District of Texas, the largest district in the state.

E. (Kika) de la Garza (1927–)

D-Texas

Congressman Kika de la Garza was born on September 22, 1927, in the Mexican border town of Mercedes, Texas. He comes from a family with roots in the Rio Grande Valley that go back to the 1700s. After graduating from high school, de la Garza, by struggle and perseverance, obtained his education at Edinburg Junior College and St. Mary's University in San Antonio. His education was interrupted by the Korean War, in which he served as an artillery officer from 1950 to 1952. He then earned his B.A. degree from St. Mary's in 1952 and later received his law degree from St. Mary's Law School. With heavily Mexican-American Hidalgo County as his base of support, de la Garza was elected to the Texas House of Representatives in 1952. He was reelected for another five terms.

De la Garza was first elected to Congress in 1964 as a Democrat from the 15th District in the Rio Grande Valley. His election was a milestone for Texas Mexican Americans. De la Garza is chairman of the House Agricul-

Henry Bonilla.

ture Committee and an ex officio member of all its subcommittees. He is also a member and former chairman of the Congressional Hispanic Caucus. He is an active member of the League of United Latin American Citizens (LULAC) and a host of other organizations. In 1978 Mexican President José López Portillo awarded de la Garza Mexico's highest award to a foreigner, the order of the Aztec Eagle.

Rep. E. de la Garza holds up a chart during a news conference, July 1993, to discuss NAFTA and its effects on agriculture.

Ron de Lugo
(1930–)

D-Virgin Islands

The de Lugo family migrated from Puerto Rico to the Virgin Islands in 1879. Ron de Lugo was born on August 2, 1930, in Saint Thomas. He attended school in the Virgin Islands and Puerto Rico. In 1968, De Lugo was elected at-large as the first representative from the Virgin Islands and was reelected to that post in 1970. In 1972, he was elected as the Virgin Islands's first seated delegate in the U.S. Congress. Now in his tenth term as the Virgin Islands's delegate to Congress, De Lugo is chairman of the House Subcommittee on Insular and International Affairs, with jurisdiction over the Caribbean and Pacific island areas associated with the United States. De Lugo is a member of the House Interior and Insular Affairs Committee and the House Public Works and Transportation Committee. De Lugo is also a member of the Congressional Hispanic Caucus.

Lincoln Diaz-Balart
(1954–)

R-Florida

Lincoln Diaz-Balart was born in Cuba in 1954, and fled the country with his family upon the arrival of communism in 1959. He received a degree in international relations from New College of the University of South Florida, and a diploma in British politics in Cambridge, England. He went

on to earn a law degree from Ohio's Case Western Reserve University. As a lawyer in Miami, Diaz-Balart served as an assistant state attorney in the office of then-state attorney and the current U.S. Attorney General, Janet Reno. He went on to serve in the Florida State House and State Senate.

In 1992, Diaz-Balart was elected to the U.S. House of Representatives from Florida's newly created 21st District, which encompasses much of western Dade County. He won the Republican primary election with 69 percent of the vote and ran unopposed in the general election. Congressman Diaz-Balart serves on the Foreign Affairs Committee, the Committee on Merchant Marine and Fisheries, and chairs the Housing Task Force of the Congressional Hispanic Caucus.

Henry B. González
(1916–)
D-Texas

Henry González was born on May 3, 1916, in San Antonio, Texas, to Mexican refugees. He grew up in a family that stressed education and intellectual pursuits. González received his early education in San Antonio public schools. He went on to attend San Antonio Junior College and the University of Texas at Austin, where he received his bachelor's degree. He then attended St. Mary's University Law School, where he received his law degree in 1943. After graduation, González worked at a variety of jobs, including teaching and social services.

In 1950 González entered the political arena and ran for San Antonio City Council. He lost narrowly, but won in his second bid three years later. González fought for a city ordinance ending segregation in city facilities. In 1956, he was elected to the Texas Senate. González was the first Mexican-American Texas state senator in 110 years. He attracted national attention as an outspoken advocate of equal rights for minorities and as an opponent of racist legislation. In 1960 González was elected to Congress for the first time, as a Democrat representing the 20th District of Texas. He has been overwhelmingly reelected to Congress for each subsequent term. Congressman González is currently the chairman of the influential House Banking, Finance and Urban Affairs Committee and is also chairman of the Housing and Community Development Subcommittee.

The first Texan of Mexican descent to serve in the U.S. House of Representatives, he has fervently defended civil rights, distinguishing himself nationally as a liberal Democrat during the 1960s and 1970s. He was chairman of the Viva Kennedy campaign in 1960 and the Viva Johnson campaign in 1964. In 1964, he contributed significantly to the termination of the infamous Mexican Bracero Program.

Luis Gutierrez was born to Puerto Rican parents in Chicago, Illinois, on December 10, 1953. He received a B.A. degree from Northeastern Illinois University in 1974. Gutierrez worked as a social worker and a teacher before being elected to the Chicago City Council in 1986. In 1992 Gutierrez became the first Hispanic to represent Illinois in Congress. He won 78 percent of the vote in Illinois's newly created 4th District, which is 66 percent Hispanic. Gutierrez now serves on the House Banking, Finance and Urban Affairs Committee and the Veterans Affairs Committee.

**Luis Gutierrez
(1953–)**

D-Illinois

Matthew Martínez was born on February 14, 1929, and resides in Monterey Park, California. Martínez attended the Los Angeles Trade Technical School and was involved in small business prior to his election to the U.S. Congress. He is also a veteran of the U.S. Marine Corps. Martínez was mayor of Monterey Park, California, from 1974 to 1975. He was a member of the California legislature from 1980 to 1982. Martínez was first elected to Congress as a Democrat in 1981, representing the 30th District of California. He is a member of the important House Education and

**Matthew G.
Martínez (1929–)**

D-California

Rep. Matthew Martínez at a press conference, 1988, about a fact-finding mission to Costa Rica and Nicaragua. With him is Rep. Esteban Torres.

Labor Committee and is chairman of its Human Resources Subcommittee. Martínez is also a member of the House Government Operations Committee and the House Select Committee on Children, Youth, and Families. In January 1991, Congressman Martínez was elected vice chairman of the Congressional Hispanic Caucus.

Robert Menendez

(1954–)

D-New Jersey

Robert Menendez was born in New York City on January 1, 1954. He received his B.A. degree from St. Peter's College in New Jersey in 1976, and his law degree from New Jersey's Rutgers Law School in 1979. At 20, Menendez was the youngest elected member of New Jersey's Union City School Board. After working as an attorney, Menendez served as mayor of Union City from 1986 to 1992. He also served on the New Jersey State Assembly and the State Senate. He is chairman of the New Jersey Hispanic Leadership Program. Menendez currently serves on the House Foreign Affairs Committee, the Public Works Committee, and the Transportation Committee. Menendez is the first Hispanic whom New Jersey has ever sent to Congress, as well as the first Democratic Cuban American to serve in the House. His district is 43 percent Hispanic.

Solomon P. Ortiz

(1937–)

D-Texas

Solomon Ortiz was born on June 3, 1937, in Robstown, Texas. He attended Del Mar College in Texas. Ortiz was first elected to office in 1964 as Nueces County constable. Four years later he was elected Nueces County commissioner and was reelected to that post in 1972. In 1976 Ortiz was elected Nueces County sheriff and was reelected in 1980. In 1982 Ortiz won his first bid for national office. Congressman Ortiz is a member of the Congressional Hispanic Caucus and was elected chairman of the caucus in January 1991. He sits on the powerful House Armed Services Committee, the Merchant Marine and Fisheries Committee, and the Select Committee on Narcotics Abuse and Control.

Ed Lopez Pastor

(1943–)

D-Arizona)

Born June 28, 1943, in Claypool, Arizona, Ed Pastor received his B.A. and J.D. from Arizona State University. He worked as a chemistry teacher before becoming deputy director of the Guadalupe Organization in 1969. Pastor was the director of affirmative action for the State of Arizona, 1975–77, and the Maricopa County county supervisor, 1977–91. He sits on the Appropriations Committee and is a member of the Congressional Hispanic Caucus.

Rep. Bill Richardson (second from left), in 1993 discussing NAFTA with Rep. Jim Kilbe (R-AZ), Treasury Sec. Lloyd Bentsen, and House Minority Whip Newt Gingrich of Georgia.

William B. Richardson (1947–)

D-New Mexico

Bill Richardson was born on November 15, 1947, and lives in Santa Fe, New Mexico. Richardson attended Tufts University and received a master's degree from the Fletcher School of Law and Diplomacy. Richardson was first elected to Congress in 1982 to represent New Mexico's newly created 3d District, one of the largest in square miles and one of the most ethnically diverse in the country: 40 percent Anglo, 40 percent Hispanic, and 20 percent Native American. Congressman Richardson rose relatively quickly to become a member of the House leadership and serves as Chief Deputy Majority Whip. He is a member of the House Energy and Commerce Committee, the House Interior and Insular Affairs Committee, the House Select Committee on Aging, the House Select Committee on Intelligence, and the Democratic Steering and Policy Committee.

Ileana Ros-Lehtinen (1952–)

R-Florida

Ileana Ros-Lehtinen was born on July 15, 1952, and resides in Miami, Florida. She attended Florida International University, where she received both a bachelor's and a master's degree. After graduating from college, Ros-Lehtinen taught at a private school in Miami that she owned and op-

erated. In 1982 Ros-Lehtinen was elected to the Florida legislature. In 1986 she was elected to the Florida state senate, where she served until 1989. Congresswoman Ros-Lehtinen was elected in 1989 to the U.S. Congress for the 18th District in Florida. She is a member of the critical House Foreign Affairs Committee and the House Government Operations Committee and serves as the ranking minority member of the House Employment and Housing Subcommittee. Ros-Lehtinen has also been elected twice to the post of secretary-treasurer of the Congressional Hispanic Caucus.

Lucille Roybal-Allard (1941–)

D-California

Born in Los Angeles, California in 1941, Roybal-Allard is the eldest daughter of former Congressman Edward R. Roybal of California, and the first Hispanic woman to directly follow her father into Congress. She received her B.A. degree from California State University in 1965. In 1987, she was elected to the California State Assembly, where she served until 1992. She was elected to the U.S. House of Representatives in 1992, representing the newly created 33d District. Roybal-Allard is deeply committed to environmental and women's issues. She has won numerous awards in recognition of her work in these areas, including the 1992 Feminist of the Year Award from the Feminist Majority Foundation, the 1991 Legislator of the Year Award from the National Organization for Women, and the 1990 and 1991 Highest Legislative Rating from the League of Conservation Voters.

Carlos Romero-Barcelo (1932–)

D/NP-Puerto Rico

Born in San Juan, Puerto Rico, on September 4, 1932, Carlos Romero-Barcelo earned a B.A. degree from Yale University and both a J.D. and an LL.B. from the University of Puerto Rico. He then worked as an attorney until he was elected mayor of San Juan in 1969. He went on to the governership of Puerto Rico in 1977, and then served in Puerto Rico's senate from 1986 to 1989. He was elected Resident Commissioner of Puerto Rico in 1992, as a Democratic/New Progressive Party candidate.

José E. Serrano (1943–)

D-New York

José Serrano was born in Mayaguez, Puerto Rico, on October 24, 1943. His family moved to the South Bronx in 1950. Serrano attended public schools and went to the City University of New York. He was a New York state assemblyman from 1974 until he was elected to Congress in 1990. He represents the 18th District in New York. Congressman Serrano is a member of the influential House Education and Labor Committee and the

Jose Serrano after capturing a House seat in the impoverished South Bronx in a special election, 1990.

House Small Business Committee. He is also a member of the Congressional Hispanic Caucus.

Frank Tejeda (1945–)

D-Texas

Frank Tejeda was born in San Antonio, Texas, on October 2, 1945. He received a B.A. degree from St. Mary's University, a J.D. from the University of California at Berkeley, an M.P.A. from Harvard University, and an LL.M. from Yale Law School. Tejeda served in the U.S. Marine Corps from 1963 to 1967, and then worked as an attorney. He was elected to the

Texas State House of Representatives in 1977 and went on to serve in the Texas State Senate in 1987. He was elected to the U.S. House of Representatives in 1992.

Tejeda represents Texas's newly created 28th District, which includes some of the poorest counties in the nation. A Vietnam veteran, Tejeda supports a strong military and sits on the Armed Services and Veterans Affairs Committees. His district contains two military bases. A fiscal conservative, Tejeda nevertheless takes a more liberal stance on the social issues of health care, job creation and training, and public education.

Esteban E. Torres
(1930–)

D-California

Esteban Edward Torres was born on January 27, 1930, in Miami, Arizona, where his Mexican-born father was a miner. When his father was deported in 1936 as a result of his union-organizing activities, the family moved to East Los Angeles, where Torres received his early education. After graduating from high school in 1949, he joined the army and served during the Korean War. After being discharged in 1954, Torres took a job on an assembly line at Chrysler and attended California State University at night, receiving his B.A. degree in 1963. Torres was a supporter of the United Auto Workers Union.

In 1974, Torres narrowly lost his first bid for the Democratic nomination for the U.S. House of Representatives. In 1977, President Jimmy Carter appointed Torres as the U.S. representative to UNESCO, with diplomatic rank. President Carter also appointed Torres as his special assistant for programs and policies concerning Mexican Americans. After President Reagan took office in 1981, Torres returned to California. The next year, he was elected to Congress as a Democrat representing the 34th District in California. He is a member of the House Banking, Finance and Urban Affairs Committee and is chairman of its Consumer Affairs Subcommittee. Torres is also a member of the House Small Business Committee and a member of the Congressional Hispanic Caucus.

Robert A.
Underwood
(1948–)

D-Guam

Robert Underwood was born in Tamuning, Guam, on July 13, 1948. He received both his bachelor's and master's degrees in history from California State University. He earned a doctorate in education from the University of Southern California in 1987. Prior to his election to the U.S. House of Representatives in 1992, Underwood had built a career in education.

He was an administrator and curriculum writer for Guam public schools, then a full professor of education at the University of Guam. Underwood serves on the House Armed Services and Natural Resources Committees.

Nydia Velazquez was born in Yabuoca, Puerto Rico, on March 23, 1953. In 1992, Velazques, the daughter of a sugar cane worker and a professor by trade, became the first Puerto Rican woman ever elected to serve in the U.S. House of Representatives. She defeated long-term incumbent Stephen Solarz in a hotly contested race. Velazquez received a B.A. degree from the University of Puerto Rico in 1974, and a master's degree from New York University in 1976. She then worked as a professor and in 1984 became the first Puerto Rican woman to serve on the City Council of New York City. In 1989 she was appointed Director of the Department of Puerto Rican Community Affairs in the United States.

Nydia M.
Velazquez
(1953–)

D-New York

♦ ♦ ♦ SELECTED HISPANIC MEMBERS OF CONGRESS, 1822–1992

As of the 1992 elections, fifty-seven Hispanic Americans have been members of the U.S. House of Representatives, serving constituents in California, Florida, Louisiana, New Mexico, New York, Texas, Illinois, and New Jersey. This includes seventeen nonvoting members from Puerto Rico, Guam, and the Virgin Islands.

Two members of the House of Representatives, Dennis Chavez and Joseph Manuel Montoya, both of New Mexico, became the only Hispanics to serve in the U.S. Senate.

House of Representatives

Name	Party and State	Years Served
Joseph Marion Hernández	W-Florida	1822-1823
Jose Manuel Gallegos	D-New Mexico	1871-1873
Miguel Antonio Otero, Sr.	D-New Mexico	1856-1861
Francisco Perea	R-New Mexico	1863-1865
Jose Francisco Chaves	R-New Mexico	1865-1867
Trinidad Romero	R-New Mexico	1877-1879
Mariano Sabino Otero	R-New Mexico	1879-1881
Romualdo Pacheco	R-California	1879-1883
Tranquillino Luna	R-New Mexico	1881-1884
Francisco Manzanares	D-New Mexico	1884-1885
Pedro Perea	R-New Mexico	1899-1901
Julio Larringa	U-Puerto Rico*	1905-1911
Luis Muñoz Rivera	U-Puerto Rico*	1911-1916
Ládislas Lázaro	D-Louisiana	1913-1927
Benigno Cárdenas Hernández	R-New Mexico	1919-1921
Felix Córdova Dávila	U-Puerto Rico*	1917-1932
Nestor Montoya	R-New Mexico	1921-1923
Dennis Chávez	D-New Mexico	1931-1935
Joachim Octave Fernández	D-Louisiana	1931-1941
José Lorenzo Pesquera	NP-Puerto Rico*	1932-1933
Santiago Iglesias	C-Puerto Rico*	1933-1939
Bolívar Pagán	C-Puerto Rico*	1939-1945
Antonio Manuel Fernández	D-New Mexico	1943-1956
Jesús T. Piñero	PD-Puerto Rico*	1945-1948
Antonio Fernós-Isern	PD-Puerto Rico*	1949-1965
Joseph Manuel Montoya	D-New Mexico	1957-1964
Henry B. González	D-Texas	1961-present
Edward R. Roybal	D-California	1962-1992
E. (Kika) de la Garza	D-Texas	1965-present
Santiago Polanco-Abreu	PD-Puerto Rico*	1965-1969
Manuel Luján, Jr.	R-New Mexico	1969-1988
Jorge Luis Córdova	NP-Puerto Rico*	1969-1973
Herman Badillo	D-New York	1971-1977
Ron de Lugo	D-Virgin Islands	1981-present
Jaime Benítez	PD-Puerto Rico*	1973-1977
Baltasar Corrada	NP-Puerto Rico*	1977-1984
Robert García	D-New York	1978-1989
Matthew G. Martínez	D-California	1982-present
Solomon P. Ortiz	D-Texas	1983-present
William B. Richardson	D-California	1983-present
Esteban Edward Torres	D-California	1983-present
Ben Blaz	R-Guam*	1985-1992
Albert G. Bustamante	D-Texas	1985-1992
Jaime B. Fuster	D-Puerto Rico*	1985-1992
Ileana Ros-Lehtinen	R-Florida	1989-present
Ed Pastor	D-Arizona	1991-present
José E. Serrano	D-New York	1991-present
Xavier Becerra	D-California	1993-present
Henry Bonilla	R-Texas	1993-present
Lincoln Diaz-Balart	R-Florida	1993-present
Luis Gutierrez	D-Illinois	1993-present
Robert Menendez	D-New Jersey	1993-present
Lucille Roybal-Allard	D-California	1993-present
Carlos Romero-Barcelo	D/NP-Puerto Rico*	1993-present
Frank Tejeda	D-Texas	1993-present
Robert A. Underwood	D-Guam*	1993-present
Nydia M. Velazquez	D-New York	1993-present

Senate

Dennis Chávez	D-New Mexico	1935-1962
Joseph Montoya	D-New Mexico	1964-1977

Source: Congressional Hispanic Caucus. *Nonvoting member of Congress.
Party Affiliation: D=Democrat; R=Republican; C=Congress; PD=Popular Democratico;
NP=Nuevo Progresista; U=Unida; W=Whig.

The first Puerto Rican ever elected as a voting member of Congress, Herman Badillo was born in Caguas, Puerto Rico. Orphaned at age 5, he was sent to live with relatives in New York City in 1940. He attended the City College of New York, where he graduated with honors, then attended the Brooklyn Law School at night.

In 1961, Badillo entered politics, narrowly losing a race for the state assembly. After serving in several local appointed positions, he ran unsuccessfully for mayor of New York. Badillo gained popularity as a result of his strong showing in the mayoral election and later won election to Congress in 1970. Badillo served as a U.S. congressman from New York for four terms, representing the 21st District.

After serving in Congress for seven years, Badillo resigned in 1978 to accept an appointment as deputy mayor of New York City under Mayor Edward Koch. Badillo went into the practice of law in New York after leaving the deputy mayor's office. In 1986, he ran for the post of New York state comptroller. He lost the statewide race, but carried 61 percent of the New York City vote. Many in the New York Hispanic community suggest that Badillo may again run for mayor.

Herman Badillo (1929–)

Ben Blaz was born on February 14, 1928, and resides in Ordot, Guam. Blaz lived in Guam during the two-year Japanese occupation of that island during World War II. He regards the liberation of Guam by the U.S. Marines as the most exciting experience of his life. Blaz attended college at the University of Notre Dame and received a master's degree in business administration at George Washington University. Blaz also attended the Naval War College and served in the U.S. Marine Corps in both Korea and Vietnam. He reached the rank of brigadier general before retiring from the service. Blaz was first elected to Congress as a Republican delegate representing the island of Guam in 1984, and served until 1992.

Ben Blaz (1928–)

Albert Bustamante was born on April 8, 1935, and resides in San Antonio, Texas. Bustamante attended college at Sul Ross State University. Bustamante was elected to Congress as a Democrat representing the 23rd District of Texas from 1984 to 1992.

Albert G. Bustamante (1935–)

José Francisco Chaves (1833–1904)

José Chaves was born in what is today Bernalillo County, near Albuquerque, New Mexico. His father, Mariano Chaves, was an important political figure in the Mexican government in the late 1830s. After his early education in New Mexico and Chihuahua, Chaves was sent to school in Saint Louis by his father so that he might better cope with the westward flood tide of American frontiersmen. After returning to New Mexico during the U.S. war with Mexico, Chaves went to New York to complete his education.

When his father died, Chaves returned to New Mexico to manage the family ranch. During the 1850s, he was involved in various Indian campaigns to preserve cattle ranges. His participation in the Indian campaigns proved useful in the Civil War, in which he reached the rank of lieutenant colonel in the New Mexico infantry.

After the war, Chaves studied law and entered the New Mexico political arena. He was elected New Mexico territorial delegate in several bitter, brawling campaigns and served three terms between 1865 and 1871 as a Republican. In 1875, he was elected to the New Mexico territorial legislature and reelected until his death thirty years later. Chaves was a dynamic political leader, fighting the Sante Fe Ring and strongly supporting New Mexico Governor Miguel Otero, Jr.

On the night of November 26, 1904, Chaves was assassinated by an unknown assailant at Pinos Wells, New Mexico. The murder was rumored to be politically motivated and connected to his opposition to the infamous Santa Fe Ring. Despite a $2,500 reward offered by the legislature, his murderer was never identified.

Dennis Chávez (1888–1962)

Dennis Chavez was a member of the U.S. House of Representatives and the first Hispanic U.S. senator. Chávez was born as the third of eight children in a village west of Albuquerque, New Mexico, to a poor family. The family moved to Albuquerque seven years later and Chávez attended school there, but family poverty forced him to drop out of school in the eighth grade to work delivering groceries for the next five years. He continued to educate himself in the evenings at the public library.

From 1906 to 1915, he worked for the Albuquerque city engineering department. In 1912, Chávez worked as a Spanish interpreter for the successful Democratic candidate for U.S. Senate, Andrieus Jones. Jones obtained a clerkship in the Senate for Chávez, who entered law school at Georgetown University in Washington, D.C. In 1920, Chávez was awarded a law degree.

Chávez then returned to New Mexico, where he began a successful law practice and ran for public office in the classic pattern of American political advancement. As Chávez rose in Democratic party ranks, he successfully ran for a seat in the New Mexico legislature. In 1930, Chávez defeated the incumbent Republican and won a seat in the U.S. House of Representatives. He was reelected to the House in 1932.

In the 1934 elections, Chávez ran for the U.S. Senate seat held by the powerful Republican Bronson Cutting and was defeated by a narrow margin. Chávez challenged the validity of Cutting's reelection, charging vote fraud, and took the challenge to the floor of the U.S. Senate. While the challenge was pending, Cutting was killed in an airplane crash. Chávez was appointed by the governor of New Mexico to the U.S. Senate. Chávez was reelected easily in the 1936 elections.

As a Democratic senator, Chávez was a staunch supporter of President Roosevelt's New Deal. As chairman of the Public Works Committee, Chávez obtained federal funding for irrigation and flood control projects in New Mexico. As a Western isolationist, he opposed U.S. entry into World War II and argued that the country should follow a policy of strict neutrality. Serious attempts to unseat him at home were halted by the loyalty of New Mexico supporters who sustained him politically.

During the years after the war, Chávez did some of his best work in the Senate. Perhaps his greatest contribution to Hispanic Americans, and to the nation, was his support of education and civil rights. Cháavez drafted a bill to create the federal Fair Employment Practices Commission and fought tirelessly for its enactment.

In all, Senator Chávez was elected to the Senate five times. A champion of civil rights and full equality for all Americans to the last, the long and distinguished national career of this son of New Mexico was ended by a heart attack in mid-November 1962.

**Jaime B. Fuster
(1941–)**

Jaime Fuster was born on January 12, 1941, in Guayama, Puerto Rico. He graduated from the University of Notre Dame in 1962 and received his law degree from the University of Puerto Rico in 1965. During 1980 and 1981, Fuster was U.S. deputy assistant attorney general, U.S. Department of Justice, in Washington, D.C. He later served as president of Catholic University of Puerto Rico. Fuster was first elected to Congress as the resident commissioner of Puerto Rico in 1984, and served until 1992.

**José Manuel
Gallegos
(1815–1875)**

Jose Gallegos was a territorial delegate to the U.S. Congress for New Mexico. Gallegos was born in northwest New Mexico in present-day Rio Arriba County, in the town of Abiquiu. He hailed from a prominent family and was educated in Taos and later went to the College of Durango, Mexico, to study for the priesthood. Upon graduation in 1840, he was ordained a priest. He first went to southwestern New Mexico to work among the people of San Juan, and later to Albuquerque and Santa Fe.

While in Santa Fe, Gallegos began to get involved with politics. In 1843, he was elected to the New Mexico provincial legislature on the eve of the American conquest and served until 1846 in that assembly. After New Mexico became part of the United States by the Treaty of Guadalupe Hidalgo, he was elected to the first territorial council in 1851.

In 1853, Gallegos was elected territorial delegate to the U.S. Congress as a Democrat. He lost his bid at reelection in 1855 to Miguel Otero, Sr., in a hotly disputed campaign. He returned to service in the territorial legislature in 1860 and was named Speaker of the House. He again made a bid for territorial delegate two years later but lost.

Meanwhile, the Civil War broke out, and Gallegos, a staunch Unionist, was imprisoned in 1862 by invading Texan Confederate forces. At the end of the war, he was appointed territorial treasurer, where he served from 1865 to 1866. At the end of his term, he again won election to the territorial legislature.

In 1870, Gallegos again ran for territorial delegate to the U.S. Congress and won. His bid for reelection two years later was unsuccessful. He returned to Santa Fe and after a short illness died in April 1875.

Benigno Hernández was born in Taos, New Mexico, during the Civil War and was educated there in public schools. He began his business career as a store clerk in the 1880s. Ten years later he began a stock-raising business and in 1896 opened his own general store in Lumberton in Rio Arriba County.

Hernandez entered politics in 1900 and served as Rio Arriba County's probate clerk, recorder, sheriff, treasurer, and tax collector over the following ten years. Very active in Republican politics, Hernandez was elected to the U.S. House of Representatives in 1914 and was reelected in 1918. His bid for a third term was unsuccessful.

After the end of his second term in 1921, President Warren G. Harding appointed Hernández collector of Internal Revenue for the state of New Mexico. Hernández held that post until 1933, when President Franklin D. Roosevelt took office. He was then age 71. He later served on the Selective Service Board of New Mexico during World War II. In the 1950s, Hernández moved to Los Angeles, where he died at age 92.

Benigno Cárdenas Hernández (1862–1954)

Joseph Montoya was born in the small village of Pena Blanca, New Mexico, where his father was county sheriff. Montoya's parents were descendants of eighteenth-century Spanish immigrants to New Mexico. After graduating from high school in 1931, he attended Regis College in Denver, Colorado. In 1934, he entered Georgetown University Law School in Washington, D.C.

In 1936, during his second year of law school, Montoya was elected as a Democrat to the New Mexico House of Representatives at age twenty-one, the youngest representative in the state's history. Two years later, he received his LL.B. degree from Georgetown University and was reelected to the state legislature. In 1940, Montoya was elected to the state senate; at age twenty-five, he was the youngest senator in the state's history. He served a total of twelve years in the state legislature. He then served four terms as lieutenant governor of New Mexico, from 1946 to 1950 and from 1954 to 1957.

In 1957, at age 42, Montoya was elected as a Democrat to the first of four consecutive terms in the U.S. House of Representatives. He established a reputation as a hardworking legislator and loyal party man. He followed a

Joseph M. Montoya (1915–1978)

moderate political course and was regularly returned to Congress with well over 60 percent of the vote.

When Senator Dennis Chavez (D-New Mexico) died in 1962 leaving a Senate seat vacant, Montoya won election to the Senate. He also won a second term to the Senate in 1970. One of the most influential senators in Washington, he was a member of the Appropriations Committee and the Public Works Committee. However, in the early 1970s Montoya's popularity at home waned, and he was defeated in his bid for reelection in 1976 by former astronaut Harrison Schmitt. Montoya's health declined rapidly following the 1976 election. After undergoing surgery for cancer, he died of complications in June 1978.

Nestor Montoya (1862–1923)

Nestor Montoya was born in Albuquerque, New Mexico, on April 14, 1862. He was educated in Albuquerque public schools and then graduated from St. Michael's College in Santa Fe. After college, he worked in the Santa Fe post office and the U.S. Treasury office there. In 1889, Montoya founded *La voz del pueblo,* a Spanish-language newspaper. Montoya founded a second paper in 1900 called *La bandera americana.*

In addition to his journalistic activities, Montoya was also involved in New Mexico politics. In 1892, he was elected to the New Mexico territorial legislature's lower house and was repeatedly reelected, serving until 1903. The following year Montoya was elected to the legislature's upper house and in 1910 was elected a delegate to the New Mexico Constitutional Convention. He worked hard for the rights of Hispanics at the convention and gained the respect of many across the state. In 1920, Nestor Montoya was elected as New Mexico's representative to the U.S. Congress. He died in 1923 before his term ended.

Mariano S. Otero (1844–1904)

Mariano Otero was born in the tiny town of Peralta, New Mexico, on August 29, 1844, during the last years of Mexican control. As a member of the powerful Otero clan, he attended local parochial and private schools and later studied at Saint Louis University in Missouri. After college, Otero became a banker.

In the early 1870s, he was appointed probate judge of Bernalillo County. In 1874, he turned down the Democratic nomination for congressional delegate. In 1878, however, he accepted the Republican nomination for congressional delegate and won. He declined to run for reelection in 1882 and returned to his banking business. Between 1884 and 1886, Otero twice ran for Congress but was defeated. In the 1890s, Otero moved to Albuquerque to continue his banking activities. He died there in 1904 at age 59.

Born in Valencia, New Mexico, on June 21, 1829, Miguel Otero was the son of Vicente Otero, an important local leader during both the Spanish and Mexican eras. After completing his early education in Valencia, Otero was sent to Missouri in 1841 to attend Saint Louis University. Six years later, he went to Pingree's College in New York. He later taught there and then began the study of law. In 1851, he returned to Saint Louis, where he continued his legal studies and was admitted to the bar.

Miguel A. Otero, Sr. (1829–1882)

Returning to New Mexico in 1852 to practice law in Albuquerque, Otero became private secretary to territorial Governor William C. Lane and immediately plunged into politics. That same year, Otero was elected to the territorial legislature. Two years later, he was appointed New Mexico attorney general. Otero's political experience and wide family connections (his older brother Antonio Jose Otero was chief justice at the time) worked to his advantage, and in 1855 he was nominated by the Democratic party for the office of territorial delegate to Congress. Otero won the election and went on to win reelection to Congress, serving a total of six terms.

In Congress, Otero's efforts ensured that the transcontinental railroad would cross through New Mexico, giving great promise to the state's future. By doing so, he aligned himself with other Southern states that also favored a southern route for the railroad. As a result of Otero's influence, New Mexico legislated a slave code in 1859. The following year he supported a compromise to avoid civil war by extending slavery to the territories south of the 36th parallel, including New Mexico.

The outbreak of the Civil War greatly reduced Otero's political influence. He did not support the Confederacy, but he did support a separate confederation of western states. President Lincoln offered the post of minister to Spain to Otero, but he declined it in favor of the nomination of secretary of the Territory of New Mexico. The U.S. Senate did not confirm him because of his political views.

After the Civil War ended, Otero pursued banking and land business interests with the coming of the railroad. He founded and was the first president of the San Miguel National Bank. He was also part of the business group that purchased the immense Maxwell Land Grant in 1870. He was a director of the Maxwell Land Grant and Railroad Company and was also a director of the Atchinson, Topeka, and Santa Fe Railroad. The first terminal of the Santa Fe Railroad was named Otero in his honor.

In 1880, despite his failing health, Otero made a last bid for territorial delegate to Congress but was defeated. His health continued to deteriorate rapidly, and in 1882 he died at the age of 53.

Romauldo Pacheco
(1831–1899)

Romualdo Pacheco was born in Santa Barbara, California, on October 31, 1831. He was the son of an aide to the Mexican governor of California, Manuel Victoria. Pacheco's father was killed in battle shortly after his birth. His mother remarried and Pacheco's stepfather sent him to Honolulu to be educated at an English missionary school. When he returned to California at age 15, Pacheco began working on his stepfather's ships.

After the U.S. takeover of California, Pacheco left the sea to manage the family's large estate and began to show an interest in politics. During the 1850s, Pacheco was successively elected county judge and state senator as a Democrat. Having switched from the Democratic party to the Union party (and later to the Republican party) at the outbreak of the Civil War, Pacheco was reelected to the state senate, and from 1863 to 1867 he served as state treasurer. In 1871 he was elected lieutenant governor and became governor of California in 1875 when then-Governor Newton Booth was appointed to the U.S. Senate. In the next election he failed to secure the Republican nomination for Governor.

In 1876, Pacheco was elected to the U.S. House of Representatives, and was reelected in 1879 and 1881. He was not known as an aggressive congressman, but did serve on the influential Public Expenditures Committee and the Committee on Private Land Claims. In 1883, he did not seek reelection and returned to his family business interests in California.

In 1890, he was named minister plenipotentiary to Central America by President Benjamin Harrison. He remained at that post until Democratic President Grover Cleveland took office in 1893. Pacheco then returned to his California home and died in 1899.

Francisco Perea was born in the small New Mexico town of Los Padillas, near Albuquerque, to Juan Perea and Josefa Chavez, descendants of two important families. Having completed his early education in Los Padillas and Santa Fe, he was sent to study with the Jesuits at Saint Louis University in Missouri from 1843 to 1845. After the U.S. takeover of New Mexico, he went to New York and studied at the Bank Street Academy between 1847 and 1849.

In 1850, Perea returned to New Mexico to engage in stock trading. He became a commercial success by transporting sheep to California to sell to meat-hungry miners. His family and his commercial success helped him in 1858 to be elected to the New Mexico territorial legislature's upper house. After the Civil War broke out, he was twice reelected as an active supporter of the North.

Perea was also active in the military and formed "Perea's Battalion," which he commanded as lieutenant colonel. The battalion took part in the defeat of Confederate invaders of New Mexico at Glorieta Pass in 1862.

After the victory at Glorieta Pass, Perea was elected to the U.S. Congress as territorial delegate for New Mexico. His bid for reelection two years later was unsuccessful. He returned to New Mexico and opened a resort hotel at Jemez Springs, which he owned and operated until 1905. Perea then moved to Albuquerque,where he remained until his death in 1913.

Francisco Perea (1830–1913)

Pedro Perea was born April 22, 1852, in the central New Mexico town of Bernalillo in Sandoval County. After his early education there, he was sent to Saint Michael's College in Santa Fe, then to Georgetown University in Washington, D.C. In 1871 he graduated from Saint Louis University in Missouri.

Like many sons of prominent New Mexican families of the era, he returned to New Mexico to engage in stock raising and business. From 1890 to 1894, he was president of the First National Bank of Santa Fe. He also began to take an interest in New Mexico politics at this time.

Between 1889 and 1897, he served three terms in the New Mexico territorial legislature's upper house as a Republican. In 1898, he was elected

Pedro Perea (1852–1906)

territorial delegate to the U.S. Congress. He chose not to run for reelection and returned to New Mexico at the end of his term in 1900 to resume his banking activities. He died in 1906.

Edward R. Roybal

(1916–)

Edward Roybal was born on February 10, 1916, in Albuquerque, New Mexico, into a middle-class Mexican-American family. When he was four, his family moved to the Boyle Heights area of Los Angeles. After graduating from high school he began working for the Civilian Conservation Corps. Later he continued his education at the University of California and Southwestern University. Roybal took a position as a health care educator beginning in the late 1930s. He served in World War II during 1944—45, and returned to Los Angeles to continue to work in health care.

Following World War II, a group of concerned Mexican Americans formed a group to elect a Mexican American to the Los Angeles City Council, and Roybal was their choice for candidate. In 1947, he ran and was defeated. Instead of giving up, Roybal and the group intensified their efforts to get out the vote in East Los Angeles, and in his second bid for city council in 1949 Roybal was elected. He was the first Mexican American on the council since 1881. Roybal was reelected several times and served on the council for thirteen years.

Roybal was first elected to Congress in 1962 as a Democrat from the 25th District of California. During his three decades in Congress, Roybal worked for social and economic reforms. In 1967, he introduced legislation that became the first federal bilingual education act. In 1982 as chairman of the Congressional Hispanic Caucus, he led the opposition to employer sanctions for hiring the undocumented, which ultimately was enacted as the Immigration Reform and Control Act of 1986. Throughout his tenure, Congressman Roybal consistently advocated greater citizen participation in party politics and in the federal and local government.

HISPANICS IN THE EXECUTIVE BRANCH ♦ ♦ ♦ ♦ ♦ ♦ ♦ ♦ ♦ ♦ ♦

President Clinton has appointed twenty-three Hispanics to notable positions in his administration, twenty-one of which required Senate confirmation. They join the eighty Hispanics in the Senior Executive Service of the federal government. They include: Aida Álvarez, Director, Federal Housing Enterprise Oversight, Department of Housing and Urban Development; Antonio C. Amador, Member, Merit Systems Protection Board; Tony Armendaríz, Member, Federal Labor Relations Authority; Mary Azcuenaga, Commissioner, Federal Trade Commission; Jim Baca, Director, Bureau of Land Management, Department of the Interior; Norma Cantu, Assistant Secretary for Civil Rights, Department of Education; Gil Casellas, General Counsel, Air Force; Henry Cisneros, Secretary, Department of Housing and Urban Development; Nelson Díaz, General Counsel, Department of Housing and Urban Development; Maria Echeveste, Administrator, Wage and Hour Division, Department of Labor; Enrique Esquivel, Assistant Secretary, Natural Resources and Environment, Department of Agriculture; Tony Gallegos, Acting Chair, Equal Employment Opportunity Commission; Eduardo González, Director, U.S. Marshals Service, Department of Justice; Michael Huerta, Associate Deputy Secretary, Intermodalism, Department of Transportation; Kathy Elena Jurado, Assistant Secretary, Public and Intergovernmental Affairs, Veterans Administration; Victor Marrero, U.S. Representative, U.N. Economic and Security Council; Velma Montoya, Commissioner, Occupational Safety and Health Review Commission; George Muñoz, Assistant Secretary, Management, Chief Financial Officer, Department of Treasury; Federico Peña, Secretary, Department of Transportation; Peter Romero, Ambassador to Ecuador, State Department; Isabelle Tapia, Director, Presidential Advance, White House; Fernando Torres-Gil, Assistant Secretary for Aging, Department of Health and Human Services; and Joe Velásquez, Deputy Director, Political Affairs, White House.

♦ ♦ ♦ ♦ SELECTED PROMINENT HISPANIC FEDERAL OFFICIALS

Henry G. Cisneros (1947–)

Henry Cisneros was named Secretary of the Department of Housing and Urban Development by President Clinton in 1992. Cisneros was born in a west-side Mexican barrio of San Antonio to a civil servant. He was educated in the city's parochial schools and attended Texas A&M University, where he received a B.A. degree and a master's degree in urban planning in 1970.

In 1971 Cisneros moved to Washington, D.C., where he worked for the National League of Cities and began full-time graduate studies in public administration at George Washington University. During 1971, at age 24,

Henry Cisneros.

Cisneros became the youngest White House fellow in U.S. history. When his fellowship ended, he earned a second master's degree, in public administration, at Harvard University. He then went on to complete his work at George Washington University and received a Ph.D. degree in public administration. He then returned to San Antonio and taught government at the University of Texas.

Cisneros ran for the city council on the Good Government League ticket in 1975 and won. He gained a reputation as a bright, young politician, and in 1977 he was reelected in a landslide. In 1981, Cisneros ran for mayor of San Antonio, the ninth-largest city in the United States, and won with 62 percent of the vote. In 1983, he was reelected with 94 percent of the vote, again reelected in 1985 with 72 percent, and reelected in 1987 with twice as many votes as his closest opponent.

After he left office as Mayor of San Antonio, Cisneros founded Cisneros Asset Management. Today the business has more than $500 million of pension funds under management. Cisneros is widely viewed as a coalition builder who is working to reform HUD regulations and programs to make the department's services more accessible to the poor.

Gil Coronado

Coronado, a retired air force colonel from San Antonio, Texas, was named Deputy Assistant Secretary of Veterans Affairs for Legislative Affairs in the Clinton administration in May 1994.

Nelson Díaz

A former Philadelphia Court of Common Pleas Judge, Díaz now serves as general counsel at the Department of Housing and Urban Development.

Maria Echaveste

Maria Echaveste serves as administrator at the Wage and Hour Department in the Department of Labor. Echaveste received a degree in anthropology from Stanford University and later earned a law degree from the University of California at Berkeley. She served on a board with Hillary Clinton before assuming the role of deputy director of personnel of the Clinton transition team.

Jack Otero

Jack Otero was appointed Deputy Undersecretary of Labor for International Affairs in July 1993. Otero is the former vice president of the AFL-CIO. He aslo served as international vice president of the Transportation and Communications International Union, and as vice chair of the Democratic National Committee.

Federico Peña (1947-)

Named Secretary of the Department of Transportation by President Clinton in 1992, Federico Peña was born in Laredo, Texas. Peña was raised in Brownsville, Texas, and received his early education there. He attended the University of Texas at Austin, where he received both an undergraduate degree and a law degree. Peña follows in a tradition of public service in his family. One of his great grandfathers served as mayor of Laredo during the Civil War and another was a member of that city's first school board. Peña's grandfather held the office of alderman in Laredo for almost a quarter of a century.

In 1983, at age 36, Peña was elected Denver's thirty-seventh mayor. He was reelected to a second term in 1987. At the time he entered office, he was among the youngest chief executives in Denver history. Mayor Peña's efforts to strengthen Denver's economy placed the city in the national spotlight. The U.S. Conference of Mayors recently selected Denver over one hundred other cities as the winner of its prestigious City Liveability Award. Peña did not seek a third term in 1991.

Peña is viewed as a visionary for his leading role in the building of a multi-billion dollar airport on the outskirts of Denver. As Secretary of Transportation, he has a budget of $36 billion a year, with which he must oversee the growth and maintenance of the national infrastructure, including the nation's ailing airline and maritime industries. He must upgrade the U.S. highway system to facilitate trade between Mexico and Canada under the North American Free Trade Agreement. In 1992, Peña became director of President Clinton's transition team, and was subsequently appointed to Clinton's Cabinet.

José Villareal   Villareal, who served as deputy campaign manager of the Clinton/Gore campaign, was appointed to the Board of Directors of the Federal National Mortgage Association (Fannie Mae) in March 1994. Villareal grew up in a poor east Chicago neighborhood with nine brothers and sisters. He attended Purdue University on a scholarship and earned a law degree at Indiana University. As a civil rights lawyer working with the Southwest Voter Registration Project, Villareal championed the rights of poor tenants against unfair treatment by their landlords.

SELECTED PROMINENT HISPANIC FORMER FEDERAL OFFICIALS

Everett Álvarez, Jr. (1937–)   Former deputy administrator of the U.S. Veterans Administration, Everett Álvarez was born in Salinas, California, of farm worker parents from Mexico. His parents emphasized hard work and education as the way to succeed. Álvarez was awarded an engineering degree from the University of Santa Clara in 1960. Álvarez was a navy pilot during the Vietnam War and was shot down over the Gulf of Tonkin. He was held prisoner by the Viet Cong for more than eight years. After his release in 1973, Álvarez went back to school and received a law degree from George Washington University and practiced law as a patent attorney. In 1981 President Reagan appointed Álvarez deputy director of the Peace Corps. In 1982 the president appointed Álvarez deputy administrator of the Veterans Administration.

Archuleta served as U.S. Indian agent under President Abraham Lincoln. Born of a prominent family in the Rio Arriba country of New Mexico during the Mexican war for independence, Archuleta was educated at the seminary at Durango, Mexico. In 1840, he returned to New Mexico and from 1843 to 1845 served as representative from New Mexico at the National Congress in Mexico City. When American forces invaded New Mexico in 1846, Archuleta gave no resistance to General Stephen Kearny's army. Disappointed at not being made part of the new American government in New Mexico, Archuleta took a leading role in two unsuccessful Taos rebellions in 1846 and 1847.

Archuleta later took the oath of allegiance to the United States and sought to use American institutions to his advantage. During the 1850s, he was repeatedly elected to the New Mexico state assembly, and in 1857 he was named U.S. Indian agent to the Utes and Apaches, in which capacity he served until the Civil War broke out. He became a brigadier general in the New Mexico militia during the war and was reappointed U.S. Indian agent by President Abraham Lincoln. After the war Archuleta returned to service in the New Mexico state assembly, where he served until his death in 1884.

Diego Archuleta (1814–1884)

The first Mexican American and the sixth woman to hold the post of treasurer of the United States, Bañuelos was born in Miami, Arizona, of undocumented Mexican parents. During the Great Depression, she was forced at age 6 to accompany her parents when they were repatriated to Mexico in 1931. She grew up in Mexico and at age 19 moved back to the United States and settled in Los Angeles.

In 1949, she started a small tortilla factory with $400. Over the following twenty years, she developed Romana's Mexican Food Products into a $12 million per year business, employing hundreds of workers and producing dozens of food items. She also helped to establish the Pan American National Bank in Los Angeles, of which she was a director and chairwoman.

In 1971, President Nixon appointed Bañuelos treasurer of the United States. She served as treasurer from December 1971 until February 1974. While retaining some interest in politics, she has since devoted herself principally to her business activities.

Romana Acosta Bañuelos (1925–)

**Arturo Morales
Carrión
(1913–1989)**

Former deputy assistant secretary of state under President John F. Kennedy, and the first Puerto Rican to be appointed to such a high State Department position, Arturo Carrión was born in Havana, Cuba, on November 16, 1913. He earned a B.A. degree from the University of Puerto Rico in 1935, an M.A. degree from the University of Texas in 1936, and a Ph.D. degree from Columbia University in 1950. Carrión taught at the University of Puerto Rico and became chairman of the history department. He then went into politics and served as undersecretary of Puerto Rico's State Department, in charge of external affairs.

He joined the Kennedy administration in 1961 as deputy assistant secretary of state for inter-American affairs, serving until the assassination of President Kennedy in 1963. Carrión was a member of the Kennedy administration's Latin American Study Group, which warned of a Communist threat to Latin America. After leaving the State Department, Carrión became special assistant to the secretary general of the Organization of American States. He later returned to Puerto Rico to become president of the University of Puerto Rico. Carrión died in San Juan in 1989 at age 75.

**Leonel J. Castillo
(1939–)**

Former director of the U.S. Immigration and Naturalization Service (INS), Leonel Castillo was born in Victoria, Texas, where he grew up and attended school. He graduated from St. Mary's University in San Antonio, Texas, in 1961. Castillo joined the Peace Corps after graduation and served in the Philippines from 1961 to 1965. Upon his return to the United States, he attended the University of Pittsburgh, where he received his master's degree in social work in 1967. Castillo then returned to Texas and lived in Houston, where he took an active role in local politics. In 1970, he won a surprise victory in his election as Houston city comptroller against a twenty-five-year incumbent. In 1974, he was named treasurer of the Texas Democratic party.

President Jimmy Carter appointed Castillo to head the INS in 1977. After thirty months of trying to modernize the INS, to reduce violence on the border, and to emphasize service rather than enforcement, he resigned in 1979. Castillo then returned to Houston to head Castillo Enterprises.

**Fernando E. Cabeza
de Baca (1937–)**

Former special assistant to President Gerald Ford and a direct descendant of the famous Spanish explorer Alvar Núñez Cabeza de Baca (often spelled "Vaca"), Fernando Cabeza de Baca was born in Albuquerque, New Mexico.

He received his early education in New Mexico, and at the end of the 1950s he received a degree in public administration from the University of New Mexico in Albuquerque. He also studied at the University of New Mexico School of Law. During the Vietnam War, he served in the U.S. Army and returned from the war disabled and decorated. In the late 1960s and early 1970s de Baca held high-ranking positions with the New Mexico Department of Transportation, the Civil Service Commission, and the Department of Health, Education and Welfare. He then became chairman of the Federal Regional Council for the Western United States.

In 1974 President Gerald Ford appointed de Baca as special assistant to the president. In this role, at age 37, he became both the youngest and the highest-ranking federal executive of Hispanic descent. De Baca returned to New Mexico to pursue business activities after Ford left the presidency in 1976. He remains deeply involved in veterans affairs and is active in the New Mexico Republican party.

Lauro F. Cavazos (1927–)

Former U.S. secretary of education and the first Hispanic named to a cabinet-level position, Lauro Cavazos left a distinguished career as the president of Texas Tech University in Lubbock, Texas, to join President Reagan's cabinet in 1988. Previously, Cavazos had been the dean of Tufts University School of Medicine. Appointed secretary of education by President Reagan in 1988 and reappointed by President Bush in 1989, Cavazos was instrumental in persuading President Bush to sign the executive order creating the President's Council on Educational Excellence for Hispanic Americans. Cavazos's leadership and sensitivity raised the awareness of Congress regarding the educational needs of Hispanics in the United States. Secretary Cavazos resigned in December 1990, and Lamar Alexander was appointed to replace him.

Tirso del Junco, M.D.

A member of the board of governors of the U.S. Postal Service in Washington, D.C., del Junco was born in Havana, Cuba, received a medical degree in 1949 from the Havana School of Medicine, and became a U.S. citizen in 1963. He is a member of the board of regents of the University of California and was a delegate to the Republican National Conventions for the past six presidential elections. In 1983 he was a U.S. delegate to the Twenty-second conference of UNESCO in Paris. Del Junco is the founder and former chairman of the Los Angeles National Bank and is a member of the Queen of Angels Hospital Clinic and Research Foundation. Del Junco was a captain in the U.S. Army and chief of surgery at the Camp

Howland Army Hospital from 1955 to 1957. In 1948, del Junco was a member of the Cuban Olympic team and participated in the crew competition.

Cari M. Domínguez
(1949–)

Cari Domínguez was born in Havana, Cuba, in 1949. Her family immigrated to the United States and she was raised in Takoma Park, Maryland. She holds a bachelor's degree and a master's degree from American University in Washington, D.C. In 1974, Domínguez joined the Office of Federal Contract Compliance Programs, where she held a variety of positions until 1983. In 1984, she left the Department of Labor and began working for the Bank of America in San Francisco, where she served as corporate manager of equal opportunity programs. In 1986, she was promoted to vice president and director of executive programs, in charge of executive compensation and benefits programs, succession planning, development, and staffing services. In 1989, President Bush appointed Domínguez director of the Office of Federal Contract Compliance Programs of the U.S. Department of Labor.

Raymond
Emmanuel González
(1924–)

Born in Pasadena, California, on December 24, 1924, González received his B.A. and M.A. degrees from the University of Southern California in 1949 and 1950, respectively, and became a career diplomat for the United States. He served in various diplomatic capacities throughout Latin America and Washington, D.C., Belgium, and Italy, until finally serving as American ambassador to Ecuador from 1978 to 1982, at which time he retired. Since 1983, he has served as senior inspector, Office of the Inspector General in Washington, D.C. In 1970, he was the recipient of the Department of State Meritoriuos Award, and, in 1988, the Department of State Wilbur J. Carr Award.

Jimmy Gurulé

Jimmy Gurulé grew up in Utah. He received both his bachelor's degree and his law degree from the University of Utah. Prior to joining the Department of Justice, Gurulé was an associate professor of law at the University of Notre Dame Law School. He is a former president of the Hispanic National Bar Association.

Gurulé was appointed assistant attorney general by President George Bush and was sworn in on August 3, 1990. He was the highest-ranking Hispanic in the history of the Department of Justice. As assistant attorney general for the Office of Justice Programs, Gurulé was responsible for co-ordinating policy, management, and priorities within the Office of Justice Programs in Washington, D.C., and its five program bureaus and field offices. He worked to form partnerships among federal, state, and local government officials to improve administration of justice, combat violent crime and drug abuse, meet the needs of crime victims, and find innovative ways to address problems such as narcotics trafficking, gang-related crime, white-collar crime, and corruption. Gurulé was awarded the Attorney General's Distinguished Service Award in 1990 for his excellence as an assistant U.S. attorney in prosecuting the killers of Drug Enforcement Administration Special Agent Enrique Camarena, who had been working in Guadalajara, Mexico.

Edward Hidalgo

(1912–)

Former secretary of the navy, Edward Hidalgo was born in Mexico City. His family immigrated to the United States. in 1918 and he was naturalized in 1936. He holds law degrees from both countries, a J.D. degree from Columbia University, which he received in 1936, and a similar degree from the University of Mexico, which was conferred in 1959. During World War II, Hidalgo was special assistant to Secretary of the Navy James Forrestal in 1945—46 and was a member of the Eberstadt Commission on the Unification of the Military Services in 1945. After the war, he returned to private practice as an attorney. In 1965, Hidalgo was named special assistant to Secretary of the Navy Paul Nitze. From 1977—79 he served as assistant secretary of the navy. Hidalgo was appointed secretary of the navy by President Carter in 1979 and remained there until 1981.

Manuel Luján, Jr.

Luján grew up in Santa Fe, New Mexico, and earned his B.A. degree from the College of Santa Fe. After college, Luján was a partner in a family insurance and real estate business. Luján served as a Republican congressman and represented the 1st District of New Mexico in the U.S. House of Representatives from 1969 to 1989. In Congress, Luján was the ranking minority member of the House Interior Committee. In 1989, President Bush appointed Luján as the forty-sixth secretary of the interior.

Robert Martínez (1934–)

Robert Martínez was born in Tampa, Florida, on December 25, 1934. He received his bachelor's degree in education from the University of Tampa in 1957 and a master's degree in labor and industrial relations from the University of Illinois in 1964. Martínez went into business following college and owned and operated a restaurant in Tampa until 1983. He became involved in local politics in the late 1970s and was elected to two terms as a Republican mayor of Tampa from 1979 to 1987. In 1988, Martínez was elected governor of Florida and served one term. During his tenure as governor, President Reagan named Martínez to the White House Conference on a Drug-Free America. Martínez was appointed by President Bush as director of the Office of National Drug Control Policy in 1991.

Julián Nava (1927–)

Born on June 19, 1927, in Los Angeles, California, to a family that had fled Mexico during the Mexican Revolution, Nava grew up in East Los Angeles. He served in the Navy Air Corps during World War II and, upon return, obtained an education through the G.I. Bill. Nava graduated from Pomona College with an A.B. degree in 1951 and from Harvard University with a Ph.D. degree in 1955. Since graduation he has served as a lecturer and professor at various universities in Colombia, Venezuela, Puerto Rico, Spain, and California, where he is still a tenured professor of history at California State University at Northridge. In 1967, Nava was elected to the Los Angeles school board and later served as president of the board. Nava served as ambassador to Mexico from 1979 to 1981; he is the first Mexican American to ever hold that post.

Antonia C. Novello (1944–)

The first woman and first Hispanic surgeon general of the United States, Antonia Novello was born in Fajardo, Puerto Rico, on August 23, 1944. She received a B.A. degree in 1965 and an M.D. degree in 1970 from the University of Puerto Rico. Novello was awarded her master's degree in public health from Johns Hopkins University in 1982. Novello joined the U.S. Public Health Service in 1978 after working in the private practice of pediatrics and nephrology. She served in various capacities at the National Institutes of Health (NIH) beginning in 1978, including serving as deputy director of the National Institute of Child Health and Human Development. In 1990, President Bush appointed Novello as the fourteenth surgeon general. She was the first Hispanic to ever hold that post.

Katherine D. Ortega (1934–)

Katherine Ortega was born in rural south-central New Mexico. She received her early education in Tularosa, New Mexico. From her early years, she excelled in mathematics and accounting. After high school, Ortega worked at the Otero County Bank for two years until she saved enough money to go to college. She graduated from the Eastern New Mexico State University at Portales in 1957, with honors. After college, she began her own accounting firm in New Mexico. In 1969, she moved to Los Angeles to work as a tax supervisor and later became a vice president of the Pan American National Bank. She then became the first woman president of a California bank when she was named president of the Santa Ana State Bank in 1975. In 1978, she returned to New Mexico with her family and became active in the Republican party. In 1983, President Reagan appointed Ortega as U.S. treasurer. She remained at that post throughout the Reagan presidency. Ortega then returned to New Mexico and is still active in politics.

Born in Santa Fe, New Mexico, on March 14, 1926, Francis Ortiz received his B.S. degree from the School of Foreign Service at Georgetown University in 1950 and went on to pursue a career in diplomacy. He later attained an M.S. degree in 1967 from George Washington University and also studied at the National War College. His career in the foreign service took him to posts in Ethiopia, Mexico, Peru, Uruguay, Argentina, Barbados, and Grenada from 1953 to 1979. In 1979, he became the ambassador to Guatemala; from 1981 to 1983, the ambassador to Peru; and from 1983 to 1986, the ambassador to Argentina. His honors include the 1952 Honor Award from the State Department, the 1964 and 1973 Superior Award, the 1980 Gran Cruz de Mérito Civil from Spain, and the 1964 U.S./Mexican Presidential Chamizal Commemorative Medal. From 1944 to 1946, Ortiz served in the U.S. Air Force; he received the Air Medal for his service.

Francis V. Ortiz, Jr. (1926–)

Villalpando was born April 1, 1940, in San Marcos, Texas, and is a graduate of Southwest Texas State University. Villalpando joined Communications International, a multinational telecommunications systems integrator, and became a senior vice president. From 1985 until her executive appointment, Villalpando directed all public relations and marketing for the company's northeast region, based in Washington, D.C. Villalpando served as White House special assistant for public liaison to President Ronald Reagan from 1983 to 1985. Prior to assuming her duties at the White House she served as liaison director for the Republican party of Texas. In 1989, President Bush appointed Villalpando as the thirty-ninth treasurer of the United States.

Catalina Vásquez Villalpando (1940–)

PROMINENT HISPANIC POLITICIANS IN STATE GOVERNMENT ◆

**Toney Anaya
(1941–)**

Former Democratic governor of New Mexico from 1983 to 1986, Toney Anaya was one of ten children born to New Mexican parents in Moriarty, New Mexico. He spent his childhood in an adobe house with a dirt floor and no electricity or plumbing. Although his parents had no more than a couple of years of schooling, they encouraged their children to get a good education. Anaya attended the New Mexico Highlands University, on a Sears Foundation scholarship.

Anaya moved to Washington, D.C., where he graduated from Georgetown University. In 1967, he received his law degree from American University. While he was attending American University, he worked for Senator Dennis Chavez, and following graduation worked for Senator Joseph Montoya.

In 1970, Anaya returned to New Mexico. He ran for attorney general of New Mexico in 1974 and won, serving until 1978. Anaya then ran for the Senate, but lost a close election to incumbent Pete Domenici. In 1982, Anaya was elected governor of New Mexico, where he served until 1986.

**Jerry Apodaca
(1934–)**

Former governor of New Mexico, Jerry Apodaca was born and raised in Las Cruces, New Mexico, where his family had lived for over one hundred years. He graduated from the University of New Mexico in 1957 and worked as a teacher and businessman. In 1966, Apodaca entered politics and was elected to the New Mexico state senate as a Democrat. After eight years in the state legislature, Apodaca, at age 40, was elected in 1974 as the first Hispanic governor of New Mexico in over fifty years (Governor Octaviano Larrazolo had served from 1918 to 1920). After Apodaca's term as governor ended, President Carter appointed him as chairman of the President's Council on Physical Fitness and Sports. Apodaca has since resumed his business interests and is currently on the board of directors of the Philip Morris Company.

**Polly Baca-
Barragán (1941–)**

The first Hispanic woman to be elected state senator to the Colorado legislature, Polly Baca-Barragán was born in La Salle, Colorado. In 1963 she graduated from Colorado State University. During the 1960's, she was active in the Democratic party and worked on the Presidential campaigns of

President John F. Kennedy, President Johnson and Senator Robert F. Kennedy. From 1971 to 1972 she was Director of Spanish Speaking Affairs for the Democratic National Committee. In 1974 Baca-Barragán made a successful bid for State Representative to the Colorado legislature. In 1978 she became the first Hispanic woman to be elected to the Colorado State Senate and was reelected in 1982.

Casimiro Barela (1847–1920)

A delegate to the Colorado State Constitutional Convention and a Colorado state senator, Casimiro Barela was born in Embudo, New Mexico, and was educated in Mora by Archbishop Jean B. Salpointe. Barela's family moved to Colorado in 1867, where they raised cattle. In 1869, Barela was elected justice of the peace and over the next six years held several elected posts, including county assessor and sheriff.

In 1875, Barela was elected as a delegate to the state constitutional convention, in which he took a leadership role. He secured a provision in the constitution protecting the civil rights of Spanish-speaking citizens as well as publication of laws in both Spanish and English, but this provision was limited to twenty-five years. Barela was elected to the first Colorado senate in 1876 and served until 1916. He was twice elected president of the Colorado senate.

Stephanie Gonzales (1950–)

Secretary of state for New Mexico, Stephanie Gonzales was born in Santa Fe, New Mexico. She is a graduate of Loretto Academy for Girls in Santa Fe. From 1987 to 1990, Gonzales was the deputy secretary of state under then-secretary Rebecca Vigil-Giron. In 1990, Gonzales, a Democrat, was elected secretary of state of New Mexico.

Art Torres

(1941–)

State senator for California, Art Torres was born and raised in East Los Angeles. He received his B.A. degree from the University of California, Santa Cruz, and a J.D. degree from the University of California, Davis, Law School. He later served as a John F. Kennedy teaching fellow at Harvard University.

In 1976, Torres was first elected to the California Senate and has been reelected for each subsequent term. As state senator, Torres has worked to improve education at all levels, particularly through legislation to prevent attrition of high school students. Torres was recently elected to the Council on Foreign Relations of New York. He also participates on the National Commission on International Migration and Economic Development, which recommends to Congress and the president the economic policies the United States should implement in Latin America.

PROMINENT HISPANIC METROPOLITAN LEADERS ♦ ♦ ♦ ♦ ♦ ♦

Ygnacio D. Garza

(1953–)

Mayor of Brownsville, Texas, Ygnacio Garza, the son of U.S. Federal Court of Appeals Judge Reynaldo G. Garza, was elected mayor of the city of Brownsville in 1987 and served in that capacity until 1991. By law, the mayor of Brownsville is nonpartisan, and Garza is not affiliated with any political party. Brownsville's population is 85 percent Hispanic, and Garza believes that Hispanics are adequately represented in this border town: the mayor, all the city council members, and the majority of the school board members are Hispanic. However, Garza believes that the Hispanic population is not adequately represented nationally, and that the United States still has a long way to go in equalizing the balance of political power.

Ana Sol Gutiérrez

(1942–)

A member of the Montgomery County, Maryland, Board of Education and the first Hispanic to be elected to any office in Maryland history, Ana Gutiérrez was born in El Salvador in 1942. Her father, Jorge Sol Castellanos, was El Salvador's first finance minister. Her family moved to Montgomery County, Maryland, in 1945. She attended the University of Geneva in Switzerland and lived in South America briefly following graduation. She then returned to Maryland and became active in local politics. In 1990,

Gutierrez ran successfully for a seat on the Board of Education of Montgomery County, one of Maryland's most affluent counties. Gutierrez was named by U.S. Senator Barbara Mikulski (D-Maryland) to serve on the senator's Academic Review Board, which advises her on national and state educational issues. Many in the Hispanic community regard Gutierrez as someone to watch and a possible contender for a seat in the U.S. Congress.

County supervisor of Los Angeles, Gloria Molina was born in Los Angeles on May 13, 1948 to Mexican parents who had immigrated to the United States the year before. She grew up and received her early education in the small town of Pico Rivera, California, and then attended East Los Angeles College. In 1967, an accident suffered by her father forced her to become the full-time provider for the family at age 19. Her job as a legal assistant did not prevent her from continuing her education, and she received a bachelor's degree from California State University in Los Angeles.

Gloria Molina (1948–)

Taking a vigorous role in community affairs, Molina served on the board of United Way of Los Angeles and was active in the Latin American Law Enforcement Association. In 1973, she was the founding president of the Comision Femenil de Los Angeles and served as national president from 1974 to 1976. She is also a founding member of Hispanic American Democrats, the National Association of Latino Elected and Appointed Officials, and Centro de Ninos. Molina was first elected to office in 1982 as state assemblywoman for the 56th District of California.

In 1987, she was elected to the Los Angeles City Council, on which she served as councilwoman of the 1st District until 1991. In 1991, she was elected to the Los Angeles County Board of Supervisors. Molina is the first Hispanic American in history elected to the California state legislature, the Los Angeles City Council, and the Los Angeles County Board of Supervisors. Prior to being elected to public office, Molina served in the Carter White House as a deputy for presidential personnel. After leaving the White House, she served as deputy director for the U.S. Department of Health and Human Services in San Francisco. With a reputation for candor and independence, Molina is known for her strong, issue-oriented style and her commitment to community empowerment.

Manuel Requena (1802–1876)

Mayor of Los Angeles in 1856, Manuel Requena was born and raised in Mexico and moved to Los Angeles in 1834. Active in the shipping business, he quickly became an important business and political figure. Avoiding conflict when U.S. forces invaded California during the Mexican-American War, Requena was elected to the Los Angeles City Council in 1850 as a member of the Democratic party. He was reelected to four more terms, serving most of the time as president of the council. In 1852, he was elected to the first Los Angeles County Board of Supervisors. Losing his 1855 bid for reelection to the city council, he ran again in 1856 and was reelected to a sixth term, and was again elected president.

When the Los Angeles mayor resigned that year, Manuel Requena became mayor until an election was held eleven days later. He thus was briefly the only Mexican American to serve as mayor of Los Angeles during the American period.

Prior to the Civil War, Requena switched from the Democratic to the Republican party and openly supported the candidacy of Abraham Lincoln. At the time, Los Angeles was heavily Democratic and Requena did not win election to the city council again until 1864, when he was elected to a seventh term; subsequently he was reelected to an eighth term. During the 1860s, he continued his business interests, served on the school board, and founded an orphanage.

Louis E. Saavedra (1933–)

Mayor of Albuquerque, New Mexico, Louis Saavedra was born in Socorro, New Mexico. Saavedra's family has lived within thirty miles of Albuquerque since the 1600s. Saavedra received a B.A. degree and an M.A. degree from Eastern New Mexico University in Portales. Saavedra is the former president of the Albuquerque Technical Vocational Institute, a community college with an enrollment of fifteen thousand. He has held high-ranking positions with the institute since 1965. Saavedra also served on the Albuquerque City Commission between 1967 and 1974. From 1973 to 1974, he was chairman of the city commission. In 1989, Louis Saavedra was elected mayor of Albuquerque, a post he still holds. Saavedra has been active in Latin American politics and has worked in eleven Latin American countries and seven countries in the West Indies.

Mayor of Miami, Florida, Xavier Suarez attended Villanova University, studying engineering, and graduated first in his class. Suárez went on to Harvard Law School and the John F. Kennedy School of Government at Harvard, where he obtained the joint degrees of J.D. and master of public policy in 1975. He also holds an honorary law degree from Villanova University School of Law. After graduation, Suárez moved to Miami and began to practice law with the firm of Shutts & Bowen.

**Xavier L. Suárez
(1949–)**

In 1985, Suárez was elected mayor of Miami, and was reelected to second and third terms in 1987 and 1989. President Bush appointed Suárez to the board of directors of the Legal Services Corporation. Suárez states that Hispanic American voters have made a significant impact on Miami politics, but remaining impediments are large electoral districts for county commission and school board elections.

♦ ♦ ♦ ♦ ♦ ♦ ♦ ♦ ♦ ♦ ♦ HISPANIC JUDGES IN FEDERAL COURTS

Almost all Hispanic judges currently sitting on the bench at all levels of the judiciary received their appointments in the last three decades. Hispanics now sit on both the U.S. district courts and the U.S. courts of appeals. However, no Hispanic has yet sat on the U.S. Supreme Court.

According to the *Directory of Hispanic Judges of the United States,* there were 85 Hispanic members of federal tribunals in 1991, but this includes judges in the District of Columbia and Puerto Rico as well as U.S. magistrates and administrative law judges.

Today, five Hispanic judges sit on the court of appeals, the second-highest federal court in the United States. The Honorable Juan R. Torruella sits on the U.S. Court of Appeals for the First Circuit, which has jurisdiction over Massachusetts, Rhode Island, Maine, New Hampshire, Puerto Rico, and the Virgin Islands. The Honorable Reynaldo G. Garza and the Honorable Emilio M. Garza sit on the U.S. Court of Appeals for the Fifth Circuit, which has jurisdiction over Texas, Louisiana, and Mississippi. The Honorable Arthur L. Alarcón and the Honorable Ferdinand Francis Fernández sit on the U.S. Court of Appeals for the Ninth Circuit, which has jurisdiction over California, Arizona, Nevada, Washington, Oregon, Idaho, Montana, Alaska, Hawaii, Guam, and the Northern Mariana Islands.

Twenty-two Hispanic judges sit on U.S. District Courts in Arizona, California, Connecticut, Florida, Indiana, Michigan, Missouri, New Jersey, New Mexico, New York, Rhode Island, Texas, and Puerto Rico.

Additionally, eight Hispanic judges serve as U.S. magistrates, four serve on the U.S. Bankruptcy Court, and forty-three currently serve as administrative law judges for various federal agencies, such as the Executive Office for Immigration Review (special inquiry officers), the Social Security Administration, and the Federal Communications Commission (FCC).

HISPANIC JUDGES IN STATE COURTS ♦ ♦ ♦ ♦ ♦ ♦ ♦ ♦ ♦ ♦ ♦ ♦ ♦ ♦

The growing number of Hispanic judges can be attributed to the increasing Hispanic population as well as to favorable legislation such as the Civil Rights Act of 1964 and the Voting Rights Act of 1965, which have enabled Hispanics to become full participants in the U.S. political and judicial process.

Hispanic Americans have made the greatest inroads at the state, county, and municipal court levels, where hundreds have been appointed or elected to these courts. Hispanic judges have served on state courts throughout the history of the United States, but almost always at the lowest levels. In recent years this trend has changed, as large numbers of Hispanics have been both appointed and elected to all levels of state courts.

Today, Hispanics serve on some of the highest state courts in the nation. Five Hispanics are state supreme court justices, in Colorado, Michigan, New Mexico, and Texas. Fourteen Hispanics serve as state appeals court judges in the states of Arizona, California, Colorado, New Mexico, New York, and Texas.

Most dramatic are the large numbers of Hispanic Americans serving in lower state courts. Six hundred twenty-five Hispanics serve on various state trial courts.

Critics of the process of selecting judges charge that the system is subject to a wide range of problems and abuses, including discrimination against minorities. The appointment process, critics charge, is also subject to political interference from special interest groups, influence peddling, and highly inflammatory campaigning by opposition groups. The nominee's qualifications are rarely the test of whether he or she should be a judge. For example, a 1988 analysis of U.S. Supreme Court appointments published in *Texas Lawyer* found that of twenty-seven failed nominations to the Court, only five were denied because of qualifications or ethical concerns. Political concerns were the primary reasons the other nominees were not confirmed.

Discrimination is a serious problem in the appointive system. The Mexican American Legal Defense and Educational Fund (MALDEF) recently concluded that the appointive system is discriminatory. According to MALDEF, approximately 97 percent of all individuals making judicial appointments are White, which consequently tends to limit the opportunities for minority nominees. (MALDEF states that the elective system is of the greatest benefit to Hispanics and other minorities.) Instead of taking politics out of the system, the appointive process takes the voter out of the system.

Fortunately, today the majority of states select judges through the election process. Eight states choose all their judges in partisan elections; twelve use nonpartisan elections. One state, Virginia, uses legislative election exclusively to select its judges. Another thirteen states have variable procedures, appointing judges to certain courts and electing them to others.

SELECTED PROMINENT HISPANICS AT THE FEDERAL AND
◆ **STATE JUDICIAL LEVELS**

**Raymond L. Acosta
(1925–)**

Raymond Acosta was born in New York City and grew up in Teaneck, New Jersey. After graduating from high school in 1943, Acosta joined the U.S. Navy during World War II and took part in the Normandy invasion. He returned to New Jersey after the war and graduated from Princeton University in 1948. Acosta received his law degree in 1951 from Rutgers University Law School in Newark, New Jersey. From 1951 to 1954, he was in private practice in Hackensack, New Jersey, and worked for the Federal Bureau of Investigation in Washington, D.C., from 1954 to 1958. In 1958, he moved to Puerto Rico to serve as assistant U.S. attorney there. From 1962 to 1980, he was in the private sector, practicing law in San Juan, Puerto Rico, with the firm of Igaravídez & Acosta, and held posts with various real estate and banking interests. From 1980 to 1982, Acosta was the U.S. attorney for Puerto Rico. In 1982, President Reagan appointed Acosta to the U.S. District Court for the District of Puerto Rico.

Robert P. Aguilar

(1931–)

Former judge of the U.S. District Court for the Northern District of California, Robert Aguilar attended the University of California, Berkeley, where he received his B.A. degree in 1954. He then went on to receive his law degree from the University of California Hastings College of Law. He practiced law with the firms of Mezzetti & Aguilar, Aguilar & Aguilar, and Aguilar & Edwards from 1960 to 1979.

In 1979 Aguilar was appointed a California Superior Court judge for Santa Clara County. He was later appointed to the U.S. District Court for the Northern District of California by President Jimmy Carter in 1980. In 1991 he withrew from hearing cases while he appeals his November 1990 conviction on two charges: illegally disclosing a wiretap to its subject and lying to the FBI to obstruct a grand jury probe.

Arthur L. Alarcón

(1925–)

Arthur Alarcón received his B.A. degree in 1949 and his LL.B. degree in 1951, both from the University of Southern California. President Carter appointed him to the U.S. Court of Appeals for the Ninth Circuit in 1979, where he is now serving as a senior judge.

John Argüelles

(1927–)

Former supreme court justice for the state of California, John Argüelles was born in Los Angeles, California, to Arturo Argüelles, a Mexican American who graduated from Columbia University with an accounting degree, and Eva Powers, the daughter of an Oklahoma judge.

Argüelles was educated in public schools in Los Angeles and went on to UCLA where he received a degree in economics in 1950. He continued his education at the UCLA law school and received his degree in 1954. Argüelles practiced law in East Los Angeles and Montebello, California, from 1955 to 1963. During that time he was president of the local bar association and was elected to the Montebello City Council with the largest vote in that city's history.

In 1963 Governor Edmund G. Brown, Sr. appointed Argüelles municipal court judge for the East Los Angeles Municipal Court. He was then elevated to the Los Angeles Superior Court by Governor Ronald Reagan in 1969. Argüelles was appointed to the California Court of Appeal for the Second District in 1984 by Governor George Deukmejian. Three years later, Deukmejian named Argüelles to the California Supreme Court, where he served until his retirement in 1989. At the end of 1989, Argüelles joined the law firm of Gibson, Dunn & Crutcher.

New Mexico Supreme Court Justice Baca was born in Albuquerque, New Mexico, in 1936 to Mexican-American parents. He graduated from the University of New Mexico in 1960 with a degree in education. He studied law at George Washington University in Washington, D.C., and received his degree in 1964.

Baca served as assistant district attorney in Santa Fe from 1965 to 1966, then as special assistant to the attorney general of New Mexico from 1966 to 1972. He also established a private law practice in Albuquerque during this time.

In 1972 Baca was appointed by Governor Bruce King to fill a vacancy in the New Mexico District Court for the Second District in Albuquerque. Baca was elected to six-year terms in 1972, 1978, and 1984. In 1988, Baca was elected to an eight-year term as justice of the New Mexico Supreme Court, and has served there since 1989.

Joseph Francis Baca

(1936–)

Juan Burciaga attended the U.S. Military Academy at West Point, where he received his B.S. degree in 1952. He then served in the U.S. Air Force from 1952 to 1960. He received his law degree from the University of New Mexico School of Law in 1963. Burciaga was in private practice from 1964 to 1979 with the firm of Ussery, Burciaga & Parrish. In 1979 President Jimmy Carter appointed Burciaga to the U.S. District Court for the District of New Mexico. Burciaga became chief judge of that court.

Juan C. Burciaga

(1929–)

Born in Mayagüez, Puerto Rico, José Cabranés is the first native Puerto Rican appointed to the federal court within the continental United States. Cabranés moved with his family to New York from Puerto Rico when he was only five. After attending public schools in the Bronx and Flushing, Queens, he graduated from Columbia College in 1961. He received his law degree from Yale University Law School in 1965, and an LL.M. degree in international law from the University of Cambridge in Cambridge, England, in 1967.

Cabranés served as general counsel of Yale University from 1975 to 1979. Previously he had practiced law at the firm of Casey, Lane & Mittendorf in New York City from 1967 to 1971; taught law at Rutgers University School of Law in New Jersey from 1971 to 1973; and served as special counsel to the governor of Puerto Rico and as administrator, Office of the Commonwealth of Puerto Rico, Washington, D.C.

José A. Cabranés

(1940–)

He also served in the administration of President Jimmy Carter as a member of the President's Commission on Mental Health from 1977 to 1978; as a member of the U.S. delegation to the Belgrade Conference on Security and Cooperation in Europe from 1977 to 1978; and as consultant to U.S. Secretary of State Cyrus Vance in 1978. In 1979, Carter appointed Cabranés to the U.S. District Court for the District of Connecticut; he is now its Chief Judge.

In December 1988 U.S. Supreme Court Chief Justice William H. Rehnquist named Judge Cabranés as one of five federal judges for the fifteen-member Federal Courts Study Committee, created by an act of Congress "to examine problems facing the federal courts and develop a long-range plan for the future of the federal judiciary." Cabranés was seriously considered as a possible nominee for appointment to the United States Supreme Court when Justice Harry Blackmun retired in 1994.

**Santiago E. Campos
(1926-)**

Santiago Campos served in the U.S. Navy during World War II. He attended Central College in Fayette, Missouri, and received his law degree from the University of New Mexico in 1953. Campos was assistant attorney general for the state of New Mexico from 1954 to 1957. He was a New Mexico district judge from 1971 to 1978. President Carter appointed Judge Campos to the U.S. District Court for the District of New Mexico in 1978. He retired from that court in 1993.

**John M. Cannella
(1908-)**

Cannella is a Colombian American and played professional football for the New York Giants from 1933 to 1935. He attended Fordham University, where he received his B.A. degree in 1930 and his law degree in 1933. Cannella was assistant U.S. attorney for the Southern District of New York from 1940 to 1942. In 1963 President Kennedy appointed him to the U.S. District Court for the Southern District of New York, where he is now a Senior Judge.

**Carmen C. Cerezo
(1940-)**

Carmen Cerezo attended the University of Puerto Rico, where she received his B.A. degree in 1963 and his LL.B. degree in 1966. She was a judge on the Puerto Rico Court of Inter Appeals from 1976 to 1980, and was on the Superior Court of Puerto Rico from 1972 to 1976. President Carter appointed Judge Cerezo to the U.S. District Court for the District of Puerto Rico in 1980.

Born in Houston, James DeAnda received his B.A. degree from Texas A&M University and his J.D. degree from the University of Texas in 1950. He was in private practice from 1951 until 1979. In 1979, Judge DeAnda was appointed to the U.S. District Court for the Southern District of Texas where he subsequently became chief judge. He retired on October 1, 1992.

James DeAnda (1925–)

Ferdinand Fernández attended the University of Southern California and was awarded his B.A. degree in 1958 and his J.D. degree in 1962. He was in private practice from 1964 to 1980 with the law firm of Allard, Shelton & O'Connor in Pomona, California. Fernández was on the U.S. District Court for the Central District of California from 1985 to 1989. In 1989, Judge Fernández was appointed to the U.S. Court of Appeals for the Ninth Circuit by President Bush. Judge Fernández was reportedly considered as a potential replacement for retiring U.S. Supreme Court Justice Thurgood Marshall.

Ferdinand Francis Fernández (1937–)

José Fuste attended the University of Puerto Rico, where he received his B.A. degree in 1965 and his LL.B. degree in 1968. He was in private practice from 1968 to 1985 with the law firm of Jiménez and Fuste. Fuste was appointed to the U.S. District Court for the District of Puerto Rico by President Reagan in 1985.

José Antonio Fuste (1943–)

President Bush appointed Gaitán to the U.S. District Court for the Western District of Missouri in 1991.

Fernando J. Gaitán, Jr.

Edward García attended the Sacramento City College and graduated in 1951. He received his law degree from the McGeorge School of Law in 1958. García was deputy district attorney for Sacramento County from 1959 to 1964, supervising deputy district attorney from 1964 to 1969, and chief deputy district attorney from 1969 to 1972. He was a Sacramento Municipal Court judge from 1972 until 1984. President Reagan appointed Judge García to the U.S. District Court for the Eastern District of California in 1984.

Edward J. García (1928–)

Frank García served in the U.S. Army during World War II. He then attended St. Mary's University, where he received his B.A. degree in 1949 and his LL.B. degree in 1951. He was a Texas county court judge from

Hipolita Frank García (1925–)

1964 to 1980. In 1980 President Carter appointed García to the U.S. District Court for the Western District of Texas.

Emilio M. Garza

(1947–)

Emilio Garza attended the University of Notre Dame and was awarded his B.A. degree in 1969 and M.A. degree in 1970. He received his law degree from the University of Texas in 1976. He was in private practice from 1976 to 1987 with the law firm of Clemens, Spencer, Welmaker & Finck. Garza was a judge for the U.S. District Court for the Western District of Texas from 1988 to 1991. President Bush appointed Judge Garza to the U.S. Court of Appeals for the Fifth Circuit in 1991.

Reynaldo G. Garza

(1915–)

Reynaldo Garza was born in Brownsville, Texas. His parents were both born in Mexico and had immigrated to the United States in 1901. Garza attended the University of Texas, where he received his law degree in 1939. He practiced law in Brownsville as a solo practitioner until he joined the air force during World War II. After the war, he resumed his private practice until 1950, when he joined the firm of Sharpe, Cunningham & Garza.

President Kennedy in 1961 appointed Garza to the U.S. District Court for the Southern District of Texas; in 1974 he became chief judge of that court. In 1979, Garza was appointed to the U.S. Court of Appeals for the Fifth Circuit by President Jimmy Carter. In 1987, U.S. Supreme Court Chief Justice William H. Rehnquist appointed Garza to the Temporary Emergency Court of Appeals of the United States. He was later named by Rehnquist as chief judge of that court.

Garza has often been recognized for his active role in education, community affairs, and the law. He was honored when a small law school opened its doors in Edinburg, Texas, and was named the Reynaldo G. Garza School of Law. Pope Pius XII twice decorated Garza for his work with the Knights of Columbus, conferring on him the Medal Pro Ecclesia et Pontifice in 1953 and recognizing him as a Knight of the Order of St. Gregory the Great in 1954. Garza received the American Association of Community and Junior Colleges Alumnus of the Year Award in 1984, and in 1989 he was given the Distinguished Alumnus Award of the University of Texas.

President Carter offered the position of attorney general of the United States to Judge Garza. Garza declined the cabinet post because he would have had to resign from his position as a federal judge, which is a lifetime appointment.

Gierbolini attended the University of Puerto Rico, where he received his B.A. degree in 1951 and his LL.B. degree in 1961. He was a captain in the U.S. Army and served during the Korean War from 1951 to 1957.

Gilberto Gierbolini (1926–)

Gierbolini served as assistant U.S. attorney for Puerto Rico from 1961 to 1966, as a superior court judge from 1966 to 1969, as assistant secretary of justice for Puerto Rico from 1969 to 1972, and as solicitor general of Puerto Rico from 1970 to 1972. Gierbolini was in the private practice of law between 1972 and 1980. In 1980, President Carter appointed Judge Gierbolini to the U.S. District Court for the District of Puerto Rico.

Ricardo Hinojosa attended the University of Texas, where he received his B.A. degree in 1972. He received his law degree from Harvard University Law School in 1975. He was in private practice as a partner in the law firm of Ewers & Toothaker in McAllen, Texas, from 1976 until 1983. In 1983, Hinojosa was appointed by President Reagan to the U.S. District Court for the Southern District of Texas.

Ricardo H. Hinojosa (1950–)

Judge Laffitte was born in Ponce, Puerto Rico. Laffitte received his B.A. from the Interamerican University in 1955, his law degree from the University of Puerto Rico in 1958 and his LL.M. degree from Georgetown University in 1960.

Héctor M. Laffitte (1934–)

Laffitte was the Civil Rights Commissioner for the commonwealth of Puerto Rico from 1969 to 1972. He was in private practice from 1972 to 1983 with the firm of Laffitte, Domínguez & Totti. President Reagan appointed Laffitte to the U.S. District Court for the District of Puerto Rico in 1983.

George La Plata

(1924-)

George La Plata was born in Detroit to Mexican-American parents. He attended Wayne State University, where he received his B.A. degree in 1951. He received his law degree from the Detroit College of Law in 1956. La Plata also served in the U.S. Marine Corps during World War II, reaching the rank of colonel.

La Plata, in conjunction with George Menéndez, adviser to the Republic of Mexico, helped pioneer the representation of migrant workers in Michigan, Ohio, and Indiana during the 1950s.

From 1956 to 1979, La Plata was in private practice. La Plata served as a Michigan county judge from 1979 to 1985. When appointed to that position in 1979, he became the first Hispanic judge in Michigan history. President Reagan appointed Judge La Plata to the U.S. District Court for the Eastern District of Michigan in 1985. He remains active in providing pro bono services to Hispanics in his community.

Rudolpho Lozano

(1942-)

Rudolpho Lozano attended Indiana University, where he received his B.A. degree in 1963 and his law degree in 1966. He was in private practice with the law firm of Spangler, Jennings, Spangler, & Dougherty in Merrillville, Indiana, from 1966 to 1988. In 1988 President Reagan appointed Lozano to the U.S. District Court for the Northern District of Indiana.

Alfredo C. Márquez

(1922-)

Alfredo Márquez served in World War II as an ensign in the U.S. Navy. After the war, he attended the University of Arizona, where he received his B.S. degree in 1948 and his law degree in 1950. Márquez served as assistant attorney general for the state of Arizona from 1951 to 1952, as prosecutor for the city of Tucson and assistant county attorney for Pima County from 1953 to 1954, and as an aide to Congressman Stewart Udall (D-Arizona) in 1955.

Márquez was in private practice with the firm of Mesch, Márquez & Rothschild from 1957 until 1980. Márquez was appointed by President Carter in 1980 to the U.S. District Court for the District of Arizona, where he is now a Senior Judge.

Harold R. Medina,

Sr. (1888-1991)

Former U.S. circuit court judge, Harold Medina was born in Brooklyn, New York, of Mexican-American and Dutch-American parents. His father, Joaquín Medina, came to the United States as a refugee from a bitter civil and race war in the Yucatan Peninsula. Harold Medina attended Princeton University, where he graduated with honors in 1909. He went on to Columbia University Law School and received his law degree in 1912. Medina began practicing law and also lectured at Columbia Law School at the invitation of Dean Harlan Fiske Stone.

In 1918, Medina formed his own law firm and specialized in appeals. The most famous case argued by Medina was the Cramer treason case during World War II. Anthony Cramer, of Brooklyn, was accused of helping two Nazi spies who had landed from a submarine. Medina initially lost the case in the lower courts but won it on appeal to the U.S. Supreme Court.

After World War II ended, Medina was appointed to the U.S. District Court for the District of New York by President Harry Truman. In 1951 President Truman appointed Judge Medina to the U.S. Court of Appeals for the Second Circuit.

Federico A. Moreno, Sr. (1952–)

Federico Moreno was born in Caracas, Venezuela, and immigrated to the United States with his family in 1963. In 1974, Moreno graduated from the University of Notre Dame, where he received his B.A. degree in government. He worked as a janitor and in restaurants to pay his way through college. After graduating, he taught at the Atlantic Community College in Mays Landing, New Jersey, and at Stockton State College in Pomona, New Jersey, in 1975 and 1976. In 1978, Moreno received his law degree from the University of Miami School of law.

Moreno was an associate with the law firm of Rollins, Peeples & Meadows in 1978 and 1979, and served as an assistant federal public defender from 1979 to 1981. He was a partner in the law firm of Thornton, Rothman & Moreno from 1982 to 1986. He served as Dade County judge in 1986 and 1987. Moreno was a Florida Circuit Court judge from 1987 until 1990. President Bush appointed Judge Moreno to the U.S. District Court for the Southern District of Florida in 1990.

Philip Newman (1916–)

The first Mexican-born U.S. judge, Newman was born in Mexico City to a German-American father and a Mexican mother. His family fled Mexico in the 1920s during the Mexican civil war and settled in California. Arriving destitute in the United States, Newman's father put himself through law school at night and became an attorney. Newman also became an attorney in 1941. He won landmark cases protecting the rights of individuals against unwarranted searches and seizures and leading to changes in immigration law. He was the founder of the Community Services Organization in Los Angeles. In 1964, Newman was appointed by Governor Edmund G. Brown to a Los Angeles municipal judgeship, where he remained until his retirement in 1982.

Juan M. Pérez-Giménez (1941-)

Juan Pérez-Giménez received his B.A. degree in 1963 and his LL.B. degree in 1968 from the University of Puerto Rico; his M.B.A. degree was conferred by George Washington University in 1965. He was an assistant U.S. attorney for Puerto Rico from 1971 to 1975. President Carter appointed Pérez-Giménez to the U.S. District Court for the District of Puerto Rico in 1979.

Jaime Pieras, Jr. (1924-)

Jaime Pieras served in the U.S. Army during World War II. He received his B.A. degree from Catholic University in 1945 and his J.D. degree from Georgetown University in 1948. Pieras was in private practice from 1949 until 1982. In 1982, Judge Pieras was appointed to the U.S. District Court for the District of Puerto Rico by President Reagan.

Edward C. Prado (1947-)

Edward Prado attended the University of Texas, where he received his B.A. degree in 1969 and his J.D. degree in 1972. In 1984, President Reagan appointed Prado to the U.S. District Court for the Western District of Texas.

Raul Anthony Ramírez (1944-)

After receiving his law degree from the University of the Pacific, McGeorge School of Law, Ramírez went into private practice. He served as a municipal court judge in Sacramento from 1977 until 1980. In 1980, he was appointed by President Carter to the U.S. District Court for the Eastern District of California. He resigned in 1990.

Manuel L. Real (1924-)

Manuel Real's parents immigrated to the United States from Spain. His mother was born in Albunol, Granada, Spain, and his father was born in Sierra de Yegas, Malaga, Spain. Real was educated in California and received his B.S. degree from the University of California in 1944 and his

LL.B. degree from Loyola University in 1951. Real also served as assistant U.S. attorney from 1952 to 1955 for the Southern District of California. He was in private practice from 1955 to 1964 in San Pedro, California, and was assistant U.S. attorney for the Southern District of California from 1964 to 1966.

In 1966, Real was appointed to the U.S. District Court for the Central District of California by President Johnson. He was named chief judge of that court in 1982.

Former state supreme court justice for California, Cruz Reynoso was born on May 2, 1931, of farm worker parents in the small town of Brea, California, where he was raised and received his early education. He attended Fullerton Junior College and Pomona College, where he earned his B.A. degree in 1953. From 1953 to 1955, he served in the U.S. Army. After his discharge, Reynoso entered the study of law at the University of California, Berkeley, and was awarded his degree in 1958. That same year he began the private practice of law in El Centro, California.

**Cruz Reynoso
(1931–)**

During the 1960s, Reynoso acted as assistant chief of the Division of Fair Employment Practices for California. From 1967 to 1968, he was associate general counsel to the Equal Employment Opportunity Commission in Washington, D.C., returning to California to become the first deputy director and then director of California Rural Legal Assistance. In 1972, he accepted a position at the University of New Mexico Law School, where he served for four years.

In 1976, Reynoso was appointed to the California Court of Appeal in Sacramento as an associate justice. Governor Jerry Brown then appointed him to the California Supreme Court in 1982. Reynoso became the first Hispanic on the court and served until 1986. In 1987, he entered private practice with the firm of O'Donnell & Gordon in Los Angeles and subsequently was of counsel to Kaye, Scholer, Fierman, Hays & Handler in Sacramento.

Reynoso has been honored by appointment to four presidential commissions, including the Select Commission on Immigration and Refugee Policy and the UN Commission on Human Rights. He was appointed to the law faculty of the University of California, Los Angeles, in 1990.

Dorothy Comstock Riley (1924–)

Supreme court justice for the state of Michigan, Dorothy Riley was born to Hispanic parents in Detroit. She attended Wayne State University, where she received both her B.A. degree in politics and her law degree. She went into private practice in 1950 and established the firm of Riley and Roumell in 1968.

Riley sat on the Michigan Court of Appeals from 1976 until 1982, when she was elevated to the Michigan Supreme Court as an associate justice. Judge Riley was named chief justice in 1987 and remains in that position.

Joseph H. Rodríguez (1930–)

Rodriguez received his B.A. degree from LaSalle University in 1955 and his J.D. degree from Rutgers University in 1958. He was in private practice from 1959 to 1982 with the firm of Brown, Connery, Kulp, Wille, Purcell, & Greene and was also an instructor at Rutgers University School of Law from 1972 to 1982.

In 1982, Rodriguez was appointed New Jersey public advocate, a state cabinet position, and served until 1985. He litigated landmark cases in the areas of education and housing. President Reagan appointed Judge Rodriguez to the U.S. District Court for the District of New Jersey in 1985. Judge Rodriguez has always been involved in community affairs and continues to be active today.

Luis D. Rovirá (1923–)

Supreme court justice for the state of Colorado, Luis Rovirá was born in San Juan, Puerto Rico. His family moved to Colorado, where he was educated. Rovirá attended the University of Colorado and received both B.A. and law degrees. He was in private practice with the firm of Rovirá, DeMuth & Eiberger until 1976.

In 1976, Rovirá was appointed to the Colorado District Court for the second district. In 1979, he was elevated to the Colorado Supreme Court as an associate justice and became chief justice in 1990.

Ernest Torres graduated from Dartmouth College in 1963 and received his law degree from Duke University School of Law in 1968. He was in private practice from 1968 to 1974. In 1975, Torres was elected to the Rhode Island House of Representatives, where he served until 1980. After leaving the state house, he went into private practice. Torres was appointed by President Reagan in 1988 to the U.S. District Court for the District of Rhode Island.

Ernest C. Torres
(1941–)

Juan Torruella received his B.A. degree from the University of Pennsylvania in 1954 and his LL.B. degree from Boston University in 1957. He was appointed by President Ford to the U.S. District Court for the District of Puerto Rico in 1974 and was chief judge of that court from 1982 to 1984. In 1984, President Reagan appointed Judge Torruella to the U.S. Court of Appeals for the First Circuit.

Juan R. Torruella
(1933–)

Vazquez received both her B.A. and her law degree from the University of Notre Dame. She began her career as a public defender for the State of New Mexico, and then went into private practice, becoming a partner in her Sante Fe firm in 1984. President Clinton appointed Vazquez to the U.S. District Court for the District of New Mexico in 1993.

Martha A. Vazquez
(1953–)

Vela graduated from the University of Texas and received a J.D. degree from St. Mary's University in 1962. He was in private practice from 1962 to 1975 and also served as an attorney for the Mexican American Legal Defense and Educational Fund (MALDEF) from 1962 to 1975. He was a Texas district court judge from 1975 to 1980. President Carter appointed Vela to the U.S. District Court for the Southern District of Texas in 1980.

Filemón B. Vela
(1935–)

◆ ◆ ◆ ◆ ◆ ◆ ◆ ◆ ◆ ◆ ◆ ◆ **HISPANICS IN THE PUBLIC INTEREST**

A great number of Hispanic attorneys have chosen a career in the public interest. Many serve at government posts or with nonprofit legal organizations established to aid underprivileged and disenfranchised clients. Many attorneys who enter service in the public interest do so because they have a desire to aid other Hispanic Americans with legal, social, and cultural problems.

In public interest service, Hispanic attorneys have the opportunity to make gains for not only themselves and their community but also all Americans. They take pride in the victories made in the struggle for equal rights at a time when the tide is running against civil rights efforts of minorities. Public interest firms often act as watchdogs that monitor government action to see that public resources are effectively channeled into the Hispanic community. By monitoring these agencies, they can ensure that programs they devise realistically account for the needs of Hispanics. However, public interest firms and organizations are plagued by insufficient funding and staff. Despite these limitations, those people who join the public interest have achieved a great deal in this country.

Issues often monitored by public interest groups include immigration, employment, education, housing, voter registration and elections, public funding, discrimination, and civil rights. In the past two decades, there has been dramatic growth in the number of public interest organizations specifically created to assist Hispanics with legal problems and to advocate political involvement. Some of the most well known and effective national public interest groups in the United States include local offices funded by the Legal Services Corporation; Migrant Legal Action Program; Mexican-American Legal Defense and Educational Fund; Puerto Rican Legal Defense and Education Fund; and the National Immigration Law Center.

SELECTED PROMINENT HISPANIC ATTORNEYS AND LAW PROFESSORS ◆

Michael J. Aguirre

(1949–)

Attorney

Born in San Diego, California, on September 12, 1949, Aguirre was educated in California, attained a bachelor of science degree at Arizona State University in 1971, a law degree from the University of California, Berkeley, in 1974, and a master of public administration degree from Harvard University in 1989. He has worked as deputy legislative counsel for the California legislature, 1974—1975; as assistant U.S. attorney, 1975—76; assistant counsel for the U.S. Senate Subcommittee on Investigations, 1976—77; and as special reports legal counsel for the CBS network, 1977. Since that time he has worked in private practice. Since 1980, he has been the president of his own law firm, Aguirre & Meyer, A.P.C., which specializes in civil litigation. He has also been an adjunct professor and lectured in law at the University of California, San Diego, and at the

University of Southern California. Aguirre is active in the community and has also been the author of various laws passed by the California legislature. His awards include the Wille Velásquez Community Service Award, given by the Chicano Federation in San Diego in 1989. In 1987, he was voted the most distinguished name in the San Diego legal community by the readership of the *San Diego Daily Transcript*.

Blancarte was born in 1953 in Pomona, California, and graduated from Pomona College. He received his law degree from the University of California School of Law and was admitted to the bar in 1979. Blancarte's current areas of practice are litigation and entertainment and business law. Blancarte was president of the Mexican American Bar Association of Los Angeles in 1983 and was president of the western region of the Hispanic National Bar Association in 1988. He is currently a partner with the firm of Mitchell, Silberberg & Knupp in Los Angeles.

James E. Blancarte (1953–)

Litigation Attorney

Caraballo was born in Yabucoa, Puerto Rico, in 1947 and grew up in a tough neighborhood of New York City. Caraballo attended St. Joseph's University and went on to New York University Law School and received his law degree in 1974. He then worked the streets of New York City as a community activist and a legal aid lawyer. Caraballo was also active in the Puerto Rican Legal Defense and Education Fund. In 1975, he joined Seton Hall Law School in Newark, New Jersey, as a clinical professor. During his fifteen years at Seton Hall, Caraballo specialized in teaching contract, commercial, and bankruptcy law. He was a visiting professor at New York University, the City University of New York, and Pace College law schools. In 1982 he was named associate dean of Seton Hall Law School.

Wilfredo Caraballo (1947–)

Former Public Advocate/Public Defender, State of New Jersey

Caraballo took a leave of absence in 1990, when New Jersey Governor James Florio appointed Caraballo to the Office of Public Advocate and Public Defender, a cabinet post. Caraballo states that one of the reasons he was so enthusiastic about becoming New Jersey's fourth public advocate is that the post gives him an opportunity to deal with the same kinds of public interest problems he faced firsthand as a young man growing up on the streets of Brooklyn and the South Bronx. Caraballo served as public advocate until 1992.

Daniel P. García

(1947–)

Attorney

Daniel García was born in Los Angeles in 1947. He was educated in Los Angeles and attended Loyola University, where he received a degree in business in 1970. He went on to the University of Southern California and earned his M.B.A. in 1971. García then attended UCLA School of Law and was awarded a law degree in 1974. García joined the prestigious firm of Munger, Tolles & Olson in Los Angeles where he is now a partner. He is a member of the board of the Mexican-American Legal Defense and Education Fund and has been active in Los Angeles politics. García was a member of the Los Angeles Planning Commission from 1976 to 1988 and was its president from 1978 to 1988. Of Hispanic participation in the legal profession, García believes that in recent years Hispanic attorneys have done much better in breaking barriers to join the nation's largest firms. García himself is among that group.

Antonia Hernández

President and General Counsel, Mexican-American Legal Defense and Educational Fund (MALDEF)

Born in Coahuila, Mexico, Hernández earned her B.A. at UCLA, a teaching credential at the university's School of Education, and her law degree at the UCLA School of Law in 1974. Hernández began her legal career as a staff attorney with the Los Angeles Center for Law and Justice that same year. In 1977, she became the directing attorney for the Legal Aid Foundation office in Lincoln Heights. An expert in civil rights and immigration issues, Hernández worked with Senator Edward M. Kennedy and the U.S. Senate Committee on the Judiciary in 1979 and 1980. She was also the Southwest regional political coordinator of the Kennedy for President campaign in 1980. Active in community affairs, she presently serves on the board of directors of several organizations, including the National Hispanic Leadership Conference, the Latino Museum of History, Art & Culture, and the Independent Sector.

Hernández has been the president and general counsel of MALDEF since 1985, served as its vice president from 1984 to 1985, as employment program director from 1983 to 1984, and as an associate counsel from 1981 to 1983. As president of MALDEF, she directs all litigation and advocacy programs, manages a $4.5 million budget and a 65-person staff, and is responsible for the organization's long-range plans and goals.

Gerald P. López

(1948–)

Law Professor

López attended the University of Southern California. He received his law degree from Harvard Law School in 1974. López then served as law clerk to U.S. District Court Judge Edward Schwartz from 1974 to 1975 in San Diego. López has taught at California Western School of Law, UCLA Law

School, and Harvard Law School. He has been a professor at Stanford School of Law since 1985.

Martínez is a partner in the firm of Munger, Tolles & Olson in Los Angeles. Martínez was born in San Antonio, Texas, in 1943. She attended the University of Texas and went on to Columbia University Law School, where she received her law degree in 1967. As general counsel of MALDEF from 1973 to 1982, Martínez was an influential advocate during the congressional hearings for the Voting Rights Act of 1975, which opened the door to greater access to political participation by Hispanics. Martínez also served as a consultant to the U.S. Commission on Civil Rights from 1969 to 1973.

Vilma S. Martínez (1943–)

Former General Counsel, Mexican American Legal Defense and Educational Fund (MALDEF)

Méndez-Longoria attended Texas Southmost College and received his law degree from George Washington University Law School in 1968. Méndez-Longoria served as a law clerk for the U.S. Court of Claims in Washington, D.C., from 1968 to 1969. He then was legal assistant to U.S. Senator Alan Cranston (D-California) from 1969 to 1971. Méndez-Longoria was a staff attorney for the Mexican American Legal Defense and Educational Fund (MALDEF) in San Francisco from 1971 to 1972 and was deputy director of California Rural Legal Assistance in San Francisco from 1972 to 1974. Méndez-Longoria served as deputy public defender for Monterey County, California, from 1975 to 1976. Since 1976, Méndez-Longoria has taught law at the University of Santa Clara Law School, University of California at Berkeley Law School (Boalt Hall), Vermont Law School, University of San Diego Law School, and Stanford University Law School. He has been a professor at Stanford University Law School since 1984.

Miguel Angel Méndez-Longoria (1942–)

Professor

Born in San Antonio, Texas, Obledo attended the University of Texas, where he was awarded a degree in pharmacy. After serving in the Korean War, he returned to Texas and received his law degree from St. Mary's University Law School in 1961. Obledo has been active in Hispanic affairs for over thirty years: Cofounder, Hispanic National Bar Association (HNBA) and Mexican-American Legal Defense and Educational Fund (MALDEF); Past President, the League of United Latin American Citizens (LULAC). In LULAC he has held local, district, state, and national offices, including the presidency. He was also active in the Southwest Voter Registration Project. Obledo has been active in government and is a former Secretary of the California Health and Welfare Agency, where he was instrumental in bringing thousands of Hispanics into state government.

Mario G. Obledo (1932–)

Obledo was also assistant attorney general for the state of Texas and has lectured at Harvard Law School. Currently, Obledo is chairman of the National Rainbow Coalition. He has offices in Austin, Texas, Sacramento, California, and Washington, D.C., where he remains active in national politics.

Michael A. Olivas

(1951–)

Professor

Olivas attended Pontifical College in Columbus, Ohio, where he was awarded a B.A. degree in 1972 and an M.A. degree in 1974. He then went on to Ohio State University and received his Ph.D. in 1977. Olivas received his law degree from Georgetown University Law School in 1981. Olivas served as director of resources for the League of United Latin American Citizens (LULAC) Education Resource Center in Washington, D.C., from 1979 to 1982. In 1982, he began teaching law at the University of Houston Law School. He is director of the Institute for Higher Education Law and Governance there and was named associate dean in 1990.

Leo M. Romero

(1943–)

Dean, University of New Mexico Law School

Romero is the only Hispanic dean in the United States. He attended Oberlin College and received his J.D. degree from Washington University Law School in St. Louis, Missouri, and his LL.M. degree from Georgetown University Law School in Washington, D.C. Romero was associate editor of the *Washington University Law Quarterly* and was editor-in-chief of the *Urban Law Review* at Washington University. Romero has taught law at Dickinson University Law School, the University of Oregon Law School, and the University of New Mexico Law School. He became associate dean at the University of New Mexico Law School in 1989 and was named dean in 1991.

Gerald Torres

(1952–)

Professor

Torres was born in Victorville, California. He attended Stanford University, where he received his B.A. in 1974. He received his J.D. degree from Yale Law School in 1977 and his LL.M. degree from the University of Michigan Law School in 1980. He was admitted to the bar in 1978. Torres was staff attorney for the Children's Defense Fund in Washington, D.C., from 1977 to 1978. He began teaching law in 1980 and has taught at the University of Pittsburgh Law School, the University of Minnesota Law School, and Harvard Law School. He now teaches jurisprudence, environmental law, property law, and agricultural law, at the University of Texas School of Law.

Valdez was born in Floresville, Texas, and attended Texas A&M University. He received a J.D. degree from Baylor University Law School and an LL.M. degree from Harvard Law School. He was admitted to the bar in 1970. Valdez served as an aide to President Lyndon Johnson from 1965 to 1967. He was an attorney for the Overseas Private Investment Corporation from 1971 to 1973 and was general counsel for the Inter-American Foundation from 1973 to 1975. Under President Carter, Valdez was assistant administrator of the Latin American and Caribbean region for the U.S. Agency for International Development from 1977 to 1979. He served as U.S. ambassador and chief of protocol for the White House from 1979 to 1981. In 1981, Valdez joined the law firm of Laxalt, Washington, Perito & Dubuc in Washington, D.C., where he is a partner. Valdez's areas of law are administrative, regulatory, and international law.

Gilbert Paul Carrasco

Abelardo López Valdez (1942–)

Attorney, Former Presidential Aide, and Government Official

Media

The treatment of one ethnic group by another is quite often influenced by economic or political factors in their nation, state, or region. This is certainly true regarding the relations between Anglos and Latinos. The conflict and cooperation between these groups has been shaped by the political and economic relations between the United States and other Spanish-American countries.

The general market mass media—including newspapers, magazines, television, and radio—which so often reflect the prevalent perspectives of the dominant groups in society, have historically replicated those views in their treatment of Hispanics. Therefore, an avenue for partially understanding contemporary Hispanic life is the assessment of messages that the media disseminate about them. First, at all levels of society, general mass market media are the most pervasive sources of news and information. For many people they are also the most relied-upon source for entertainment. Second, the messages presented by the media may have significant effects on the audience, especially regarding events, topics, and issues about which the audience has no direct knowledge or experience. Thus, for millions of people, a significant part of the information they receive and the notions they develop about Hispanics may often be products of mass media messages.

TREATMENT OF HISPANICS IN GENERAL MARKET MEDIA ✦ ✦ ✦

Two qualifications are critical to a discussion of the general market media's treatment of Hispanics. One of those conditions occurs when viewers do not have other sources of information or experiences that provide a standard against which to assess the media messages. To the extent that non-Hispanics live segregated lives with limited opportunities to interact effectively with a variety of Hispanics in constructive or productive ways, the media images of Hispanics will be among the only sources for non-Latinos to learn and interpret who Hispanics are and how they think. Another factor that increases media's influence occurs when the values or views presented by them are recurrent. To date, the values and views presented about Latinos are predominantly negative and recurrent across media and time.

Furthermore, the treatment of Latinos in general market media has its impact on Hispanics, who suffer the consequences of the recurring negative imagery. For example, they face the psychological pain that emerges from the negative portrayals and lack of recognition of their own people and values. They also have to endure the social scorn that emerges when the treatment they receive from other people, and sometimes from those of their own ethnic background, is consciously or unconsciously based on stereotyped notions disseminated by the media.

GENERAL MARKET NEWSPAPERS ✦ ✦ ✦ ✦ ✦ ✦ ✦ ✦ ✦ ✦ ✦ ✦ ✦ ✦

General market newspapers were probably the first major means of mass communication through which fragmented and distorted news, information, and images of Hispanics were created and promoted. While much has changed from the early depictions, the treatment and employment of Hispanics in newspapers is still far from adequate in this media institution.

The Anglo image of the Mexican as a bandit is largely an outgrowth of the Manifest Destiny policy of the 1800s. English-language American newspapers in California and Texas reveal how circumstantial events related to economic and political relations between the people who inhabited the expansive Mexican territories of the Southwest and the Anglo-European settlers and gold prospectors led the latter group to create stereotypes of the former to justify the conquest of that region. The political, religious, and economic beliefs of Anglo-European superiority were constantly betrayed as they depicted the Native American and Mexican inhabitants as people destined to be conquered and unworthy of keeping their lands and resources.

After the conquests of the southwestern territories, the general market press of the early twentieth century continued a pattern of false depictions of Hispanic people, or simply ignored their experiences.

Changing journalistic standards over the years increased professionalism, balance, and objectivity, which diminished such blatant anti-Mexican racism. Yet negative, limited, or inadequate portrayals of Hispanics in newspapers of the latter half of this century have been systematically documented. One of the first studies in this area was a 1969 analysis of Puerto Ricans in *The New York Times* and *The Post* compared with coverage in the Spanish-language dailies *El Diario* and *El Tiempo*. The English-language dailies showed little interest in Puerto Ricans, who were referred to with negative attributes and covered primarily in terms of their community needs or problems (for which solutions were infrequently offered). The same was not true in the Spanish dailies, which featured more positive and solution-oriented stories.

Negative and biased coverage of Mexican Americans was also evident in research regarding pretrial criminal news reporting and general reporting, and comparing immigration and deportation news in the *Los Angeles Times* and the Spanish-language daily *La Opinión* during the 1930s, 1950s, and 1970s, which found that the plight of Mexicans was covered much more sympathetically and humanistically in the latter paper.

Yet some improvements have been made, at least according to two recent studies of the general market press. In a 1983 study of the coverage of Hispanic Americans in the English-language dailies of Santa Fe, Tucson, Salinas, San Bernardino, Stockton, and Visalia, researchers conclude that

Portrayals

The most blatant act of negative stereotyping occurred during the 1940s through exploitation of social and economic tensions between Hispanics and Anglos in Los Angeles. The general market press gave undue prominence to Mexican Americans in crime news. Alarmist headlines and stories blaming these Hispanics for many of the city's social ills were part of the 1943 "zoot suit" riots and their aftermath.

sports news and photo coverage get high marks for their inclusion of local Hispanics and that local news coverage exclusive of sports gets a passing grade—good, not excellent, but better than it is currently receiving credit for. However, editorial coverage and bulletin listings of Hispanic people and activities are below average and in need of considerable attention.

The most promising assessment comes from a 1989 study of the Albuquerque *Journal* and the San Antonio *Express-News,* which revealed some examples of parity in the inclusion of Hispanics and conclude that Hispanics and Hispanic issues are present in the newspaper in proportion to their presence in the population. Also, in comparison to stories about Anglos, Hispanic stories were adequately treated in terms of length and placement. However, as was the case in previously cited studies, Hispanics were much too prominently reported as "problem people," for example, in judicial and crime news, news of riots, and accident and disaster news.

In spite of this, the prognosis of Hispanic treatment in general market newspapers has consistently remained culturally insensitive and nonsupportive. From his observations and personal experiences, Charles A. Erickson, founder and editor of *Hispanic Link, Inc.,* in 1981 summarized that "the relationship between 20 million Americans crowded under the umbrella Hispanic and the nation's establishment print media sprawls across the spectrum from nonexistent to quaint, to precarious, to outright antagonistic." Erickson identified six dimensions of general market press irresponsibility: the press will not allow Hispanics to be authorities on general issues; the press will not even allow Hispanics to be authorities on issues where Hispanics have the obvious expertise; the press still views the Hispanic community in stereotype; the press fails to provide Hispanics with information of critical interest and importance to their welfare and progress; the press does not hire enough Hispanics or other reporters and editors with Hispanic cultural awareness and expertise; and the press tends to smother those Hispanics they do hire.

Regarding the press's viewing the Hispanic community in stereotype, Erickson states, "Traditionally, non-Hispanic reporters have attached negative adjectives to the word 'barrio.' For example, Houston's barrios were described in a series one of its papers ran some months ago as places where shoppers haggle and Latin rhythms blare. A Chicago reporter described New York's Spanish Harlem as 'grim, rat-infested.' A *Christian Science Monitor* writer chose the words '[t]he often-steamy barriors [sic] of East Los Angeles.'"

A decade following Erickson's critique of the general market press, David Shaw's 1990 nine-article series in *The Los Angeles Times* assessing the status of reporting about and hiring minorities found many of the same situations and problems discussed by Erickson. The headline of the first story summarized the issue: "Negative News and Little Else." The story went on to say that "by focusing on crime, poverty and aberrant behavior newspapers fail to give a complete portrait of ethnic minorities." An example of continued stereotyping presented by Shaw is the use of the word "aliens" (which can make Latinos seem "inhuman—strange outcasts from another world") instead of "illegal immigrants" or "undocumented workers."

In trying to understand some of the reasons that lead to the continued fragmentation and distortion of news about Hispanics and other minorities, those who have written on this subject would probably agree that the lack of Hispanics in the newsrooms and in their management is one of the major factors to be considered.

Employment

When the first counts of minority participants in the general market press were conducted in the early 1970s, these groups constituted less than 2 percent of the total. About a decade later, in 1984, the total had only made it to 5.8 percent among the approximately 1,750 daily newspapers in the nation. As low as these figures are, one must realize that they are for all minorities, which means that the situation for Hispanics is more dismal. This is a problem that continues even today, according to the most recent surveys of the National Association of Hispanic Journalists (NAHJ) and the American Society of Newspaper Editors (ASNE).

According to an NAHJ survey, Hispanics accounted for a mere 3.2 percent of this labor force in general; only 2 percent were managers. According to an ASNE survey, approximately 1,349 Hispanics were employed in those newspapers and constituted a scant 2.4 percent of the work force of about 55,714.

In addition to the problem of low employment, Hispanics who have succeeded in gaining employment in journalism encounter various burdens often related to their ethnicity. Hispanic reporters face unwarranted challenges of their latitude and credibility as professional journalists. While too often Hispanics are considered to lack the intellect to write about issues other than ethnic problems or strife, they are also perceived as too partial for "objective" in-depth reporting about educational, economic, and other types of policy issues of importance to their community. Moreover, many Hispanic journalists are burdened with requests to be translators in situations beyond their reporting duties; for example, to assist in answering Spanish-language business calls or correspondence not related to their responsibilities. Yet, these bilingual abilities usually are exploited without compensatory pay.

Given these current employment figures and practices, one can understand some of the factors related to the inadequate treatment of Hispanics in newspapers. Unfortunately, given the slow progress in newsroom integration and the limited sensitivity of many Anglo reporters and editors, it will be some time before Hispanics make sufficient inroads to professional positions, which is necessary to help improve the portrayal of their communities.

In the late 1980s some newspapers, such as The Los Angeles Times *and the* Fresno Bee, *began publishing weekly supplements in Spanish. This practice has been going on with mixed success since the 1840s in various locations, especially in border towns.*

However, many newspapers have been hiring more Latino and other ethnic minority journalists and improving their working environment, especially with respect to training, promotions, and distribution of assignments. These efforts have also included second-language courses (especially Spanish) and racial and ethnic awareness workshops for all employees of the newspaper.

The concerted efforts of organizations such as the National Association of Hispanic Journalists, the National Hispanic Media Coalition, the Hispanic Academy of Arts and Sciences, and the National Association of Hispanic Publications have been major factors in the push for positive changes and will undoubtedly contribute to improving both the portrayal and employment of Hispanics in the media.

GENERAL MARKET TELEVISION ♦ ♦ ♦ ♦ ♦ ♦ ♦ ♦ ♦ ♦ ♦ ♦ ♦ ♦ ♦ ♦

While newspapers were the first mass medium to widely disseminate images of Hispanics, their circulation and influence were limited when compared with films or television. Since the inception of moving pictures, stereotypes of minority and ethnic groups have been a standard feature. For a more extensive survey, see the Film chapter.

Not surprisingly, the treatment of Hispanics on general market television has not been sharply different from that in the film industry. Although there have been occasional breaks with stereotypical imagery, in some respects the portrayal has been more critical of Hispanic culture and life. In addition, the situation is worse in the number of Hispanics employed in front or behind cameras. This conclusion is quite evident from even cursory watching of American television.

The masters of television images have been less than fair in their portrayals of Hispanics. The first "prominent" Hispanic male on television was on the "I Love Lucy" show (CBS 1951–61), where Lucille Ball's husband, Desi Arnaz, played Ricky Ricardo, the good-looking, excitable, short-tempered Cuban band leader who spoke with an accent and occasionally rattled off expletives in Spanish. Interestingly, in "Desi and Lucy: Before the Laughter," a television biography, he is portrayed as an irresponsible Latin lover.

Portrayals

Other Hispanic male buffoons include Pancho, the sidekick to the Cisco Kid in the syndicated series "The Cisco Kid" (1951–56); José Jiménez, the Puerto Rican bumbling doorman and elevator operator in "The Danny Thomas Show" (NBC 1953–71); and Sgt. García in the "Zorro" series (ABC, 1957–59). The last of the successful (in terms of ratings and continuity) Hispanic male buffoons on network television was probably Freddie Prinze, who in "Chico and the Man" (NBC, 1974–78) played Chico, a streetwise kid working in a garage with a bigoted old man.

With such exceptions as "Chico and the Man," which was terminated shortly after Prinze's suicide, Hispanics as major comic characters in successful network programs have been few. CBS came up with an innovative strategy to market its "Latino Odd Couple" sitcom "Trial and Error" (1988). It was simulcast in Spanish on Spanish-language radio stations. The show centered around two unlikely roommates: Tony (Paul Rodríguez), a T-shirt salesman on Los Angeles's Olvera Street, and John (Eddie Vélez), a newly graduated Puerto Rican lawyer working in an established law firm. The comedy was strained and the series never gained acceptance. Much more noteworthy was the short-lived "I Married Dora," which had a brief run on ABC during the fall 1987 season. An admirable attempt to center a situation comedy around a Salvadoran woman, it reversed cultural fields by making Dora (Elizabeth Peña) smart and self-assured and her uptight, "open-minded" Anglo husband the butt of many jokes because of his stereotypical ideas about Hispanics. The series dealt meaningfully with Latino immigration to the United States and the misconceptions the two cultures often have about one another. Sadly, it was canceled before establishing a consistent tone and finding an audience.

The Hispanic bandidos—bandits, criminals, and lawbreakers—were also adapted promptly and prominently by television. The stock bandido, spitfire or peon was common in innumerable western cowboy series. Also, the numerous urban counterparts have been constantly present, starting with "Dragnet" (NBC 1951–59; 1967–70) and "Naked City" (ABC 1958–59; 1960–63), as part of the detective and police dramas. Most recently, they were quite prominent in the underworld activities (especially regarding drug traffic and dealings) in "Hill Street Blues" (NBC 1981–86) and "Miami Vice" (ABC 1984–89).

General market television has allowed a few law-enforcer or lawmaker Hispanic stereotypes. "The Cisco Kid," "Zorro," "CHiPs," "Miami Vice," and "L.A. Law" have included some relatively positive Hispanic male figures. One notable early example was Walt Disney's "The Nine Lives of Elfago Baca" (1958). Based on the exploits of the legendary Mexican-American lawman, the miniseries was an all-too-rare instance of television depicting a Chicano hero. More often, Hispanics have been cast in secondary or insignificant roles. For example, on "Hill Street Blues" the Hispanic lieutenant who is second in command is often given little to do and is generally dull.

Most attempts at centering a law enforcement series around a Hispanic character have been disappointing. "Juarez" (1988) was conceived as a gritty portrayal of the life of a Mexican-American border detective. ABC lost confidence in the project, however, and suspended production shortly after only two episodes were completed. NBC's "Drug Wars: the Kiki Camarena Story" (1990) was replete with updated bandido stereotypes and so offensive to Mexicans that Mexico issued formal complaints about the mini-series—which went on to win an Emmy. Paul Rodríguez's private investigator in "Grand Slam" resulted in little more than yet another instance of the comic buffoon.

In contrast, Edward James Olmos's Lieutenant Martin Castillo in "Miami Vice" is one of the most positive Hispanic characters in television history. Olmos was initially reluctant to take the part (he turned down the role several times before finally accepting), and the show's producers ultimately gave him control over the creation and realization of Castillo. He fashioned a dignified, honorable character of quiet strength and considerable power, thereby helping to offset the show's facile stereotyping of villainous Latin American drug smugglers. Another major impact was in the formidable presence of Jimmy Smits playing Victor Sifuentes on "L.A. Law," who provided the law firm (and the series) with a healthy dose of social consciousness.

Other stereotypes of Hispanics on television could be examined, as could the occasions when some Hispanic actors (for example, Ricardo Montalbán) and actresses (for instance, Rita Moreno) have been called upon to play a variety of roles beyond the usual stereotypes. What has been most neglected, however, is regular positive roles for Hispanic women and, equally important, the Hispanic family. This is one area in which Hispanics on television have been worse off than in film.

During the early 1950s Elena Verdugo starred in the comedy series "Meet Millie," but not as a Hispanic woman. Instead, she played an "all-American girl." The image of the Hispanic woman has been usually relegated to the overweight *mamacita,* the spitfire or señorita, the suffering mother, or gang member's girlfriend. Images of strong, self-reliant, attractive, all-knowing Hispanic females were notable in Linda Cristal's role as Victoria Cannon in "The High Chaparral" (NBC 1967–71) and Elena Verdugo as nurse Consuelo in "Marcus Welby, M.D." (ABC 1969–76). More recently this shortage of strong Latina characters remains the predominant pattern. Notable exceptions are Elizabeth Peña's roles on the previously discussed "I Married Dora" (ABC 1987) and "Shannon's Deal" (NBC 1989–90) and the character of Pilar in "Falcon Crest" (CBS 1987–89). The latter managed to be more than a simple one-dimensional love interest and was a forceful businesswoman.

Hispanic families have also been absent from the center stages of general market network television. In "The High Chaparral," a Mexican cattle-ranching family was portrayed alongside the gringo family. After that series, consequential inclusions of Hispanic families have eluded long runs on the small screen. "Viva Valdez," a poorly conceived and received situation comedy about a Chicano family living in East Los Angeles, was aired on ABC during the summer of 1976.

It was not until the spring of 1983, when ABC aired "Condo," that a middle-class urban Hispanic family was first introduced to TV viewers in the United States. That situation comedy series featured a stereotyped WASP and an upwardly mobile Hispanic who find themselves as condominium neighbors on opposite sides of almost every question, but who are faced with impending family ties. This modern-day Romeo and Juliet—in the very first episode the oldest Anglo son and a Hispanic daughter elope—was also short-lived as its quality declined and ratings faltered against the competition of CBS's "Magnum, P.I." and NBC's "Fame." Yet during "Condo's" twelve episodes, another TV first was set as the featured Mexican-American family was shown interacting as equals with an Anglo family that sometimes acceptingly participated with them as Hispanics.

The wealthiest urban Hispanic family ever featured was in another sitcom, "Sánchez of Bel Air," on the USA Cable Network. In this program, the nouveau riche Sánchez family faced numerous social class and cultural challenges after they moved up from the barrio to live in one of the most upscale areas of Los Angeles. The program ran only thirteen episodes between 1986 and 1987.

In March 1984 ABC tried Norman Lear's "a.k.a. Pablo," another situation comedy centered on Hispanic comedian Paul Rodríguez. This show also featured his working-class family. Unfortunately, Pablo's pungent jokes, often about Mexicans and Hispanics in general, irked enough Hispanics and others whose strong protest to the network contributed to the show's cancellation after only six episodes. As of this writing, general market network television has no Hispanic Huxtables, Windslows, or even Jeffersons.

Until very recently, the absence of notable Hispanic female figures and families was also evident in the daytime soap opera genre, which generally neglect Blacks, Latinos, and most other ethnic minorities. "Santa Barbara" was the only ongoing contemporary soap with recurring roles for Hispanics. That show made a commitment to have a Hispanic family to reflect the large numbers of Latinos in Santa Barbara.

Studies originating from government, academic, and professional circles corroborate the previous findings and reveal additional shortcomings about the treatment of Hispanics on general market television. In 1977 and 1979, the U.S. Commission on Civil Rights published two reports on the portrayals and employment of women and minorities in television. While many results were reported with aggregated data on all minorities, specific findings about "people of Spanish origin" [sic] were noted in the 1977 report. For example, from the content analysis of one sample week of programming during the fall of 1973 and 1974, only three Hispanics, all males, were found in "major" roles; twelve Hispanic males and one female were found playing minor roles. The highest-status occupation shown was a lawyer in a minor role.

The first academically based systematic analysis of this subject examined sample weeks of commercial fictional programming during three television seasons (1975–78). Among the 3,549 characters with speaking roles observed in the 255 episodes coded, they were able to find only 53 different individuals who could reliably be identified as Hispanics—slightly less than 1.5 percent of the population of speaking TV characters. Those characters were hard to find; mostly males of dark complexion, with dark hair, most often with heavy accents; women were absent and insignificant; the characters were gregarious and pleasant, with strong family ties, that half work hard, half are lazy, and very few show much concern for their futures; and most have had very little education, and their jobs reflect that fact.

General market television's neglect of Hispanics was similarly documented in a report commissioned by the League of United Latin American Citizens (LULAC) and prepared by Public Advocates, Inc. In the Public Advocates audit of all sixty-three prime-time shows during the first week of the fall 1983 television season, Hispanics played 1/2 of 1 percent (3 characters out of 496) of the significant speaking roles and only 1 percent (10 characters out of 866) of the those who spoke one or more lines. With the exception of Geraldo Rivera, there was an absence of positive Hispanic characters. On ABC, two-thirds of all speaking parts for Hispanics were criminals; on CBS, no Hispanics were in any significant speaking roles; and on NBC only one of its 189 (1/2 of 1 percent) significant roles included a Hispanic.

The very low percentage of Hispanic participation in television was also found in a study analyzing 620 episodes of prime-time series randomly selected from the Library of Congress's holdings from 1955 to 1986. Findings showed that since 1975, nearly one in ten characters have been Black (from a low of under 1 percent in the 1950s), while Hispanics have hovered around the 2 percent mark for three decades. Furthermore, in almost every comparison made of the social background (for example, education, employment) and plot functions (starring role, positive/negative portrayal, having committed a crime, and so on) of the White, Black, and Latino characters, the latter group was consistently worst off.

Public television has fared just slightly better than the commercial networks. "Sesame Street," "3-2-1 Contact," and "The Electric Company," programs produced by the Children's Television Workshop for PBS, regularly feature Hispanic role models, adults as well as children. PBS also has featured Latino themes, dramas, and films such as Jesús Salvador Treviño's *Seguín,* Robert M. Young's *Alambrista,* Moctezuma Esparza and Robert M. Young's *The Ballad of Gregorio Cortéz,* and Gregory Nava's *El Norte.*

Happily, this trend has continued. More recently, PBS has broadcast Luis Valdez's *Corridos!* (1987), dramatizations of traditional Mexican narrative ballads; Jesús Salvador Treviño's *Birthright: Growing Up Hispanic* (1989), interviews with leading Hispanic writers; Isaac Artenstein's *Break of Dawn* (1990), a docudrama based on the life of singer and Los Angeles radio personality Pedro J. González; and Héctor Galán's hard-hitting documentaries *New Harvest, Old Shame* (1990), *Los Mineros* (1991), and *In Search of Pancho Villa* (1993). However, exemplary series such as "Villa Alegre," "Carrascolendas," and "Qué Pasa, U.S.A." have been canceled due to lack of funds or low ratings. The lack of funding is certainly at the core of the problem as only about 2 percent of funds for television production allocated by the Corporation for Public Broadcasting in the past fourteen years have gone to produce programs specifically geared to the Hispanic communities.

The final area of interest regarding the images of Hispanics in general market television is news coverage. Ironically, researchers of media news content have themselves shown little concern for this population. Among the scores of articles published about the characteristics and biases of television news, not even one has given systematic attention to the portrayal of Hispanics in newscasts. For studies that have focused on the major network news, part of the problem may be the few stories broadcast about Hispanics.

One view is that in essence, it seems that general market television has yet to do much with, or for, the Hispanic either as a television character or as a viewer. It might be improper to characterize them as invisible, but the portrayal is blurred or certainly hard to follow.

Employment
Behind the cameras and in the offices, the treatment of Hispanics is likewise inadequate. From the first reports of the U.S. Commission on Civil Rights (1977, 1979) to more recent configurations of minority employment in the broadcasting industry, Hispanic participation has been and continues to be extremely small, much below Hispanic population proportions, and it is inferior to that of Afro-Americans.

A 1987 study of 375 television stations across the U.S. showed the average for Hispanic females on news staffs was .9 percent, while for males it was 2.2 percent. On the "talent track," minority women are as likely as non-minority men and women to be reporting or anchoring. But minority men are much less likely than minority women to have jobs that put them on the air as reporters or anchors. So although Black, Hispanic and other minority women are visible on the talent track but not on the managerial track, minority men (including Hispanics) are underrepresented in both pipelines to advancement in broadcast news.

In spite of the bleak picture summarized in this synopsis of Hispanic portrayals and employment in general market television, there is evidence that some changes have taken place throughout the years. One of the forces contributing to the gradual changes has been the complaints and protests of concerned individuals and organizations.

As in the general market film industry of the United States, Hispanics have been neglected and poorly depicted in a television industry oriented to the dominant society. The future treatment of Latinos in this medium may be contingent on some inroads that individual actors and actresses make. It may also depend on the continued process of organized activities being carried out by advocacy and Latino community groups.

◆ **ADVERTISING**

For years Hispanics have been practically invisible in general market advertising and by extension in employment in this industry. When Hispanics have been included in ways palatable to the Anglo majority society, their images have often been quite offensive to fellow Hispanics.

Perhaps the most controversial advertisement with a "Hispanic character" was the Frito Bandito—the Mexican bandit cartoon figure utilized repeatedly by the Frito-Lay Corporation in its television and print promotions of corn chips. In discussions about advertising racism and mistreatment of Hispanics, this example is often cited because of the complaints it generated, especially among Chicano activist and civic groups. Thanks in part to the public protests against Frito-Lay and activists threatening boycotts of television stations airing the commercials, the Frito Bandito figure was discontinued in 1971. The public objections by Hispanics during the 1970s led to some positive changes in the media during the 1970s, just at the dawn of the so-called Hispanic decade. As advertising and marketing companies began to recognize the profitability of this growing sector of society, Hispanic-oriented strategies began to emerge in these industries.

HISPANIC-ORIENTED PRINT MEDIA ✦ ✦ ✦ ✦ ✦ ✦ ✦ ✦ ✦ ✦ ✦ ✦ ✦ ✦

Unlike other ethnic groups, Hispanics have had a broad range of mass media directed at them. Beginning with the border newspapers of the 1800s up to present-day inroads in telecommunications, Hispanics have worked hard at establishing and maintaining print and electronic channels through which they can be informed and entertained in ways more relevant to their particular populations and cultures. While most of the Hispanic-oriented media have been in the Spanish language, many have been bilingual and in more recent times, fully English-language products specifically directed at Latinos. Likewise, Hispanics have been owners and producers of a number of mass media institutions oriented to them. However, a significant part of such media have been wholly or partially owned and operated by Anglo individuals or corporations. Whatever the language or ownership, one of the common aspects of all these media is that in their portrayals via images or words, and in their general employment practices, Latinos have been treated much more adequately. In these media, Hispanic life in the United States has been and continues to be presented and reflected more thoroughly, appropriately, and positively.

HISPANIC-ORIENTED NEWSPAPERS ✦ ✦ ✦ ✦ ✦ ✦ ✦ ✦ ✦ ✦ ✦ ✦ ✦

The Spanish-language press within the U.S. had its beginnings in 1808 in New Orleans, Louisiana, with *El Misisipí*, a four-page commercial-and trade-oriented publication. The paper, which was started by the Anglo firm of William H. Johnson & Company, appeared to be a business venture, its content was heavily influenced by events outside the United States, and it was directed toward Spanish-speaking immigrants—characteristics that were similar to those of other Hispanic-oriented publications that followed.

After the inauguration of *El Misisipí*, dozens of Spanish-language newspapers and periodicals, founded by Mexican pioneers of the times, were published in the southwestern territories, which belonged to Mexico until the 1850s. In fact, the very first printing press in the Americas was brought to Mexico from Spain in 1535.

At present, nine Spanish-language newspapers are published daily—two in New York, two in Miami, one in Los Angeles, one in Chicago, and three in El Paso, Texas. Additionally, Hispanics are served by one hundred thirty-three community newspapers throughout the country.

La Opinión (Los Angeles) began publishing on September 16, 1926. It was founded by Ignacio E. Lozano, Sr., a Mexican national who wanted to provide news of the native homeland as well as of the new country for the growing Mexican population in southern California. Lozano went to Los Angeles after working during four years for two Texas newspapers and owning and editing his own paper—*La Prensa* of San Antonio—from 1913 to 1926. The move to California was the result of Lozano's view that there were greater Mexican readership needs and opportunities on the West Coast.

From its beginning, *La Opinión* was owned and operated by Lozano and his family, which in 1926 formed Lozano Enterprises, Inc. This company also publishes *El Eco del Valle*, a weekly tabloid distributed in the San Fernando Valley since 1985. On September 28, 1990, 50 percent interest in Lozano Enterprises was purchased by the Times Mirror Company. This major media conglomerate has interests in broadcasting and cable television, and book and magazine publishing; it publishes *The Los Angeles Times*, *Newsday* (New York), and five other newspapers nationwide. With this association, *La Opinión* has acquired financial resources to enable it to continue improving its product. In spite of this new financial affiliation, the Lozano family maintains a majority on the board of directors and continues its full editorial policy and operational control. *La Opinión*'s circulation is approximately 109,000.

El Diario/La Prensa (New York) started in the summer of 1963 from the merger of two newspapers, *La Prensa* and *El Diario de Nueva York*. The former had been operating since 1913 under the ownership of José Campubrí, a Spaniard who kept the paper until 1957, when it was purchased by Fortune Pope. Pope, whose brother was the owner of *The National Enquirer,* was also the owner of the New York Italian paper *Il Progreso* and of WHOM-AM which later became WJIT-AM, one of the most popular

Contemporary Papers

For more than four centuries, "Hispanic" publications have circulated in this part of the world; some have lasted various decades while others only issued an edition or two. Among the Hispanic-oriented newspapers, the majority have been published in Spanish but many have been bilingual and a few have been in English but specifically directed at the regional or national Hispanic populations.

Spanish-language radio stations in New York. In 1963, Pope sold *La Prensa* to O. Roy Chalk, who bought *El Diario de Nueva York* in 1961 from Porfirio Domenicci, a Dominican who had started the paper in 1948.

With both papers under his control, Chalk, president of Diversified Media, merged *El Diario* and *La Prensa.* In 1981, he sold it to Gannett, which at the time owned a chain of ninety English-language papers. In 1989 El Diario Associates, Inc. was formed by Peter Davidson, a former Morgan Stanley specialist in newspaper industry mergers and acquisitions. This new company then bought *El Diario/La Prensa* from Gannett in August 1989 for an estimated 20 million dollars. Carlos D. Ramírez, a Puerto Rican from New York who had been publisher of this newspaper since 1984, stayed on board to participate as a partner of El Diario Associates.

Since their beginnings, *La Prensa* and *El Diario de Nueva York* had been primarily directed at the Puerto Rican, Spanish, and Dominican communities in New York. Presently, *El Diario/La Prensa* caters to a more diverse Hispanic population that, although still principally Puerto Rican, is increasingly more Dominican and Central and South American. Its current circulation is approximately 48,000.

Noticias del Mundo (New York) began publishing on April 22, 1980 under the ownership of News World Communications, Inc., which also publishes the *Washington Times,* the *New York City Tribune,* and various other publications, including *Ultimas Noticias,* a daily newspaper in Uruguay. *Noticias del Mundo*'s circulation hovers around 32,000 in the New York metro area.

El Nuevo Herald (Miami) was started on November 21, 1987, as a new and improved version of *El Miami Herald,* which had been continuously published since March 29, 1976, as an insert to *The Miami Herald.* Both the Spanish-language and the English-language newspapers are owned by The Miami Herald Publishing Company, a subsidiary of the Knight-Ridder newspaper chain, which has holdings in twenty-nine newspapers across the United States.

In 1987, The Miami Herald Publishing Company recognized the geometric growth of the Hispanic populations in south Florida and, with the support and approval of the Knight-Ridder Corporation, began assessing what Hispanic readers wanted in their Spanish-language daily. The outcome of the study was *El Nuevo Herald*, which moved to a separate build-ing from that of its English-language counterpart to begin publishing from a location closer to the Hispanic community. Other improvements in-cluded a 150 percent increase of the daily news space, better coverage of the Cuban and Latin American events and communities, and the use of color with modern format, graphics, and layout.

As might be expected, given the demographics of Miami and southern Florida, since its beginnings the principal readers of *El Nuevo Herald* have been immigrant Cuban and Latin American populations residing in that area. This broadsheet paper, in contrast to its New York counterparts, reaches the majority of its readers via home delivery. Its daily circulation is approximately 102,000 and its Sunday circulation is 126,000.

Aside from the news gathering by its own staff, *El Nuevo Herald* can bene-fit from the work of its English-language partner, including the use of translated stories from the international correspondents. For major sto-ries, *El Nuevo Herald* may send its own reporters to Latin America. Thus, *The Miami Herald* may use stories gathered by *El Nuevo Herald*'s foreign or local reporters.

El Diario de las Américas (Miami) was founded on July 4, 1953, by Horacio Aguirre, a Nicaraguan lawyer who had been an editorial writer for a Pana-manian newspaper, *El Panamá-América,* directed by Harmodio Arias, a former president of that country. Part of the financial support needed for starting *El Diario de las Américas* was made possible thanks to a Venezue-lan builder-investor and two Pensacola, Florida, road builders who also believed in the founder's mission. The paper is published by The Ameri-cas Publishing Company, which is owned by the Aguirre family. *El Diario de las Américas* remains the only Spanish-language daily owned and oper-ated by Hispanics without full or partial partnership by Anglo corpora-tions. The Cuban and Latin American interests of their readership are evi-dently reflected in the strong international—particularly Latin American—news coverage of the paper. Its circulation is currently ap-proximately 70,000.

In addition, other daily publications serve Hispanic communities. The oldest is the Spanish-language page of *The Laredo Morning Times*. This daily news page has been published continuously since 1926. Also pro-duced in the U.S. is *El Heraldo de Brownsville* (Texas), published seven

Dozens of Spanish-language newspapers from Spain, Mexico, Puerto Rico, Venezuela, Colombia, Chile, and numerous other Latin American countries reach the newsstands in U.S. cities with large Hispanic populations. They are important sources of information widely sought and read.

days a week by *The Brownsville Herald*. This edition was inaugurated on November 11, 1934, by Oscar del Castillo, who was the founder and editor from its beginning until his death on January 19, 1991. Marcelino González is the current director of this paper serving the Texas Rio Grande Valley region.

Other daily publications include *El Fronterizo, El Mexicano,* and *El Continental*—respectively the morning, afternoon, and evening editions published by the Compañia Periodística del Sol de Ciudad Juárez. *El Fronterizo,* published since 1943, is the largest of the three, with six daily sections each of approximately eight pages. As of mid-1991, its circulation was approximately 36,000 Monday through Sundays. *El Mexicano,* published since 1950, is more condensed and contains about ten pages; its circulation figures are 29,000 Monday through Saturdays. *El Continental*, founded in 1933, has only eight pages and a Monday through Saturday circulation of 8,000. While all three newspapers have as major clients the Mexicans and Hispanics in El Paso and surrounding communities, they are published in Ciudad Juárez by the Organización Editorial Mexicana, representing seventy-eight newspapers in that country.

Additionally, *El Mañana* is the daily paper serving Chicago. It was founded in May 1971 by Gorki Tellez, who at the time was a community activist and owner of a small truck catering business. Its current circulation is around 20,000.

HISPANIC-ORIENTED MAGAZINES AND PERIODICALS ◆ ◆ ◆ ◆ ◆

Long before the turn of the century, a variety of publications that can be classified as Hispanic-oriented magazines have been produced. The rich history of these publications can be observed in the holdings of major libraries such as the Benson Mexican American collection at the University of Texas at Austin and the Chicano Studies Collections of the University of California, Berkeley, Los Angeles, and Santa Barbara. While a comprehensive anthology of all such publications is still lacking, even a cursory review of the titles shows that culturally-oriented magazines have abounded, as have many with political, social, education, business, and entertainment topics. More than eighty consumer magazines circulate throughout the U.S.

Of current Spanish-language magazines, the oldest is *Temas,* founded in November 1950. It circulates more than 110,000 copies per month. *Temas* features articles on culture, current events, beauty, fashion, home decoration, and interviews with personalities of various artistic and academic backgrounds of interest to Hispanics. This general interest, family-oriented magazine was founded by publisher and editor José de la Vega, a Spaniard, who has indicated that *Temas* is the only national magazine published in Castilian Spanish without trendy "idioms." Given this editorial style, many of its articles are widely reprinted in high school and university reading packages across the country.

Another notable magazine, *Réplica,* was founded in 1963 by Alex Lesnik, a Cuban immigrant. From its base in Miami, this monthly magazine has a circulation of 111,000 nationwide, of which approximately 96 percent was controlled—targeted to reach bilingual, bicultural, affluent opinion makers and other influential Hispanics in the United States. It includes a variety of articles on topics such as travel, fashion, sports, entertainment, and news events related to Latin America and the Caribbean Basin.

Three English-language magazines of particular note are *Hispanic, Hispanic Business,* and *Hispanic Link.* Founded in 1988, *Hispanic's* major focus is on contemporary Hispanics and their achievements and contributions to American society. Thus, the stories cover a broad range of topics, such as entertainment, education, business, sports, the arts, government, politics, literature, and national and international personalities and events that may be of importance and interest to Hispanics in the United States. A family company of chairman and founder Fred Estrada, a native of Cuba, his son, Alfredo, is the current publisher. The first publisher was Jerry Apodaca, a Mexican American and former governor of New Mexico. Published monthly, its circulation is approximately 150,000.

Hispanic Business is run by editor and publisher, Jesús Chavarría, a Mexican American who started the magazine in 1979 as a newsletter. In 1982 it became a monthly publication; current circulation is approximately 166,000. One of its regular departments covers news related to "Media/Marketing." Special monthly topics include, among others, statistics and trends in the Hispanic media markets (December); the Hispanic "Business 500"—the annual directories of the leading Hispanic-owned corporations in the United States (June); and Hispanics in the general market television, film, music, and related entertainment businesses (July).

Another English-language Hispanic-oriented publication is *Hispanic Link.* Although it is a newsletter, it is an influential publication that provides a succinct summary of the major issues and events related to education, immigration, business, legislative, political, policy, and economic concerns of the Hispanic populations. Weekly summary columns include "Arts and Entertainment" and a "Media Report." *Hispanic Link* was founded by Mexican American Charles A. Erickson in February 1980 as a column service for newspapers. In September 1983 it became a regular newsletter. Although it only claims approximately 1,200 subscribers, its circulation and readership is much higher as it reaches many libraries, Hispanic organization leaders, people in corporations with major responsibilities toward Hispanics, journalists, Hispanic advocacy groups, and influential government officials working with or interested in legislation and policy issues related to Hispanics. *Hispanic Link* solicits columns from various journalists and experts on subjects concerning Hispanics and provides those articles as a syndicated service of three columns per week to more than eighty-five newspapers across the country via the *Los Angeles Times* syndicated news service.

Two notable bilingual magazines are *Vista* and *Saludos Hispanos* (Regards, Hispanics). *Vista* started in September 1985 as a monthly supplement insert to selected Sunday newspapers in locations with large Hispanic populations. Although *Vista* was published in English on a weekly basis from late 1989 through June 1991, financial problems resulting from the general national economic situation, particularly insufficient advertising support, made it return to its monthly schedule. Since June 1991, in addition to its English-language articles, it has incorporated "mosaico"—a Spanish-language supplement with three stories. *Vista* is aimed at informing, educating, and entertaining Hispanic American readers with stories that focus on Hispanic role models, positive portrayals of Hispanics, and their cultural identity. As of July 1994, *Vista* was inserted in thirty-eight different newspapers in seven states—Arizona, California, Florida, Illinois, New Mexico, New York, and Texas. Its current circulation is more than 1 million. In 1991 the magazine was purchased by Fred Estrada and his Hispanic Publishing Corporation.

Saludos Hispanos, "the official publication of the United Council of Spanish Speaking People," is owned by Rosemarie García-Solomon, a Mexican American. A significant part of its approximately 300,000 circulation goes to about three thousand schools, universities, and various institutions in California, Florida, Illinois, New York, and Texas, which use the magazine for educational purposes. One reason for *Saludos Hispanos*'s educational value is that it publishes side-by-side Spanish and English versions of most of its stories. Furthermore, it stresses positive role models for and about Hispanics. In addition to articles on the feature topic, the regular departments include, among others, role models, music, careers, earth watch, university profile, fashion, law and order, museums, and food.

Another educational distinction of this publication company is its *Saludos Hispanos Video Magazín*—a three-part video program that has been used by over four thousand schools and organizations for recruitment and retention of Hispanic youth in the educational system. The video, available in English and a Spanish-language dubbed version, is designed to motivate Hispanic youth to stay in school, to improve relationships, and to stress the importance of cultural pride and self-esteem as keys to success.

Dozens of Spanish-language consumer magazines cover specialized topics related to parenthood, fashion, hobbies, and social, cultural, and political interests. All are readily available in the United States via subscriptions or magazine racks in Hispanic communities in major cities. Examples of these are *Buenhogar, Cosmopolitan, Geomundo, Hombre del Mundo, Harper's Bazaar en Español, Mecánica Popular, Selecciones del Reader's Digest, Tu Internacional,* and *Vanidades Continental,* just to name a few of the most popular. As can be observed by the titles, some are Spanish-language editions of English-language publications. Regardless of where these are produced, be it Spain, the United States, or Latin America, they have as primary clients any and all Spanish-speaking populations.

Other specialized magazines in Spanish and/or English are produced with the Hispanic as the primary client, for example, *Automundo, Buena Salud, Career Focus* (also targeted to Afro-Americans), *Embarazo, Hispanic American Family, Hispanic Youth-USA, Mi Bebé, Ser Padre, Teleguía, TV y Novelas USA, Una Nueva Vida,* the northeastern U.S. edition of *Imagen,* and the Hispanic youth-oriented automobile publication *Lowrider.*

Furthermore, there are journals with specialized topics related to academia, professions, and organizations. Among the current academic journals are *Aztlán, The Americas Review,* the *Bulletin of the Centro de Estudios Puertorriqueños,* the *Hispanic Journal of Behavioral Sciences, Journal of Hispanic Policy,* and the *Latino Studies Journal.*

And finally, there are state and regional publications aimed at the respective Hispanic or Spanish-speaking populations. Examples of these are

Adelante (Washington, D.C.), *Avance Hispano* (San Francisco), *Cambio!* (Phoenix), *La Voz de Houston* (Houston), *La Voz* (Seattle), *Miami Mensual*, and *Bienvenidos a Miami, Tele Guía de Chicago* and *Lea* (directed at Colombians residing in the United States). In these cities and dozens of others with large Hispanic concentrations, one can even find Spanish and/or Hispanic yellow pages—the telephone-type directories.

HISPANIC-ORIENTED ELECTRONIC MEDIA ♦ ♦ ♦ ♦ ♦ ♦ ♦ ♦ ♦ ♦ ♦

Today hundreds of Spanish-language radio stations, a couple of Hispanic commercial and public radio owners' associations, various specialized news services, and at least five major advertising representatives target this expanding market.

The number of stations, companies, and organizations related to Spanish-language radio and television in this country has grown, as has the content they offer. Radio, for example, not only offers *rancheras* and *salsa*, but also Top 40, mariachi, *norteña*, Tex-Mex, Mexican hits, adult contemporary, contemporary Latin hits, international hits, Spanish adult contemporary, romantic, ballads, traditional hits and oldies, folkloric, regional, *boleros*, progressive *tejano*, *merengue*, and even bilingual contemporary hits. Television is no longer song-and-dance shows with some novelas and old movies. It is also drama, talk shows, comedy, news, investigative journalism, sports, contemporary movies, entertainment magazines, dance videos, and many specials from all over the world. All of these options have been brought by the search for new markets by both Hispanic and Anglo entrepreneurs, and the combined growth of the Hispanic population and its purchasing power.

In some markets the Hispanic audience for selected Spanish-language radio and television stations is larger than that of many well-known English-language stations; for example, in Los Angeles, KLVE-FM and KWKW-AM have more listeners than KNX-AM and KROQ-FM. Radio directed especially to the Hispanic market has grown from an occasional voice heard on isolated stations in the Southwest and on big city multilingual stations to a multimillion-dollar segment of the broadcast industry.

Radio:
The Early Years

Spanish-language radio programs transmitted from within the boundaries of the United States began as early as the mid-1920s—almost immediately after the inauguration of commercial broadcasting in this country. While Hispanic-oriented radio is now quite diversified and can be found in almost every community with an established Hispanic population, its development has been and difficult. Spanish-language radio started in the mid-1920s when English-language radio stations began selling time slots to Latino brokers. During the early days of radio, the stations that sold these slots and the time frames that were made available to brokers depended on the local market competition among stations and the profitability of the various airtimes. Invariably, space for foreign-language programming was provided primarily during the least profitable time (early mornings or weekends) and by stations seeking alternative avenues for revenue.

One of the most well known pioneers of Spanish-language radio in California was Pedro J. González, about whom two films have been made: the documentary *Ballad of an Unsung Hero* (1984, Paul Espinosa, writer and producer) and the full-length feature *Break of Dawn* (1988, Isaac Artenstein, director). Between 1924 and 1934 González was responsible for shows such as "Los Madrugadores" (The Early Birds). This program was broadcast from 4:00 to 6:00 A.M., primarily on Los Angeles station KMPC, which thanks to its 100,000-watt power could be heard at that time all over the Southwest—even as far as Texas—thus reaching thousands of Mexican workers as they started their day. The dynamics of González's show and his progressive political stands made him a threat to the establishment, resulting in trumped-up rape charges against him in 1934. He was convicted and condemned to six years in San Quentin prison, released in 1940, and immediately deported to Mexico. In Tijuana he reestablished and continued his radio career until the 1970s, when he retired to the United States. Many others across the Southwest followed Pedro's footsteps in the new medium.

Even through the early brokerage system, Spanish-language radio thrived. By the late 1930s, numerous stations carried Spanish-language programs either full-time or part-time. In response to the market demands, in 1939 the International Broadcasting Company (IBC) was established in El Paso, Texas, to produce and sell Spanish-language programming to various stations and brokers across the country. As a result of the efforts of services like the IBC and the work by dozens of independent brokers, by 1941 it was estimated that 264 hours of Spanish were being broadcast each week by U.S. broadcasters.

In Texas, Raúl Cortez was one of the earliest Chicano brokers and eventually was successful enough to establish and operate his own full-time Spanish-language station—KCOR-AM, a 1,000-kilowatt "daytime only"

At Spanish-language broadcast stations, almost all the announcers came from Latin America, in spite of the growth of the Hispanic audiences. While no research has been done to explain this, it is perhaps because station managers perceived that the Spanish of Hispanics was of poorer quality.

station in San Antonio—which went on the air in 1946. Nine years later, Cortez ventured into the Spanish-language television industry. After World War II, Anglo station owners and Hispanic brokers saw increasing opportunities in the Hispanic market via Spanish-language radio. This allowed some brokers to follow Cortez's lead and become owners of full-time stations. Most, however, were made employees of the stations they had been buying time from.

From the 1950s to the 1970s, Spanish-language radio was in transition. During those decades, this radio format continued to grow but began moving away from the brokerage system in favor of the more independent, full-time stations in AM and subsequently in FM—many transmitting up to twenty-four hours per day. In terms of the content, the early "broker" years were characterized by poetry, live drama, news, and live music programming. Most of the live music was "Mexican" and the majority of the news was from foreign countries, predominantly Mexico. As musical recordings became more common, this less expensive form of programming replaced the live music, allowing brokers and the stations to keep more of their profits for themselves. During the transition years, "personality radio" was at its best; brokers and announcers who had control over their programs and commercials became popular themselves. By the late 1960s, the format became more tightly packaged and was less in the hands of individual radio stars. Music was selected by the station management to give a consistent sound throughout the programs. These broadcasts had less talk than before and were very much like other music-oriented English-language programs. In the 1970s, the stations' growth also brought increased attention to format programming on the air and to sophisticated marketing techniques on the business side.

Contemporary Spanish Radio

Currently, approximately 35 AM and 115 FM radio stations are broadcasting full-time Spanish-language programming. An additional 75 AM and 15 FM stations dedicate a significant part (but not the majority) of their broadcast time to Spanish programming. Spanish-language radio is a powerful and growing medium in the United States.

While these numbers attest to a remarkable growth of the Hispanic-oriented radio industry, Hispanic *ownership* of these radio stations has not followed similar patterns. In 1980 of the 64 primary Spanish-language radio stations identified in their study, only 25 percent were owned by Latinos. In the top ten markets (for example, New York, Los Angeles,

Chicago, Miami, San Antonio), Latinos owned only about 10 percent of these types of stations. Primary Spanish-language radio (PSLR) stations are those that transmit in Spanish 50 percent or more of their broadcast day. Additionally, PSLR stations are owned and operated predominantly by Anglos.

An important issue about the ownership of Hispanic-oriented radio is the trend toward concentration of various stations, particularly the most profitable ones, under major corporate groups. The oldest and largest of these is Tichenor Media System, Inc., a family-owned private company based in Dallas, Texas, which presently owns eleven full-time Spanish-language radio stations in the following locations: New York (WADO-AM), Miami (WQBA-AM and FM), Chicago (WIND-AM and WOJO-FM), San Antonio (KCOR-AM), Houston (KLAT-AM), Brownsville-Harlingen-McAllen (KGBT-AM and KIWW-FM), and El Paso (KBNA-AM and FM). Tichenor also has partial ownership of another Spanish-language station in Corpus Christi (KUNO-AM).

This company was started in 1940 by McHenry Tichenor, a successful Anglo newspaperman who in 1941 bought his second radio station in south Texas, which at the time broadcast half a day in English and half a day in Spanish. This was the family's first venture into the Hispanic market. The expansion into the Spanish radio field began in 1984 with the formation of Tichenor Spanish Radio. At that time, the non-Spanish-language broadcast properties, including television, were divested to allow for the new ventures into the Hispanic market. In 1990, Spanish Radio Network was formed in partnership with SRN Texas, Inc. (a wholly owned subsidiary of Tichenor Media System) and Radio WADO, Inc., in order to purchase the Miami and the New York stations.

The second-largest group owner of Spanish-language radio stations is Spanish Broadcasting System (SBS), which was started in 1983 by Raúl Alarcón, Jr. This company, the only radio group company whose proprietors are Hispanics, now owns six stations in the top three Latino markets: New York (WSKQ-AM and FM), Los Angeles (KSKQ-AM and FM), and Miami (WCMQ-AM and FM), plus a station in Key Largo, Florida (WZMQ-FM), that retransmits the Miami station's signals. In addition to its own stations, SBS is the national sales representative for six stations in Texas, six in California, and three in Illinois. The company also develops revenues from its SBS Promotions (for example, of concerts, sporting events, supermarket tie-ins, and on-air contests) and from Alarcón holdings in real estate. In 1993, SBS's combined capital of $42 million made it the fifty-seventh-largest Hispanic company.

Lotus Communications Corporation owns a third group of Spanish-language radio stations. The flagstaff operation is KWKW-AM, a station that has been serving the Hispanic community in Los Angeles and vicinities since 1942. It was purchased by Lotus in 1962 for approximately one million dollars. The price was a reflection of the large audience it attracts, especially among the Mexican and Mexican-American populations of that region. A recent audience estimate placed the number of listeners at over one million (at least during one "day-part," that is, time segment), making it among the largest in the United States and a few Latin American cities. Other Spanish-language stations owned by Lotus are KOXR-AM in Oxnard, California (bought in 1968), WTAQ-AM in Chicago (since 1985), and KGST-AM in Fresno (since 1986). All four of these stations are identified as La Mexicana in their respective markets because the music, programming, and the disc jockeys follow a Mexican format in idioms and accents. Another distinctive programming feature of these stations is that they broadcast Los Angeles Dodger baseball games and retransmit these to 148 stations in Mexico. Lotus owns ten other radio outlets in the United States, all of which are English-language stations. In addition, under Lotus Hispanic Reps, this company is sales representative to approximately one hundred Spanish-language radio stations in the United States. The president of Lotus Communications is Howard Kalmenson; the vice president is Jim Kalmenson. Both are Anglos, as are the other owners of the company. The executive vice president is Joe Cabrera; he is Hispanic, as are the respective station managers. In 1993, billings for KWKW on its own totaled $14 million, making it the single most profitable Spanish-language station in the country. According to Kalmenson, the success of this station has helped fund the growth of the entire company, which continues its operations with no capital debt.

A fourth Spanish-language radio group is *Radio América*, founded in 1986 when brothers Daniel and James Villanueva, of Mexican heritage, bought stations KBRG-FM in the San Francisco Bay Area. In 1988, they acquired station KLOK-AM in the San Jose/San Francisco area. Villanuevas, under a separate company called Orange County Broadcasting, purchased station KPLS-AM in Los Angeles. A distinctive characteristic of this station, with 20 percent ownership by Fernando Niebla, also of Mexican descent, is that it is the first "all talk" Spanish-language station in the Los Angeles and southern California area (there are four "talk" stations in the Miami market). Daniel Villanueva also has minority (20 percent) interests in Washington, D.C.'s Los Cerezos Broadcasting Company, which owns WMDO-AM and WMDO-TV Channel 48—a Univisión affiliate.

Yet another Spanish-language radio group is the *Viva América* company, which was started in 1989 with 49 percent owned by Heftel Broadcasting and 51 percent owned by Mambisa Broadcasting Corporation. Heftel owns stations in Los Angeles (KLVE-FM and KTNQ-AM). Mambisa is divided among Amancio V. Suárez, his son Amancio J. Suárez, and cousin Charles Fernández, all of whom are of Cuban descent. In Miami, the Viva America Media Group owns two stations (WAQI-AM and WXDJ-FM). In addition, under the corporate heading of the Southern Media Holding Group, presided over by Amancio V. Suárez, it is also linked to *Mi Casa*—a monthly Spanish-language newspaper. In spite of its recent entry into the market, Viva América earned $10.1 million in billings in 1991, almost doubling the figure of the previous year; the two Heftel stations were the top in the Spanish-language radio market, totaling $16.3 million for the same year.

A final group of stations that are especially distinct from the aforementioned ones are administered by the nonprofit Radio Bilingüe (Bilingual Radio) network in California. Efforts to establish this network date to 1976, when Hugo Morales, a Harvard Law School graduate of Mexican Mixtec Indian heritage, and Lupe Ortiz y Roberto Páramo, in collaboration with a group of Mexican peasants, artists, and activists sought to use radio to improve life and sustain the cultural identity of farm workers of the San Joaquin Valley. With the significant backing of a grant from a Catholic charity, KSJV-FM was launched in Fresno, California, on July 4, 1980. It transmits a variety of music programs, plus a diversity of information related to health, education, immigration, civic action, and the arts. Supported primarily by donations from community members, businesses, and some foundations, the Radio Bilingüe network now reaches across central California via KSJV and two retransmitting stations in Bakersfield and Modesto. In southern California, some of the network's programs are also aired by affiliate KUBO-FM, which started in El Centro on April, 1989, producing some of its own independent programming. Radio Bilingüe also sponsors the "Viva El Mariachi" (Long Live the Mariachi), a music festival that serves as an important fund-raiser for the network. One of the distinctive features of this network is the operational and programming support it receives from innumerable volunteers who produce diverse music and public service programs in English, Spanish, and bilingual format.

Due to increased pressures in the commercial and public radio markets, two organizations serving the interests of this sector were established in 1991. The first was the American Hispanic-Owned Radio Association (AHORA), which started with fifty-five Hispanic station owners concerned with competition for the Hispanic market and with the rapid pace at which Spanish-language radio stations are being bought by non-Hispanics. AHORA, under the direction of Mary Helen Barro (majority owner of KAFY-AM in Bakersfield, California), seeks to increase the number of business opportunities for Hispanic broadcasters and to attract more Hispanic talent to broadcasting; its agenda also includes encouraging the government to include Spanish-language radio stations in government media buys.

With June 1991 as its organization date, another professional radio group is Hispanics in Public Radio (HPR). This nonprofit professional organization is designed to provide a forum for the expression of the needs and interests of Hispanic Americans involved with public radio and proposes to represent the interests of Hispanic-controlled public radio stations with the goal of improving the financial resources of the stations.

Radio News and Other Program Providers

Although some stations produce everything they broadcast, including news and commercials, many stations depend on various companies dedicated to packaging programs for the Spanish-language radio market. Two types of providers merit special attention: those that provide news services and the ones that provide "full service."

Among the major news service providers, the oldest is *Spanish Information Systems* (SIS), inaugurated in 1976. From its headquarters in Dallas, Texas, it distributes via satellite Spanish-language news programs. They also transmit "SIS al Día" (SIS to Date), a fifteen-minute radio magazine that includes segments on current affairs, cooking, health, and sports. SIS is a division of Command Communications, Inc., an Anglo-controlled company that also owns Texas State Network—a nationwide English-language information service and sports news network.

Another radio news provider is Radio Noticias (News Radio), which began in 1983 as a division in Spanish of United Press International (UPI), once one of the major wire services in the world. From its base in Washington, D.C., Radio Noticias distributes its news program on an hourly basis.

A third news provider is Noticiero Latino, produced by Radio Bilingüe in Fresno, California. This news service, which began in 1985, is unique in that it is the only Spanish news service produced by a nonprofit network in the United States whose proprietaries and coordinators are Latino residents of this country. It is also unique because it is exclusively dedicated to informing and helping to interpret events in the United States, Latin America, and the Caribbean that are related to Hispanics, for example, immigration, civil rights, health, education, culture, and successes of Hispanics. Using information gathered by its local reporters and network of correspondents in the United States, Mexico, and Puerto Rico, Noticiero Latino offers a daily news program. Noticiero Latino's news services are used by stations in the United States, Puerto Rico, and Mexico.

Among the "full service" providers of Spanish-language programming, the oldest and largest is Cadena Radio Centro (CRC)—a network founded in 1985 in Dallas, Texas. CRC is a subsidiary of Organización Radio Centro, a Mexican company controlled by the Aguirre family. In the United States the president of Cadena Radio Centro is Barrett Alley, and the vice chairman is Carlos Aguirre—a controlling family heir. This U.S. radio network offers its news services to affiliated Spanish-language stations linked via satellite.

With its starting date in March 1991, Hispano U.S.A., claims to be the first Hispanic-owned and -operated Spanish network service. According to a company informational brochure, Hispano U.S.A. sells "Spanish radio programming for the 90's, designed for cost-efficient station operations which benefits resident as well as absentee ownership." The programming, which is transmitted via satellite, features "top 40 Hispanic dance tunes," and national and international news, including sports and weekend special reports.

Another major provider of Spanish-language radio programs is CBS Hispanic Radio Network (CBSHRN), which focuses on sports and entertainment special events. CBS Hispanic Radio Network started its Spanish-language programming in Latin America in the mid-1970s with baseball specials. When it began in the United States, it was affiliated with Caballero Hispanic media representatives to provide such programs to the stations represented by Caballero, but in 1990 it established its own syndication network.

Hispanic-Oriented Television

As was the case for radio, Spanish-language television transmissions started almost as soon as they began in the English-language medium. Since the 1940s, entrepreneurs have found a significant market and profits transmitting to the Hispanic populations in the United States. Spanish-language television has grown enormously from the early days of a few brokered hours on some English-language stations in San Antonio and New York. In 1993, over $324 million in advertising was spent in national network and local Spanish-language television.

The Early Years

The first Spanish-language television station in the United States was San Antonio's KCOR-TV Channel 41, which began some evening programs in 1955. But a few years before KCOR and similar stations started, several Spanish-language radio entrepreneurs recognized the potential of the Spanish-speaking television audiences and pioneered the way by producing special TV programs. Following the pattern used in the early stages of Spanish-language radio, time was brokered for these programs in the nascent English-language stations in selected cities.

During the 1960s, part-time Spanish-language programs on English-language stations emerged in various cities with large concentrations of Hispanics, such as Los Angeles, Houston, Miami, Phoenix, Tucson, and Chicago. Most often such programs—sponsored primarily by a local company—would be the outcome of personal efforts of Hispanic entrepreneurs, many of whom had experience with radio. Some stations provided time for these in order to seek alternative sources of profits or to comply with Federal Communications Commission (FCC) requirements of public service programs.

From Spanish International Network to Univisión

The experiences of Hispanic entrepreneurs and their part-time Spanish-language television programs eventually led the way to establishing separate stations especially directed at Hispanic viewers. The pioneer behind the KCOR effort was Raúl Cortez, the same owner of KCOR-AM, which was itself the first Hispanic-owned and operated Spanish-language radio station in the United States. KCOR-TV began in 1955, broadcasting from 5:00 P.M. to midnight. Emilio Nicolás, one of the first general managers of the station, recalls that approximately 50 percent of the programs were live variety and entertainment shows that featured a host of the best available talent from Mexico. Many of these shows took place in the studios of

Cortez's radio station, which aired these programs simultaneously. Movies and other prerecorded programs imported primarily from Mexico accounted for the rest of the early offerings of Channel 41.

Although the station was very popular among the Mexican and other Spanish-speaking residents of San Antonio and vicinities, Nicolás recalls that advertisers did not acknowledge this market and failed to use it extensively for commercial promotions. During those early years of the medium, Hispanic viewers were not accounted for in the standard ratings services. One reason for this, according to Nicolás, was that in the 1940s and 1950s Mexicans were cautious in either acknowledging their heritage or exposure to Spanish-language media for fear of blatant discriminatory practices. Thus, Cortez, after spending heavily on the live talent imported from Mexico and receiving limited financial support from the advertising agencies, was forced to sell the television station to an Anglo. He kept the KCOR call letters for his radio station, but the television station's were changed to KUAL. The station continued some Spanish-language programs, and in 1961 these call letters changed again to KWEX when Channel 41 was sold to Don Emilio Azcárraga Vidaurreta and his financial partners, who then went on to establish the first Spanish-language television network.

Until his death in 1972, Don Emilio Azcárraga Vidaurreta was the most prominent media magnate in Mexico. With his family, he owned and operated a significant part of the country's commercial radio system and the emerging Telesistema Mexicano S.A. (Sociedad Anónima), broadcasting empire. In the United States, Don Emilio, his son Emilio Azcárraga Milmo, and Reynold (René) Anselmo became central figures in not only the purchase of San Antonio's Channel 41 but also in the establishment of the largest and most influential businesses related to Spanish-language television broadcasting.

The most significant development of Spanish-language television in the United States began when Spanish International Communications Corporation (SICC) was initiated and organized by René Anselmo and bankrolled by Azcárraga Vidaurreta, along with minority investors having U.S. citizenship. Since SICC (which at one point was called Spanish International Broadcasting Corporation, SIBC) was to hold the licenses of the stations, the corporation was structured so that Azcárraga Vidaurreta, a Mexican citizen, would own only 20 percent of the company. Most of the other partners were U.S. citizens so as to conform with Federal Communication Act Section 310, which "prohibits the issuing of broadcast li-

Spanish-language radio stations, whether owned by Hispanics or Anglos, could be heard in practically every region of the United States. In some major metropolitan cities with large concentrations of Hispanics (New York, Los Angeles, Miami, Chicago, San Antonio, and Houston), Hispanics have a variety of such stations to choose from, each with a distinct format and music to please almost any of the major Latin American and United States Hispanic musical traditions. Through the news and other programming services, Spanish-speakers in the United States also have many opportunities to keep ties to their countries of origin, enjoy the diversity of entertainment shows, and be part of the news and cultural events in this country as well as around the Hispanic world.

Anselmo, a Boston-born Italian and associate of Azcárraga's Mexican media, was the main U.S. partner in the ensuing enterprises. Among other principal U.S. citizens of SICC at the time were Frank Fouce, owner of Los Angeles Spanish-language movie houses, including the famous Million Dollar Theater, and Edward Noble, an advertising executive in Mexico City. After obtaining KWEX, the SICC with the assistance of a few other partners bought Los Angeles station KMEX Channel 34 in 1962.

censes to aliens, to the representatives of aliens, or to corporations in which aliens control more than one-fifth of the stock."

Although there is a limitation in the amount of stock a foreign national can hold in a broadcast license, there apparently is no such restriction on U.S. television networks. Thus, in 1961 Don Emilio and Anselmo established the sister company Spanish International Network (SIN) to purchase and provide programming, virtually all of which originated from Azcárraga's production studios at Telesistema (later known as Televisa) in Mexico. The other function of SIN was to provide advertising sales for the SICC stations.

Over the next ten years the licensee corporation went through a series of expansions, mergers, and reorganizations as it added three other stations: WXTV Channel 41 in New York (1968); WLTV Channel 23, Miami (1971); and KFTV Channel 21, Fresno/Hanford (1972). The network was also extended with stations owned by some principals of SICC/SIN: under the Bahía de San Francisco company it was KDTV Channel 14, San Francisco (1974), and under Legend of Cibola (later known as Seven Hills Corporation) it was KTVW Channel 33, Phoenix (1976). In addition, SIN had the affiliation of five stations owned and operated by corporations not related to SIN/SICC; these were located in Albuquerque, Chicago, Corpus Christi, Houston, and Sacramento. Furthermore, SIN had four stations owned and operated by this company's parent corporation, Televisa, S.A. From their locations on the Mexican border at Juárez, Mexicali, Nuevo Laredo, and Tijuana, these stations served U.S. cities at, respectively, El Paso, El Centro, Laredo, and San Diego.

Until the mid-1970s, most of these stations shared the programming, which primarily came from Mexico's Productora de Teleprogramas (Pro-Tele, S.A.), a company created and controlled by Televisa as its export subsidiary. SIN imported and licensed taped shows, movies, and other programs that were transported to the Los Angeles station, sent to San Antonio, and then passed along in a "bicycle type network" to the other owned and affiliated stations. In September 1976, SIN became the first major broadcasting company, preceding CBS, ABC, and NBC, to distribute programming directly to its affiliates via domestic satellite.

In 1979, as cable connections became more readily available, another precedent was established as SIN began paying cable franchise operators to carry its satellite signals. Then in early 1980, SIN's outlets expanded further as the network was granted permission to establish low-power television (LPTV) stations (those whose signals only reach a radius of approximately twelve to fifteen miles). Altogether, by 1983 the Spanish-language television stations represented by SIN/SICC were reaching over 3.3 million Hispanic households across the United States. Advertising for the stations was sold in the United States, Mexico, and other Latin American countries.

Most of the programming broadcast by Univisión has been provided by Mexico's Televisa, with additional programs imported from Venezuela, Spain, Agrentina, and Brazil, and occasionally from Puerto Rico and other countries. *Telenovelas* continue to be very popular with the Latino audiences in the U.S. and elsewhere. However, game and variety shows, music festivals, comedies, and sports are also big attractions in this network. Since 1970, Univisión has had exclusive rights to broadcast the World Cup soccer championship in the U.S. Spanish-language market.

From the 1960s to the 1970s, Hispanic programs made within the United States usually consisted of public affairs programming and local newscasts, some of which were acclaimed for their excellent coverage of issues of concern to the local Hispanic communities.

A notable accomplishment of SIN (and Univisión) news has been its coverage of U.S. and Latin American political developments. The first U.S. national election night coverage in Spanish was in 1968; similar reports followed in subsequent years. Starting with the 1981 elections in Miami, in which two Hispanic candidates were finalists for mayor of that city, "Noticias 23" (News 23) and "Noticiero SIN" at the national level began giving ample time to present and analyze in Spanish the campaigns, issues, and personalities of the time. Pre- and postexit polls were also conducted by the stations and the network to share their projections and predictions of the electoral outcomes, especially among the Hispanic populations. At each station and at the network level, there was also a very strong campaign for voter registration.

In 1984, SIN launched "Destino '84" (Destiny '84), which further promoted voter registration and, through a series of special programs and reports, gave ample coverage to the presidential elections in the United States. Since then, Univisión produces "Destino" programs for every presidential and congressional election year. Reporters follow up the trends in Hispanic voting at the national level. Similar coverage is given to elections in Latin America, including polling activities beginning with the 1984 congressional and presidential elections in El Salvador, where their surveys were quite accurate in predicting the voting results. In subsequent years ample coverage was given to and more exit polls were conducted of elections in Guatemala, Peru, Honduras, Colombia, Costa Rica, and many other locations.

Most of the SICC stations did not operate in the black until a decade or more after they began operations. Nevertheless, the Azcárragas and their fellow investors recognized the growth potential of the Spanish-speaking television audience and market in the U.S., and were willing to subsidize the station group. When SICC did eventually generate profits, many of them found their way back to Mexico through the SIN pipeline. A falling out between Frank Fouce, one of SICC's principal investors, and René Anselmo, one of the creators and president of both SICC and SIN, led to a long, bitter stockholder derivative lawsuit that took more than ten years to settle. A second legal action against SICC was initiated at the FCC in 1980 when a group of radio broadcasters (the now-defunct Spanish Radio Broadcasters Association) charged that the company was under illegal foreign control. In January 1986, a judge appointed by the FCC ruled not to renew the licenses of the thireen SICC stations and ordered their transfer to U.S.-based entitites. This decision was followed by numerous legal appeals and challenges.

An intense and controversial bidding war in the same court that had heard the stockholder suit culminated in July 1986. Hallmark Cards, Inc., and its 25 percent partner, First Captial Corporation of Chicago, won with a $301.5 million bid for the SICC licenses and properties. The losing bidder was TVL Corporation, directed by a group of Hispanic investors who submitted a higher bid ($320 million) but whose financing was less secure. Legal challenges of the sale process brought by losing bidders were not resolved until April 1991.

As various appeals were being deliberated in federal court and at the FCC, SIN, and SICC were renamed Univisión on January 1, 1987. In Februrary, the cable service Galavisión, which was not included in the deal, split from Univisión and remained under the control of Televisa and Univisa. Univisa was Ascárraga's new enterprise established to house Galavisión and his remaining U.S. companies. In July of that year, Hallmark and First

Capital paid $286 million for the five original SICC stations and in August obtained actual control of the channels. Later, San Francisco station KDTV was purchased for an additional $274.5 million. With the transition, both the station group and the network continued operations under the name Univision Holdings, Inc., of which Hallmark became sole owner February 15, 1988.

In spite of its expansions and changes, by late 1991 Hallmark Cards Corporation was dissatisfied with its returns on its investments. Thus, in the spring of 1992 it sold the network to a group comprised of A. Jerrold Perenchio (a previous owner of the Spanish-language station WNJU in New Jersey, and an unsuccessful bidder for Univisión when Hallmark purchased it in 1986) and two of the richest and most influential media magnates in Latin America, Emilio Ascárraga Milmo (the controlling owner of the Mexican media conglomerate Televisa) and Gustavo and Ricardo Cisneros (of the powerful Venezuelan broadcast coporation Venevision). The arrangement was announced in April 1992 and approved by the FCC in September 1992. Perenchio had 76 percent ownership of the television station gorup and fifty percent ownership of the network, with Azcárraga and the Cisneros each holding 12 percent of the station group (to conform with U.S. foreign ownership laws) and 25 percent of the network.

This ownership change caused protest within and outside the industry and led to numerous changes among the top executives of Univisión. For example, network president Joaquín Blaya had not been forewarned of the sale, and within two months left his post to become president of Telemundo.

As of this writing, the Univisión-owned and operated Spanish-language television group is in the process of purchasing two new stations: WGBO Channell 66 in Chicago, and KXLN Channel 45 in Houston. It will then consist of thirteen full-power and one low-power stations. The network also has about a dozen affiliated UHF stations plus more than 600 cable carriers in all markets across the U.S. Its continuous programming reaches an estimated 92 percent of Hispanic households. Univisión programs are also seen in more than 18 countries in Latin America and Spain. Univisión Television Network's principal executives include Jaime Dávila, chairman and CEO; Ray Rodriguez, president and COO; Alina Falcón, director of news; and Mario Rodriguez, director of programming. For the television group, the executives are: A. Jerrold Perenchio, chairman and CEO; and Carlos Barba, president and COO.

Telemundo

While SIN and SICC were developing their powerful and far-reaching dominion, the growth and market potential of the Hispanic audience was being recognized by other interested parties, such as Saul Steinberg, chairman of the board and chief executive officer (CEO) of Reliance Capital Group, L.P., and Henry Silverman, the eventual president, CEO, and director of Telemundo. Together with their investment partners, they founded the Telemundo Group, Inc., which is currently the second-largest Spanish-language television network in the United States.

The organization of the Telemundo Group began in May 1986, when Reliance Capital Group acquired John Blair & Company, a diversified communications business. Blair had fallen prey to corporate raiders after an attempt at expansion left it overburdened with debt. Telemundo, as the successor to Blair, thus obtained stations WSCV Channel 51 in Miami and WKAQ Channel 2 in San Juan, Puerto Rico, which had been purchased by Blair in 1985 and 1983, respectively. Prior to its acquisition by Blair, WSCV was an English-language subscription television station. The station in Puerto Rico had been a major component of the Fundación Angel Ramos media enterprises and had its own islandwide retransmitter and affiliation network under the name adopted for the U.S. group—Cadena Telemundo. The change of name to Telemundo Group, Inc., was officially established on April 10, 1987. The company went public with offerings of common stock and bonds during the summers of 1987 and 1988.

Prior to forming the Telemundo Group, Reliance had entered the Hispanic media market in April 1985 with its ownership interests in Estrella Communications, Inc., which had been formed in January of that year for the purpose of buying Channel 52 in Los Angeles. Under the call letters KBSC and the corporate name SFN Communications, Inc., this station was owned by Columbia Pictures and A. Jerrold Perenchio, who had launched it in the late 1970s to compete with KMEX for Los Angeles's Hispanic audience. At the time, KBSC split its broadcast schedule, offering approximately ninety-five hours a week in Spanish. The remaining hours were sold to other programmers. In 1980 KBSC offered a pay-television service (ON-TV) in English at night and switched to full-time Spanish-language programs during the day. Much of that station's Spanish-language programming was supplied by government station Channel 13, of Mexico. When KBSC was put on the market in 1985, Reliance Capital, a large shareholder of Estrella Communications, purchased a greater proportion of the stock for $38 million and began operating the station with the new call letters KVEA. By December 1986, Reliance had spent $13.5 million to buy out the remaining minority holders of Estrella Communications, including some shares held by Hallmark Cards.

The third major component of the Telemundo Group was WNJU Channel 47, licensed in Linden, New Jersey, and serving the metropolitan New York area. It was because of the strength of its Spanish-language programs and Hispanic audience that WNJU was bought for approximately $75 million in December 1986 by Steinberg and his Reliance Capital Group.

The growth of Steinberg's television network continued in August 1987, when Telemundo bought out (for $15.5 million) National Group Television, Inc., the license holder of station KSTS Channel 48, serving the San Jose and San Francisco area. For the Houston/Galveston market, Telemundo invested $6.428 million to obtain the outstanding stock of Bluebonnet, which operated KTMD Channel 48 in that area in 1988. Another significant Hispanic market penetration came that year when Telemundo won over the affiliation, of Chicago's WSNS Channel 26, which had been associated with Univisión. Until then, Telemundo's link to Chicago had been WCIU Channel 26. A year later, entry was made into San Antonio with the affiliation, of KVDA Channel 60. In August, 1990, Telemundo paid $2.975 million to purchase 85 percent of the stock of Nueva Vista, which operated KVDA. With these stations, its affiliations and cable linkages, the Telemundo network was firmly established and available to more than 80 percent of Hispanic households.

As of this writing, the Telemundo-owned and operated Spanish-language television group consisted of 7 full-power stations (including the only VHF station, located in Puerto Rico) and 8 low-power stations. The network also counted on the affiliation of 12 full-power stations (three of these located in border cities in Mexico) and 24 low-power stations plus 470 cable carriers in the U.S. Approximately 135.5 hours of programming are broadcast weekly, reaching an estimated 85.4 percent of the Hispanic television households. In addition to Joaquín Blaya and Gustavo Pupo-Mayo, other executives of Telemundo are Peter Housman, Jr., president of business and corporate affairs; and José Cancela, president of the station group.

Galavisión

A third major player in Spanish-language television in the United States is Galavisión. This television company was launched in 1979 under parent

One of the distinct characteristics of this network's programming was the prompt venture to make local productions a large percentage of the offerings. In addition to news programming, Telemundo has continued its efforts of producing Hispanic-oriented as well as Latin American-oriented programs from its U.S. facilities. Joachin Blaya has made this one of his primary goals for the network, which presently produces more than fifty percent of its programming. The main types of programs are telenovelas, movies, news, talk shows, and game and variety shows.

company Univisa, Inc., a subsidiary of Mexico's Televisa. At that time, Galavisión was a premium cable service, offering recently produced Spanish-language movies along with coverage of select sporting events and special entertainment shows. In early 1988, it had only 160,000 subscribers. But in September of that year, after the entry of the Telemundo network and the consolidation of Hallmark's Univisión network, Univisa started to convert Galavisión's cable operations to an advertising-based basic cable service. This change expanded Galavisión's audience substantially as potentially 2 million cable subscribers were able to receive Galavisión's programs.

The new format offered continuous programming via a network feed provided by the Galaxy I and Spacenet 2 satellites. Galavisión expanded to over-the-air offerings when it affiliated stations KWHY Channel 22 in Los Angeles, KTFH Channel 49 in Houston, KSTV Channel 57 in Santa Barbara, and low-power retransmitters in seven other cities. KWHY and KTFH were converted from English-language stations; KSTV was licensed for the first time for Galavisión.

Galavisión, operating under the separate entity of SIN, Inc., was not included in the sales of SICC and SIN to Hallmark. Shortly after Televisa regained control of Univisión, Galavisión was placed under the management of Univisión. To avoid competition with its new sister network, contracts were terminated with the few stations that carried Galavisión over ther air (except the Houston broadcast affiliate); it thus became an almost exclusively cable delivery service. In May 1993 Galavisión announced its move to the Galaxy 1-R satellite as well as the addition of four new Spanish-language cable-exclusive netowrks: Telehit, a pop music video network; Telenovelas, a continuous soap operal channel; ECO, a 24-hour news channel, and Ritmosón, a video channel featuring nonstop Latin dance hits.

As of this writing, Galavisión broadcasts continuously, reaching approximately 28 percent (1.5 million) Hispanic households via 300 cable affiliates and its broadcast affiliate, KTFH Channel 49 in Houston. Executives include J. Manuel Calvo, vice-president and general manager, and Maria Elena Dieguez, director of programming.

Other Hispanic-Oriented Television Companies and Program Ventures

It can be expected that the aforementioned networks will capture the majority of the Hispanic audience in terms of general programming. However, several companies are seeking their own niche in this market. One of them is International TeleMúsica, Inc., which produces a show featuring international music videos, entertainment news, promotions and life-style segments. The programs, hosted by Alex Sellar, a Spaniard, and Pilar Isla, a native of Mexico, are produced in Hollywood using various California landscapes for settings. The target audience is Hispanic and Latin American youth. In 1990, Jesus Garza Rapport, executive vice president of Telemusica, started the company with full financial backing from Radio Programas de México (RPM). A Mexican company, RPM owns thirty and operates fifty radio stations in that country, and also owns one television station in Guadalajara, Mexico.

Viva Television Network, Inc., "the first U.S.-Latino owned national cable television network," as proclaimed in an informational brochure of the company, is also seeking its niche in the Hispanic market. Viva's goal was to provide sixteen-hour daily Spanish-language (and some English-language) programs, such as documentaries, public affairs, music, sports, comedy, news, children's shows, art films, and movies catering to the eighteen- to forty-nine-year-old Hispanic audience. The chief executive officer and one of the founders is Mark Carreño, a native of Cuba who has served as executive director of the Latino Consortium, a nationally syndicated network based at KCET-TV, Los Angeles's Public Broadcasting Station. Other founders and executive staff include chief operating officer Guillermo Rodríguez, a native of Puerto Rico who has worked with KMEX-TV and Lorimar Telepictures, and the vice president of international operations, Esteban de Icaza, of Mexican heritage, who was president of Azteca films, the foreign distribution company of the Mexican government. De Icaza's connections with that company and Imevisión, the Mexican government's educational television company, helped Viva obtain exclusive rights for telecasting selections from these companies' movie and video libraries, as well as Imevisión's newscasts. For program delivery, Viva subleased a transponder from the General Electric cable satellite and has agreements with multisystem cable operators in major Hispanic markets. The expected potential audience numbers from 300,000 to 1.5 million cable subscribers in the United States and Puerto Rico.

Home Box Office's Selecciones en Español (Selections in Spanish) is another significant venture to capture a niche in the U.S.-Hispanic television audience. In January 1989, this service was inaugurated to provide to HBO and Cinemax cable subscribers the option of Spanish-language audio for the telecast motion pictures and even some sporting events, such as boxing matches. This service is the brainchild of Lara Concepción, a native of Mexico, who after eight years of trying was able to persuade HBO's executives that there was a viable Hispanic market for such a service. The turning point for Concepción came shortly after the box office success of the Hispanic-theme movie La Bamba. Following a market study that further convinced HBO that it could expand its business with the Spanish-speaking audience, HBO scheduled about ten Spanish-dubbed movies per month in 1989. At first, Selecciones en Español was provided to twenty HBO and Cinemax cable operators in five cities: El Paso, Miami, New York, San Antonio, and San Diego. Shortly thereafter, the service was requested by an additional thirty-five cable firms and later by another fifteen. By the end of 1989, HBO expanded its dubbed activities and was offering an average of twenty movies per month in Spanish. In 1991, Selecciones en Español was carried by 182 cable systems within the United States. HBO and Cinemax cable operators have three methods for delivering this service: a channel dedicated to Selecciones, a Second Audio Program (SAP) channel available for stereo television sets or videocassette recorders with multiple channel television sound (MTS), and an FM tuner in which the affiliates can transmit the second audio feed via an FM modulator (that is, cable subscribers listen to the Spanish soundtrack on their FM radio).

Folowing up on its formidable success with the U.S. Spanish-speaking audience, HBO in October 1991 launched HBO-Olé pay-cable service in Latin America and the Caribbean Basin. This allows cable subscribers in more than twenty Latin American countries prompt access in Spanish to HBO's movies and other shows, which are supplied by Warner Brothers, 20th Century Fox, and Columbia TriStar International Television, which provides feature films from Columbia Pictures and TriStar Pictures.

Long before HBO started applying the Sanish-language audio and related technologies to establish their particular niches in the Hispanic market, other Anglo television businesses had successfully used SAP to provide selected programs to their audiences. In Los Angeles, one of the most successful ventures with Second Audio Program was Fox affiliate KTLA Channel 5. This station, now owned by the Tribune Broadcasting Company, was the pioneer in taking advantage of the Federal Communication Commission's 1984 rule authorizing broadcasters and cable providers to split up the single soundtrack into four audio channels. Henceforth, the first track was for the English audio, the second for stereo, the third for any alternate language, and the fourth for data transmission. In October 1984 KTLA broadcast the movie *2001: A Space Odyssey* and began offering the "The Love Boat," "McMillan & Wife," "Columbo," and "McCloud" in Spanish via the third audio channel. Dubbed editions of these programs were readily available because some Hollywood producers had a long-standing policy of dubbing many of their programs for their Latin American markets. Then, in February 1985, KTLA hired Analía Sarno-Riggle to be the Spanish interpreter of the "News at Ten," which airs Monday through Friday from 10:00 to 11:00 P.M. While in 1984 the pilot program with three other interpreters had not succeeded, the public response to Sarno-Riggle was formidable, as she developed an accurate technique to provide the Spanish-speaking viewers an adequate representation of what they were getting on the screen. She also strived to establish her own "audio personality," not just mimic the people she was interpreting.

Given her success, especially as evidenced by ratings among Hispanic viewers, by July 1985, KTLA had made Sarno-Riggle a regular staff employee and committed to continue the service. Sarno-Riggle, a native of Argentina, considers her own simulcast interpretations an alternative to Univisión's and Telemundo's news. She believes it offers access to a larger and more diverse amount of local news, which may be preferred by some assimilated Hispanics, or by those who simply wish to be informed on the same issues their neighbors are tuned into. Subsequently, KTLA assigned her to the Hollywood Christmas parade and various other specials. The station also expanded its offerings of Spanish-language audio for more of its prime-time programs, such as "Airwolf," "Magnum P.I.," and "Knight Rider." These programs were also among those dubbed for foreign distribution by their producers. Currently, KTLA schedules approximately twenty hours per week of Spanish-language audio.

The Hispanic audience ratings of KTLA did not go unnoticed by other stations and networks in Los Angeles and elsewhere. Second Audio Program has already been adopted by various other Anglo broadcasters in large Hispanic markets, including the Tribune Broadcasting Company's Chicago and New York stations WGN Channel 9 and WPIX Channel 11. Even some nonprofit stations began this language option. For example, KCET Channel 28 hired Sarno-Riggle for ten months to do the Spanish-language audio for "By the Year 2000," a weekly half-hour public affairs program for southern California. Also, under Sarno-Riggle's guidance, on January 14, 1991, New York station WNET Channel 13 began the second audio for "The MacNeil/Lehrer News-Hour." Presently, Bolivian native Oscar Ordenes is the Spanish-language voice for this show, which in the United States is carried by thirty-three Public Broadcasting System stations either via Second Audio Program or as a separate show repeated later in the evening. In addition, thirty-two cities in twenty-six Latin American countries receive videos of this version of the "MacNeil/Lehrer News Hour" by way of the United States Information Agency's Worldnet information program.

Finally, English-language musical programs specifically oriented toward Hispanics are also making their debut. In June 1991, MTV launched "Second Generation," a half-hour mix of videos, comedy, and entertainment news aimed primarily at second-generation Hispanics in the United States. Hosted by New York Puerto Rican Andy Panda and Colombian Tony Moran, this program is being broadcast by thirty-one primarily English-language stations from the east to the west coast.

Federico A. Subervi-Vález

SELECTED HISPANICS IN MEDIA ♦ ♦ ♦ ♦ ♦ ♦ ♦ ♦ ♦ ♦ ♦ ♦ ♦ ♦ ♦

Mary Helen Barro

(1838–)

Radio Broadcasting

Born on June 17, 1938, in Culver City, California, Barro was educated in California, received a degree in management systems and procedures from the University of California at Los Angeles in 1967, and began a career in radio broadcasting. After working at various on-air and management positions in radio and television, from 1985 to 1986 she served as the general manager of the King Videocable Corporation. In 1986, she became a founder and partner of MC Gavren-Barro Broadcasting Corporation, serving as vice president and general manager. She has been an outstanding figure in broadcasting and a pioneer in creating emergency broadcasting procedures for the Spanish-speaking in the Los Angeles area. He honors include the Mexican American Opportunity Foundation's Woman of the Year Award in 1972 and resolutions honoring her achievements from the city of Los Angeles (1972) and the California state legislature (1976).

Harry Caicedo

(1928–)

Journalism

Born on April 1, 1928, in New York City to Colombian parents, Caicedo was educated in the United States, received his bachelor of journalism from the University of Missouri in 1954, and has developed an outstanding career in journalism as an editor and director in various media. From 1955 to 1958, he served as associate editor of *Latin American Report* magazine; from 1958 to 1959, he was the chief of the *Miami Herald* news bureau, and from 1961 to 1978, he served the U.S. Information Agency and the Voice of

America in various positions in the United States and in Latin America. In 1984, he became president of Inter American Editorial Services. From 1984 to 1991, he served as the founding editor of the nation's first Hispanic mass circulation magazine, *Vista*. Since 1991, he has been a media consultant.

Born in Phoenix, Arizona, Lynda Carter began her show business career as a nightclub singer and dancer after finishing high school; she later attended Arizona State University. In 1970, she was crowned Miss World USA, which led her to Hollywood. She has since become a successful television actress. Her most famous role was Wonder Woman, from 1976 to 1979; she has also starred in various made-for-television movies, including *Stillwatch* and *Born to Be Sold* in 1981, *Rita Hayworth* and *The Love Godess* in 1983. During the 1980s, Carter also starred in her own variety shows, which highlight her singing and dancing: "Lynda Carter Celebration," "Lynda Carter: Body and Soul" and "Lynda Carter: Street Life." She is the founder of Lynda Carter Productions, which continues to launch new television programs. Included among her honors are the Golden Eagle Award for Consistent Performance in Television and Film and Mexico's Ariel Award as International Entertainer of the Year.

Lynda Córdoba Carter

Television, Film

Born on October 25, 1955, in San Juan, Texas, Pérez was educated in south Texas, receiving her B.A. degree from the University of Texas-Pan American in 1980. Since 1979, she has embarked on a career in television journalism, working at KGBT-TV in Harlingen, Texas, as a reporter, then as producer and anchor. In 1982, she became a morning anchor and reporter for KMOL-TV in San Antonio, and in 1984, she held a similar position at an Austin station. From there she worked as a reporter in stations in Dallas and Phoenix. From 1987 to 1992, she worked as a reporter and anchor for KTLA-TV in Los Angeles. In 1992, she joined KTRK Channel 13 in Houston, Texas, as a weekend anchor and reporter. Pérez's outstanding work has been acknowledged through various awards: the Spot News Coverage Associated Press Media Award in 1987; an Emmy nomination for Best Host of a Community Affairs Program; and a Golden Mike Media Award, both in 1990; and others.

Minerva Pérez (1955–)

Television Journalism

Born on July 4, 1943, in New York City, Rivera studied at the University of Arizona and Brooklyn Law School and received his law degree from the University of Pennsylvania and a degree in journalism from Columbia University. Rivera went on to become one of the nation's most celebrated

Geraldo Miguel Rivera (1943–)

Journalism, Television

and respected investigative television journalists, writing and producing various award-winning documentaries. He has won a Peabody Award and ten Emmys for distinguished broadcast journalism. After beginning his career as a reporter for WABC-TV in New York in 1970, he went on to become a reporter, producer, and host for various television news and entertainment shows. Since 1987, he has hosted and produced his own "Geraldo" talk show, which is nationally syndicated. Rivera is also the author of books, including his very controversial autobiography, which was published in 1991. Today, Rivera is one of the most visible and successful Hispanics in media and entertainment.

Paul Rodríguez

Entertainment

Paul Rodríguez is the most recognized and popular Hispanic comedian in the United States. Born in 1977 in Mazatlán, Mexico, Rodríguez came to the United States as the son of immigrant farm workers. "My family never thought that being a comedian or an actor was an obtainable goal. Being farmworkers, all they wanted for their children was a steady job. But I knew I had to give it a chance." In 1977, after a stint in the air force, Rodríguez entered Long Beach City College on the G.I. Bill, where he received and associate arts degree, and then he enrolled in California State University, Long Beach, with the objective of becoming an attorney. During theater classes at the university, Rodriguez's comic talent became obvious to his professor, who led him to become associated with the Comedy Store in Los Angeles, and thus his standup comic career was launched. Currently, Paul Rodríguez has worked in three television major network sitcom series and various movies. He is the host and star of immensely popular "El Show de Paul Rodríguez" on the Univision Spanish-language network. Rodríguez is the head of his own company, Paul Rodríguez Productions, which produced the one-hour special "Paul Rodríguez behind Bars," which aired nationally on the Fox Network in 1991. His earlier special "I Need a Couch" had one of the highest ratings in the history of HBO comedy specials. In addition to his film and television work, Rodríguez is a comedy headliner at Las Vegas and Atlantic City, and in 1986 released his first comedy album, "You're in America Now, Speak Spanish."

Luis Santeiro
(1947–)

Television Writer, Playwright

Born on October 9, 1947, in Havana, Cuba, Santeiro immigrated to Miami with his parents in 1960. He received a B.A. degree in sociology from Villanova University in 1969 and an M.A. degree in communications from Syracuse University in 1970. He became a free-lance writer and, since 1978 has served as a writer for the award-winning Children's Television Workshop and as the producer of "Sesame Street." Among the many shows he has written for television are thirty episodes of the bilingual comedy "Qué Pasa, USA?" (1977-80), and numerous episodes of the PBS series "3-2-1 Contact!", "Oye, Willie!", "Carrascolendas," and the ABC "After School Specials." Santeiro is among the most recognized Hispanics on television; he has won six Emmy Awards for his writing on "Sesame Street." Santiero is also a recognized dramatist with plays successfully produced in New York and Miami.

Born on January 29, 1948, in Havana, Cuba, into a distinguished family of journalists, Cristina Saralegui's grandfather, Francisco Saralegui, was known throughout Latin America as the "paper czar"; he initiated his granddaughter into the world of publishing through such popular magazines as *Bohemia*, *Carteles*, and *Vanidades*. In 1960, she immigrated to Miami's Cuban exile community, but continued to develop the family profession by majoring in mass communications and creative writing at the University of Miami. In her last year at the university, she began working for *Vanidades*, the leading ladies' service magazine in Latin America. By 1979, she was named editor-in-chief of the internationally distributed *Cosmopolitan-en-Español*. In 1989, she resigned that position to become the talk show host for "The Cristina Show," which has become the number one rated daytime show on Spanish-language television in the United States. Since 1991, Saralegui has also been the host for a daily nationally syndicated radio show, "Cristina Opina" (Cristina's Opinions) and the editor-in-chief of a new monthly magazine, *Cristina-La Revista* (*Cristina-The Magazine*), published by Editorial América in Miami. Through radio and television, Cristina reaches 6.5 million Hispanics daily throughout the United States and in twelve Latin American countries.

Cristina Saralegui (1948-)

Television, Journalism

Born in Havana, Cuba, on May 5, 1928, Suárez received his primary and secondary education there. He obtained a bachelor's degree in economics and finance from Villanova University in 1949. After returning to Havana, from 1959 to 1960 he was active in real estate, construction and finance. In 1962, he went to work for *The Miami Herald* as a part-time mailer. He advanced to controller of the Knight-Ridder subsidiary operations. In 1972, he joined Knight Publishing Company in Charlotte, North Carolina, as controller and was named vice president and general manager in 1978. He was named president in 1986. In 1990, he assumed his present position as president of *The Miami Herald* and Publisher of *El Nuevo Heraldo*, the Spanish-language newspaper published by *The Miami Herald*

Robert Suárez (1928-)

Journalism

since 1987. His awards include the 1989 Gold Medal for Excellence for being the most distinguished executive of al Knight-Ridder companies, the 1990 Hispanic Alliance Heritage Award for Media, and the 1991 Leadership Award from ASPIRA.

Art

What is Hispanic art? What are its sources? When and where did it begin? What are its characteristics? How has it changed over time? What forces altered or determined its direction? How does it differ from the art of other groups of people? These and related questions are examined here in order to provide a historical framework for the art of Hispanics.

Each region in Spanish America developed its own variant of Hispanic culture because of local conditions, resources, and people. Mountains, jungles, and other natural barriers isolated settlements and affected communications between them. The cultural differences were also the result of differences in the size of the indigenous populations and their level of civilization at the time of European contact. Finally, the history of the areas determined how the peoples of Spanish America developed as nations following their independence from Spain in the early nineteenth century. The result is that Hispanic cultures have been tempered by European, indigenous, and African peoples, and their art reflects those conditions.

THE SOURCES OF HISPANIC ART ◆ ◆ ◆ ◆ ◆ ◆ ◆ ◆ ◆ ◆ ◆ ◆ ◆ ◆ ◆ ◆

The sources of Hispanic art in the United States are found primarily in Mexico and the Caribbean basin as well as in the regions where most Hispanics reside (Texas, Colorado, New Mexico, Arizona, California, New York, and Florida). The countries or territories to the immediate south of the United States—Mexico, Puerto Rico, and Cuba—have had a greater influence on the art of Hispanic Americans than others because of their geographical proximity and the result of wars between Spain, Mexico, and the United States in the nineteenth century. There are fewer people from other parts of Latin America, and, as a result, their impact on Hispanic art in the United States has not been as great.

Mexico, the largest country south of the border, is the place of origin for the vast majority of Hispanics in the United States, who identify themselves as Mexican Americans, Hispanos (Spanish Americans), or Chicanos. They are found primarily in the Southwest, Pacific Southwest and Pacific Northwest, and Great Lakes regions. They are related to the people of Mexico and share their history, religion, and culture. They identify with Mexican history, which began with the Indian civilizations of the pre-Columbian epoch and continued through the colonial period under Spanish rule, which lasted three centuries. The modern period began in 1821 with Mexican independence from Spain and the rise of a civilization that combines Indian and Spanish roots. Thus, the overriding Spanish influence in the northern territory was tempered by the Mexican experience, which began with Mexican independence and continued into the twentieth century with constant immigration caused by economic necessity and the Mexican Revolution of 1910. Anglo-American influence began in the middle of the nineteenth century and has continued unabated throughout the area.

Continued American expansion toward the end of the nineteenth century led to the acquisition of Puerto Rico following the war between the United States and Spain in 1898. By 1917 Puerto Ricans were made citizens of the United States and thus were able to travel freely and to settle in the United States without any immigration restrictions. Cubans have lived in the United States since the nineteenth century, but extensive Cuban immigration began after the takeover of Cuba by Fidel Castro and his partisans in 1959 and the failed Bay of Pigs invasion of 1962. They and other groups from all over Latin America have continued to immigrate to the United States. Thus, the largest groups of Hispanics in the northeastern and southeastern parts of the United States are from Puerto Rico, Cuba, and other nations in the Caribbean area, and to a lesser extent from the rest of Latin America. What brings these disparate groups together? How do they differ? What distinguishes one from the other?

♦ ♦ ♦ ♦ ♦ ♦ NEW SPANIARDS AND MEXICANS: 1599 TO 1848

The Missions

The missions built from Texas to California in the seventeenth and eighteenth centuries were intended to serve as Christianizing outposts as well as economic, social, and political units. The Franciscan friars in charge of the northernmost missions were sometimes the sole Europeans along the frontier. The missions, therefore, had to serve the many assigned functions and be relatively independent, self-contained units.

The northern missions are related to the architectural complexes built by the friars in central New Spain in the sixteenth century. These complexes, known as *conventos*, always included a single-nave church and the various units associated with it, such as the sacristy (a small room next to the altar for storage of religious vestments), the friars' quarters, the cloister, the refectory or dining room, the kitchen, and other areas. The friars also included a large open space in front of the church, known as the *atrio* (atrium), with small chapels called *posas* at each of the four corners and a cross in the center. The posas were used for religious processions and the cross was used to teach the Indians about the new religion.

The seventeenth- and eighteenth-century missions in the Indian pueblos of New Mexico follow the same arrangement used in the conventos of central New Spain. Examples are found in New Mexico at the Indian pueblos of Laguna (San José, about 1700) and Acoma (San Esteban del Rey, 1629–1641).

By the eighteenth and early nineteenth centuries, the standard arrangements seen in the sixteenth-century conventos were no longer strictly followed in the northern territories. They varied from region to region. The church no longer seemed to be the focal point of the complex, since the various units were not clustered around it as in central New Spain, nor did they have the standard east-west orientation of the earlier churches. Most churches had Latin cross plans, which also correspond to examples

Figure 1. Bell wall, San Juan Capistrano Mission, 1760–87. San Antonio, Texas.

found in central New Spain. Examples are seen in the churches of Nuestra Señora de la Purísima Concepción (1755) in San Antonio, Texas, San Xavier del Bac (1783–97), south of Tucson, Arizona, San Juan Capistrano (1796–1806) in California, and San Francisco de Assís (1813–15) in Ranchos de Taos, New Mexico.

The facades of the mission churches also followed examples seen in the churches of central New Spain. The early convento churches have a vertical extension of the facade sometimes used as a belfry (*espadaña*), as in the churches of the Indian pueblos of Laguna and Picuris, New Mexico, and in the San Francisco de la Espada church in San Antonio. Another type of belfry is the bellwall (*campanario*), a wall with one or more openings for bells. A campanario was added to one of the walls of the nave of the San Juan Capistrano church in San Antonio (Figure 1). Another was built as an independent tower or wall adjacent to the facade but not part of it as in the churches of the San Diego, San Gabriel, and Santa Inés missions in California.

The bell towers of the later colonial period and a dome over the crossing of the nave and transept are seen in the San José and Concepción churches in San Antonio, and the San Xavier church in Arizona. Bell towers but not the domes are seen in the Acoma and Ranchos de Taos churches in New Mexico, and the Santa Barbara, Carmel, San Buenaventura, and San Luis Rey churches in California.

Although the missions of the Southwest have *espadañas*, campanarios, bell towers, and domes, each region or mission field has its own characteristics due to the local conditions and the time the building programs began. The style of the New Mexico missions, built in adobe, remained unchanged over a period of several hundred years. The others differ only slightly, owing to the differences in style (baroque in Texas and Arizona and neoclassical in California) and distance from the central part of New Spain.

The primary function of the mission churches and chapels was to provide an area for religious celebratons carried out on a daily, weekly, and annual basis. The images on the exterior portal facades and the altarpieces placed inside these sacred areas were meant to be viewed and experienced for their religious meaning, with the devout using them for veneration and supplication purposes. Thus, purpose and function were related to the religious content and meaning the images conveyed, rather than their being created for purely artistic or aesthetic reasons.

The best examples of portal facades with figural and architectural sculptures are found in the mission churches of San José y San Miguel de Aguayo (1768–82) in San Antonio and San Xavier del Bac (1783–97) near Tucson. Figural sculptures are placed in niches framed by columnar supports, known as *estipites*, at San Xavier and on pedestals placed within niche-pilasters at San José. The pilaster is so named because it functions as a background for the sculptures.

San José and San Miguel de Aguayo

The architectural frame of the San José church portal has a single bay that spans its two stories. The entablature of the first story establishes its width and the niche-pilasters provide its outer frame. Inner pilasters extend up to the entablature beyond the jambs of the doorway, which has a mixtilineo arch. The second-story bay, narrower than the first, has an entablature with supporting pilasters and a choir window, which are in line with the inner dimensions of the main doorway. The pedestals with sculptures

Figure 2. Facade, San José y San Miguel de Aguayo Mission, 1768–82. San Antonio, Texas.

are in line with the inner pilasters of the first story. Mixtilineo brackets provide the frame for the ensemble and a transition to the cornice topped by a stone cross.

Figural sculptures are on each side of the doorway, and above it under the cornice of the entablature. The same arrangement is seen around the choir window of the second story (Figure 2).

Figure 3. Saint Joachim *portal sculpture (left side of the doorway), 1768–82, San José y San Miguel de Aguayo Mission.*

The main doorway is flanked by sculptures of Saint Joachim on the left and Saint Anne on the right (Figures 3 and 4). A sculpture of Our Lady of Guadalupe is seen over the doorway. There is a sculpture of Saint Dominic on the left side of the choir window and one of Saint Francis on the right. A sculpture of Saint Joseph holding the Christ Child is seen above the choir window. The arrangement of the sculptures by threes at each level of the portal is in keeping with other similar ones found throughout New Spain. There is no other example like this one in the mission churches of New Mexico, Arizona, or California. The closest to this

Figure 4. Saint Anne.

arrangement is found at San Xavier, where the sculptures are located in niches on each side of the door and choir window. However, there are no sculptures along the central axis.

San Xavier del Bac

The estipite columns and the entablatures of the San Xavier portal are arranged in a rectangular grid (Figure 5). This is contrasted by the third story, framed by the curvilinear frame known as a reretted cornice. There

Figure 5. Facade, 1783–97,
San Xavier del Bac Mission.
Tuscon, Arizona.

is a sculpture of Saint Francis of Assisi in the central part of the cornice, known as a chamfered center. The sculptures on either side of the door-way are Saint Catherine of Siena on the left and Saint Lucy on the right (Figure 6). The sculptures on the second story are Saint Barbara on the left and Saint Cecilia on the right. These are much smaller in relation to their surrounding spaces than those at San José.

Figure 6. Saint Lucy.

Other Mission Church Portals

The few sculptures that may have been placed in the portal niches of the California mission churches have long since disappeared. As an example, the three sculptures on the portal of the Santa Barbara church are modern replacements of those that were destroyed by an earthquake in 1925. The sculptures of the San Luis Rey church have disappeared. Those that were undoubtedly on the portal of the San Juan Capistrano church were destroyed by the earthquake of 1812. And finally, the sculpture in a niche on the portal of the San Gabriel church is a modern addition.

The mission churches of New Mexico did not have figural or architectural sculptures on the facades, owing to the use of adobe, which does not lend itself to this type of decoration. The primary focus in these churches was on the interior walls used for paintings and individual panels hung as pictures. Every church had an altar screen, known as a *reredos* in New Mexico (and *retablo* in Mexico), on the back wall of the sanctuary and numerous freestanding sculptures of holy images, known as *santos* (literally, saints), placed in front of it on altar tables.

Architectural Polychromy

Some of the mission churches also had painted decorations on the exterior surfaces to enhance their appearance, particularly in those cases where it was too expensive to add architectural and figural sculptures on the portals. A good example of this practice is seen on the facade of Nuestra Señora de la Purísima Concepción de Acuña Mission (1755) in San Antonio (Figure 7). All the windows and the portal and tower bases and the belfries were painted to simulate stone masonry frames and belfry arches. Simulated masonry was also painted on each side of the portal to give the illusion of tower bases. Simulated fluted pilasters were painted near the corners of each side of the belfry towers. Finally, a sun and a moon were painted on the upper part of the portal with the letters "AE" (Ave María). Other examples are found at San José mission church, where a quatrefoil pattern was painted over the entire facade along with simulated block frames on the tower base windows and zig-zags on the dome (Figure 8). Examples of architectural painting in California are seen in the mission churches of Santa Clara de Assís (1822–23) and Santa Inés.

The use of colors on the facades of the Texas and California churches reflects the interest in creating dramatic effects of light and color seen in the churches of central Mexico (New Spain), where glazed tiles were used on

Figure 7. Main Portal, 1755,
Nuestra Señora de la
Purísima Concepción de
Acuña Mission.
San Antonio, Texas.

domes and, on occasion, on facades as well. The best example of this practice is seen at the church of San Francisco Acatepec, Puebla.

Altarpieces

Few of the mission churches in Texas and California have sculptures or paintings on canvas that are original or date from the mission period. Those seen in some of the churches may not be from that period but are recent additions. Others that are from the mission period, as in the case of

Figure 8. Polychromy (reconstruction, 1948), south tower, 1768–82, San José y San Miguel de Aguayo Mission. San Antonio, Texas.

Most of the sculptures and paintings of the altarpieces in Texas and California were probably brought in from central New Spain where they were produced. Some wood sculptures originally located in altarpieces or altar areas of the Texas mission churches are now placed on pedestals (altars), in museum exhibitions, or in storage. There are also isolated sculptures and paintings in the California mission churches and museums. Some are placed in modern altarpieces.

the San Antonio missions, are no longer in their original locations because the altarpieces in which they were placed disappeared in the nineteenth century.

Only the church of San Xavier del Bac and others in New Mexico have their original altar screens in place. Those at San Xavier cover the altar area and the transepts (the arms of a Latin cross). The apostles are represented in the nave and chancel (the area in front of the altar at the crossing of the transepts and the nave). The focus is on human salvation (entrance to the chancel), and within the chancel are references to the missionary work of Saint Francis Xavier, the birth of the Virgin Mary, the earthly experience of Adam's offspring, and God the Father giving his benediction.

The altarpieces of the New Mexico mission churches were painted by local artisans in a folk art style. The sculptures made of wood and painted in different colors were also done by local artisans. Some mission altar screens are now found in the Museum of New Mexico (Santa Fe) and Taylor Museum (Colorado Springs, Colorado).

Alteration and Restoration of the Mission Churches

Many of the original churches have been altered over the years as a result of neglect and, in some cases, restorations carried out in the nineteenth and twentieth centuries. In the nineteenth century, some of the New Mexico churches were altered when Victorian-style decorations were added to the adobe structures. Most of these additions were removed in the twentieth century and efforts made to restore the churches to their original configurations. Unfortunately, the need to continually maintain the adobe surfaces because of the fragile nature of the material has led to unintended changes in the details of the structures.

More durable materials were used in Texas and Arizona, and to some extent in California. It is on the portal facades of these structures that figural and architectural sculptures are more apt to be found than on the adobe churches of New Mexico. However, these sculptures have suffered as a result of abandonment and vandalism in the nineteenth century. This began when the missions were secularized a few years after Mexico gained its independence from Spain in 1821. Political turmoil and war between Texas and Mexico eventually led to the partial destruction of some of the sculptures found on these facades. Some of them have been restored in the twentieth century.

The relatively isolated New Mexicans developed a folk art independent of academic models far to the south during the first half of the nineteenth century. That style, generally dated from 1810 to 1850, is characterized by the work of holy image makers known as *santeros* (literally makers of saint images—sculptures and paintings). The paintings on panels were called *retablos;* the sculptures were called *bultos.* However, they were not totally isolated. Works by masters from the metropolitan cities were available in such places as the church at Pecos Pueblo and the church of Our Lady of Guadalupe in Santa Fe. In addition, the earlier paintings and sculptures produced in New Mexico during the eighteenth century are derivative of academic styles.

New Mexico Santeros

The Laguna Santero

The unique style of painting and sculpture in New Mexico began with the work of the anonymous Laguna santero who worked there from 1796 to 1808. The design of his altar screens and paintings indicate that he may have been from the provinces of Mexico. His work is clearly derived from Mexican provincial sources, specifically paintings and engravings, but is simplified to such an extent (all the forms are flattened out) that the figures appear weightless. The facial expressions are neutral in contrast to the more animated baroque examples from central New Spain. The baroque image and its variety of poses and expressions was meant to accentuate the ecstasy or other states of the saintly or holy person portrayed. The expression of religious piety in the works by the Laguna santero are closer to the images of medieval Europe.

A good example of the santero's work is the Laguna altar screen, dated 1800 to 1808. It has three bays on the first story and a single one on the second story. Solomonic columns frame each of the side bays and solomonic balusters top the two outer columns on the second story. (Other santeros painted altar screens in a similar style, that is, they emphasized the architectural frame for the images as in the examples found in central New Spain.) Altar screens attributed to the Laguna santero are found in Pojoaque (about 1796–1800), Santa Fe (around 1796 and 1798), Zia and Santa Ana (both about 1798), and Acoma (1802). The altar screens have three bays and usually two stories.

The Laguna santero had several followers, among them Molleno, who may have worked in the santero's workshop. Among Molleno's works is the altar screen at the church in Rio Chiquito (1828). Another santero, known as the Quill Pen Santero, was a follower of Molleno. These two artists, like the Laguna santero, emphasized the linear treatment of all forms and details.

José Aragón

José Aragón differed from the other santeros because he could read and write, and this ability was reflected in his work. He used engravings as models for his paintings, signed them, and even included lengthy prayers in them. While his work can be considered folk in style, it has a relationship to academic sources. It is sophisticated in its definition of form and the proportions of the human figure.

A good example of Aragón's *reredos* (altar screen) paintings is the one of Our Lady of Guadalupe, now in the Taylor Museum in Colorado Springs. The iconographic program is clearly based on the well-known conventional sources, but Aragón emphasized the formal rather than the narrative qualities of the image. There is a fine linearity that permeates all of the narrative panels and the spaces between them as well as the frame that contains them all. The Virgin is represented in the center, and her appearance to Juan Diego and the events subsequent to it are depicted in the four corners of the painting. Christ is seen in the top center, and the church that the Virgin ordered built in her honor is seen at the bottom center.

The Truchas Master

Another of the anonymous santeros working in the first quarter of the nineteenth century was initially identified as the Dot-Dash Painter, then later as don Antonio Fresques, and more recently as the Truchas Master. Works by this artist are dated between 1790 and 1830.

The reredos painting of Our Lady of Guadalupe, now in the Taylor Museum in Colorado Springs is also a good example of the Truchas Master's work. This painting is unlike most representations of the Virgin, which are based on the original in the basilica of Guadalupe near Mexico City. The artist ignored the standard proportions of the slender figure of the Virgin and did away with all semblance of naturalism in the depiction of her downward gaze. The eyes are simple crescent shapes and each iris is indicated by a black dot. The other features are defined with an equal economy of means. The figure and the slender form of the original have been transformed into a schematic rendition in which there is an emphasis on the colors and the vigorous line used to outline all forms.

José Rafael Aragón (1796?–1862)

José Rafael Aragón was born in 1796 or 1797 and died in 1862. His earliest dated altar screen (1825) is found in the pueblo church of San Lorenzo de Picuris. Other works are in Chimayo, Taos, Talpa, and the Cordoba/Santa Cruz area.

Aragón was the major artist from around 1820 to 1860, and his reredos panel paintings, altar screens, and sculptures are the finest examples of the local folk art style.

Aragón took all the abstracting tendencies of his predecessors and created even finer examples of this type of art. His work is known for his bold use of line and pure color, and although he used late baroque models, his work was not dependent on them. Typical of his mature work is the altar screen originally in the chapel of Our Lady of Talpa (near Taos) and now in the Taylor Museum. It was completed in 1838. The style is softer than his earlier works. The faces tend to be round instead of elongated ovals, and the figures are relatively static in presentation.

A fine example of Aragón's sculpture is a *bulto* (religious sculpture) from the Talpa chapel, now in the Taylor Museum collection of Our Lady of Talpa. She is crowned and holds the Christ Child in her left arm. As in the retablo and altar screen paintings, the artist created a fine balance between the decorative and figural elements in the sculpture.

HISPANIC ART FROM 1848 TO 1920 ✦ ✦ ✦ ✦ ✦ ✦ ✦ ✦ ✦ ✦ ✦ ✦ ✦

There is little information on the art of Hispanos and Mexican Americans dating from the period immediately following 1848, when the northern-most territories of Mexico became part of the United States. The process of bringing the entire area into the economic, political, and cultural life of the United States was begun at this time and continued during the re-mainder of the nineteenth century and the first two decades of the twenti-eth. The area became known as the Southwest and Pacific Southwest of the United States. Its incorporation into the country's economic system was hastened by the building of railroads in the area. Cultural changes were eventually brought about by the people who began to go into the area from the eastern seaboard and other parts of the country.

Modernization in Mexico and the United States during the last decades of the nineteenth century led to a period of consolidation on both sides of the border. There were no great movements of people in either direction. On the American side, the modernization affected various regions of the area during the second half of the nineteenth century. The most apparent changes took place in New Mexico, where new churches were built on American and European models, and the old ones were changed with the addition of wood siding, pointed spires, and a general refurbishing con-sistent with the eclectic tastes of the nineteenth century. Plaster saints and inexpensive religious prints were also introduced into the area. The latter supplanted the retablo painting tradition but the former did not stop the production of bultos. A few of the artists who continued to produce san-tos were "discovered" in the twentieth century.

The production of santos in New Mexico declined in number and style, as well as technical quality, after the 1850s. The changes were the result of a change in patronage of the church, first under the Spanish Crown and later Mexico, and the importation of plaster saints and inexpensive prints after 1848. The few santos produced for Spanish Americans in the isolated communities of northern New Mexico are the work of less technically proficient artists. Santos were made for the oratories and *moradas* (meeting houses) and were used by the Penitente Brotherhood for the first time in 1833, when they were condemned by the Mexican Church. The Penitentes eventually became the first of many groups of Hispanics who sought to retain the integrity of their culture against the attacks of Protestant Americans and the Catholic Church in the 1850s. Although the Penitentes had been condemned by the Mexican Catholic Church, their persecution by American Catholics and Protestants in the mid-1850s eventually led to their activities becoming more and more secretive. The Penitentes provided the patronage as well as the selection of certain subjects that were an essential part of their religious observances and practices. The subjects most often represented were the death figures and the suffering Christ of the Passion.

Santos and Santeros

Miguel Herrera, a resident of Arroyo Hondo in Taos County, was among the several santeros serving the needs of the Penitentes and others in the area. He worked in the 1870s, 1880s, and possibly later as a bulto maker. (No retablos are known to have been produced by him, but this is not surprising, since religious prints were readily available.) The tall figures with attention paid only to the head and hands were meant to be dressed in fabric clothing. His santos are noted for small seashell ears set too low on the head. Much of his work was done for the moradas of the Penitentes. A fine example of his work is the *Christ in the Holy Sepulchre*, in the Taylor Museum collection. It is life-size and its knees, shoulders, neck, and jaw are articulated.

Miguel Herrera (1835–1905)

José Benito Ortega traveled from town to town, a true itinerant artist, to seek out potential patrons. He was one of several such artists serving the needs of the Hispanos in northern New Mexico. When Ortega received an order, he stayed in the town until he finished the work. He also made death figures for use in the moradas. His santo figures are very simple and stylized with sharply defined Spanish features and painted in bright colors.

José Benito Ortega (1858–1941)

An example of Ortega's work is *San Isidro Labrador (Saint Isidro the Farmer)* in the Denver Art Museum, made of wood and gesso, and painted. The work is modeled on the traditional representations of this saint in the tin paintings of northern Mexico, in which the size of the figures is based on their importance rather than on how they would appear in nature. The saint towers over all the other figures in the group. The winged angel behind the plow is slightly less than half the size of Saint Isidor! The oxen are also less than half the size of the angel, thereby creating a pronounced distortion of scale in the work.

TRADITIONAL ARTS FROM 1920 TO THE PRESENT ♦ ♦ ♦ ♦ ♦ ♦

By the 1920s, the Hispanic communities in various parts of the Southwest had begun to change as a result of American cultural dominance in the area and the increased immigration from Mexico following the political and economic chaos caused by the Mexican Revolution of 1910. The most immediate changes occurred in northern New Mexico following World War I, when the traditional arts of santo making were brought to an end as a result of economic changes in the area. They were revived but in different form and to serve other than religious purposes.

However, the traditional arts were strengthened in other parts of the Southwest by the new arrivals from Mexico. Their strong devotion to the saints and Our Lady of Guadalupe, to whom they prayed for salvation and assistance in resolving problems, led to the creation of private oratories, known as yard shrines and home altars. The latter have inspired contemporary Chicano artists who call themselves *altaristas* (altar makers). The former have inspired contemporary santeros in New Mexico. Both are expressions of the Hispanic experience in the Southwest and Pacific Southwest.

The new emphasis on santo making was created by a number of American artists who began to arrive in Santa Fe and Taos in the 1920s. The craftsmen were encouraged to continue making furniture and other domestic products as well as sculptures that were similar to the traditional santos of the nineteenth century. Unlike the earlier pieces, however, the new santos were not painted in different colors, nor were they intended for chapels or churches. They were produced for collectors and tourists who acquired such objects as mementos of a trip through the area. Another change was seen in the production of the santos. Entire families were now involved in making santos, in contrast to the production of works by single artists in the past.

The revival of santo making took place primarily in the small community of Cordoba, New Mexico. However, the impetus for it can be found in Santa Fe, where the needed mechanisms were instituted starting in 1919 with the "revival" of the Santa Fe Fiesta and culminating in 1929 with the incorporation of the Spanish Colonial Arts Society, which had an impact on the making of santos in northern New Mexico. An annual fiesta exhibition was adopted in the late 1920s in which the works of Hispanic craftsmen were included. These exhibitions were variously called Spanish Colonial Handicrafts, Spanish Fair, and Spanish Arts and Crafts Exhibition. In 1929 the Spanish Arts Shop was established by the Spanish Colonial Arts Society in Sena Plaza, Santa Fe. During the time it lasted, through the early 1930s, it served as an impetus to some of the santeros, such as José Dolores López and others, who began to concentrate on the production of objects that were acceptable to Anglo patrons. As patrons, the Anglos determined questions of quality and originality of craftsmanship. Santos were no longer produced on the basis of the Hispanics' own understanding of their heritage.

One of the most important of the new santeros was José Dolores López, whose works date from about 1929 to 1937, the year of his death. He was primarily a furniture maker from 1917 to about 1929. He also did carpentry work—window and door frames, roof beams and corbels, crosses for grave markers, coffins, and chests—and made small wooden figures, primarily for relaxation and as gifts for neighbors and relatives. He began to carve birds and animals as well as santos after 1929 because he could no longer earn a living from his fields and livestock and his carpentry work. This new endeavor coincided with the emerging interest in Hispanic culture and handicrafts generated by a few Anglo artists. They were interested in revitalizing Hispanic "traditional," "colonial," and "Spanish" crafts. These external factors created new markets for Hispanic crafts and competition between artists. At the same time, the new patrons taught the Hispanic artists to be "selective" in their work, that is, to produce objects for the non-Hispanic market.

José Dolores López (1868–1937)

López made several changes in his work during the period of transition from an older Hispanic tradition to the new one created by Anglo patrons. The furniture he produced in painted and unpainted versions was changed exclusively to the latter because the painted pieces were too "gaudy" for Anglo patrons. He then turned to making unpainted santos at the prodding of Frank Applegate, who was in charge of arts and crafts for the Spanish Colonial Arts Society. Another reason for the change had to do with the success of the image carvings by Celso Gallegos, who was awarded several prizes for his work in 1926 and 1927. Gallegos, a santero from Agua Fria who was slightly older than López, carved sacred images and animals in stone and wood and, like López, served as *sacristan* (caretaker) for his church. He was among the last of the pious santeros. Both santeros were deeply religious.

The santos by López demonstrate an interest in narrative content, which differs from the emphasis on local prototypes of favored saints and other religious figures represented in the traditional santos. López used several sources for his images, among them an old book of French drawings that he displayed with pride to visitors. He was also influenced by the work of José Rafael Aragón, which he saw in the Cordova church in the course of his work as a sacristan of the sanctuary. He is known to have overpainted and repaired several worn traditional images during that period.

Among the subjects López portrayed in his work are Saint Anthony, Saint Peter, Saint Michael with the dragon, a *nacimiento* (nativity) in which all the

Figure 9. José Dolores López. Expulsion from the Garden of Eden.

appropriate figures are included, a *muerte* (death cart), and Adam and Eve, in which the Garden of Eden and the Tree of Life with the serpent are included. The latter is a formal extension of earlier trees with birds made by the artist. A good example of the Adam and Eve theme is the piece in the Taylor Museum collection titled *Adam and Eve in the Garden of Eden*. It is made up of three separate units that can be moved around to create different arrangements. The figures of Adam and Eve are placed on a long, narrow base, which allows a frontal presentation of the two figures. Behind them is a stylized representation of the garden, composed of vertical plants inserted onto a similar base, which is used as a backdrop for Adam and Eve. To the side is the Tree of Life with the forbidden fruit and the serpent. "The Tree of Life of the Good and the Bad" is inscribed on its base in English and Spanish. López made other elaborate santos, such as *The Expulsion from the Garden of Eden* (Figure 9), in the collections of the Museum of International Folk Art (Santa Fe); *Michael the Archangel and the Dragon*, in the Taylor Museum; *The Expulsion from Paradise*, in the collections of the Museum of International Folk Art; and in the same museum, the *Flight into Egypt*.

Patrocino Barela (1908–1964)

The work of Patrocino Barela, a Taos wood carver, was supported by the Federal Art Project (FAP), part of the Works Progress Administration, from 1936 to 1943. He began to carve santos in 1931, and his work was later exhibited nationally under the auspices of the FAP. His benefactors had an even greater impact on his work than was the case with the López family. Barela broke away from the santero tradition and began to carve figurative works that have an overall organic quality usually suggested by the grain of the woods he used for his works.

A good example of Barela's work is *Saint George*, in the National Museum of American Art (Washington, D.C.). It was carved from a single piece of cedar. The helmetlike nose and brow of the saint form one continuous shape that is echoed by the figure's crown, just as the V-neck of the tunic mirrors the shape created by the position of the figure's legs. The saint's expression is characterized by a stern projecting chin and the gentle slit of the mouth, set off to one side. Through a dynamic series of directions and counterdirections—created by the play between positive and negative form and space—Barela adroitly depicted the slaying of the dragon.

George López

The increased markets and competition between artists led to an increase in the number of people making santos in the 1930s. The children of José

Dolores López began to make santos at this time. Among them was George López, who began carving objects in 1925 but was not able to devote full time to it until 1932. Eventually, his work became more widely known than that of the other Cordova santeros. By the 1960s, he was considered the best of the santeros.

Outdoor Shrines and Home Altars

The yard shrines or private oratories found in the barrios of the Southwest are similar to the folk art produced in New Mexico in terms of genesis, purpose, function, and meaning. These private oratories are called *capillas* (chapels) in San Antonio, *nichos* (niches) in Tucson, and *grutas* (grottoes) in Los Angeles. They express the deeply held religious beliefs of the people who made them. In their genesis they are related to the *exvotos* of northern New Mexico painted in the nineteenth century. Both are responses to a time of crisis experienced by individuals who promised to paint an image (exvoto) as an offering or as a testament of their salvation or to build a shrine (oratory) for similar reasons, if their prayers were answered. The words in Spanish for these acts of devotion and thanksgiving are *promesa* (promise) and *manda* (gift, offering).

The exvoto paintings and the shrines testify to relief from an illness, a malady, financial problems, accidents, robberies, pursuit by enemies or the police, and so on. The nature of the problem determined the manner of supplication: through prayer at the time and place of the natural or man-made catastrophe or in a formal setting, such as a church, for a long-standing illness, or prayer coupled with the use of milagros placed on the saint selected for the occasion. *Milagros* are small sculptures made of various metals (brass, tin, nickel, silver, or gold) into numerous configurations (natural and man-made objects) that can be used to point to the problem. All the body parts are represented, as are the human figure, animals, automobiles, houses, and so forth. The images were used for relief from some illness, such as an arthritic arm, leg, or other part of the body, or a financial problem, such as an outstanding debt or a pending mortgage on a house.

Milagros have been used traditionally in Latin American and some European countries where Catholicism is practiced. Parishioners routinely place milagros on favored saints found in the chapels. Devout parishioners continue to use milagros in some of the mission churches of the Indian pueblos, such as San Xavier del Bac. Mexican Americans use milagros in the shrines and home altars, which are usually comprised of a small sacred image on a shelf or framed for placement on a wall.

San Antonio

As of the early 1980s, there were over 175 oratories in the west side of San Antonio. Some were built as early as the 1940s. Many of them have deteriorated because the younger residents have not maintained them when the owners or builders died. Some have suffered from vandalism. Enough remain, however, to demonstrate the survival of a strong tradition of religious folk art.

The oratories are made of concrete, wood, mirror fragments, tile, brick, stone, pebbles, aluminum, plexiglass, seashells, cement, or other materials. The sacred images placed inside them can be lighted with Christmas lights, plain light bulbs, or even neon light. In most cases, the oratory was built from scratch by the person who made the promise; in other cases, the individual embellished a ready-made oratory available in west-side shops that also sell figurines and flowerpots. In both cases, the individuals placed the sacred image of the saint to whom it was dedicated along with other sacred images inside the shrine. These were decorated with plants, flowers (real, paper, or plastic), candles, seashells, and assorted Christmas decorations.

The shrines vary in size from relatively small constructions (no more than one foot high) to highly elaborate structures (twelve feet high, nine feet wide, and eight feet deep), in which the sacred image was placed. The two most popular images used, were Our Lady of Guadalupe and Our Lady of San Juan de los Lagos. Oratories for the latter were modeled on the miraculous statue in the town of San Juan de los Lagos in the state of Jalisco, Mexico.

A good example of the shrines in San Antonio is the one dedicated to Our Lady of San Juan, built in the mid-1950s by Ramiro Rocha as a manda (offering) to the Virgin. The shrine had a statue of Our Lady in the front central part of the niche, and statues in the corners in the back—the Sacred Heart, left, and San Martín de Porres, right. An electric light was suspended directly above the Virgin. The niche was protected by a glass door. Rocha built the shrine on the property of Elia González, who paid for the materials (the reason is unknown, since Rocha is deceased). González, who allowed her mother, María Garza, to live there, maintained the shrine by looking after it and repainting and cleaning it. González was also responsible for the neon that spelled out the name of the Virgin as follows: "San Juanita de los Lagos," with "viva" in front of it. The shrine was, therefore, appropriately identified by its makers and its location as the Garza/González/Rocha shrine. The property was later sold, and the shrine was destroyed.

Tucson

The private oratories in Tucson are called *nichos* by the residents of the barrio. Most of them have representations of Our Lady of Guadalupe in them. Some of the yard shrines are as elaborate as the shrines of San Antonio. Most were built of brick or stone, and on occasion embellished with tiles added to enhance the appearance of the image placed inside the shrine.

There is an unusual example in which holy images are placed inside a square niche and on a shelf above it (Figure 10). The shrine was built out of a discarded refrigerator in 1957 on Theodora Sánchez's front lawn by her husband as a fulfillment of a promise made to Saint Dymphna, the patron saint of lunatics. This was in response to their prayers to the saint to

Figure 10. Theodora Sánchez. Nicho (Yard Shrine), dedicated to Saint Dymphna. 1957. Tucson, Arizona.

save their son's girlfriend, who went crazy when she visited his grave five years after his death in Korea in the early 1950s. When she got well, they fulfilled their promise to build the shrine.

Framed pictures of Our Lady of Guadalupe are propped up in each corner of the lower niche, in which the statue of Saint Dymphna is placed. On the top shelf there is a statue of Saint Francis Xavier lying in a glass box. This shrine is reminiscent of the work *Christ in the Holy Sepulchre*, by Miguel Herrera, in the Taylor Museum collection.

Austin

In Austin, the yard shrines differ from the small oratories constructed inside the home, appropriately called home altars by those who study them, and *altares* (altars) or *altarcitos* (little altars) by those who build them. The former are "public" and the result of a manda (offering), the latter are "private" and are not tied down to a specific promise given in a time of "need." Both serve a religious function and can be equally complex. Home altars, however, are probably found over a wider area.

The most frequently used image in the Austin home altars is Our Lady of Guadalupe, although other sacred images are also used. The altars include votive candles, flowers, milagros (small sculptures), family photographs, ceramic birds, shells, stones, stuffed animals, bottles full of buttons, ribbons, tea cups, and even photographs of John Kennedy and Bobby Kennedy (both martyred) and other political figures. The altars, therefore, provide the focus for religious as well secular concerns.

♦ ♦ ♦ ♦ ♦ ♦ ♦ HISPANIC ARTISTS: 1920S THROUGH THE 1950S

Throughout the period from World War I through the 1950s, most Spanish-American, Mexican-American, and other Hispanic artists were part of general market art in the United States. Their work was part of the figurative and regionalist traditions that dominated such art in the 1920s through the 1940s. Among the noted artists whose works are characteristic of the period are the Mexican-American artists Octavio Medellín, Antonio García, José Aceves, and Edward Chávez. Other important Hispanic artists of the period are Francisco Luis Mora, born in Uruguay, and Carlos

López, born in Cuba. Among the Spanish-born artists are José Moya del Pino and Xavier González. The latter two are also associated with Mexico, González through immigration before entering the United States, and Moya del Pino through the subjects and style of his work.

The Mexican-American artists were primarily found in the Southwest, and other Hispanics lived in the Great Lakes and northeastern regions. Medellin, García, and Aceves were based in Texas; Chavez in New Mexico, Colorado, and New York; López in Michigan; and Mora in New York and Connecticut. González was initially based in Texas and later in Louisiana, and Moya del Pino in California.

Mexican-American Artists

The subject matter of most of the works by Mexican-American and other Hispanic artists was primarily American, particularly in the murals they painted in the 1930s under the auspices of the Works Progress Art Project (WPAP). However, some of the Mexican-American artists focused on their Mexican as well as American background in their work.

From the 1940s through the 1950s, Mexican-American artists continued to reflect regional concerns in their work in a figurative or realistic style. Others worked in the abstract and nonfigurative styles of the same period. An emphasis on regionalism was evident in the landscapes of the New Mexican artist Margaret Herrera Chávez and the Texas bluebonnet painter Porfirio Salinas. Other regionalists, such as Pedro Cervantes of New Mexico, painted still lifes.

Herrera Chávez was born in Las Vegas, New Mexico, in 1912. Salinas, born in Bastrop, Texas, in 1912, was raised in San Antonio, where he died in 1973. Cervantes, born in Wilcox, Arizona, in 1915, has spent most of his life in Clovis, New Mexico.

Chelo González Amezcua, a contemporary of Antonio García and Octavio Medellín, devoted the last ten to twenty years of her life to her art and poetry. Most of her work was based on a highly personal ichnography in which there are depictions of numerous birds and exotic places and personages. Amezcua was born in Ciudad Acuña, Mexico, in 1903, but lived most of her life in Del Rio, Texas, where she died in 1975.

José Aceves painted murals (framed oil paintings) for the post offices in Borger and Mart, Texas (both in 1939). The mural in Borger, titled *Big City News*, deals with the mail service's delivering news to the most re- mote and isolated regions of the country. The mural in Mart, titled *McLen- nan Looking for a Home*, focuses on the arrival in 1841 of Neil McLennan and his family in the Bosque River Valley, eight miles east of Waco, Texas. The latter is typical of the idealized portrayals of the pioneers in the Southwest seen in post office murals of that period. Aceves was influenced by the muralist Edward Holsag in the development of the western subject matter in the Mart painting.

Aceves was born in Chihuahua, Mexico, in 1909, and moved with his family to El Paso in 1915 as a result of the chaos created by the Mexican Revolution. He studied art at the Museum of Fine Arts in Dallas and at the Chicago Art Institute in the 1930s.

José Aceves
(1909–)

Edward Chávez painted murals for post offices and other government buildings from 1939 to 1943 in Denver, Colorado, Geneva, Nebraska, Center, Texas, and Fort Warren, Wyoming. His murals deal with a direct portrayal of life and industry in each of the areas where he received com- missions for his work. He turned to abstraction in the 1950s and 1960s.

Edward Chávez
(1917–)

For the Denver Center High School panels, titled *The Pioneers* (1939), Chávez focused on the daily chores of tending the oxen on the wagon trail and chopping down trees. He chose the actual building of a sod house as the subject for his Geneva, Nebraska, mural, *Building a Sod House* (1941). He portrayed the early method of hauling logs in the lumber industry around Center, Texas, for that city's post office mural, *Logging Scene* (1941). He focused on the American Indians and the first white men in Wyoming for the mural in Fort Warren, *Indians of the Plains* (1943). All his works were painted with oil on canvas except for the one in Wyoming, which was painted with egg tempera on plywood.

The large wall of Chávez's mural in the Fort Warren Service Club mea- sures eighteen feet high by forty feet wide (Figure 11). It has double doors in the lower center and stairs on each side that break up the rectangular format of the mural. A large Indian in the central part of the mural over the doors kneels on one leg, holds a peace pipe in one hand, and gestures with the other. There are numerous scenes in which hunting and other everyday activities of the Indians are depicted in two horizontal registers

Figure 11. Edward Chávez.
Indians of the Plains. 1943.
Egg Tempera on Plywood.
18' high x 40' wide.
Service Club,
Fort Warren, Wyoming.

to the left and right of the large Indian. American soldiers standing by a tent are seen on the lowermost panel on the left, and Indians are standing by a tepee on the right.

Edward Chávez was born in New Mexico in 1917 and now lives in Woodstock, New York. Although he studied at the Colorado Springs Fine Arts Center, he considers himself to be largely self-taught as an artist. He taught at the Art Students League, New York City in 1954 and from 1955 to 1958; Colorado College, Colorado Springs in 1959; Syracuse University in New York from 1960 to 1961, and Dutchess Community College, Poughkeepsie, New York in 1963. He was appointed artist in residence at the Huntington Fine Arts Gallery in West Virginia in 1967.

Antonio García (1901–) and Octavio Medellín (1907–)

Antonio García used the Spanish Conquest of Mexico as a theme in a work titled *Aztec Advance* (1929), and a Mexican national and religious icon in a mural titled *Our Lady of Guadalupe* (1946–47). Medellín dealt with the entire scope of Mexican history, from pre-Columbian times to the revolution to the 1940s with a sculpture titled *History of Mexico*

Figure 12. Octavio Medellín.
Xtol *print.*

(1949), and treated the pre-Columbian Maya and Toltec in a series of prints titled *Xtol: Dance of the Ancient Maya People* (1962), based on research he carried out in Yucatán in 1938 (Figure 12).

Antonio García, born in Monterrey, Mexico, in 1901, moved with his family to San Diego, Texas, around 1911. He studied at the Chicago Art Institute from 1927 to 1930 and taught art at Del Mar College, Corpus Christi, Texas, from 1950 to 1970. He is retired and continues to reside in Corpus Christi.

Octavio Medellín, born in Matehuala, Mexico, in 1907, moved to San Antonio, in 1920, where he studied painting under José Arpa and drawing under Xavier González at the San Antonio School of Art from 1921 to 1928; he studied at the Chicago Art Institute in 1928. He traveled the Gulf Coast of Mexico from 1929 to 1931 and the Yucatán in 1938. He taught at North Texas State College (now the University of North Texas), Denton, from 1938 to 1942, and at Southern Methodist University, Dallas, from 1945 to 1966. In 1969 he opened his own art school in Dallas. He is retired and lives in Bandera, Texas.

Other Hispanic Artists

The murals painted by other Hispanic artists in the 1930s were similar to those painted by Aceves, Chávez, and other Mexican-American artists. The subjects portrayed invariably dealt with the history, industry, identity, or landscape of the city or region for which they were painted.

Xavier González (1898–)

In 1930 Xavier González won third prize in a national competition for murals on the subject "The Dynamic of Man's Creative Power." The winning entries were installed in the Los Angeles Museum. He later painted murals for the post offices in Hammond and Covington, Louisiana (1936 and 1939), the federal courtroom in Huntsville, Alabama (1937), and the post offices in Kilgore and Mission, Texas (1941 and 1942).

Xavier González was born in Almeira, Spain, in 1898, and received his art training at the Chicago Art Institute. He taught art in San Antonio, Texas, in the early 1920s and at Newcomb College, Tulane University, from 1929 to 1943. He presently lives in Newark, New Jersey.

Carlos López (1908–1953)

Carlos López painted murals under the WPAP from 1937 to 1942. His first mural was painted in Dwight, Illinois (1937), followed by three others in the Michigan cities of Plymouth (1938), Paw Paw (1940), and Birmingham (1942).

Throughout the 1940s, López received numerous commissions from several federal agencies and from private companies to portray various aspects of American life: American industries at war for the War Department, a pictorial record of the war for *Life* magazine, the amphibious training activities for the navy, and the project Michigan on Canvas, for the J. L. Hudson Company. After World War II, López's work turned toward fantasy and symbol, conveyed by figures that always appear to stand alone, lonely and sad.

López, born in Havana, Cuba, in 1908, spent his early years in Spain and lived in South America before immigrating to the United States when he was eleven years old. He studied at the Art Institute of Chicago and the Detroit Art Academy and taught art at the University of Michigan from 1945 until his death in 1953.

Francisco Luis Mora (1874–1940)

Francisco Luis Mora painted murals for the Orpheum Theatre in Los Angeles, the reading room of the Lynn Public Library in Lynn, Massachusetts, the central building of the Red Cross in Washington, D.C., and in Clarksville, Tennessee (1938). Among his earliest public works was a large decoration for the Missouri State Building for the Saint Louis Fair of 1904, for which he received a Bronze Medal.

Mora was born in Montevideo, Uruguay, in 1874, and his family immigrated to the United States in 1880. He studied with his father, a sculptor, and at the Museum of Fine Arts School in Boston and at the Art Students League in New York. He taught painting and drawing for many years at the Chare School and the Art Students League in New York. He died in New York City in 1940.

José Moya del Pino (1891–1969)

Throughout the 1930s, José Moya del Pino painted murals under the auspices of the WPAP and for private corporations. In 1933 he painted murals and did the decorations, in Aztec and Mayan motifs, for the rathskeller of the Aztec Brewery in San Diego, California. In the mid 1930s, he worked on the WPAP-sponsored murals painted in San Francisco's Coit Tower. He also painted murals in Stockton (1936), Redwood City (1937), and Lancaster, California (1937), and Alpine, Texas (1940).

In 1988 Moya del Pino's murals and decorations in the rathskeller of the Aztec Brewery in San Diego were threatened with destruction when the brewery was targeted for demolition to make way for the construction of a $10 million concrete warehouse. The brewery had been closed for more than thirty years. When Salvador Roberto Torres, a leading Chicano activist from the Barrio de la Logan, learned of the demolition, he sought to have the murals saved.

José Moya del Pino, born in Cordova, Spain, in 1891, studied art in his native country and settled in San Francisco in 1928. He died in Ross, outside San Francisco, in 1969. Most of his work was done in California.

Rufino Silva
(1919–)

The work of Rufino Silva, a Chicago-based artist, belongs to the Chicago school of social realism in a surrealistic vein. Silva was born in Humacao, Puerto Rico, in 1919. He studied at the Chicago Art Institute from 1938 to 1942 on a fellowship from the Puerto Rican government. He taught at the Layton School of Art, Milwaukee, from 1946 to 1947 and studied abroad for four years, from 1947 to 1951, in Europe and South America on grants from the art institute. He returned to Chicago in 1952 and joined the faculty. He retired in the 1970s.

HISPANIC ARTISTS: 1960S AND 1970S ✦ ✦ ✦ ✦ ✦ ✦ ✦ ✦ ✦ ✦ ✦ ✦

In the 1960s the art of Mexican-American and other Hispanic artists continued to reflect the many current styles of art, from figurative to abstract, from pop, op, and funk to destructive. Some of the artists who had painted murals in the 1930s and 1940s turned to abstraction, as in the case of Edward Chávez. However, he continued to make references in his abstract works to his background by using Mexican place-names, such as Xochimilco in one of his paintings.

Among the Mexican-American artists who matured in the 1960s are Michael Ponce de León of New York, Eugenio Quesada of Phoenix, Peter Rodríguez of San Francisco, Melesio Casas of San Antonio, Manuel Neri of San Francisco, Ernesto Palomino of Fresno, California, and Luis Jiménez of Hondo, New Mexico. Puerto Rican artists who matured during the same period include New York—based artists Olga Albizu, Pedro Villarini, Rafael Montañez-Ortiz (Ralph Ortiz), and Rafael Ferrer. There were many other artists from Latin America working in New York and other U.S. cities at the time, but their work falls outside the confines of this study because their formative years as artists were spent in their country of origin. Their presence, however, has not gone unnoticed by Hispanic and other American artists. Some remained in the United States for many years and then returned to their native countries. Others stayed to continue their careers.

Among those who stayed and attained national and international status for their work is the Argentine printmaker Mauricio Lasansky, who immigrated to the United States in 1943 and taught printmaking at Iowa State University, Ames. He influenced generations of American printmakers through his teaching and his work. He was born in Buenos Aires in 1914 and became a U.S. citizen in 1952. Marisol Escobar, born to Venezuelan parents in Paris in 1930, has resided in New York City since 1960. She became internationally famous in the 1960s with her sculptures of well-known personalities, such as Lyndon B. Johnson and John Wayne. Fernando Botero, known for his paintings of overblown figures used in satirical contexts, arrived in New York City in 1960. He was born in Medellín, Colombia, and now resides in New York City and Paris.

♦ ♦ ♦ ♦ ♦ ♦ ♦ ♦ ♦ ♦ ♦ ♦ ♦ ♦ ♦ ♦ **MEXICAN-AMERICAN ARTISTS**

**Melesio Casas
(1929–)**

Melesio Casas of San Antonio, was among the pioneers of the Chicano art movement. Although he began to include references to the United Farm Workers' eagle logo and pre-Columbian motifs in his work as early as 1970, the way in which these were used reflects the pop art style of the early 1960s. Typical of these works is the 1970 painting *Brownies of the Southwest*.

Casas was born in El Paso, in 1929. He attended Texas Western University, where he received his bachelor of arts degree in 1956, and the University of the Americas in Mexico City, where he received his master of fine arts degree in 1958. As a teacher and an artist at San Antonio College for almost thirty years, he had a strong impact on the training and education of many Chicano artists in San Antonio. He is retired and presently lives in southern Italy.

**Luis Jiménez
(1940–)**

Luis Jiménez, of El Paso, is primarily known for his sculptures made of resin epoxy coated with fiberglass. Jiménez paraphrased Mexican art, American Western art, and used pre-Columbian concepts in his works of the late 1960s and early 1970s. Since then, he has concentrated on the Southwest for a series of sculptures and colored-pencil drawings. Among the early works are *Man on Fire* (1969–70), *The End of the Trail* (1971), *The American Dream* (1967–69), and *Indians to Rockets* (1972).

Jiménez initially selected the many post office murals found all over the country as a source for the imagery in the *Indian to Rockets* project. The murals in the Southwest invariably deal with the history of the region or its industries. What struck the artist most was the emphasis in all of these murals on the notion of progress, exemplified by the machine. Starting in the early 1970s, he did studies on the history of the Southwest that were eventually used for a series of sculptures on that subject, titled *Progress I*, *Progress II*, and so on.

Toward the end of the 1970s, Jiménez began to concentrate more specifically on regional subjects in which the Chicano, the Anglo, and others were represented in their natural surroundings. A good example of these works is the drawing of a man and woman dancing while an onlooker watches, titled *Honky Tonk* (1981–86).

Jiménez was born in El Paso in 1940. He attended the University of Texas, Austin, where he received his bachelor of fine arts degree in 1964. He received a fellowship from the National University of Mexico. Shortly afterward, he moved to New York, where he worked and exhibited in several galleries. He now resides in Hondo, New Mexico.

Manuel Neri
(1930–)

Manuel Neri of the San Francisco Bay area was at the forefront of the art movements of the 1960s, especially funk art. Although his work was based primarily on the human figure defined in plaster and selective polychromy, he referred to pre-Columbian architectural forms, such as the pyramid, in other works.

Neri, born in Sanger, California, in 1930, received all his early schooling in Los Angeles. He studied ceramics from 1949 to 1953 at San Francisco City College, the University of California, and the Bray Foundation in Helena, Montana. He also studied at the Oakland School of Art and Crafts from 1955 to 1957 and at the California School of Art, now the San Francisco Art Institute, from 1957 to 1959. He has taught at the University of California, Davis, for many years.

Ernesto Palomino
(1933–)

Ernesto Palomino was among the first of the Chicano muralists to use pre-Columbian and Mexican as well as Chicano motifs in murals, such as the one he painted in Fresno, California, in 1971. Before he began work as a muralist, Palomino made constructions of various materials that were characteristic of the works being produced in the San Francisco Bay area in the mid-1960s.

Palomino, born in Fresno, in 1933, has spent most of his life in that city as an artist, and has been a professor at Fresno State University since 1970. He attended the San Francisco Art Institute in 1954, Fresno City College in 1957, and San Francisco State University from 1960 to 1965.

Michael Ponce de León (1922–)

The work of New York printmaker Michael Ponce de León was in keeping with the new styles of the 1960s. He used a raised surface (relief) and objects to create works that were expressive of his feelings toward words, places, conditions, and events.

Ponce de León was born in Miami, in 1922 and spent his early years in Mexico City. He joined the U.S. Air Force during World War II. After working as a cartoonist in New York in the 1940s and early 1950s, he turned to printmaking in the late 1950s. He has taught printmaking at the Pratt Graphic Center in New York.

Peter Rodríguez (1926–) and Eugenio Quesada (1927–)

Peter Rodríguez of California and Eugenio Quesada of Arizona spent several years in Mexico, and their work reflects that experience. Rodríguez used Mexican place-names in some of his abstract works, such as *Tlalpan*. In recent years, he has concentrated on making altars that have a closer relationship to his background as a Chicano in northern California. Quesada's drawings of Mexican-American children are similar in form and subject to the paintings and drawings of Mexican artists such as Raúl Anguiano.

Rodríguez was born in Stockton, California, in 1926 and received all his schooling in that city. As founder of the Mexican Museum in San Francisco in 1972, he has had a great impact on the development of the Chicano art movement in the San Francisco Bay area.

Quesada, born in Wickenburg, Arizona, in 1927, studied at Mesa Community College and Arizona State University, where he received a bachelor of arts degree. He taught at Santa Paula High School, California, in

1954, Glendale Community College, Arizona, in 1972, and has taught at Arizona State University since 1972.

PUERTO RICAN ARTISTS ✦

Olga Albizu
(1924–)

Olga Albizu is an abstract painter who became widely known for her paintings for RCA record covers for the music of Stan Getz in the late 1950s. Albizu was born in Ponce, Puerto Rico, in 1924 and has lived in the United States since 1956. She first arrived in New York City in 1948 with a University of Puerto Rico fellowship for postgraduate study. She studied with the well-known abstract expressionist Hans Hoffmann at the Art Students League from 1948 to 1951, and that experience is evident in her work. She also studied in Paris and Florence in 1951.

Rafael Ferrer
(1933–)

In the 1960s Rafael Ferrer was at the forefront of the movement in New York City that dealt with temporary installations and other ephemeral works and deemphasized "the object" as a work of art. He experimented with a variety of media and methods, from assemblages, constructions, and freestanding sculpture to lengths of chain-link fence, blocks of ice, bales of hay, and masses of dry leaves used to create environments for indoor and outdoor exhibitions. These temporary installations were related to the nonobject events of conceptual art of the early 1970s.

In the early 1970s, Ferrer began to focus on imaginary voyages and the apparatus used to carry them out—maps, kayaks, tents, and boats—in works assembled or constructed of steel, wood, and other materials.

Ferrer was born in Santurce, Puerto Rico, in 1933. He studied at the Shunton Military Academy, Virginia, from 1948 to 1951 and at Syracuse University, New York, from 1951 to 1952. He abandoned his studies at Syracuse to study art in Puerto Rico, where he was introduced to the work of the surrealists by the Spanish painter E. F. Granell. From then on he spent part of the year in Puerto Rico and part in the United States until 1966, when he settled in Philadelphia.

Ralph Ortiz
(1934–)

The work of Rafael Montañez-Ortiz (Ralph Ortiz), was part of the European and American movement known as destructive art. His best-known piece, *Piano Destruction Concert*, was performed on BBC television in 1966

Figure 13. Ralph Ortiz.
Piano Destruction Concert
Duncan Terrace. *Destruction
in Art Symposium,*
September 1966, London.

and later presented on national and local television in the United States
(Figure 13). The extreme gestures in Ortiz's work have their source in the
work of the European Dadaists, who emerged during World War I. In one
of their events, they invited viewers to use an ax placed next to a small ex-
hibit to destroy the art. This was only one of many antiart gestures of the
Dadaists. Ortiz focused on the violence itself in order to emphasize its
pervasive presence in our lives. This was unlike the "happenings" of Claes
Oldemburg, Allan Kaprow, and others, which were essentially formalist
events.

Ortiz also used pre-Columbian references in a series he called Archaeological Finds, in order to focus on his non-European roots and the destruction wrought by the first Europeans who arrived in the Americas. A typical piece in this series is an upholstered chair that was torn apart—destroyed—and titled *Tlazolteotl* (1963), a manifestation of the Aztec earth goddess.

Ortiz was born in New York City in 1934. He studied at the High School of Art and Design, the Brooklyn Museum of Art, and the Pratt Institute, where he received a bachelor of science degree and a master of fine arts degree in 1964. He received the doctorate of fine arts and fine arts higher education degrees from Columbia University in 1967. He taught at New York University in 1968, and was an adjunct professor at Hostos Community College in the Bronx in 1970.

Pedro Villarini

(1933-)

Pedro Villarini defines all the motifs in his paintings with great precision. There is a stillness and an air of calm in his painting *La Fortaleza* (1968). The peaceful effect is enhanced by the horizontal directions established by the fortress wall and the buildings in the middle ground, and by the clouds in the sky. They are balanced by the turret of the fortress on the left side of the painting.

Villarini was born in 1933 in Hato Ray, Puerto Rico, and has lived in New York City since 1947. He is a self-taught painter.

HISPANIC ARTISTS: 1970S TO THE PRESENT ♦ ♦ ♦ ♦ ♦ ♦ ♦ ♦ ♦

Chicano Artists

There were many Mexican-American artists who matured in the 1970s and 1980s. Some were muralists or public artists, others were not. Many easel painters, sculptors, printmakers, and poster artists were also interested in the Chicano movement as a source of their work. Some of them started as muralists and then turned to painting easel pictures, making altars, or creating other nonmural work.

The greatest number of Hispanic artists are found in California, followed by Texas and then the other states with sizeable Hispanic populations.

Many have received recognition for their work through regional, national, and international exhibitions that have focused on their background as Hispanics. In the late 1960s and early 1970s, exhibitions of Chicano art were strictly local and regional events. By the late 1970s, major exhibitions that included all Hispanic groups were being organized and presented in the United States and abroad.

Los Angeles

In Los Angeles numerous muralists as well as easel painters, sculptors, and printmakers were active. Those who painted murals in the 1970s concentrated more and more on nonmural work by the 1980s. Among the artists who did both are Carlos Almaraz, Gilbert Sánchez Luján (Magú), Frank Romero, John Valadez, and Gronk. Almaraz, Sánchez Luján (Magú), and Romero were members of the group called Los Four. The other member was Beto de la Rocha. They focused on Mexican icons and the Chicano political movement in their work. Gronk was a member of ASCO (nausea) along with Willie Herrón, Harry Gamboa, and Patssi Valdez. They were conceptual and performance artists as well as muralists in the 1970s.

Carlos Almaraz (1941–)

Carlos Almaraz was deeply involved with the Chicano movement in the 1970s, doing volunteer work with the United Farmworkers Union from 1972 to 1974, and graphic designs for the Teatro Campesino, which was formed to promote the farm worker cause. He was also a counselor and program director for the All Nations Neighborhood Center, helping "hard core" youth from 1974 to 1976. He also painted murals in East Los Angeles during the same period until 1978. Since the 1980s, he has concentrated on painting nonmural works of art that focus on his background as a Chicano. A good example of his nonmural work is the painting *Europe and the Jaguar* (1982), in which the two major strands of Mexican and Mexican-American or Chicano culture—the European and the indigenous—are woven into a complex pictorial statement. A woman and a jaguar walking hand in hand are in front of a backdrop full of isolated motifs—a house, a train, a quarter moon, human heads in profile—painted in an explosive style. A man between them on a lower level stands calmly smoking a cigarette. The backdrop seems to be full of multicolored sparks that give the surface a luminous effect. Almaraz was born in Mexico City in 1941. His family moved to Chicago when he was one year old, and to California when he was eight. He attended Loyola University in New Orleans, California State University, Los Angeles, East Los Angeles College, and Los Angeles Community College. He also attended the New School of

Social Research and the Art Students League in New York City. Almaraz received his master of fine arts degree from the Otis Art Institute in 1974. He exhibited as a member of Los Four in 1974 at the University of California, Irvine and the Los Angeles County Museum.

**Judy Baca
(1946–)**

Judy Baca is one of the pioneers of the mural movement in Los Angeles. She founded the first city of Los Angeles mural program in 1974, and in 1976 she cofounded the Social and Public Art Resource Center (SPARC) in Venice, California, where she served as artistic director throughout the 1970s and 1980s. Her best-known work is *The Great Wall of Los Angeles*. Painted over five summers, the half-mile long mural employed 40 ethnic scholars, 450 multicultural neighborhood youth, 40 assisting artists, and more than 100 support staff (Figure 14).

She is currently working on a mural program that addresses issues of war, peace, cooperation, interdependence, and spiritual growth. It is titled

Figure 14. Judy Baca. 350 Mexicans Deported and Dustbowl Refugees. Detail of The Great Wall of Los Angeles. 1980.

World Wall: A Vision of the Future without Fear and consists of seven portable panels that measure ten feet by thirty feet each.

Baca was born in Los Angeles in 1946. She attended California State University, Northridge, where she received her bachelor of arts degree in 1969. She also did work toward a master of art education degree and completed an intensive mural techniques course in Cuernavaca, Mexico.

Rupert García (1941-)

The precisely defined flat areas that are characteristic of the silk-screen process make the work of Rupert García immediately recognizable. The unvarying fields of color, which are also part of this process, carry over into some of his painting. This aspect of his work is so strong that a design he provided for a mural in Chicano Park, San Diego, retained the look of a silk-screen print. The pylon mural, actually painted by Víctor Ochoa and the Barrio Renovation Team, focuses on *Los Tres Grandes* (Diego Rivera, José Clemente Orozco, and David Alfaro Siqueiros) and *Frida Kahlo* (1978).

García was born in French Camp, California, in 1941. He attended Stockton College and San Francisco State University, where he received his bachelor of arts degree, in painting in 1968 and a master of arts degree in printmaking (silk-screen) in 1970. He pursued his doctoral studies in art education at the University of California, Berkeley, from 1973 to 1975, and received another master of arts degree, in the history of modern art, in 1981. He taught at San Francisco State University from 1969 to 1981; the San Francisco Art Institute from 1973 to 1980; the University of California, Berkeley from 1979 to the present; Mills College in 1981; Washington State University in 1984; and the Mexican Museum, San Francisco in 1986.

Carmen Lomas Garza (1948-)

Carmen Lomas Garza, a painter and printmaker, uses her Chicano background as the primary focus of her work. Her images, based on recollections of her childhood in south Texas, are used to heal the wounds she suffered as a result of racism and discrimination.

One of Lomas Garza's most widely known series is the one based on the game *Lotería* (The Lottery) (Figure 15). In the work, titled *Lotería—Tabla Llena*, she consciously used an exaggerated perspective, reminiscent of the works of native artists, because it allowed her to present all the thematic

Figure 15. Carmen Lomas
Garza. Lotería—Table
Llena, 1974.

elements (motifs) in the work in as clear a fashion as possible. The large table was presented as if seen from above, and everything else—the figures, the animals, furniture, plants, and trees—was represented as if seen head-on. The only exception is the walkway at the bottom of the print, also shown as if seen from above.

Garza was born in Kingsville, Texas, in 1948. She attended Texas A&I University in Kingsville, where she received her bachelor of arts degree in 1972. She attended Antioch Graduate School of Education, Juarez Lincoln Extension (Austin), where she received her master of arts degree in 1973. She received another master of arts degree from San Francisco State University in 1980. She currently resides in San Francisco.

Ester Hernández
(1944–)

Ester Hernández has used her painting and graphic work to make statements about Chicano culture and the economic forces that have had a negative impact on one segment of it: the farm-working communities in California. One of the most controversial works by Hernández is a print that was published on the cover of *En frecuencia*, a guide for public radio in Santa Rosa, California. The primary focus of the image was on Our Lady of Guadalupe, but instead of using the traditional image of the Virgin she used a woman in a karate stance to make a statement about the liberation of Chicanas.

Hernández was born in Dinuba, California, in 1944 to farm-worker parents. She moved to the San Francisco Bay area in 1971 to continue her studies. She met and worked with other Chicano artists, among them Malaquías Montoya, and became involved with *Mujeres Muralistas* (Women Muralists). She teaches at an art center for the developmentally disabled in San Francisco.

Yolanda López (1942–)

López used Our Lady of Guadalupe in a series of works that emphasize Chicano culture and identity. She substituted human figures and an Aztec deity for Our Lady of Guadalupe in several works, including her grandmother, Tonantzin (Our Mother), a small sculpture of Coatlicue (Serpents Her Skirt), an Indian woman nursing her child, and the artist herself. Her self-portraits include a performance piece and a painting. In the former, the artist was photographed moving toward the viewer armed with paint brushes and wearing blue shorts, a sleeveless undershirt with stars painted on it, and sneakers. In the latter, the artist is shown appropriating the attributes of Our Lady of Guadalupe and her pre-Columbian counterpart. She runs toward the observer with an expression of triumph while holding a serpent in one hand and a mantle with a star-studded blue field in the other.

López was born in San Diego in 1942. She received her master of fine arts degree from the University of California, San Diego in 1978. She is currently a visiting lecturer in painting at the California College of Arts and Crafts.

Amalia Mesa-Baines (1943–)

Although the altar installations by Amalia Mesa-Baines are not directly religious in content, their format has allowed her to attain a spiritual sensibility that is in tune with her personal and cultural life. She has used these altars to pay homage to ancestors and Mexican historical figures in the arts, religion, and the cinema, such as Frida Kahlo, Sor Juana de la Cruz, and Dolores del Rio.

Mesa-Baines uses Mexican symbols in her altars, such as *calaveras* (skulls), *corazones* (hearts), crosses, and images of the Virgin in her many manifestations. She also cuts her own paper *(papel picado)*, makes the altar cloths and paper flowers, and builds the *nichos* and the *retablo* boxes with the help of a carpenter. One of her major works, *Altar for San Juana Inés de la Cruz* (1981), a mixed-media construction, was shown in the Made in Aztlán exhibition at the Centro Cultural de la Raza in San Diego in 1986.

Mesa-Baines first exhibited an altar in the annual show at the Galería de la Raza in 1976 and later at the San Francisco Museum of Art in 1980. She has since exhibited altars in several national and international exhibitions. Mesa-Baines received her doctor of philosophy in psychology with an emphasis on culture and identity.

Patricia Rodríguez (1944-)

Patricia Rodríguez was one of the leading muralists in the San Francisco Bay area in the 1970s. In 1972, she organized the group known as Mujeres Muralistas, and with them painted murals from 1972 to 1977. Its members were Consuelo Méndez, Irene Pérez, and Graciela Carrillo. In 1980 she began working on box constructions, inspired by the traditional *nichos* that serve a religious function for the Chicano family. She focused on religious prejudice, cultural identity, and the world around her. The boxes or nichos, made with found and handmade objects, are based on Catholic traditions as well as on the myths, legends, and magic of Mexican culture dating all the way back to the Aztecs and the Mayans.

Rodríguez was born in Marfa, Texas, in 1944. She was raised by her grandparents, and at age eleven lived with her parents, who worked as migrants throughout the Southwest. At age thirteen, in the 1950s, she attended public schools in California. She later attended junior college and the San Francisco Art Institute on a scholarship. She taught at the University of California from 1975 to 1980.

Frank Romero (1941-)

Frank Romero, another member of the Los Four, has often focused on street scenes in his paintings, in which automobiles are prominently displayed. Sometimes he makes a statement about barrio life in Los Angeles. He works in various media other than painting and drawing—photography, graphics, ceramics, and textile design. A good example of his work is the painting *The Closing of Whittier Boulevard* (1984). The night scene includes a bird's-eye view of a street corner in East Los Angeles where the police have set up barricades to stop the flow of traffic. The two streets leading up to the corner are filled with cars with their lights illuminating the police behind the barricades, who are holding billy clubs. The toylike appearance of the figures and the cars gives the entire scene an eerie effect.

Romero was born in East Los Angeles in 1941. He attended the Otis Art Institute and California State University, Los Angeles, where he met Carlos Almaraz in the 1960s. He met Gilbert Luján and Beto de la Rocha in 1969 during a sojourn in New York (1968–69) during which he stayed with his friend Almaraz. Throughout the early 1970s, he was involved in the Chicano movement.

Gilbert Sánchez Luján (Magú) (1940–)

Sánchez Luján is known for his pastel paintings and painted wood sculptures that deal with barrio life in southern California. In some of the wood sculptures, he combines brightly colored cactus and palm trees in tableaus that include smartly dressed figures with dog faces! Their activities on the street, at the beach, or elsewhere in the barrio strike a responsive chord in the viewer who reacts to the humor in the scenes. A good example of his work is the sculpture *Hot Dog Meets La Fufu con su Poochie* (1986). The wood cutouts of the two figures, the dog, the plants, and the small fence were painted in different colors and constructed to create a whimsical street scene with two young people in the barrio reacting to each other.

Luján was born in French Camp (Stockton), California, in 1940. He attended East Los Angeles Junior College and Long Beach State College, where he received his bachelor of arts degree. He received his master of fine arts degree at the University of California, Irvine, and made a commitment to Chicano art at this time. He joined Almaraz and Romero to form the exhibiting group known as Los Four. Their first show went up at Irvine in 1974. He taught ethnic studies at Fresno City College from 1976 to 1981, and then returned to Los Angeles, where he taught at the Municipal Art Center at Barnsdall Park.

San Francisco

In San Francisco since the 1960s, artists have focused on social, political, cultural, and feminist issues in their nonmural works. Malaquías Montoya and Rupert García were two of the most active political artists in the Bay Area. Their comments against American involvement in the internal affairs of Latin American countries appeared repeatedly in their silk-screen prints, posters, and paintings of the 1970s and 1980s. Many women artists dealt with cultural and feminist issues during the same time. Yolanda López focused on the family and Our Lady of Guadalupe in her drawings, paintings, and installations of the late 1970s. Amalia Mesa Baines dealt with similar issues in her altar installations. Ester Hernández dealt with feminist and environmental issues in her prints and paintings. Patricia Rodríguez, a muralist in the 1970s, turned to cultural issues in the 1980s, with boxes that have their genesis in the home altars found in many Chicano homes. Carmen Lomas Garza focused on her childhood in south Texas in her prints and paintings of the 1970s and 1980s.

San Diego, California

Many Chicano artists in San Diego were at the forefront of the Chicano mural movement. Their struggle to create Chicano Park in the Barrio de la Logan and the Centro Cultural in Balboa Park has been recounted in numerous local, national, and international publications. The story has even been told in an hour-long video that has been telecast over National Public Television. Among the pioneers of that struggle were Salvador Roberto

Figure 16. Víctor Ochoa. Geronimo, 1981. Centro Cultural de la Raza, Balboa Park, San Diego, California.

Torres, Víctor Ochoa, David Avalos, and others who were members of the group called Toltecas en Aztlán, initially, and later Congreso de Artistas Chicanos en Aztlan. (For more information, see the section on Chicano Murals later in this chapter.)

Víctor Ochoa, one of the pioneers of the Chicano art movement in San Diego, has concentrated primarily on mural painting. A good example of his work is the mural *Gerónimo* (1981) on one part of the wall of the Centro Cultural in Balboa Park (Figure 16). It is a gigantic depiction of the late-nineteenth-century Apache warrior Gerónimo. It is a faithful rendition of a well-known photograph of the Apache leader. Ochoa saw him as a freedom fighter, with whom he identified as a Chicano fighting for his rights in his community. This is in contrast to the Anglo-American view of Gerónimo as a renegade. The other figures on either side are also rendered from photographs. There is a potter on the left and a woman in a skeletal costume on the right. Behind her is a view of Chicano Park with the kiosk where celebrations take place (Figure 17). The Coronado Bridge is seen in the background.

Víctor Ochoa
(1948–)

Figure 17. Víctor Ochoa. Chicano Park, 1981. Centro Cultural de la Raza, Balboa Park, San Diego, California.

San Antonio   Although Chicano murals were painted in San Antonio, most of the artists in the city concentrated on nonmural work as painters, sculptors, printmakers, and photographers. Among the best-known Chicano artists in San Antonio are César Martínez, Rudy Treviño, Jesse Treviño, and Adán Hernandez.

César Martínez
(1944–)   In the late 1970s César Martínez dealt with specific Chicano motifs other than the usual Huelga eagle and the Chicano triface. He was fascinated

Figure 18. Cesar Martinez.
La Pareja, *1979.*

with the pachuco (zoot suiter) as an important icon in Chicano culture. As a teenager in the 1950s and 1960s, he saw individuals who adopted the dress of the pachucos. He also included other figures in his works that he classified as *batos locos* (pachucos) and *mujeres* (women). Since he did not have any other visual information, other than his memory and photographs (snapshots and high school annual pictures), he used them as sources for some of his paintings. He was interested in these types as individuals rather than as a social phenomenon. An example of these works is *La Pareja (The Couple,* 1979) (Figure 18).

Aside from these Chicano subjects, Martínez also did a painting of Our Lady of Guadalupe under the guise of Leonardo da Vinci's *Mona Lisa;* it was a bizarre juxtaposition of motifs. The work, titled *Mona Lupe,* demonstrates the power that each of its sources has to evoke emotions and to function within several levels of meaning. First of all, there is the antiart posture first articulated by Marcel Duchamp in his work of 1919 titled *L.H.O.O.Q.* (a reproduction of Leonardo da Vinci's *Mona Lisa* with a mustache and beard added in pencil), and second, there is the entire realm of Chicano identity, exemplified by the religious, national, and political icon of Our Lady of Guadalupe. Martínez was born in Laredo, Texas, in 1944. He attended Texas A&I University in Kingsville, where he received his bachelor of science degree in 1968. He resides in San Antonio.

**Jesse Treviño
(1946–)**

Jesse Treviño used everyday scenes and places in the barrio for works that have been included in photorealism exhibitions in San Antonio and elsewhere. An example of the very matter-of-fact portrayals of the barrio is the painting *La Panadería (The Bakery)* (Figure 19).

Treviño was born in Monterrey, Mexico, in 1946. His family moved to San Antonio in 1948. He attended the Art Students League in New York City on an art scholarship and studied portrait painting under William Draper from 1965 to 1966. He attended Our Lady of the Lake University in San Antonio, where he received his bachelor of arts degree in 1974. He attended the University of Texas, San Antonio where he received his master of fine arts degree in 1979.

**Rudy Treviño
(1945–)**

Rudy Treviño worked in an abstract style in the 1960s and in a more figurative one in the 1970s and 1980s in which he used pre-Columbian, Mexican, and Chicano subjects. An example of Chicano ichnography is his work

Figure 19. Jesse Treviño.

Panadería, late 1970s.

titled *George Zapata*. The work refers to the Mexican revolutionary hero Emiliano Zapata and to the American revolutionary hero George Washington, both of which are components of Chicano culture and identity.

Brownsville, Texas

George Trúan

(1944–)

George Trúan used the altar format in the late 1970s in a series of works he called Altares Chicanos. Among those works is *Self-Portrait,* which includes a statue of Our Lady of Guadalupe in the center of the tabletop with a backdrop filled with numerous photographs of the artist taken at different ages. Next to the image of Our Lady of Guadalupe is a photograph of John Kennedy, and above that, a print of the Santo Niño de Atocha (The Christ Child of Atocha). Flowers were placed in vases on the left and right sides of the tabletop.

Trúan was born in Kingsville, Texas, in 1944. He attended Texas A&I University in Kingsville, where he received his bachelor of arts degree in 1968 and his master of arts degree in 1974. He resides in Brownsville, Texas, where he is an art professor at Southmost College.

The artists in Santa Fe are unique because they have been able to build on the santero tradition as well as the Chicano muralist movement that was central to Chicano art in the 1970s and 1980s. No other region where Chicanos reside has santeros. (For more information, see the section Chicano Murals later in this chapter.)

Santa Fe

The resurgence of the santo-making tradition dates from the 1960s when New Mexico artists looked to their own past for inspiration for their work. They ignored the work of the López family and other twentieth-century santeros and turned to the use of colors to make the pieces closer to the traditional ones produced in the nineteenth century. Among the well-known new santeros are Luis Tapia of Santa Fe and Félix A. López of Española.

Typical of the new works are the sculptures of Saint Michael by Félix A. López and Luis Tapia. *San Miguel* (1984) by López, in a private collection, shows the saint with his sword in one hand and the scales in the other. This is the traditional image of the saint. The other way in which Saint Michael was portrayed is seen in the elaborate image of *St. Michael and the Dragon* by Tapia in the collection of the Museum of International Folk Art. These and other pieces by these santeros are generally larger than the unpainted santos made in Cordova and are meant to be taken more seriously as images related to the Hispanic tradition in New Mexico.

Félix A. López (1942–) and Luis Tapia (1950–)

López was born in Gilman, Colorado, in 1942. He attended New Mexico Highlands University, where he received his bachelor's degree with a major in Spanish and a minor in German in 1965. He taught high school in Corcoran and Orange, California, in the late 1960s. He continued his studies and received his master's degree in Spanish literature in 1972 from the University of New Mexico, Albuquerque. He began making santos in 1977.

Tapia was born in Santa Fe in 1950. He attended New Mexico State University for a year and began making santos around 1970 when he became aware of the Hispanic issues related to the civil rights movement. Unlike the earlier santeros, he began to use bright colors for the figures; this was shocking to viewers in the early 1970s. He also paints altar screens in the old style.

As in other regions where Hispanics are found, Chicago is home to numerous Chicano artists who painted murals during the late 1960s through

Chicago

the 1970s and part of the 1980s and now devote their energies to producing portable objects or nonmural art. Some have turned to painting, printmaking, or sculpture. (For more information, see the section Chicano Murals later in this chapter.)

**José Gonzalez
(1933–)**

José González of Chicago is a multitalented painter, photographer, and arts administrator who has been at the forefront of the muralist movement in that city since the early 1970s. He has also worked with the publication *Revista Chicano Riqueña,* now *The Americas Review,* published in Houston by Arte Público Press. Among the designs by González for *The Americas Review* is the one titled *Barrio murals* (1976). The cover design is a photo collage composed of the many murals painted in Chicago in the early 1970s.

González, born in Iturbide, Nuevo León, Mexico, in 1933, has lived most of his life in the United States. He studied and received a diploma from the Chicago Academy of Fine Arts in the mid-1950s and continued his studies at several institutions in the 1960s: the Instituto Allende, San Miguel Allende, Mexico; the University of Chicago; the School of the Art Institute of Chicago, where he received his bachelor of fine arts degree in 1970; and the University of Notre Dame, where he received his master of fine arts degree in 1971. He devoted all his energies to the Chicano movement throughout the 1970s and 1980s as a muralist, organizer of exhibitions, and founder of organizations, such as Movimiento Artístico Chicano (MArCh) and others.

**Marcos Raya
(1948–)**

One of the most prolific painters of murals and easel pictures is Marcos Raya, who was a full participant in the Chicano mural movement in Chicago and in recent years has also made altars with secular subjects, such as *Frida and Her Nurse* (1987).

Raya's murals deal with political issues in Chicago and abroad, with particular emphasis on Central America. This is seen in his panel for the mural program *Stop World War III* (1980) (Figure 20), in which six other artists participated. The mural project was initiated by the Chicago Mural group under the leadership of John Weber. The block-long mural includes different panels framed in accordance with a series of curvilinear formats. Raya's work is seen on the upper left of the mural. The motifs include the fallen statue of a Central American dictator and a group of figures above it holding banners and flags with the image of Che Guevara and references to El Salvador and Guatemala. Raya was born in Irapuato, Guanajuato, Mexico, and moved to Chicago in 1964. He studied drawing and painting for two years with Allan Thiekler.

Figure 20. Marcos Raya.
Stop World War III. *Mural.*
Chicago, Illinois.

Other Hispanic Artists

Puerto Ricans in the United States, Cuban Americans, and non-Mexican Hispanics are found primarily in New York, New Jersey, Miami, and Chicago. Their work is varied and represents the many styles that are found in the United States, Europe, and Latin America. It is difficult, therefore, to distinguish their work as being distinctively Puerto Rican, Cuban, and so forth.

Carlos Alfonso (1950–)

Carlos Alfonso, a Miami-based Cuban-American artist, draws his images from the Afro-Cuban religious tradition. Among the motifs he uses is the knife, which stands for protection against the evil eye. The knife through the tongue is intended to keep evil quiet. He uses such motifs for their connotations as well as for formal reasons. His paintings include numerous references to the human figure presented in simplified configurations that recall the jungle paintings (1943) of Wifredo Lam. They are shown within a flattened-out visual field full of crescent shapes that can be used to define large mouths with toothy grins, tongues, large leaves, and eye masks.

Alfonso was born in Cuba in 1950. He studied painting, sculpture, and printmaking at the Academia de Bellas Artes San Alejandro in Havana from 1969 to 1973 and art history at the University of Havana from 1974 to 1977. He began a teaching career at the Academia San Alejandro as instructor in art history from 1971 to 1973, and then taught studio courses in art schools of the Ministry of Culture during 1973 and 1980. He immigrated to the United States in 1980 for ideological and professional reasons.

Luis Cruz Azaceta (1942–)

The Cuban-American artist Luis Cruz Azaceta, like other Hispanic artists in New York, has been concerned with the brutalizing effects of violence in his work, in which cartoonlike characters are often presented as victims. According to Azaceta, "My art takes the form of violence, destruction, cruelty, injustice, humor, absurdity and obscenity, as a revolt against our condition and man's evil instincts. I want my paintings and drawings to be an outcry, to awaken man's deepest feelings. Feelings of love, nobility and brotherhood."

Azaceta, born in Havana, Cuba, in 1942, arrived in the United States in 1960 and settled in Hoboken, New Jersey. He began to take life-drawing lessons at an adult center in Queens in the mid-1960s. While working nights as a clerk in the library of New York University, he enrolled in the School of Visual Arts in 1966 and received the equivalent of a bachelor of arts degree in 1969. He has taught at the University of California, Davis in 1980, Louisiana State University, Baton Rouge in 1982, the University of California, Berkeley i in 1983, and Cooper Union, New York in 1984. He lives in Queens, New York.

Rafael Colón-Morales (1941–)

Rafael Colón-Morales was a member of Borinquen 12, an artists' group formed to find venues for their work. The artists did not have a unifying goal in their work other than a practical aim to have their art exhibited, and the group no longer exists. Colón-Morales's early work was primarily geometric abstraction. His later works bear a resemblance to the Cuban surrealist painter Wifredo Lam, with crescent shapes and spiked projections within a dense thicket of forms. An example is *Apestosito (Stinker)* (1969). Colón-Morales was born in 1941 in Trujillo Alto, Puerto Rico. He has lived in New York since 1970.

Arnaldo Roche Rabell (1955–)

Arnaldo Roche Rabell, a Chicago-based Puerto Rican artist, has a unique style of painting in which the figures and their surroundings are almost overwhelmed by a densely painted surface. An overall furlike effect is the result of the paint being applied and then scratched with a sharp instrument. Rubbings and projections are the two methods he uses in his work. He lays a piece of canvas or paper over a model or an object that has been smeared with paint. He then rubs it and elaborates upon the distorted image. His projections of face-only self-portraits are presented in frontal view.

Roche was born in Puerto Rico in 1955. He studied architecture but gave it up for painting. He studied at the Chicago Art Institute, where he received a bachelor of fine arts degree and later a master of fine arts degree in 1984. He continues to live much of the year in Chicago.

Jorge Soto of New York became identified with the Taller Boricua (Puerto Rican Workshop), established in the barrio, where he distinguished himself as an artist. Like many self-taught artists, Soto defines his forms with very elaborate linear patterns. A good example is an untitled work on canvas painted in acrylic and ink. The two meticulously defined nude figures, a female and a male, are armless and shown standing in a frontal position on a green field with a few tropical plants around their legs. He is concerned with recovering an African and Taino Indian aesthetic in his works. Soto was born in New York City in 1947.

**Jorge Soto
(1947–)**

◆ **CHICANO MURALS**

Although there is great diversity in the works of the Chicano muralists, they shared a desire to paint walls in the barrios where large numbers of Hispanics reside. Their aim was to provide images that were acceptable to that community. Finally, they all had an affinity for the Mexican muralists of the 1920s through the 1950s.

Chicano murals are found over a vast area in the barrios of the Southwest, Pacific Southwest, Northwest, and the Great Lakes region. The number of murals in each community varies from just a few in some cities, like Houston, to the many hundreds in Los Angeles. Only a few of the most representative murals are included in this discussion because of limited space. The intent is to give the reader an understanding of the form, content, and meaning of the murals rather than a full survey of all the murals that were painted from the late 1960s through the early 1990s. The murals selected for discussion are among the most complex in thematic and formal terms. They are not the best, nor do they represent all the regions, but they span the decade of the 1970s, the period of greatest activity in the mural movement. Many of the artists have since worked on easel paintings and other portable works.

Diagrams of the murals are provided in the text, where appropriate, with captions listing the motifs used by the artists. The murals are discussed in chronological order as follows:

1. *History and Heroes,* by Congreso de Artistas Chicanos en Aztlán and Toltecas en Aztlán; 1973, Chicano Park, San Diego.

2. *Black and White Mural,* by Willie Herron and Gronk; 1973 and 1978, Los Angeles.

3. *History of the Mexican American Worker,* by Vicente Mendoza, José Nario, and Raymond Patlán; 1974—75, Blue Island, Illinois.

4. *La Raza Cosmica (The Cosmic Race),* by Raúl Valdez; 1977, Austin.

5. *En la lucha . . . ponte trucha (In the struggle . . . Beware),* by Rogelio Cárdenas; 1978, Hayward, California.

6. *Multicultural Mural,* by Gilberto Garduño and others; 1980, Santa Fe.

San Diego   Some of the earliest murals were painted in the San Diego area known as Chicano Park, in the Barrio de la Logan, and at the Centro Cultural de la Raza in Balboa Park, near downtown. Although murals were painted in other barrios of the city, it is in these two places that most of the murals were painted by local artists as well as by those who came in from other parts of California over a period of ten years in the 1970s.

Chicano Park exemplifies the mural movement, in which the community, artists' groups, students, and others were involved in efforts to give the area cohesiveness, direction, and meaning. The story behind the movement, which began in earnest in 1970 in the Barrio de la Logan (named after the street that runs through it), was reported in the local press and in several books.

The Barrio de la Logan was first altered when a freeway was built through its center in a north-south direction in the early 1960s. By 1969 the completion of the Coronado Bridge, running in an east-west direction, fragmented it further. Many residents lost their homes as a result of such massive construction. In spite of these changes, Salvador Roberto Torres, a former resident and a graduate of the Oakland School of Arts and Crafts, returned to the barrio in 1968 and began planning the concept he had been formulating to turn the area under the bridge into a Chicano Park. The plan was to make it a green corridor all the way to the waterfront and thereby open up the area to the sky and the bay for the people. In order to achieve this, the refuse dump under the bridge had to be cleaned up and murals painted along the way. The waterfront itself also had to be cleaned up.

By early 1970 Torres, along with other Chicano artists who called themselves Toltecas en Aztlán, began to discuss ideas regarding the bridge, the community, and their role as artists in it. This led to the discussion of murals in Chicano Park. Among those involved in the planning were Guillermo Aranda, Mario Acevedo, Víctor Ochoa, Tomás Castañeda, and Salvador Barajas.

While Torres and others were continuing with their plans to revitalize the barrio, an event that was to activate the entire community took place in April 1970. The California Highway Patrol moved in with a bulldozer to clear the topsoil under the bridge for the construction of a parking lot for thirty patrol cars. In addition, Chicano artists found out that the highway patrol had plans for a small brick building once used by the bridge engineer, which they wanted for themselves. The response was immediate. Artists, students, families, and children occupied the Ford Building in Balboa Park to emphasize the need for a Chicano cultural center. The area under the bridge was eventually turned over to the community piece by piece, and an abandoned water tank in Balboa Park was turned over to the group for a cultural center in 1971.

Chicano Park has more than eighteen concrete pillars, which have been painted on both sides since 1973. The area is bounded by the approaches to the bay bridge connecting Coronado Island to the mainland and Interstate Highway 5, and the freeway running perpendicular to it. Over thirty individual panels were painted during the 1970s and early 1980s by artists from San Diego and other California cities. The pillars supporting the bridge approaches are T-shaped and of varying heights. Almost all the pillars on the various ramps between National and Logan Avenues have been painted.

History and Heroes

The *History and Heroes* painting program began on the easternmost side of the area on two of the off-ramps flanking Logan Avenue. The triangular-shaped ramps were painted during the months of March and April 1973 by artists and people from the community. Both murals were coordinated by Congreso de Artistas en Aztlán and Toltecas en Aztlán. Among the artists who worked on both panels were Guillermo Aranda, Víctor Ochoa, Abraham Quevedo, Salvador Barajas, Arturo Román, Guillermo Rosete, Mario Acevedo, Tomas Castañeda, and Salvador Roberto Torres.

The off-ramp mural on the west side of Logan Avenue is typical of what was painted in the early 1970s in the Chicano barrios everywhere. It includes references to all three Mexican epochs (pre-Columbian, colonial, and modern) and recent Chicano history. In addition, there are references to contemporary events, such as space travel and civil rights demonstrations. It is immediately apparent that the entire mural was painted by several different artists. There are sharp lines of demarcation, with panels having little or no relation to others on either side, and the themes are not fully articulated.

The people represented along the upper portion of the mural represent historical as well as contemporary figures and are the work of several artists. The first four heads were painted by Guillermo Aranda: Pablo Picasso, included because he died when the mural was being painted; Jose Clemente Orozco and David Alfaro Siqueiros, two of the Mexican muralists most admired by the Chicano artists; and *La Niña Cosmica*, or the Cosmic Child, a reference to the people of Mexican descent and their future.

Carlos Santana, the rock music star, and Che Guevara, the Cuban-based Communist leader, were painted by an unknown artist, possibly Guillermo Rosete.

Víctor Ochoa painted César Chávez, the head of the United Farmworkers Union, and Joaquín Murrieta, a folk hero and bandit in nineteenth-century California. Chávez was a key figure in the Chicano movement for equal rights along economic, political, and educational lines.

The next heads were painted by Salvador Barajas. Rubén Salazar, a well-known journalist, was accidentally killed by police during the National Chicano Moratorium demonstration against the Vietnam War that took place in East Los Angeles on August 29, 1970. Salazar was considered the first martyr of the Chicano movement. Ramón Ortiz, born in Santa Fe, New Mexico (1813–1896), was a diplomat and priest who worked for better U.S.-Mexican relations during the 1840s. He was also appointed to oversee the removal of those New Mexicans who wished to live in Mexico after the war between Mexico and the United States. The next heads represent heroes of Mexican history: Miguel Hidalgo y Costilla and José Guadalupe Morelos, heroes of the War of Independence (1810–1821); Benito Juárez, the leading figure during the War of Reform of the 1850s and in the struggle against the French occupation of the 1860s; and the key figures of the Mexican Revolution of 1910: Venustiano Carranza, Francisco Villa, Rojas, and Emiliano Zapata.

There are panels from the extreme left to right beneath the heads appearing on the upper register. The first one on the left, painted by Guillermo Aranda and Guillermo Rosete, is a reference to the conquest of Mexico by the Spaniards. Skeletal figures wearing Spanish helmets are engulfed by flames and a jaguar is shown in their midst. The jaguar refers to the pre-Columbian peoples of Mexico. The flames, a paraphrase of José Clemente Orozco's murals in Mexico and the United States, refer to destruction as well as regeneration or rebirth. The skeletal figures are also a reference to Mexican art in general and to the work of José Guadalupe Posada in particular.

The next set of panels, also painted by Guillermo Aranda, focus on the future, the present, and the past. The first panel deals with outer space with some celestial bodies, and the present—the Chicano struggle for economic parity with other Americans—directly below it with the inclusion of the United Farmworkers' eagle symbol. The pyramid refers to the ancient past of Mexico, with which Chicanos identify.

The next two panels, painted by Arturo Román, focus on Chicano identity and the struggle to save the Barrio de la Logan from destruction by local and state authorities. Our Lady of Guadalupe, a reference to Mexican and Chicano identity, has religious as well as political meaning. The demonstration by barrio residents includes banners of Our Lady of Guadalupe and United Farmworkers flags. The stylized rainbow and workers in the fields above the demonstration scene were painted by Guillermo Rosete.

The Olmec collosal head was painted by Víctor Ochoa, and the two *soldaderas* (female soldiers of the Mexican Revolution) were painted by Arturo Román. The final two motifs, the man on horseback and the flag were painted by Guillermo Rosete and Sal Barajas. The man on horseback started out as a portrait of Francisco Villa carrying a Mexican flag and was later changed to a member of the Brown Berets, a paramilitary group of young Chicano militants, and the triface motif in the center of the flag is a reference to the mestizo, part Spanish, part Indian.

Los Angeles   Hundreds of murals were painted in Los Angeles over an extremely large area and on every conceivable type of surface (brick, wood, stucco, and concrete) and building (end walls of housing project buildings, back alleys, concrete stairways, park pavillions, side walls of grocery stores, pharmacies, launderettes, cultural centers, and many structures). Although most were painted in East Los Angeles, some were painted in other parts of the city, such as the Tujunga Wash murals by Judy Baca, miles away from the barrio. The earliest murals date from 1972 and are found in Estrada Courts and at the Mechicano Art Center.

Among the many artists who painted murals in East Los Angeles, starting in 1972, were Leonard Castellanos, who directed the Mechicano Art Center on Whittier Boulevard, and Charles Félix, who was associated with the Goez Gallery and others. Judy Baca, mentioned earlier, founded and headed the arts organization known as SPARC (Social and Public Art Resource Center) for many years. Many of the artists worked as members of groups such as ASCO (Distasteful), Los Dos (The Two) Streetscapers, Los Four (The Four), and others.

Castellanos was committed to finding ways to initiate and implement programs emanating from the Mechicano Art Center and introducing them into the barrio. The murals were part of the center's stated reasons for being. Eventually twenty-five murals were painted in Echo Par and fifteen in Ramona Gardens, a federal housing project of six hundred families.

The most extensive mural project at one location in the barrios of East Los Angeles is found at the Estrada Courts housing complex. The work, under the direction of Charles Félix, was begun in the summer of 1973. Materials for the project were provided by the Los Angeles City Housing Authority and the Los Angeles Fire Department, initially, and also by the Board of Public Works.

The murals designed by Charles Félix and other community artists were painted by youths living in the housing complex and surrounding community. About 125 of the more than 150 Hispanic youth who partici-

Figure 21. Willie Herrón and
Gronk. Black and White
Mural, *1973 and 1978.*
Estrada Courts,
Los Angeles, California.

pated in the project during the first summer were paid by the Los Angeles Housing Authority with funds from the Neighborhood Youth Corps.

The Estrada Courts murals display great variety. The subjects portrayed range from the usual pre-Columbian references to historical and contemporary ones relating to Mexico and the United States. The subjects had to be approved by a group of residents, organized under the name of Residentes Unidos (United Residents). Among the artists who painted murals at the courts are Willie Herron and Gronk, and Mario Torero of San Diego, as well as other members of the San Diego artist's group Congreso de Artistas Chicanos en Aztlán. Nearly sixty panels were painted by 1977. Many others were painted after that date.

Black and White Mural

Black and White Mural (Figures 21 and 22), by Willie Herron and Gronk, has various narratives and is composed of heads and massed figures that were placed in interlocking squares and rectangular units. There are long views of street scenes, as in the upper central part interspersed with other smaller units in which groups of figures are also shown at various eye levels. These are contrasted with individual heads that fill up the square formats and extreme close-ups of only the eyes of a human head presented upside down and right side up to the right of center.

The artists focused on their community, the Chicano movement, and their own lives—as well as on their own artwork—in the mural. The panels were

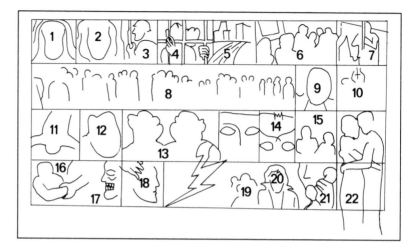

Figure 22. Willie Herrón and Gronk. Diagram for Black and White Mural, 1973 and 1978. Estrada Courts, Los Angeles, California.

evenly distributed in terms of space allotted to each artist. Herron painted a baboon (1) on the upper left, and Gronk painted a head of a long-haired youth (2) next to it. The rest of the panels on this register and most of the next one below it deal with East Los Angeles in general and the National Chicano Moratorium in particular. Herron painted a Los Angeles street scene (5), demonstrators carrying placards (7), and the largest panel, in which the demonstration itself is depicted (8). Gronk presents a helmeted soldier with rifle (3), figures behind bars (4), and women and children who may have sat and stood on the sidelines during the demonstration (6).

The remaining panels on the second through the fourth registers deal with terror, religion, death, Chicano art, portraiture, and the family in the barrio. Herron painted the remaining two panels of the second register from the top, which represent a terror-struck screaming woman (9) and the Catholic Sacred Heart (10). He also painted two panels in the third register, which represent a work performed by members of ASCO in the early 1970s, known as the *Walking Mural* (13), and a self-portrait with his sister based on a photograph taken of them when they were children (15). Herron also painted panels on the fourth register. On the extreme lower left a figure is being pulled by another by the arm (16), and next to it there is a long-haired head in profile with skeletal attributes (17). Toward the right there are demonstrators reacting to tear gas (19), a portrait of Patssi Valdés (20), a member of ASCO (Herron, Gronk, and Harry Gamboa were the other members), and a woman using a telephone (21).

On the extreme left of the third register, Gronk painted a sprawled dead figure (11) seen from above and only from the waist up, and the face of a clown (12) next to it. To the right of center on the same register, he painted two different views of the same set of eyes framed by barbed wire and a crown of thorns (14). On the fourth register, he painted a profile head (18), which has a somber aspect. The young couple (22) seen on the extreme right is the only vertical format used in the mural.

Gronk's young couple embracing each other and Herron's self-portrait with his sister were added in the late 1970s. They worked on the mural for the last time in 1980. The mural remains untitled. (The title *Black and White Mural* is used for convenience only.)

In Chicago most of the artists were grouped around three organizations: The Public Art Workshop, The Chicago Mural Group, and Movimiento Artistico Chicano (Chicano Artistic Movement, MArCH).

Chicago and Blue Island, Illinois

The first Hispanic murals were painted in 1968 and 1969 by Mario Castillo, a Mexican-born artist. He used pre-Columbian references in both murals, which are essentially nonfigurative works. In the first mural, *Metafísica*, the artist used enamel paints on a brick wall. In the second mural, *Wall of Brotherhood*, he used acrylic paints.

Raymond Patlán was an early muralist who painted on the inside and outside walls of Casa Aztlán (Aztlán House) cultural center. The murals deal with Mexican and Mexican-American history. The first was painted by the artist in the auditorium of Casa Aztlán during 1970 to 1971. Titled *From My Fathers and Yours,* it deals with Mexican history from the time of the Spanish conquest of Mexico to the Revolution of 1910 and with Mexican-American history in the United States. The narrative is carried primarily by the portraits of historical figures, such Moctezuma, Hernán Cortes, Miguel Hidalgo y Costilla, Emiliano Zapata, César Chávez, and Rodolfo "Corky" González. There are thematic references to the War of Independence, the Revolution of 1910, and the Mexican-American worker. The latter is conveyed by three figures in procession wearing hardhats, blue pants, work shoes, no shirts, and holding tools of their trade in the right hand, while the one leading the trio points with his left. The viewer's attention is drawn to a portrait of César Chávez shown in profile and placed in a cartouche.

History of the Mexican American Worker

One of the most ambitious murals in thematic and formal terms was painted in Blue Island (a suburb of Chicago), Illinois, by Raymond Patlán, Vicente Mendoza, and José Nario in 1974 and 1975. *History of the Mexican American Worker* (Figures 23 and 24) has allegorical and historical figures, Mexican and Chicano icons, medicine, and a pre-Columbian life-death symbol along the upper register. Farm workers, steelworkers, and meatpackers were represented along the lower register. The discussion of the themes and motifs corresponds to the numbers shown in the diagram.

There is a gigantic figure on the extreme upper left of the mural shown lunging forward (1). Only the upper half of the figure, from the waist up, is represented. Its greatly foreshortened arms and hands hold two cog wheels with interlocking sprocketed gears in which there are representations of Our Lady of Guadalupe (greatly simplified) and the Huelga eagle. The large figure is reminiscent of the many lunging figures in the works of the Mexican muralist David Alfaro Siqueiros.

The next cluster of motifs to the right of the lunging figure is comprised of an open book (2) flanked by two gigantic figures presented in bust form (head and shoulders only). The two figures presented in frontal view have their arms around each other as evidenced by the hands shown on each figure's shoulder. The man is a blue-collar worker and the woman is his counterpart. The open book has quotes from the writings of Abraham Lincoln and José Vasconcelos, who was the minister of education in Mex-

Figure 23. Raymond Patlán and others. History of the Mexican American Worker, *1974–75. Blue Island, Illinois.*

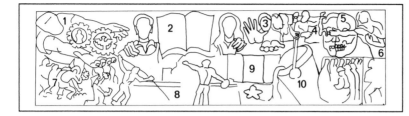

Figure 24. Raymond Patlán and others. Diagram for History of the Mexican American Worker, *1974–75. Blue Island, Illinois.*

ico (1921–1924) and the man responsible for the government support that helped initiate the mural movement in Mexico.

To the right of center there is a large hand shown in the open position with fingers spread apart and, directly below it, the other one shown extended toward the viewer (3). These are the hands of Benito Juárez, the president of Mexico who led the fight against French intervention in the 1860s. Right next to him is a three-quarter view of Abraham Lincoln's face.

A profile head next to Lincoln draws the viewer's attention to the last scene on the right side of the mural. It includes a physician on the left side holding a newborn child by the ankles with his left hand and a nurse behind him (5). The physician extends his arm in a gesture of offering to a woman in white on the right side who appears to be reaching for the baby (6). There is an American flag behind the physician and the nurse, and a very large life-death head in the midst of the offering scene.

Mexican-American workers picking grapes in the fields are seen on the extreme left of the lower register (7). A railroad worker and machinist are seen to the immediate right below a man and woman flanking an open book (8). A Mexican flag and the American Bicentennial logo (9) are seen below Benito Juárez. Molten steel spills out of a tilted vat (10), and next to it are the meat-packers (11) and other workers (12) that complete the scene on the right side of the mural.

History of the Mexican American Worker generated controversy even before it was completed. This was not unusual; opposition to murals led to confrontations all over the Southwest. Opposition, regardless of the reasons for it, was expressed through direct action (vandalism and defacement of murals), by pressure through the press or local governments, by petitions, and even by legal action. Such opposition occurred in Santa Barbara, California, Santa Fe, Denver, Pueblo, and Houston.

The Blue Island muralists have the distinction of having been enjoined by the city council of that industrial suburb of Chicago to stop painting under the threat of arrest because they were in violation of a city ordinance that prohibited the use of advertising on public walls. The focus of the controversy was on the Huelga eagle seen in the upper left side of the mural. No arrests were made, but painting stopped pending a decision by U.S. District Court Judge Richard B. Austin. This followed action by the ACLU (American Civil Liberties Union) to keep the city council from prohibiting the artists from working on the mural. Judge Austin ruled in favor of the artists, citing First Amendment rights of freedom of expression. The judge ruled that the mural dealt with ideas rather than advertising and should therefore not be destroyed. This precedent-setting decision established the Blue Island murals as an example of the muralist's freedom to work without outside interference.

The mural was defaced by vandals in May 1975, but the artists continued their work on it in the following two months. The mural was dedicated on July 19, 1975.

La Raza Cósmica

One of the most elaborate mural programs of the Chicano art movement is found in Austin. Raúl Valdez and those who assisted him painted on every available surface of the Pan American Center outdoor stage and its adjacent buildings in 1977. Discussion of the mural follows a left-to-right numbering of the ten scenes (even though this is not the thematic order of the mural program). This should be kept in mind as the historical themes are discussed in chronological order. (Figures 25 and 26–28.)

The focus of the mural program is found on the stage area, with the United Farmworkers eagle dominating the entire central area (6). The long horizontal band in the upper section was painted in the center to create the profile head and wings of the eagle. The suspended sound deflectors directly below and above the stage area function as the stepped wings associated with this emblem. On the stage wall, there are two bodiless hands presented in a welcoming gesture. They float over a large expanse of space whose depth is defined by linear perspective. There is a large celestial body in the center (instead of the head for the implied figure) with outstretched arms.

Various panels on each side are taken up with references to the history of Mexico. To the immediate left side of the stage area there is an elaborate

Figure 25. Raúl Valdez and others. La Raza Cósmica, *1977. Austin, Texas.*

scene of battle between the Spaniards and the Aztecs with a pyramid and temple in the background (5). The entire scene is enveloped by flames. Next to it on the left is the violently gesturing figure of Miguel Hidalgo y Costilla (4). The word *independencia* (independence) is lettered on a banner seen directly below the half-figure, modeled on the leader of Mexican independence painted by José Clemente Orozco in the state government palace stairway in Guadalajara, Jalisco, Mexico.

A figure corresponding to the Mexican Revolution of 1910 is seen to the immediate right of the stage area (7). He is backed up by a woman fighter and other fighters of that conflict. The artist included multiple arms for the main figure because the single arm proved insufficient visually to encompass the available space.

References to modern barrio life and culture were portrayed on the walls of the small building adjacent to the stage on the left side. The artist in-

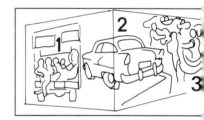

Figure 26.

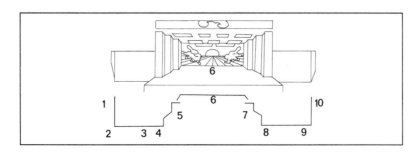

Figure 27. Raúl Valdez and others. Diagram for La Raza Cósmica, *1977. Austin, Texas.*

corporated two windows right under the flat roof of the end wall in his depiction of the back of a truck with figures seated on the back of it (1). A red 1950s Chevrolet, next to it, was foreshortened to enhance the illusion of a single flat surface for the painting, which actually encompasses the meeting of the two walls at the corner of the building (2). There are folk dancers to the right of the Chevrolet (3). The mural continues all the way around the building to the right of the stage area in a series of violent scenes, some of which are shown with buildings in flames (9 and 10).

Finally, on the rear wall of the stage panel, but on the back, is a representation of a figure with outstretched arms designed by Pedro Rodríguez of San Antonio. It was based on the New Democracy Freeing Herself figure painted by David Alfaro Siqueiros in the Palace of Fine Arts in Mexico City.

En la lucha . . . ponte trucha

Rogelio Cárdenas and assistants designed and painted a large mural in 1978 on the side of a tortilla factory in Hayward, California (Figures 29 and 30). It has elements of Chicano culture as well as references to several Latin American countries. The numbers assigned to the various motifs in the mural read from left to right on the top register and then in similar fashion on the lower one.

The mural is dominated by a monumental figure with outstretched arms that paraphrases the New Democracy figure by Alfaro Siqueiros in the Palace of Fine Arts (3). The Cárdenas woman, however, has a triface and long flowing hair. An eagle is enveloped protectively under her hair on the left side (2) and a serpent on the right (4). The serpent bares its fangs as it coils around the chain that contains the two creatures. The chain is behind the woman's neck and above her shoulders and arms. She holds a hammer in her right hand (1) and her left hand turns into a flaming circular shield with a Greek cross superimposed on it (5). The hammer has a United Farmworkers eagle within a circle inscribed on its side. The flags

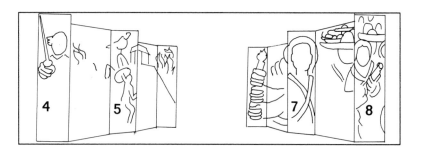

Figure 28. Raúl Valdez and others. Diagram for La Raza Cósmica, 1977. Austin, Texas.

Figure 29. Rogelio Cárdenas. En la lucha... ponte trucha, 1978. Hayward, California.

of Mexico, Cuba, Pan-Africa, and Puerto Rico are on the inner circle (running clockwise from the upper right) of the shield. Native American peace symbols are in the center of the cross.

References to Chicano identity and barrio culture are seen along the lower register. In the center over the monumental figure's chest is a representation of Our Lady of Guadalupe painted on the lower part of a Latin cross with the caption "Hayward, Califas" (California) above and the artist's name Rogelio Cárdenas below (7). A lowrider Chevrolet is seen under each arm of the woman. The one on the left dates from the late 1940s (6), and the one on the right from the mid-1950s (8). There is a corn plant and a pre-Columbian Indian on the extreme lower right of the mural (9). There are stencil-like representations of roses on a bordered band all the way across the bottom of the mural (10). This is a reference to the roses that miraculously appeared on the *tilma* (vest) of Juan Diego, along with the image of Our Lady of Guadalupe engraved on it, when he appeared before Fray Diego de Zumárraga, bishop of Mexico, in 1531.

Figure 30. Rogelio Cárdenas. Diagram for En la lucha... ponte trucha, 1978. Hayward, California.

The left side of the wall contains several motifs, among them skulls, a large hand, and flames around the actual windows. The title of the mural, its dedication, and the names of those who worked on it are listed on the adjacent wall to the left.

Santa Fe   The mural activity in Santa Fe was dominated by the Leyba brothers, who painted their first murals in the early 1970s. They and other artists identified themselves under the name of Artes Guadalupanos de Aztlán (Guadalupe Arts of Aztlán). Members of the group were Samuel, Carlos, and Albert Leyba, Gilberto Garduño, Gerónimo Guzmán, and Pancho Hunter.

One of the first murals painted by the Artes group dates from 1971. It was painted on the exterior wall of a building in the barrio used for the Clínica de Gente (The People's Clinic). The mural was later painted over. It had an Indian figure clothed in white in the center of a long wall. It was presented in cruciform fashion with wings attached to the arms and a United Farmworkers eagle attached to the head. A patient was wheeled into an operating room by a Chicano doctor and an Indian on the left side of the mural. Several patients were depicted on the right side.

Multicultural Mural

Multicultural Mural (Figures 31 and 32) was painted on the side of the New Mexico State Records Center in Santa Fe. Its main theme deals with the multicultural history of the state of New Mexico. The numerous fig-

Figure 31. Gilberto Garduño and others. Multicultural Mural, *1980. Santa Fe, New Mexico.*

Figure 32. Gilberto Garduño and others. Diagram for Multicultural Mural, *1980. Santa Fe, New Mexico.*

ures are presented in different scales and symmetrically arranged within an elaborate landscape. Each thematic section has been numbered from left to right in the mural diagram. Each number from 1 to 6 encompasses an area filled from top to bottom with several motifs and themes.

The scene on the left side of the mural is dominated by a large bull amidst red flowers below and Indians wielding batons above (1). This is the coming together of the Hispanic and Indian cultures. The next scene includes a train in the middle ground shown in foreshortened position (2). The train appears to be moving toward the viewer. In the foreground are workers busily repairing the tracks. Below them are two figures holding onto tools that resemble handlebars. One is an Anglo, the other is an American Indian.

The central scene is dominated by the Indian with outstretched arms holding the instruments of technology in each hand (3). In the middle ground are Spanish dancers framed by a gnarled tree on the left and one with foliage on one side only on the right. Spectators are seen on each side of the dancers. The Mount Rushmore-type heads in the background represent the peoples that have settled New Mexico: Indians, Hispanics, Anglos, and Afro-Americans. The males are seen on the left side, the females on the right.

The Mexican national emblem emblazoned on the Mexican flag is seen next to the left hand of the native American figure with outstretched arms (4). A mountain lion peering at the viewer from behind cactus and prickly pears is seen on the lower right side of the mural (6). Three flying figures appear to be reaching for the sun above it. Ravines are seen in the middle ground.

The background of the entire mural is composed of the mountains and high plains that are characteristic of the northern part of New Mexico.

Jacinto Quirarte

*L*iterature

Hispanic literature of the United States is the literature written by Americans of Hispanic descent. It includes the Spanish-language literature of what became the U.S. Southwest before this territory was incorporated through war and annexation. It thus incorporates a broad geographic and historical space, and even includes the writings of early explorers of the North American continent as well as Spanish-speaking immigrants and exiles who made the United States their home. It is a literature that reflects the diverse ethnic and national origins of Hispanics, and thus includes writers of South and Central American, Caribbean, and Spanish descent, as well as writers of Afro-Hispanic and Indo-Hispanic literatures; it may also include writers of Sephardic (exiled Spanish Jews) origins who identified themselves as Hispanic, should their works be brought to light in the future. Finally, Hispanic literature also reflects the linguistic diversity of the people and has been written and published in both Spanish and English and even bilingually.

THE COLONIAL PERIOD ♦ ♦ ♦ ♦ ♦ ♦ ♦ ♦ ♦ ♦ ♦ ♦ ♦ ♦ ♦ ♦ ♦ ♦ ♦

The roots of Hispanic literature were planted north of the Rio Grande quite some time before the landing of the Mayflower at Plymouth Rock. Juan de Oñate's 1598 colonizing expedition up from central Mexico into what is today New Mexico is doubly important as the beginning of a written and oral literary tradition in a European language, Spanish. The written tradition is represented by the landmark epic poem *La conquista de la Nueva México (The Conquest of the New Mexico),* by one of the soldiers on the expedition, Gaspar Pérez de Villagrá. The oral Spanish literary tradition was introduced with the improvised dramas, songs, ballads, and poetic recitations of the soldiers, colonists, and missionaries, some of which have survived in New Mexico and the Southwest to this date.

The Northeast of what is today the United States, on the other hand, can point to its earliest written and oral expression in Spanish with the founding of the colony of Sephardic Jews in New Amsterdam in 1654. Both the Northeast and Southwest can boast an unbroken literary tradition in Spanish that predates the American Revolutionary War. Much of this early literary patrimony from the colonial period has been lost or has not been collected and studied; the same can be said of all periods of the literature except for contemporary Hispanic literature in the United States. A missionary and colonial literature of historical chronicles, diaries, and letters and an oral literature developed in the Southwest until the Mexican-American War of 1846–48.

THE NINETEENTH CENTURY ♦ ♦ ♦ ♦ ♦ ♦ ♦ ♦ ♦ ♦ ♦ ♦ ♦ ♦ ♦ ♦ ♦

Following the Mexican-American War and up to 1910, the foundation was really laid for the creation of a true Mexican-American literature, a U.S. Hispanic literature, with the resident population of the Southwest adapting to the new U.S. political and social framework. It was the period when many Spanish-language newspapers began publishing throughout the Southwest and when they and the creative literature they contained became an alternative to Anglo-American information and cultural flow. During this period the important commercial centers of San Francisco and Los Angeles supported numerous newspapers, which, besides fulfilling their commercial and informational functions, also published short stories, poetry, essays, and even serialized novels, such *Las aventuras de Joaquín Murieta (The Adventures of Joaquín Murieta)*, a novel of the legendary California social bandit, published in 1881 by the Santa Barbara newspaper *La gaceta*. Among the more important newspapers in California were Los Angeles's *El clamor público (The Public Clamor)* and *La estrella de Los Angeles (The Los Angeles Star)*, issued in the 1850s, and *La crónica (The Chronicle)*, from the 1870s to the 1890s, and San Francisco's *La voz del Nuevo Mundo (The Voice of the New World)*, *La sociedad (Society)*, *La cronista (The Chronicles)*, and *La República (The Republic)*, issued during the last four decades of the century. In New Mexico, *El clarín mexicano (The Mexican Clarion)* and *El fronterizo (The Frontier)*, in the 1870s, *El nuevomexicano (The New Mexican)*, from the 1850s to the turn of the century, and *El defensor del pueblo (The People's Defender)*, in the 1890s, were important. Among Texas's contributions during this period were San Antonio's *El bejareño (The Bejar County)* during the 1850s, El Paso's *Las dos Américas (The Two Americas)* in the 1890s, and *El clarín del norte (The Northern Clarion)* in the 1900s. These were but a few of the literally hundreds of newspapers that provided for the cultural enrichment and entertainment of the Mexican-American communities while they provided information, helped to solidify the community, and defended the rights of Mexican Americans in the face of the growing influence of Anglo-American culture.

During the latter part of the nineteenth century various literary authors were published in book form. In southern California, Pilar Ruiz de Burton was one of the first writers to contribute important novels in the English language. Writing under the pseudonym C. Loyal, she published *The Squatter and the Don* in 1881, a novel that effectively exploits the genre of the romance to document the loss of family lands by many Californios to squatters and other interests supported by the railroads, corrupt bankers, and politicians in the newly acquired American territory of California. From a wealthy Californio family herself, she underwrote the cost of publication of *The Squatter* and of her other novel, *Who Would Have Thought It* (1872), which she published under her own name.

Also in 1881, New Mexican Manuel M. Salazar published a novel of romantic adventure, *La historia de un caminante, o Gervacio y Aurora (The History of a Traveler on Foot, or Gervacio and Aurora)*, which creates a colorful picture of the pastoral life in New Mexico at this time. Another New Mexican, Eusebio Chacón (1869–1948) published two short novels in 1892 that are celebrated today: *El hijo de la tempestad (Child of the Storm)* and *Tras la tormenta la calma (The Calm after the Storm)*. New Mexican

Miguel Otero

Eusebio Chacón

Miguel Angel Otero (1859–1944) issued a three-volume autobiography, *My Life on the Frontier* (1935), in English, in which he covers his life from age 5 until just after his term as governor of New Mexico ended in 1906.

During the late 1870s California bookseller and historian Hubert H. Bancroft had numerous autobiographies transcribed from oral dictation in his research for writing the history of California. In the process, some fifteen Hispanic women of early California were able to dictate their autobiographies, some of which are literary documents that reveal women's perspectives on life, culture, politics, and gender roles. Notable among those autobiographies are those of María Inocenta Avila's *Cosas de California* (*Things of California*), Josefa Carillo de Fotch's *Narración de una californiana* (*Narration by a California Woman*), Apolinaria Lorenzana's *Memorias de la Beata* (*Memories of a Pious Woman*), Eulalia Pérez's *Una vieja y sus recuerdos* (*An Old Woman and Her Memories*), and Felipa Osuna de Marrón's *Recuerdos del pasado* (*Memories of the Past*).

Apolinaria Lorenzana was a woman who came to Alta California as an orphan, worked as a servant in various homes and as an adult worked at the San Diego Mission up until the time of the United States invasion and occupation of California. At the mission she became a teacher, nurse, and supervisor of the Indian seamstresses, and came to own three ranches herself. Similarly, Eulalia Pérez was the housekeeper for the richest mission in California, the San Gabriel Mission, where she was in charge of all of the Indian domestic workers and oversaw the distribution of provisions for the mission. Both of their autobiographies are especially important because of their perspective of self-made and important women who functioned in positions of power in a society dominated by men.

Poetry in this era was primarily lyric, amorous, and pastoral and appeared regularly in the newspapers, with very few authors ever collecting their works in books.

Among the most frequently published poets were the Texan E. Montalván in *El bejareño*, Felipe Maximiliano Chacón and Julio Flores in New Mexico papers, and Dantés in Santa Barbara's *La gaceta* (*The Gazette*). One of the most interesting poets of the turn of the century was Sara Estela Ramírez, who published her poems and some speeches in Laredo's *La crónica* (*The Chronicle*) and *El demócrata* (*The Democrat*) and in her own literary periodicals, *La corregidora* (*The Corrector*) and *Aurora*, between the years 1904 and 1910. In her life and in her literary works, Ramírez was an activist for the Mexican Liberal Party in its movement to overthrow dictator Porfirio Díaz, and for workers' and women's rights. But much work needs to be done in collecting and analyzing Ramírez's works and the thousands upon thousands of other poems that were published throughout the Southwest during the nineteenth century.

On the other hand, the late nineteenth century is the period when the Mexican *corrido* (a folk ballad related to the romance introduced by the Spanish colonists and missionaries) came into maturity and proliferated throughout the Southwest. The corrido increased its popularity in the twentieth century and became a living historical and poetic document that records the history of the great Mexican immigrations and labor struggles between the two world wars.

During the nineteenth century, the New York area sustained various Hispanic literary activities and cultural institutions. Again the newspapers came to play a key role in providing a forum for literary creation for a community that at that time was made up principally of Spaniards and Cubans. During the late 1820s and 1830s such newspapers as *El menasajero semanal* (*The Weekly Messenger*) and the weekly *El mercurio de Nueva York* (*The New York Mercury*) published news of the homeland, political commentary and poetry, short stories, essays, and even excerpts of plays. Two other early newspapers were *La crónica* (*The Chronicle*) and *La voz de América* (*The Voice of America*), appearing in the 1850s and 1860s, respectively. Among the poets publishing at this time were Miguel Teurbe Tolón (1820–58), who was born in the United States, educated in Cuba, and became a conspirator for Cuban independence from Spain. One of the few books of poetry in Spanish was published in 1828: *Poesías de un mexicano* (*Poems by a Mexican*), by Anastacio Ochoa y Acuña.

In particular, the border ballad, which chronicled the adventures of social bandits, like Joaquín Murieta, Aniceto Pizaña, and even Billy the Kid, became a popular anvil on which was forged a Mexican-American identity.

But it was not until the late nineteenth century that newspaper, magazine, and book publishing really began to expand, because of increased immigration and the political and cultural activity related to the Cuban, Puerto Rican, and Dominican independence movements and the Spanish-American War. In this regard, the most noteworthy institution was the Cuban newspaper *La patria*, in whose pages could be found essays by the leading Cuban and Puerto Rican patriots. Furthermore, numerous essays, letters, diaries, poems, short stories, and literary creations by some of Puerto Rico's most important literary and patriotic figures were written in New York while they worked for the revolution. Included among these were Eugenio María de Hostos, Ramón Emeterio Betances, Lola Rodríguez de Tió, and Sotero Figueroa. Active as well in literature and political organizing were the revolutionary leaders Francisco González "Pachín" Marín, a Puerto Rican, and the Cuban José Martí. Marín, a typesetter by trade and an important figure in Puerto Rican poetry for his break with romanticism, left us an important essay, "Nueva York por dentro; una faz de su vida bohemia" ("New York on the Inside; One Side of Its Bohemian Life"), in which he sketches New York from the perspective of a disillusioned immigrant; this is perhaps the earliest document in Spanish that takes this point of view and can be perhaps considered the beginning of Hispanic immigrant literature. Martí was an international literary figure in his own right, and his writings are still studied today in Latin American literature classes throughout the world; he has left us a legacy of many essays and other writings that relate directly to his life in New York and elsewhere in the United States.

Also of importance as the most widely circulated weekly was *Las novedades (The News)*, (1893–1918), whose theater, music, and literary critic was the famed Dominican writer Pedro Henríquez Ureña. An early Puerto Rican contribution was *La gaceta ilustrada (The Illustrated Gazette)*, edited in the 1890s by writer Francisco Amy. Many of the Spanish-language literary books published in New York were also related to the Cuban independence struggle, such as Luis García Pérez's *El grito de Yara (The Shout at Yara*, 1879) and Desiderio Fajardo Ortiz's *La fuga de Evangelina (The Escape of Evangelina*, 1898), the story of Cuban heroine Evangelina Cossío's escape from incarceration by the Spaniards and her trip to freedom and the organizing effort in New York.

José Martí

◆ ◆ ◆ ◆ ◆ ◆ ◆ ◆ ◆ ◆ ◆ ◆ ◆ ◆ **THE EARLY TWENTIETH CENTURY**

The turn of the century brought record immigration from Mexico to the Southwest and Midwest because of the Mexican Revolution of 1910. During the period from 1910 until World War II, immigrant workers and upper-class and educated professionals from Mexico interacted with the Mexican-origin residents of the Southwest, who had been somewhat cut off from the evolution of Mexican culture inside Mexico. During this period Hispanic newspaper and book publishing flourished throughout the Southwest. Both San Antonio and Los Angeles supported Spanish-language daily newspapers that served diverse readerships made up of regional groups from the Southwest, immigrant laborers, and political refugees from the revolution. The educated, political refugees played a key role in publishing, and in light of their upper social class, they created an ideology of a Mexican community in exile, or *"México de afuera"* (Mexico on the outside).

The Southwest

In the offices of San Antonio's *La prensa (The Press)* and Los Angeles's *La opinión (The Opinion)* and *El heraldo de México (The Mexican Herald),* some of the most talented writers from Mexico, Spain, and Latin America earned their living as reporters, columnists and critics. These included Miguel Arce, Esteban Escalante, Gabriel Navarro, Teodoro Torres, Daniel Venegas, and many others, who wrote hundreds of books of poetry, essays, and novels. Many of these were published in book form and marketed by the newspapers themselves via mail and in their own bookstores. Besides the publishing houses related to these large dailies, there were many other smaller companies, such as Laredo Publishing Company, Los Angeles's Spanish American Printing, and San Diego's Imprenta Bolaños Cacho Hnos.

The largest and most productive publishers resided in San Antonio. Leading the list was the publishing house founded by the owner of *La prensa* and Los Angeles's *La opinión,* Ignacio Lozano. The Casa Editorial Lozano was by far the largest publishing establishment ever owned by a Hispanic in the United States. Among the San Antonio publishers were the Viola Novelty Company, probably a subsidiary of P. Viola, publisher of the satiric newspapers *El vacilón (The Joker)* and *El fandango (The Fandango),* active from 1916 until at least 1927; the Whitt Company; and the Librería Española, which still exists today as a bookstore. Many of the novels produced by these houses were part of the genre known as "novels of the

Mexican Revolution"; the stories were set within the context of the revolution and often commented on historical events and personalities. In the United States, the refugees who wrote these novels were very conservative and quite often attacked the revolution and Mexican politicians, which they saw as the reason for their exile. Included among these were Miguel Bolaños Cacho's *Sembradores de viento* (*Sewers of the Wind*, 1928), Brígido Caro's *Plutarco Elías Calles: dictador volchevique de México* (*Plutarco Elías Calles: Bolshevik Dictator of Mexico*, 1924), and Lázaro Gutiérrez de Lara's *Los bribones rebeldes* (*The Rebel Rogues*, 1932). The most famous author of this genre has become Mariano Azuela, author of the masterpiece that is one of the foundations of modern Mexican literature, *Los de abajo* (*The Underdogs*), which was first published in 1915 in a serialized version in El Paso's newspaper *El paso del norte* (*The Northern Pass*) and was issued later by the same newspaper in book form.

Authors of the very popular genre of novels of the Mexican Revolution included Miguel Arce, Conrado Espinosa, Alfredo González, Esteban Maqueo Castellanos, Manuel Mateos, Ramón Puente, and Teodoro Torres.

Although most of the novels published during these years gravitated toward the political and counterrevolutionary, there were others of a more sentimental nature and even some titles that can be considered forerunners of the Chicano novel of the 1960s in their identification with the working-class Mexicans of the Southwest, their use of popular dialects, and their political stance in regard to U.S. government and society. The prime example of this new sensibility is newspaperman Daniel Venegas's *Las aventuras de Don Chipote o Cuando los pericos mamen* (*The Adventures of Don Chipote or When Parakeets May Suckle Their Young*, 1928), a humorous account of a Mexican immigrant, Don Chipote, who travels through the Southwest working here and there at menial tasks and running into one misadventure after the other, suffering at the hands of rogues, the authorities, and his bosses while in search of the mythic streets of gold that the United States is supposed to offer immigrants. *Don Chipote* is a novel of immigration, a picaresque novel, and a novel of protest all wrapped into one, and furthermore, it is the one clear forerunner of today's Chicano literature.

One of the most important literary genres that developed in the newspapers at this time was *la crónica* (chronicle). It was a short satirical column that was full of local color, current topics, and observation of social habits. In the Southwest it came to function and serve purposes never before thought of in Mexico or Spain. From Los Angeles to San Antonio, Mexican moralists satirized the customs and behavior of the colony whose very existence was seen as threatened by the dominant Anglo-Saxon culture. It was the *cronista's* (cronicler's) job to enforce the ideology of México de afuera and battle the influence of Anglo-American culture and the erosion of the Spanish language caused by the influence of speaking English. The cronistas, using such pseudonyms as El Malcriado (The Spoiled Brat—Daniel Venegas), Kaskabel (Rattler—Benjamín Padilla), Az.T.K. (Aztec), and Chicote (The Whip), were literally whipping and stinging the community into conformity, commenting on or simply poking fun at the common folks' mixing of Spanish and English and Mexican women's adapting American dress and more liberalized customs, such as cutting their hair short, raising the hemlines, and smoking.

First and foremost behind the ideology of the crónica writers and the owners of the newspapers was the goal of returning to the homeland; as soon as the hostilities of the revolution ended, the immigrants were supposed to return to Mexico with their culture intact. Quite often the target of their humorous attacks were stereotyped country bumpkins, like Don Chipote, who were having a hard time getting around in the modern American city. They also poked fun at the Mexican immigrants to the United States who became impressed with the wealth, modern technology, efficiency, and informality of American culture, to the extent that they considered everything American superior and everything Mexican inferior. In some of his chronicles, Jorge Ulica satirized women who made much to do about throwing American-style surprise parties and celebrating Thanksgiving, and criticized their taking advantage of greater independence and power at the expense of men's machismo. The cronistas quite often drew from popular jokes, anecdotes, and oral tradition to create these tales. Two of the most popular cronistas, who saw their columns syndicated throughout the Southwest, were the aforementioned Benjamín Padilla, an expatriate newspaperman from Guadalajara, and Julio Arce, who was also a political refugee from Guadalajara and used the pseudonym Jorge Ulica for his *"Crónicas Diabólicas"* (Diabolical Chronicles). So popular was this type of satire that entire weekly newspapers, usually of no more than eight pages in length, were dedicated to it. Daniel Venegas's weekly *El Malcriado (The Brat)* and P. Viola's *El vacilón (The Joker)* are prime examples of these.

Clustered around the publication of newspapers in the Southwest were communities of women intellectuals who not only aimed their journalism at the service of the Mexican Revolution and women's empowerment, but also penned and published some of the most eloquent editorials, speeches, and poems in support of their liberal causes. Most noteworthy were Sara Estela Ramírez's newspapers and magazines, mentioned above; Andrea and Teresa Villarreal's *El obereo (The Worker),* founded in San Antonio in 1910; Isidra T. de Cárdenas's *La voz de la mujer (The Woman's*

> La crónica *owes its origins to Addison and Steele in England and José Mariano de Lara in Spain, but the form was cultivated extensively throughout Mexico and Latin America.*

Voice), founded in El Paso in 1907; and *Pluma Roja (Red Pen)*, edited and directed by Blanca de Moncaleano from 1913 to 1915 in Los Angeles. In the anarchist *Pluma Roja* there was a consistent editorial articulation of re-configuring the role of women in society as central to the struggle for so-cial, political, and economic freedom; it was presented as an integral part of the ideal of anarchism. Blanca de Moncaleano addressed both men and women, urging them to free women of their enslavement and to encour-age their education and politicization. In a February 1, 1914, editorial en-titled "Hombre, educad a la mujer" (Man, Educate Women), she pleads for men to allow women to obtain an education.

One of these women activists, Leonor Villegas de Magnón (1876–1955), was born and raised in Mexico but emigrated to Laredo, Texas. She pro-vided one of the very few autobiographies of the Mexican Revolution to be written by a woman: *The Rebel*, which was finally published posthu-mously in 1994 after the author was unsuccessful in having it published in her Spanish or English versions during her lifetime. Villegas de Magnón was associated with the ideological precursors of the Revolution, the Brothers Flores Magón, and in fact spent her inherited fortune in support of the Revolution. Villegas was the founder of a women's nursing corps, made up mostly of women from the Texas side of the border, which tended to the wounded in Venustiano Carranza's army. As such, she worked side-by-side with the future victor of the Revolution and presi-dent of the republic. Upon seeing how fast official sources had ignored the women's contribution, she specifically created her two autobiographies to document the role of women in Mexico's cataclysmic insurgency. Villegas was both an heroic figure and a dramatic writer, one who wrote with doc-umentary care, but with literary style and flair.

Much of this literary activity in the Mexican-American Southwest came to an abrupt halt with the Great Depression and the repatriation, forced or voluntary, of a large segment of that society back to Mexico. Some writers during the Depression, like Américo Paredes, began to write in both Span-ish and English and to express a very pronounced and politicized Mexi-can-American sensibility. His English novel *George Washington Gómez* was written from 1936 to 1940 (but not published until 1990), and during the 1930s and 1940s he was a frequent contributor of poetry in Spanish, Eng-lish, and bilingual format to newspapers in Texas, including *La prensa*. In 1937 at age 22 he published a collection of poems, *Cantos de adolescencia (Songs of Adolescence)*, but it was not until 1991 that his collected poems were issued under the title *Between Two Worlds*, which contained works selected from his writings from the late 1930s to the 1950s.

Another very important literary figure who emerged during the Depression and began to publish poetry and tales based on New Mexican folklore was Fray Angelico Chávez. A Franciscan monk, Chávez's poetry books are principally made up of poems to Christ and the Virgin Mary: *Clothed with the Sun* (1939), *New Mexico Triptych* (1940), *Eleven Lady Lyrics and Other Poems* (1945), *The Single Rose* (1948), and *Selected Poems with an Apologia* (1969). From the 1930s to the 1950s there appeared a number of short story writers who succeeded in publishing their works in general market English-language magazines. Most of these, such as Texas's Josefina Escajeda and Jovita González, based their works on folktales, oral tradition, and the picturesque customs of Mexicans in the Southwest. Robert Hernán Torres, who published some of his stories in *Esquire* magazine, focused his works on the cruelty and senselessness of the revolution in Mexico. Despite the significance of Chávez, Paredes, and others, it was not until the 1960s that there was a significant resurgence of Mexican-American literary activity, except that by the end of that decade it was called Chicano literature.

Fray Angélico Chávez

Josephina Niggli was successful in having a number of her works published by general market presses in the United States. While writing as an adult, Niggli was able to vividly re-create the small town settings of her rural upbringing in Mexico. Although born in 1910, she was somewhat of a nineteen-century regionalist in her descriptions and evocations. Her *Mexican Village* (1945), for example, portrays the power of land and locale over individuals and community, in this case a fictional town on the northern border of Mexico. Like many of the New Mexico writers, Niggli was also concerned with tradition and the passage of customs and worldview from one generation to the other.

Another prose writer in English who experienced relative success was Josephina Niggli: she focused many of her novels and short stories on life in Mexico after the revolution.

Emerging in the English-language literary world at the same time as Angélico Chávez was a group of New Mexican women writers who sought to examine the colonial and territorial past and preserve the folkways and customs that were fast passing away. Their contributions ranged from fiction and literary folklore to personal narrative and social history. Included among their works are: Nina Warren Otero's *Old Spain in Our Southwest* (1936); Cleofas Jaramillo's *The Genuine New Mexico Tasty Recipes: Old and Quaint Formulas for the Preparation of Seventy-five Delicious Spanish Dishes* (1939), a kind of culinary autobiography; Aurora Lucer White Lea's *Literary Folklore of the Hispanic Southwest* (1953); Fabiola Cabeza de Vaca's *The Good Life: New Mexico Traditions and Food* (1949) and *We Fed Them Cactus* (1954). Many of the personal reminiscences in these books are framed within the traditional practices of telling stories within the family, of passing recipes down from mother to daughter and relating them to life experiences and family history, of preserving the songs and other oral lore of the family and the region. In these women, we find a somewhat nostalgic re-creation of the past that is an embryionic resistance to the Anglo-American ways that were eroding traditional New Mexican culture.

An English-language short fiction writer, María Cristina Mena (1893–1965), was also born and raised in Mexico and moved to the United States at age fourteen. In New York from 1913 to 1916, Mena published a series of short stories in *The Century Illustrated Monthly Magazine.* In 1927, many of these stories, along with new ones, were published in a collection under her husband's name, Henry K. Chambers, a dramatist and journalist. In the 1940s she developed into a prolific novelist: *The Water Carrier's Secret* (1942), *The Two Eagles* (1943), *The Bullfighter's Son* (1944), *The Three Kings* (1946), and *Boy Heroes of Chapultepec: A Story of the Mexican War* (1953). Behind all of her writings was the desire to inform the public in the United States of the history and culture of Mexico, proposing to correct the negative image that Mexico has held in the popular media.

The Northeast   In New York, the period from the turn of the century up into the Great Depression was also one of increased immigration and interaction of various Hispanic groups. It was a period of increased Puerto Rican migration, facilitated by the Jones Act, which declared Puerto Ricans to be citizens of the United States, and later of immigration of Spanish workers and refugees from the Spanish Civil War. Artistic and literary creation in the Hispanic community quite often supported the Puerto Rican nationalist movement and the movement to reestablish the Spanish republic. At the turn of the century, Cuban and Spanish writers and newspapers still dominated the scene. The first decade of the century witnessed the founding of *La prensa (The Press),* whose heritage continues today in *El diario-La prensa (The Daily-The Press),* born of a 1963 merger. Also publishing during the decade were *Sangre latina (Latin Blood),* out of Columbia University, *Revista Pan-Americana (Pan American Review),* and *La paz y el trabajo (Peace and Work),* a monthly review of commerce, literature, science, and the arts. Even places as far away as Buffalo began to support their own publications, such as *La hacienda (The State),* founded in 1906.

Spanish-language literary publishing did not begin to expand until the late 1910s and early 1920s. By far the most interesting volume that has come down to us from the 1910s is an early example of the immigrant novel. Somewhat similar in theme to *Don Chipote*, Venezuelan author Alirio Díaz Guerra's *Lucas Guevara* (1917) is the story of a young man who comes to the city seeking his fortune, but is ultimately disillusioned. While *Lucas Guevara* was probably self-published at the New York Printing Company, there were Spanish-language publishing houses functioning during the 1910s in New York. One of the most important and long-lived houses, Spanish American Publishing Company, began issuing titles at this time and continued well into the 1950s. It too was an early publisher of books on the theme of Hispanics in New York, such as Puerto Rican playwright Javier Lara's *En la metrópoli del dólar (In the Metropolis of the Dollar)*, circa 1919. *Las novedades* newspaper also published books, including Pedro Henríquez Ureña's *El nacimiento de Dionisos (The Birth of Dionysus)* (1916).

Although during the 1920s the Spanish American Publishing Company, Carlos López Press, The Phos Press, and others were issuing occasional literary titles, it was not until the late 1920s and early 1930s that there was an intensification of activity. To begin with, various specialized newspapers began to appear. Probably as an outgrowth of the very active theatrical movement that was taking place in Manhattan and Brooklyn, *Gráfico (Graphic)* began publishing in 1927 as a theater and entertainment weekly newspaper under the editorship of the prolific writer Alberto O'Farrill, who was also a playwright and a leading comic actor in Cuban blackface farces *(teatro bufo cubano)*. As was also the custom in the Southwest, *Gráfico* and the other newspapers and magazines published numerous poems, short stories, literary essays, and crónicas by the leading New York Hispanic writers. Among the most notable cronistas were those unknown writers using the pseudonyms Maquiavelo (Machiavelli) and Samurai; O'-Farrill himself was an important contributor to the tradition, signing his columns "Ofa." As in the Southwest, these cronistas labored in their writings to solidify the Hispanic community, which in New York was even more diverse than in the Southwest, drawing from many ethnic and national backgrounds. They too were protecting the purity of Hispanic culture against the dangers of assimilation, as they voiced the political and social concerns of the community and corrected and satirized current habits. While in the Southwest the cronistas promoted a México de afuera, in New York they often attempted to create a *Trópico en Manhattan* (A Tropical [or Caribbean] Culture in Manhattan).

Unlike in the Southwest, there were no massive repatriations and deportations disrupting the cultural life in the Hispanic community during the Great Depression. In fact, New York continued to receive large waves of

For the Caribbean peoples there is an immense repository of lyric and narrative poetry that is to be found in their songs, such as the décimas, plenas, *and* sones, *and in the popular recorded music of such lyrical geniuses as Rafael Hernández, Pedro Flores, and Ramito, whose compositions began appearing on recordings in the 1930s and continue to influence Puerto Rican culture on the island and in New York to the present. Of course, the compositions of Hernández and Flores have influenced Hispanic popular music around the world.*

Hispanics during the Depression and World War II: refugees from the Spanish Civil War, workers for the service and manufacturing industries flown in from Puerto Rico during World War II in the largest airborne migration in history, and Hispanics from the Southwest. Newspapers were founded that reflected this renewed interest in Spanish, Puerto Rican, and working-class culture: *Vida obrera (Worker's Life,* 1930), *Alma boricua (Puerto Rican Soul,* 1934–35), *España libre (Free Spain,* 1943), and *Cultura proletaria (Proletariat Culture,* 1943). The pages of these newspapers are valuable sources of an important body of testimonial literature that reflected the life of the immigrant. They frequently took the form of autobiographical sketches, anecdotes, and stories, quite often in a homey, straightforward language that was also replete with pathos and artistic sensibility. Despite the many sources available in print, a large part of Puerto Rican, Cuban, Dominican, and Spanish literature in New York is an oral literature, a folk literature, completely consistent with and emerging from the working-class nature of the immigrants.

As the Puerto Rican community grew in the late 1920s and into World War II, Puerto Rican literature began to gain a larger profile in New York, but within a decidedly political context. It also seems that the literature with the most impact for the Puerto Rican community was the dramatic literature, if published books are a measure. Poet Gonzalo O'Neill (1867–1942) was a businessman who during the 1920s and 1930s was at the hub of Puerto Rican and Hispanic cultural life, not only as a writer, but as a cultural entrepreneur, investing his money in the theater and protecting and offering support to other writers. O'Neill began his literary training and career in Puerto Rico as a teenager in association with a magazine, *El palenque de la juventud (The Young People's Arena),* which featured the works of some of the most important writers in Puerto Rico, such as Luis Muñoz Rivera, Lola Rodríguez de Tió, Vicente Palés, and many other notables. O'Neill's first published book was a dramatic dialogue in verse, more appropriate for reading aloud than staging: *La indiana borinqueña (The Puerto Rican Indians,* 1922). Here O'Neill revealed himself to be intensely patriotic and interested in Puerto Rican independence from the United States. His second published book was the three-act play *Moncho Reyes,* named after the central character, issued by Spanish American Publishing in 1923. In 1924, O'Neill published a book of nationalistic poetry, *Sonoras bagatelas o sicilianas (Sonorous Bagatelles or Sicilian Verses),* for which Manuel Quevedo Baez stated in the prologue that "Gonzalo is a spontaneous and ingenuous poet.... He is a poet of creole stock, passionate, tender, and as melancholic as Gautier Benítez" (Gautier Benítez was Puerto Rico's greatest poet to date). Although all of his plays, even *La indi-*

ana borinqueña, enjoyed stage productions, it was his third play, *Bajo una sola bandera (Under Only One Flag,* 1928), that went on to critical acclaim and various productions on stages in New York as well as in Puerto Rico. *Bajo una sola bandera* examines the political options facing Puerto Rico, as personified by down-to-earth flesh-and-blood characters. (A more extensive study of O'Neill's plays is in the Theater chapter.) A glowing review in San Juan's *La democracia (Democracy)* on April 16, 1929, marveled at O'Neill's conserving perfect Spanish and his Puerto Rican identity, despite having lived in the United States for forty years. O'Neill certainly continued to write, although the remainder of his work is unknown or has been lost. Newspapers report that another play of his, *Amoríos borincanos (Puerto Rican Loves),* was produced for the stage in 1938.

Following the example of Gonzalo O'Neill, there were many other Puerto Ricans who wrote for the stage and even published some of their works from the late 1920s to the 1940s, such as Alberto M. González, Juan Nadal de Santa Coloma, José Enamorado Cuesta, Frank Martínez, and Erasmo Vando. But one poet-playwright stands out among the rest as a politically committed woman, although the major portion of her work has been lost: Franca de Armiño. Franca de Armiño (probably a pseudonym) wrote three works that have been lost and are inaccessible today: *Luz de tienieblas (Light of Darkness),* a book of poems on various themes; *Aspectos de la vida (Aspects of Life),* philosophical essays; and *Tragedia puertorriqueña (Puerto Rican Tragedy),* a comedy of social criticism. Her one published and available play, *Los hipócritas: comedia dramática social (The Hypocrits: A Social Drama),* self-published in 1937 at the Modernistic Editorial Company, is a major work that demands critical attention. Dedicated to "the oppressed and all those who work for ideas of social renovation," the work is set in Spain during the time of the republic and is openly anti-Fascist and revolutionary, calling for a rebellion of workers. *Los hipócritas,* which begins with the 1929 stock market crash, deals with a daughter's refusal to marry her father's choice, the son of a duke. Rather, she is romantically involved with a son of the working class, Gerónimo, whom her father calls a Communist and who has led her into atheism. The plot is complicated, with Gerónimo organizing workers for a strike, a Fascist dictatorship developing in Spain, and a corrupt priest trying to arrange for Gloria to become a nun so that the church will receive her dowry. The play ends with Gloria and Gerónimo together, the traitors unmasked, and the workers' strike prevailing over police, who attack them brutally. While full of propaganda and stereotyped characters, *Los hipócritas* is a gripping and entertaining play that reflects the tenor of the times, as far as the Great Depression, labor organizing, and the Spanish Civil War are concerned.

Bernardo Vega

A cigar roller who settled in New York in 1916, Bernardo Vega reconstructed life in the Puerto Rican community during the period between the two great wars. Written in 1940, his *Memorias de Bernardo Vega* was published in 1977, and its translation was published in English as *The Memoirs of Bernardo Vega* in 1984. Valuable as both a literary and a historical document, Vega's memoirs make mention of numerous literary figures, such as poet Alfonso Dieppa, whose works were either not published or are lost to us. Vega is an important forerunner of the Nuyorican writers of the 1960s because he wrote about New York as a person who was there to stay, with no intention to return to live in Puerto Rico.

Luisa Capetillo proved to be a profound thinker and a passionate writer and a precursor of many of the sentiments soon to be expressed in English by Jesús Colón.

A figure similar to the women activists of the Hispanic Southwest was Luisa Capetillo, who came to New York from Puerto Rico in 1912 and wrote for various labor publications. In *Cultura Obrera (Worker Culture)*, she consistently built a case for women's emancipation. She reemerged in the cigar factories of Tampa and Ybor City and continued her intellectual as well as her activist life. In Tampa she published the second edition of her book, *Mi opinión (My Opinion*, 1913), and published a new book of essays, *Influencia de las ideas modernas (The Influence of Modern Ideas*, 1916).

The literature of this period is also represented by a newspaper columnist who wrote in English and was very active in the Communist party: Jesús Colón, author of columns for the *Daily Worker*. Colón's was a heroic intellectual battle against the oppression of workers and racial discrimination; he nevertheless wrote about and supported Puerto Rican culture and literature, even to the extent of founding a small publishing company that has the distinction of issuing some of the first works of the great Puerto Rican novelist and short story writer José Luis González. In 1961, Colón selected some of the autobiographical sketches that had appeared in newspapers and published them in book form in *A Puerto Rican in New York*, which was perhaps the one literary and historical document that was accessible to young Nuyorican writers and helped to form their literary and social awareness, as well as stimulate their production of literature. Colón, a black Puerto Rican, had created a document that, tempered with his political ideology, presented insight into Puerto Rican minority status in the United States, rather than just immigrant or ethnic status. In this it was quite different from all that had preceded it.

◆ ◆ ◆ ◆ ◆ ◆ ◆ ◆ ◆ ◆ ◆ ◆ ◆ ◆ ◆ **WORLD WAR II TO THE PRESENT**

Scholars consider the year 1943 as the beginning of a new period in Mexican-American history and culture. This is the year when the so-called Zoot Suit Riots occurred in the Los Angeles area; they mark a stage in the cultural development of the Mexican American in which there was a consciousness of not belonging to either Mexico or the United States, and there was an attempt to assert a separate independent identity, just as the zoot suiters in their own subculture were doing by adopting their style of dress, speech, and music. Then, too, Mexican-American veterans serving in and returning from World War II, where they proportionately suffered more casualties and won more medals for valor than any other group in U.S. society, now felt that they had earned their rights as citizens of the United States and were prepared to assert that citizenship and to reform the political and economic system so that they could participate equitably. Thus the quest for identity in modern American society was initiated, and by the 1960s, a younger generation made up of the children of the veterans not only took up this pursuit of democracy and equity in the civil rights movements but also explored the question of identity in all of the arts.

Because of the interruption caused by the Depression, repatriation, and World War II, and the decreased production of literature that ensued during the 1940s and 1950s, the renewed literary and artistic productivity that occurred during the 1960s has often been considered to be a Chicano renaissance. In reality it was an awakening that accompanied the younger generation's greater access to college and its participation in the civil rights movements, the farmworker labor struggle and the protest movement against the Vietnam War. For Chicano literature the decade of the 1960s was characterized by a questioning of all the commonly accepted truths in the society, foremost of which was the question of equality. The first writers of Chicano literature in the 1960s committed their literary voices to the political, economic, and educational struggles. Their works were frequently used to inspire social and political action, quite often with poets reading their verses at organizing meetings, at boycotts, and before and after protest marches. Of necessity many of the first writers to gain prominence in the movement were the poets who could tap into an oral tradition of recitation and declamation, such as Abelardo Delgado, Ricardo Sánchez, and Alurista (Alberto Urista), and create works to be performed orally before groups of students and workers, in order to inspire them and raise their level of consciousness.

Chicano Literature

Zoot suiters were Mexican-American youth who used as symbols of their subculture the baggy pants and long, feathered, wide-brimmed hat that made up a zoot suit.

The most important literary work in this period that was used at the grass roots level as well as by university students to provide a sense of history, mission, and Chicano identity was an epic poem written by an ex-boxer in Denver, Colorado: Rodolfo "Corky" González's *I Am Joaquín/Yo Soy Joaquín* (1964). The short, bilingual pamphlet edition of the poem was literally passed from hand to hand in the communities, was read from at rallies, dramatized by street theaters, and even produced as a slide show on film with a dramatic reading by Luis Valdez, the leading Chicano director and playwright. The influence and social impact of *I Am Joaquín* and poems such as "Stupid America," by Abelardo Delgado, which was published and reprinted in community and movement newspapers throughout the Southwest, then cut out of those papers and passed hand to hand, is inestimable. "Stupid America" was included as well in Abelardo's landmark collection, *Chicano: 25 Pieces of a Chicano Mind* (1969). This period was one of euphoria, power, and influence for the Chicano poet, who was sought after, almost as a priest, to give his blessings in the form of readings at all cultural and Chicano movement events.

The 1960s was an era of intense grass roots organizing and cultural fermentation, and along with this occurred a renewed interest in publishing small community and workers' newspapers and magazines, such as the California farm workers' *El Malcriado (The Brat)* and Houston's *Papel Chicano (Chicano Newspaper)*, which were now quite often published bilingually. During the late 1960s and early 1970s, literary magazines proliferated, from the academic, such as Berkeley's *El grito (The Shout [for independence])*, to the grass roots type printed on newsprint and available for twenty-five cents, such as San Antonio's *Caracol (Shell)*, to the artsy, streetwise, avant-garde, and irreverent, such as Los Angeles's *Con Safos (Safety Zone)*.

In 1967 appeared the most influential Chicano literary magazine, *El grito*, which initiated the careers of some of the most prominent names in Chicano literature and, along with the publishing house Editorial Quinto Sol, which it established in 1968, began to delineate the canon that is the official identity of Chicano literature by publishing those works that best exemplified Chicano culture, language, themes, and styles. The very name of the publishing house emphasized its Mexican/Aztec identity, as well as the Spanish language; the "quinto sol" (fifth sun), referred to Aztec belief in a period of cultural flowering that would take place some time in the future, in a fifth age that conveniently coincided with the rise of Chicano culture. Included in its 1968 anthology, *El espejo/The Mirror*, edited by the owners of Quinto Sol, Octavio Romano and Herminio Ríos, were such writers as Alurista, Tomás Rivera, and Miguel Méndez, who are still models of Chicano literature. *El espejo* recognized the linguistic diversity and the erosion of Spanish literacy among the young by accompanying works originally written in Spanish with an English translation; it even included Miguel Méndez's original Yaqui-language version of his short story "Tata Casehue." In *El espejo* and in later books that Quinto Sol published, there was a definite insistence on working-class and rural culture and language, as exemplified in the works of Tomás Rivera, Rolando Hinojosa, and most of the other authors published in book form. Also, there was not only a tolerance but a promotion of works written bilingually and in *caló,* the code of street culture, switching between both English and Spanish and various social dialects of each one in the same literary piece, as in the poems of Alurista and the plays of Carlos Morton.

In 1970, Quinto Sol reinforced its leadership in creating the concept of Chicano literature by instituting the national award for Chicano literature, Premio Quinto Sol (Fifth Sun Award), which carried with it a one-thousand-dollar prize and publication of the winning manuscript. The first

Abelardo Delgado, Ron Arias, and Rolando Hinojosa at the Second National Latino Book Fair and Writers Festival, Houston, Texas, 1980.

three years of prizes went to books that today are still seen as exemplary Chicano novels and, in fact, are still among the best-selling Chicano literary texts: Tomás Rivera's *...y no se lo tragó la tierra (...And the Earth Did Not Part,* 1971), Rudolfo Anaya's *Bless Me, Ultima* (1972), and Rolando Hinojosa's *Estampas del valle y otras obras/Sketches of the Valley and Other Works.* Rivera's outwardly simple but inwardly complex novel is much in the line of experimental Latin American fiction, demanding that the reader take part in unraveling the story and in coming to his own conclusions about the identity and relationships of the characters, as well as the meaning. Drawing upon his own life as a migrant worker from Texas, Rivera constructed a novel in the straightforward but poetic language of migrant workers in which a nameless central character attempts to find himself by reconstructing the over-heard conversations and stories as well as events that took place during a metaphorical year, which really represents his whole life. It is the story of a sensitive boy who is trying to understand the hardship that surrounds his family and community of migrant workers; his path is first one of rejection of them only to embrace them and their culture dearly as his own at the end of the book. In many ways, *...y no se lo tragó la tierra* came to be the most influential book in the Chicano search for identity.

Rivera, who became a very successful university professor and administrator—he rose to the position of chancellor of the University of California, Riverside, before his death in 1984—wrote and published other stories, essays, and poems. Through his essays, such as "Chicano Literature: Fiesta of the Living" (1979) and "Into the Labyrinth: The Chicano in Literature" (1971), and his personal and scholarly activities, he was one of the prime movers in the promotion of Chicano authors, in the creation of the concept of Chicano literature, and in the creation of Chicano literature and culture as legitimate academic areas in the college curriculum. In 1989, his stories were collected and published under the title *The Harvest,* which was also the title of one of his stories, and in 1990 his poems were collected and published under the title *The Searchers,* both by Arte Público Press, which has also kept his first novel in print and has recently published *Tomás Rivera: The Complete Works* (1990). In 1987, *...y no se lo tragó la tierra* was given a liberal translation into Texan dialect under the title *This Migrant Earth* (1987) by Rolando Hinojosa; the translation that accompanies the Arte Público bilingual edition was done by poet Evangelina Vigil-Piñón. By any accounts, Tomás Rivera remains the most outstanding and influential figure in the literature of Mexican peoples in the United States, and he deserves a place in the canon of Spanish-language literature in the world.

Evangelina Vigil-Piñón,
reciting at the Third
National Hispanic Book Fair,
Houston, 1987.

Rudolfo Anaya's *Bless Me, Ultima* is a straightforward novel about a boy's coming of age. Written in a poetic and clear English, it has reached more readers, especially non-Chicano readers, than any other Chicano literary work. In *Bless Me, Ultima*, again we have the search for identity, but this time the central character, Antonio, must decide between the more Spanish heritage of the plainsman-rancher or the more Indian heritage of the farmer; he is guided and inspired in his attempts to understand good and evil and his role in life by a larger than life folk healer, Ultima, who passes on many of her secrets and insights about life to Antonio. Anaya puts to good use his knowledge of the countryside of New Mexico, its romance and picturesque qualities, in fashioning this novel full of mystery and references to the symbols and folk knowledge of American Indian, Asian, and Spanish culture.

Anaya went on to become celebrated in his home state and to head the creative writing program at the University of New Mexico. His subsequent novels, all dealing with Chicano/Indian culture in New Mexico, have not been as well received by the critics: *Heart of Aztlán* (1976), *Tortuga (Tortoise)* (1979), *The Silence of the Llano* (1982), and *Lord of the Dawn: The Legend of Quetzalcoatl* (1987). As can be seen from these titles, Anaya is a promoter of the concept of Aztlán, the mythical place of origin of the Aztec, supposedly located in what has become the five states of the Southwest. He and numerous other Chicano writers have derived both poetic inspiration and a sense of mission in reviving the cultural glories of Mexico's indigenous past. For Anaya and especially for poets and playwrights such as Alurista and Luis Valdez, the Aztec and Mayan past has been a source of imagery, symbols, and myths that have enriched their works.

Rolando Hinojosa is the most prolific and probably the most bilingually talented of the novelists, with original creations in both English and Spanish published in the United States and abroad. His Quinto Sol Award-winning *Estampas del valle y otras obras/Sketches of the Valley and Other Works* is a mosaic of the picturesque character types, folk customs, and speech of the bilingual community in the small towns along Texas's Rio Grande valley. His sketches and insights at times reminiscent of the local color of the *crónicas* of the 1920s, Hinojosa's art is one of the most sophisticated contributions to Chicano literature.

Estampas was just the beginning phase of a continuing novel that has become a broad epic of the history and culture of the Mexican Americans and Anglos of the valley, centered in the fictitious Belken County and around two fictitious characters and a narrator—Rafa Buenrostro, Jehú Malacara, and P. Galindo—all of whom may be partial alter egos of Hinojosa himself. What is especially intriguing about Hinojosa's continuing novel, which he calls the Klail City Death Trip Series, is his experimentation with various forms of narration—derived from Spanish, Mexican, English, and American literary history—in the respective installments of the novel. *Klail City y sus alrededores (Klail City and Surroundings,* 1976) owes much to the picaresque novel; *Korean Love Songs* (1980) is narrative poetry; *Mi querido Rafa (Dear Rafe,* 1981) is part epistolary novel and part reportage; *Rites and Witnesses* (1982) is mainly a novel in dialogue; *Partners in Crime* (1985) is a detective novel; *Claros varones de Belken (Fair Gentlemen of Belken,* 1986) is a composite; and *Becky and Her Friends* (1990) continues the novel in the style of reportage, but with a new unnamed narrator, P. Galindo having died.

While there have been translations by others of his works, Hinojosa has penned and published re-creations in English and Spanish of all of these books, except for the English titles *Korean Love Songs, Rites and Witnesses,* and *Partners in Crime. Mi querido Rafa* is especially important because it represents the first novel to experiment with bilingual narration and demands of the reader a good knowledge of both English and Spanish and their south Texas dialects.

Because of his many awards—including the international award for Latin American fiction given in Cuba, Premio Casa de las Americas, 1976—his academic background and doctorate in Spanish, and the positive response to his sophisticated art from critics and university professors, in particular, Hinojosa is one of the few Hispanic writers in the country to teach in creative writing programs at a high level. In holding the distinguished title Ellen Clayton Garwood Professor of English and Creative Writing at the University of Texas, Hinojosa is the most recognized and highest-ranking Chicano/Hispanic author in academia.

It was not until 1975 that the Quinto Sol Award was given to a woman, Estela Portillo Trambley, for her short story collection *Rain of Scorpions,* and it marked the ascendancy of women's voices in Chicano literature, which had been too dominated by males. Portillo Trambley's strong feminist and irreverent stories did much both to sensitize the publishing powers in Chicano literature and to encourage a new generation of women writers to persevere in getting their works published; their works were soon to change the character of Chicano literature in the 1980s.

In nine finely crafted stories and a novella Portillo Trambley presents a series of female characters who draw from an inner strength and impose their personalities on the world around them. In the novella that gives title to the collection, a fat and unattractive central character overcomes her own dreams of beauty and the set roles that society has for her to prevail as a woman who from behind the scenes controls and determines the action around her. She has chosen her life and how to live it; it will not be imposed upon her by others. In the most feminist of the short stories, "If It Weren't for the Honeysuckle," the eldest of three women being oppressed and enslaved by a drunk and irrational male succeeds in poisoning him and in freeing the women. In this as in the other stories, as well as in her books to follow—*The Day of the Swallows* (1971), the collection of plays *Sor Juana* (*Sister Juana*, 1983), and the novel *Trini* (1986)—Portillo Trambley has created strong women who prevail in a male-dominated world. Her latest work, *Trini*, is the story of a Tarahumara woman who leaves her Indian life behind and, after numerous tragedies and betrayals, crosses the border to give birth to her child in the United States, where she is able to control her life for herself and even become a landowner. In all of her work Portillo Trambley has demonstrated an uncompromising pursuit for equality and liberation for women.

By the end of the 1970s most of the literary magazines and Chicano literary presses had disappeared, including Editorial Quinto Sol and *El grito*. Fortunately, since 1973 a new Hispanic magazine, *Revista Chicano-Riqueña* (*Chicano-Rican Review*), edited by Nicolás Kanellos and Luis

Helena María Viramontes

Luis Dávila, Co-Editor
of Revista Chicano-Riqueña,
at the First National
Latino Book Fair,
University of Illinois—
Chicago Circle, 1979

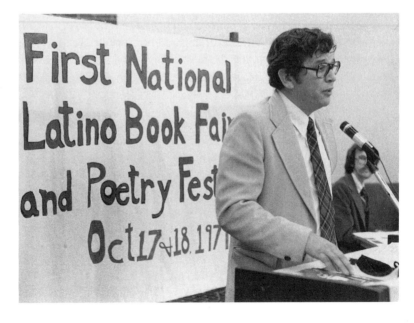

Dávila in Gary, Indiana, had been operating and making greater incursions into academia than any other Hispanic literary publication. In 1979, Kanellos founded Arte Público Press as an outgrowth of the magazine and relocated both to Houston, Texas, just in time to carry on where Quinto Sol had left off and to assume the leadership in publishing the works of a blossoming Hispanic women's literary movement. During the 1980s, Arte Público published books of poetry by San Antonio poets Evangelina Vigil and Angela de Hoyos, Chicago poets and prose writers Ana Castillo and Sandra Cisneros, San Francisco Bay Area novelist and poet Lucha Corpi, Los Angeles short story writer and former editor of the magazine *ChismeArte* Helena María Viramontes, and New Mexico novelist and playwright Denise Chávez, who were to produce some of the best-selling and most highly reviewed Chicano books of the decade.

Along with Arte Público and *Revista Chicano-Riqueña,* which in 1987 became *The Americas Review* and was edited by Julián Olivares and Evangelina Vigil, another magazine/book publisher was founded in Indiana in 1980 and relocated to the University of California, Berkeley, in 1985: *Third Woman,* directed by Norma Alarcón. Around the same time, another Hispanic book publisher with an academic base, *Bilingual Review Press,* also relocated, from Binghamton, New York, to the Southwest, to Arizona State University in Tempe. Supported by these three establishments and various other presses that were occasionally issuing women's titles, this first full-blown generation of Chicana writers flourished, finding a welcome space for their books in the academic curriculum, not only in Chicano literature courses but also in women's studies programs and American literature courses. The majority of the women were more educated than the 1960s and 1970s writers; most of them were college graduates. Two of its representatives, Denise Chavez and Sandra Cisneros, had even obtained master's degrees in creative writing. Most of the women write English, thus the Spanish language was no barrier to their works' entering literature courses and becoming accessible to broader circles of the reading public. As a whole, they were thoroughly versed in the general feminist movement while preserving their own Chicana identities and culture and developing their literature from it.

At the close of the decade, general market textbook publishers were finally responding to the reform movements occurring in academia and to the new demographic statistics relating to the public school markets in the most populous states, which convincingly showed overwhelming Hispanic enrollments then and into the next century. As a result, most of the textbook publishers have begun to desperately search out and include His-

Ana Castillo

panic writers. In 1990, the nation's largest textbook publisher, Harcourt Brace Jovanovich, in fact, even went so far as to issue a high school English anthology titled *Mexican American Literature,* which includes selections of works from the colonial period to the present in its more than seven hundred pages. Some of the most successful writers in being chosen for the general American literature textbooks and for such canonizing texts as *The Norton Anthology of American Literature* include Pat Mora and Denise Chávez. Mora is the author of three books of poetry, her first two winning the Southwest Book Award: *Chants* (1984), *Borders* (1986), and *Communion* (1991). Drawing upon the desert landscape and a Mexican Indian sensibility, *Chants* is a richly textured exploration, in beautiful whispered tones, of the desert as a woman and of women as holders of the strength and endurance of the desert. In *Borders,* Mora, an El Paso native, continues in the same vein, drawing upon folk customs and the insight of healers as she explores all types of borders: the political and cultural ones between the United States and Mexico, the borders between the sexes, and so forth. Her latest book, *Communion,* is about communion with other women, other peoples of the earth, as she expands her vision to Asia and Africa.

Pat Mora

Denise Chávez is a talented actress and a prolific playwright, but it is as a novelist that she has gained a deserved place in Chicano and American literature as a whole. For Chávez, as for Rolando Hinojosa, literature is very much the art of writing about lives, about individuals, and about the stories they have to tell. Both of her novels, *The Last of the Menu Girls* (1986) and *Face of an Angel* (1993), present series of lives and characters talking for themselves within a loose biographic structure. In the case of her first novel, the unifying structure is the life of Rocío Esquivel, who, through a series of interconnected stories gains maturity by rebelling against the social roles created for her. *Face of an Angel,* on the other hand, centers on the life of a waitress and the unfortunate and tragicomic amorous relationships that she has with men; in the midst of the narration are brought in various types of unlikely elements, such as a manual on how to become a good waitress that the protagonist is writing. Both Mora and Chávez have won attention from the world that was previously off-limits to Chicano writers: the pages of the *New York Times Book Review* and the Norton anthologies, important fellowships, and awards.

While women were ascending in the world of Chicano literature, so was a younger generation of male writers who were the products of creative writing programs at universities, through which they gained access to opportunities for study, travel, and publishing never before had by Chicanos (nor Chicanas). To date, theirs is the only Chicano poetry that has begun to become part of the American literary establishment. Of this new cadre of American poets who no longer speak or write in Spanish and no longer derive sustenance from the oral tradition, recitation, and political action, the most famous and prolific is Gary Soto, currently a tenured associate professor in creative writing and ethnic studies at the University of California, Berkeley. He is the winner of numerous prestigious awards, including the Academy of American Poets Prize (1975), the *Discovery*-Nation Award (1975), a Guggenheim Fellowship (1979), an American Book Award, and many other prizes. His poetry is finely crafted, down-to-earth, and rigorous, mostly inspired by the life of the common working man in the fields and factories.

Quite often, as in his book *The Elements of San Joaquin,* published, as are most of his other poetry books, by the prestigious University of Pittsburgh Press poetry series, his work is a recollection of growing up in Fresno. While dealing with very real and concrete pictures of life in a particular time and setting, such as his youth in the agricultural San Joaquin Valley, Soto frequently approaches his subject from a classical frame of reference.

Gary Soto and Evangelina Vigil-Piñón at the Third National Hispanic Book Fair and Writers Festival in Houston, Texas, 1987.

For instance, in the second section of the book, the Valley is envisioned according to the four universal elements of the Greek philosophers: earth, air, water, and fire. He takes these elements and transforms them into the particular sights, smells, and labors of the Valley.

Among Soto's other books of poetry are *The Tale of Sunlight* (1978), *Where Sparrows Work Hard* (1981), *Black Hair* (1985), and *Who Will Know?* (1990). In 1985, Soto also began publishing autobiographical prose essays, which have met with a great deal of success, his first three books winning an American Book Award: *Living Up the Street* (1985), *Small Faces* (1986), and *Lesser Evils: Ten Quartets* (1988).

Among other writers who have made it into university creative writing programs as professors are Arizonan Alberto Rios and Californians Ernesto Trejo and Lorna Dee Cervantes. Cervantes did not follow the usual trek through master of fine arts programs in creative writing for entrance into her career. She was very much a product of the 1970s and the Chicano literary movement of those days, in which she began reading her poetry in public at a theater festival in 1974, published her first works in *Revista Chicano-Riqueña* in 1975, and shortly thereafter founded and edited a literary magazine, *Mango*, which was free-form and experimental and not limited to publishing Chicanos. By 1981, her first book of poems, *Emplumada (Plumed)*, was published by the University of Pittsburgh Press. Despite many publications in magazines and success as a performer of poetry, it was not until 1986 that she finished her B.A. degree. In 1990, she earned a Ph.D. in the history of consciousness at the University of California, Santa Cruz. She currently teaches creative writing at the University of Colorado.

Perhaps better than anyone yet, Lorna Dee Cervantes has described the pain of separation from the tongue and culture of family in such poems as "Refugee Ship" and "Oaxaca, 1974." Her work also deals with the dehumanizing landscape and the dehumanization that is caused by racism and sexism. Today she is still very much a hard-driving poet who takes risks and is not afraid to deal with taboo topics and violence, whether it be racist, sexist, or psychological, as can be seen in her book *From the Cables of Genocide* (1991).

Today, as greater opportunities in academia have opened up for both Hispanic students and writers, the larger commercial world of publishing is beginning to open its doors to a few more Chicano writers. Under the leadership of writer-scholars, like Tomás Rivera and Rolando Hinojosa, and publishers like Arte Público Press and Bilingual Review Press, Chicano literature has created a firm and lasting base for itself in academia. The larger society of readers and commercial publishing represent the new frontier for the 1990s. A strong beginning is represented by the publication in 1991 of Victor Villaseñor's generational family saga, "the Chicano *Roots*," entitled *Rain of Gold*, which is currently under development as a five-part television miniseries by the Corporation for Public Broadcasting. In 1975, Villaseñor's novel *Macho* was published but barely promoted by Bantam Books; in 1991, it was reprinted by Arte Público Press and made into a feature film for commercial release. In 1990, the commercial publisher Chronicle Books issued two books of poetry by Chicanos, Gary Soto and Francisco Alarcón, and Random House in 1991 issued two books by Sandra Cisneros. Finally, in 1991 the long-awaited filming of *Bless Me, Ultima* began, with Luis Valdez as director.

Nuyorican Literature

In 1898, Puerto Rico became a colony of the United States; since 1917, Puerto Ricans have been citizens of the United States. Since that latter date, Puerto Ricans have never really been immigrants to the United States, but migrants. Puerto Ricans on the island and those on the continent, despite graphic separation, hold in common their ethnicity, history, and their religious and cultural traits and practices. They also both deal with the confrontation of two languages and cultures. Thus, whether they reside in the continental United States or on the island of Puerto Rico, Puerto Ricans are one people. That is true whether they prefer the Spanish language or English, whether they were born on the island or not. The island experience and the experience on the continent are two sides of the same coin. Thus, most attempted divisions of the people are for vested interests, whether political or prejudicial.

Puerto Rican culture today is the product of the powerful political, economic, and social forces that descend on small native populations and attempt to evangelize, assimilate, decimate, or otherwise transform them. In the case of Puerto Rico, in 1493 Christopher Columbus initiated the process that forever would make the island's people a blend of the cultures and races of Europe, Africa, and the Americas. It was this act of "discovery" that also resulted in Puerto Rico's becoming a colony in the Spanish Empire until 1898, when it passed into the possession of the next empire to dominate the hemisphere: the United States. It is therefore a land that has been and still is subject to overseas rule—politically and economically, as well as artistically.

Despite being an island geographically cut off from the rest of Latin America and despite being ruled as a colony and not enjoying complete self-determination, Puerto Rican literature has been rich, for it has developed out of the many cultures and experiences that make up its peoples. From the middle of the nineteenth century, it first assumed a creole, Hispanic-American identity, emphasizing the new speech and customs and history of people in this hemisphere as opposed to the Spanish in Europe— Puerto Rico and Cuba were among the very last remnants of Spain's colonial empire, the rest of Spanish America having gained its independence at the beginning of the century. After 1898, Puerto Rico emphasized its Latin American, Spanish-speaking identity as separate from the Anglo-American United States. While the reaction of Puerto Rican artists to the Spanish identity and tastes was to create a nationalism or an ethnic identity based on *mestizaje,* a blending of the cultures and the values of the New World, the reaction to the powerful presence of the United States has come as an insistence on the use of the Spanish language itself and on the relationship to Latin America and its cultures and arts.

At the turn of the century, the island's literature was developing along the lines of Latin American modernism, which was heavily influenced by French, peninsular Spanish, and Latin American models. As was the case in Mexico, Peru, Argentina, and Cuba, the artists and writers of Puerto Rico turned to the indigenous people of the island, their folklore, and national models in an effort to discover the true identity of the national culture. The mestizo highlander, or *jíbaro,* and the black and mulatto became cultural types that related Puerto Rico to the other island cultures of the Caribbean and thus created a space that was identifiable as home, while it challenged the imposition of the English language—which was done officially under U.S. military rule of the island—and the purported benefits of Yankee customs and economic power.

Although he was one of Puerto Rico's master poets, Luis Llorens Torres (1878–1944) was a European-educated intellectual who adapted the verse forms of the plaintive mountain songs (*décimas*) and folk speech of the jíbaros in poems that took pride in rural life and its values rather than in the sophistication and modern advances of the city. His jíbaros were always skeptical and unmoved by the bragging and showing off of Americanized Puerto Ricans who believed in Yankee ingenuity and progress. Puerto Rico's greatest and most universally studied poet, Luis Palés Matos (1898-1959), was the first Puerto Rican literary figure to achieve a lasting impact on the evolution of Latin American literature, principally through the development of a poetic style that was inspired by the rhythms and language of Africa and the black Caribbean. His landmark book, *Tun tun de pasa y grifería* (1937), whose onomatopoic title has no translation, openly claimed a black African heritage and presence for the cultural makeup of Puerto Rico. But the primitivism, vigor, and freedom of his black verses was only a point of departure for his critical stance toward Europe and the United States. In Palés Matos's master poem, "La plena de menéalo" ("The Dance of Shake It"), Puerto Rico is personified by a seductive *mulata* who sweats rum as she erotically dances close to, but just out of reach of, a drooling Uncle Sam.

Julia de Burgos

Two figures are essential in recognition of the transition of Puerto Rican literature from the island to the continent: Julia de Burgos (1914–1953) and René Marqués (1919–1979). The former cultivated beautiful, sensuous verses, odes to her beloved countryside, only to die tragically on the streets of New York. Her lyricism served the parallel desires for personal as well as national liberation. René Marqués, the most widely known Puerto Rican playwright, spent time in New York as well, and was able to capture the true meaning of the dislocation of the native populations from Puerto Rico and their relocation to foreign lands and values. Even more moving than John Steinbeck's *Grapes of Wrath* is the plight of the family of displaced mountain folk in Marqués's *La carreta (The Oxcart)*, which was first produced on stage in New York in 1953 and then published in Spanish in 1961 and in English in 1969. *La carreta*, which dramatizes the tragic life of this family as they are forced to move from their farm to a San Juan slum and then to New York, ends with an appeal to Puerto Ricans not to leave their homeland and to return to the island and the values of the countryside.

To a great extent, today's major Puerto Rican writers on the island still draw upon Marqués's spirit, style, and message in their attempt to preserve the integrity of the Puerto Rican culture and in their call for the political independence of the island. Prose writers like José Luis González, Pedro Juan Soto, Luis Rafael Sánchez, and Jaime Carrero satirize the complacency of the Americanized middle class, which would like Puerto Rico to become a U.S. state. They also develop the themes of Puerto Rico's past as Edenic and the *jíbaro* as a child of nature, with his intense code of honor and decency. Most of today's island novelists, while romanticizing the island's past, have, however, also created a one-dimensional image of Puerto Ricans in New York, only focusing on the tragedy of the rootlessness, poverty, and oppression of the second-class citizens who seem to be lost in the labyrinth of the monster city.

Puerto Rican writing in New York dates back to the end of the nineteenth century, and writing in English begins about the time that Jesús Colón was writing his columns for the *Daily Worker*. This seems to be a rather appropriate beginning, given that most of the Puerto Rican writers in English that followed identify with the working class. Unlike the writers of the island, who largely are members of an elite, educated class and many of whom are employed as university professors, the New York writers, who came to be known as Nuyoricans, are products of parents transplanted to the metropolis to work in the service and manufacturing industries. These writers are predominantly bilingual in their poetry and English-dominant in their prose; they hail from a folk and popular tradition heavily influenced by roving bards, reciters, storytellers, salsa music composers, and the popular culture and commercial environment of New York City.

Jesús Colón

Thus Nuyoricans are typically the children of working-class Puerto Rican migrants to the city; they are generally bilingual and bicultural, and so is their literature. During the search for ethnic roots and the civil rights movements of the 1960s, young Puerto Rican writers and intellectuals began using the term *Nuyorican* as a point of departure in affirming their own cultural existence and history as divergent from that of the island of Puerto Rico and that of mainstream America, much as the Chicanos were doing. A literary and artistic flowering in the New York Puerto Rican community ensued in the late 1960s and early 1970s as a result of greater access to education for Puerto Ricans raised in the United States and as a result of the ethnic consciousness movement. Although the term "Nuyorican" was first applied to literature by playwright-novelist Jaime Carrero in his poem "Neo-Rican Jetliner/Jet neorriqueño" in the late 1960s when he resided in New York, and the term finds some stylistic and thematic development in his plays *Noo Jall* (a blending of the Spanish pronunciation of "New York" and the word "jail") and "Pipo Subway no sabe reír" ("Pipo Subway Doesn't Know How to Laugh"), it was a group of poet-playwrights associated with the Nuyorican Poets' Café in the lower East Side of New York who later really defined and exemplified Nuyorican literature in their works. Included in the group were Miguel Alagarín, Lucky Cienfuegos, Tato Laviera, and Miguel Piñero. Two members of the group, Cienfuegos and Piñero, were ex-convicts who had begun their writing careers while incarcerated and associating with Afro-American convict-writers; they chose to concentrate on prison life, street life, and the culture of poverty and to protest the oppression of their peoples through their poetry and dramas. Algarín, a university professor and owner and operator of the Nuyorican Poets' Café, contributed more of a spirit of the avant-garde for the collective and managed to draw into the circle such well-known poets as Alan Ginsberg. Tato Laviera, a virtuoso bilingual poet and performer of poetry (*declamador*), contributed a lyricism and a folk and popular culture tradition that derived from the island experience and the Afro-Caribbean culture but was cultivated specifically in and for New York City.

It was Miguel Piñero's work (and life), however, that became most celebrated, his prison drama, *Short Eyes,* having won an Obie and the New York Drama Critics Award for Best American Play in the 1973-74 season. His success, coupled with that of the autobiography of fellow Nuyorican writer and ex-convict Piri Thomas and that of poet Pedro Pietri, who developed the image of a street urchin always high on marijuana, resulted in Nuyorican literature and theater's often being associated with crime, drugs, abnormal sexuality, and generally negative behavior. Thus, many writers who in fact were affirming Puerto Rican working-class culture did not want to become identified with the movement. Still others wanted to hold onto their ties with the island and saw no reason to emphasize differences, but, rather, wanted to stress similarities. What exacerbated the situation was that the commercial publishing establishment in the early 1970s was quick to take advantage of the literary fervor in the Puerto Rican community by issuing a series of ethnic autobiographies that insisted on the criminality, abnormality, and drug culture of New York Puerto Ricans. Included in this array of mostly paperbacks was, of course, Piri Thomas's *Down These Mean Streets* (1967, issued in paper in 1974), Thomas's *Seven Long Times* (1974), Thomas's *Stories from El Barrio* (1978, issued in paper in 1980), Lefty Barreto's *Nobody's Hero* (1976), and a religious variation on the theme: Nicky Cruz's *Run Nicky Run.*

Ed Vega's *The Comeback* is the story of a confused college professor who creates for himself the identity of a Puerto Rican-Eskimo ice hockey player; he suffers a nervous breakdown and is treated for the classical symptoms of an identity crisis. Throughout the novel are satirized all types of characters that populate the barrio as well as popular culture, such as Puerto Rican revolutionaries, psychiatrists, and a Howard Cosell-type sportscaster. In his interrelated collection of stories told by fictitious narrator Ernesto Mendoza, *Mendoza's Dreams* (1987), Vega surveys the human comedy of everyday barrio life and relates tales of success in small ways in reaching for the American Dream. In his collection *Casualty Report* (1991), he shows us the inverse: the physical, psychological, and moral death of many who live within the poverty and deprivation of the Puerto Rican barrio, as well as in the larger ghetto of a racist society.

More than anything else, the first generation of Nuyorican writers was one that was dominated by poets, many of whom had come out of an oral tradition and had honed their art through public readings; thus the creation of the Nuyorican Poets' Café was a natural outcome of the need to create a specific space for the performance of poetry. Among the consummate performers of Nuyorican poetry were Victor Hernández Cruz, Tato Laviera, Miguel Piñero, and Miguel Algarín. Like his fellow poets, Cruz's initiation into poetry was through popular music and street culture; his first poems have been often considered to be jazz poetry in a bilingual mode, except that English dominated in the bilingualism and thus opened the way for his first book to be published by a general market publishing house: *Snaps: Poems* (Random House, 1969). It was quite a feat for a twenty-year-old from an impoverished background. Already announced in *Snaps* were the themes and styles that would dominate and flourish in his subsequent books. In all of Hernández Cruz's poetry of sound, music and performance are central. He always experiments with bilingualism as oral poetry [and written symbols of oral speech,] and he searches for identity through these sounds and symbols. Thus, his next two books are odysseys that take the reader back to Puerto Rico and primordial Indian and African music and poetry (*Mainland,* 1973) and across the United States and back to New York, where the poet finds the city transformed by its Caribbean peoples into their very own cultural home (*Tropicalization,* 1976). *By Lingual Wholes* (1982) is a consuming and total exploration of the various linguistic possibilities in the repertoire of a bilingual poet, and *Rhythm, Content and Flavor* (1989) is a summary of his entire career.

Tato Laviera has said in a 1980 interview with the author of this chapter, "I am the grandson of slaves transplanted from Africa to the Caribbean, a man of the New World come to dominate and revitalize two old world languages." And, indeed, Laviera's bilingualism and linguistic inventiveness have risen to the level of virtuosity. Laviera is the inheritor of the Spanish oral tradition, with all of its classical formulas, and the African oral tradition, with its wedding to music and spirituality; in his works he brings both the Spanish and English languages together as well as the islands of Puerto Rico and Manhattan—a constant duality that is always just in the background. His first book, *La Carreta Made a U-Turn* (1979) was published by Arte Público Press, which has become the leading publisher of Nuyorican literature, despite its location in Houston. *La Carreta Made a U-Turn* uses René Marqués's *Oxcart* as a point of departure and redirects back to the heart of New York, instead of back to the island, as Marqués had desired; Laviera is stating that Puerto Rico can be found here too. His second book, *Enclave* (1981) is a celebration of diverse heroic personalities, both real and imagined: Luis Palés Matos and salsa composers, the neighborhood gossip and John Lennon, Miriam Makeba and Tito Madera Smith, the latter being a fictional, hip offspring of a jíbara and a southern American black. *AmeRícan* (1986) and *Mainstream Ethics* (1988) are surveys of the lives of the poor and marginalized in the United States and a challenge for the country to live up to its promises of equality and democracy.

Sandra María Esteves

One of the few women's voices to be heard in this generation is a very strong and well-defined one, that of Sandra María Esteves, who from her teen years has been very active in the women's struggle, Afro-American liberation, the Puerto Rican independence movement, and, foremost, the performance of poetry. In 1973, she joined El Grupo, a New York-based touring collective of musicians, performing artists, and poets and the cultural wing of the Puerto Rican Socialist party. By 1980, she had published her first collection of poetry, *Yerba Buena,* which is a search for identity of a colonized Hispanic woman of color in the United States, the daughter of immigrants from the Caribbean. All three of her books, *Yerba Buena, Tropical Rains: A Bilingual Downpour* (1984), and *Mockingbird Bluestown Mambo* (1990), affirm that womanhood is what gives unity to all of the diverse characterizations of her life.

The most productive and recognized Nuyorican novelist is Nicholasa Mohr. Her works, *Nilda* (1973), *El Bronx Remembered* (1975), *In Nueva York* (1977), *Felita* (1979), and *Going Home* (1986) were all published in hardback and paperback by major commercial publishing houses and are all still in print, three of them having been reissued by Arte Público Press. Her books have entered the general market as have few other books by Hispanic authors of the United States. They have won such awards as the New York Times Outstanding Book of the Year, the *School Library Journal* Best Children's Book, and many others, including a decree honoring her by the state legislature of New York. Her best-loved novel, *Nilda,* traces the coming of age of a young Puerto Rican girl in the Bronx during World War II. Unlike many other such novels of development, Nilda gains awareness of the plight of her people and her own individual problems by examining the racial and economic oppression that surrounds her and her family, in a manner that can be compared to Tomás Rivera's central character in *...y no se lo tragó la tierra.*

In two of her other books, *In Nueva York* and *El Bronx Remembered,* Mohr examines through a series of stories and novellas various Puerto Rican

Nicholasa Mohr, Nicolás Kanellos, and Ed Vega, 1985

neighborhoods and draws sustenance from the common folks' power to survive and still produce art, folklore, and strong families in the face of oppression and marginalization. *Rituals of Survival: A Woman's Portfolio* (1985), in five stories and a novella, portrays six strong women who take control of their lives, most of them by liberating themselves from husbands, fathers, or families that attempt to keep them confined in narrowly defined female roles. *Rituals* is the book that the general market houses would not publish, wanting to keep Mohr confined to what they saw as immigrant literature and children's literature, as in her *Felita* and *Going Home*.

While not banding together with groups and collectives, Mohr has been one of the most influential of the Nuyorican writers out of sheer productivity and accomplishment. She has also led the way to greater acceptance of Nuyorican and Hispanic writers in creative writing workshops, such as the Millay Colony, in Poets, Editors and Novelists (PEN), and on the funding panels of the National Endowment for the Arts and the New York State Council on the Arts.

Another Nuyorican writer who has not participated in nor benefitted from collective work is Judith Ortiz Cofer, who grew up in Paterson, New Jersey, and has lived much of her adult life in Georgia and Florida. Cofer is one of the few Nuyorican products of the creative writing programs, and much of her early poetry was disseminated through establishment small presses in the South that may have been intrigued by the exoticism of her Puerto Rican subjects, packaged in finely crafted verses, with a magic and mystery that is similar to that of Pat Mora's poetry.

Her first book of poems, *Reaching for the Mainland* (1987), is a chronicle of the displaced person's struggle to find a goal, a home, a language, and a history. In *Terms of Survival* (1987), she explores the psychology and social attitudes of the Puerto Rican dialect and how it controls male and female roles; in particular she carries on a dialogue with her father throughout the poems of the book. In 1989, Cofer published a highly reviewed novel of immigration, *Line of the Sun,* through the University of Georgia Press and in 1990 an even more highly reviewed book, made up of a collection of autobiographical essays, in the style of Virginia Wolf, *Silent Dancing: A Remembrance of Growing Up Puerto Rican,* through Arte Público Press.

In 1988, Cofer and five other writers discussed earlier—Nicholas Mohr, Tato Laviera, Rolando Hinojosa, Alberto Ríos, and Lorna Dee Cervantes— were featured reading and performing their works in a historic documentary, *Growing Up Hispanic,* directed by Jesús Treviño, presented on national television by the Corporation for Public Broadcasting. The future of Hispanic literature in the United States promises to be very fruitful, and more and more segments of the population are getting the message.

As mentioned previously, Cuban culture and literature in the United States dates back to the nineteenth century when writer-philosopher José Martí and other patriots plotted from the U.S. mainland for Cuban independence from Spain. During the first half of the twentieth century, Cubans and Spaniards dominated Hispanic arts and media in New York. While Cuban culture was on the ascendancy in New York, its island literature had already joined that of Mexico and Argentina in the leadership of Spanish American letters since the nineteenth century, with such internationally acknowledged masters as Gertrudis Gómez de Avellaneda, José Echeverría, Julián del Casal, and José Martí, and in the twentieth century with such leaders as patriarch Nicolás Guillén, who has taken Spanish American poetry from a markedly Afro-Caribbean to a Pan Hispanic vi-

Cuban-American Literature

sion in support of universal socialist revolution. Cuban writers who have contributed to the Latin American literary boom include Alejo Carpentier, José Lezama Lima, and Gabriel Cabrera Infante.

It is no wonder then that the inheritors of such a rich and dynamic tradition would contribute so greatly to Hispanic culture in the United States, especially given the fact that their mass immigration took place so recently, beginning in 1959 as refugees from the Cuban Revolution. In contrast, whereas Puerto Rican mass migration really had begun during World War II, when the American economy drew heavily on its island territory for workers, the Cubans came as political refugees from a land that had never been a colony of the United States, although it had been a protectorate and an economic dependent since the Spanish-American War. Most of the Puerto Ricans had come as workers and generally did not have the level of education nor the financial resources and relocation services that the Cubans did. This first mass of Cubans came with an outstanding written tradition well intact. And the Cuban literary aesthetic, unlike the Puerto Rican one, had never been so obsessed with protecting the Spanish language and Hispanic culture while defending itself against Anglo-American culture and language. Numerous writers and intellectuals immigrated to the United States as refugees; many of them were able to adapt to and become part of Hispanic and general U.S. cultural institutions.

Virgil Suárez

Today, after three decades of new Cuban culture in New York, New Jersey, Miami, and dispersed throughout the United States—in contrast to the older Cuban communities in New York City and Tampa—a Cuban-American literary and artistic presence has developed. Younger writers are no longer preoccupied with exile, with eyes cast only on the island past; instead they are looking forward to participating in general English-language society or serving the intellectual and cultural needs of the U.S. Cuban and Hispanic communities. Thus there has developed a definite separation of purpose and aesthetics between the younger writers—Roberto Fernández, Iván Acosta, Virgil Suárez, and Oscar Hijuelos, for instance—and the older writers of exile—Lydia Cabrera, Matías Montes Huidobro, José Sánchez Boudy, and so on. Also, there continues to be an influx of exiled writers, disaffected with Cuban communism, like Heberto Padilla, who must be viewed differently from the earlier generation of exiles who have already created for themselves a solid niche within Hispanic and general market institutions such as publishing houses and universities.

What we have seen during the last decades is first a literature that almost exclusively attacked the Cuban Revolution and Marxism. The novel of exile became another weapon in the struggle. Following the first antirevolutionary novel, *Enterrado vivo* (*Buried Alive*), published in Mexico in 1960 by Andrés Rivero Collado, were a host of others published in the United States and abroad by minor writers, such as Emilio Fernández Camus, Orlando Núñez, Manuel Cobo Souza, Raúl A. Fowler, Luis Ricardo Alonso, and many others. When they were not openly propagandistic and rhetorical, they were nostalgic for the homeland to the point of idealization. Poetry and drama followed the same course, for the most part. Later, political verse would come to form a special genre of its own, what has been called by critic Hortensia Ruiz del Viso "poesía del presidio político" (political prisoner poetry), as in the works of Angel Cuadra, Heberto Padilla, and Armando Valladares, who resides in Spain but is quite active in the United States.

A key figure in providing a new direction for Cuban literature in the United States has been Celedonio González, who, beginning with *Los primos* (*The Cousins*, 1971), changed his focus to concentrate on Cuban life and culture in the United States. Later, in *Los cuatro embajadores* (*The Four Ambassadors*, 1973) and *El espesor del pellejo de un gato ya cadáver* (*The Thickness of the Skin on a Cat Already a Corpse*, 1978), he not only examined culture shock and conflict between Cubans and Americans, but he also treated a very taboo topic: criticism of the economic system of the United States, especially in its exploitation of Cuban workers. González presents us with Cubans who do not yet see themselves as Americans but who are also conscious that Cuba is no longer theirs.

Ironically, one of the most important writers in forging a Cuban-American literature and in breaking new ground in his use of the English language is a professor of Spanish, Roberto Fernández. Through his novels, Fernández not only touches upon all the taboo subjects in the Cuban community of Miami—the counterrevolutionary movement in the United States, racism, acculturation, and assimilation—but also helps the community to take them in a less serious vein and to laugh at itself. In his two open-form mosaiclike novels, *La vida es un special* (*Life Is on Special*, 1982) and *La montaña rusa* (*The Roller Coaster*, 1985), Fernández presents a biting but loving satire of a community transformed by the materialism and popular culture of the United States, but somewhat paralyzed by the nostalgia and political obsession with a Communist Cuba. In 1988, Fernández continued the community saga in English, with the publication of *Raining Backwards*, which has become his most known and highly regarded novel. Here as in his other works, the hilarious parade of characters, language styles—with quite a bit of bilingual humor—and diverse social events are aimed at encouraging the community to take stock of its present circumstances and reckon with a future here in the United States.

One of the most influential literary magazines of Cuban literature in the United States has been *Linden Lane,* which is published in Spanish. Published by writer Heberto Padilla and edited by poet Belkis Cuza Malé, who is a professor at Princeton University, the magazine has created a forum for the whole Cuban writing community, both the generation of exile and the new Cuban-American generation. In 1990, the magazine formally announced the advent of a Cuban-American literature with its publication of an anthology containing works in both English and Spanish and entitled *Los atrevidos: Cuban American Literature,* edited by Miami poet Carolina Hospital, also an editor of *Linden Lane.* In 1991, Arte Público Press published an anthology that also proclaimed a Cuban-American identity, *Cuban American Theater,* edited by critic Rodolfo Cortina. Both collections draw upon writers dispersed throughout the United States, not just from the Miami and New York communities.

Among the new generation of Cuban-American writers growing up in the United States, there are a few who have gone through creative writing programs at universities and who thus have had access to general market publishing opportunities. A graduate of the important writing program at Louisiana State University, Virgil Suárez has had two novels published, *Latin Jazz* (1989) by Morrow and *The Cutter* (1991) by Ballantine Books. His third book, a very fine collection of short stories, *Welcome to the Oasis,* was not accepted by commercial publishers who prefer novels; it was published in 1991 by Arte Público Press. *Latin Jazz* is a somewhat different type of ethnic biographical novel, portraying a whole Cuban family, instead of just one individual; in alternate chapters devoted to each of the family members, Suárez provides their respective histories, hopes, and desires as they wait for a missing family member to arrive in Miami with the Mariel boat-lift.

Probably the most important of the Cuban-American writers to come out of the creative writing schools is Oscar Hijuelos, who is not the son of refugees from the Cuban Revolution, but of earlier immigrants to New York. Nevertheless, Hijuelos's first offering, *Our House in the Last World* (1983), is a typical ethnic autobiography and may be seen as a symbol of Cuban assimilation in that it is one of the few novels that negatively portrays the island culture, as personified by an alcoholic and machistic father, while it develops the tried-and-true theme of the American dream in the United States. His novel *The Mambo Kings Play Songs of Love* (1990) made history; it is the first novel by a Hispanic writer of the United States to win the Pulitzer Prize. It is also the first time that a major publishing house, Simon and Shuster, has ever invested heavily in a novel by a Hispanic writer, bringing it out at the top of its list and promoting the book very heavily. *The Mambo Kings* is the story of two musician brothers during the heyday of the mambo and during the time when at least one Cuban had captured the attention of the United States: Desi Arnaz on the "I Love Lucy" show. The novel thus has a historical background that lends it a very rich texture; it allows us to see a portion of American popular culture history through the eyes of two performers very wrapped up in the euphoria of the times and then the waning of interest in things Latin in the United States. The story of the tragic ending of the duo is very touching, but offers hope for the potential of Hispanic culture to influence the general society. In fact, Hijuelo's book and the recognition that it has won offer the hope of opening the door to mainstream publishing for other Hispanic writers.

◆ ◆ ◆ ◆ ◆ ◆ ◆ ◆ OUTSTANDING HISPANIC LITERARY FIGURES

A native of Santurce, Puerto Rico, Miguel Algarín grew up in a hardworking family that loved music and the arts and gave to their children an early appreciation of opera and classical music; Miguel's father taught him to play the violin. The Algaríns moved to New York City in the early 1950s and settled in Spanish Harlem for a while, and then moved to Queens. Miguel Alagarín began his higher education at City College and finished his B.A. degree at the University of Wisconsin in 1963; in 1965, he graduated with a master's degree in English from the Pennsylvania State University. After teaching English literature at Brooklyn College and New York University for a time, Algarín went on to teach at Rutgers, where he is an associate professor in the English department.

Miguel Algarín (1941–)

Miguel Algarín is the founder and proprietor of the Puerto Rican Poets' Café, which is dedicated to the support of writers performing their art orally. It was especially important as a gathering place of young writers during the early 1970s when Nuyorican literature was being defined. Algarín played an important leadership role in that definition by also compiling, with Miguel Piñero, an important anthology, *Nuyorican Poetry: An Anthology of Puerto Rican Words and Feelings* (1975). He also founded a

Miguel Algarín reciting his poetry at the First National Latino Book Fair, Chicago, 1979

short-lived publishing house, the Nuyorican Press, which only issued one book, his own *Mongo Affair* (1978). One year later, he took part in the launching of Arte Público Press, which became the leading publisher of Nuyorican literature.

Algarín has written plays, screenplays, and short stories, but is principally known as a poet. His books include *Mongo Affair, On Call* (1980), *Body Bee Calling from the 21st Century* (1982), and *Time's Now/Ya es tiempo* (1985). Algarín's poetry runs the gamut from jazz-salsa poetry to the mystical and avant-garde. He is one of the foremost experimenters with English-Spanish bilingualism and has even penned trilingual works that incorporate the French language. In 1976, Algarín published translations of the poetry of Chilean Nobel Prize winner Pablo Neruda, under the title *Canción de gesta/A Song of Protest.*

Alurista (Alberto Baltazar Urista) is considered one of the pioneers of Chicano literature. He was one of the first poets to support the Chicano movement through his poetry, a writer and signer of important manifestoes of the movement, a founder of the Moviemiento Estudiantil de Aztlán (MECHA, Chicano Student Movement of Aztlán) in 1967, and one of the first to establish the concept of Aztlán in literature, which forecasts a return to the glories of Aztec civilization by the Chicanos in the mythic homeland of the Aztecs, what is today roughly the five states of the Southwest.

Born in Mexico City on August 8, 1947, Alberto Baltazar Urista spent his early years in the states of Morelos and Guerrero. At age 13 he immigrated to the United States with his family, which settled in San Diego, California. He began writing poetry at an early age and was a restless and widely-read student. He began Chapman College in 1965 and transferred to and graduated from San Diego State University in 1970 with a B.A. degree in psychology. He later obtained an M.A. degree from that institution and a Ph.D. degree in literature from the University of California, San Diego, in 1983. Around 1966, he began writing poetry seriously for publication and assumed the pen name Alurista, which is virtually the only name he uses now.

Alurista is a consummate reader and performer of his poetry, which has led to many travels to fulfill invitations nationally and internationally to read his works. He was the founder and coeditor, with his wife, Xelina, of the literary magazine *Maize* and the publishing house associated with it; both ceased to exist after he began his present employment as professor of Spanish at California State University, San Luis Obispo, in 1987. Alurista is a prolific and talented poet, a pioneer of bilingualism in Chicano poetry. Throughout his career his study of the Nahuatl and Mayan languages and mythology have enriched his poetic works and inspired his promotion of the ideology of Aztlán. But it is his bilingualism that has opened new frontiers in poetry, with his free experimentation in combining the sounds, meanings, and graphic representations of Spanish and English in the same poem, quite often achieving surprising and beautiful effects.

Alurista has published the following books of poetry: *Floricanto en Aztlán* (1971), *Nationchild Plumaroja, 1967–1972* (1972), *Timespace Huracán: Poems, 1972–1975* (1976), *A'nque* (1979), *Spik in Glyph?* (1981), and *Return: Poems Collected and New* (1982).

Rudolfo A. Anaya was born in the village of Pastura, New Mexico, in surroundings similar to those celebrated in his famous novel about growing up in the rural culture of New Mexico: *Bless Me, Ultima*. He attended pub-

Alurista (1947–)

Rudolfo A. Anaya (1937–)

lic schools in Santa Rosa and Albuquerque and earned both his B.A. (1963) and his M.A. (1968) degrees in English from the University of New Mexico. In 1972, he also earned an M.A. degree in guidance and counseling from the same university. From 1963 to 1970, he taught in the public schools, but in 1974 he became a member of the English department of the University of New Mexico. With the success of his writing career, Anaya has risen to become the head of the creative writing program at the University of New Mexico. Included among his many awards are the following: an honorary doctorate from the University of Albuquerque, the New Mexico Governor's Award for Excellence, the President's National Salute to American Poets and Writers in 1980, and the Premio Quinto Sol in 1972 for his novel *Bless Me, Ultima.* Anaya is also a fellow of the National Endowment for the Arts and the Kellogg Foundation through whose auspices he has been able to travel to China and other countries for study.

Anaya is very much a believer and promoter of a return to pre-Columbian literature and thought through the reflowering of Aztec civilization in Aztlán, the mythic homeland of the Aztecs, which corresponds to the five states of today's Southwest. He sees his role in literature as that of the shaman; his task as a storyteller is to heal and reestablish balance and harmony. These ideas are present throughout his works, but are most successfully represented in his prize-winning novel *Bless Me, Ultima,* in which the folk healer Ultima works to reestablish harmony and social order in the life of the Mares family and to bring psychological well-being to Antonio, the protagonist, who is struggling to understand the roles of good and evil in life. Anaya's other books are *Heart of Aztlán* (1976), *Tortuga* (1979), *The Silence of the Llano* (1982), *The Legend of La Llorona* (1984), *The Adventures of Juan Chicaspatas* (1985), *A Chicano in China* (1986), *The Farolitas of Christmas* (1987), *Lord of the Dawn: The Legend of Quetzalcoatl* (1987). He is also the author of plays and screenplays and has coedited three literary anthologies: with Simon Ortiz, *Ceremony of Brotherhood, 1680-1980* (1980); with José Griego y Maestas, *Cuentos: Tales from the Hispanic Southwest* (1980), and with Antonio Márquez, *Cuentos Chicanos (Chicano Stories,* 1980).

Angélico Chávez (1910-)

Fray Angélico Chávez is one of the most renowned religious poets in the United States. The author of some nineteen books, Chávez is also a historian of his order, the Franciscan brothers, and of the Catholic church in New Mexico. Born on April 10, 1910, in Wagon Mound, New Mexico, he was named Manuel Chávez by his parents. Chávez was raised in Mora and attended St. Francis Seminary in Cincinnati, Ohio, and colleges in the Midwest. In 1937, he became the first New Mexican to become a Franciscan friar. From the time of his ordination at age 27 until age 62, he served as a pastor in several towns and Indian pueblos of New Mexico.

What unifies Chávez's large output as a poet and historian is his interest in New Mexico's past, the work of his order in New Mexico, and his own Catholicism. Beginning as essentially a religious poet, he later took an interest in historical fiction and, finally, in the history of the region itself, as in his most famous historical essay, *My Penitente Land: Reflections on Spanish New Mexico* (1974). Other historical writings by Chávez also were intended to provide an accurate understanding of Hispanic New Mexico; these include *Our Lady of the Conquest* (1948), *Origins of New Mexico Families in the Spanish Colonial Period* (1954), *Coronado's Friars* (1968), *But Time and Chance: The Story of Padre Martínez of Taos, 1793–1867* (1981), and other edited books.

His works of historical fiction include *New Mexico Triptych: Being Three Panels and Three Accounts: 1. The Angel's New Wing, 2. The Penitente Thief, 3. Hunchback Madonna* (1940), *La Conquistadora: The Autobiography of an Ancient Statue* (1954), *From an Altar Screen/ El retablo: Tales from New Mexico* (1957), and *The Lady from Toledo* (1960).

Chávez's reputation as a creative writer rests upon an important body of poetic works that include *Clothed with the Sun* (1939), *Eleven Lady Lyrics, and Other Poems* (1945), *The Single Rose; the Rose Unica and Commentary of Fray Manuel de Santa Clara* (1948), and *The Virgin of Port Lligat* (1959). Although Chávez's poetry and all of his works are grounded in New Mexico Catholicism, his poems are not local-color pieces celebrating New Mexico's picturesque landscape; instead they depict Chávez's inner life. In *The Single Rose,* Chávez was so intent on communicating the poems' inner religious meaning that he included commentary in the book, which studies the rose as an allegorical figure for human and divine love. Chávez's last poetry collection was *Selected Poems, With an Apologia* (1969), which brought together some of his most successful poems along with an apologia that announced that he would no longer publish poetry, due to changing fashions in poetry and his loss of excitement in writing verse.

Denise Chávez

(1948–)

Denise Chávez is a novelist, playwright, and poet who, through her writings, has brought to life entire populations of memorable characters of the Southwest, both Mexican-American and Anglo-American. Born on August

15, 1948, in Las Cruces, New Mexico, Chávez was raised principally by her mother, Delfina, a teacher, because her father had abandoned the family while she was still young. After attending schools and colleges in Las Cruces, Chávez obtained a master's degree in theater arts from Trinity University in San Antonio, Texas, in 1974, and a master's degree in creative writing from the University of New Mexico in Albuquerque in 1984. During her career she has taught and been a writer in residence at numerous institutions in New Mexico and elsewhere. In 1988, she became a professor in the drama department of the University of Houston.

Denise Chávez has won numerous awards and fellowships, including Best Play award for *The Wait* from New Mexico State University in 1970, the Steele Jones Fiction Award in 1986 for her story "The Last of the Menu Girls," two fellowships from the National Endowment for the Arts in 1981 and 1982, a Rockefeller Foundation Fellowship in 1984, and the Creative Writing Arts Fellowship from the Cultural Arts Council of Houston in 1990.

As a playwright, Chávez has written and seen produced numerous unpublished plays, including *Novitiates* (1971), *Elevators* (1972), *The Mask of November* (1977), *Nacimiento* (*Birth*, 1979), *Santa Fe Charm* (1980), *Sí, Hay Posada* (*Yes, There Is Room*, 1980), *El Santero de Córdova* (*The Saintmaker of Córdova*, 1981), *Hecho en México* (*Made in Mexico*, 1982) (with Nita Luna) *The Green Madonna* (1982), *La Morenita* (*The Little Brown Girl*, 1983), *Francis!* (1983), *How Junior Got Throwed in the Joint* (1981), *Plaza* (1984), *Novena Narrativa* (*A Narrative Novena*, 1986), *The Step* (1987), *Language of Vision* (1987), and *The Last of the Menu Girls* (1990). She has also seen three of her children's plays produced on stage: *The Adobe Rabbit* (1979), *El Más Pequeño de Mis Hijos* (*The Smallest of My Children*, 1983), and *The Flying Tortilla Man* (1975), which was also published in a high school textbook, *Mexican American Literature*, edited by Charles Tatum (1990). Chávez has also edited an anthology of plays, *Plays by Hispanic Women of the United States* (1991).

Despite Chávez's high productivity as a playwright, it is her published works of fiction that have contributed most to her national reputation. Chávez has published short stories in magazines and has two novels in print, *The Last of the Menu Girls* (1986) and *Face of an Angel* (1993). The first of these is a series of stories centering on the coming of age of Rocío Esquivel that come together to form a novel. As Rocío compares her own life to that of her mother and as she encounters a wide range of characters in her neighborhood and at work, she begins to formulate her own identity. By the end of the book, we realize that we have been participating in the making of a novelist, and that what we have been reading is the product of Rocío's creative and psychological exploration. While still centering on the life of a female central character and her development, *Face of an Angel* is completely different from her first novel. It is unrestrained, bawdy, irreverent, and hilariously funny as it explores some of the major themes of the women's liberation movement as represented in the life of a waitress, who is an author in her own right (of a manual on waitressing, which is included in the novel). Soveida Dosamantes, it seems, is one of those people who are destined to repeat over and over the same mistakes in their choice of a male partner. The novel thus consists of her experiences with a number of lazy, good-for-nothing men who are irresistible to her. But *Face of an Angel* is also populated with a host of other humorous and tragic figures that represent a cross section of life in the Southwest.

Lorna Dee Cervantes (1954–)

Of Mexican and Amerindian ancestry, Lorna Dee Cervantes was born into a very economically deprived family, but she discovered the world of books at a very early age. Born on August 6, 1954, in the Mission District of San Francisco, at age 5 she moved with her mother and brother to San Jose to live with her grandmother when her parents separated. Lorna began writing poetry when she was six years old; poems written when she was fourteen were eventually published in a magazine after Cervantes had established her career as a writer. Cervantes later attended college, but did not finish her B.A. degree from California State University until after she had initiated her writing career; in 1990 she obtained a Ph.D. degree from the University of California, Santa Cruz, where she studied philosophy and aesthetics. She then went on to teach creative writing at the University of Colorado in Denver.

Emplumada (*Plumed,* 1981), Cervantes's first collection of poems, is made up of works published in literary magazines throughout the Southwest. The book's popularity has made it the best-selling title in the University of Pittsburgh's prestigious poetry series. *Emplumada* presents a young woman coming of age, discovering the gap that exists in life between one's hopes and desires and what life eventually offers in reality. The predominant themes include culture conflict, oppression of women and minorities, and alienation from one's roots. Cervantes's poetry is very well crafted and has the distinction of using highly lyrical language while at the same time being direct and powerful. The same can be said of her second book, *From the Cables of Genocide,* which is very much the work of a mature poet dealing with the great themes of life, death, social conflict, and poverty.

Judith Ortiz Cofer

(1952–)

Judith Ortiz was born in Puerto Rico in 1952 into a family that was destined to move back and forth between Puerto Rico and Paterson, New Jersey. Her father, Jesús Ortiz Lugo, was a navy man, first assigned to the Brooklyn Navy Yard and then other points around the world. In Puerto Rico, the young Judith attended San José Catholic School in San Germán, and in Paterson she went to public schools at first and then to Saint Joseph's Catholic School. In 1968, after her father had retired from the navy with a nervous breakdown, the family moved to Augusta, Georgia, where she attended high school and Augusta College. She met John Cofer at the college and they were married. After graduation and the birth of her daughter, they moved to West Palm Beach, Florida, and she earned an M.A. degree at Florida Alantic University. She was also awarded a scholarship to do graduate work at Oxford University by the English-Speaking Union of America. Included among many other awards were fellowships from the Florida Arts Council (1980), the Bread Loaf Writers Conference (1981), and the National Endowment for the Arts (1989).

While teaching English in south Florida colleges, Ortiz Cofer began writing poetry, and her works were soon appearing in such magazines as the *New Mexico Humanities Review, Kansas Quarterly, Prairie Schooner, Revista Chicano-Riqueña, Southern Humanities Review, Southern Poetry Review,* and elsewhere. Her collections of poetry include four chapbooks—*Latin Women Pray* (1980), *Among the Ancestors* (1981), *The Native Dancer* (1981), *Peregrina* (1986)—and two full-length books—*Reaching for the Mainland* (1987) and *Terms of Survival* (1987). Her well-crafted poetry reflects her struggle as a writer to create a history for herself out of the cultural ambiguity of a childhood spent traveling back and forth between the United States and Puerto Rico. Through her poetry she also explores from a feminist perspective her relationship with her father, mother, and grandmother, while also considering the different expectations for the males and females in Anglo-American and Hispanic cultures. In particular, her book of autobiographical essays, *Silent Dancing: A Remembrance of a Puerto Rican Childhood* (1990), pursues this question. Her novel *The Line of the Sun* (1990) is based on her family's gradual immigration to the United States and chronicles the years from the Great Depression to the 1960s.

Jesús Colón

(1901–74)

Jesús Colón's writings are considered to be landmarks in the development of Puerto Rican literature in the continental United States because he is one of the first writers to become well known through his use of English, because of his identification with the working class, and because of his ideas on race. These three factors in the essays that he was already writing in the 1940s and 1950s make him a clear forerunner of the Nuyorican writers who began to appear two decades later.

Colón was born into a working-class family in Cayey, Puerto Rico. At age 16, he stowed away on a ship that landed in Brooklyn. In New York, he worked in a series of jobs that exposed him to the exploitation and abuse of lower-class and unskilled workers. He became involved in literary and journalistic endeavors while working as a laborer, trying to establish a newspaper and writing translations of English-language poetry. As he strived to develop his literary and journalistic career, he encountered racial prejudice, mainly because of his skin color, for Colón was of Afro-Puerto Rican heritage. Despite discrimination, Colón became active in community and political activities. He became a columnist for the *Daily Worker,* the publication of the national office of the Communist party, as an outgrowth of these activities and his literary interests. Colón also founded and operated a publishing house, Hispanic Publishers (Editorial Hispánica), which published history and literary books, as well as political information in Spanish. In 1952 and 1969, he ran for public office on the Communist party ticket, but was unsuccessful.

A selection of Colón's newspaper columns and essays was collected and published in 1961 in book form under the title *A Puerto Rican in New York and Other Sketches.* In this work, Colón's major themes are (1) the creation and development of a political consciousness, (2) his own literary development and worth, (3) advocacy for the working-class poor, and (4) the injustices of capitalist society in which racial and class discrimination is all too frequent and individual worth does not seem to exist. The collection as a whole is richly expressive of a socially conscious and humanistic point of view.

Victor Hernández Cruz (1949–)

Victor Hernández Cruz is the Nuyorican poet most recognized and acclaimed by the mainstream. Born on February 6, 1949, in Aguas Buenas, Puerto Rico, he moved with his family to New York's Spanish Harlem at age 5. Cruz attended Benjamin Franklin High School, where he began writing poetry. In the years following graduation, his poetry began to appear in *Evergreen Review, New York Review of Books, Ramparts, Down Here,* and in small magazines. In 1973, Cruz left New York and took up residence in San Francisco, where he worked for the U.S. Postal Service. In 1989, he moved back to Puerto Rico, where he currently resides.

Victor Hernández Cruz's poetry books include *Papo Got His Gun* (1966), *Snaps* (1969), *Mainland* (1973), *Tropicalization* (1976), *By Lingual Wholes*

Victor Hernandez Cruz.

(1982), and *Rhythm, Content and Flavor* (1989). Classifying his poetry as Afro-Latin, Cruz has developed as a consummate bilingual poet and experimenter who consistently explores the relationship of music to poetry in a multiracial, multicultural context. Cruz has often been considered a jazz poet or an Afro-American poet. The April 1981 issue of *Life* magazine included Cruz among a handful of outstanding American poets.

Abelardo Delgado

(1931–)

Abelardo "Lalo" Delgado is one of the most renowned and prolific Chicano poets, a pioneer of bilingualism in Hispanic poetry and a consummate oral performer of his works. Delgado was born in the small town of La Boquilla de Conchos in northern Mexico on November 27, 1931. At age 12 he and his mother immigrated to El Paso, Texas. In El Paso, he lived in a poor Mexican barrio until 1969. Despite early problems in school with the English language, Delgado excelled as a student, and by graduation in 1950 from Bowie High School, he had become vice president of the National Honor Society chapter there. He went on to college while working at a variety of jobs and graduated from the University of

Abelardo Delgado.

Texas, El Paso, in 1962. Since that time he has earned his living as a counselor for migrant workers and as a teacher in Texas and later in Colorado.
During the late 1960s and throughout most of the 1970s, Delgado was
also one of the most popular speakers and poetry readers in the Southwest, which translated into a life of frequent tours and engagements. This
was the height of the Chicano movement, and Delgado was one of its
most celebrated animators and poet laureates.

Besides writing numerous poems, essays, and stories that have been published in literary magazines and anthologies nationwide, Delgado is the author of some fourteen books and chapbooks; many of these were published through his own small printing operation known as Barrio Press. Delgado's first book, *Chicano: 25 Pieces of a Chicano Mind* (1969), is his best known, containing many of the poems that were performed personally in the heat of the protest movement and that subsequently received widespread distribution through small community newspapers and hand-to-hand circulation throughout the Southwest. Poems such as his "Stupid America" not only embodied the values of life in the barrio but also called for the types of social reform that became anthems for the Chicano movement. Other noteworthy titles include *It's Cold: 52 Cold-Thought Poems of Abelardo* (1974), *Here Lies Lalo: 25 Deaths of Abelardo* (1979), and his book of essays, *Letters to Louise* (1982), which ponder the feminist movement and the social roles of women and men and was awarded the Premio Quinto Sol, the national award for Chicano literature. In all, Delgado is a remarkably agile bilingual poet, an outstanding satirist and humorist, an undaunted and militant protester and pacifist, and a warmhearted and loving narrator and chronicler of the life and tradition of his people.

Roberto Fernández
(1951–)

Roberto Fernández is in the vanguard of Cuban-American literature, having made the transition from the literature of exile to a literature very much of the culture and social conditions of Cubans in the United States, and having made the transition from producing works in Spanish to writing in English. Born in Sagua la Grande, Cuba, on September 24, 1951, just eight years before the Cuban Revolution, he went into exile with his family at age 11. His family settled in southern Florida, not in the Cuban community of Miami but in areas where Anglo-American culture was dominant. This led to periods of adjustment to what seemed like a hostile environment to the young boy, an impression that accounts for some of the culture conflict that is narrated in his writings. The Fernández family nevertheless maintained close ties with the Miami community, and this too became subject matter for the writer. Fernández became interested in writing as an adolescent, and this interest led him to college and graduate school. In 1978, he completed a Ph.D. degree in linguistics at Florida State University; by that time he had already published two collections of stories, *Cuentos sin rumbo* (*Directionless Tales*, 1975) and *El jardín de la luna* (*The Garden of the Moon*, 1976). At this point he also began his career as an academic, teaching linguistics and Hispanic literature at Florida State University in Tallahassee.

Roberto Fernández is the author of three open-formed novels that have created for him the reputation of being a satirist and humorist of the Miami Cuban community. In all three, he is also a master at capturing the nuances of Cuban dialect in Spanish and English. *La vida es un special (Life Is on Special,* 1982), *La montaña rusa (The Roller Coaster,* 1985), and *Raining Backwards* (1988) are all mosaics made up of monologues, dialogues, letters, phone conversations, speeches, and other types of oral performance that, in the composite, make up a continuing tale of the development of the exile community and its younger generations of increasingly acculturated Cuban Americans. Through the pages of these books the author charts the goings-on at social clubs and coming-out parties, follows counterrevolutionary guerrilla movements in the Florida swamps and the emergence of a Cuban pope, plots a mystery novel, discusses a poetry and art contest, and gives many other episodic bits and pieces that create a broad and epic spectrum of a dynamic community caught between two cultures, two sets of values, two languages, and two political systems. *Raining Backwards,* Fernández's first book to be published in English, became somewhat of a small press hit, receiving outstanding reviews from coast to coast in major newspapers and magazines (*The New York Times, USA Today, San Francisco Chronicle,* to name a few), and was optioned to become a feature film.

Lionel G. García is a novelist who has created some of the most memorable characters in Chicano literature in a style that is well steeped in the traditions of Texas tall-tale and Mexican-American folk narrative. Born in San Diego, Texas, in 1935, García grew up in an environment in which Mexican Americans were the majority population in his small town and on the ranches where he worked and played. His father was a paint-and-body man and his mother was a teacher, so García lived a middle-class background; he did so well in school that he was one of the very few Mexican Americans admitted to Texas A&M University, where he majored in biology, but was also encouraged by one of his English professors to write. After graduating he attempted to become a full-time writer but was unsuccessful in getting his works published. He served in the army, and after being discharged honorably, he returned to Texas A&M and graduated from that institution in 1969 as a doctor of veterinary science. Since then he has developed a successful career as a veterinarian.

Lionel G. García (1935-)

Throughout this time he has continued to write. In the early 1980s, he once again attempted to publish, and he found that there were many more opportunities at hand. In 1983, he won the PEN Southwest Discovery

Award for his novel in progress, *Leaving Home,* which was published in 1985. This and his second novel, *A Shroud in the Family* (1987), draw heavily on his family experiences and small-town background. In part, *A Shroud in the Family* also demythologizes the "great" Texas heroes, such as Sam Houston and Jim Bowie, who have become symbols of Anglo-Texans' defeat of and superiority over Mexicans; this was García's contribution to the Texas sesquicentennial celebrations. His novel *Hardscrub* (1989) is a departure from his former works; it is a realistically drawn chronicle of the life of an Anglo child in an abusive family relationship. García has also published short stories in magazines, newspapers, and anthologies.

Celedonio González (1923-)

Celedonio Gonzalez has been known as "el cronista de la diáspora" (the chronicler of the Cuban diaspora or flight from Cuba). Of all of the Cuban exile novelists, he is the one who has turned his attention most to the trials, tribulations, and successes of the Cuban refugees and their children in the United States. Born on September 9, 1923, in the small town of La Esperanza in central Cuba, González began his education in the neighboring city of Santa Clara at a Catholic school and later graduated from a Protestant high school in the city of Cárdenas. Upon returning to La Esperanza he began working in his family's farming enterprises, which he eventually came to manage. He was a supporter of progressive causes and of Castro's revolution, but by 1960 he had become disillusioned with the revolution and was imprisoned for two months as a counterrevolutionary. Upon release, he immigrated to the United States with his wife and children. In Miami he eked out a living at a number of odd jobs. In 1965, he and his family resettled in Chicago in search of a better living.

It was there that he began writing, but it was not until his return to Miami at age 41 that he wrote his first successful novel, *Los primos* (*The Cousins,* 1971), a mirror of Cuban life in Miami during the 1960s. The same year, his short stories depicting the loneliness of Cuban exile life in the United States, *La soledad es una amiga que vendrá* (*Solitude Is a Friend Who Will Come*), were published in book form. His novel *Los cuatro embajadores* (*The Four Ambassadors,* 1973) criticizes American capitalism and the dehumanization in American life. His greatest work to date is his *El espesor del pellejo de un gato ya cadáver* (*The Thickness of Skin of a Dead Cat,* 1978), a call for Cubans to give up their dreams of returning to the island of their birth and to make the best of life in the United States. González's short stories also deal with life in the United States from the vantage point, quite often, of the Cuban laboring classes and small-scale shopkeepers.

Oscar Hijuelos is the first Hispanic writer to win the Pulitzer Prize for Fiction (1990). Born on August 24, 1951, to Cuban-American working-class parents in New York City, Hijuelos was educated in public schools and obtained a B.A. degree in 1975 and an M.A. degree in 1976, both in English, from City College of the City University of New York. While at City College he studied creative writing with and was guided by the noted novelist Donald Barthelme. Hijuelos is one of the few Hispanic writers to have formally studied creative writing and to have broken into the Anglo-dominated creative writing circles, participating in prestigious workshops such as the Breadloaf Writers Conference and benefiting from highly competitive fellowships, such as the American Academy in Rome Fellowship from the American Academy and the Institute for Arts and Letters (1985), the National Endowment for the Arts Fellowship (1985), and the Guggenheim Fellowship (1990).

Hijuelos is the author of various short stories and two novels, *Our House in the Last World* (1983) and *The Mambo Kings Play Songs of Love* (1989), the latter won the Pulitzer Prize. His first novel follows in the tradition of ethnic autobiography and the novel of immigration, as it chronicles the life and maladjustment of a Cuban immigrant family in the United States during the 1940s. *The Mambo Kings Play Songs of Love,* more than just a story of immigration, examines a period in time when Hispanic culture was highly visible in the United States and was able to influence American popular culture: the 1950s during the height of the mambo craze and the overwhelming success of Desi Arnaz's television show, "I Love Lucy." Written in a poetic but almost documentary style, the novel follows two brothers who are musicians trying to ride the crest of the Latin music wave. While providing a picture of one segment of American life never seen before in English-language fiction, the novel also indicts, as does *Our House in the Last World,* womanizing and alcoholism as particularly Cuban flaws.

Rolando Hinojosa is the most prolific and bilingual of the Hispanic novelists of the United States. Not only has he created memorable Mexican-American and Anglo characters, but he has completely populated a fictional county in the lower Rio Grande Valley of Texas through his continuing generational narrative that he calls the Klail City Death Trip Series.

Born in Mercedes, Texas, on January 21, 1929, to a Mexican-American father and a bilingual Anglo mother, his paternal ancestors arrived in the

Oscar Hijuelos (1951–)

Rolando Hinojosa (1929–)

lower Rio Grande Valley in 1749 as part of the José Escandón expedition. Hinojosa was educated at first in Mexican schools in Mercedes and later in the segregated public schools of the area where all his classmates were Mexican Americans. He only began integrated classes in junior high. It was in high school that Hinojosa began to write, with his first pieces in English published in an annual literary magazine, *Creative Bits*. Hinojosa left the valley in 1946 when he graduated from college, but the language, culture, and history of the area form the substance of all his novels. The ensuing years saw a stretch in the army, studies at the University of Texas, reactivation into the army to fight in the Korean War (an experience that informs his poetic narrative *Korean Love Songs*), graduation form the University of Texas in 1954 with a degree in Spanish, and back to Brownsville as a teacher, among a variety of other jobs, and finally on to graduate school. In 1969 he obtained his Ph.D. degree in Spanish from the University of Illinois and returned to teach at Texas colleges. Hinojosa has remained in academia in a variety of positions at several universities; today he serves as Ellen Clayton Garwood Professor of English and Creative Writing at the University of Texas.

Although he has continued writing throughout his life, Rolando Hinojosa did not publish a book until his *Estampas del Valle y otras obras* (which he recreated in English and published as *The Valley* in 1983) was published in 1973. The book won the national award for Chicano literature, Premio Quinto Sol. From that time on he has become the most prolific Chicano novelist, publishing one novel after another in his generational narrative that centers around the lives of two of his alter egos, Rafa Buenrostro and Jehú Malacara, in individual installments that vary in form from poetry and dialogue to the picaresque novel and the detective novel. His titles in English alone include *Korean Love Songs* (1980), *Rites and Witnesses* (1982), *Dear Rafe* (1985), *Partners in Crime: A Rafe Buenrostro Mystery* (1985), *Claros varones de Belken/Fair Gentlemen of Belken County* (1986, bilingual edition), *Klail City* (1987), and *Becky and Her Friends* (1989). His original Spanish version of *Klail City*, entitled *Klail City y sus alrededores* (1976), won an international award for fiction, Premio Casa de las Américas, from Cuba in 1976; it was issued there under this title and a year later a version was published in the United States under the title *Generaciones y semblanzas*. The book was also published in German two years later. Hinojosa has also published short stories and essays widely, as well as installments of a satirical running commentary on life and current events in the United States, known as "The Mexican American Devil's Dictionary," supposedly created by another of his alter egos who is also one of the narrators of the Klail City Death Trip Series: P. Galindo (meaning "right on target" in Spanish).

Hinojosa has been hailed as a master satirist, an acute observer of the human comedy, a Chicano William Faulkner for his creation of the history and people of Belken County, a faithful recorder of the customs and dialects in Spanish and English of both Anglos and Mexicans in the lower Rio Grande Valley. Hinojosa is one of the best-loved and most highly regarded Hispanic writers; he is totally committed to the novelistic world that he has created and that has helped us to understand Mexican-American life so well.

Tato Laviera (1950–)

Jesús Abraham "Tato" Laviera is the best-selling Hispanic poet of the United States, and he bears the distinction of still having all his books in print. Born in Santurce, Puerto Rico, on September 5, 1950, he migrated to New York at age 10 with his family, which settled in a poor area of the lower East Side. After finding himself in an alien society and with practically no English, Laviera was able to adjust and eventually graduate high school as an honor student. Despite having no other degrees, his intelligence, aggressiveness, and thorough knowledge of his community led to his developing a career in the administration of social service agencies. After the publication of his first book *La Carreta Made a U-Turn* (1979), Laviera gave up administrative work to dedicate his time to writing. Since 1980, his career has included not only writing but touring nationally as a performer of his poetry, directing plays, and producing cultural events. In 1980, he was received by President Jimmy Carter at the White House gathering of American poets. In 1981, his second book, *Enclave,* was the recipient of the American Book Award of the Before Columbus Foundation.

All Tato Laviera's books have been well received by critics, most of whom place him within the context of Afro-Caribbean poetry and U.S. Hispanic bilingualism. *La Carreta Made a U-Turn* is bilingual, jazz- or salsa-poetry that presents the reader with a slice of life drawn from the Puerto Rican community of the lower East Side. As such, it examines both oppression of the migrant community and its alienation through such popular culture forms as soap operas; it probes crime and drug addiction while affirming the spiritual and social values of the community and the place of art, poetry, and music in what many may consider to be the unlikeliest of social environments. Laviera, here as in the rest of his books, acknowledges and supports the existence of a true Puerto and Latino culture within the heart of the metropolis and within the very belly of the United States. He further affirms that there is no need to return to a homeland on an island or south of the border, for Latinos have made their home here and are transforming not only mainstream culture in the United States, but throughout the hemisphere.

In *Enclave,* Laviera celebrates such cultural heroes, both real and imagined, as Alicia Alonso, Suni Paz, John Lennon, Miriam Makeba, the fictitious half-southern black, half-Puerto Rican Tito Madera Smith, the barrio gossip Juana Bochisme, and the neighborhood tough Esquina Dude. As in *La Carreta Made a U-Turn,* Laviera acknowledges his debt to Afro-Caribbean music and poetry in his eulogies of salsa composer Rafael Cortijo, the famed poetry reciter Juan Boria, and master poets Luis Palés Matos and Nicolás Guillén. *AmeRícan* (1986), published on the occasion of the centennial celebration of the Statue of Liberty, is a poetic reconsideration of immigrant life in New York City and the United States. *Mainstream Ethics* (1988) proposes transforming the United States from a Eurocentric culture to one that is ethnically and racially pluralistic in its official identity. *Continental* (1992), published during the Columbus quincentenary, extends these themes and imperatives to the whole hemisphere.

Despite Laviera's outstanding publishing record, the sophistication of his vision, and his artistic bilingualism, he is an oral poet, a consummate performer of his poetry, which slowly but surely is constituting a living epic of the Hispanic peoples of the United States. Even Laviera's written and published poems have been created out of a process that attempts to re-create as much as possible the oral performance. For Laviera, part of that oral tradition and performance are the structures, spirit, and rhythms of popular and folk music, especially those drawn from Afro-Puerto Rican music.

Nicholasa Mohr
(1935–)

To date, Nicholasa Mohr is the only Hispanic woman to have developed a long career as a creative writer for the major publishing houses. Since 1973, her books for such publishers as Dell/Dial, Harper & Row, and Bantam Books, in both the adult and children's literature categories, have won numerous awards and outstanding reviews. Part and parcel of her work is the experience of growing up a female, a Hispanic, and a minority in New York City.

Born on November 1, 1935, in New York City, Nicholasa Mohr was raised in Spanish Harlem. Educated in New York City schools, she finally escaped poverty after graduating from the Pratt Center for Contemporary Printmaking in 1969. From that date until the publication of her first book, *Nilda* (1973), Mohr developed a successful career as a graphic artist. *Nilda,* a novel that traces the life of a young Puerto Rican girl confronting prejudice and coming of age during World War II, won the Jane Addams Children's Book Award and was selected by *School Library Journal* as a Best

Book of the Year. After *Nilda*'s success, Mohr was able to produce numerous stories, scripts, and the following titles: *El Bronx Remembered* (1975), *In Nueva York* (1977), *Felita* (1979), *Rituals of Survival: A Woman's Portfolio* (1985), and *Going Home* (1986). Selections from all these story collections have been reprinted widely in a variety of anthologies and textbooks.

Mohr's works have been praised for depicting the life of Puerto Ricans in New York with empathy, realism, and humor. In her stories for children, Mohr has been able to deal with the most serious and tragic of subjects, from the death of a loved one to incest, in a sensitive and humane way. Mohr has been able to contribute to the world of commercial publishing—where stereotypes have reigned supreme—some of the most honest and memorable depictions of Puerto Ricans in the United States. In this and in her crusade to open the doors of publishing and the literary world to Hispanics, Nicholasa Mohr is a true pioneer.

Cherríe Moraga (1952–)

The works of Cherríe Moraga have opened up the world of Chicano literature to the life and aesthetics of feminism and gay women. Moraga's works are well known in both feminist and Hispanic circles for their battles against sexism, classism, and racism. Born in Whittier, California, on September 25, 1952, to a Mexican-American mother and an Anglo father, Moraga was educated in public schools in the Los Angeles area, after which she graduated from college with a B.A. degree in English in 1974. While working as a teacher she discovered her interest in writing, and in 1977 moved to the San Francisco Bay Area, where she became acquainted with the Anglo lesbian literary movement. In part to fulfill the requirements for a master's degree at San Francisco State University, Moraga collaborated with Gloria Anzaldúa in compiling the first anthology of writings by women of color, *This Bridge Called My Back: Writings by Radical Women of Color* (1981), which has become the most famous and best-selling anthology of its kind and has inspired a movement of Hispanic feminist and lesbian writers. In her writings here and in other books, Moraga explains that her understanding of racial and class oppression suffered by Chicanas only came as she experienced the prejudice against lesbians. In 1983, Moraga edited another ground-breaking anthology with Alma Gómez and Mariana Romo-Carmona, *Cuentos: Stories by Latinas*. *Cuentos* attempts to establish a poetics or a canon of Hispanic feminist creativity, a canon where there is room for, and indeed, respect for, the insights of lesbianism. In 1983, Moraga published a collection of her own essays and poems dating back to 1976, *Loving in the War Years: (lo que nunca pasó por sus labios)*, in which she explores the dialectical relationship between sexuality and cultural identity. Her conclusion here, as elsewhere, is that women must be put first. Moraga is also a playwright whose work *Giving Up the Ghost* was produced in 1984 and published in 1986. Her latest produced play, *The Shadow of a Man,* was published in 1991. To date, Moraga remains one of the most controversial of the Hispanic literary figures.

Alejandro Morales (1944–)

Alejandro Morales is one of the leading Chicano novelists, having published substantial novels in both Spanish and English in the United States and Mexico and having created through them a better understanding of Mexican-American history, at least as seen from the vantage point of working-class culture. Born in Montebello, California, on October 14, 1944, Morales grew up in East Los Angeles and received his B.A. degree from California Sate University, Los Angeles. He went on to complete an M.A. degree (1973) and a Ph.D. degree (1975) in Spanish at Rutgers University in New Jersey. Today Morales is a full professor in the Spanish and Portuguese department at the University of California, Irvine.

Morales is at once a recorder of the Chicano experience, basing many of his narratives on historical research, and he is also an imaginative interpreter of that experience by creating memorable and dynamic characters and language. His first books were written in Spanish and published in Mexico, due to the lack of opportunity here in the United States. *Caras viejas y vino nuevo* (1975, translated as *Old Faces and New Wine,* 1981), examines the conflict of generations in a barrio family. *La verdad sin voz* (1979, translated as *Death of an Anglo,* 1988) is a continuation of the earlier novel, but is created against the backdrop of actual occurrences of Chicano-Anglo conflict in the town of Mathis, Texas. The novel also includes autobiographical elements in the form of a section that deals with racism in academia, which comes to a head when a Chicano professor goes up for tenure. *Reto en el paraíso* (*Challenge in Paradise,* 1983) is based on more than a hundred years of Mexican-American history and myth, as it centers on a basic comparison of the decline of the famed Coronel family of Californios and the rise of the Irish immigrant Lifford family. The novel charts the transfer of power and wealth from the native inhabitants of California to the gold-and land-hungry immigrants empowered by Manifest Destiny. *The Brick People* (1988) traces the development of two families connected with the Simons Brick Factory, one of the largest enterprises of its type in the country. Again, Morales uses the technique of comparing the lives of two families, those of the owners of the factory and those of an immigrant laborer's family. Morales's novel *The Rag Doll Plagues* (1991), while still incorporating a historical structure, follows the development of a plague and a Spanish-Mexican doctor who is forever caught in mortal battle with this plague in three time periods and locations: colonial Mexico, contemporary Southern California, and the future in a country made up of Mexico and California united together.

In all, Morales is a meticulous researcher and a creator of novelistic circumstances that are symbolic of Mexican-American history and cultural development. His novels have an epic sweep that are cinematic and highly literary.

Josephina Niggli (1910–)

Josephina Niggli demonstrated many of the sensibilities that would develop into a full-blown literary movement in the 1960s and 1970s. Born on July 13, 1910, in Monterrey, Mexico, she came to the United States with her parents in 1913 during the Mexican Revolution. Educated in American schools, she attended a Catholic high school in San Antonio, received her B.A. degree from Incarnate Word College (1931), and an M.A. degree from the University of North Carolina (1937). During her adolescence she began her writing career, publishing short stories and poems in such magazines as *Ladies' Home Journal* and *Mexican Life*. By age 18, she had published her first collection of poetry, *Mexican Silhouettes* (1928). She later received training in playwriting and had various of her plays produced and some screenplays made into Hollywood films. The following plays have been published in anthologies: *Soldadera* (1938), *This Is Villa* (1939), *Red Velvet Goat* (1938), *Sunday Costs Five Pesos* (1939), *Miracle at Blaise* (1942), *The Ring of General Macías* (1943), and *This Bull Ate Nutmeg* (1945). In 1945, the University of North Carolina Press published her novel *Mexican Village*. The press had already published her collection of *Mexican Folk Plays* in 1938; from 1942 on, Niggli embarked upon a career as an instructor and later professor of radio, television, theater arts, and speech at the University of North Carolina. Today she is still a professor emeritus of that institution. While working as a professor at the University of North Carolina, Niggli also published another novel, *Step Down, Elder Brother* (1947), distributed by the Book-of-the-Month Club. In 1964, she published a young adult book, *A Miracle for Mexico*.

Niggli's writings reveal a thorough knowledge of Mexican customs, traditions, and history. Some of her works also analyze the role of women in Mexican life, especially from her bicultural perspective. All of her work together that is set in Mexico can been seen as a mosaic of Mexican life and character types; her depiction of the Mexican Revolution is realistic and epic in nature, acquainting her readers with the struggles that would bring about the birth of modern Mexico.

Pedro Pietri
(1943–)

Pedro Pietri is famous for the literary persona of street urchin or skid-row bum that he has created for himself. His works are characterized by the consistent perspective of the underclass in language, philosophy, and creative and psychological freedom. Pietri was born in Ponce, Puerto Rico, on March 21, 1943, just two years before his family migrated to New York. He was orphaned of both parents while still a child and raised by his grandmother. Pietri attended public schools in New York City and served in the army from 1966 to 1968. Other than his having taught writing occasionally and participated in workshops, very little else is known about this intentionally mysterious and unconventional figure.

Pietri has published collections of poems and poetry chapbooks: *The Blue and the Gray* (1975), *Invisible Poetry* (1979), *Out of Order* (1980), *Uptown Train* (1980), *An Alternate* (1980), and *Traffic Violations* (1983). Nevertheless, it was his first book of poetry, *Puerto Rican Obituary* (1971), that brought him his greatest fame and a host of imitators. In 1973, a live performance by him of poems from this book was recorded and distributed by Folkways Records. In 1980, Pietri's short story *Lost in the Museum of Natural History* was published in bilingual format in Puerto Rico. Pietri has also had numerous unpublished, but produced, plays and one published collection, *The Masses Are Asses* (1984). Always a master of the incongruous and surprising, Pietri has created unlikely but humorous narrative situations in both his poetry and plays, such as that in his poem "Suicide Note from a Cockroach in a Low Income Housing Project" and in a dialogue between a character and her own feces in his play *Appearing in Person Tonight—Your Mother*. Pietri's work is one of a total break with conventions, both literary and social, and it is subversive in its open rejection of established society and its hypocrisies.

Ricardo Sánchez
(1941–)

Ricardo Sánchez is one of the most prolific Chicano poets, one of the first creators of a bilingual literary style, and one of the first to be identified with the Chicano movement. Born the youngest of thirteen children on March 21, 1941, he was raised in the notorious Barrio del Diablo (Devil's Neighborhood) in El Paso, Texas. He became a high school dropout, an army enlistee, and later a repeat offender sentenced to prison terms in Soledad Prison in California and Ramsey Prison Farm Number One in Texas; at these prisons he began his literary career before his last parole in

1969. Much of his early life experience of oppressive poverty and over-whelming racism, as well as his suffering in prisons and his self-education and rise to a level of political and social consciousness, is chronicled in his poetry, which although very lyrical, is the most autobiographical of all the Hispanic poets'. Once his writing career was established and Sánchez began to publish his works with both mainstream and alternative literary presses, he assumed various visiting appointments as a professor or writer in residence at various universities. He was a founder of the short-lived Mictla Publications in El Paso, editor of various special issues of literary magazines, such as *De Colores* and *Wood/Ibis,* a columnist for the *San Antonio Express,* a bookseller, and a migrant worker counselor, and he is still an active performer of his poetry on tours in the United States and abroad.

Sánchez's poetry is characterized by an unbridled linguistic inventiveness that not only calls upon both English and Spanish lexicon but also is a source of neologisms and surprising combinations of the sounds and symbols of both languages in single works. His work can be virile and violent at one moment and delicate and sentimental at the next, as he follows the formulas and dictates of a poetry written for oral performance. His is often the exaggerated gesture and emotion of the *declamador* (poetic orator), whose works are performed to inspire a protest rally, inaugurate a mural, celebrate a patriotic holiday, or eulogize the dead. Most of all, Sanchez is the autobiographical poet who casts himself as a Chicano Everyman participating in the epic history of his people through his poetry. His bilingual facility and immense vocabulary and inventiveness are legendary in Chicano literature.

Besides publishing hundreds of poems in magazines and anthologies, Sánchez is author of the following collections: *Canto y grito mi liberación (y lloro mis desmadrazgos)* (*I Sing and Shout for My Liberation (and Cry for My Insults)* (1971)), *Hechizospells: Poetry/Stories/Vignettes/Articles/Notes on the Human Condition of Chicanos & Pícaros, Words & Hopes within Soulmind* (1976), *Milhuas Blues and Gritos Norteños* (1980), *Amsterdam cantos y poemas pistos* (1983), and *Selected Poems* (1985).

Gary Soto (1952–)

In academic and creative writing circles, Soto is considered the most outstanding Chicano poet; he is certainly the most widely known Hispanic poet in the Anglo-American poetry establishment, as represented by creative writing departments, magazines, and workshops. Born to Mexican-American parents in Fresno, California, on April 12, 1952, Soto was raised in the environs of the San Joaquin Valley and attended Fresno City College and California State University in Fresno, where he came under the guidance of poet Philip Levine and his creative writing career was born. Soto graduated magna cum laude from California State University in 1975, and in 1976 he earned an M.F.A. degree in creative writing from the University of California, Irvine. In 1977, he began teaching at the University of California, Berkeley; today he is a tenured associate professor in the English and Ethnic Studies departments of the University of California, Berkeley.

Soto has more prestigious awards than any other Hispanic poet in the United States, including the Academy of American Poets Prize in 1975, the *Discovery*-Nation Award in 1975, the United States Award of the International Poetry Forum in 1976, the Bess Hopkins Prize from *Poetry* magazine in 1977, the Guggenheim Fellowship in 1979, the National Association Fellowship in 1981, the Levinson Award from *Poetry* magazine in 1984, and the American Book Award from the Before Columbus Foundation in 1984.

Soto's books of poetry include the following: *The Elements of San Joaquin* (1977), *Father Is a Pillow Tied to a Broom* (1980), *Where Sparrows Work Hard* (1981), *Black Hair* (1985), and *Who Will Know Us?* (1990). Soto has also published three collections of autobiographical essays and stories: *Living Up the Street: Narrative Recollections* (1985), *Small Faces* (1986), and *Lesser Evils: Ten Quartets* (1988). His most recent book is a young adult novel, *Baseball in April* (1990).

All of Soto's works are highly autobiographical and characterized by a highly polished craft. In his poetry and prose, there is also a great attention paid to narration and characterization; whether he is writing a poem or an essay, Soto is always cognizant of telling a story. Critics have always stated that Soto has something important and human to say, and it is poignantly said in well-crafted writing. While writing from his particular ethnic stance and worldview, he also maintains that there are certain values, experiences, and feelings that are universal.

Piri Thomas
(1928–)

Piri Thomas is one of the most widely known cultivators of ethnic autobiography; his *Down These Mean Streets* (1976) was so successful as a powerful chronicle of growing up in the barrio that it spawned a host of Puerto Rican imitators. Piri (John Peter) Thomas was born on September

30, 1928, in New York City, to a Puerto Rican mother and a Cuban father. Thomas grew up during the Great Depression, facing both poverty and racism in New York's East Harlem. American society perceived Thomas as black, while his family perceived him as Puerto Rican and encouraged his identity with the island that he had never seen. However, out on the streets and later in prison, he began to identify and take pride in an Afro-American identity, even becoming a Black Muslim for a while. Thomas entered a life of theft, gang violence, and criminality in adolescence, and he met his inevitable fate of imprisonment. After serving seven years of a fifteen-year term, he was paroled at age 28. While in prison he had obtained his high school equivalency diploma and also had begun to learn to express himself in writing; he also developed a sense of dignity and self-respect. After returning to his old neighborhood and then to his family, who now lived in Long Island, he worked at a variety of jobs, but eventually developed his career as a writer.

All of Thomas's literary works are highly autobiographical, dealing mostly with his upbringing in the poverty, racism, and culture conflict of the barrio. In addition to his well-known *Down These Mean Streets,* Thomas also wrote a sequel, *Saviour, Saviour Hold My Hand* (1972), and a book on his seven-year imprisonment, *Seven Long Times* (1974). He has also had published a collection of stories, *Stories from el Barrio* (1978). In addition, Thomas has written numerous published articles and essays and has written plays that have been produced on stage. Thomas's work is important for having been one of the first to break through to the mainstream, with all of his books having been issued by major publishers, and *Down These Mean Streets* was so highly reviewed that it projected Thomas into the television talk-show circuit and instant celebrity. A powerful and charming speaker, Thomas became an important spokesperson for the Puerto Rican community. In his books and in his public presentations he became identified with the search for identity, and to many readers and critics of the time this became the most important characteristic of Hispanic literature in the United States.

Estela Portillo Trambley (1936–)

Estela Portillo Trambley is one of the first women writers to successfully publish prose in the early male-dominated stages of the Chicano literary movement. Born in El Paso, Texas, on January 16, 1936, she was raised and educated in El Paso, where she attended high school and the University of Texas, El Paso, for her B.A. degree (1957) and her M.A. degree (1977). After graduation from college, she became a high school English teacher and administrator. Since 1979, she has been affiliated with the Department of Special Services of the El Paso Public Schools. From 1970 to 1975, she served as dramatist in residence at El Paso Community College.

Estela Portillo Trambley was the first woman to win the national award for Chicano literature, Premio Quinto Sol, in 1973, for her collection of short stories and novela *Rain of Scorpions and Other Writings*. Besides stories and plays published in magazines and anthologies, Portillo Trambley has written a collection of plays, *Sor Juana and Other Plays* (1981), and a novel, *Trini* (1983). In both her prose and drama, Portillo Trambley develops strong women who resist the social roles that have been predetermined for them because of their sex. In her fiction, women command center stage and achieve a level of self-determination and control over social and cultural circumstances. The culmination of her pursuit of strong women is represented in her exploration of the life of the eighteenth-century poet and essayist Sor Juan Inés de la Cruz in her play *Sor Juana*. The protagonist of her novel, *Trini,* is a fictional character who struggles against poverty and adversity to make her way in life; she eventually leaves Mexico and crosses the border illegally to find the power over her own life for which she has been searching.

Sabine Ulibarrí
(1919–)

Short story writer, poet, and essayist Sabine Ulibarrí has had one of the longest and most productive literary careers in Chicano literature. He is a well-known and highly respected chronicler of the way things once were in his beloved New Mexico. Born on September 21, 1919, in the small village of Tierra Amarilla, New Mexico, he was raised on a ranch by his parents, both of whom were college graduates. Besides learning the ways of rural life and the rugged countryside, Ulibarrí also experienced firsthand the folk culture of the area, which included not only the full repository of oral literature but also a strong connection to the language and oral literature of Spain and the Spanish-speaking Americas. His early love for the Spanish language and Hispanic literature took Ulibarrí to college and eventually to a Ph.D. degree in Spanish. Over the years he taught at every level, from elementary school to graduate school, except during World War II, when he flew thirty-five combat missions as an air force gunner. Today he is a professor emeritus of the University of New Mexico, where he spent most of his academic career as a student and professor.

Among Ulibarrí's awards are the following: Governor's Award for Excellence in Literature (1988), Distinguished Alumni Award and Regents' Medal of Merit, University of New Mexico (1989), and the White House Hispanic

Heritage Award (1989). Ulibarrí has had published two books of poems, *Al cielo se sube a pie* (*You Reach Heaven on Foot*, 1966), and *Amor y Ecuador* (1966, *Love and Ecuador*), and the following collections of short stories in bilingual format: *Tierra Amarilla: Stories of New Mexico/Tierra Amarilla: Cuentos de Nuevo México* (1971), *Mi abuela fumaba puros y otros cuentos de Tierra Amarilla/ My Grandma Smoked Cigars and Other Stories of Tierra Amarilla* (1977), *Primeros encuentros/First Encounters* (1982), *El gobernador Glu Glu* (*Governor Glu Glu*, 1988), and *El Cóndor and Other Stories* (1989).

In all of his work, Ulibarrí preserves a style, narrative technique, and language that owes much to the oral folk tradition. Through his works he has been able to capture the ethos and the spirit of rural New Mexico before the coming of the Anglo. His works memorialize myths and legends and such distinctive characters of the past as cowboys, sheriffs, folk healers, penitents, and just the common everyday folk. Quite often writing two versions of the same story, in English and Spanish, in all of modern Chicano literature his works are among the most direct and accessible to broad audiences.

Ed Vega (1936–)

Ed Vega is a Puerto Rican fiction writer who bases many of his works on life in New York City's Spanish Harlem. Edgardo Vega Yunqué was born in Ponce, Puerto Rico, on May 20, 1936, where he lived with his family until they moved to the Bronx, New York, in 1949. He was raised in a devout Baptist home, his father having been a minister of that faith; today, Vega and his wife and children have adopted the Buddhist faith. As a child, books were very accessible at home, and he began both his education and writing at an early age in Spanish in Puerto Rico. After moving to New York and going through the public education system of the city, he served in the air force and studied at Santa Monica College in California under the G.I. Bill. In 1963, Vega almost graduated as a Phi Beta Kappa from New York University with a major in political science; he was short three hours of credit and did not actually graduate until 1969. He did not return to finish until that date because he had become disillusioned after personally experiencing racism at the university. After leaving there in 1963, he worked in a variety of social service programs. In 1969, he returned to academic life as a lecturer for Hunter College and thereafter assumed various other lecturing and assistant professor positions at other colleges. From 1977 to 1982, he worked at such community-based education programs as ASPIRA of New Jersey. From 1982 to the present, he has been a full-time writer.

Vega is one of the most prolific Hispanic prose writers, although much of his work remains unpublished. In 1977, his short stories began to be published by Hispanic magazines, such as *Nuestro, Maize,* and *Revista Chicano-Riqueña.* His novel *The Comeback,* a rollicking satire of ethnic autobiography and the identity crisis, as personified by a half-Puerto Rican, half-Eskimo ice hockey player who becomes involved in an underground revolutionary movement for Puerto Rican independence, was published in 1985. A collection of interconnected short stories, *Mendoza's Dreams,* narrated by a warmhearted observer of the human comedy, Alberto Mendoza, was published in 1987. An additional common thread holding these barrio stories together is their charting of various Puerto Ricans on the road to success in the United States; thus, once again we have a Puerto Rican interpretation of the American dream. Vega's third book, *Casualty Report* (1991), is just the opposite; for the most part the collection of stories included here chronicle the death of dreams, as characters faced with racism, poverty, and crime succumb to despair in many forms: violence, alcohol and drug abuse, withdrawal, and resignation.

Daniel Venegas

Daniel Venegas was a harbinger of today's Chicano writers not only in openly proclaiming a Chicano identity and pursuing working-class language but also in generating a style and a literary attitude that would come to typify the Chicano novels of the late 1960s and the 1970s. Very little is known of his life. Born and raised in Mexico, his level of formal education is uncertain. In Los Angeles, he maintained an active life in the world of Mexican journalism and the theater during the 1920s and 1930s. There he founded and edited a weekly satirical newspaper, *El malcriado (The Brat),* from 1924 into the 1930s. He was the director of a popular vaudeville theatrical company and the author of numerous plays, short stories, and one novel that relates to the language, customs, and values of working-class Mexican immigrants, who at that time were known as *chicanos.*

All of his theatrical works have been lost, only one issue of *El malcriado* has been located (this containing two short stories by Venegas), and his novel, *Las aventuras de Don Chipote o Cuando los pericos mamen* (1928, *The Adventures of Don Chipote or When Parakeets Suckle Their Young),* was rediscovered and reissued in 1985. *Don Chipote* is the humorous tale of the trials and tribulations of one Don Chipote, who immigrates to the United States from Mexico believing naively that he can shovel up the gold from the streets and send it back to his family. The novel becomes a picaresque story of Chipote's struggle to survive in the alien environment while facing oppression and exploitation from foremen and representatives of industry and the legal authorities and while serving as a target for con men and other underworld characters bent on fleecing him. The satirical tale ends with a moral that warns Mexicans not to come to the United States in search of riches. What is important about *Don Chipote* is the identification of the author-narrator with Chicanos and his having as ideal readers the Chicanos themselves. Not only does it imply that a good portion of those workers knew how to read, but also that those workers, like the author himself, were capable of producing literature and art.

Victor Villaseñor is a novelist and screenwriter who has brought Chicano literature to the widest of audiences through his novel of immigration, *Macho!,* issued in 1973 by the world's largest paperback publisher, Bantam Books; through the epic saga of his own family in *Rain of Gold* (1991); and through the television screenplay *The Ballad of Gregorio Cortez,* the miniseries *Rain of Gold,* and the feature film, *Macho.* Born on May 11, 1940, in Carlsbad, California, the son of Mexican immigrants, Villaseñor was raised on a ranch in Oceanside and experienced great difficulty with the educational system, having started school as a Spanish-speaker and dyslexic. He dropped out of high school and worked on the ranch and in the fields and as a construction worker. After attempting college at the University of San Diego for a brief period, he again dropped out and went to live in Mexico, where he discovered the world of books and learned to take pride in his identity and cultural heritage. From then on he read extensively and taught himself the art of writing fiction. During years of work in California as a construction worker, he completed nine novels and sixty-five short stories, all of which were rejected for publication, except for *Macho!,* which launched his professional writing career. His second publishing venture was the nonfiction narrative of the life and trial of a serial killer, *Jury: The People versus Juan Corona* (1977). Negative experiences with stereotyping and discrimination of Hispanics in the commercial publishing world led Villaseñor to publish his most important literary effort with a small, not-for-profit Hispanic press, Arte Público Press of Houston.

Victor Villaseñor (1940–)

Macho! tells the tale of a young Mexican Indian's illegal entry into the United States to find work, along the classic lines of the novel of immigration; however, it departs from the model in that, upon return to his hometown in central Mexico, the protagonist has been forever changed, unable to accept the traditional social code, especially as it concerns *machismo.* *Rain of Gold,* on the other hand, is the nonfiction saga of various generations of Villaseñor's own family and how they experienced the Mexican Revolution and eventually immigrated to establish themselves in California. The saga is narrated in a style full of spiritualism and respect for myths and oral tradition, derived not only from Villaseñor's growing up in the bosom of his extended working-class family but also from the years of interviews and research that he did in preparing the book. The popularity of *Rain of Gold* has brought to millions of Americans the family stories of the social, economic, and political struggles that have resulted in Mexican immigration to the United States, where new stories of racism, discrimination, and the triumph over some of these barriers continue to develop in the epic of Mexican-American life.

Nicolás Kanellos

*T*heater

The roots of Hispanic theater in the United States reach back to the dance-drama of the American Indians and to the religious theater and pageants of medieval and Renaissance Spain. During the Spanish colonization of Mexico, theater was placed at the service of the Catholic missionaries, who employed it in evangelizing the Indians and in instructing them and their mestizo descendants in the mysteries and dogma of the church. But the story of Hispanic theater in the United States is not just one of a folk theater, but also of the development and flourishing of professional theater in the areas most populated by Hispanics: throughout the Southwest, New York, Florida, and even the Midwest.

HISPANIC THEATER IN THE UNITED STATES: ORIGINS TO 1940 ♦

The Southwest

In 1598 Juan de Oñate led his colonizing mission into what is today New Mexico. The missionaries introduced religious theater, and Juan de Oñate's soldiers and colonists brought along the roots of secular drama. It has been recorded that while camped at night the soldiers would entertain themselves by improvising plays based on the experiences of their journey. They also enacted the folk play that has been spread wherever Spaniards have colonized, Moros y cristianos, which is the heroic tale of how the Christians defeated the Moors in northern Spain during the Crusades and eventually drove them from the Iberian Peninsula.

Throughout the seventeenth and eighteenth centuries in Mexico developed a hybrid religious theater, one that often employed the music, colors, flowers, masks, even the languages of the Indians of Mexico while dramatizing the stories from the Old and New Testaments. In Mexico and what eventually became the Southwest there developed a cycle of religious plays that, while dramatizing these stories from the Bible, nevertheless became so secular and entertaining in their performances that church authorities finally banned them from church grounds and from inclusion in the official festivities during feast days. They thus became folk plays, enacted by the faithful on their own and without official sanction or sponsorship by the church.

At the center of this cycle of folk plays that dealt with Adam and Eve, Jesus lost in the desert, and other favorite passages of the Holy Scriptures was the story of the Star of Bethlehem announcing the birth of Jesus Christ to humble shepherds, who then commence a pilgrimage in search of the newborn Christ Child. On the way to Bethlehem Satan and the legions of hell attempt to waylay and distract the shepherds, and a battle between good, represented by the Archangel Michael, and evil takes place. Among the other various dramatic elements in this shepherd's play, or *pastorela* as it is called in Spanish, are the appearance of a virginal shepherdess, a lecherous hermit, and a comic bumbling shepherd named Bato. Pastorelas, presented by the common folk from central Mexico to northern California, are still performed today, especially in rural areas during the Christmas season. Originally the whole cycle of mystery plays was performed from December 12, when the play that dramatized Las Cuatro Apariciones de Nuestra Señora de Guadalupe (the four appearances of Our Lady of Guadalupe) was presented, through the Easter season and its pageants. The famed *Las posadas* is a Christmas pageant dealing with Mary and Joseph looking for shelter, and originally belongs to this cycle as well.

In one form or another these folk plays are still with us today and have especially influenced the development of Mexican-American theater in the United States. The most noteworthy parts of the legacy of the pastorelas and other religious drama have been their missionary zeal, their involvement of the community of grass roots people, their use of allegory and masks, their totally mestizo nature, and their sense of comicality and slapstick.

This secular folk theater gave rise to such New Mexican plays in the eighteenth and early nineteenth centuries as *Los comanches* and *Los tejanos,* both of which deal with military conflict in an epic manner. As late as the early twentieth century, reenactments of *Moros y cristianos*—even performed on horseback—have been documented in New Mexico, which, perhaps because of its rural culture, seems to be the state that has most preserved its Hispanic folk traditions.

The origins of the Spanish-language professional theater in the United States are to be found in mid-nineteenth-century California, where troupes of itinerant players began touring from Mexico to perform melodramas accompanied by other musical and dramatic entertainments for the residents of the coastal cities that had developed from earlier Franciscan missions—San Francisco, Los Angeles, and San Diego. These three cities were more accessible from Mexico than San Antonio, Texas, for instance, because of the regularity of steamship travel up and down the Pacific coast.

Evidence suggests that plays were being performed as early as 1789; the manuscript copy of a three-act cloak-and-dagger play, *Astucias por heredar un*

The Mason Theatre, a movie and vaudeville house in Los Angeles.

sobrino a su tío (The Clever Acts of a Nephew in Order to Inherit His Uncle's Wealth) bears that date and shows evidence of having been toured through the California settlements. Records of professional theatrical performances become more numerous some decades later. In the 1840s, various troupes of itinerant players visited the ranches and inns around the San Francisco and Monterey areas of northern California, performing in Spanish for both Spanish- and English-language audiences. During this time at least one semiprofessional theater house existed in Los Angeles. In 1848, don Antonio F. Coronel, later to become mayor of Los Angeles, opened a theater that seated three hundred people as an addition to his house. It included a covered stage with a proscenium, a drop curtain, and a good supply of scenery. In the following decades various other theaters opened to accommodate both Spanish- and English-language productions: Don Vicente Guerrero's Union Theater existed from 1852 to 1854, don Abel Stearn's Hall from 1859 to 1875, and don Juan Temple's Theater from 1859 to 1892. In the 1860s and 1870s, the Hispanic community also frequented the Teatro de la Merced, Teatro Alarcón, and Turn Verein Hall. In the 1880s, Spanish-language productions were even held in the Grand Opera House in Los Angeles.

By the 1860s, the professional stage had become so established and important to the Spanish-speaking community that companies that once toured the Mexican republic and abroad began to settle down as resident companies in California. Such was the case of the Compañía Española de la Familia Estrella, directed by the renowned Mexican actor Gerardo López del Castillo, in its choosing of San Francsico for its home. The company was typical of those that toured interior Mexico in that it was composed of Mexican and Spanish players, was organized around a family unit, into which López del Castillo had married, staged mostly Spanish melodrama, and held its performances on Sunday evenings. Each program was a complete evening's entertainment that included a three- or four-act drama; songs, dances, and recitations; and a one-act farce or comic dialog to close the performance. The full-length plays that were the heart of the program were mostly melodramas by peninsular Spanish authors, such as José Zorrilla, Mariano José de Larra, and Manuel Bretón de los Herreros. Productions by this and the other companies that settled in or toured California were seen as wholesome entertainment appropriate for the whole family, and a broad segment of the Hispanic community, not just the elite, subscribed and attended. This departs somewhat from the English-language tradition and Protestant attitudes at that time, especially west of the Mississippi, which considered the theater arts to be improper for women and immoral, even to the extent of using such euphemisms as "opera house" in naming theaters. In the Hispanic community actors were quite often seen

California Theater.

as upstanding citizens, at times even as community leaders, as was the case of López del Castillo, who was elected president of one of the most important Mexican organizations in San Francisco: Junta Patriótica Mexicana (The Mexican Patriotic Commission).

Among the twelve or fourteen companies that were resident or actively touring California during the 1870s and 1880s, the Compañía Dramática Española, directed by Pedro C. de Pellón, and the Compañía Española de Angel Mollá were two resident companies in Los Angeles that extended their tours to Baja California and up to Tucson, Arizona; from there they would return to Los Angeles via stagecoach. During this time Tucson boasted two Spanish-language theater houses: Teatro Cervantes and Teatro Americano. In 1878 Pellón established himself permanently in Tucson, where he organized the town's first group of amateur actors, Teatro Recreo. Thus, the 1870s mark Arizona's participation in Hispanic professional theater. It is in this decade as well that troupes began to tour the Laredo and San Antonio axis of Texas, first performing in Laredo and then San Antonio in open-air markets, taverns and later in such German-American settings as Meunch Hall, Krish Hall, and Wolfram's Garden in San Antonio; but it is only at the turn of the century and afterward that companies touring from Mexico began making San Antonio and Laredo their home bases.

The last decade of the nineteenth century experienced a tremendous increase in Mexican theatrical activity in the border states. More and more companies that had previously only toured interior Mexico were now establishing regular circuits extending from Laredo to San Antonio and El Paso, through New Mexico and Arizona to Los Angeles, then up to San Francisco or down to San Diego. It was the advent of rail transportation and the automobile that was bringing the touring companies even to smaller population centers after the turn of the century. Between 1900 and 1930, numerous Mexican theaters and halls were established in order to house Spanish-language performances all along this circuit. By 1910, even some smaller cities had their own Mexican theaters with resident stock companies. The more mobile tent theaters, circus theaters and smaller makeshift companies performed in rural areas and throughout the small towns on both sides of the Rio Grande valley.

Theatrical activities expanded rapidly when thousands of refugees took flight from the Mexican Revolution and settled in the United States from the border all the way up to the Midwest. During the decades of revolution, many of Mexico's greatest artists and their theatrical companies came to tour and/or take up temporary residence; however, some would never return to the homeland.

Mexican and Spanish companies and an occasional Cuban, Argentine, or other Hispanic troupe toured the Southwest, but they found their most lucrative engagements in Los Angeles and San Antonio. They at times even crisscrossed the nation, venturing to perform for the Hispanic communities in New York, Tampa, and the Midwest. By the 1920s, Hispanic theater was becoming big business, and important companies like Spain's Compañía María Guerrero y Fernando Díaz de Mendoza had its coast-to-coast tours into major Anglo-American theaters booked by New York agents, such as Walter O. Lindsay. The company of the famed Mexican leading lady Virginia Fábregas was of particular importance in its frequent tours because it not only performed the latest serious works from Mexico City and Europe, but also because some of the troupe members occasionally defected to form their own resident and touring companies in the Southwest. Virgina Fábregas was also important in encouraging the development of local playwrights in Los Angeles by buying the rights to their works and integrating the plays into her repertoire.

Teatro Puerto Rico.

The two cities with the largest Mexican populations, Los Angeles and San Antonio, became theatrical centers, the former also feeding off the important film industry in Hollywood. In fact, Los Angeles became a talent pool for Hispanic theater. Actors, directors, technicians, and musicians from throughout the Southwest, New York, and the whole Hispanic world were drawn there looking for employment. Both Los Angeles and San Antonio went through a period of intense expansion and building of new theatrical facilities in the late teens and early 1920s. Los Angeles was able to support five major Hispanic theater houses with programs that changed daily. The theaters and their peak years were Teatro Hidalgo (1911–34), Teatro México (1927–33), Teatro Capitol (1924–26), Teatro Zendejas (later Novel; 1919–24), and Teatro Principal (1921–29). As many as twenty other theaters were operating at one time or another during the same time period.

San Antonio's most important house was the Teatro Nacional, built in 1917 and housing live productions up through the Great Depression. Its splendor and elite status was not shared by any of the other fifteen or so theaters that housed Spanish-language productions in San Antonio during this period. While it is true that in the Southwest, as in Mexico, Spanish drama and *zarzuela,* the Spanish national version of operetta, dominated the stage up until the early 1920s, the clamor for plays written by Mexican playwrights had increased to such an extent that by 1923 Los Angeles had developed into a center for Mexican playwriting unparalleled in the history of Hispanic communities in the United States. While continuing to consume plays by Spanish peninsualr authors, such as Jacinto Benavente, José Echegaray, Gregorio Martínez-Sierra, Manuel Linares Rivas, and the Alvarez Quintero brothers, the Los Angeles Mexican community and its theaters encouraged local writing by offering cash prizes in contests, lucrative contracts, and lavish productions. Various impresarios of the Spanish-language theaters maintained this tradition throughout the 1920s, offering at times as much as two hundred dollars in prize money to the winners of the playwriting contests. It was often reported in the newspapers of the time that the Hispanic theaters drew their largest crowds every time they featured plays by local writers.

The period from 1922 to 1933 saw the emergence and box office success of a cadre of playwrights in Los Angeles composed mainly of Mexican theatrical expatriates and newspapermen. At the center of the group were four playwrights whose works not only filled the theaters on Los Angeles's Main Street, but were also contracted throughout the Southwest and in Mexico: Eduardo Carrillo, an actor; Adalberto Elías González, a novelist; Esteban V. Escalante, a newspaperman and theatrical director; and Gabriel Navarro, poet, novelist, composer, orchestra director, columnist for *La Opinión* newspaper, and editor of the magazine *La Revista de Los Angeles.* At least twenty other locally residing writers saw their works produced on the professional stage, not to mention the scores of authors of vaudeville revues and lighter pieces.

The serious full-length plays created by these authors addressed the situation of Mexicans in California on a broad, epic scale, often in plays based on the history of the Mexican-Anglo struggle in California. Eduardo Carrillo's *El proceso de Aurelio Pompa (The Trial of Aurelio Pompa)* dealt with the unjust trial and sentencing of a Mexican immigrant; it was performed repeatedly on the commercial stage and in community-based fund-raising events. Gabriel Navarro's *Los emigrados (The Emigrées)* and *El sacrificio (The Sacrifice)* dealt, respectively, with Mexican expatriate life in Los Angeles during the revolution and with the history of California around 1846, the date of the outbreak of the Mexican-American War.

By far the most prolific and respected of the Los Angeles playwrights was Adalberto Elías González, some of whose works were not only performed locally, but also throughout the Southwest and Mexico, and made into movies and translated into English. His works that saw the light on the stages of Los Angeles ran the gamut from historical drama to dime-novel sensationalism.

Two of González's plays dealt with the life and culture of Mexicans in California: *Los misioneros* (*The Missionaries*) and *Los expatriados* (*The Expatriates*). The sensationalist *La asesino del martillo o la mujer tigresa* (*The Assassin with the Hammer or Tiger Woman*), was based on a real-life crime story reported in the newspapers in 1922 and 1923. A dozen other plays dealt with love triangles and themes from the Mexican Revolution, including *La muerte de Fancisco Villa* (*The Death of Francisco Villa*) and *El fantasma de la revolución* (*The Ghost of the Revolution*).

Adalberto Elías González and these other authors addressed the needs of their audiences for reliving their history on both sides of the border and for reviving the glories of their own language and cultural tradition with the decorum and professionalism befitting the type of family entertainment that the community leaders believed served the purposes of reinforcing Hispanic culture and morality while resisting assimilation to Anglo-American culture. But with the rise of vaudeville and the greater access of working-class people to theatrical entertainment, vaudeville-type revues and variety shows became more and more popular and gradually displaced more serious theater. But Mexican vaudeville and musical comedy did not avoid the themes that were so solemnly treated in three-act dramas. Rather, the Mexican stage had developed its own type of revue: the *revista*. Revistas were musical revues that had developed in Mexico under the influence of the Spanish zarzuela and the French *revue* and vaudeville, but had taken on their own character in Mexico as a format for piquant political commentary and social satire. Also, like the zarzuela, which celebrated Spanish regional customs, music, and folklore, the Mexican revista also created and highlighted the character, music, dialects, and folkore of the various Mexican regions. Under the democratizing influence of the Mexican Revolution, the revista highlighted the life and culture of the working classes. During the revolution, the *revista política* in particular rose to prominence on Mexico City stages, but later all revista forms degenerated into a loose vehicle for musical and comedic performance in which typical regional and underdog characters, such as the *pelado* (literally, skinned or penniless), often improvised a substantial part of the action.

The Los Angeles stages hosted many of the writers and stars of revistas that had been active during the time of formation of the genre in Mexico,

The most famous of Adalberto Elías González's plays, Los amores de Ramona (The Loves of Ramona), was a stage adaptation of Helen Hunt Jackson's novel about early California, Ramona: A Story; it broke all box office records when it was seen by more than fifteen thousand people after only eight performances, and soon it became a regular item in many repertoires in the Southwest.

including Leopoldo Beristáin and Guz Aguila. In the theaters of Los Angeles and the Southwest were staged most of the revistas that were popular in Mexico and that were of historical importance for the development of the genre. Such works as *El tenorio maderista* (*The Maderist Tenorio*), *El país de los cartones* (*The Country Made of Boxes*) and *La ciudad de los volcanes* (*The City of Volcanoes*) and numerous others were continuously repeated from Los Angeles to Laredo. Such innovators of the genre as Guz Aguila was for a time a perennial attraction at the Los Angeles theaters. Even important composers of scores for the revistas, such as Lauro D. Uranga, graced the Los Angeles Hispanic stages. With their low humor and popular music scores, the revistas in Los Angeles articulated grievances and poked fun at both the U.S. and Mexican governments. The Mexican Revolution was satirically reconsidered over and over again in Los Angeles from the perspective of the expatriates, and Mexican-American culture was contrasted with the "purer" Mexican version. This social and political commentary was carried out despite the fact that both audiences and performers were mostly immigrants and thus liable to deportation or repatriation. The Los Angeles writers and composers were serving a public that was hungry to see itself reflected on stage, an audience whose interest was piqued by revistas relating to current events, politics, and the conflict of cultures that was produced while living in the Anglo-dominated environment. The revistas kept the social and political criticism leveled at the authorities, be they Mexican or American, within the light context of music and humor in such pieces as Guz Aguila's *México para los Mexicanos* (*Mexico for the Mexicans*) and *Los Angeles vacilador* (*Swinging Los Angeles*), Gabriel Navarro's *La ciudad de irás y no volverás* (*The City of You Go There Never to Return*), and Don Catarino's *Los efectos de la crisis* (*The Effects of the Depression*), *Regreso a mi tierra* (*The Return to My Country*), *Los repatriados* (*The Repatriated*), *Whiskey, morfina y marihuana*, and *El desterrado* (*The Exiled One*).

It is in the revista that we find a great deal of humor based on the culture shock typically derived from following the misadventures of naive, recent immigrants from Mexico who have difficulty in getting accustomed to life in the big Anglo-American metropolis. Later on in the 1920s, and when the depression and repatriation took hold, the theme of culture shock was converted to one of outright cultural conflict. At that point Mexican nationalism became more intensified as anti-Mexican sentiments become more openly expressed in the Anglo-American press as a basis for taking Mexicans off the welfare rolls and deporting them. In the revista, the Americanized, or *agringado* and *renegado*, became even more satirized, and the barbs aimed at American culture become even sharper. It is also in the revista that the raggedly dressed underdog, the *pelado,* comes to the fore with his low-class dialect and acerbic satire. A forerunner of characters like Cantinflas the pelado really originates in the humble tent theaters that evolved in Mexico and existed in the Southwest of the United States until the 1950s. With roots in the circus clown tradition, and a costume and dialect that embody poverty and marginality, the pelado was free to improvise and exchange witticism with his audiences that often embodied working-class distrust of societal institutions and the upper classes. Although the pelado or *peladito,* as he was affectionately called, was often

Actress Rosalinda Melendez (left) as a shoe-shine boy during the Depression.

criticized for his low humor and scandalous language, theater critics today consider the character to be a genuine and original Mexican contribution to the history of theater.

But the most prominent author of revistas was Antonio Guzmán Aguilera, who went by the stage name Guz Aguila. Unlike Tirado, who settled in Los Angeles expressly to become a theater impresario and movie producer, Aguila became a journalist for *El Heraldo de México* newspaper, but still managed to tour his theatrical company as far south as Mexico City and as far west as San Antonio. Aguila rose to fame in Mexico City as a newspaperman and prolific revista author, but as a result of a falling out with President Obregón and subsequent imprisonment, Aguila went into exile in Los Angeles in 1924. His production has been estimated as high as five hundred theatrical works, none of which were ever published, but many of his revistas were reworked, renamed, and recycled to accommodate different current events, locations, and audiences. An abundance of laughter, color, patriotic symbolism, and naturalism is what Aguila gave his audiences by pulling out and producing his most famous and time-proven revistas: *Alma tricolor (Three-Colored Soul), La huerta de Don Adolfo (Don Adolfo's Garden;* a reference to President Adolfo de la Huerta), and *Exploración presidencial (A Presidential Exploration).* After presenting many of his well-known works, Aguila began to produce new revistas based on culture and events in Los Angeles: *Los Angeles vacilador (Swinging Los Angeles), Evite peligro (Avoid Danger),* and *El eco de México (The Echo from Mexico).* Aguila returned to the stages of Mexico City in 1927, but he never regained the level of success that he had previously experienced there. He continued to tour the republic and the Southwest in the years that followed.

Eusebio Pirrín decided on his stage name, don Catarino, while in Los Angeles after developing his acts from childhood in his family's tent theater. It was on the Los Angeles stage during his teens that Pirrín gained prominence, principally in the role of a tiny old man with a bushy moustache. Pirrín was so small that women from the chorus line would pick him up like a baby. Pirrín directed and starred in his family show, which became a perennial presence on the Los Angeles stages in the late 1920s and early 1930s; he somehow even managed to get bookings during the Great Depression. All of the revistas, songs, and dance routines of the Pirríns were original, most of them creations of the enormously innovative Pirrín. Although don Catarino's role was that of a little old ranchero, much of the humor, settings, and situations for his work truly represented urban culture through picaresque adventures. In his numerous revistas, all built around the character of don Catarino, Pirrín explored the themes of Los

One actor who played the pelado to perfection was not even a Mexican but a Spaniard: Romualdo Tirado. He is without a doubt the most important figure in the history of the Hispanic stage of this period. Tirado was an impresario, director, singer, actor, and the author of numerous revistas. Tirado had immigrated to Mexico around the turn of the century and developed a career on the stage there for fifteen years before resettling in Los Angeles in the late teens. In the City of Angels Tirado became a prime mover in the Hispanic theatrical and cinematic industries as a theater owner and movie producer, and, just as important, he was also one of the catlysts that brought about the writing and staging of local plays and revistas.

Angeles night life, culture conflict, and amorous adventures, but he did not shy away from the real-life dramas of the depression, exile, and repatriation in his generally lighthearted works.

Unlike Los Angeles, the stages of San Antonio did not attract or support the development of local playwrights, and while they hosted many of the same theatrical companies and performers, such as don Catarino and Los Pirríns, as did the California stages, theater in the Alamo City did not support as many resident companies. While the story of Los Angeles's Hispanic theater is one of proliferation of Spanish-language houses, companies, and playwrights, the story of San Antonio is one that illustrates the persistence of resident companies, actors, and directors in keeping Hispanic drama alive in community and church halls after being dislodged by vaudeville and the movies from the professional theater houses during the depression. San Antonio's is also the story of the rise of a number of vaudevillians to national and international prominence. Finally, San Antonio also became a center for another type of theater, one that served an exclusively working-class audience: tent theater.

Circus and theater had been associated together since colonial days in Mexico, but during the nineteenth century there developed a humble, poor man's circus that traveled the poor neighborhoods of Mexico City and the provinces. It would set up a small tent, or *carpa,* to house its performances; later these theaters were called carpas by extension of the term. It was in the carpa during the revolution that the Mexican national clown, the pelado developed. In general, besides offering all types of serious and light theatrical fare, the carpa came to be known for satirical revistas that often featured the antics and working-class philosophy and humor of the pelado. The carpas functioned quite often as popular tribunals, repositories of folk wisdom, humor, and music, and were incubators of Mexican comic types and stereotypes. They continued to function in this way in the Southwest, but particularly in San Antonio, which had become, especially after the outbreak of the revolution, a home base and wintering ground for many of the carpas.

Probably because of their small size, bare-bones style, and organization around a family unit, the carpas could manage themselves better than large circuses or theatrical companies. Furthermore, they were able to cultivate smaller audiences in the most remote areas. The carpas became in the Southwest an important Mexican-American popular culture institution. Their comic routines became a sounding board for the culture conflict that Mexican Americans felt in language usage, assimilation to American tastes and lifestyles, discrimination in the United States, and *pocho,* or Americanized status, in Mexico. Out of these types of conflicts in popular entertainment arose the stereotype of the *pachuco,* a typically Mexican-American figure. Finally, the carpas were a refuge for theatrical and circus people of all types during the Great Depression, repatriation, and World War II. More important, their cultural arts were preserved by the carpas for the postwar generation that was to forge a new relationship with the larger American culture.

From the turn of the century through World War II, San Antonio was home to many carpas. Two of the most well-known resident tent shows of San Antonio were the Carpa García and the Carpa Cubana, whose descendants still reside in the Alamo City. The Carpa García was founded by Manuel V. García, a native of Saltillo, Mexico. He relocated his family to San Antonio in 1914, after having performed with the Carpa Progresista in Mexico. Featured in his Carpa García was the famed *charro* (Mexican-style cowboy) on the tightrope act. In Latin American and U.S. circus history, the Abreu name appears frequently at the end of the nineteenth century and beginning of the twentieth. The Abreu company, directed by Virgilio Abreu, owned and operated the Carpa Cubana—also known as the Cuban Show and the Circo Cubano—that made San Antonio its home base in the 1920s and 1930s. But before that various members of the family had appeared as acrobats, tumblers, and wire walkers with such famous shows as Orrin, Barnum and Bailey, Ringling Brothers, John Robinson, and Sells-Floto. In San Antonio the Cuban circus included trapeze artists, rope walkers, jugglers, clowns, dancers, and its own ten-piece band. Although based in San Antonio, the company toured as far as California and central Mexico by truck and train, but mostly limited its tours to the Rio Grande valley in the south and Austin to the north during the 1930s.

New York City   It was during the 1890s in New York that regular amateur and semiprofessional shows began, as the Hispanic community, made up mostly of Spaniards and Cubans, was growing in size, reflecting once again the patterns of internal conflict in the homeland and immigration to the United States that would be repeated time and again during the development of Hispanic communities and culture in the United States. Of course, the diaspora brought on by the Mexican Revolution more than any other factor characterized the theater in the Southwest during the first half of the twentieth century. In the 1890s New York became an organizing and staging center for Cuban, Puerto Rican, and Dominican expatriates seeking the independence of their homeland from Spain. Later in the century, heavy migration of Puerto Ricans, now U.S. citizens, and the Puerto Rican nationalist movement in pursuit of independence from the United States, also manifested itself on the city's Hispanic stages, as did the efforts by exiled Spanish Republicans fighting fascism during the Spanish Civil War in the mid-1930s.

Documentary evidence of the Hispanic stage in New York begins in 1892 with *La patria* newspaper reporting on the dramatic activities of actor Luis Baralt and his company. Until 1898, the year of the Spanish-American War, this newspaper, which supported the Cuban revolutionary movement, occasionally covered performances by Baralt and his troupe, which included both amateurs and actors with professional experience. The company had an irregular performance schedule in such auditoriums and halls as the Berkeley Lyceum and the Carnegie Lyceum, where it presented standard Spanish melodramas as well as Cuban plays, such as *De lo vivo a lo pintado (From Life to the Painted Version)*, by Tomás Mendoza, a deceased hero of the revolutionary war, and *La fuga de Evangelina (The Escape of Evangelina)*, by an unknown author, the dramatization of the escape from prison by a heroine of the independence movement. The last performance reported took place at the Central Opera House on January 16, 1899; funds were raised for the sepulcher of the great Cuban philosopher-poet and revolutionary José Martí. After this last performance, no further mention is made in surviving newspapers of theatrical performances in Spanish until the advent of a truly professional stage some seventeen years later in 1916.

Unlike the theatrical experience of Los Angeles, San Antonio, and Tampa, in the mid-teens of the new century the New York Hispanic community could not claim any theaters of its own. Rather, a number of impresarios rented available theaters around town, but mainly those located in the Broadway area, from midtown Manhattan up to the eighties: Bryant Hall, Park Theater, Amsterdam Opera House, Leslie Theater, Carnegie Hall, and so forth. The first impresario to lead companies on this odyssey through New York theater houses was a Spanish actor-singer of zarzuelas who had made his debut in Mexico City in 1904: Manuel Noriega. Noriega became a figure in New York who in many ways was comparable to Romualdo Tirado in Los Angeles. Like Tirado, he was a tireless and enthusiastic motivator of Hispanic theater, and for a number of years he had practically the sole responsibility for maintaining Spanish-language theatrical seasons. Like Tirado, he became one of the first impresarios to establish a Hispanic motion picture company. Also like Tirado, Noriega's genius as a comic actor could always be relied upon to bring in audiences during difficult financial straits. Noriega found his way to New York in 1916 from the Havana stage to perform with another singer, the famous and charming María Conesa, at the Amsterdam Theater. That very same year he founded the first of his many theatrical companies, Compañía Dramática Española, which performed at the Leslie Theater from June to September and then went on to other theaters in the city. In Noriega's repertoire was the typical fare of Spanish comedies, zarzuelas, and comic afterpieces. During the first two years, Noriega had difficulty in getting the Hispanic community out to the theater, so much so that a community organization, the Unión Benéfica Española, had to have a fund-raiser for his poverty-stricken actors. It was in 1918 at the Amsterdam Opera House that Noriega's company began finding some stability, performing each Sunday, with an occasional special performance on Thursdays. By November of that year the company was so successful that it added matinee showings on Sundays, and by December it began advertising in the newspaper for theatrical artists. As Noriega hired on more actors, mostly Cuban, Spanish, and Mexican, the nature of the company began to change, at times highlighting Galician or Catalonian works, at others Cuban blackface comedy. In 1919 Noriega formed a partnership with Hispanic, Greek, and Anglo-American businessmen to lease the Park Theater and make it the premier Hispanic house, rebaptizing it El Teatro Español. After a short performance run all the parties concerned bailed out of the bad business deal; the Noriega company went on to other theaters to perform in its usual manner until 1921, when Noriega slipped from sight.

The 1920s saw a rapid expansion of the Hispanic stage in New York, which was now regularly drawing touring companies from Cuba, Spain, Mexico, and the Southwest and which had also developed many of its own resident companies. Most of the companies followed the pattern of renting theaters for their runs and relocating afterward to different neighborhoods or to Brooklyn, New York, Bayonne, or Jersey City, New Jersey, or even Philadelphia. Beginning in 1922 the Hispanic community was able to lay claim to several houses on a long-term basis, at times even renaming the theaters in honor of the Hispanic community. The first two theaters that began to stabilize Hispanic theater culture in New York were the Dalys and the Apollo. After 1930, the Apollo no longer offered Hispanic fare; the leadership then passed in 1931 to the San José/Variedades, in 1934 to the Campoamor, and finally in 1937 to the most important and longest-lived house in the history of Hispanic theater in New York: El Teatro Hispano.

As in the Southwest, these houses also experienced the same evolution of Hispanic theater in which melodrama and zarzuela reigned at the beginning of the 1920s to be gradually displaced by musical revues and vaude-ville, while in the 1930s artists of serious drama took refuge in clubs and mutualist societies—rarely in church auditoriums as in the Southwest. However, the kind of musical revue that was to rein supreme in New York was not the Mexican revista, but the *obra bufa cubana,* or Cuban blackface farce, which featured the stock character types of the *negrito* (blackface), *mulata,* and *gallego* (Galician) and relied heavily on Afro-Cuban song and dance and improvised slapstick comedy. Like the revistas, the obras bufas cubanas often found inspiration in current events, neighborhood gossip, and even politics.

The bufo genre itself had been influenced in its development during the second half of the nineteenth century by the *buffes parisiennes* and the Cuban circus. Under the Spanish in Cuba the bufos were particularly re-pressed for being native Cuban, causing many of them to go into exile in Puerto Rico, Santo Domingo, or Mexico.

Beginning in 1932 the Mt. Morris Theater (inaugurated in 1913) began serving the Hispanic community under a series of various impresarios and names, first as the Teatro Campoamor, then the Teatro Cervantes, and on August 19, 1937, finally metamorphosing into El Teatro Hispano, which lived on into the 1950s. A somewhat mysterious Mexican impresario who never used his first names, Señor del Pozo, surfaced at the head of a group of backers made up of Hispanic and Jewish businessmen. Del Pozo admin-istered the theater and directed the house orchestra. Under Del Pozo, be-sides movies, the Teatro Hispano offered three daily shows at 2:00, 5:30, and 9:00, except Sundays, which featured four shows. To maintain the in-terest of his working-class audiences, Del Pozo instituted a weekly sched-ule that included bonuses and surprises: Tuesdays and Fridays, banco was played at the theater and prizes were awarded; Wednesday audiences par-ticipated in talent shows broadcast over radio WHOM; Thursdays gifts and favors were distributed to audiences; and Saturday mornings featured a special children's show. Occasionally, beauty contests, turkey raffles, and such were held. Weekly programs changed on Friday evenings and were billed as debuts. Del Pozo used the radio, his weekly playbills, and per-sonal appearances to promote the theater as a family institution and him-self as a great paternal and kindly protector of the community.

Upon opening in August 1937, Del Pozo immediately began to elaborate the formula of alternating shows relating to the diverse Hispanic national-ities represented in the community. For one week he played to the Puerto

The most famous of all the bufos, Arquimides Pous, who played in New York in 1921, was the creator of more than two hundred of these obras, many of which were kept alive by his followers after his death in Puerto Rico in 1926. Pous, who always played the negrito, was famous for his social satire and especially his attacks on racism.

Ricans with the revue *En las playas de Borinquen (On the Shores of Puerto Rico)*; then he followed in September with an Afro-Caribbean revue, *Fantasía en blanco y negro (Fantasy in Black and White)* and then *De México vengo (I Come from Mexico)*; this was followed by the Compañía de Comedias Argentinas, then a week celebrating Puerto Rico's historic proclamation of independence, El Grito de Lares; by the end of September Del Pozo was again announcing Cuban week, featuring a *Cuba Bella (Beautiful Cuba)* revue. Each week a movie was shown to coincide with the country featured in the revue or plays.

In the months and years that ensued, numerous revues and an occasional zarzuela were staged, always balancing out the ethnic nationality represented. The Puerto Rican negrito Antonio Rodríguez and the Cuban negrito Edelmiro Borras became very popular and were ever present. The cast at the Teatro Hispano was constantly being reinforced by refugees from the Spanish Civil War, such as Rosita Rodrigo of the Teatro Cómico de Barcelona, and artists from the failing stages of the Southwest, like La Chata Noloesca and even Romualdo Tirado. By 1940 the Teatro Hispano had fixed its relationship to the predominantly working-class community, which by now was becoming Puerto Rican in majority.

Unlike the theaters in Los Angeles, the Teatro Hispano and the other theaters did not sponsor playwriting contests nor support the development of a local dramatic literature. While the dramatic activity was intense in New York City, the Big Apple did not support a downtown center where five or six major Hispanic houses located side by side competed with each other on a daily basis, as did the theaters in Los Angeles. Unlike the communities in the Southwest, the community of Hispanic immigrants in New York was not cognizant of a resident Hispanic tradition. And, while the relationship between journalism and playwriting had been well established in Mexico and the Southwest, this was not the case in Cuba, Puerto Rico, or Spain. Then, too, many playwrights had been drawn to Los Angeles to work in the Hispanic film industry. And finally, the New York Hispanic public was not as large as Los Angeles's during the 1920s and could not support so large a business as the theater represented in the City of Angels.

By far the most productive playwrights and librettists in New York were the Cubans, especially those riding the crest of poularity of the irreverent, bawdy, satirical obras bufas cubanas. Of these, the most prolific and popular were Alberto O'Farrill and Juan C. Rivera. The former was a successful blackface comic and literary personality who edited the weekly *Gráfico* newspaper and produced zarzuelas and obras bufas cubanas based on Afro-Cuban themes. All of them debuted at the Apollo Theater. Juan C. Rivera was a comic actor who often played the role of the gallego and is known to have written both melodramas and revistas. Only a few of the works by these authors are known by name; it is assumed that they produced a considerable body of works to be staged by the companies in which they acted.

While it is true that Cubans and Spaniards made up the majority of theater artists in New York City and that their works dominated the stage in the 1920s and 1930s, it is also true that Puerto Rican drama emerged at this time and, it seems, accounts for a more serious and substantial body of literature. Two of the first Puerto Rican playwrights appear to have been socialists whose dramas supported the Spanish republican cause and working-class movements: José Enamorado Cuesta (1892–1976) and Franca de Armiño (a pseudonym). Of the former, all that is known is that *La prensa* on May 22, 1937, called him a revolutionary writer when it covered his play *El pueblo en marcha (The People on the March)*. Of Franca de Armiño, all we have is her published drama *Los hipócritas (The Hypocrits)*, whose notes and introduction reveal that she was the author of various other plays, essays, and poems, and that *Los hipócritas* was staged in 1933 at the Park Palace Theater.

While Franca de Armiño and José Enamorado Cuesta were calling for a workers' revolution, Gonzalo O'Neill was championing Puerto Rican nationalism and independence from the United States. Immediately upon graduation from Puerto Rico's Instituto Civil, O'Neill moved to New York, where he became a very successful businessman and somewhat of a protector and godfather to newly arrived Puerto Rican immigrants. A published poet and literary group organizer as a youth in Puerto Rico, he continued his literary vocation in New York by writing poetry and plays, some of which he published. From his very first published dramatic work, *La indiana borinqueña (The Indians of Puerto Rico)* (1922), O'Neill revealed himself to be intensely patriotic and interested in Puerto Rican independence. His second published play, *Moncho Reyes* (1923), was a three-act biting satire of the current colonial government in Puerto Rico. Although both of these works enjoyed stage productions, it was his third play, *Bajo una sola bandera (Under Just One Flag)* (1928), which debuted at the Park Palace Theater in New York in 1928 and at the Teatro Municipal in San Juan in 1929, that deserves the greatest attention for its artistry and thought, which also made it a popular vehicle for the Puerto Rican na-

In Bajo una sola bandera *the political options facing Puerto Rico are personified in down-to-earth flesh-and-blood characters. The plot deals with the daughter of a middle-class Puerto Rican family residing in New York who must choose between a young American second lieutenant— the personification of the United States and military rule—and a young native Puerto Rican, whom she really loves. Both parents oppose each other in their preferences. Of course, the Puerto Rican youth wins the day and the play ends with sonorous, patriotic verses that underline the theme of independence for Puerto Rico.*

tionalist cause. Although O'Neill is sure to have written other plays, the only other title that is known, *Amoríos borincanos (Puerto Rican Episodes of Love)*, appeared at the Teatro Hispano in 1938; O'Neill was one of the investors in the theater.

Tampa

In the late nineteenth century, the Tampa area witnessed the transplant of an entire industry from abroad and the development of a Hispanic enclave that chose the theater as its favorite form of art and culture. To remove themselves from the hostilities attendant on the Cuban war for independence from Spain, to come closer to their primary markets and avoid import duties, and to try to escape the labor unrest that was endemic to this particular industry, various cigar manufacturers from Cuba began relocating to Tampa. In the swampy, mosquito-infested lands just east of Tampa, Ybor City was founded in 1886. By the 1890s, the Spanish and Cuban tobacco workers had begun establishing mutual aid societies and including theaters as centerpieces for the buildings they constructed to house these societies. Many of these theaters eventually hosted professional companies on tour from Cuba and Spain, but, more important, they became the forums where both amateurs and resident professionals entertained the Hispanic community for more than forty years without interruption. These theaters were also the training grounds where numerous tobacco workers and other community people developed into professional and semiprofessional artists, some of whom were able to make their way to the Hispanic stages of New York, Havana, and Madrid. Also, Tampa played a key role in one of the most exciting chapters of American theater history: it was the site of the Federal Theater Project's only Hispanic company under the Works Progress Administration.

Poster from a popular play.

Unlike Los Angeles, San Antonio, and New York, very little truly commercial theater was active in the Tampa-Ybor City communities. The six most important mutual aid societies—Centro Español, Centro Español de West Tampa, Centro Asturiano, Círculo Cubano, Centro Obrero, and Unión Martí-Maceo—each maintained a *comisión de espectáculos* (show committee) to govern the use of their theaters, a task that included renting the theater to touring companies and others, scheduling events, hiring professional directors, scenographers and technicians, and even purchasing performance rights to theatrical works. Along with this comisión, which obviously took on the theater management role, most of the societies also supported a *sección de declamación*, or amateur theatrical company, made up mostly of the society's members. For a good part of each year the company rehearsed on weeknights and performed on Sundays.

Full house at Centro Asturiano.

For the most part, the audiences were made up of tobacco workers and their families.

The tobacco workers prided themselves on their literary and artistic tastes; they were considered an intellectual or elite labor class that had gained an informal education from the professional *lectores* (readers) they hired to read aloud to them from literary masterpieces, newspapers, and other matter while they rolled cigars. Neither the demanding audiences nor the managing committees were satisfied by strictly amateurish renditions, especially since they could compare performances with those of the professional companies that often visited their theaters. It therefore became the custom to recruit and hire professional actors and directors from Havana to train and direct the resident sección de declamación, which was paid for its performances. Over the years numerous professional artists either settled in Tampa or were recruited to become part of the companies. But Tampa's Hispanic societies also prepared such important actors as Manuel Aparicio, Cristino R. Inclán, and Velia Martínez, who later abandoned the cigar factories to dedicate themselves completely to the world of the footlights and marquees. By the 1920s, a good number of the local artists considered themselves professionals and demanded reasonable salaries for their performances.

Of the six societies, the Centro Asturiano was the most important and the longest-lived; in fact, it is still functioning today as a theater, hosting theater and even opera companies. While the Centro Español of Ybor City was the oldest society—founded in 1891 (the Asturiano in 1902)—and for a time the most prestigious, the Asturiano held the distinction of hosting in its twelve-hundred-seat, first-class theater some of the greatest names in Hispanic theater in the world and even opera companies from New York and Italy during the period before World War II; and it was to the Centro Asturiano that Spain's first lady of the stage, María Guerrero, took her company in 1926. That was a stellar year in which, besides producing the works of its own stock company directed by Manuel Aparicio, the Asturiano also hosted the Manhattan Grand Opera Association. But the socially progressive, even liberal, Centro Asturiano—it extended its membership to all Latins, even Cubans and Italians—held the further distinction of housing the only Spanish-language Federal Theater Project (FTP).

It was during the tenure of the FTP, for eighteen months in 1936 and 1937, that the Centro Asturiano made American theater history by housing the only Hispanic unit of the Works Progress Administration's (WPA's) national project. It is a chapter in which the two theatrical traditions, the Hispanic and the Anglo-American, which had existed side by side for so long, finally intersected to produce at times exciting theater but also examples of cultural misunderstanding. From the start the FTP administration's attitude seems to have been a model of condescension and, ultimately, the Hispanic unit had to disband because of congressional xenophobia.

It is somewhat ironic that Hispanic units were not created in Los Angeles or New York, sites of far greater Hispanic theatrical activity of a professional nature and more in line with the main purposes of the WPA. But all of the documents of the FTP make no mention of Hispanic theater outside Tampa and there seems to have been no awareness at all of the remarkable activities documented previously. The project's basic objective of creating work-relief theater of a relevant nature would best have been served where the full-time professionals were suffering unemployment, not in Tampa, where many of the artists still gained a good part of their living rolling cigars. Commercial Hispanic companies were suffering the ravages of the Great Depression in Los Angeles, San Antonio, and to some extent New York; Hispanic actors were hungry in these cities and many of them could not even raise the money to return to their homeland.

The activities sponsored under the FTP were not much different from what was already ongoing in Tampa's Hispanic theater. The project hired Manuel Aparicio to direct the Hispanic unit in the production of what was for the most part a repertoire of well-worn zarzuelas and revistas. The

Manuel Aparicio (center) directing a rehersal of Sinclair Lewis's It Can't Happen Here *in Spanish at the Centro Asturiano.*

greatest difference was brought about, however, by the infusion of capital for scenery, properties, and costumes, which were all new and first-rate. And, even more significant, the Hispanic actors became integrated for the first time into the shows of the Tampa FTP vaudeville unit and, in general, began to associate more and more with non-Hispanic artists and personnel. It must be stated, however, that when it came time for that integrated vaudeville unit to perform at the Centro Asturiano, the FTP was not able to get Anglos to cross the tracks to see the show. In all, the Hispanic unit of the FTP produced fourteen shows in Spanish in forty-two performances for more than twenty-three thousand spectators. The unit achieved its greatest success with *El mundo en la mano* (*The World in His Hand*), a revista written by Aparicio and the entire company, which was a musical tour through Spain, Cuba, Italy, Mexico, and China.

The Hispanic community was very proud of its unit and of its leading man and director, Manuel Aparicio, who was selected to attend a conference of FTP directors in Poughkeepsie, New York. But the FTP administrators, who always referred to the Hispanic unit as one of the strongest in the South, took pride in having successfully "brought" theater to the Hispanics; they also decried the Spanish-speakers backwardness, or fawned at their quaint habits. Ultimately, because of language differences and misunderstandings about citizenship, the Hispanic unit lost twenty-five of its members in 1937 when Congress passed the ERA Act (Emergency Relief Administration), which effectively removed "foreigners" from the WPA. Included among these was director Manuel Aparicio. Other members, such as Chela Martínez, were lost when they were decertified because their family income was too high. The remaining citizens were integrated into the "American" vaudeville company of the federal project. The Hispanic unit had met its end.

A unique theatrical experience was that of the Unión Martí-Maceo, Tampa's Afro-Cuban mutual aid society, whose very existence resulted from the doubly segregationist forces of the Jim Crow South and Cuba's own racism. While the union hosted many of the same theater companies touring to Tampa and also sponsored performances by its own and the other society's *secciones de declamación,* the union's theatrical and cultural activities were rarely covered in the press, rarely attracted audiences from the Hispanic "white" population, and, on the whole, were hardly integrated into the social life of the Hispanic, the Anglo-American, or the African American communities. In the archives of the union, however, are plays and fragments of plays that provide some interesting glimpses into the nature of the theatrical performances of this society. Two of these works, a one-act play, *Hambre (Hunger)*, and the obra bufa cubana *Los novios (The Betrothed)*, are notable for their relevance to the social and economic ambience of the Martí-Maceo. *Hambre* is a gripping and angry social drama that protests the poverty and hunger suffered by the working class while the rich enjoy the life of luxury. *Los novios*, a much lighter and more entertaining play with mistaken identities and ridiculously complex love triangles, also deals with the supposed trespassing of race and class barriers and miscegenation.

Another society that offered a unique theatrical experience was the Centro Obrero, the headquarters for the Union of Tampa Cigarmakers, which served as a gathering place for workers and as a vehicle to promote their culture. Through its various classes, workshops, publications, and other activities, the Centro Obrero promoted unionism and, quite often, socialism. While the Centro Obrero also hosted touring and local companies and even frivolous shows of obras bufas cubanas, it was within its halls and auspices that plays were developed and shown that promoted workers' interests, using their dialect and ideology. In the Centro's weekly newspapers, *El Internacional* and *La Federación*, various of these plays were published, including *Julia y Carlota (Julia and Carlota)*, in which Julia exhorts Carlota to break the bonds of family and religion that are meant to keep women in their place, oppressed, and divorced from politics so that they do not help to reform evil laws. Other works were clearly agitational and propagandistic, attempting to inspire workers to action. Finally, the Centro Obrero went all out to support the republican cause in the Spanish Civil War. It sponsored numerous fund-raising performances of such plays as *Milicianos al Frente (Militia to the Front)*, *Abajo Franco (Down with Franco)*, and *Las luchas de hoy (The Struggles of Today)*, all of unknown authorship.

Tampa's Hispanic theatrical experience was unique in that it provided a successful example of deep and lasting community support for theater arts, so deep and so strong that private enterprise could not compete with the efforts of the mutual aid societies. And because the Hispanic stage had become such a symbol of achievement, that legacy lives on today in the memory of the Tampeños, in the Hispanic theatrical groups that still exist there, and in such actresses as Velia Martínez who still are enjoying careers on the stage and in film.

Many parallels can be drawn between the Tampa Hispanic stage and the Hispanic theater as it flourished in the Southwest and New York: the relationship of the theater to politics and to patterns of immigration; the dominance of the Spanish zarzuela and melodrama, eventually ceding to more popular forms, such as the revista and the obra bufa cubana; the effects of the Great Depression; the role theater played in protecting Hispanic cultural values and the Spanish language and in the education of the youth; and the isolation of Hispanic culture and theater from the larger society.

POST–WORLD WAR II TO THE PRESENT ✦ ✦ ✦ ✦ ✦ ✦ ✦ ✦ ✦ ✦ ✦ ✦

The Southwest   The post–World War II period has seen the gradual restoration of the amateur, semiprofessional, and professional stages in the Hispanic communities of the Southwest. From the 1950s on, repertory theaters have appeared throughout the Southwest to produce Latin American, Spanish, and American plays in Spanish translations. In San Antonio, the extraordinary efforts of such actors as Lalo Astol, La Chata Noloesca, and her daughter Velia Camargo were responsible for keeping plays and vaudeville routines alive in the communities, even if they had to be presented for free or at fund-raisers. Actors like Lalo Astol made the transition to radio and television, usually as anouncers, at times as writers and producers. Astol even wrote, directed, and acted in locally produced television drama during the 1950s and 1960s. In Los Angeles veteran actor-director Rafael Trujillo-Herrera maintained a theater group, almost continuously during the war and through the 1960s, made up of his drama students and professionals, who quite often performed at a small theater house that he bought, El Teatro Intimo.

While a few stories remain of valiant theater artists managing to keep Hispanic theater alive during the war and postwar years, in most cases the tale is of theater houses that once housed live performances becoming cinemas forever, or at least phasing out live performances during the war and through the 1950s by occasionally hosting small troupes of vaudevillians or subscribing to the extravagant *caravanas de estrellas,* or parades of recording stars, that were syndicated and promoted by the recording companies. Through these shows prominaded singers and matinee idols, with former peladitos and other vaudevillians serving as masters of ceremonies and comic relief. Vestiges of this business strategy still survive today in the shows of Mexican recording and movie stars of the moment, which are produced, not at movie houses, but at convention centers and sports and entertainment arenas of large capacity.

The most remarkable story of the stage in the Southwest is the spontaneous appearance in 1965 of a labor theater in the agricultural fields, under the directorship of Luis Valdez, and its creation of a full-blown theatrical movement that conquered the hearts and minds of artists and activists throughout the country. Under the leadership of Luis Valdez's El Teatro Campesino, for almost two decades Chicano theaters dramatized the political and cultural concerns of their communities while crisscrossing the states on tour. The movement, largely student- and worker-based, eventually led to professionalism, Hollywood and Broadway productions, and the creation of the discipline of Chicano theater at universities.

In 1965 the modern Chicano theater movement was born when aspiring playwright Luis Valdez left the San Francsico Mime Troupe to join César Chávez in organizing farm workers in Delano, California. Valdez organized the workers into El Teatro Campesino in an effort to popularize and raise funds for the grape boycott and farm-worker strike. From the humble beginning of dramatizing the plight of farm workers, the movement grew to include small, agitation, and propaganda theater groups in communities and on campuses around the country and eventually developed into a total theatrical expression that would find resonance on the commercial stage and screen.

By 1968 Valdez and El Teatro Campesino left the vineyards and lettuce fields in a conscious effort to create a theater for the Chicano nation, a people which Valdez and other Chicano organizers of the 1960s envisioned as working-class, Spanish-speaking or bilingual, rurally oriented, and with a very strong heritage of pre-Columbian culture. By 1970 El Teatro Campesino had pioneered and developed what would come to be known as *teatro chicano*, a style of agitprop theater that incorporated the spiritual and presentational style of the Italian Renaissance commedia dell'arte with the humor, character types, folklore, and popular culture of the Mexican theater, especially as articulated earlier in the century by the vaudeville companies and tent theaters that had toured the Southwest.

El Teatro Campesino's *Los vendidos (The Sell-Outs),* a farcical attack on political manipulation of Chicano stereotypes, became the most popular and imitated of the actos; it could be seen performed by diverse groups from Seattle to Austin. The publication of *Actos* by Luis Valdez y El Teatro Campesino in 1971, which included *Los vendidos,* placed a ready-made repertoire in the hands of community and student groups and also supplied them with several theatrical and political canons: (1) Chicanos must be seen as a nation with geographic, religious, cultural, and racial roots in Aztlán. Teatros must further the idea of nationalism and create a national theater based on identification with the Amerindian past. (2) The organizational support of the national theater must be from within, for "the *corazón de la Raza* (the heart of our people) cannot be revolutionized on a grant from Uncle Sam." (3) Most important and valuable of all was the principle that "the teatros must never get away from La Raza.... If the Raza will not come to the theater, then the theater must go to the Raza. This, in

Theater groups quickly sprang up throughout the United States to continue along Luis Valdez's path. In streets, parks, churches, and schools, Chicanos were spreading a newly found bilingual-bicultural identity through the actos, *one-act pieces introduced by Valdez that explored all of the issues confronting Mexican Americans: the farm-worker struggle for unionization, the Vietnam War, the drive for bilingual education, community control of parks and schools, the war against drug addiction and crime, and so forth.*

the long run, will determine the shape, style, content, spirit, and form of el teatro Chicano."

El Teatro Campesino's extensive touring, the publicity it gained from the farm-worker struggle, and the publication of *Actos* all effectively contributed to the launching of a national teatro movement. It reached its peak in the summer of 1976 when five teatro festivals were held to commemorate the Anglo bicentennial celebration. The summer's festivals also culminated a period of growth that saw some of Campesino's followers reach sufficient a aesthetic and political maturity to break away from Valdez. Los Angeles's Teatro Urbano, in its mordant satire of American heroes, insisted on intensifying the teatro movement's radicalism in the face of the Campesino's increasing religious mysticism. Santa Barbara's El Teatro de la Esperanza was achieving perfection, as no other Chicano theater had, in working as a collective and in assimilating the teachings of Bertolt Brecht in their plays *Guadalupe* and *La víctima (The Victim)*. San Jose's El Teatro de la Gente had taken the corrido-type acto, a structure that sets a mimic ballet to traditional Mexican ballads sung by a singer-narrator, and perfected it as

A scene from El Teatro de la Esperanza's production of Rodrigo Duarte Clark's Brujerias.

its innovator, El Teatro Campesino, had never done. El Teatro Desengaño del Pueblo from Gary, Indiana, had succeeded in reviving the techniques of the radical theaters of the 1930s in their *Silent Partners,* an expose of corruption in a local city's construction projects.

The greatest contribution of Luis Valdez and El Teatro Campesino was their inauguration of a true grass roots theater movement. Following Valdez's direction, the university students and community people creating teatro held fast to the doctrine of never getting away from the raza, the grass roots Mexican. In so doing they created the perfect vehicle for communing artistically within their culture and environment. At times they idealized and romanticized the language and the culture of the *mexicano* in the United States. But they had discovered a way to mine history, folklore, and religion for those elements that could best solidify the heterogeneous community and sensitize it to class, cultural identity, and politics. This indeed was revolutionary. The creation of art from the folk materials of a people, their music, humor, social configurations, and environment, represented the fulfillment of Luis Valdez's vision of a Chicano national theater.

While Campesino, after leaving the farm worker struggle, was able to experiment and rediscover the old cultural forms—the carpas, the corridos, the Virgin of Guadalupe plays, the peladito—it never fully succeeded in combining all the elements it recovered or invented into a completely refined piece of revolutionary art. *La gran carpa de la familia Rascuachi (The Tent of the Underdogs)* was a beautiful creation, incorporating the spirit, history, folklore, economy, and music of la raza. However, its proposal for the resolution of material problems through spiritual means (a superimposed construct of Aztec mythology and Catholicism) was too close to the religious beliefs and superstitions that hampered la raza's progress, according to many of the more radical artists and theorists of people's theater.

The reaction of critics and many Chicano theaters playing at the fifth Chicano theater festival, held in Mexico, was so politically and emotionally charged that a rift developed between them and El Teatro Campesino that has never been healed. El Teatro Campesino virtually withdrew from the theater movement, and from that point on the Chicano theaters developed on their own, managing to exist as agitation and propaganda groups and raggle-taggle troupes until the end of the decade. The more successful theaters, such as El Teatro de la Esperanza, administered their own theater house, created playwriting workshops, and took up leadership of TENAZ, the Chicano theater organization, while taking over El Teatro

Campesino's former role as a national touring company. Other groups, such as Albuquerque's La Compañía, set down roots and became more of a repertory company.

The decade of the 1980s saw many Chicano theater groups disbanding, as some of their members became involved in local community theaters, with their own performance spaces and budgets supplied by state and local arts agencies. Although the grass roots, guerrilla, and street theater movement among Chicanos disappeared, these were the years when greater professionalization took place and greater opportunity appeared for Chicano theater people to make a living from their art in community theaters, at universities, and even in the commercial media—the latter facilitated, of course, by the great rise of the Hispanic population and its spending power.

The decade of the 1980s also saw the emergence of a corps of Chicano and Latino playwrights in communities from coast to coast, as the repertory theaters in the Southwest, New York, and Miami began clamoring for works dealing with Hispanic culture and written in the language of Hispanics in the United States. Numerous playwriting laboratories, workshops, and contests, such as Joseph Papp's Festival Latino in New York, sprung up from New York to Los Angeles. In the mid-1980s, a major funding organization, the Ford Foundation, took official interest in Hispanic theater and began funding, in a very significant way, not only the theater companies in an effort to stabilize them (including El Teatro de la Esperanza) but also the efforts by mainstream companies and theaters, such as the South Coast Repertory Theater and the San Diego Repertory Theater, to produce Hispanic material and employ Hispanic actors.

New York   During the war years and following, serious theater in the Hispanic community waned. First vaudeville drove it from the commercial stage, as it did the Teatro Hispano, and then, as in the Southwest, the movies and the caravans of musical recording stars began to drive even vaudeville from the stage. Under the leadership of such directors as Marita Reid, Luis Mandret, and Alejandro Elliot, full-length melodramas and realistic plays were able to survive in mutualist societies, church halls, and lodges during the 1940s and 1950s, but only for smaller audiences and for weekend performances. With such attractions as La Chata Noloesca's Mexican company and Puerto Rican vaudevillians, including famed recording star Bobby Capó, vaudeville survived into the early 1960s, playing to the bur-

A scene from
Beautiful Senoritas.

geoning working-class audiences of Puerto Ricans. One notable and valiant effort was that of Dominican actor-director Rolando Barrera's group Futurismo, which for a while during the 1940s was able to stage four productions a year of European works in Spanish translation at the Master's Auditorium. Beginning in 1950, Edwin Janer's La Farándula Panamericana staged three and four productions a year of classical works, as well as contemporary Spanish, Puerto Rican, and European works at the Master's Auditorium and the Belmont Theater.

In 1953 a play was staged that would have the most direct and lasting impact ever of any theatrical production in New York's Hispanic community. A young director, Roberto Rodríguez, introduced to a working-class audience at the Church of San Sebastian *La carreta (The Oxcart),* by an as yet unknown Puerto Rican writer, René Marqués, after its first production in Puerto Rico. The play effectively dramatized the epic of Puerto Rican migration to the United States in working-class and mountain dialect.

Roberto Rodríguez joined forces with stage and screen actress Miriam Colón to form El Nuevo Círculo Dramático, which was able to administer a theater space in a loft, Teatro Arena, in Midtown Manhattan. Although other minor and short-lived companies existed, it was El Nuevo Círculo Dramático, along with La Farándula Panamericana, that dominated the New York Hispanic stage into the early 1960s, when two incursions were made into the mainstream: in 1964 Joseph Papp's New York Shakespeare Festival began producing Shakespearean works in Spanish, and in 1965 an off-Broadway production of *La carreta* was mounted, starring Miriam Colón and Raúl Juliá.

René Marqués went on to celebrity and many more plays and productions in Puerto Rico and the continental United States, but his La carreta *became a key for building a Puerto Rican and Hispanic theater in New York in that it presented serious dramatic material based on the history, language, and culture of the working-class communities.*

The 1960s announced the introduction of improvisational street theater similar to Latin American people's theater and Chicano theater, which attempted to raise the level of political consciousness of working-class Hispanics. Among the most well-known, although short-lived groups were the following ensembles, which usually developed their material as a collective: El Nuevo Teatro Pobre de las Américas (The New Poor People's Theater of Americas), Teatro Orilla (Marginal Theater), Teatro Guazabara (Whatsamara Theater), and Teatro Jurutungo. But the most interesting of the improvisational troupes, and the only one to survive to the present, has been the Teatro Cuatro, named so for its first location on Fourth Avenue in the lower East Side and made up at first of a diverse group of Puerto Ricans, Dominicans, and other Latin Americans. Under the directorship of an Argentine immigrant, Oscar Ciccone, and his Salvadoran wife, Cecilia Vega, the Teatro Cuatro was one of the most serious troupes, committed to developing a true radical art and to bringing together the popular theater movement of Latin America with that of Hispanics in the United States. As such Teatro Cuatro became involved with TENAZ and the Chicano theater movement and with *teatro popular* in Latin America, and sponsored festivals and workshops in New York with some of the leading guerrilla and politically active theatrical directors and companies in the hemisphere. During the late 1970s Teatro Cuatro became officially associated with Joseph Papp's New York Shakespeare Festival and began to organize the biennial Festival Latino, a festival of Hispanic popular theater. Today, Ciccone and Vega manage the Papp organization's Hispanic productions, including the festival and a playwriting contest, while the Teatro Cuatro has gone its own way, functioning as a repertory company in its own remodeled firehouse theater in east Harlem.

The type of theater that has predominated in New York's cosmopolitan Hispanic culture since the 1960s is that which more or less follows the patterns established by the Nuevo Círculo Dramático and the Farándula Panamericana mentioned previously, in which a corps of actors and a director of like mind work as a repertory group in producing works of their choosing in their own style. Styles and groups have proliferated, so that at any one time over the last twenty to twenty-five years at least ten groups have existed with different aesthetics and audiences. Among these theaters, many of which have their own houses today, are International Arts Relations (INTAR), Miriam Colón's Puerto Rican Traveling Theater, Teatro Repertorio Español, Nuestro Teatro, Duo, Instituto Arte Teatral (IATE), Latin American Theater Ensemble (LATE), Thalia, Tremont Arte Group, and Pregones. In addition to the reason that New York has over 1 million Hispanic inhabitants, another reason that so many organizations are able to survive—although many of them do not flourish—is that the state, local, and private institutions that provide financial support for the arts have been generous to the theaters. Compared with that in other cities and states, the financial support for the arts, and theater in particular, in the capital of the U.S. theater world, has been excellent.

The three most important theater companies have been the Puerto Rican Traveling Theater (PRTT), Teatro Repertorio Español, and INTAR. The PRTT, founded in 1967 by Miriam Colón, takes its name from its original identity as a mobile theater that performed in the streets of Puerto Rican neighborhoods. At first it performed works by some of the leading Puerto Rican writers, such as René Marqués, José Luis González, and Pedro Juan Soto, alternating Spanish-language performances with English-language ones. The company also produced Latin American and Spanish works and in the early 1970s pioneered productions of works by Nuyorican (New York Rican, discussed later in this chapter) and other U.S. Hispanic authors, such as those of Jesús Colón and Piri Thomas. In addition to its mobile unit, the theater maintained a laboratory theater and children's the-

Pregones, a Puerto Rican theater company from the Bronx.

ater classes. Its most important development came in 1974 when it took over and remodeled an old firehouse in the Broadway area, on Forty-seventh Street, and opened its permanent theater house. To this day, the PRTT provides the stage, audience, and developmental work for New York Hispanic playwrights, such as Jaime Carrero, Edward Gallardo, Manuel Ramos Otero, Pedro Pietri, and Dolores Prida.

Founded in 1969 as an offshoot of Las Artes by exiled members of Cuba's Sociedad Pro Arte, the Teatro Repertorio Español has grown into the only Hispanic theater in the nation specializing in the production of both classical Spanish works, such as Calderon's *La vida es sueño* and Zorrilla's *Don Juan Tenorio,* and works by contemporary authors from Latin America. It is also one of the few companies in the nation to also stage nineteenth-century zarzuelas. Operating today out of the Gramercy Arts Theater, which has a tradition of Spanish-language performances that goes back to the 1920s, the Teatro Repertorio Español caters both to educational as well as community-based audiences, with productions in both Spanish and English. It is the only New York Hispanic theater to tour around the country.

INTAR was founded in 1967 as ADAL (Latin American Art Group), dedicated to producing works by Latin American authors. By 1977, under the name INTAR, the company had achieved equity status as a professional theater. After converting a variety of structures into theater spaces, the company currently occupies a theater on West Forty-second Street near the Broadway theater district. Under the direction of Max Ferra, the company has offered workshops for actors and directors, and staged readings for playwrights and a children's theater. Today INTAR is known for its production of classical works in new settings and innovative directing, such as María Irene Fornés's *La vida es sueño (Life Is a Dream)* and Dolores Prida's *Crisp,* based on Jacinto Benavente's *Los intereses creados (Vested Interests).* INTAR also presents works in English, including some standard non-Hispanic fare. INTAR has been particularly instrumental in developing Hispanic playwriting through its playwright's laboratory and readings, quite often following up with full productions of plays by local writers.

While the Hispanic theatrical environment in New York has been of necessity cosmopolitan and has lent itself to the creation of companies with personnel from all of the Spanish-speaking countries, there have been groups that have set out to promote the work and culture of specific nationalities, such as the Puerto Ricans, Cubans, Dominicans, and Spaniards. Most notable, of course, has been the Puerto Rican Traveling Theater, but also the

Centro Cultural Cubano was instrumental in the 1970s in developing Cuban theatrical expression, most significantly in producing the work of Omar Torres and Iván Acosta. Acosta's play *El super (The Super),* has been the biggest hit to ever come out of a Hispanic company and even led to a prize-winning film adaptation. And, in general, Cuban-American theater is well represented in almost all the Hispanic companies of New York, with Dolores Prida, Iván Acosta, Manuel Martín, and Omar Torres included among the most successful playwrights.

Puerto Rican playwriting is also well represented at most of the Hispanic companies, but during the 1960s an important new focus developed among New York Puerto Ricans that had long-lasting implications for the creation of theater and art in Hispanic working-class communities; it was called Nuyorican (New York Rican), meaning that it emerged from the artists born or raised among New York's Puerto Rican working classes.

Nuyorican theater is not a specific form of theater per se. It has included such diverse theatrical genres as collectively created street theater as well as works by individual playwrights produced in such diverse settings as the Puerto Rican Traveling Theater, the Henry Street Settlement's New Federal Theater, Joseph Papp's New York Shakespeare Festival, and on Broadway itself. Although the term was first applied to literature and theater by playwright-novelist Jaime Carrero in the late 1960s and finds some stylistic and thematic development in his plays *Noo Jall* (a wordplay on the Spanish pronunciation of "New York" and "jail") and *Pipo Subway no sabe reír (Pipo Subway Doesn't Know How to Laugh),* it was a group of playwright-poets associated with the Nuyorican Poets' Café and Joseph Papp that first defined and came to exemplify Nuyorican theater.

Included in the group were Miguel Algarín, Lucky Cienfuegos, Tato Laviera, and Miguel Piñero, all of whom focused their bilingual works on the life and culture of working-class Puerto Ricans in New York. Two members of the group, Lucky Cienfuegos and Miguel Piñero, were ex-convicts who had begun their writing careers while incarcerated, and they chose to develop their dramatic material from prison, street, and underclass culture. Algarín, a university professor and proprietor of the Nuyorican Poets' Café, created a more avant-garde aura for the collective, while the virtuoso bilingual poet Tato Laviera contributed lyricism and a folk and popular culture base. It was Piñero's work (and life), however, that became most celebrated; his prison drama *Short Eyes* won an Obie and the New York Drama Critics Best American Play Award for the 1973–74 season. His success, coupled with that of fellow Nuyorican writers ex-convict Piri Thomas and street urchin Pedro Pietri, often resulted in Nuyorican literature and theater's being associated with a stark naturalism and the themes of crime, drugs, abnormal sexuality, and generally aberrant behavior. This led to a reaction against the term by many writers and theater companies that were in fact emphasizing Puerto Rican working-class culture in New York.

Today a new generation of New York Puerto Rican playwrights is at work who were nurtured on the theater of Piñero and the Nuyoricans and who have also experienced greater support and opportunities. They quite often repeat and reevaluate many of the concerns and the style and language of the earlier group, but with a sophistication and polish that has come from drama workshops, playwright residencies, and university education. Among these are Juan Shamsul Alam, Edward Gallardo, Federico Fraguada, Richard Irizarry, Yvette Ramírez, and Cándido Tirado.

Florida   Today Hispanic theater still finds one of its centers in Florida. However, most of the theatrical activity in Tampa has disappeared, with only the Spanish Repertory Theater continuing to perform in the old playhouses (Centro Asturiano) with a fare that varies from the standard zarzuelas to Broadway musicals in Spanish. With the exodus of refugees from the Cuban Revolution of 1959, Hispanic theater in Florida found a new center in Miami, where the Cuban expatriates—many from middle-class or upper-class backgrounds and used to supporting live theater in Cuba— founded and supported theater companies and laid fertile ground for the support of playwrights. During the last thirty years the type of theater that has predominated in Miami has produced standard works from throughout the Spanish-speaking world and from the theater of exile, which is burdened with attacking communism in Cuba and promoting a nostalgia for the pre-Castro past. While the Cuban playwrights of New York, many of whom have been raised and educated in the United States, have forged an avant-garde and openly Cuban-American theater, the Miami playwrights have been more traditional in form and content and, of course, more politically conservative. Most frequent in the exile theater is the form and style inherited from the theater of the absurd, from theatrical realism, and, to some extent, from the comic devices and characters of the teatro bufo cubano; however, the predominant attitude among Cuban exile playwrights is the intellectual one, the creation of a theater of ideas. The exile playwrights whose works are most produced in Miami are Julio

Matas, José Cid Pérez, Leopoldo Hernández, José Sánchez Boudy, Celedonio González, Raúl de Cárdenas, and Matías Montes Huidobro.

Overall, the theatrical fare in Miami is eclectic, with audiences able to choose from a variety of styles and genres, from vaudeville to French-style bedroom farce, serious drama, Broadway musicals in Spanish, and Spanish versions of classics, such as Shakespeare's *Taming of the Shrew* and *Othello*. The theater companies offering the most "serious" fare have included the Teatro Bellas Artes, the Teatro La Danza, Grupo Ras, and Pro Arte Gratelli. Among the longest-lasting theaters in Miami are Salvador Ugarte's and Ernesto Cremata's two locations of Teatro Las Máscaras, which for the most part produce light comedy and vaudeville for mostly working-class audiences. Two of impressario Ernesto Capote's three houses, the Martí Theater and the Essex Theater, have a steady lineup of comedies and vaudeville; and his third house, the Miami Theater, provides an eclectic bill, including such hard-hitting dramas as *The Boys in the Band* in Spanish. The Teatro Miami's stage also serves for the taping of soap operas for television. The theater, which plays more to the working

Romeo and Juliet *being performed in Spanish in Miami.*

classes in Miami, as exemplified by some of the Miami theaters named above and by some that use movie houses after the showing of the last films, produces a type of reincarnation of the teatro bufo cubano that uses working-class language and culture and uses comic style and characters from the bufo tradition to satirize life in Miami and Cuba under Castro. Here, comic characterizations of Fidel and his brother Raúl (Raúl Resbaloso-Slippery Raúl) join some of the traditional character types, such as *Trespatines* (Three Skates) and *Prematura* (Premature). This theater is the most commercially successful Cuban theater, while the other, more artistically elite and intellectual theater often begs for audiences and depends on grants and university support for survival.

OUTSTANDING FIGURES IN HISPANIC THEATER ✦ ✦ ✦ ✦ ✦ ✦ ✦ ✦

Iván Acosta
(1943–)

Iván Mariano Acosta is an outstanding playwright and filmmaker. Born in Santiago de Cuba on November 17, 1943, he immigrated to the United States with his parents as a result of the Cuban Revolution. He is a graduate in Film Direction and Production of New York University (1969), and has worked as a playwright and director at the Centro Cultural Cubano and the Henry Street Settlement Playhouse. His play *El super (The Super)*, produced at the Centro Cultural Cubano, is probably the most successful Hispanic play to come out of an ethnic theater house; it not only was highly reviewed and won awards but also was adapted to the screen by Acosta in a feature film that has won twelve awards for best script and best director. *El super* was published in book form in 1982, and four other plays were published in his anthology *Un cubiche en la luna y otras obras* in 1989.

Manuel Aparicio

Manuel Aparicio was a Tampa cigar-roller, who in the 1920s and 1930s rose to become an outstanding actor and director in Hispanic theater in Tampa and New York. From the humble beginnings of acting in amateur performances at the mutualist societies in Tampa, Aparicio went on to head up his own theatrical companies and take them on tour to Havana and New York. Tampa remained his home base, even during the Great Depression, which was the economic cataclysm that eventually resulted in his name going down in Hispanic theater history, for he became the only director of a Hispanic company under the U.S. Government Works Progress Administration's (WPA's) Federal Theater Project (FTP). In this role he led one of the FTP's most successful theater companies and was even selected for the FTP's conference of directors in Poughkeepsie, New York, in 1937. The Hispanic troupe of the FTP produced some of its own collectively created material, such as the revue *El Mundo en la Mano,* under his directorship and including his acting and singing talents. Like some twenty-five other actors, Aparicio lost his job when Congress passed the ERA Act of 1937, which prohibited the employment of aliens under the WPA.

Miriam Colón is the first lady of Hispanic theater in New York. She is the founder and artistic director of the Puerto Rican Traveling Theater and a genuine pioneer in bringing Hispanic theater to broad audiences. Born in Ponce, Puerto Rico, and raised in Ponce and in New York, Colón attended the University of Puerto Rico and the Erwin Piscator Dramatic Workshop and Technical Institute, as well as the famed Actors Studio, both in New York. Colón developed a long and distinguished career on New York stages and in Hollywood films and television series. Included among her stage credits are *The Innkeepers* (1956), *Me, Cándido!* (1965), *The Oxcart* (1966), *Winterset* (1968), *The Passion of Antígona Pérez* (1972), *Julius Caesar* (1979), *Orinoco* (1985), and *Simpson Street* (1985). In 1989 she was made an honorary doctor of letters by Montclair (New Jersey) State College; she also received the White House Hispanic Heritage Award in 1990.

**Miriam Colón
(1945–)**

Known by her stage name, La Chata Noloesca (a rearranged spelling of Escalona), Beatriz Escalona became the greatest stage personality to come out of U.S. Hispanic communities. Born on August 20, 1903, in San Antonio, Escalona was discovered while working as an usherette and box office cashier at the Teatro Nacional. She became associated with the Spanish-Cuban troupe of Hermanos Areu—she married José Areu—and played everything from melodrama to vaudeville with them, beginning in 1920, when she made her stage debut in El Paso. Over the course of the 1920s Escalona developed and perfected her comic persona of the streetwise maid, a *peladita* or underdog character who maintained a spicy and satirical banter. By 1930 La Chata Noloesca had split from the Areus and formed her own company, Atracciones Noloesca, and continued to tour the Southwest and northern Mexico. In 1936 she reformed her company in her native San Antonio and set out to weather the depression by performing in Tampa, Chicago, and New York—as well as Puerto Rico and Cuba—as the Compañía Mexicana. La Chata's novel idea was to take to the Cubans, Puerto Ricans, and others Mexican vaudeville, music, folklore, and her own brand of humor. In 1941, the company set down roots in New York for a stretch of nine years, during which time it was a main-

**Beatriz Escalona
(1903–1980)**

stay on the Hispanic vaudeville circuit made up of the Teatro Hispano, the Teatro Puerto Rico, the Teatro Triboro, and the 53rd Street Theater. Back in San Antonio, she periodically performed for special community events until her death.

José Ferrer

(1912–)

José Ferrer is one of the most distinguished actors of Hispanic background to have made a career in mainstream films and on stage in the United States. The star of numerous Hollywood films and many stage productions, he was born in Santurce, Puerto Rico, on January 8, 1912. Raised and educated in Puerto Rico, he graduated from Princeton University in 1933. As an actor and/or director, his stage credits include *Let's Face It* (1942), *Strange Fruit* (1945), *Design for Living* (1947), *Twentieth Century* (1950), *Stalag 17* (1951), *Man of La Mancha* (1966), and *Cyrano de Bergerac* (1975), among many others. As an actor, director, or producer, he has been associated with some of the most famous Hollywood films, including *Joan of Arc* (1947), *Moulin Rouge* (1952), *The Caine Mutiny* (1954), *Return to Peyton Place* (1962), *Lawrence of Arabia* (1962), *Ship of Fools* (1966), and others. His awards include the Gold Medal from the American Academy of Arts and Sciences (1949), the Academy Award for Best Actor in *Cyrano de Bergerac* (1950), induction into the Theater Hall of Fame (1981), among many others.

María Irene Fornés

(1930–)

María Irene Fornés is the dean of Hispanic playwrights in New York, having enjoyed more productions of her works and more recognition, in the form of six Obie awards, than any other Hispanic. Born on May 14, 1930, in Havana, Cuba, she immigrated o the United States in 1945 and became a naturalized citizen in 1951. This sets her off considerably from most of the other Cuban playwrights who immigrated to the United States as refugees from the Cuban Revolution. Since 1960 she has been a playwright, director, and teacher of theater with Theater for New York City (1973–78) and various other workshops, universities, and schools. In the theater, Fornés has had more than thirty plays produced, including adaptations of plays by Federico García Lorca, Pedro Calderón de la Barca, and Chekhov. Her plays have been produced on Hispanic stages, on mainstream off-off-Broadway, off-Broadway, Broadway, in Milwaukee, Minneapolis, Claremont, California, London, and Zurich. Fornés's works, although at times touching upon political and ethnic themes, generally deal with human relations and the emotional lives of her characters. Her plots tend to be unconventional, and at times her characters are fragmented, in structures that vary from musical comedy to the theater of ideas to very realistic plays. Many of her plays have been published in collections of her work: *Promenade and Other Plays* (1971), *María Irene Fornés: Plays* (1986), and *Lovers and Keepers* (1986).

Leonardo García Astol (1906–)

Leonardo García Astol was born into a theatrical family in Mexico and as a child began touring with his mother, a famous actress divorced from his father, and with the companies of his father and his brother in northern Mexico and later in the Rio Grande valley of the United States. Prepared as an actor of the grand melodramatic tradition, Astol had to accommodate his considerable acting talents throughout his life in the United States to the needs of the moment, which were usually dictated by economic conditions and working-class audience demands. He began performing in the United States in 1921 and from that time on was associated with many of the most popular theatrical companies and with the famed Teatro Nacional in San Antonio. As the Great Depression hit, he continued to work with one company after another, at times managing the companies. For years he survived doing vaudeville, especially with the role he created of Don Lalo, a comic hobo, for which he is still remembered in communities of the Southwest. In 1938, Astol became a member of the stock vaudeville company for the Teatro Nacional and the Teatro Zaragoza in San Antonio, and during this time he began doing comic dialogues on Spanish-language radio. By 1940, he had become the emcee of an hour-long Mexican variety show on the radio; this later led to his doing soap operas on the radio in the 1950s, as well as other dramatic series. In the late 1950s and early 1960s, Astol broke into television and even wrote, directed, and acted in a serial entitled "El Vampiro" ("The Vampire"). While developing the various phases of his career, Astol was always active in maintaining serious theatrical performances for the community, usually staged at church halls and community centers for little or no remuneration. Over the years, Astol's has been a heroic effort to keep Hispanic theater alive in the United States.

Adalberto Elías González

Adalberto Elías González was by far the most prolific and successful playwright ever in the Hispanic communities of the United States. A native of Sonora, Mexico, who probably immigrated to Los Angeles in 1920 to further his education after graduating from the Escuela Normal in Hermosillo, he is known to have worked as a newspaperman and professional playwright there at least until 1941. Because of the subject matter of various of his plays, it is assumed that he also had military experience in Mexico before moving to the United States. By 1924 González had steady employment as a movie critic for *El Heraldo de México* newspaper in Los Angeles and had four new plays debut that year. By 1928 his fame as a playwright was so great that in that one year alone his works were staged in Hermosillo, Mexicali, El Paso, Nogales, and, of course, Los Angeles. González's works ran the gamut from historical drama to dime-novel sensationalism. The most famous of his plays was *Los Amores de Ramona* (*The Loves of Ramona*), a stage adaptation of Helen Hunt Jackson's California novel, *Ramona: A Story*. His second most successful work, *La Asesino del Martillo o La mujer tigresa* (*The Hammer Assassin or The Tiger Woman*), was based on news stories of 1923 and 1924. González also wrote historical drama, based both on Mexican history in California and on the Mexican Revolution, such as his *La Conquista de California* (*The Conquest of California*), *Los Expatriados* (*The Expatriates*), *La Muerte de Francisco Villa* (*The Death of Francisco Villa*), and *El Fantasma de la Revolución* (*The Ghost of the Revolution*). In all, González is known to have written some fourteen or fifteen plays that were successfully produced in Los Angeles during the 1920s and 1930s.

Antonio Guzmán Aguilera (1894–?)

Antonio Guzmán Aguilera, whose pen name was Guz Aguila, was one of Mexico's most prolific and beloved librettists and composed scores of popular theatrical revues. Born in San Miguel del Mesquital on March 21, 1894, Guzmán studied in Mexico City at the Jesuit Instituto Científico de México, and by 1916 had his first play produced at the Teatro Juan Ruiz de Alarcón. After that he began developing his career as a journalist at various newspapers; while still a journalist he became a famous author of revistas that commented on current events. He became the friend of presidents and politicians and suffered the ups and downs of these associations, so much so that he was arrested when a political rival became president (Obregón); he later went into exile in Los Angeles in 1924. At the Teatro Hidalgo he wrote and debuted one of his only full-length plays, *María del Pilar Moreno, o la Pequeña Vengadora* (*María del Pilar Moreno or the Tiny Avenger*), based on the story of a young girl recently exonerated of murder in Mexico City. While contracted by Hidalgo he also wrote and staged the following new revues based on culture and events in Los Angeles: *Los Angeles Vacilador* (*Swinging Los Angeles*), *Evite Peligro* (*Avoid Danger*), and *El Eco de México* (*The Echo from Mexico*). In 1927 Guz Aguila returned to the stages of Mexico City, but he never regained the level of success that he had experienced there earlier.

Gerardo López del Castillo

Gerardo López del Castillo was a leading man and director of the Compañía Española, a Spanish-Mexican theatrical company that first toured and then became a resident company in San Francisco in the mid-nineteenth century. A native of Mexico City, López del Castillo was a professional actor from age fifteen. Today he is known as the first Mexican actor to take companies on tour outside Mexico. By the time he arrived in California, he was already well known throughout Mexico, the Caribbean, and Central and South America. An intensely patriotic individual, López del Castillo often used theatrical performances to raise funds for Zaragoza's and Juárez's liberation armies, and he interrupted his theatrical career on various occasions to serve Mexico as a soldier. He is also known as a great promoter of the creation of a national dramatic art for Mexico. By 1862 López del Castillo and his theatrical company had made San Francisco their home. From there the company occasionally ventured out on tours up and down the coast of California and Baja California, but it mostly performed its melodramas at Tucker's Music Academy, the American Theater, and other San Francisco stages. News of the López del Castillo troupe in California exists until 1867; by 1874, he and his family company had resurfaced in Mexico City, where he was actively promoting the creation of a national dramatic literature.

Julio Matas (1931–)

Julio Matas is a playwright, poet, and fiction writer. Born in Havana, Cuba, on May 12, 1931, Matas was encouraged to follow in the steps of his father, a judge, and he thus obtained his law degree from the University of Havana in 1955. But he never practiced as an attorney. He had enrolled in the University School for Dramatic Arts and by the time of his graduation in 1952, he had already organized a drama group, Arena. In his youth he worked on literary magazines and film projects with some of the figures who would become outstanding in these fields, such as Roberto Fernández Retamar, Néstor Almendros, and Tomás Gutiérrez Alea. In 1957 Matas enrolled at Harvard University to pursue a Ph.D. in Spanish literature; however, he remained active as a director, returning to Cuba to work on stage productions. It was during the cultural ferment that accompanied the first years of the Communist regime in Cuba that Matas saw two of his first books published there: the collection of short stories *Catálogo de imprevistos (Catalog of the Unforeseen)* (1963), and the three-act play *La crónica y el suceso (The Chronicle and the Event)* (1964). In 1965 Matas returned to the United States to assume a position in the Department of Hispanic Languages and Literatures at the University of Pittsburgh, a position that he still holds today.

René Marqués (1919–1979)

René Marqués is considered Puerto Rico's foremost playwright and writer of short fiction. Born in Arecibo, Puerto Rico, on October 4, 1919, to a family of agrarian background, Marqués studied agronomy at the College of Agriculture in Mayagüz and actually worked for two years for the Department of Agriculture. But his interest in literature took him to Spain in 1946 to study the classics. Upon his return, Marqués founded a little-theater group dedicated to producing and furthering Puerto Rican theater. In 1948 he received a Rockefeller Foundation Fellowship to study playwriting in the United States, which allowed him to study at Columbia University and at the Piscator Dramatic Workshop in New York City. After his return to San Juan, he founded the Teatro Experimental del Ateneo (the Ateneum Society Experimental Theater). From that time on, Marqués maintained a heavy involvement not only in playwriting, but also in development of Puerto Rican theater. He also produced a continuous flow of short stories, novels, essays, and anthologies.

While Marqués's best-known work is still the all-important play *La carreta (The Oxcart)* (debuted in 1953, published in 1961), he has been writing since 1944, when he published his first collection of poems, *Peregrinación (Pilgrimage)*. His published plays include *El hombre y sus sueños (Man and His Dreams)* (1948), *Palm Sunday* (1949), *Otro día nuestro (Another of Our Days)*, (1955), *Juan Bobo y la Dama de Occidente (Juan Bobo and the Western Lady)* (1956), *El sol y los MacDonald (The Sun and the MacDonalds)* (1957), and a collection, *Teatro* (1959), which includes three of his most important plays: *Los soles truncos (The Fan Lights)*, *Un niño azul para esa sombra (A Blue Child for that Shadow)*, and *La muerte no entrará en palacio (Death Will Not Enter the Palace)*. Many are the other published plays, novels, collections of short stories, and essays. Marqués is one of the few Puerto Rican writers who has had international audiences and impact; he is truly one of the high points of all Latin American drama. The style, philosophy, and craft of his works, as produced in New York, have had long-lasting influence on the development of Hispanic theater in the United States.

Matías Montes Huidobro (1931–)

Matías Montes Huidobro is a prolific writer of plays, fiction, and poetry, and he has been a theatrical producer and scriptwriter for television and radio. Born in Sagua la Grande, Cuba, Montes was educated there and in Havana. In 1952 he obtained a Ph.D. degree in pedagogy from the University of Havana, but from 1949 on he had already begun publishing creative literature and literary criticism. He served as a professor of Spanish literature at the National School of Journalism in Havana, at which point he had a falling out with the political powers and immigrated to the United States. In 1963 he became a professor of Spanish at the University of Hawaii, a position he holds to this date.

The dramas of Matías Montes Huidobro vary in style, theme, and format, ranging from expressionism to surrealism, from the absurd to the allegorical and political. His published plays include *Los acosados (The Accosted)* (1959), *La botija (The Jug)* (1959), *Gas en los poros (Gas in His Pores)* (1961), *El tiro por la culata (Ass-Backwards)* (1961), *La vaca de los ojos largos (The Long-Eyed Cow)* (1967), *La sal de los muertos (Salt of the Dead)* (1971), *The Guillotine* (1972), *Hablando en chino (Speaking Chinese)* (1977), *Ojos para no ver (Eyes for Not Seeing)* (1979), *Funeral en Teruel (Funeral in Teruel)* (1982), and *La navaja de Olofé (Olofé's Blade)* (1982). Montes has also published important novels, including *Desterrados al fuego (Exiled into the Fire)* (1975) and *Segar a los muertos (To Blind the Dead)* (1980).

Carlos Morton (1947–)

Carlos Morton is the most published Hispanic playwright in the United States. Born on October 15, 1947, in Chicago, to Mexican-American parents, Morton received his education in various states, as his father's assignments in the army as a noncommissioned officer changed. Morton obtained a bachelor's degree from the University of Texas, El Paso (1975), an M.F.A. degree in theater from the University of California, San Diego (1979), and a Ph.D. degree in drama from the University of Texas, Austin (1987), after which he embarked on a career as a professor of drama. Today he is an associate professor at the University of California, Riverside. His writing career began much earlier, with the publication of his first chapbook of poems, *White Heroin Winter,* in 1971, followed by the publication of his most famous play, *El Jardín (The Garden)* in an anthology in 1974. The majority of his plays have been produced on stages at universities and Hispanic community arts centers, with *Pancho Diablo* being produced by the New York Shakespeare Festival and *The Many Deaths of Danny Rosales* by Los Angeles's Bilingual Foundation for the Arts. Most of his plays are contained in two published collections, *The Many Deaths of Danny Rosales and Other Plays* (1983) and *Johnny Tenorio and Other Plays* (1991).

Juan Nadal de Santa Coloma

One of the grandest Puerto Rican theatrical figures in the 1920s and 1930s was Juan Nadal de Santa Coloma, the leading actor, singer, director, and impresario. The overriding theme of his life was the development of a Puerto Rican national theater. Born and raised in Puerto Rico at the end of the nineteenth century, Nadal left his engineering studies at San Juan's Instituto Civil to begin a career on the stage. He worked his way through various touring companies in Puerto Rico and South America, and by 1902 was directing his own company, the Compañía de Zarzuela

Puertorriqueña. For the next couple of decades he toured continuously in Latin America and Spain, and he even for a while managed Mexico City's Teatro Principal and Madrid's Teatro Eslava. From 1927 through 1934, he was on and off New York and San Juan stages, with his Compañía Teatral Puertorriqueña, promoting Puerto Rican theater. In 1930, he wrote and staged his musical comedy *Día de Reyes (The Day of the Magi)*, which had 156 performances in New York City alone. In 1935, he returned to Puerto Rico after what he described as "the cold shower" that was New York, and on the island he continued to direct several companies during the rest of the decade.

Gabriel Navarro   Originally from Guadalajara, Gabriel Navarro moved to Los Angeles as an actor and musician in 1922 in the Compañía México Nuevo. In Los Angeles he developed into a playwright; he also worked as a journalist and theater critic. During the Great Depression and the demise of the theater industry, he became a movie critic. In 1923 he launched a magazine, *La revista de Los Angeles (The Los Angeles Magazine)*; it is not known how long it lasted. In 1925 he became associated with a newspaper in San Diego, *El Hispano Americano (The Hispano American)*, which that same year published his novel, *La señorita Estela (Miss Estela)*. As a playwright and composer, Navarro experimented with all of the popular dramatic forms, from drama to musical revue. Navarro's favorite genre was the revista; it allowed him to put to use his talents as a composer and writer, in addition to the technical knowledge he had accrued as an actor and director. In the revista, Navarro was the celebrant of Hollywood nightlife and the culture of the Roaring Twenties. His known works include the following revues: *Los Angeles al día (Los Angeles to Date)* (1922), *La Ciudad de los extras (The City of Extras)* (1922), *Su majestad la carne (Her Majesty the Flesh)* (1924), *La ciudad de irás y no volverás (The City of To Go and Never Return)* (1928), *Las luces de Los Angeles (The Lights of Los Angeles)* (1933), *El precio de Hollywood (The Price of Hollywood)* (1933), *Los Angeles en pijamas (Los Angeles in Pajamas)* (1934), and *La canción de Sonora (The Song of Sonora)* (1934). His dramas include *La Señorita Estela* (1925), *Los emigrados (The Emigrées)* (1928), *La sentencia (The Jail Sentence)* (1931), *El sacrificio (The Sacrifice)* (1931), *Loco amor (Crazy Love)* (1932), *Alma Yaqui (Yaqui Soul)* (1932), and *Cuando entraron los dorados (When Villa's Troupes Entered)* (1932). Navarro's serious works draw upon his experience growing up in Guadalajara and his twelve years in the Mexican army in Veracruz and Sonora during the Mexican Revolution. *El sacrificio* and *La sentencia* use California as a setting; the latter play examines the expatriate status of Mexicans in Los Angeles and shows the breakdown of family and culture, with an Anglo-Mexican intermarriage ending in divorce and bloody tragedy.

Manuel Noriega was the first director and impresario to really try to develop Hispanic theater in New York by founding various companies, renting and/or buying theaters, and even establishing a motion picture studio. Noriega was a Spanish singer-actor of *zarzuelas* (operettas) who made his debut at the Teatro Principal in Mexico City in 1904. Noriega found his way to New York in 1916 via the Havana stage. That same year he founded the Compañía Dramática Española, which began touring theater houses in the city for the next few years. In 1919 he formed a partnership with various businessmen and opened the first Spanish-language theater house in New York, El Teatro Español, but because of poor financial management, it closed its doors almost as soon as it opened. Noriega continued to direct companies until 1922, when he left New York. He resurfaced in Los Angeles in 1927, where he had been developing his career in film.

Manuel Noriega

Alberto O'Farrill was born in Santa Clara, Cuba, in 1899 and had begun his career as an actor and playwright in Havana in 1921 before emigrating to the United States. In New York O'Farrill was the ubiquitous negrito of *obras bufas cubanas* and Cuban zarzuelas who made a career playing all the major Hispanic stages in New York's stock and itinerant companies. O'Farrill was also an intensely literate man who had been the editor of *Proteo*, a magazine in Havana, and had become in 1927 the first editor for New York's *Gráfico* newspaper, which he led in becoming the principal organ for the publication and commentary of literature and theatre. In *Grafico*, O'Farrill also published various stories and essays of his own. Despite his literary interests, as of 1926 none of O'Farrill's dramatic works had been published. O'Farrill debuted two zarzuelas at the Teatro Esmeralda in Havana in 1921: *Un negro misterioso (A Mysterious Black Man)*, and *Las pamplinas de Agapito (Agapito's Adventures in Pamplona)*. His other known works were all debuted at the Apollo Theatre in 1926: one *sainete* (comedy), *Un doctor accidental (An Accidental Doctor)*, and the four zarzuelas *Los misterios de Changó (The Mysteries of Changó)*, *Un negro en Adalucía (A Black Man in Andalusia)*, *Una viuda como no hay dos (A Widow like None Other)*, and *Kid Chocolate*. In most of these, as in his acting, he was concerned with Afro-Cuban themes.

**Alberto O'Farrill
(1899–?)**

Gonzalo O'Neill was a key figure in the cultural life of the Puerto Rican community in New York during the 1920s and 1930s. While a young man on the island of his birth, Puerto Rico, he began his literary career as a poet and as a founder of the literary magazine *Palenque de la juventud (Young People's Forum)*, which published the works of many who would

Gonzalo O'Neill

become Puerto Rico's leading writers. A graduate of Puerto Rico's Instituto Civil, he moved to New York City and soon became a prosperous businessman, but he also maintained his love of literature, culture, and his drive for Puerto Rican independence from the United States. The latter is seen in all his known published dramatic works: *La indiana boirinqueña (The Indians of Puerto Rico)* (1922), a dramatic dialogue in verse; *Moncho Reyes* (1923), a biting satire of the colonial government in Puerto Rico, named after the fictional governor; and *Bajo una sola bandera (Under Just One Flag)* (1928), a full-length drama examining the political options for Puerto Rico as personified by a young girl's choice of betrothed. O'Neill was a type of godfather who offered assistance to writers and Puerto Rican immigrants and who invested in cultural institutions, such as the Teatro Hispano. Various of his plays were staged at this theater, including one that was not published: *Amorios borincanos (Puerto Rican Loves)* (1938). It is certain that O'Neill wrote many other works, including other plays, poetry, and possibly essays, but they are as yet lost today. The works that do exist have been preserved probably because he was wealthy enough to underwrite their publication.

Miguel Piñero (1946–1988)

Miguel Piñero is the most famous dramatist to come out of the Nuyorican school. Born in Gurabo, Puerto Rico, on December 19, 1946, he was raised on the lower East Side of New York, the site of many of his plays and poems. Shortly after moving to New York, his father abandoned the family, which forced them to live on the streets until his mother could find a source of income. Piñero was a gang leader and involved in petty crime and drugs while an adolescent; he was a junior high school dropout and by the time he was twenty-four he had been sent to Sing Sing Prison for armed robbery. While at Sing Sing, he began writing and acting in a theater workshop there.

By the time of his release, his most famous play, *Short Eyes* (published in 1975), had already been prepared in draft form. The play was produced and soon moved to Broadway after getting favorable reviews. During the successful run of his play and afterward, Piñero became involved with a group of Nuyorican writers in the lower East Side and became one of the principal spokespersons and models for the new school of Nuyorican literature, which was furthered by the publication of *Nuyorican Poets: An Anthology of Puerto Rican Words and Feelings,* compiled and edited by him and Miguel Algarín in 1975. During this time, as well, Piñero began his career as a scriptwriter for such television dramatic series as "Barreta," "Kojac," and "Miami Vice." In all, Piñero wrote some eleven plays that were produced, most of which are included in his two collections, *The Sun Always Shines for the Cool, A Midnight Moon at the Greasy Spoon, Eulogy for a Small-Time Thief* (1983) and *Outrageous One-Act Plays* (1986). Piñero is also author of a book of poems, *La Bodega (Sold Dreams)* (1986).

Eusebio Pirrín

Eusebio Pirrín (Pirrín was a stage name, the real family name possibly being Torres) was born into a circus and vaudeville family that toured principally in the U.S. Southwest and somewhat in South America. Born in Guanajuato, Pirrín developed his famous Don Catarino act on the Los Angeles stage; Catarino was named for a character in a comic strip that ran in Los Angeles's newspaper *El Heraldo de México*. Although Eusebio was only a teenager at the time, Don Catarino was a tiny old many with a bushy moustache. Don Catarino became so famous that he spawned many imitators of his dress, speech, and particular brand of humor throughout the Southwest and in Mexico. The Pirrín family troupe enjoyed great fame and fortune and was able to continue performing in the Southwest from the early 1920s through World War II, even surviving the Great Depression. Although Don Catarino was a rural, ranch type, most of his humor was urban; Pirrín created all of the revues and music in which Don Catarino took center stage. Eusebio Pirrín's revues are too numerous to list, but many of them celebrated urban nightlife in Los Angeles, while others commented on and satirized such important political and social themes as the depression, deportations, exile, and the use of alcohol and drugs.

Dolores Prida
(1943–)

Dolores Prida is a playwright and screenwriter whose works have been produced in various states and in Puerto Rico, Venezuela, and the Dominican Republic. Born on September 5, 1943, in Caibairén, Cuba, Prida emigrated with her family to New York in 1963. She graduated from Hunter College in 1969 with a major in Spanish-American literature. Upon graduation she began a career as a journalist and editor, first for Collier-Macmillan and then for other publishers, quite often using her bilingual skills. In 1977 her first play, *Beautiful Señoritas,* was produced at the Duo Theater. Since then approximately ten of her plays have been produced. Prida's plays vary in style and format and include adaptations of international classics, such as *The Three Penny Opera;* experiments with the Broadway musical formula, as in her *Savings* (1985); and her bilingual play, *Coser y cantar (To Sew and to Sing)* (1981). Her themes involve an examination of the phenomenon of urban gentrification, as in *Savings;* and the generation gap and conflict of culture, as in *Botánica* (1990). Prida's plays, which are written in Spanish or English or bilingually, have been collected in *Beautiful Señoritas and Other Plays* (1991). Prida is also a talented poet who was a leader in the 1960s of New York's *Nueva Sangre* (New Blood) movement of young poets. Her books of poems include *Treinta y un poemas (Thirty-One Poems)* (1967), *Women of the Hour* (1971), and, with Roger Cabán, *The IRT Prayer Book*.

Marita Reid

Marita Reid was one of the most famous actresses in New York's Hispanic theater, and she was a tireless promoter of serious drama in the Hispanic community during the difficult years of the Great Depression and World War II. Born in Gibraltar, Spain, to a Spanish mother and an English father, Marita Reid grew up bilingual and began her life on the stage at age seven. Her early experience was performing on tours in extreme southern Spain. She began performing in New York in the early 1920s in Spanish-language companies. In 1922 she formed her own company, and during the 1930s and 1940s her leadership was crucial as she headed up a number of companies that kept Spanish-language theater alive by performing in the mutualist societies and clubs, as well as in conventional theaters. For nearly three decades she was the leading lady of the Hispanic stage in New York and one of its leading directors. Because of her English background, Reid was able to cross over to American, English-language mainstream theater. Her career extended to Broadway, cinema, and television, including live television drama in the "Armstrong Circle Theater," "The U.S. Steel Hour," and "Studio One." Reid was also the author of four unpublished plays: *Patio gilbraltareño (Gibraltar Patio)*, *Luna de mayo (May Moon)*, *El corazón del hombre es nuestro corazón (The Heart of Man Is Our Heart)* (1933), and *Sor Piedad (Sister Piety)* (1938).

Gustavo Solano

Gustavo Solano, whose pen name was El Conde Gris (The Grey Count) was a prolific Salvadoran playwright, poet, and prose writer. In addition to his extensive record as a creative writer, Solano led a very fruitful career as a journalist, beginning in his native El Salvador and later developing in New Orleans, where he was the managing editor of the *Pan American Review* and the founder and editor of the bilingual weekly *La Opinión (The Opinion)* from 1911 to 1912. In 1912, he moved to Laredo, Texas, to become the editor of *El Progreso (The Progress)*, then later to Saltillo, Mexico, as founder and editor of *La Reforma (The Reform)*. During the late teens he was a soldier in the Mexican Revolution and in 1916 he also served time in the penitentiary in Mexico City for his political activities. In 1920 he began a long relationship with Los Angeles's *El Heraldo de México (The Mexican Herald)* as an editorial writer. While in Los Angeles, he was under contract to at least two of the theater houses as a playwright charged with producing original material. He remained in Los Angeles until 1929; during this time he also maintained relationships with various publications in Mexico.

Of all the Los Angeles playwrights, Solano had the greatest number of works published. In his book of poems *Composiciones escogidas (Selected Compositions)* (1923), Solano lists the following published works: *Verso, Fulguraciones, Trinidad de arte (poesía) (Verses, Ponderings, Trinity of Art (poetry))*, *Nadie es profeta en su tierra (No One Is a Prophet in His Own Land,* a play), *Apóstoles y judas (Apostles and Judases,* an allegorical play of the Mexican Revolution) (1915), and *La sangre, Crímenes de Estrada Cabrera (The Blood, Crimes of Estrada Cabrera,* a play satirizing the Salvadoran dictator). In *Uno más—Prosa y verso (One More—Prose and Verse)* (1929), he added the following: *México glorioso y trágico (Revolución Mexicana en escena—Prosa y verso) (Glorious and Tragic Mexico (The Mexican Revolution Onstage—Prose and Verse))* and *Con las alas abiertas (Prosa) (With Wings Spread Open (Prose))*; he also mentioned various other works of drama, poetry, and prose about to be published. In his *Volumen de una vida (Volume of a Life)* (1932), are included four of the plays that were staged in Los Angeles: *El homenaje lírico a la raza (The Lyric Homage to Our People), La casa de Birján (Birján's House), Las falsas apariencias (Mistaken Impressions),* and *Tras Cornudo, Apaleado (Beaten on top of Being Cuckolded).*

Romualdo Tirado

The most important figure in the history of the Los Angeles Hispanic stage was the great impresario, director, singer, and actor Romualdo Tirado, who was also the author of numerous librettos for revues. Tirado was a Spaniard who had immigrated to Mexico and developed a career on the stage there during his fifteen years of residence. From the time of his arrival in Los Angeles in the late teens, Tirado was a prime mover in the Hispanic theater and movie industries, and he was also the catalyst that brought about the writing and staging of local plays. Tirado celebrated the highs of the 1920s and stayed on for the lows of the Los Angeles stage during the Great Depression. During the 1940s, however, he was able to obtain some work in Puerto Rico and in New York at the Teatro Hispano.

Tirado developed many of his own musical revues around his own comic persona in various satirized situations, such as *Clínica moderna (The Modern Clinic)* (1921), *Tirado dentista (Tirado the Dentist)* (1921), *Tirado bolshevique (A Bolshevik Tirado)* (1924), and *Tirado en el Polo Norte (Tirado at the North Pole)* (1925). In 1930 Tirado and Antonieta Díaz Mercado wrote a full-length play based on Mariano Azuela's novel of the Mexican Revolution, *Los de abajo (The Underdogs)*, but it was a complete flop. None of Tirado's compositions is available today.

Omar Torres (1945–)

Omar Torres is an actor, playwright, poet, and novelist. Born and raised in Las Tunas, Cuba, he immigrated to Miami with his family in 1959. There he attended both junior and senior high school. The family moved to New York and there he attended Queens College for a while, only to drop out to study on his own. He later took acting classes at the New York Theater of the Americas and subsequently graduated from the International Television Arts School. He has had an active career in radio, television, and movies. In 1972 he co-founded, with Iván Acosta, the Centro Cultural Cubano, and in 1974 he founded the literary and arts journal *Cubanacán* (a nonsense word meaning "Cuba" here). Torres's produced plays include *Abdala-José Martí* (1972), *Antes del Vuelo y la Palabra (Before the Flight and the Word)* (1976), *Cumbancha cubiche (Cumbancha Low Class Cuban)* (1976), *Yo dejo mi palabra en el aire sin llaves y sin velos (I Leave My Word in the Air without Keys and without Veils)* (1978), *Latinos* (1979), and *Dreamland Melody* (1982). Torres is the author of three novels—*Apenas un bolero (Just a Bolero)* (1981), *Al partir (Upon Leaving)* (1986), and *Fallen Angels Sing* (1991)—and five books of poetry: *Conversación primera (First Conversation)* (1975), *Ecos de un laberinto (Echoes from a Labyrinth)* (1976), *Tiempo robado (Stolen Time)* (1978), *De nunca a siempre (From Never to Always)* (1981), and *Línea en diluvio (Line in the Deluge)* (1981).

Rafael Trujillo Herrera (1897–)

Rafael Trujillo Herrera is a prolific playwright, drama teacher, and impresario. Born in Durango, Mexico, Trujillo immigrated to Los Angeles and remains there to this day. In the late 1920s and early 1930s, he began writing plays for the stage and for the radio; in 1933 he began directing his own radio show. In 1940 Trujillo became associated with the Works Progress Administration (WPA), for which he wrote a play, *Bandido (Bandit)*; it was later published under the title of *Revolución (Revolution)*. During the 1960s, Trujillo published numerous works in various genres in Los Angeles, Mexico, and elsewhere, including some through his own publishing house, Editorial Autores Unidos (United Authors Publishing). All told, Trujillo claims to have written some fifty one-act plays, two in four acts, and twelve in three acts. During these years he also directed at least five theater groups. In 1974 he opened the doors to his own little theater, the teatro Intimo, in Los Angeles. Trujillo's most famous three-act plays are *Revolución, Estos son mis hijos (These Are My Children)*, *La hermana de su mujer (His Wife's Sister), Cuando la vida florece (When Life Flourishes),* and *A la moda vieja (Old Style).*

**Luis Valdez
(1940–)**

Luis Valdez is considered the father of Chicano theater. He has distinguished himself as an actor, director, playwright, and filmmaker; however, it was in his role as the founding director of El Teatro Campesion, a theater of farm workers in California, that his efforts inspired young Chicano activists across the country to use theater as a means of organizing students, communities, and labor unions. Luis Valdez was born into a family of migrant farm workers in Delano, California. The second of ten children, he began to work the fields at age six and to follow the crops. Valdez's education was continuously interrupted; he nevertheless finished high school and went on to San Jose State College, where he majored in English and pursued his interest in theater. While there he won a playwriting contest with his one-act "The Theft" (1961), and in 1963 the drama department produced his play *The Shrunken Head of Pancho Villa.*

After graduating from college in 1964, Valdez joined the San Francisco Mime Troupe and learned the techniques of agitprop (agitation and propaganda) theater and Italian *commedia dell'arte* (comedy of art), both of which influenced Valdez's development of the basic format of Chicano theater: the one-act presentational *acto.* In 1965 Valdez enlisted in César Chávez's mission to organize farm workers in Delano into a union. It was there that Valdez brought together farm workers and students into El Teatro Campesino to dramatize the plight of the farm workers. The publicity and success gained by the troupe led to the spontaneous appearance of a national Chicano theater movement. In 1967 Valdez and El Teatro Campesino left the unionizing effort to expand their theater beyond agitprop and farm worker concerns. From then on Valdez and the theater have explored most of the theatrical genres that have been important to Mexicans in the United States, including religious pageants, vaudeville with the down-and-out *pelado* (underdog) figure, and dramatized *corridos* (ballads). During the late 1960s and the 1970s, El Teatro Campesino produced many of Valdez's plays, including *Los vendidos (The Sell-Outs)* (1967), *The Shrunken Head of Pancho Villa* (1968), *Bernabé* (1970), *Dark Root of a Scream* (1971), *La carpa de los Rascuachis* (1974), and *El fin del mundo* (1976). In 1978 Valdez broke into mainstream theater in Los Angeles, with the Mark Taper Forum's production of his *Zoot Suit* and the 1979 Broadway production of the same play. In 1986 he had a successful run of his play *I Don't Have to Show You No Stinking Badges* at the Los Angeles Theater Center.

Valdez's screenwriting career began with early film and television versions of Corky González's poem "I Am Joaquín" (1969) and "Los vendidos," and later with a film version of *Zoot Suit* (1982). But his real incursion into major Hollywood productions and success came with his writing and directing of *La Bamba* (the name of a dance from Veracruz), the screen biography of Chicano rock-and-roll star Ritchie Valens. Valdez's plays, essays, and poems have been widely anthologized. His only collection of work still in print is *Luis Valdez—The Early Works* (1990), which includes the early actos that he developed with El Teatro Campesino, his play *Bernabé,* and his narrative poem "Pensamiento Serpentino."

Carmen Zapata (1927–)

Carmen Zapata is an actress and producer of Mexican heritage. Born on July 15, 1927, in New York City, she was raised and educated in New York, and later attended the University of California, Los Angeles, and New York University. Zapata has had a very successful career in Hollywood films and on television, including children's television. She is most important, however, as the founder and director of the Bilingual Foundation for the Arts in Los Angeles, which is a showcase for Hispanic playwrights, actors, and directors and has resulted in introducing new talent to the television and movie industries. Included among her awards are the National Council of La Raza Rubén Salazar Award (1983), the Women in Film Humanitarian Award (1983), Hispanic Women's Council Woman of the Year (1985), best Actress Dramalogue (1986), and an Emmy (1973).

Nicolás Kanellos

F*ilm*

Depictions of Hispanics by the American film industry generally have been less than realistic or sympathetic. A host of early trends and personal contributions combined to create an extraordinarily harsh American style of racial and ethnic characterization, which was reinforced in the 1920s and 1930s with the conglomeration of the American film industry in a fashion that emphasized theatrical distribution, the assembly line production of many films, the star system, and production formulas that were later turned into a production code.

The early cinematic portrayal of Hispanics embodied the prevailing stereotypes of bandidos, buffoons, dark ladies, caballeros, and gangsters. However, the changes in the representation of Hispanics and other minority groups brought about by the Great Depression, World War II, and the advent of the "Hollywood social problem film" are quite remarkable. Hispanic-focused films and Hispanic actors and filmmakers carved a niche in the industry against the backdrop of important social developments such as the emergence of the civil rights movement and the decline of the production code.

Since the early 1980s the emergence of Hispanic film consciousness has broadened, with an emphasis on Chicano productions and films made in Puerto Rico (often with Mexican or Hollywood control) or by Puerto Ricans both on the island and in the continental United States. The filmmaking climate of the 1990s indicates that the future of Hispanic cinema is a bright one, with Hispanic talent and issues continuing to gain prominence.

DEPICTION OF MINORITY GROUPS IN EARLY AMERICAN FILM ✦

During a period of a few years, primarily between 1903 and 1915, several technological, aesthetic, economic, and cultural developments in the United States came together that were important in determining how American cinema was to depict race and ethnicity for decades to come. An unfortunate filmic style emerged that was much harsher in its depiction of race and ethnicity than the cinema of other nations. American cinema delighted in the depiction of such stereotypes as "chinkers," "Micks," "darkies," "Hebrews," "greasers," "redskins," and "guineas," and actually used these epithets in the titles and publicity or in the films themselves.

Five governing factors converged and interacted with one another around the turn of the century to produce a definable style of racial stereotyping in American cinema: (1) the developing technological sophistication of filmmaking, particularly in projection and editing, (2) the developing philosophy of illusionism that began to gain ascendancy in film aesthetics, (3) the economic necessity in the U.S. film industry to produce westerns and to produce epic, prestige pictures of middle-class appeal, (4) the attitudes toward race and ethnicity that prevailed in society and that governed the popular novel of the period, and (5) the racial attitudes of the most prominent filmmakers of the period, especially D. W. Griffith.

In 1903 Edwin S. Porter produced the landmark film *The Great Train Robbery*. Significantly, the film was a western and reigned for about ten years as the most important American cinematic production, until the emergence of D. W. Griffith's features. *The Great Train Robbery* was of epic proportions for its time, an incredible twelve minutes. Yet, by 1915 technological advances and artistic will had stretched the concept of epic to three hours with Griffith's *The Birth of a Nation*. It is in the nature of epics that they deal with race and ethnicity; and it was no coincidence that Griffith's most famous epic was the most ambitious attempt to date, a flawed and racist depiction of ethnic and racial types: tender and sensitive Southern Whites, vain White Northern liberals, vicious or brutal Blacks, merciless Northern soldiers, heroic Ku Klux Klansmen, and evil mulattoes, the result of deplorable mixing of the races. Griffith's films, through their depiction of kidnappings, attempted rapes, destruction of homesteads or Indian villages, and most of all, war, were able to bring forth feelings of outrage, simultaneous horror, and titillating anticipation, pity, and remorse more intensely than other available media—theater, fiction, poetry, or journalism.

The earliest period of cinema, which had its roots in magic and lantern shows and in vaudeville, emphasized the illusionism of special effects (trains, horses, running water, flights to the moon, and so on). However, as the result of rapid advances in technology that permitted longer and more sophisticated films, together with the increasing staleness of purely optical effects such as waves beating against a pier, cinema began to both borrow from and more closely approximate the stage. The early film directors, Edwin S. Porter, Stuart Blackton, Sidney Olcott, and others, quickly discovered that film had a distinct advantage over the stage in presenting melodrama. The devices available to film could have a reality that was impossible to attain on the stage. For example, the count of Monte Cristo need not escape from his prison through a canvas sea; the film showed a real ocean.

Moreover, the early filmmakers, Griffith the leader among them, soon made changes in style based on the aesthetics of illusionism. Film moved from a style based on special optical effects (where the cameraman was supreme) to a photographic record of legitimate theater, to an emotionally heightened superrealism where the auteur/director reigned supreme.

The conscious economic policy of attempting to raise the social respectability of films and consequently attract a middle-class audience also had an important ideological and aesthetic consequence, propelling film toward the classical narrative style of illusionism and, in turn, the depiction of ethnic and racial stereotypes in the distinctive American manner. In 1908 the Motion Picture Patents Company (MPPC) was established with the goals of establishing a controlling monopoly of film distribution and achieving acceptance of the "flickers" by the middle class.

The early years of cinema witnessed an explosion of technology similar to that of the contemporary computer industry. Advances in film technology were instrumental in determining the art of the possible for the emerging American cinematic filmmakers of the period, such as Edwin S. Porter, D. W. Griffith, Mack Sennett, Thomas H. Ince, William S. Hart, and Charles Chaplin. The development of more powerful projection and editing technologies permitted the production of what audiences of that period perceived to be more realistic films. These films included epics that lent themselves to the depiction of minority group types, including Mexicans, African Americans, Asians, and Native Americans, in a way that was not technologically possible before.

The push to make film respectable (that is, acceptable to the middle class) opened on two basic fronts: censorship of film content and improvement of the theaters in which the films were shown. Film censorship had two aims: to "improve" film content and therefore attract a "better class" of audience, and to keep censorship out of the hands of the government and the clergy, which might deal more harshly with the films than the producers wanted. Of course, the goal was to make films that still catered to the working class (many of them recently arrived immigrants from western and, increasingly, eastern Europe), even as they attracted the middle class.

To woo the middle class, filmmakers began to produce films with more complicated narrative plots and characterization, films with "educational" or "instructive" values or a "moral lesson," and films with happy endings. These initiatives lent themselves to the creation of racial antagonists (Mexicans, Blacks, American Indians), whose interactions with white males and females, however simplistic and formulistic by contemporary standards, were considerably more complex from a narrative and psychological point of view. Moreover, their defeat could be the basis of a moral lesson for both the character on-screen and the audience, and for happy endings evoking the moral and physical superiority of Anglo values over the degenerate or primitive mores of other cultures. The central impetus behind the production of vast numbers of westerns, many using Mexicans or Indians as foils to Anglo heroes and heroines, was a ready international market for such films. The genre became proprietary to the American film industry.

It appears that the filmmakers' racial attitudes that were introduced in westerns were readily passed into American cinema style. These attitudes were embedded in D. W. Griffith's film technique. They were integral to the way he developed many of his plots and the way he developed several of his epic films. American cinema took not only the technical (relatively content-free) contributions from Griffith and other early filmmakers, but also the content-intensive ones. What emerged, partially as a contribution of these racial attitudes and their narrative and thematic elaboration in film, partially from the convergence of technological, aesthetic, economic, and sociocultural factors, was a distinctively American style of racial and ethnic depiction, one that was uniquely derogatory.

CONGLOMERATION OF THE FILM INDUSTRY AND THE
◆ **PRODUCTION CODE**

The first wave of ethnic stereotyping that so distinguishes American film from the silver screen of other nations was further reinforced by the development of film as big business. Capital investment in the American film industry became centered not in production but in distribution, particularly in the form of movie theaters. By the early 1930s, power rested with a mere eight major, vertically structured corporations that had consolidated production, distribution, and exhibition in monopolistic fashion: MGM, Warner Brothers, Paramount, Twentieth Century Fox, Universal, RKO, Columbia, and United Artists. A steady turnover of product was needed to ensure revenue at the box office, which was dependent on regular attendance at many theaters on a continual basis, not on high attendance for any one movie during a single run. From an industry point of view, then, making good pictures was secondary to making a large quantity of pictures.

This assembly line methodology or homogenization of craft, which governed the "high technology" of the early twentieth century and had a profound influence on the stylistic, thematic, and performance components of U.S. film, is usually known as the Hollywood Formula. With respect to style, film was produced and marketed to the public by genre: western, musical, screwball comedy, horror, gangster, or woman's film. The easily identifiable genres provided variations on familiar movie experiences and made moviegoing a sort of ritual. Repetition of this sort ensured a basically effortless participation by the audience. For example, they absolutely trusted that the hero would prevail and get the girl. It was just a matter of how and when. With respect to performance, typecasting (the human resource analog to the production of standard fenders or automobile bodies) led to the highly salesworthy star system. After several films, the public came to know a star very well, so much so that it became difficult for actors to stray very far beyond their normal range.

Given the circumstances of marketing by the star system, it is small wonder that Hispanic film actors and actresses had the option of either retaining their Hispanic identity and being typecast negatively or denying their Hispanic identity by what the industry euphemistically calls "repositioning" themselves.

The influence of the Hollywood Formula on the development of movie themes or messages did extreme damage to minority groups, including Hispanics. The two fundamental thematic components of the formula were that the movie should communicate Americanism and that it should provide wish fulfillment. Often films combined both notions—nationalism and hedonism—at the deleterious expense of minorities.

Two actors who identified as Hispanic were Leo Carrillo, who played his stereotype faithfully as a gambling, murdering, extorting, pimping, border bandido in some thirty films; and Lupe Vélez, who played to perfection the stereotype of the Hispanic "dark lady" with her hip swinging and her amusing difficulties with the English language. Lupe would invariably go down to defeat when confronted with female Anglo-Saxon competition in the struggle to infatuate an Anglo male star.

As a result, in American film the ethnic *other* strictly and almost invariably played the outcast or the evildoer. Film, and for that matter, television in its early period, was an instrument of socialization that took as its guiding premise the assimilation of all racial, ethnic, and religious differences into the harmonizing credo of the American melting pot. No room whatsoever was allowed for divergence from this requirement. Even more painful, those races and ethnicities that could not be readily assimilated because of their difference of color and physiognomy—which would be readily apparent on the black-and-white celluloid—for example, African Americans, Hispanics, and Native Americans, were drummed into the fold of evildoers and outcasts, a priori and without recourse. These and other ethnic groups consequently functioned as the slag in the melting-pot alchemy of American film. The usual components of wish fulfillment, such as romance and true love, destroying evil (even as we relish evil actions fiendishly depicted on the screen), rewarding good, happy endings, and so on, ensured that Hispanic and other minority characters would perform for the assembly line the roles of vamps, seductresses, greasers, gangsters, and the like, ad nauseam.

The formula became Hollywood law in 1934 with the introduction of the production code. The code states in pontifical and hypocritical fashion the moral value system behind the Hollywood Formula, decrying criminal violence and intimate sexuality, upholding the sanctity of marriage and the home and other traditions that had already become heartily compromised in the movies. The code stated that entertainment is "either helpful or harmful to the human race." Because of this, "the motion picture...has special moral obligations" to create only "correct entertainment" that "raises the whole standard of a nation" and "tends to improve the race, or at least to re-create or rebuild human beings exhausted with the realities of life."

In a very broad sense, an ideological vision of the world was acted out in each formula movie. Each individual—of the correct ethnic background, that is—can aspire to success. You are limited only by your own character and energies (if you are of the correct ethnic background, of course).

Wealth, status, and power are possible for everyone (Anglo, that is) in America, the land of opportunity where the individual (Anglo) is rewarded for virtue. Such Americana as home, motherhood, community, puritanical love, and the work ethic are all celebrated. All issues are reduced to a good versus evil, black-and-white conflict, an us-against-them identification process where good equals the American (Anglo) values and social system ("us"). "Them," the villains, are defined as those who reject and seek to destroy the proper set of American (Anglo) values. Conflict is always resolved through the use of righteous force, with American (Anglo) values winning out. "Them" not only includes Blacks, Hispanics, and Native Americans—that is, those ethnics whose color and racial features overtly identify them as "others"—but usually any ethnic group when it is depicted ethnically.

Examples of the "repositioned" actor include Margarita Cansino and Raquel Tejada, who changed their images to Rita Hayworth and Raquel Welch, respectively, in order not to be typecast as Hispanic dark ladies.

FIRST DECADES: THE BANDIDO, BUFFOON, DARK LADY,

◆ ◆ ◆ ◆ ◆ ◆ ◆ ◆ ◆ ◆ ◆ ◆ ◆ ◆ ◆ ◆ **CABALLERO, AND GANGSTER**

During the first two decades of U.S. filmmaking, the Hispanic stereotypes were the bandido, the buffoon, and the dark lady. By the 1920s, two additional roles were added to the repertoire, the caballero and the gangster. Typically, in accordance with the traditional role of minorities in American film, the Hispanic was one to be killed, mocked, punished, seduced, or redeemed by Anglo protagonists.

The earliest westerns generally followed the conventions of that period's dime novels, with two differences. One is that in some films the greaser was allowed to reform or redeem himself, usually by saving a beautiful Anglo heroine. *The Greaser's Gauntlet* and *Tony, the Greaser* cultivate the theme of Hispanic redemption through obeisance to the physical and moral splendor of an Anglo-Saxon beauty.

The second way films were different from the dime novels reflected the historical reality of the Mexican Revolution (1910–1920), which the American film industry depicted with the customary quality of cinematic exaggeration, but occasionally showing no Americans at all. These films actually depicted the emergence of revolutionaries from the peon class and treated them as heroes. Thus, in *The Mexican Joan of Arc*, where only

Mexican characters are featured, a woman whose husband and son are arrested and murdered by the *federales* becomes a rebel leader. In a similar film, *The Mexican Revolutionists*, a rebel named Juan is captured but escapes the *federales* only to help the revolutionaries capture Guadalajara. Films of this type were rare, however. As has been described earlier, American film needed to operate on the basis of stark moral conflicts where whites represented good and nonwhites represented evil. Thus, even the Mexican Revolution provided the backdrop for the famous early actor Tom Mix. In his movies, such as *An Arizona Wooing* and *Along the Border,* the plot features rebels who are really bandidos in masquerade interested in kidnapping a beautiful blonde and providing her with a "fate worse than death." The plot required an Anglo hero to outwit them and give them a suitable punishment.

Maria Montez

The Caballero's Way in 1914 marked the first of the Castilian caballero films, promoting personages such as Zorro, Don Arturo Bodega, and later the Cisco Kid. The formula for this cycle of films is very much within the convention of how American film treated ethnicity, since the heroes of these movies, by virtue of their pure Spanish ancestry or Caucasian blood, are able to put down the degraded mestizos who inhabit the Mexican California setting. The caballero cycle owed its inspiration to the North Carolina-born writer O. Henry (pen name of William Sidney Porter). The Cisco Kid was directly modeled on the writer's story "The Caballero's Way" (1907). O. Henry, whose colorful life included several years in Austin and Houston and a jail sentence for embezzlement from an Austin bank, presented Mexicans in a prejudicial and stereotypical manner. His usual method when writing about the West, aptly reflected in the caballero film cycle, was to spice up his stories with Spanish characters and motifs and to have pure-blooded Castilians thwart the mestizos and Indians. O. Henry's short stories, extremely popular at the time, were ideal for movies. While today we may see them as a type of formula fiction based on contrived plots, shallow characterization, strange turns of events, and surprise endings, Porter was innovative in his time and did much to further short story writing as a craft and an art. Many of his stories were turned into films.

The gay caballero had a few minor variations. The Cisco Kid cycle was the most popular. It began in the silent era with films such as *The Caballero's Way* and *The Border Terror* (1919), and during the sound era large numbers were made. Warner Baxter starred (typically with Hollywood, Anglos first portrayed the role, Hispanics only later) in three such films from 1929 to 1939. César Romero did six between 1939 and 1941, Duncan Renaldo did eight between 1945 and 1950, and Gilbert Roland did six between 1946 and 1947. The Cisco character stressed the amorous side of the gay caballero, a charming brigand who prized a beautiful woman as a gourmet savors a vintage wine (from a contemporary perspective he was a plain and simple cad). Like his Anglo counterparts of similar western series, his method was to ride in, destroy evil, and ride out, leaving a broken heart or two. If Cisco flirted with Anglo women, his status as a serial hero made marriage inconceivable—it would end the series! The formula worked tremendously on television as well, and this syndicated serial garnered the largest receipts of its time.

Even before the demise of the gay caballero series, the popularity of this type of film was outstripped by the appearance of the dark lady films, particularly the Mexican spitfire in the person of Lupe Vélez, who elevated the stereotype from a minor role to star billing. Rita Hayworth also got her start this way. Born Margarita Carmen Cansino of a Spanish-born dancer father and his Ziegfield Follies partner Volga Haworth, she was discovered at thirteen dancing at Mexican night spots in Tijuana and Agua Caliente. Her early movies, under the name Rita Cansino, included work in the "Three Mesquiteers" series (a takeoff on both the *Three Musketeers* and the mesquite plant), a seemingly unending cycle of movies featuring trios of cowboys. Everyone did them, including John Wayne, Bob Steele, Tom Tyler, Rufe Davis, Raymond Hatton, Duncan Renaldo, Jimmy Dodd, Ralph Byrd, Bob Livingston, Ray (Crash) Corrigan, and Max Terhune. Rita played, of course, the dark lady, and she was notable in dancing a barroom "La Cucaracha" in *Hit the Saddle* (1937). It was that year that she married the shrewd businessman Edward Judson, who helped her see that being a Hispanic limited her to work as a cinematic loose woman. Under his guidance she changed her name to Rita Hayworth and was transformed from a raven-haired Hispanic dark lady into an auburn-haired sophisticate. By the early 1940s she attained Anglo recognition as the hottest of Hollywood's love goddesses. Her picture in *Life* magazine was so much in demand that it was reproduced in the millions and adorned the atomic bomb that was dropped on Bimini. Raquel Welch (formerly Raquel Tejada) had a similar career as a non-Hispanic and was therefore more acceptable as a love goddess to the mainstream.

Lupe Vélez went the other way and was dead at age thirty-six. Born Guadalupe Vélez de Villalobos in San Luis Potosí, Mexico, in 1910, she was the daughter of an army colonel and an opera singer. Her arrival in Los Angeles was auspicious. She did eight movies in the "Mexican Spitfire" series, had a tempestuous romance with Gary Cooper, married

Another facet of representation has been animated cartoons with Hispanic figures. Mice Speedy González and Slowpoke Rodríguez can still be viewed on television today. These insensitive cartoon images are animated versions of the greaser buffoon, as earlier depicted in Cisco's sidekick. Slowpoke, for example, is the stereotypical sleepy, lazy Mexican. And while Speedy González is energetic enough, neither his frenetic activity accompanied by shouts of ¡Arriba, arriba, arriba! nor his triumphs over cats and coyotes ever overcome his greaser image. Children may not be aware of it, depending on their age, but his name evokes countless obscene jokes focusing on Mexican sexuality.

Johnny Weismuller, with whom she had celebrated rows, and committed suicide, reportedly because she could not face the shame of bearing a child out of wedlock to a man she felt bore her no love (actor Harold Ramond). She was five months pregnant. Ironically, her last film was *Mexican Spitfire's Blessed Event* (1943).

In the early 1930s Hollywood began to produce a number of gangster films, and as one might have predicted, there quickly appeared a greaser-gangster subgenre. The greaser gangster differed from the dark heroes of Prohibition and the Great Depression (such as James Cagney, George Raft, and the early Humphrey Bogart) in crucial ways. He was a treacherous coward, oily, ugly, crude, overdressed, unromantic, and with no loyalty even to his criminal peers. Leo Carrillo played the stereotype faithfully as a gambling, murdering, extorting, pimping, often border bandido in some twenty-five or thirty films. In *Girl of the Río* (1932), he attempted to steal the hand of the glamorous Dolores del Río, a cantina dancer called the Dove. That particular film earned a formal protest on the part of the Mexican government, especially because it portrayed Mexican "justice" as a reflection of who could pay the most for the verdict of their liking.

Ironically, one of the most positive things to happen on behalf of Hispanics with respect to animation was the advent of World War II and the need to be sensitive to Hispanics during wartime. During World War II, Nelson D. Rockefeller's Office for Coordination of Inter-American Affairs asked Walt Disney to make a goodwill tour of Latin America in support of the Good Neighbor policy. The result was two films, *Saludos amigos* (1943), oriented toward Brazil, and *The Three Caballeros* (1945), set in Mexico. The latter film featured Panchito, a sombrero-wearing, pistol-packing rooster. A bit of the stereotype remained in Panchito, but he was a likable, fun-loving, and highly assertive type who showed *el pato Pascual* (a Hispanic Donald Duck) and José Carioca (a Brazilian parrot from *Saludos amigos*) the wonders of Mexico, such as piñata parties, Veracruzan jarochos (dances), posadas (Christmas pageant), and other celebrations of Mexican folklore. Mexico had never been given such a benign, positive image by Hollywood, wherein in the persons of Donald, José, and Panchito, the United States, Brazil and Mexico were three pals, none more equal than the others. Latin American audiences were enchanted by both of these films.

HISPANICS IN FILM DURING THE 1930S AND THE ERA OF

♦ ♦ ♦ ♦ ♦ ♦ ♦ ♦ ♦ ♦ ♦ ♦ ♦ ♦ ♦ ♦ ♦ **SOCIAL CONSCIOUSNESS**

The Great Depression brought with it the gangster movie genre, which produced a new spate of negative Hispanic stereotypes. The depression also brought with it a new genre as well, the "Hollywood social problem film." For the first time, Hispanics were portrayed in a somewhat different, and occasionally radically different, light in these Hollywood movies.

The economic breakdown represented by the Depression, the rise of fascism and other totalitarianism movements worldwide, the war against these political forms of oppression, and the idealistic vigor of the post–World War II years (up to the advent of McCarthyism) all fostered concern with social conditions, an impulse toward political change. The theater of Clifford Odets, the novels and screenplays of John Steinbeck, and the songs of Woody Guthrie all found a large public response to their criticism of American society, government, and business during the period.

This era of social consciousness also found reflection in Hollywood social problem films, which usually were produced in accordance with the conventions of the Hollywood Formula. The Hollywood conventions were that America is a series of social institutions that from time to time experience "problems" that, like those of an automobile, need to be tinkered with and corrected. For the most part, the films attacked such problems in order to inspire limited social change or restore the status quo to an "ideal" level of efficiency. While the Hollywood social problem genre places great importance on the surface mechanisms of society, only an indirect or covert treatment is given to the broader social values (those of the family, sexuality, religion, and so on) that function behind and govern the mechanisms.

In depicting Chicanos, Mexicans, and other Hispanics, the social problem vehicle produced some noteworthy if flawed films, but a review of the overall film production reveals that the positive depiction of Hispanics was still the exception rather than the rule. *Bordertown* (1935, starring Paul Muni in brownface and Bette Davis in her standard performance as a lunatic) is the first Hispanic social problem film. The central concern is not the oppression of Chicanos but rather who committed a murder.

What social comment exists functions as a sedative against militancy by Hispanics. The filmic creation of Johnny Ramírez was certainly a more complex one than the standard Hollywood border type. Relative psychological complexity aside, the soothing conventions of the Hollywood Formula determine the finale. The film ends with Ramírez, disillusioned over the corruption and meanness of success, returning to his barrio home. He says his confession to the priest, prays with his mother, and all three walk down the church aisle. The padre asks, "Well, Johnny, what are you going to do now?" and Johnny gives the expected reply, "Come back and live among my own people where I belong." *Bordertown* hypothesizes that for a Chicano, success is fruitless and undesirable, that true virtue lies in accepting life as it is. Ramírez has learned the padre's lesson of patience and no longer holds impractical ambitions. *Bordertown* celebrates stoic acquiescence to the status quo and denigrates the aspiration for social change.

Despite the limitations of the social problem film, it is certainly true that psychologically complex and occasionally resolute and strong characters emerged from this genre. Among them are several Chicano protagonists in *Giant* (1956), including the proud and dedicated nurse María Ramírez, who experiences the racism of Texans; the family of Leo Mimosa, who is buried alive in a New Mexico cave in Billy Wilder's notable *The Big Carnival* (1951), which depicts a tragic act of God turned into a public relations event; and Katy Jurado and Pina Pellicer, the women in *One-Eyed Jacks* (1961, starring Marlon Brando). Occasionally the strong and resolute character is also "evil," as in *Washington Masquerade* (1932), one of the earliest of the "political machine and country crusader" series of films that include *Washington Merry-Go-Round* (1932) and the Frank Capra series: *Mr. Deeds Goes to Town* and *You Can't Take it With You* (1938), *Mr. Smith Goes To Washington* (1939), and *Meet John Doe* (1941). *Washington Masquerade* proclaims that "the running of the U.S. has fallen into bad hands!" and proceeds to identify clearly whose hands they are—Hispanic ones! Unbelievable as this may be, given the lack of political visibility, much less power, of Hispanics in the real world of 1932, the villain is an oily, Latin-like (and hence un-American) lobbyist whose influence extends through all levels of government.

The socially conscious era of the Great Depression and its aftermath brought in a new wave of Anglo Good Samaritans who acted on behalf of innocent and defenseless Mexicans. Some of this character development and plot existed in the silent era as well: *Mexicans on the Río Grande* (1914), *A Mexican's Gratitude* (1909), *Land Baron of San Tee* (1912). In films such as *Border G-Man* (1938), *Durango Valley Raiders* (1938), and

Rose of the Rancho (1936), or for that matter in the pertinent films of Hopalong Cassidy, Gene Autry, the Lone Ranger, Roy Rogers, and Tex Ritter (*In Old Mexico* (1938), *Song of Gringo* (1936), *South of the Border* (1939), and numerous others), the emphasis changes from the hero as implacable and brutal conqueror of greasers to the hero as implacable and devoted defender of Mexican rights, typically as he tramps touristlike through the exotic local Hispanic community, whether it be north or south of the border. Often the Anglo is fighting bad Mexicans on behalf of good, defenseless, passive Mexicans. The acts of these Good Samaritans strongly reinforce the stereotype of Mexicans as people who are unable to help themselves.

The most daring and best realized of the Hispanic-focused social problem films are *The Lawless* (1950) and *Salt of the Earth* (1954). The former was a low-budget independent released through Paramount, while the latter was made outside the studio system altogether by blacklisted artists, including writer Michael Wilson, producer Paul Jarrico, and director Herbert Biberman. It is precisely because neither was made within the confines of the studio that a profounder and more artistically elaborated interpretation of racial oppression is realized. In contrast to the usual treatment, which views racial prejudice against minorities as the product of a white sociopath or other such deranged troublemaker who is then blamed for inciting a mostly ingenuous but somewhat blameless populace, the lynch mob violence in *The Lawless* and the vicious labor strife in *Salt of the Earth* are deemed to be typically middle American. In these films, by stereotyping "spics" as lazy and no-good, people find a scapegoat for their hatreds and a rationale for injustice.

Closely aligned to the social problem films were the historical "message" pictures such as Warners' Paul Muni biography cycle initiated with *The Life of Emile Zola* (1937), which devoted considerable attention to the Dreyfuss affair (but only fleetingly alluded to the anti-Semitic element). Two major films focused on Mexico emerged from this cycle, *Juárez* (1939) and the renowned *Viva Zapata!* (1952). *Juárez* featured Paul Muni in the title role, Bette Davis as Carlotta, and John Garfield as a youthful Porfirio Díaz learning Lincolnesque democracy at the master's feet. This was another film marked by renewed efforts on the eve of the war by Franklin Roosevelt's administration to enhance the Good Neighbor policy. The passage of the years has not been good to *Juárez*, but despite its faults, which include the cultural chauvinism of an omnipresent Lincoln, the film rises far above the standard degrading stereotypes of Hollywood. *Juárez* reflects relatively accurate documentation of Mexican history and society, and it impressed not only the American audience for whom it was intended, but the Mexican public as well.

The clear masterpiece of the "message" biographies, *Viva Zapata!* (screenplay by John Steinbeck, direction by Elia Kazan, and starring Marlon Brando and Anthony Quinn) is also one of the best Hollywood Hispanic-focused films. The film is not free of problems and stereotypes, many of which relate to turning Zapata into a Hollywood-style "hero" at the expense of historical veracity; nevertheless, it is the most comprehensive and attentive Hollywood film ever produced about the Mexican Revolution—with the possible exception of *Old Gringo* (1988), which is not accurately a "Hollywood" film. One of the reasons for the enduring popularity of the film is precisely the nature and complexity of the message. The film is not only about power and rebellion but also about the ways of corruption and how easy it is for a social movement to be debased. Zapata resists the corruption of his brother, the power-hungry Fernando, who betrays the revolution and goes to the side of Huerta, and he even resists the tendency of the *campesinos* to look for heroes or leaders to whom they can abdicate their own responsibilities.

In addition to *Viva Zapata!*, John Steinbeck did several other treatments of Hispanic material. His other contributions make for a mixed, but on balance, positive record. In 1941 he wrote the screenplay and collaborated with director/producer Herbert Kline to film *The Forgotten Village*, an artistic semidocumentary about science versus superstition in a small Mexican mountain village. This film, which was done outside the studio system, won numerous prizes as a feature documentary but played only in small independent art theaters because it did not benefit from studio distribution. In 1954 Steinbeck helped write the screenplay for *A Medal for Benny*, adapted from one of his paisano (rustic Hispanic) short stories. Starring Arturo de Córdova and Dorothy Lamour, this comedy treats the hypocrisy of town officials who exploit the posthumous awarding of the Congressional Medal of Honor to a brawling paisano. It contains many of the stereotypes of Hispanics (drunkenness, immaturity, brawling, but also a chivalric sense of honor), that mark the novel *Tortilla Flat* which was also adapted into a film (1942, starring Spencer Tracy, John Garfield, Hedy Lamarr, Akim Tamiroff, and Academy Award nominee for supporting actor Frank Morgan), but without Steinbeck's participation. *Benny* was a critical and box office success, and Steinbeck and his cowriter received Academy Award nominations. This film, however, is hardly his best effort at depicting Hispanics.

The 1948 production *The Pearl* was cowritten by Steinbeck, Emilio "El Indio" Fernández, and Jack Wagner (who also cowrote *Benny*). In addition, "El Indio" Fernández directed it, and it starred Pedro Armendáriz. *The Pearl* was in fact a Mexican movie, the first to be widely distributed (by RKO) in the United States. The film, an adaptation of the novella, is a well-made, sensitive, and genuine treatment of Mexican fishermen, as might be expected of the Mexican director and crew. The plot itself is a parable of a poor Mexican fisherman who learns that wealth brings corruption and death. The critical response and the box office receipts on this film were respectable, but it has not endured.

Even as significant Hispanic films of the social problem and historical message varieties were being produced, in parallel fashion other films of the earlier genres continued unabated. Enormous numbers of westerns were produced in the period between the Great Depression and the civil rights movement. A small fraction of those containing significant Hispanic elements include the following, in chronological order, concentrating on the more notable westerns: *Billy the Kid* (1930, King Vidor, director), *The Ox-Bow Incident* (1943, William Wellman, director; Anthony Quinn, Henry Fonda), *The Outlaw* (1943, Howard Hughes, director; Jane Russell), *My Darling Clementine* (1946, John Ford, director; Linda Darnell, Victor Mature), *Treasure of the Sierra Madre* (1947, John Huston, director; Humphrey Bogart, Alfonso Bedoya), *The Fugitive* (1947, John Ford, director; Henry Fonda, Pedro Armendáriz, Dolores del Río), *The Furies* (1950, Barbara Stanwyck, Gilbert Roland), *Branded* (1951, Alan Ladd), *High Noon* (1952, Gary Cooper, Katy Jurado), *Rancho Notorious* (1952, Fritz Lang, director; Marlene Dietrich), *Ride Vaquero* (1953, Anthony Quinn), *Veracruz* (1954, Robert Aldrich, director; Gary Cooper, Sarita Montiel), *The Burning Hills* (1956, Tab Hunter, Natalie Wood), *The Sheepman* (1958, Glenn Ford), *The Left-Handed Gun* (1958, Arthur Penn, director; Paul Newman), and *Río Bravo* (1959, Howard Hawks, director; John Wayne, Dean Martin, Ricky Nelson).

Billy the Kid, The Outlaw, The Left-Handed Gun, and much later *Pat Garrett and Billy the Kid* (1973) form part of the cycle on that folk hero; each of these films perpetuates the legend of the Kid as the friend of oppressed Hispanos and the foe of the Anglo cattle barons.

Most of these films perpetuate the three major Hispanic stereotypes of the western—dark lady, bandido, and buffoon. The more substantial dark lady roles of the westerns of the 1930s through the 1950s have been assigned to mistresses of white gunmen. This is the case in such films as *My Darling Clementine, Veracruz,* and, above all, the classic *High Noon,* which is undoubtedly the best of these films.

While some opportunities for Hispanics to work in the film industry remained in the western genre between the Great Depression and 1960, notwithstanding the fact that even here many of the parts were played by Anglos, in other genres the Hispanic presence was, in fact, greatly diminished. Some World War II movies contained a bit part from time to time for a Hispanic character, presumably to promote patriotism, a sense of unity, and the brotherhood (not yet sisterhood in these self-satisfied times) of races against the fascist menace.

DECLINE OF THE PRODUCTION CODE, EMERGENCE OF THE CIVIL RIGHTS MOVEMENT, AND NEW DEVELOPMENTS IN FILM: 1960S AND 1970S ♦

The 1960s witnessed two important social developments that had significant impact on filmmaking: a liberalizing or loosening of social values, often referred to as the sexual revolution, and the emergence of the civil rights movement. The first phenomenon was a factor in the decline of the production code. Beginning in the 1960s, films became much bolder in their depiction of sex, including interracial sex, and violence. However, this was a double-edged sword for Hispanics and other minorities because often they were cast in roles where their villainy was far more graphic and horrifying than the snarling but ineffective criminal or would-be rapist of blander times. In this sense, the stereotypes of many Hispanic characters were actually intensified by the relaxation of Hollywood moral codes.

The 1960s and 1970s were marked by far more diversity in films but also by a group of films that featured even more serious, racially damaging putdowns of Hispanics. For example, the bandidos were often engaged in visually explicit and gory violence, and the torrid Hispanas were now engaged in R-rated loose sex with Anglo heroes or an occasional black superstud. The Hispano became the toy of Anglo producers, directors and audiences, all competing in the effort to create for Anglos ever more titillat-

audiences, all competing in the effort to create for Anglos ever more titillating and vicariously experienced films. As a result, new subgenres of film emerged, such as the fiendish group of plotters (particularly the group western), featuring casual brutality and other actions that Anglos stereotypically and inaccurately identify under the rubric of "macho." The word "macho" entered the Anglo lexicon in a way that is ungrammatical in Spanish as an abstract quality in adjective form ("mucho macho" could be heard from time to time in bars or seen on T-shirts around the nation).

Moreover, by the 1960s there emerged the "good-bad bandidos." An example is Clint Eastwood in *The Good, the Bad, and the Ugly* (1967), where the Anglo hero teams up with the Mexican bandit, Tuco the Terrible (Eli Wallach), to steal gold. In this film, typical of the new, amoral western, both Anglos and Mexicans are equally evil from the moral perspective and good becomes merely identified with technical skills such as a quick draw or creative thievery.

While in *The Good, the Bad, and the Ugly* the Anglo descends to the level of the stereotypical greaser, the converse is true in the extremely popular group western, *The Magnificent Seven* (1960) (which spawned sequels: *Return of the Seven*, 1966, and *Guns of the Magnificent Seven*, 1969). Unfortunately for Hispanic actors in this film, which is about the defense of a Mexican village against a Mexican bandit, the stereotypical greaser role is not even played by a Hispanic, but by Eli Wallach, who was to become the new Leo Carrillo, replaying the greaser-style performance in a number of Italian and Spanish-based "spaghetti" westerns.

This trend toward amorality reached its extremes in the 1960s and 1970s films that revolved around the Mexican Revolution of 1910, taking the image of Hispanics and the understanding of those events a giant step backward from the peak that was established by *Viva Zapata!* In the amoral westerns of director Sergio Leone—*A Fistful of Dollars* (1967), its sequel, *For A Few Dollars More* (1967), and *Duck, You Sucker* (1972)—the viewer is given no moral guidelines to measure or judge the revolution. Both the *federales* and the rebels are repulsive. If the former are sadistic, pretentious, class-conscious, and stupid, the latter are sadistic, filthy, promiscuous, contemptuous, and stupid.

The cycle of Pancho Villa movies displays the same sort of denigration. The first Villa film of the sound era, *Viva Villa!* (1934), presented the revolutionary hero as a sadistic Robin Hood. Subsequent films, *Villa!* (1958) and *Villa Rides* (1968), stray little from this general depiction. The latest film to depict Villa, *Old Gringo* (1989), based on a novel by Mexican novelist Carlos Fuentes and produced by Jane Fonda with the avowed intention of injecting realism into the relationship between the United States and Mexico, stands in marked positive contrast to the rest of the cycle.

Set against the simplistic, amoral standard of most of the other westerns of these years, the work of Sam Peckinpah, particularly *The Wild Bunch* (1969), *Pat Garrett and Billy the Kid* (1973), and *Bring Me the Head of Alfredo García* (1974), developed a more sophisticated view of Hispanics, particularly in the context of the Mexican Revolution in the case of *The Wild Bunch*. In that film the two Mexicos of the revolution are rendered in the contrast between Angel, the morally pure *villista* who represents Mexican village life, and Mapache, the degenerate revolutionary. In a film that is, ironically, one of the most violent on record, Angel occupies a pivotal role in that by his Christlike example he turns the drifting, amoral Anglo mercenaries to good purpose and sacrifice, thus redeeming them. *The Wild Bunch* is one of the most memorable films of the period, combining outsized violence and explicit sex with a certain sense of high moral purpose and interethnic camaraderie. In its own way, it is a distinctively realized combination of the decline of the moral code and the rise of civil rights.

Sporadic examples of Hispanic avenger types existed during the silent period, although not usually directed against Anglos but rather against *federales* of the Mexican government. The first major appearance of the type is in the western *The Ox-Bow Incident* (1943). Here Anthony Quinn plays a Mexican who is hanged along with two Anglos for murdering a Nevada cowboy. Of the three, he is the only one to die with his dignity and honor intact, subverting the stereotypical role of the cowardly and inept greaser. These pre-civil rights examples, however, have a quite different tone about them, primarily because they were pitched to a non-Hispanic audience. This is the case, as well, of the films *Death of a Gunfighter* (1969) and *The Outrage* (1964), which also depict assertive Hispanics, even though they are not part of the Hispanic exploitation model. In *Death of a Gunfighter* the aging white marshall (Richard Widmark) has become an embarrassment to a prospering Kansas town that no longer needs him. In the final, shocking scene, the shopkeepers and bankers gun him down, leaving his Chicana mistress without a husband after a last-minute wedding ceremony.

Even with the emergence of the Hispanic avenger, which somewhat reflected the atmosphere of the civil rights movement, and the emergence of a more sexually titillating dark lady, which primarily reflected the relaxation of the Hollywood production code, the film industry continued to grind out westerns with buffoons and bandidos. *The Sheepman* (1958) provided a comic sidekick to the Anglo played by Glenn Ford, and in *Río Bravo* (1959) we view the antics of Carlos and Consuela, a comedy couple. In *The Train Robbery* (1973), John Wayne's gun quickly turns a Mexican railroad engineer from a "¡No! ¡No!" stance to a "¡Sí! ¡Sí!"

The role of the bandido took on certain variations that reflected Hollywood's exploitation of attitudinal changes. On the one hand, there existed the straight evil bandido, the continuation of the type from the earliest period, except that with the relaxation of the Hollywood morality codes this character suddenly became more "competent." Whereas the earliest version was usually a tame utterer of incomplete curses or hisses who was incapable of really delivering evil, at least on screen—he might tie the girl to the railroad track or inside a house he would set on fire, but the deed was never consummated—the new breed practiced mayhem, sadism, and sex. Anthony Quinn in *Ride Vaquero!* (1953) enjoys killing men and raping women and maims a cattleman for life in a sadistic shooting. The earlier, classic performance of Alfonso Bedoya and his gang, who brawl over their victims' boots in *Treasure of the Sierra Madre* (1947) is another of the same variety. A xenophobic variation on the same theme was John Wayne's (director and star) *The Alamo* (1961). This film, which takes egregious liberties with the facts, not only depicts Mexicans as violent and inept, but was promoted by means of a shamelessly ultrapatriotic advertising campaign. In 1969, Hollywood took another crack at the Alamo with *Viva Max*, starring Peter Ustinov as a bumbling Mexican buffoon who retakes the historic site from the Anglos in contemporary times. This film, without a single Hispanic in any significant role, was hardly as offensive as the Wayne vehicle, and pitted inept Americans against incompetent Mexicans. In contrast to the patriotic froth associated with *The Alamo*, however, the latter film inspired minor demonstrations in several cities where it played, a good index of the progress of the civil rights movement over the 1960s.

Beginning in the 1960s and intensifying in the 1970s, changes in American society and consequently American film and television made the roles of dark lady and Latin lover considerably less important. One of these changes related to ethnicity. Particularly in the 1970s, Hollywood and other media centers rediscovered the significance of ethnicity, both from the point of view of plot and of box office. However, the primary ethnicity that was cultivated was the Italian American, and secondarily the Jewish American, Slavic, and Afro-American. This period witnessed the rise to stardom of such actors as Robert De Niro, Sylvester Stallone, Al Pacino, Barbra Streisand, and others. However, the cultivation of various U.S. cultures and ethnicities primarily reflected English-speaking groups, not Spanish or other non-English-speakers. In the increased attention to multi-ethnicity, the Hispanic variety played a limited role.

The phenomenon of increased multiculturalism in plots and acting styles combined with yet another factor to the detriment of hispanidad in film, namely, the expectation of increased sexuality on the part of actors and actresses, irrespective of their culture. While this expectation produced degrading stereotypes, it also provided considerable work for Hispanic actors and actresses, who consistently had roles exposing their "hot-blooded" nature. In contrast to the earlier traditions of Anglos and some of the other ethnicities who were expected to be aloof, glacial, and dispassionate, the film expectations of the 1960s to this day cultivate unabashed carnality and hot-bloodedness on the part of all actors and actresses, whatever their national origin.

The civil rights period beginning in the 1960s also marked an important change in hiring patterns in the film industry with respect to directors, camera crew, and other production people. For the first time, an effort was made to bring Hispanics into production, and it was this cadre of professionals who were the primary group to go on to make Hispanic films. However, the introduction of Hispanic avenger films, group westerns, and other Hispanic-focused subgenres usually did not carry with it more work for Hispanic actors. The 1960s and 1970s were not particularly advantageous for Hispanics in acting roles, since more often than not, non-Hispanic actors were awarded the roles of Hispanic characters. For example, George Chakiris and John Saxon, respectively, got the Hispanic leading parts in *West Side Story* (1961) and *Death of a Gunfighter*, and Burt Lancaster, Charles Bronson, and Paul Newman were the respective leads in *Valdez is Coming, Mr. Majestyk*, and *The Outrage*. *The Young Savages* (1961), starring Burt Lancaster, was about gang war between Italians and Puerto Ricans, the latter played by non-Hispanic actors. *The Professionals* (1966) featured Claudia Cardinale as a "María" and Jack Palance as Jesús Raza, who kidnaps her and sweeps her off her feet. *Villa Rides* (1968) featured Yul Brynner as Pancho Villa and Charles Bronson and Herbert Lom in the other significant Hispanic roles. *Che!* (1969) starred Omar Sharif and Jack Palance in the incongruous roles, respectively, of Che Guevara and Fidel Castro. *Night of the Iguana* (1964), starring Richard Burton, Deborah Kerr, and Ava Gardner all in Anglo roles, exemplified the Hollywood trend of filming on Latin location, but mostly for the purpose of local color, preferring stories reflecting non-Hispanic characters.

Despite successes in having some stereotypes eliminated, they remained abundant. In addition to the more intensive violence and sadism of Hispanic characters prevalent in the westerns of the period, gang films also abounded during the 1960s and 1970s. It was probably a factor in a spate of either Hispanic-focused exploitation, juvenile delinquent or gang films or films with other premises that brought in Hispanic gang members for their recognition value, such as *The Pawnbroker* (1965), *Change of Habit* (1969), *Badge 373* (1973), *Assault on Precinct Thirteen* (1976, a multiethnic gang, director, John Carpenter), *Boardwalk* (1979), *Boulevard Nights* (1979, Richard Yñiguez, Danny de la Paz), *Walk Proud* (1979, featuring blue-eyed Robby Benson in contact lenses as a Hispanic), *The Exterminator* (1980), and many others. With the aid of feverish media attention dedicated to gangs, the cycle has been running strong to the present day.

The urban violence (primarily juvenile gang) film has been exploitative of Anglo willingness to pay for explicit sex and brutality—both premeditated and mindless—and the pleasures of vicariously induced but moviehouse-controlled fear of the alien. These films play upon the baser assumptions about Hispanic youth and mostly do damage to racial relations in our society. To add insult to injury, Hispanic actors do not even get the top parts in these films. *Boulevard Nights* did, however, rise above the pap. While the film is not without its defects, particularly an inaccurate understanding in some respects of Chicano mores by the Japanese-American screenwriter, Desmond Nakomo, it does have an all-Latino cast, reasonably successful use of Chicano and pachuco dialect, and a serious theme and plot development that includes Hispanic violence against Hispanics—an all-too-real phenomenon of gang life. It deserves recognition, within B movie limitations, as one of the better Hollywood achievements in Chicano-focused film.

In *Badge 373* (1973), a minor follow-up to *The French Connection*, Robert Duvall singlehandedly fights the Mafia as well as Puerto Ricans who are blamed for all sorts of evil and wrongdoing. Whatever might be thought of *Colors* (1988), also starring Duvall, it represents a major advance in the Hollywood understanding of gang psychology. *The Warriors* (1978), although its artistry demands more respect than most of the others, primarily perpetuates the usual stereotypes.

West Side Story (directed by Robert Wise with Natalie Wood, Richard Beymer, George Chakiris, and Rita Moreno), the cinematic adaptation of the Broadway musical, was a groundbreaking film that won numerous Academy Awards. Unfortunately, only one Hispanic, Rita Moreno, had a major role in the film. The updating of Romeo and Juliet had a major influence on the musical genre, but in drawing attention to Hispanic gangs, its greatest impact appears to have been in helping to turn the juvenile delinquent or gang film away from blacks primarily (for example, The Blackboard Jungle, 1955, Glenn Ford, Sidney Poitier) in the direction of Hispanics.

George Chakiris as Bernardo in a scene from the movie West Side Story.

Revolution in Latin America became a common topic of films in the 1970s. Curiously enough, in contrast to the serious and solemn 1980s (*Salvador, Prisoner Without a Name, Cell Without a Number, Old Gringo, Latino, Missing, Under Fire, Romero,* and so on), many of these films were screwball comedies, a long-standing Hollywood genre now attached to a new environment. In addition to Woody Allen's *Bananas* (1971) were *The In-Laws* (1979), starring Peter Falk. Brothers Luis and Daniel Valdez both had parts in the Richard Pryor comedy *Which Way Is Up?* (1977). In a more common mode, *Viva Max!* appeared in 1969, describing, in opera-buffa style, the Chicano retaking of the Alamo. When Hollywood attempted contemporary Latin American revolutionary topics or other Latin American material in a serious fashion during this period, as in *Che* and *Night of the Iguana*, the results were more uninspired than the comic attempts. *Iguana* was particularly disappointing in its turning of the admittedly minor Mexican characters into mere cutout figures of sexuality.

♦ ♦ ♦ ♦ ♦ ♦ ♦ ♦ ♦ ♦ ♦ ♦ ♦ ♦ ♦ **HOLLYWOOD FILMS SINCE 1980**

The period from 1980 to the present has been a relatively exhilarating one for Hispanics in the film industry, especially over the last few years, primarily because of three sets of closely interrelated events or trends. The first is the increased appreciation of the importance of Hispanic culture and the Hispanic population in the United States. It became generally understood that demographics projected that Hispanics were to become the largest minority group in the United States some time early in the twenty-first century. This underlying fact of population power and consequently political, economic, and cultural importance spurred all sorts of film, television, and video initiatives for and by Hispanics. It even underlay their national promotion, as exemplified by an extended article in *Time* magazine that featured Edward James Olmos on its cover, the first time in memory that any Hispanic, much less an actor and filmmaker, had achieved such recognition.

A second factor, somewhat encouraged by the Hollywood appreciation of Hispanic box office potential, was the emergence of a considerable number of actors and filmmakers who attained star status or national recognition during the contemporary period. These included Edward James Olmos, Raúl Juliá, Andy García, and Emilio Estévez. Similarly, film figures who had labored under less recognized conditions in the 1970s also made quantum leaps with respect to their weight in the film industry, including Moctezuma Esparza, Luis Valdez, Ricardo Mestre, and Martin Sheen.

Finally, with more interest in the U.S. in Hispanic themes and market penetration and more power and recognition of Hispanic actors and film-

John Singleton's Boyz in the Hood *and Joseph Vásquez's* Hangin' With the Homeboys *(both 1991) are gang films in a class by themselves. Essentially created outside of the Hollywood system, Columbia distributed the former and the latter was released through New Line Cinema.*

A scene from Boulevard Nights.

makers, came more control of product within Hollywood. For the first time a Hispanic, Ricardo Mestre of Disney, was to run a major studio. Similarly, Moctezuma Esparza coestablished Esparza/Katz Productions, raising tens of millions of dollars for a variety of projects, some but not all Hispanic-focused. Edward James Olmos, Andy García, Joseph P. Vásquez, and the comedian Paul Rodríguez all entered the film production business, with considerable diversity in their level of affiliation with or independent from traditional Hollywood sources of backing. Both the number of production outlets and either realized or pending film deals and the number of actors and other filmmakers with national recognition has never been greater, surpassing even a few "silver" years of the silent period when Latin lovers and hot-blooded Latinas were in great demand, albeit with virtually no control over their acting roles. On the other hand, it should be noted that Afro-American filmmakers made even greater strides during the current period, led by Spike Lee, John Singleton, and many others.

The current period also marked the strong emergence of a phenomenon called Hispanic Hollywood by the mass media. Although Chicano films such as *Zoot Suit* had been released by the mainstream industry before, between the summer of 1987 and spring of 1988 Hollywood released four films that depicted the Chicano experience: *La Bamba* (1987), *Born in East L.A.* (1987), *The Milagro Beanfield War* (1987), and *Stand and Deliver* (1988). The Hispanic directors, producers, and writers who made these films had typically been in very junior roles in the film and television industry and then began to work as principals in the conceptualization, development, and execution of alternative, independent Hispanic films, such as *Seguín, Alambrista!* (Fence Jumper), and *Once in a Lifetime*. Now they entered the mainstream as well (although not necessarily giving up their commitments to independent, alternative films), bringing Hollywood production values to the creation of strong Hispanic images that also had (or at least were intended to have) box office appeal and arranging for distribution through mainstream outlets. The cross-pollination and collaboration inherent in the Hispanic Hollywood phenomenon ran the gamut—from *The Milagro Beanfield War,* where Anglos carried most of the picture (directed by Robert Redford, the script was based on the novel by Anglo connoisseur of New Mexican culture John Nichols) and consequently Hispanics had secondary, although highly significant, roles—to *Stand and Deliver*, where essentially the entire film, including scripting, producing, financing, directing, and acting, was conducted by Hispanics until the point of distribution, when the appeal of the film earned it release through mainstream industry channels.

Since 1980, several films have focused on Latin America, reflecting the political situation of the region or drug-running or both. These include *Missing* (1982), starring Jack Lemmon and Sissy Spacek, which takes place during the overthrow of Salvador Allende in Chile; *Under Fire* (1983), starring Nick Nolte and Joanna Cassidy as journalists in the midst of the 1979 Sandinista revolution in Nicaragua; *Salvador* (1986), cowritten and directed by Oliver Stone, featuring Jim Belushi; *Latino* (1985), directed by Haskell Wexler, about the anti-Samoza uprising; *Under the Volcano* (1984), featuring Jacqueline Bisset and Albert Finney, an adaptation of Malcom Lowry's classic novel; and *Havana* (1991), a failed movie starring Robert Redford as a gambler with a heart of gold who becomes embroiled in plots to overthrow dictator Batista in 1959. The poorly done but financially successful *Scarface* (1983), directed by Brian de Palma, starring Al Pacino, more or less feeds at the same trough, although it also focuses on Hispanic drug runners in the U.S.

The 1980s witnessed several films dealing with the *indocumentado* (undocumented worker). Undocumented immigration from Mexico became a movie theme as early as the 1932 *I Cover the Waterfront*, but the undocumented were Chinese being smuggled by sea from Mexico to San Diego. This theme continued into the 1940s; the 1941 *Hold Back the Dawn* dramatized the desperate efforts of European refugees living temporarily in Tijuana to enter the United States. Not until the post–World War II era did films like *Border Incident* (1949), *Borderline* (1950), *The Lawless* (1950), and *Wetbacks* (1956) begin to deal with Mexican immigrants, although the immigrants usually functioned as passive pawns to incite Anglo crime and Anglo crime–fighting. *Border Incident* (1949, directed by Anthony Mann, starring Ricardo Montalbán) is a quite violent, well-made crime story of the social problem era, also rife with the usual stereotypes, as was the original *Borderline* (1950, Fred MacMurray, Claire Trevor), with an unlikely plot featuring law enforcers tracking down dope smugglers on the Mexican border. During the past two decades, as undocumented immigration has become a more widely debated public issue, a new wave of films has emerged: *Blood Barrier* (1979, Telly Savalas, Danny de la Paz), *Borderline* (1980, Charles Bronson), and *The Border* (1982, Jack Nicholson, Harvey Keitel, Valerie Perrine, Elpidia Carillo). Nevertheless, the theme of passive Mexican immigrants being saved by noble Anglos has continued to dominate. None of these Hollywood films has ever risen above the mediocre. The films of the 1980s have scarcely improved upon the first of the lot in terms of veracity, character development, or aesthetics. Hollywood *indocumentado* pictures have never surpassed the limitations of the social problem genre as originally conceived in the 1930s and 1940s.

In contrast to the stock characterizations of the Hollywood versions, two independently produced Hispanic works *Alambrista!* (1979) and *El Norte* (*The North*, 1983) shine because of their strong and distinctive plot developments and intriguing characters. Similarly, Cheech Marín's *Born in East L.A.* (1987) shines as a Hispanic Hollywood exception to the bleakness of the rest, precisely because it combined Hispanic expertise and sensitivity to Hollywood production values.

In the area of comedy, the current period has been marked by the films of the comic team Richard "Cheech" Marín and Thomas Chong, who began by adapting their nightclub act to film in *Cheech and Chong's Up in Smoke* (1978), featuring stoned hippy routines. The film became the highest-grossing film of the year and spurred a number of 1980s sequels, includ-

Carmen Miranda in one of the hats she made famous.

ing *Cheech and Chong's Next Movie* (1980), *Cheech and Chong's Nice Dreams* (1981), *Things are Tough All Over* (1982), *Yellowbeard* (1983), and *Cheech and Chong's The Corsican Brothers* (1984).

Despite some innovations during the current period that brought Hispanic actors and filmmakers to the fore, the industry continued, as it has always done, to create more exploitative films. Among these, *Salsa* (1988) was a Hispanic version of *Dirty Dancing* (1987) that attempted to "out-dirty" it. *The Penitent* (1988, Raúl Juliá, Julie Carmen) was a muddle that featured the eternal triangle set against the local color of New Mexican *penitentes*. *Moon Over Parador* (1988, Richard Dreyfuss, Sonia Braga, Raúl Juliá) made liberal use of the usual stereotypes about Latin America and its dictators for uninspired humor. *The Believers* (1987, Martin Sheen, Jimmy Smits) abused Santería in order to make a horror/thriller. *Young Guns* (1988, Emilio Estévez, Lou Diamond Phillips, Charlie Sheen) updated the Billy the Kid cycle, having us believe that the Kid whips up the inherent violence of six young punks, including Hispanic members. *Bad Boys* (1983, Sean Penn, Esai Morales) weighs in among the newest gang films. This one, in which both Sean Penn and Morales are superb, features a personal vendetta within prison walls. Morales, who has been badly typecast merely as a Hispanic gang member, got to do his repartee also in *The Principal* (1987), featuring Jim Belushi overpowering the Hispanic youth warlord, somewhat reminiscent of the way honest Anglo do-gooders used to bring down Hispanic and other alien powerbrokers in the 1940s films. On the other hand, the gang film *Colors* (1988), directed by Dennis Hopper and starring Sean Penn, Robert Duvall, María Conchita Alonso, Rudy Ramos and Trinidad Silva, is a superior version of the genre, with the notable exception of the misuse of the Alonso romantic subplot. Trinidad Silva is excellent in this film, as he is in *The Night Before* (1988), an offbeat comedy about a young man on a senior prom who wakes up in an East Los Angeles alley.

THE EMERGENCE OF HISPANIC FILMS ♦ ♦ ♦ ♦ ♦ ♦ ♦ ♦ ♦ ♦ ♦ ♦

Chicano Cinema   In a certain sense, the emergence of Chicano cinema has been the result of new, energetic actions on the part of the film industry to increase the participation of Chicanos and other minorities in the craft of filmmaking. In that sense, it was perhaps unexpected—at least by industry executives— and due more to prodding by the courts, by certain sectors of society, such as college students, and above all by the civil rights movement. The film corporations did hire Chicanos, but for general work in the profession and not necessarily for the production of Chicano films.

As Chicano actors, filmmakers, and other professionals began entering the industry and, particularly, receiving their apprenticeships through the production of documentaries on varied subject matter, their sensitivities inevitably turned to the Chicano experience, primarily because the *raza* story was there, beckoning and untold.

First Films

The Chicanos who entered the studios on the production side were soon producing and directing a series of politically aware documentaries on the Chicano experience. Among the most significant of these are David García's *Requiem-29* (1971), which describes the East Los Angeles riot of 1970 and the circumstances surrounding the suspicious death of Chicano reporter Rubén Salazar. Jesús Treviño's *América Tropical* (1971) is about the whitewashing of a Siquieros mural in Los Angeles. Severo Pérez's *Cristal* (1975) is about Crystal City, "Spinach Capital of the World" and birthplace of the Raza Unida party. Jesús Treviño's *Yo soy chicano* (*I Am Chicano*, 1972) was the first Chicano film to be nationally televised and to deal with the Chicano movement from its roots in pre-Columbian history to the activism of the present. José Luis Ruíz's *Cinco vidas* (*Five Lives*, 1972) glosses over the lives of five Chicanos and Chicanas of varied backgrounds and experiences. Jesús Treviño's *La raza unida* (*The United People*, 1972) covers the 1972 national convention of the Raza Unida party. Ricardo Soto's *A la brava* (*With Courage*, 1973) describes the condition of Chicano convicts at Soledad prison. Rick Tejada-Flores's *Sí se puede* (*Yes It Can Be Done*, 1973) records César Chávez's twenty-four-day fast in Arizona to protest proposed antistrike legislation. José Luis Ruíz's *The Unwanted* (1974) depicts the difficulties of the *indocumentado* population, and Ricardo Soto's *A Political Renaissance* (1974) examines the contemporary emergence of Chicano political power.

From 1975 to the present, the pace of Chicano documentary cinema has accelerated enormously. Scores of films have been produced. Following are brief notations of some of the most significant documentary productions.

Anthropological and Folkloric Films

Among the most notable documentaries of the anthropological or folkloric type are Esperanza Vázquez and Moctezuma Esparza's *Agueda Martínez* (1977), nominated for an Academy Award in 1978, and Michael Earney's *Luisa Torres* (1981). Both documentaries depict the lifestyles of elderly women in northern New Mexico. Also outstanding are Les Blank's *Chulas fronteras* (*Beautiful Border*, 1976), and its sequel, *Del mero corazón* (*From the Heart*, 1979), which beautifully evoke the *norteña* or *conjunto* music prevalent in the Texas-Mexico border region and throughout the Southwest.

Homer A. Villarreal's *Expression: The Miracle of Our Faith* (1978) is about the practices of *curanderismo* (faith healing) in San Antonio and elsewhere in southern Texas. Daniel Salazar's *La tierra* (*The Land*, screened at the 1981 San Antonio Cine Festival), describes the Chicano lifestyle in Colorado's San Luis Valley. Luis Reyes's *Los Alvarez* (*The Alvarez Family*, also screened at the 1981 San Antonio Cine Festival), depicts the hopes and dreams of a family living in California's Salinas Valley. Alicia Maldonado and Andrew Valles's *The Ups and Downs of Lowriding* (screened at the 1981 San Antonio Cine Festival) is an investigation of lowriding through the eyes of the cruisers themselves, the general public, and the police department.

Ray Téllez's *Voces de yerba buena* (*Voices of Mint*, screened at the 1981 San Antonio Cine Festival) traces the Hispanic historical foundations of the San Francisco area and evokes the contemporary Latino influence in the area today. Ken Ausubel's *Los remedios: The Healing Herbs* (screened at the 1983 San Antonio Cine festival) is a review of herbal medicine in the Southwest. Rhonda Vlasak's *Between Green and Dry* (screened at the 1983 San Antonio festival) examines the impact of accelerated economic change in the New Mexican village of Abiquiu. Paul Espinosa's *The Trail North* (1983) follows Dr. Robert Alvarez and his ten-year-old son, Luis, as they recreate the journey their familial ancestors made in immigrating to California from Baja California. Toni Bruni's *Los vaqueros* (*The Cowboys*, screened at the 1983 San Antonio festival) is about Chicano cowboys, particularly those who participate in the Houston Livestock Show and Rodeo. Rich Tejada-Flores, producer and director of *Low 'N Slow: The Art of Lowriding* (screened at the 1984 San Antonio Cine Festival), both explains the lowriding phenomenon and makes a case for it as an important form of modern industrial folk art. Jack Ballesteros, producer and director of *Mt. Cristo Rey* (screened at the 1984 San Antonio festival), has created a documentary about a priest in a small mining community near El Paso and how he erected a huge sandstone cross and statue of Christ. Toni Bruni's *Long Rider* (1986) is an English-language version of his 1983 *Los vaqueros*. Jesús Salvador Treviño and Luis Torres's *Birthwrite: Growing Up Hispanic* (1989) is a docudrama that recreates the themes of growing up and self-identity in the writing of several Hispanic writers; and *Del Valle* (*From the Valley,* 1989), directed by Dale Sonnenberg and Karl Kernbergber, evokes traditional and popular Mexican and New Mexican music performed in the central Río Grande Valley of New Mexico.

Films With Political Content

On the matter of politics and the emerging Chicano political movement, several valuable films have been produced. Marsha Goodman's *Not Gone and Not Forgotten* (screened at the 1983 San Antonio festival) depicts how the community of Pico Union in Los Angeles successfully fought the mayor, the city council, and powerful business interests in order to maintain the integrity of its neighborhood. Richard Trujillo's *Tixerina: Through the Eyes of the Tiger* (1983) is an interview with Reies López Tixerina reviewing the famous courthouse raid of 1967 in Tierra Amarilla and related events. National Education Media's *Decision at Delano* (screened at the 1982 Eastern Michigan University Chicano Film Festival), documents the historic Delano grape workers' strike. Centro Campesino Cultural's *El Teatro Campesino* (screened at the 1982 Eastern Michigan University festival) traces the theater from its beginnings in the fields, boosting the morale of striking farm workers and winning over scabs, to its role as a theater committed to social change. Paul Espinosa and Isaac Artenstein's extraordinary documentary *Ballad of an Unsung Hero* (1984) evokes the political consciousness of an earlier era, depicting the life history of the remarkable Pedro J. González, a pioneering radio and recording star who was jailed on trumped-up charges by the Los Angeles district attorney's office in the midst of the Great Depression.

Coproduced by directors Jesús Salvador Treviño and José Luis Ruíz, *Yo soy (I Am,* 1985) reviews the progress that Chicanos have made during the last two decades in politics, education, labor, and economic development and summarizes the variety of ways that Chicanos are responding to contemporary challenges. *Graffiti* (1986) by Diana Costello, producer, and Matthew Patrick, director, is about a nocturnal wall-sketcher in a militaristic South American country. *Maricela* (1986), by Richard Soto, producer, and Christine Burrill, director, is the story of a thirteen-year-old Salvadoran girl who immigrates to Los Angeles with her mother seeking to find a new home and a better life. *The Lemon Grove Incident* (1986), by Paul Espinosa, producer, and Frank Christopher, director, is a docudrama that examines the response of the Mexican-American community in Lemon Grove, California, to a 1930 school board's attempt to segregate their children in a special school.

Watsonville on Strike (1989), by producer-director Jon Silver, describes an eighteen-month strike by cannery workers that virtually paralyzed a rural California town. Marilyn Mulford and Mario Barrera's *Chicano Park* (1989) is a compelling and moving visual history of the struggle of one community, Barrio Logan, to stake out a place for itself in the metropolis of San Diego. The film shows the process through which Logan residents begin to effect positive changes in their lives and their community by using the richness of their cultural heritage as the basis around which to educate themselves to gain political power.

Film Portrayals of Undocumented Workers and Migrant Workers

The plight of *indocumentados* and migrant labor generally has seen extensive filmic treatment during the last decade and a half, including Ricardo Soto's films *Cosecha (Harvest,* 1976), about migrant labor, *Migra* (1976), on the arrest of *indocumentados, Al otro paso (To Another Pass,* 1976), on the economy of the border, and *Borderlands* (1983), which once again explores the complex interrelations of the Mexican-U.S. border. F. X. Camplis's *Los desarraigados (The Uprooted,* 1977) is about the early problems of undocumented workers. Jesús Carbajal and Todd Darling's *Año Nuevo (New Year,* screened at the 1979 San Antonio Cine Festival and 1981 winner of the Eric Sevareid Award for best information program, Academy of Television Arts and Sciences) is about the nearly unprecedented court struggle by twenty-two undocumented workers against their employer, the Año Nuevo Flower Ranch. Jim Crosby's *Frank Ferree: El amigo* (screened at the 1983 San Antonio Cine Festival) depicts this man from Harlingen, Texas, known as the Border Angel, who spent most of his adult life in an untiring effort to aid the poor and dispossessed along the Texas border with Mexico. The Learning Corporation of America's *Angel and Big Jose,* an Academy Award winner for short dramatic film, starring Paul Scorvino, is an outstanding film that depicts the friendship and ultimate parting of a migrant worker youth and a lonely Anglo telephone repairman. The United Farm Workers' *The Wrath of Grapes* (1986) is a documentary that depicts the plight of California farm workers exposed to deadly pesticides. Producer-director Susan Ferris has used historical footage, clippings, interviews, and other realia to trace the history of the farm worker's union and to chronicle the experiences of Mexican farm workers in California in *The Golden Cage: A Story of California's Farmworkers* (1989). Paul Espinosa has produced and directed *Vecinos desconfiados (Uneasy Neighbors,* 1989), evoking the growing tensions between the migrant worker camps and affluent homeowners in the San Diego area.

Public Education on the Big Screen

The Chicano experience in public education has been an important topic and concern of *raza* filmmakers. Documentaries on bilingual education include the series by Adolfo Vargas, *Una nación bilingüe (A Bilingual Nation,* 1977), *Bilingualism: Promise for Tomorrow* (1978), and its sequel, *Consuelo ¿Quiénes somos? (Consuelo, Who Are We?,* 1978), one of the best of its genre, perhaps because of the excellent screenwriting by Rudolfo Anaya. Elaine Sperber's *Overture* (screened at the 1981 San Antonio Cine Festival) uses the school setting to explore the potential for friendship and antagonism between Vietnamese and Chicanos living in a hostile urban environment. In addition, José Luis Ruíz's *Guadalupe* (1975) is a screen adaptation of the play of the same title by El Teatro de la Esperanza; it is a docudrama about conditions in Guadalupe, California, especially the deplorable educational situation. In a stirring docudrama, *Vida (Life,* 1980), directed by Elsie Portillo, the issue of sexual relationships, changing norms, attitudes, and behaviors, such as the use of condoms, is set against the issue of AIDS. Southwestern Bell's *America's Time Bomb: The Hispanic Dropout Rate* (1986), narrated by Edward James Olmos, is an instructive documentary on the dropout rate among Latino students. It includes an interview with then-mayor of San Antonio Henry Cisneros. *At Risk* (1989), produced by Daniel Matta and directed by Warren Asa Maxey, based on an original stage play by Carlos Morton, portrays a variety of issues, prejudices, and misconceptions about AIDS.

Chicano Art, Poetry, Music, and Culture

Numerous documentary films have been produced that either describe or highlight Chicano art, poetry, music, culture, and the like. Among the more notable are José Valenzuela's Chicano poetry *Segundo encuentro (Second Encounter,* 1978), about a gathering of writers and artists in Sacramento; Juan Salazar's *Entelequia (Entelechy,* 1978), which evokes the life and poetry of Ricardo Sánchez, ex-convict and current Ph.D.; and William Greaves's *In Search of Pancho Villa* and *Voice of La Raza* (both screened at the 1978 San Antonio Cine Festival), the former an interview with Mexican-American actor Anthony Quinn about the Mexican Revolution and contemporary U.S. politics and social change and the latter also with Anthony Quinn and, in addition, Rita Moreno and other vocal members of the Hispanic community concerned with issues of discrimination, culture, and language. Sabino Garza's *La llorona (The Crying Woman,* screened at the 1978 San Antonio Cine Festival) is a film depiction of the traditional folktale. Jeff and Carlos Penichet's *El pueblo chicano (The Chicano Peoples): The Beginnings* and *El pueblo chicano: The Twentieth Century* (both 1979) are panoramic overviews of Chicano cultural roots and contemporary issues. Chale Nafus's *Primo Martínez, santero (Primo Martínez, Saint Carver,* screened at the 1979 San Antonio Cine Festival) is about a young man in Austin, Texas, who carves statues of the Virgin Mary from wood. Francisco Torres's *Chuco (Pachuco,* 1980) and Joe Camacho's *Pachuco* (1980) treat the 1941 Zoot Suit Riots in Los Angeles through the art of José Montoya. Efraín Gutiérrez's *La onda chicana (The Chicano Wave,* screened at the 1981 San Antonio Cine Festival) is a review of a 1976 Chicano concert featuring Little Joe y la Familia, Los Chanchos, La Fábrica, and other groups. Juan Salazar's *Mestizo Magic* (screened at the 1981 San Antonio Cine Festival) is about a fantasy trip through Aztlán exploring the world of Chicano art from its ancient past through its living musicians, sculptors, painters, dancers, and writers.

Keith Kolb's *Southwest Hispanic Mission* (screened at the 1981 San Antonio Cine Festival) features noted Chicano art historian Jacinto Quirarte, who describes the technology and aesthetics of mission buildings. Teena Brown Webb's *¡Viva la causa!* (*Long Live the Cause!* screened at the 1981 San Antonio Cine Festival) depicts the popular wall mural movement in Chicago. Paul Venema's *Barrio Murals* (screened at the 1983 San Antonio Cine Festival) documents the creation of the Cassiano Homes murals in San Antonio's west side. Gary Greenberg's *Dale Kranque (Crank It Up): Chicano Music and Art in South Texas* (screened at the 1983 San Antonio Cine Festival) profiles leading Texas Chicano musicians and artists. Beverly Sánchez-Padilla's *In Company of José Rodríguez* (screened at the 1983 San Antonio festival) is a visual history and conversation with the founder and artistic director of La Compañia de Teatro de Albuquerque. Directed by Sylvia Morales, *Los Lobos: And A Time to Dance* (screened at the 1984 San Antonio Cine Festival) is a documentary on Los Lobos, including segments of a live performance, interviews with the musicians, and montages that evoked their fusion of music forms. *Jesse Treviño: A Spirit Against All Odds* (1985) is a stirring documentary about one of San Antonio's best-

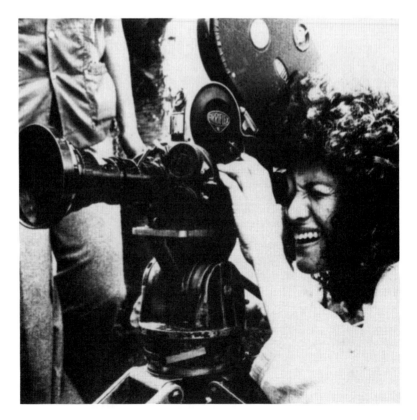

Director and cinematographer Sylvia Morales.

known artists, who while serving in Vietnam lost a right arm and shattered his left leg, yet was still able to pursue his career.

Popol Vuh (1989), directed by Patricia Amlin, is an animated film of the Sacred Book of the Quiche Maya. Lourdes Portillo and Susana Muñoz have produced and directed *La ofrenda (The Offering): The Days of the Dead* (1989), an exploration of the pre-Hispanic roots of *El día de los muertos* (The Day of the Dead) and the social dimensions of death. *The Other Side of the Coin* (1989), by producer-director Sean Carrillo, evokes the work of three East Los Angeles visual and literary artists: Simone Gad, Marisela Norte, and Diana Gamboa.

Hecho en Cuba (Made in Cuba, 1989), by Uberto Sagramoso, is a documentary on Cuban music that goes from the African rhythms that gave it birth to contemporary sounds. Graciela I. Sánchez has produced and directed *No porque lo diga Fidel Castro (Not Because Fidel Castro Says So,* 1988), which is an insightful look into gay life in Cuba, evoking both traditional and more contemporary attitudes. *The Return of Rubén Blades* (1985), by producer-director Robert Mugge, is a music documentary about the passion and commitment, art, and politics of the well-known singer, songwriter, and actor. Producer (also codirector) Eduardo Aguiar's *Federico García Lorca in New York* (1986) is an evocation of the Spanish writer's experiences and work set in New York.

The Detroit Institute of Art's haunting Rivera: The Age of Steel, *describes Diego Rivera's extraordinary Detroit murals of the 1930s and the equally extraordinary political reactions that this art aroused in the automobile and allied industries. A new contribution to the same topic is* Rivera in America *(1988), by producer-director Rick Tejada-Flores, who traces the artist's stay in the United States during the 1930s and examines his works.*

Gangs, Youth, and Domestic Violence

The circumstances of gangs specifically and youth generally have been the subject of Efraín Gutiérrez's *El Juanio* (*Johnny,* screened at the 1979 San Antonio Cine Festival), about the drug problems (mostly paint sniffing) faced by youngsters in the barrios of San Antonio, Texas. Ray Téllez's *Joey* (1980) evokes the problems of identity and of adolescence of a sixteen-year-old Chicano youth. Terry Sweeney, S.J.'s *Streets of Anger, Streets of Hope* (screened at the 1981 San Antonio Cine Festival), is an interview documentary in which members tell what attracts them to gangs. Patt Connelly, S.J.'s *El grito de las madres dolorosas (The Scream of the Mother Dolorasas,* 1981) is one of the most moving accounts of gang violence (in unincorporated East Los Angeles) and what a church brother teamed together with a group of concerned mothers attempted to do about it. Director Bill Jersey's *Children of Violence* (screened at the 1984 San Antonio Cine Festival) treats four brothers in the Oakland, California, barrio, and *Dolores* (1989), produced and directed by Pablo Figueroa, portrays the problem of domestic violence within the Latino community. Jesús Salvador Treviño won the Director's Guild of America Award (1989) in the dramatic daytime show category for his CBS special, *Gangs*.

Chicano Features   A significant and growing number of Chicano features have been produced since the distribution of what might be considered the first Chicano feature, *Los vendidos (The Sellouts,* 1972), a film adaptation of one of the finest of El Teatro Campesino's actos. On the other hand, some of what has been produced, such as the works of Efraín Gutiérrez, have fallen into complete obscurity. If we include some of the dramatic films that were aired on television (*Seguín*) or originally planned for television (*Stand and Deliver*), in addition to the films made for theatrical distribution, the Chicano features include the following, directors noted: *La Vida* (1973, Jeff Penichet), *Please Don't Bury Me Alive! (Por favor ¡No me entierren vivo!,* 1977, Efraín Gutiérrez), *Alambrista!* (1977, Robert M. Young and Moctezuma Esparza), *Amor Chicano es para siempre (Chicano Love Is Forever,* 1978, Efraín Gutiérrez), *Only Once in a Lifetime* (1978, Alejandro Grattan), *Raíces de sangre (Roots,* 1978, Jesús Salvador Treviño), *Run, Junkie (Tecato, Run,* 1979, Efraín Gutiérrez), *Zoot Suit* (1981, Luis Valdez), *The Ballad of Gregorio Cortéz* (1982, Robert M. Young), *Seguín* (1982, Jesús Salvador Treviño), *Heartbreaker* (1983, Frank Zúñiga), *El Norte* (1983, Gregory Nava), *Stand and Deliver* (1988, Ramón Menéndez), *Break of Dawn* (1988, Isaac Artenstein), and Puerto Rican filmmaker Joseph B. Vásquez's *Hangin' With the Homeboys* (1991). The Hispanic Hollywood films (combining Hispanic expertise and often control with Hollywood production values and distribution) usually are more closely affiliated with Chicano independent film than with the average Hollywood production that makes use of Chicano material. This is certainly the case of *La Bamba* (1987) and *Born in East L.A.* (1987).

Chicano feature films have contrasted greatly with contemporary films about Chicanos made by Hollywood directors and producers, even as they have shared some themes, situations or genres, such as the problems at the U.S.-Mexican border, the western genre, or teenage groups. Some salient characteristics of Chicano film not usually seen in the Hollywood product have been a meticulous attention to the authentic cultural and social conditions of Chicano life, the use of Spanish to produce a bilingual film with considerable switching between languages, the recuperation of Chicano history (in period pieces), close attention to the political dimensions of the topics that are cultivated on screen, commitment to dealing with issues above considerations of box office, and a willingness to employ considerable numbers of Hispanic actors and Hispanic production people. Chicano pictures feature plots that may or may not appeal to the mainstream audience, but are definitely designed for Chicano filmgoers. They feature Hispanic actors in genuine situations, usually filmed on location in authentic settings and speaking or singing in a natural, often bilingual environment.

In contrast to the conventional Hollywood pap of the border, Chicano productions such as *Raíces de Sangre (Roots [of Blood])*, *Alambrista!, El Norte*, and *Break of Dawn* (depicting a radio announcer and singer deported to Tijuana), have all evoked the situation at the border with sociological depth and creative distinction. The quality of verisimilitude, heightened by the bilingual (or in the case of *El Norte*, trilingual) script, have caused these movies to stand head and shoulders above their Hollywood contemporaries, such as *Blood Barrier, The Border*, and *Borderline*.

Luis Valdez's productions *Zoot Suit* (1981) and *La Bamba* (1987), as well as *Stand and Deliver* (1988, Ramón Menéndez, Tom Musca, and Edward James Olmos) and *Hangin' With the Homeboys* (1991), all deal with various aspects of Chicano or Puerto Rican juvenile and domestic life in the United States. Valdez's works, both of which have an important historical dimension, are fine examples of Chicano filmmaking, with Hollywood support and distribution. The Chicano juvenile films are light-years ahead of Hollywood products such as *Streets of L.A.* (1979) and *Walk Proud* (1981). The Hollywood films are invariably exploitive in their approach. Whether the Chicanos in these films are a menace to whites or to themselves, it is strictly the prospect of violence and its description on screen that carries these Hollywood juvenile films. In contrast, *Stand and Deliver* is a stirring story that barely even evokes gang violence. It is primarily about an extraordinary Bolivian mathematics teacher who helps Hispanic high school students in East Los Angeles learn college-level calculus and get admitted into selective universities. *Hangin' With the Homeboys* (1991), by Puerto Rican director-writer Joseph P. Vásquez, the most recent contribution to the cycle, was the cowinner of a screenwriting award at the Sundance Film Festival. *Homeboys* evokes the coming of age of four young male friends, two Puerto Rican, two Afro-American, out on the town during a night in which their futures and relationships with each other are tested.

Puerto Rican Films

Both the film industry in Puerto Rico and Puerto Rican films deserve considerably more attention than they have been given to date. Puerto Rican film dates at least from 1916, with the establishment of the Sociedad Industrial Cine Puerto Rico by Rafael J. Colorado and Antonio Capella (in

1912 Juan Emilio Viguié Cajas took the first known shots in Puerto Rico, of Ponce). This production company's first work had a *jíbaro* (Puerto Rican rural highlander) focus and was titled *Por la hembra y el gallo* (For Women and Fighting Cocks (1916), which was followed by *El milagro de la virgen* (The Miracle of the Virgin, 1916) and *Mafia en Puerto Rico* (The Mafia in Puerto Rico, 1916). Because of lack of funds and competition from U.S. film, the Sociedad Industrial was bankrupted, and no prints of its films are known to exist, although still photographs of *Por la hembra y el gallo* remain.

In 1917 the Tropical Film Company was organized with the participation of such well-known Puerto Rican literary figures as Luis Lloréns Torres and Nemesio Canales. Although its existence terminated with the entry of the United States into World War I, it did produce *Paloma del monte* (Mountain Dove), directed by Luis Lloréns Torres. In 1919 the Porto Rico Photoplays company was organized and produced *Amor tropical* (Tropical Love, 1920), with American actors Ruth Clifford and Reginald Denny, a melodrama produced for the North American market, but which failed to penetrate that distribution system, causing the company to go bankrupt.

Juan Emilio Viguié Cajas purchased the equipment of Photoplays and began a long and productive filmmaking career in Puerto Rico, primarily doing newsreels for continental U.S. enterprises, such as Pathé, Fox Movietone, and MGM. Among his works was a film on Charles A. Lindbergh's trip to Puerto Rico in 1927 and another on the San Ciriaco hurricane of 1928. He did many documentaries for private entities and for the government, the first of which was *La colectiva* (The Collective, 1920), about the tobacco industry. His film *Romance tropical* (Tropical Romance, 1934) was the first Puerto Rican feature of the sound period.

For the most part, film languished in Puerto Rico until 1949 when the government established a production facility in Old San Juan. Administered by the División de Educación de la Comunidad (which was part of the Departamento de Instrucción Pública), this unit was able to produce sixty-five shorts and two features by 1975, the year of publication of its last catalog. It counted on the cooperation of many of the best Puerto Rican graphic artists (Homar, Tony Maldonado, Eduardo Vera, Rafael Tufiño, Domingo Casiano, and so on) and writers (René Marqués, Pedo Juan Soto, Emilio Díaz Valcárcel, Vivas Maldonado, for instance). The unit also made considerable use of North American expertise, particularly screenwriter Edwin Rosskam, director Jack Delano, a longtime resident of

Puerto Rico, cameraman Benji Donniger, and director Willard Van Dyke. Because these films were produced by a unit of government responsible for education, they generally had a pedagogical or didactic quality. *Los peloteros (The Ballplayers,* 1951) is generally thought to be the best film from this period. Directed by Jack Delano, it is based on a script by Edwin Rosskam and features Ramón Ortiz del Rivero (the celebrated comedian Diplo) and Miriam Colón. The premise revolves around a group of children raising money to buy baseball uniforms and equipment.

Viguié Film Productions, founded in 1951 by Juan Emilio Viguié Cajas, Jr., and the journalist Manuel R. Navas, became the first large Puerto Rican film producer. In 1953 the writer Salvador Tió became a partner of the company, which had its own studio and laboratory in Hato Rey. Many filmmakers received their training here or with the División de la Educación de la Comunidad. The company produced both commercials and documentaries for the government and private firms. In 1962 the company was associated with the brothers Roberto and Marino Guastella, and what emerged ultimately in 1974 was Guastella Film Producers, currently the largest producer in Puerto Rico. Unfortunately, no film laboratory currently exists in Puerto Rico, so footage is sent to New York.

Beginning in the 1950s the production of film features accelerated somewhat. A group of investors and actors headed by Víctor Arrillaga and Axel Anderson produced a few films under the Producciones Borinquen. *Maruja* (1959) was the most successful, depicting the love life of a barber's wife and starring Marta Romero and several well-known actors and actresses from Puerto Rican television. A few films were produced in Puerto Rico by North American filmmakers for the continental market. *Machete* (1958) is the best known, primarily for its sexuality. Coproduction with Mexican interests began during the 1960s, but led to no more than the repetition of old Mexican formula films with Puerto Rican settings. Among the films produced were *Romance en Puerto Rico* (1961), which has the distinction of being the first Puerto Rican color film, *Bello amanecer (Beautiful Dawn,* 1962), *Lamento borincano (Puerto Rican Lament,* 1963), *Mientras Puerto Rico duerme (While Puerto Rico Sleeps,* 1964), which deals with the drug problem, *El jibarito Rafael* (1966), about Rafael Hernández, and *Fray Dollar (Brother Dollar,* 1970). Most of the major actors and directors were not Puerto Rican, but of Mexican or other Latin American nationality.

In 1964 Pakira Films was organized, led by the television producer Paquito Cordero and with financial backing from Columbia Pictures. It made several films based on the appearances of the television comedian Adalberto Rodríguez (Machuchal). These films were financially successful, including *El alcalde de Machuchal* (*The Mayor of Machuchal*, 1964), *Millionario a-go-go* (*Millionaire A-Go-Go*, 1965), *El agente de Nueva York* (*The New York Agent*, 1966), and *El curandero del pueblo* (*The Town Healer*, 1967). The company also produced its own Mexican formula films, called *churros* by the Mexican industry, such as *En mi viejo San Juan* (*In Old San Juan*, 1966), *Luna de miel en Puerto Rico* (*Honeymoon in Puerto Rico*, 1967), and *Una puertorriqueña en Acapulco* (*A Puerto Rican Girl in Acapulco*, 1968).

Another type of film based on criminals who had captured the popular imagination was produced by Anthony Felton, a Puerto Rican resident of New York. Popular for a while, the public eventually tired of these films with very low budgets, low production values, earthy language, and titillating situations: *Correa Coto, ¡así me llaman!* (*Correa Coto, That's What They Call Me!*, 1968), *La venganza de Correa Coto* (*The Revenge of Correa Coto*, 1969), *Arocho y Clemente* (*Arocho*, 1969), *La palomilla* (*The Gang*, 1969), and *Luisa* (1970).

In the 1970s the number of Mexican coproductions declined significantly, primarily because of political changes in the film industry. Among the few that were done were *Yo soy el gallo* (*I Am the Rooster*, 1971), featuring Puerto Rican singer José Miguel Class, *La pandilla en apuros* (*The Gang in Trouble*, 1977), *¡Qué bravas son las solteras!* (*Single Women Are Brave*), featuring *vedette* Iris Chacón, and *Isabel La Negra* (*Black Isabel*, 1979), by Efraín López Neris, the first superproduction by Puerto Rican standards, featuring José Ferrer, Henry Darrow, Raúl Juliá, and Miriam Colón. This last film is about a notorious madam of a Ponce brothel and is recorded in English. However, the production was both an artistic and financial failure.

While the number of features declined, the number of documentaries increased greatly in the 1970s, spurred in part by the intense political climate of Puerto Rico. A number of *talleres cinematográficos* (movie workshops) were established. Notable among them was Tirabuzón Rojo, which produced *Denunica de un embeleco* (*Charges Filed Against a Madman*, director, Mario Vissepó), *Puerto Rico* (1975, Cuban Film Institute and Tirabuzón Rojo), a socioeconomic analysis of present-day Puerto Rico from a nationalist point of view, and *Puerto Rico: paraíso invadido* (*Puerto Rico: Paradise Invaded*, 1977, Alfonso Beato, director), an examination of the history and present-day reality of Puerto Rico from a nationalist perspective. Independent filmmakers produced *The Oxcart* (1970, director, José García Torres), a short twenty-minute portrayal of the migration of a Puerto Rican family that is based on the famous play by René Marqués; *Culebra, el comienzo* (*Island of Culebra, the Beginning*, 1971, director, Diego de la Texera); *La carreta* (1972, José García, Spanish-language version of *The Oxcart*); *Los nacionalistas* (*The Nationalists*, 1973, José García Torres, director), which surveys the activities of the Puerto Rican Nationalist Party during the 1950s with a special focus on Don Pedro Albizu Campos; *La vida y poesía de Julia de Burgos* (*The Life and Poetry of Julia de Burgos*, 1974); *Destino manifiesto* (*Manifest Destiny*, 1977); *A la guerra* (*To War*, 1979, Thomas Sigel, director), an ode to the Puerto Rican community's war against cultural and racial discrimination in the form of a poem read by its author, Bimbo Rivas; and *The Life and Poetry of Julia de Burgos* (1979, José García Torres, director, Spanish-language version in 1974), a docudrama on the life and work of the great Puerto Rican poet.

In the 1980s, several features were produced including, *Una aventura llamada Menudo* (*An Adventure Called Menudo*, 1983, Orestes Trucco, director), featuring the famous young musical group. This film was one of the biggest box office successes in Puerto Rican history; however, its sequel, *Operación Caribe* (*Operation Caribbean*, 1984), with another very popular juvenile group, Los Chicos, was a financial flop. Also produced, all in 1986, were *Reflejo de un deseo* (*Reflection of a Desire*, Ivonne María Soto, director), about the director's mother, a poet; *Nicolás y los demás* (*Nicolás and the Others*, Jacobo Morales, director), a variation on the eternal triangle theme; and *La gran fiesta* (*The Great Fiesta*, Marcos Zurinaga, director). The first two were low-budget vehicles, done in sixteen millimeters and blown up to thirty-five. They were not financially or artistically successful. On the other hand, *La gran fiesta* was a watershed in Puerto Rican film. Produced with a high budget by local standards (about $1 million) and boasting excellent production values, this period piece with strong political dimensions evokes the handing over of the San Juan Casino to the U.S. military in 1942 amidst considerable turmoil about the possibility of a Nazi invasion, the status of Puerto Rico, and changing attitudes among the upper classes, particularly growers and merchants. This financially successful film was also the first to be produced under the new *Ley de Sociedades Especiales* (*Law of Special Societies*, 1985), which was designed to spur filmic production.

Among independent filmmakers, primarily with financial support of the Fundación Puertorriqueña de las Humanidades (Puerto Rican Humanities

Foundation), the number of documentaries were on the increase in the 1980s. *Retratos* (*Pictures*, 1980, Stewart Bird, director) chronicles the life stories of four individuals from New York's Puerto Rican community in their attempts to adjust to life in the United States. *Puerto Rico: Our Right to Decide* (1981, Stanley Nelson, director) features interviews with people from various walks of life on Puerto Rico's current problems and aspirations for its political future. *Puerto Rico: A Colony the American Way* (1982, Diego Echeverría, director), examines the island's economic relationship with the United States. *La operación* (*The Operation*, 1982, Ana María García, director) studies the sterilization of Puerto Rican women. *El arresto* (*The Arrest*, 1982, Luis Antonio Rosario Quiles, director) dramatizes a major event in the history of the Puerto Rican independence movement. *Ligía Elena* (1983, Francisco López, director), is a color animation that criticizes consumerism, snobbery, and racism, set to a salsa song by Rubén Blades. *Manos a la obra* (*Let's Get To Work*): *The Story of Operation Bootsrap* (1983, Pedro Rivera and Susan Zeig, directors) is an examination of the economic development plan, Operation Bootstrap, undertaken in the 1950s. *La herencia de un tambor* (*The Heritage of a Drum*, 1984, Mario Vissepó, director) is about Afro-Caribbean music. *Luchando por la vida* (*Fighting for Life*, 1984, José Artemio Torres, director) is about Puerto Rican tobacco workers. *Luis Muñoz Marín* (1984, Luis Molina, director) is a biography of the noted governor, and *Correjer* (1984, Antonio Segarra, director) is a portrait of the noted poet and politician.

La batalla de Vieques (*The Battle of Vieques*, 1986, Zydnia Nazario, director) examines the U.S. Navy's control and use of the small island of Vieques. *Tufiño* (1986, Ramón Almodóvar, director) evokes the life and work of this painter. *Raíces eternas* (*Eternal Roots*, 1986, Noel Quiñones, director) describes the history of Puerto Rico. *Cimarrón* (*Cimarron*, 1986, Juis Antonio Rosario, director) is a short fiction about a black slave who escapes his owner's manor and searches for his wife and child in Puerto Rico. *Machito* (1986, Carlos Ortiz, director) is an excellent biographical film that follows salsa musician Machito's career as well as the evolution of Latin jazz from the Cuba of the 1920s to contemporary New York City. *Una historia de los Reyes Magos* (*A History of the Three Wise Men*, 1988, Producciones Rodadero) is an animation that brings to life a Puerto Rican story inspired by the tradition of the Magi. *Sabios árboles, mágicos árboles* (*Wise Trees, Magic Trees*, 1988, Puerto Rico Conservation Trust) is an animation that deals with the importance of trees and with man's relationship to nature. *Las plumas del múcaro* (*The Feathers of the Múcaro*, 1989, Puerto Rico Animation Workshop) is an animated Puerto Rican folktale from the oral tradition.

♦ ♦ ♦ ♦ ♦ ♦ ♦ ♦ ♦ ♦ ♦ HISPANICS IN FILM: FUTURE DIRECTIONS

The prospects of the independent U.S. Hispanic film movement are good, but are without any perceived fundamental changes in the budgetary and distribution limitations of these films. Independent U.S. Hispanic film-makers will enjoy most of the benefits of the trends previously described, including more Hispanic viewers and more awareness of the importance of U.S. Hispanic culture; the decline in power and market control of the film studios and more recently of the television networks; more diversity in distribution, particularly through television; the existence of a small, influential number of benefactors with money or other substantive resources; and perhaps, most of all, the growing number of well-trained and recognized Hispanic production people and actors and actresses who may not want to make a career out of low-budget productions but are willing to cross over to the independent side periodically.

The outlook is relatively good for U.S. Hispanic cinema. Both the Hispanic Hollywood and the independent U.S. Hispanic film movement will expand, and their productions will tend to be more comparable to each other than to the exploitive films that will also continue to be ground out by the Hollywood film carnival industry. The cadre of hispano talent will continue to expand, fostered by all elements of the film, television and video industries, even the most crass sectors. However, once these individuals have been initiated into the field and develop their skills, they will be qualified and eager to produce, at least from time to time, a "real" movie about some aspect of U.S. Hispanic people.

Given the vast changes in the control of artistic content at Hollywood, the existence of Hispanic expertise to make genuine Hispanic films, the progressive sensibilities and interests in film as an art form among a distinct but influential minority of Hollywood figures, and the precedents of films like La Bamba *and* Stand and Deliver *that were financially and artistically successful, one would expect continued and accelerated Hispanic Hollywood productions.*

♦ ♦ ♦ ♦ ♦ ♦ OUTSTANDING HISPANICS IN THE FILM INDUSTRY

An actress, playwright, and director born in Argentina, Norma Aleandro is known best for her performance in the Academy Award-winning *The Official Story* (1985), for which she was named best actress at Cannes. She has also acted in *Gaby—A True Story* (1987), *Cousins* (1989), and *Vital Signs* (1990) and continues to do Spanish-language film.

Norma Aleandro (1941–)

Cinematographer Nestor Almendros.

Néstor Almendros (1930–19?)

A photography director born in Havana, Cuba, Néstor Almendros worked as a cameraman or director on several documentaries of the early Castro era, then moved to France where he worked for television and on film shorts. In the mid-1960s he began collaborating regularly with director Erich Rohmer and later director Francois Truffaut. He won the Academy Award for cinematography for the 1978 film *Days of Heaven*. Included among his films are *The Wild Racers* (1968), *Gun Runner* (1968), *Ma nuit chez Maud* (*My Night at Maud's*, 1969), *L'enfant sauvage* (*The Wild Child*, 1970), *Le genou de Claire* (*Claire's Knee*, 1971), *L'amour l'après-midi* (*Chloe in the Afternoon*, 1972), *L'histoire d'Adele* (*The Story of Adele H.*, 1975), and *Days of Heaven* (1978).

Trini Alvarado

Trini Alvarado debuted in pictures at the age of 11 in *Rich Kids* (1979), by Robert Young, and has done considerable work in television and films. Her credits include *Mrs. Soffel* (1984), starring Diane Keaton and Mel Gibson; *Sweet Lorraine* (1987), *Satisfaction* (1988), *Stella* (1990) opposite Bette Midler, *The Babe* (1992), and *American Friends* (1993).

Pedro Armendáriz (1912–1963)

Born May 9, 1912, in Mexico City, Pedro Armendáriz was one of Mexico's most successful film stars, appearing in over forty films, many directed by Emilio "El Indio" Fernández. He was internationally recognized for *María Candelaria* (1943) and his work with major directors, including Luis Buñuel and John Ford. His son, Pedro Armendáriz, Jr., is also an actor. Included among his films are *María Candelaria* (1943), *La Perla* (*The Pearl*) (1945), *Fort Apache* (1948), *Three Godfathers, We Were Strangers, Tulsa*

(1949), *Border River* (1954), *The Littlest Outlaw* (1955), *The Wonderful Country* (1959), *Francis of Assisi* (1961), and *Captain Sinbad* (1963).

Armida (1913–)

Born in 1913 in Sonora, Mexico, Armida became a stereotypical Latin lady of Hollywood B pictures of the 1930s and 1940s. Included among her films are *Under a Texas Moon, Border Romance* (1931), *Border Café* (1940), *Fiesta* (1941), *The Girl from Monterey* (1943), *Machine Gun Mama* (1944), *South of the Rio Grande* (1945), and *Bad Men of the Border* (1946).

Desi Arnaz (1917–1986)

The funny actor-musician Desi Arnaz (Desiderio Alberto Arnaz y de Acha III) was born on March 2, 1917, in Santiago, Cuba. In the United States from age sixteen, he became a popular singer and drummer, in 1940 marrying Lucille Ball, his co-star in *Too Many Girls,* his screen debut. The 1950s television series "I Love Lucy," in which he and Lucille Ball starred, was (and is) enormously popular. He and Ball divorced in 1960. Included among his films are *Too Many Girls* (1940), *Father Takes a Wife* (1941), *The Navy Comes Through* (1942), *Bataan* (1943), *Cuban Pete* (1946), *Holiday in Havana* (1949), *The Long Long Trailer* (1954), and *Forever Darling* (1956).

Alfonso Bedoya (1904–1957)

Born in Vicam, Mexico, Bedoya developed a considerable career as a character actor in Mexican films. He made a notable American film debut in 1948 in John Huston's *The Treasure of the Sierra Madre* as a treacherous, smiling, and mocking stereotypical Mexican bandit. His performance is both recognized and parodied in Luis Valdez's notable play *I Don't Have to Show You No Stinking Badges.* Included among his films are *La perla (The Pearl,* 1945), *The Treasure of the Sierra Madre* (1948), *Streets of Laredo, Border Incident* (1949), *Man in the Saddle* (1951), *California Conquest* (1952), *Sombrero, The Stranger Wore a Gun* (1953), *Border River* (1954), *Ten Wanted Men* (1955), and *The Big Country* (1958).

Rubén Blades (1948–)

Actor, musician, composer, and lawyer Rubén Blades was born in Panama City, July 16, 1948. Known as a leading salsa musician, in 1985 Blades

Rubén Blades as Sheriff Bernabe Montoya in The Milagro Beanfield War.

was recognized as co-writer and star of *Crossover Dreams* and has gone on to do several film performances, including the role of the sheriff in *The Milagro Beanfield War* (1988). Among his other films are *Critical Condition* (1986), *Fatal Beauty* (1987), *Homeboy* (1988), *Dead Man Out* (1989), *Disorganized Crime* (1989), *The Lemon Sisters* (1989), *The Heart of the Deal* (1990), *Mo' Better Blues* (1990), *One Man's War* (1990), *Predator 2* (1990), *Q & A* (1990), *The Two Jakes* (1990), *Crazy from the Heart* (1991), and *The Super* (1991).

Leo Carrillo (1880–1961)

Born in Los Angeles to an old California family, Leo Carrillo began as a cartoonist before becoming a dialect comedian in vaudeville and later on the stage. Debuting in Hollywood in the late 1920s, he became one of Hollywood's busiest character actors of the 1930s and 1940s. In the early 1950s, he played Pancho, Duncan Renaldo's sidekick in "The Cisco Kid" TV series. His films include *Mister Antonio* (1929), *Girl of the Rio* (1932), *Villa Villa!, Manhattan Melodrama, The Gay Bride* (1934), *In Caliente* (1935), *The Gay Desperado* (1936), *Manhattan Merry-Go-Round* (1937), *The Girl of the Golden West* (1939), *Captain Caution* (1940), *Horror Island* (1941), *Sin*

Town, American Empire (1942), *Gypsy Wildcat* (1944), *Crime Incorporated* (1945), *The Fugitive* (1947), *The Girl From San Lorenzo* (1950).

Linda Cristal (Victoria Moya) (1935–)

Born in 1935 in Buenos Aires and orphaned at thirteen, Linda Cristal played leads in Mexican films from age sixteen and debuted in Hollywood in the mid-1950s in both films and television ("High Chaparral") as a leading lady. Her U.S. films include *Comanche* (1951), *The Perfect Furlough* (1958), *Cry Tough* (1959), *The Alamo* (1960), *Two Rode Together* (1961), *Panic in the City* (1968), *Mr. Majestyk* (1974), and *Love and the Midnight Auto Supply* (1978).

Henry Darrow (1933–)

Born on September 15, 1933, in New York City, Henry Darrow starred in "The High Chaparral" TV series (1967–71); had the role of Alex Monténez (1973–74) on "The New Dick Van Dyke Show"; was Detective Lieutenant Manny Quinlan (1974–75) on "Harry-O," a TV drama series; played Don Diego de la Vega (Zorro Sr.) on "Zorro and Son," a TV comedy (1983); and was Lieutenant Rojas on "Me and Mom," a TV drama series (1985). His film credits include *Badge 373* (1973), *Attica* (1980), *Seguín* (1982), *In Dangerous Company* (1988), *L.A. Bounty* (1989), and *The Last of the Finest* (1990).

Pedro de Córdoba (1881–1950)

Born September 28, 1881, in New York to Cuban-French parents, Pedro de Córdoba began as a stage actor and later played character parts in numerous silent and sound films, usually as either a benevolent or malevolent Latin aristocrat. His films include *Carmen, Temptation* (1915), *Maria Rosa* (1916), *The New Moon* (1919), *When Knighthood Was in Flower* (1922), *The Bandolero* (1924), *Captain Blood* (1935), *Rose of the Rancho, Anthony Adverse, Ramona* (1936), *Juárez* (1939), *The Mark of Zorro* (1940), *Blood and Sand* (1941), *For Whom the Bell Tolls* (1943), *The Keys of the Kingdom* (1945), *Samson and Delilah* (1949), *Comanche Territory,* and *Crisis* (1950).

Arturo de Córdova (Arturo García) (1908–1973)

Born on May 8, 1908, in Merida, Yucatán, Mexico, Arturo de Córdova made his debut in Mexican films in the early 1930s and played Latin lovers in Hollywood during the 1940s, thereafter returning to Spanish-language film. His films include *Cielito lindo* (1936), *La zandunga* (1937),

For Whom the Bell Tolls (1943), Masquerade in Mexico, A Medal for Benny (1945), New Orleans (1947), and Adventures of Casanova (1948).

Dolores del Río

(1905-1983)

Born on August 3, 1905, in Durango, Mexico, Dolores del Río (Lolita Dolores Martínez Asunsolo López Negrete) was educated in a convent. By age sixteen, she was married to writer Jaime del Rço. Director Edwin Carewe was struck by her beauty and invited her to Hollywood where she appeared in Joanna in 1925. She became a star in many silent films, but her career suffered from frequent typecasting in ethnic and exotic roles, particularly after the advent of sound. Dissatisfied with Hollywood, she returned to Mexico in 1943 to do many important films of the 1940s, including María Candelaria (1943) and John Ford's The Fugitive (1947, filmed on location in Mexico). She finally returned to Hollywood in character parts in the 1960s. Her films include Resurrection, The Loves of Carmen (1927), Ramona, Revenge (1928), Evangeline (1929), The Bad One (1930), The Girl of the Rio (1932), Flying Down to Rio (1933), Madame Du Barry (1934), In Caliente (1935), Devil's Playground (1937), Doña Perfecta (1950), La cucaracha (The Cockroach, 1958), Flaming Star (1960), Cheyenne Autumn (1964), and The Children of Sánchez (1978).

Lou Diamond

Phillips

Lou Diamond Phillips first came to prominence as Ritchie Valens in La Bamba (1987). He subsequently distinguished himself as a calculus-proficient gang member in Stand and Deliver (1988). His credits include Dakota, Young Guns (1988), Disorganized Crime, Renegades, The First Power (1989), A Show of Force, Young Guns 2 (1990), Ambition (1991), and Shadow of the Wolf (1992).

Hector Elizondo

Hector Elizondo, active in television, theater, and film, won an Obie for his role as a Puerto Rican locker room attendant in the off-Broadway play Steambath. He made his movie debut in 1971 with Burt Lancaster in Valdez Is Coming. Other films include The Taking of Pelham 1-2-3 (1974), The Dain Curse (1978), American Gigolo, Cuba (1979), The Fan (1981), Young Doctors in Love (1982), The Flamingo Kid, Private Resort (1984), Out of the Darkness (1985), Courage, Nothing in Common (1986), Leviathan (1989), Pretty Woman (1990), Final Approach, Frankie and Johnny, Necessary Roughness (1991), Chains of Gold, Samantha, There Goes the Neighborhood (1992).

Producer and director and one of the best-known Chicano figures in the film industry, Moctezuma Esparza has been involved in feature, documentary, and educational filmmaking since 1973. He has formed a production company, Esparza/Katz, which has raised considerable funds to produce feature-length motion pictures with Latino themes, including an adaptation of the Rudolfo Anaya novel *Bless Me Ultima* (written and to be directed by Luis Valdez) and *Angel's Flight* (written by first-time feature scripter Jill Isaacs and scheduled for direction by Luis Valdez), about a Hispanic detective embroiled in a major plot to bankrupt Los Angeles's mass transit rail system to clear the way for freeways. His films include *Only Once in a Lifetime* (1978, producer), *The Ballad of Gregorio Cortez* (1983, producer), *The Milagro Beanfield War* (1988, co-producer), and *Radioactive Dreams* (1986, producer).

Moctezuma Esparza

Long affiliated with KPBS Television, San Diego, California, Paul Espinosa has produced and directed exceptional documentaries and docudramas, including *Los mineros* (*The Miners,* 1990, Héctor Galán, co-producer), a stirring view of the history of the labor struggle by Arizona Mexican-American miners from the turn of the century to the present. He is the producer for the "American Playhouse" TV drama series of a dramatic adaptation of Tomás Rivera's masterpiece, *And the Earth Did Not Part* (1992, Severo Pérez, director-writer). Others films by Espinosa are *Ballad of an Unsung Hero* (1983), about a scandalous case of discrimination and deportation of a well-known Chicano radio figure, and *The Lemon Grove Incident* (1985), about separate and unequal education of Chicanos in California.

Paul Espinosa (1950–)

Actor, director, and screenwriter Emilio Estévez was born May 12, 1962, in New York City and is the son of Martin Sheen and brother to Charlie Sheen. Estévez decided to use the original family surname. With his blond hair and blue eyes, he has been able to secure roles in mainstream pictures. His accomplishments as an actor are many and varied; much of the work has been highly recognized for its excellence. Estévez has written several screenplays and directed two of them.

Emilio Estévez (1962–)

The director and actor Emilio Fernández was born on March 26, 1904, in El Seco, Coahuila, Mexico. One of the most important figures of Mexican cinema, he was born to a Spanish-Mexican father and Indian mother (hence the nickname El Indio). At nineteen, he took part in the Mexican

Emilio "El Indio" Fernández (1904–1986)

Revolution and in 1923 was sentenced to twenty years' imprisonment. However, he escaped to California where he played bit parts and supporting roles until returning to Mexico, first as an actor, debuting in the role of an Indian in *Janitizio* (1934), and then as Mexico's most prominent director. His film *María Candelaria* (1943) won Grand Prize at Cannes, and *La Perla* (*The Pearl*, 1946) won the International Prize at San Sebastián, Spain. As a Hollywood actor, he had a few notable parts in Sam Peckinpah films. Among the films he directed are *Soy puro mexicano* (*I Am Full-Blooded Mexican*, 1942), *Flor silvestre* (*Wildflower*), *María Candelaria* (1943), *Bugambilla* (*Bougainvillea*, 1944), *La perla* (*The Pearl*, 1946), *El gesticulador* (*The Gesticulator*, 1957), and *A Loyal Soldier of Pancho Villa* (1966). His films as an actor include *The Reward* (1965), *The Appaloosa*, *Return of the Seven* (1966), *A Covenant with Death*, *The War Wagon* (1967), *The Wild Bunch* (1969), *Pat Garrett and Billy the Kid* (1973), *Bring Me the Head of Alfredo García* (1974), *Lucky Lady* (1975), *Under the Volcano* (1984), and *Pirates* (1986).

Mel Ferrer (Melchior Gastón Ferrer) (1917-)

Actor, director, and producer, Mel Ferrer was born on August 25, 1917, in New York to a Cuban-born surgeon and a Manhattan socialite. He attended Princeton University but dropped out to become an actor, debuting on Broadway in 1938 as a chorus dancer. He made his screen acting debut in 1949 and appeared in many films as a leading man. His third (1954–68) of four wives was actress Audrey Hepburn, whom he directed in *Green Mansions* (1959). His films as actor include *Lost Boundaries* (1949), *The Brave Bulls* (1951), *Rancho Notorious, Scaramouche* (1952), *Lili* (1953), *War and Peace* (1956), *The Sun Also Rises* (1957), *The World, the Flesh and the Devil* (1959), *Sex and the Single Girl* (1964), *Eaten Alive* (1977), *Guyana: Cult of the Damned* (1979), and *City of the Walking Dead* (1980). The films he directed include *The Girl of the Limberlost* (1945) and *Green Mansions* (1959).

Gabriel Figueroa (1907-)

Photography director Gabriel Figueroa was born on April 24, 1907, in Mexico. As an orphan, he was forced to seek work, yet was able to pursue painting and photography on his own. In 1935 he went to Hollywood to study motion picture photography; returned to Mexico the following year, and began a prolific career as the cameraman of over one hundred films. He worked for Buñuel, John Ford, and Emilio Fernández and ranks among the leading directors of photography in world cinema. His films (primarily Mexican) include *Allá en el rancho grande* (*Out on the Big Ranch*, 1936), *Flor silvestre* (*Wildflower*), *María Candelaria*, (1943), *Bugambilla*

(*Bougainvillea*, 1944), *La perla* (*The Pearl*, 1946), *The Fugitive* (1947), *Los olvidados* (*The Forgotten*, 1952), *La cucaracha* (*The Cockroach*, 1958), *Nazarín* (1959), *Macario* (1960), *Animas Trujano* (1961), *El angel exterminador* (*The Exterminating Angel*, 1962), *The Night of the Iguana* (1964), *Simón del desierto* (*Simon in the Desert*, 1965), *Two Mules for Sister Sara* (1970), *The Children of Sánchez* (1978), and *Under the Volcano* (1984).

Andy García (1956–)

Born in Havana, Andy García (Andrés Arturo Garci-Menéndez) worked as an actor in regional theater in the early 1960s. In *8 Million Ways to Die* (1986) he turned in a superb performance as a villain, and in 1987 in Brian De Palma's *The Untouchables* he achieved widespread recognition as an earnest FBI agent. In 1990 he achieved star status as the good cop in *Internal Affairs* and as the illegitimate nephew of Don Corleone in *The Godfather Part III*. His other films include *Blue Skies Again* (1983), *The Mean Season* (1985), *American Roulette* (1988), *Stand and Deliver* (1988), *Black Rain* (1989), *A Show of Force* (1990), *Dead Again* (1991), *Jennifer 8* (1992), *Hero* (1992), and *When a Man Loves a Woman* (1994).

Rita Hayworth (1918–1987)

Rita Hayworth (Margarita Carmen Cansino) was born October 17, 1918, in Brooklyn, New York, to Spanish-born dancer Eduardo Cansino and his Ziegfeld Follies partner Volga Haworth. Hayworth danced professionally by age thirteen in Mexican nightspots in Tijuana and Agua Caliente, where she was eventually noticed by Hollywood. She made her screen debut in 1935, playing bit parts under her real name. In 1937, she married Edward Judson, under whose guidance she changed her name and was transformed into an auburn-haired sophisticate. For the remainder of the 1930s, Hayworth was confined to leads in B pictures, but through much of the 1940s she became the undisputed sex goddess of Hollywood films and the hottest star at Columbia Studios. Her tempestuous personal life included marriages to Orson Welles, Aly Khan, and singer Dick Haymes. As Rita Cansino, her films included *Under the Pampas Moon, Charlie Chan in Egypt,* and *Dante's Inferno* (1935), *Meet Nero Wolfe* (1936), *Trouble in Texas, Old Louisiana,* and *Hit the Saddle* (1937). As Rita Hayworth, she acted in *The Shadow* (1937), *Angels Over Broadway* (1940), *The Strawberry Blonde, Blood and Sand* (1941), *Cover Girl* (1944), *Gilda* (1946),

Raúl Juliá during production
of the film Romero.

The Lady from Shanghai, The Loves of Carmen (1948), Salome, Miss Sadie
Thompson (1953), Pal Joey (1957), Separate Tables (1958), They Came to
Cordura (1959), The Happy Thieves (1962), The Money Trap (1966), The
Wrath of God (1972), and Circle (1976).

Raúl Juliá (1940–)   Raúl Juliá has become one of the best-known and popular actors in the
U.S. for his Shakespearean and other classical stage roles and for musicals
as well as film. His career was initiated on the Hispanic stages of New
York, most notably with important productions of René Marqués's *La
Carreta (The Oxcart)* with Miriam Colón. Born in San Juan, Puerto Rico,
on March 9, 1940, Juliá was raised there and attained his bachelor of arts
degree from the University of Puerto Rico. As a stage actor he has had important roles in serious theater and on Broadway, including *The Emperor
of Late Night Radio* (1974), *The Cherry Orchard* (1976), *Dracula* (1976),
Arms and the Man (1985), and various Shakespearean plays. In 1971 he
debuted in film with small parts in *The Organization, Been Down So Long It*

Looks Like Up to Me, and *Panic in Needle Park*. Juliá appeared in *The Gumball Rally* (1976) and *Eyes of Laura Mars* (1978) and achieved national attention in the notable *Kiss of the Spider Woman* (1985), adapted from the novel by Argentine Manuel Puig. His other films include *One from the Heart* (1982), *Tempest* (1982), *Compromising Positions* (1985), *The Morning After* (1986), *Florida Straits* (1986), *Trading Hearts* (1987), *Moon Over Parador* (1988), *The Penitent* (1988), *Tango Bar* (1988), *Tequila Sunrise* (1988), *Romero* (1989), *Mack the Knife* (1989), *Havana* (1990), *Presumed Innocent* (1990), *A Life of Sin* (1990), *The Rookie* (1990), *The Addams Family* (1991), *The Plague* (1992), and *Addams Family Values* (1993).

Katy Jurado
(1927–)

Born in 1927 in Guadalajara, Mexico, Katy Jurado (María Cristina Jurado García) began her Hollywood career as a columnist for Mexican publications following a Mexican film career. In Hollywood she played dark lady roles in a variety of films, most memorably *High Noon* (1952) and *One-Eyed Jacks* (1961). She was nominated for an Oscar for her supporting role in *Broken Lance* (1954). Her other films include *The Bullfighter and the Lady* (1951), *Arrowhead* (1953), *Trapeze, The Man From Del Rio* (1956), *Barabbas* (1961), *Pat Garrett and Billy the Kid* (1973), *El recurso del método* (*The Method's Resource*, 1978) and *The Children of Sánchez* (1978).

Fernando Lamas
(1915–1982)

Born on January 9, 1915, in Buenos Aires, Fernando Lamas became a movie star in Argentina. Lamas was imported to Hollywood by MGM and typecast as a sporty Latin lover in several lightweight films, some of which featured his singing. He married Arlene Dahl (1954-60) and Esther Williams (from 1967 until his death). His films include *The Avengers* (1950), *The Merry Widow* (1952), *The Diamond Queen* (1953), *Jívaro, Rose Marie* (1954), *The Violent Ones, Kill a Dragon* (1967), *100 Rifles, Backtrack* (1969), and *The Cheap Detective* (1978).

Adele Mara
(1923–)

Born on April 28, 1923, in Highland Park, Michigan, Adele Mara (Adelaida Delgado) began as a singer-dancer with Xavier Cugat's orchestra. In Hollywood she played dark lady/other woman parts in scores of low-budget films in the 1940s and 1950s, including *Navy Blues* (1941), *Alias Boston Blackie* (1942), *Atlantic City* (1944), *The Tiger Woman, Song of Mexico* (1945), *The Catman of Paris* (1946), *Twilight on the Rio Grande, Blackmail, Exposed* (1947), *Campus Honeymoon, Wake of the Red Witch, Angel in Exile* (1948), *Sands of Iwo Jima, The Avengers, California Passage* (1950), *The Sea Hornet* (1951), *Count the Hours* (1953), *Back from Eternity* (1956), and *The Big Circus* (1959).

Margo
(1917-)

Born on May 10, 1917, in Mexico City, Margo (Marie Marquerita Guadalupe Teresa Estela Bolado Castilla y O'Donnell) was coached as a child by Eduardo Cansino, Rita Hayworth's father, and she danced professionally with her uncle Xavier Cugat's band in Mexican nightclubs and at New York's Waldorf-Astoria, where they triumphed in introducing the rumba. From 1934, she became known as a dramatic actress, mostly typecast as a tragic, suffering woman. She has been married to Eddie Albert since 1945 and is the mother of actor Edward Albert, Jr. Her films include *Crime Without Passion* (1934), *Rumba* (1935), *The Robin Hood of Eldorado, Winterset* (1936), *Lost Horizon* (1937), *Behind the Rising Sun* (1943), *The Falcon in Mexico* (1944), *Viva Zapata!* (1952), *I'll Cry Tomorrow* (1955), *From Hell to Texas* (1958), and *Who's Got the Action?* (1962).

Richard "Cheech"
Marín (1946-)

Renowned comic, actor, and writer Richard Marín was born July 13, 1946, in Los Angeles. Marín began in show business as part of the comedy team Cheech and Chong in 1970, bringing stoned and hippie routines to the screen with *Cheech and Chong's Up in Smoke* (1979), which was the highest-grossing film of the year. In 1982 he wrote *Things Are Tough All Over*. Following the split-up of the duo in 1985, Cheech continued to appear in films and wrote, directed, and starred in *Born in East L.A.* (1987). His films include *Cheech and Chong's Next Movie* (1980), *Cheech and Chong's Nice Dreams* (1981), *Yellowbeard* (1983), *Cheech and Chong: Still Smokin'* (1983), *Cheech and Chong's the Corsican Brothers* (1984), *After Hours* (1985), *Echo Park* (1986), *Fatal Beauty* (1987), *Rude Awakening* (1989), and *The Shrimp on the Barbie* (1990, which he also directed). He provided a voice for the animated feature *Ferngully: The Last Rainforest* (1992).

Mona Maris (María
Capdevielle)
(1903-)

Born in 1903 in Buenos Aires and convent-educated in France, Mona Maris acted in several British and German films before embarking on a Hollywood career in the late 1920s and the 1930s in the usual sultry, exotic-type role. Her films include *Romance of the Rio Grande* (1929), *Under a Texas Moon, The Arizona Kid, A Devil With Women* (1930), *The Passionate Plumber, Once* in a Lifetime (1932), *Flight From Destiny, Law of the Tropics* (1941), *My Gal Sal, Pacific Rendezvous, I Married an Angel, Berlin Correspondent* (1942), *The Falcon in Mexico* (1944), *Heartbeat* (1946), and *The Avengers* (1950).

Born on November 19, 1893, in Tucson, Arizona, of Mexican parentage, Christopher Ysabel Ponciana Martin provided comic relief in the Cisco Kid series (as Pancho or Gordito) and many other westerns. His films include *The Rescue* (1929), *Billy the Kid* (1930), *The Cisco Kid* (1931), *South of Santa Fe* (1932), *Bordertown* (1935), *The Gay Desperado* (1936), *The Texans* (1938), *Stagecoach, The Return of the Cisco Kid* (1939), *Lucky Cisco Kid, Down Argentine Way, The Mark of Zorro* (1940), *Weekend in Havana* (1941), *Tombstone* (1942), *The Ox-Bow Incident* (1943), *Ali Baba and the Forty Thieves* (1944), *San Antonio* (1945), *The Fugitive* (1947), *Mexican Hayride* (1948), *The Beautiful Blonde From Bashful Bend* (1949), and *Ride the Man Down* (1952).

Chris-Pin Martin (1893–1953)

Born on November 25, 1920, in Mexico City, Ricardo Montalbán first played bit roles in several Broadway productions before debuting on the screen in Mexico in the early 1940s and subsequently being recruited as a Latin lover type by MGM in 1947. He was eventually given an opportunity to demonstrate a wider acting range on television, including roles in "The Loretta Young Show" and "Fantasy Island." He has been a strong force in Hollywood for the establishment of better opportunities for Hispanics. His films include *Fiesta* (1947), *The Kissing Bandit* (1948), *Neptune's Daughter, Border Incident* (1949), *Right Cross, Two Weeks With Love* (1950), *Across the Wide Missouri, Mark of the Renegade* (1951), *Sombrero, Latin Lovers* (1953), *The Saracen Blade* (1954), *A Life in the Balance* (1955), *Sayonara* (1957), *Let No Man Write My Epitaph* (1960), *Cheyenne Autumn* (1964), *The Money Trap, The Singing Nun* (1966), *Sweet Charity* (1969), *Escape from the Planet of the Apes* (1971), *Conquest of the Planet of the Apes* (1972), *The Train Robbers* (1973), *Joe Panther* (1976), and *Star Trek II: The Wrath of Khan* (1982).

Ricardo Montalbán (1920–)

Born on June 6, 1920, in Barahona, Dominican Republic, Maria Montez (María Africa Vidal de Santo Silas) became one of the most notable, exotic dark ladies. Affectionately called the Queen of Technicolor, she started her screen career in 1941 doing bit parts in Universal films. Although inordinately unskilled at acting, she nevertheless became immensely popular in a string of color adventure tales, often co-starring with fellow exotics Jon Hall, Sabu, and Turhan Bey. She remains the object of an extensive fan cult

María Montez (1920–1951)

thirsting for nostalgia and high camp. Her films include *Lucky Devils, That Night in Rio, Raiders of the Desert, South of Tahiti* (1941), *Bombay Clipper, Arabian Nights* (1942), *White Savage* (1943), *Ali Baba and the Forty Thieves, Cobra Woman, Gypsy Wildcat, Bowery to Broadway* (1944), *Sudan* (1945), *Tangier* (1946), *The Exile*, and *Pirates of Monterey* (1947).

Sylvia Morales

One of the best-recognized Chicana directors, Sylvia Morales directed the short film *Chicana* (1979), about the changing roles of women in Hispanic/Chicano society from pre-Columbian times to the present; *Los Lobos: And A Time to Dance* (1984), a short musical special produced for PBS that profiles the musical group Los Lobos; *Esperanza*, a one-hour narrative drama directed under the Women Filmmakers Program at the American Film Institute, about the story of a young immigrant girl whose mother is arrested and who has to cope on her own; *SIDA Is AIDS*, a one-hour video documentary for PBS, broadcast in both Spanish and English; *Values: Sexuality and the Family,* a half-hour documentary on health issues affecting the Latino community, broadcast in Spanish and English; and *Faith Even to the Fire,* a one-hour video documentary for PBS profiling three nuns whose conscience motivated them to speak out on issues of social justice, sexism, racism, and classism within the Catholic Church.

Antonio Moreno (1887–1967)

Born on September 26, 1887, in Madrid, Antonio Moreno (Antonio Garride Monteagudo) played a dapper Latin lover in numerous Hollywood silent films. He began his career in 1912 under D. W. Griffith and was quite popular during the 1920s, when he played leads opposite such actresses as Gloria Swanson, Greta Garbo, Pola Negri, and Bebe Daniels. His foreign accent limited his career in talkies, where he was seen mainly in character roles. He appeared in hundreds of films, including *Voice of the Million, The Musketeers of Pig Alley* (1912), *The Song of the Ghetto, The Loan Shark King, In the Latin Quarter, Sunshine and Shadows* (1914), *The Quality of Mercy, The Gypsy Trail* (1915), *My American Wife, The Spanish Dancer* (1923), *One Year to Live* (1925), *Mare Nostrum, The Temptress* (1926), *Venus of Venice, The Whip Woman* (1928), *Romance of the Rio Grande* (1929), *One Mad Kiss* (1930), *The Bohemian Girl* (1938), *Rose of the Rio Grande* (1938), *Seven Sinners* (1940), *Notorious* (1946), *Captain from Castille* (1947), *Crisis, Dallas* (1950), *Wings of the Hawk* (1953), *Creature From the Black Lagoon* (1954), and *The Searchers* (1956).

An actress, dancer, and singer, Moreno (Rosita Dolores Alverio) was born on December 11, 1931, in Humacao, Puerto Rico. A dancer from childhood, she reached Broadway at thirteen and Hollywood at fourteen. She won a 1962 Academy Award as best supporting actress for *West Side Story* and has been in several films important for understanding the Hollywood depiction of Hispanics, including *A Medal for Benny*, (1954), *The Ring* (1952), and *Popi* (1969). Her other films include *Pagan Love Song* (1950), *Singin' in the Rain* (1952), *Latin Lovers, Fort Vengeance* (1953), *Jivaro, Garden of Evil* (1954), *The King and I, The Vagabond King* (1956), *The Deerslayer* (1957), *Summer and Smoke* (1961), *Marlowe* (1969), *Carnal Knowledge*, (1971), *The Ritz* (1976), *The Boss' Son* (1978), *Happy Birthday, Gemini* (1980), *The Four Seasons* (1981), and *Life in the Food Chain* (1991). Among the many musicals and plays in which she performed are *The Sign in Sidney Brustein's Window* (1964–65), *Elmer Gantry* (1969–70), *The Last of the Red Hot Lovers* (1970–71), *The National Health* (1974), *Wally's Café* (1981), and *The Odd Couple* (1985). In addition to her Oscar, Moreno has won a Grammy (1973), a Tony, and an Emmy. She is also an activist in her profession and in the community for Hispanic rights.

Rita Moreno
(1931–)

Born on June 16, 1905, in Buenos Aires, Barry Norton (Alfedo Birabén) became a romantic lead in Hollywood's late silent and early sound films. He later appeared in Hollywood-made Spanish-language or Mexican productions, sometimes directing his own films. His Hollywood films include *The Lily, What Price Glory* (1926), *Ankles Preferred, The Wizard, The Heart of Salome, Sunrise* (1926), *Mother Knows Best, Legion of the Condemned, Four Devils* (1928), *The Exalted Flapper* (1929), *Lady for a Day* (1933), *Nana* (1934), *The Buccaneer* (1938), *Devil Monster* (1946), and *Around the World in Eighty Days* (cameo, 1956).

Barry Norton
(1905-1956)

Born on February 6, 1899, in Durango, Mexico, Ramón Novarro (Ramón Samaniegos) became a romantic idol of Hollywood silents of the 1920s. He began his career as a singing waiter and vaudeville performer before breaking into films as an extra in 1917. By 1922 he had become a star Latin lover and was overshadowed only by Rudolph Valentino in that role. He soon sought a broader range and less exotic image. His most famous part was the title role of the 1926 *Ben-Hur*. His films include *A Small Town Idol* (1921), *The Prisoner of Zenda* (1922), *Scaramouche* (1923), *The Arab, Thy Name is Woman* (1924), *A Lover's Oath* (1925), *The Student Prince* (1927), *The Pagan* (1929), *In Gay Madrid* (1930), *Call of the Flesh* (1930), *Son of India, Mata Hari* (1931), *The Barbarian* (1933), *The Sheik Steps Out* (1937), *The Big Steal* (1949), *The Outriders* (1950), and *Heller in Pink Tights* (1960).

Ramón Novarro
(1899-1968)

Edward James Olmos at the Clinton inaugural gala in Washington, D.C., 1993.

Edward James Olmos (1947-)

Actor, composer, producer, and director, Edward James Olmos was born on February 24, 1947, in Los Angeles. He began his career as a rock singer and earned a Los Angeles Drama Critics Circle Award for his performance in Luis Valdez's musical play *Zoot Suit*, which he reprised on Broadway and in the 1981 film version. He became nationally known as Lieutenant Castillo on television's "Miami Vice" (1984–89) and was nominated for an Oscar for best actor for his lead as a committed East Los Angeles high school calculus teacher in *Stand and Deliver* (1988). The film also helped propel him to the cover of *Time* magazine, perhaps the only Chicano to have attained that recognition. Additional films include *Wolfen* (1981), *Blade Runner* (1982), *The Ballad of Gregorio Cortez* (1983), *Saving Grace* (1986), *Triumph of the Spirit* (1989), *Maria's Story* (1990), *A Talent for the Game* (1991), and *American Me* (1992), which he also produced and directed.

While Elizabeth Peña began her career playing primarily mothers and live-in maids, she made a name for herself in *La Bamba* (1987). Her other credits include *Crossover Dreams* (1985), *Down and Out in Beverly Hills* (1986), *Batteries Not Included* (1987), *Vibes* (1988), *Blue Steel, Jacob's Ladder* (1990), and *The Waterdance*. On television, she was in the series "Tough Cookies," "I Married Dora," and "Shannon's Deal"; she also held a recurring guest spot as a private investigator on "L.A. Law."

Elizabeth Peña

Born on April 21, 1915, in Chihuahua, Mexico, of Irish-Mexican parentage, Anthony Quinn has lived in the United States from childhood. He entered films in 1936 and the following year married Cecil B. deMille's adopted daughter, Katherine (they are now divorced), but his father-in-law did nothing to advance Quinn's career, which did not attain star status until 1952 with his Academy Award–winning role as Zapata's brother in *Viva Zapata!* Quinn went on to win a second Academy Award for *Lust for Life* (1956), and he began playing leads that emphasized his earthy and exotic qualities. He has appeared in over one hundred films including *Parole!* (1936), *The Buccaneer, King of Alcatraz* (1938), *Texas Rangers Ride Again* (1940), *Blood and Sand* (1941), *The Ox-Bow Incident, Guadalcanal Diary* (1943), *Back to Bataan* (1945), *California, Sinbad the Sailor, Black Gold* (1947), *The Brave Bulls* (1951), *Against All Flags* (1952), *Ride Vaquero!* (1953), *Man From Del Rio* (1956), *The Black Orchid* (1958), *The Guns of Navarrone, Barabbas* (1961), *Requiem for a Heavyweight, Lawrence of Arabia* (1962), *Zorba the Greek* (1964), *A High Wind in Jamaica* (1965), *The Shoes of the Fisherman, The Magus* (1968), *The Secret of Santa Vittoria* (1969), *The Greek Tycoon, The Children of Sánchez* (1978), *The Salamander* (1981), *The Salamander, Valentina* (1983), *Ghosts Can't Do It* (1990), *Revenge* (1990), *Jungle Fever, Only the Lonely, Mobsters* (1991), and *The Last Action Hero* (1993). His plays include *Clean Beds* (1936), *Gentleman From Athens* (1947), *A Street Car Named Desire, Beckett* (1961), and *Zorba the Greek* (1983). Quinn is also a painter with numerous exhibitions and has written an autobiography, *The Original Sin* (1972).

Anthony Quinn (1915–)

A foundling thought to have been born in Spain on April 23, 1904, Duncan Renaldo arrived in the United States in the early 1920s and was a Hollywood leading man and supporting player. He debuted with MGM in

Duncan Renaldo (1904–1980)

1928 and by the early 1940s had found a niche in westerns as one of the Three Mesquiteers and subsequently as the screen's fourth Cisco Kid. His films include *Clothes Make the Woman* (1928), *The Bridge of San Luis Rey* (1929), *Zorro Rides Again* (serial, 1937), *Rose of the Rio Grande* (1938), *The Lone Ranger Rides Again* (serial), *The Kansas Terrors* (1939), *Down Mexico Way* (1941), *For Whom the Bell Tolls* (1943), *The Cisco Kid Returns* (1945), *The Gay Amigo*, *The Daring Caballero* (1949), and *Zorro Rides Again* (1959).

Gilbert Roland
(1905–1994)

Born in Júarez, Mexico, on December 11, 1905, the son of a bullfighter, Gilbert Roland (Luis Antonio Dámaso de Alonso) trained for the *corrida* (bullfight), but chose a career in film instead after his family moved to the United States. He debuted as an extra at age thirteen and subsequently played a Latin lover on both the silent and sound screens. His films include *The Plastic Age* (1925), *The Campus Flirt* (1926), *Camille, Rose of the Golden West* (1927), *The Dove* (1928), *The Last Train from Madrid* (1937), *Júarez* (1939), *The Sea Hawk* (1940), *Captain Kidd* (1945), *The Gay Cavalier, Beauty and the Bandit* (1946), *The Bullfighter and the Lady, Mark of the Renegade* (1951), *Bandido* (1956), *Cheyenne Autumn* (1964), *Islands in the Stream, The Black Pearl* (1977), and *Barbarosa* (1982).

César Romero
(1907–1994)

Born on February 15, 1907, in New York City of Cuban parentage, César Romero played a Latin lover in Hollywood films from the 1930s through the 1950s and later did suave supporting character roles. He played the Cisco Kid in the late 1930s and early 1940s. His films include *The Thin Man* (1934), *Clive of India, Cardinal Richelieu* (1935), *The Cisco Kid and the Lady* (1939), *Viva Cisco Kid, The Gay Caballero, Romance of the Rio Grande* (1940), *Ride Vaquero, Weekend in Havana* (1941), *Captain from Castile* (1948), *Vera Cruz* (1954), *Villa!* (1958), *Batman* (1966), and *The Strongest Man in the World* (1975).

Born on August 3, 1940, in Dayton, Ohio, to a Spanish immigrant father and an Irish mother, Martin Sheen (Ramón Estévez) began at the New York Living Theater and debuted on the screen in 1967. He was named as best actor at the San Sebastián (Spain) Film Festival for his role in *Badlands* (1973). His other films include *The Incident* (1967), *The Subject Was Roses* (1968), *Catch-22* (1970), *The Cassandra Crossing* (1977), *Apocalypse Now* (1979), *That Championship Season, Gandhi* (1982), *The Dead Zone, Enigma,* and *Man, Woman and Child* (1983), *The Guardian, Firestarter* (1984), *Broken Rainbow* (1985), *Siesta, The Believers, Wall Street* (1987), *Da, Judgment in Berlin* (1988), *Beverly Hills Brats* (1989), *Cadence* (1991, which he also directed), *Hearts of Darkness: A Filmmaker's Apocalypse* (1992), *Gettysburg, Hear No Evil,* and *The Grey Knight* (1993).

Martin Sheen (1940–)

Jimmy Smits

Jimmy Smits gained wide exposure as Victor Sifuentes on the "L.A. Law" TV series. He costarred as a Mexican revolutionary with Jane Fonda and Gregory Peck in *The Old Gringo* (1989). His other film credits include

Jimmy Smits, left, with Jane Fonda and Gregory Peck at the premier of their movie Old Gringo.

Running Scared (1986), *The Believers* (1987), *Vital Signs* (1990), *Fires Within* and *Switch (1991)*.

Jesús Salvador Treviño (?–)

Director, producer, and writer, Jesús Treviño is one of the best-known Chicano filmmakers. His credits include directing episodes of the ABC series "Gabriel's Fire," the NBC series "Lifestories," and the PBS series "Mathnet." His films include *Raíces de sangre (Roots [of Blood]*, 1977, with Richard Yñíguez), which evokes border life and the *maquiladoras* (twin manufacturing plants); *Seguín* (1982, with Henry Darrow and Edward James Olmos), a Hispanic perspective on the Alamo; and documentaries and docudramas, including *Salazar Inquest* (1970), *Chicano Moratorium* (1970), *America Tropical* (1971), *La Raza Unida* (1972), *Yo soy chicano (I Am Chicano,* 1972), *Have Another Drink, Ese* (1977), *One Out of Ten* (1979), and *Yo soy (I Am,* 1985).

Lupe Vélez (1908–1944)

Born on July 18, 1908, in San Luis Potosí, Mexico, Lupe Vélez (María Guadalupe Vélez de Villalobos) became one of the most famous Hispanic screen actresses of all time. Originally a dancer, she debuted in film in 1926 under Hal Roach's direction and became a star the following year as the leading lady in *The Gaucho* opposite Douglas Fairbanks. Known as a fiery leading lady, both in silent and sound films, she later made positive use of her Spanish-accented English to reposition herself as a comedienne in the Mexican Spitfire series. Her films include *Stand and Deliver* (1928), *Lady of the Pavements* (1929), *The Squaw Man, The Cuban Love Song* (1931), *Hot Pepper* (1933), *The Girl from Mexico* (1939), *Mexican Spitfire* (1940), and *Redhead From Manhattan* (1943).

Raoul Walsh (1887–1990)

Raoul Walsh was given his first directorial assignment by D. W. Griffith at Biograph, which was, in collaboration with Christy Cabanne, *The Life of General Villa* (1914), a seven-reel mixture of staged scenes and authentic footage of Pancho Villa's military campaign starring the Mexican bandit himself. Walsh's most notable appearance as an actor was in the role of John Wilkes Booth in Griffith's *The Birth of a Nation* (1915). He subsequently appeared in occasional films but largely devoted himself to a career as a director.

Raquel Welch (Raquel Tejada) was born on September 5, 1940, in Chicago to a Bolivian-born engineer and a mother of English background. Despite a very difficult and inauspicious beginning, and thanks to a phenomenally successful 1963 publicity tour in Europe devised by her second husband, former child actor Patrick Curtis, and herself, she became a major international star without having appeared in a single important film. Known first as a voluptuous sex goddess, she subsequently made a name as a comedienne. Her films include *A Swingin' Summer* (1965), *One Million Years B.C.* (1966), *The Biggest Bundle of Them All, Bandolero!* (1968), *100 Rifles* (1969), *Myra Breckinridge* (1970), *Kansas City Bomber* (1972), *The Three Musketeers* (1974), and *Mother, Jugs, and Speed* (1977).

**Raquel Welch
(1940–)**

Perhaps best known for her role as John Cusack's reluctant traveling companion in Rob Reiner's *The Sure Thing* (1985), Daphne Zuñiga also appeared in Lucille Ball's first dramatic telefilm, *Stone Pillow*. She played Princess Vespa in Mel Brooks's *Spaceballs* (1987) and was the leading lady in *The Fly II* (1989). Among her other credits are *The Dorm That Dripped Blood* (1981), *The Initiation* (1983), *Vision Quest* (1985), *Modern Girls* (1986), *Last Rites* (1988), *Staying Together, Gross Anatomy* (1989), *Eyes of the Panther* (1990), and *Prey of the Chameleon* (1991).

Daphne Zuñiga

Gary D. Keller

*M*usic

Music is a form of cultural communication. Music transmits shared feelings and values, and, when words are added, it can be the ideal vehicle for communicating ideologies. The most strongly symbolic or cultural musical forms are connected to a people's deepest sentiments about their way of life. They express the most profound feelings that those people have about their sense of identity and their everyday life rhythms. Most important, organic, culturally powerful music is generally "homegrown," in the sense that it is created by and belongs to the communities that perform. Many forms of musical expression will be explored in this chapter, from early folk traditions to the contemporary scene.

HISPANIC MUSICAL CULTURAL EXPRESSION ◆ ◆ ◆ ◆ ◆ ◆ ◆ ◆ ◆

Latinos in the United States have been witness to a multitude of styles and performers. Some are fleeting expressions that leave little trace behind. Some homegrown creations— mostly in the form of musical ensembles, their styles, and repertoires—have achieved great popularity and widespread distribution.

Among Latinos in the United States, several musical forms and styles fall into the category of organic, homegrown musical communication. They symbolize the most powerful cultural beliefs and ways of doing things for specific segments of the Latino community. They speak to challenges and problems that confront the various segments of the Latino community in the United States. Over many years these musical forms and styles have developed into cultural traditions that enjoy deep and widespread popularity among their respective audiences. *Música norteña*, the Mexican-American *orquesta*, and *salsa* are excellent examples. These traditions have all contributed in important, "organic" ways to the cultural life of the Latino groups with which they are historically associated. They represent major musical developments whose cultural power is linked to fundamental forces—social, economic, and ideological—among the various segments of the Latino community. These and other musical forms and styles speak symbolically to such issues as acculturation, intercultural conflict, and socioeconomic differences within the Latino communities.

Among the most important Latino musical creations are two ensembles that originated among the Mexicans in Texas. These are música norteña, known among Mexican Texans, or tejanos, as *conjunto,* and *orquesta tejana,* or simply orquesta. Both of these musical styles originated in the first half of the twentieth century, and both should be seen as musical responses to important economic, social, and cultural changes that take place among the Mexican Texans beginning in the 1930s. Both conjunto and orquesta had become major musical styles by the 1950s, and their influence had spread far beyond the Texas borders by the 1970s.

A type of Afro-Caribbean music that came to be known in the 1970s as salsa is another major style of Latino music in the United States. Just as conjunto and orquesta are homegrown Mexican-Texan styles, salsa likewise is the unique music of Afro-Hispanics from Puerto Rico, Cuba, and the Dominican Republic. It too is organically linked to the people who created it, and it continues to occupy a central position in the musical life of Afro-Hispanic people in the United States.

Two important types of vocal music are the Mexican *corrido* (ballad) and a hybrid between the corrido and the *canción* (song). These occupy a special place in the musical life of Mexican Americans, especially those living in

Texas, New Mexico, Arizona, and California. The corrido and the canción-corrido hybrid emerged as powerful cultural expressions in the Hispanic Southwest during the twentieth century, especially the years leading up to World War II. Through their lyrics, the corrido and canción-corrido address more directly than any of the ensemble styles (salsa, conjunto, orquesta) the social and ideological issues which Latinos face in their often difficult adjustment to American life.

A type of musical ensemble that has made a powerful impact on a large segment of Mexican Americans goes by several names—*grupos cumbieros, grupos tropicales, grupos modernos*—but it may best be defined as a Mexican working-class variant of so-called *música tropical. Música tropical* has a long history in Mexico and Latin America, but this ensemble has a history that coincides with the massive emigration from Mexico in the 1960s. Since that time, the grupo tropical/moderno has become an everyday music in the lives of many Mexicans in the American Southwest.

Two popular cousins of salsa are Latin jazz and Latin rock. Both of these related forms have produced their share of gifted performers. And the for-profit motive that drives pop music production does not completely strip it of its cultural message, especially for young people seeking separation from the older generation.

♦ ♦ ♦ ♦ ♦ ♦ ♦ ♦ ♦ ♦ ♦ THE CORRIDO AND CANCIÓN-CORRIDO

The corrido and canción are two distinct genres that have at times experienced considerable overlap, especially since the 1920s. The overlap occurs when the corrido sheds some of its most familiar features, such as the call of the *corridista* to his audience and mention of the date, place, and

Mexican musicians in California in the 1890s.

cast of characters. At the same time, many canciones composed during and after the 1920s abandon that genre's most recognizable feature—its lyrical quality—and assume a seminarrative form, thus moving them in the direction of the corrido. The result is a convergence of the two genres. Of course, this convergence is never complete; some corridos retain enough of their "classical" narrative features to stamp them unmistakably as corridos, while most canciones remain purely lyrical expressions, usually about love.

Beginning in the 1920s canción-corrido hybrids made their appearance in the Hispanic Southwest. Not coincidentally, it was at this time that the large American recording labels, such as Columbia and RCA, first moved into the Southwest and began to commercially expose Mexican-American music in all its variety. Not coincidentally, either, the first of the famous Mexican-American troubadors—singers of the canción and corrido—attained widespread popularity throughout the Southwest during the 1920s. Many of these troubadors were composers of the canción-corrido as well. Through the 1940s they produced a steady flow of canciones-cor-

Lydia Mendoza (center) with Marcelo, comic Tin Tan and Juanita Mendoza in Chicago in the 1950s.

ridos that depicted life in the Hispanic Southwest with great feeling and accuracy, describing in vivid detail both the sadness and the humor of life in the borderlands. Especially moving are those compositions that address the long-standing conflict between Anglos and Mexicans and the oppression endured by the latter.

The intervention of the major recording labels energized musicians and propelled a number of musical traditions to a higher level of innovation, and until the arrival of the wax disk, singers and their songs tended not to attain recognition beyond their immediate locale. Some of the ancient songs had, indeed, spread throughout the Southwest over the previous centuries, but newly composed songs, as well as their composer-performers, were usually confined to their immediate point of origin.

The major labels changed all that. In 1926, RCA, Columbia, Decca, and Brunswick began setting up makeshift studios in rented hotel rooms in cities like Dallas, San Antonio, and Los Angeles, and with the help of local entrepreneurs who knew the pool of musicians available, they began to record commercially a wide variety of musical forms, including the then evolving música norteña, various orquestalike ensembles, and, of course, the canción and the corrido. Women made their impact on Mexican American music at this time, with one female troubador in particular attaining immense popularity throughout the Southwest—the venerable Lydia Mendoza. Other popular troubadors include Los Hermanos Bañuelos (The Bañuelos Brothers, the first to record with the major labels, in 1926) and Los Madrugadores (The Early Birds), both groups from Los Angeles, as well as Los Hermanos Chavarría (The Chavarría Brothers) and Gaytán y Cantú (Gaytán and Cantú), from Texas.

These troubadors left a rich legacy of canciones-corridos that attests to the creative energy the Mexican Americans devoted to a music that could document the harshness of their daily life. This music was so poetically charged that its cultural power can be felt to this day. "El deportado" (The Deported One), a canción-corrido recorded by Los Hermanos Bañuelos in the early 1930s, depicts the bitter experiences of a Mexican immigrant in his encounter with the cold, exploitive system of American capitalism.

Another canción-corrido hybrid, "El lavaplatos" (The Dishwasher), also recorded by Los Hermanos Bañuelos, recounts in more humorous language the adventures of a poor Mexican who immigrates to the United

States in search of the glamorous life of Hollywood, only to find himself drifting from one backbreaking job to another.

Composers of the 1920s through the 1940s were exceptionally committed to documenting the enduring hardships for Mexicans. They utilized the canción-corrido extensively. But the corrido itself plays an even more central role, which dates back to the nineteenth century, in articulating the sociopolitical position of the Mexican folk vis-á-vis the dominant classes. The climate of intercultural conflict that grew out of the Anglo invasion and subsequent annexation of what became the American Southwest at the end of the Mexican-American War (1848) was the ideal setting for the birth of an expressive culture that would key in on this conflict.

Modern Corridos

Between 1848 and 1860, the modern corrido emerged out of an ancient musico-literary form that had been introduced from Spain in the sixteenth century—the romance. And it was evidently in Texas, and not in Michoacán, Durango, or Jalisco, as once thought, that the first corridos were composed. One of these was "Kiansis," a corrido that documents the epic cattle drives from Texas to the Kansas stockyards, which contains subtle indications of the intercultural conflict that attended Anglo-Mexican relations at the time.

"El corrido de Juan Cortina" details in stronger language the resentment that Mexicans on the border felt toward the Americans, and celebrates the exploits of Juan Nepomuceno Cortina. He was a Mexican from south Texas, a member of a wealthy landowning family with deep roots in the Texas-Mexico border region who came to resent the arrogant attitude of the Anglo newcomers, especially the fortune makers. After an incident in which he accosted a town marshal who was pistol-whipping a *vaquero* (cowboy) who worked on his mother's ranch, Cortina was declared an outlaw, and thereafter he dedicated his life to guerrilla warfare, until he was driven out of Texas by the U.S. cavalry.

"El Corrido de Juan Cortina" ushered in what has been called the hero corrido period, when the prevalent type was the corrido of intercultural conflict. This type of corrido invariably features a larger-than-life Mexican hero who single-handedly defies a cowardly, smaller-than-life gang of Anglo-American lawmen. The hero either defeats the Anglos or goes down fighting. In this way, the protagonist gains heroic status in the Mexican-American community, becoming, in effect, a kind of redeemer for the collective insults suffered by his people at the hands of the Anglos.

Hero corridos were written until the 1920s, in Texas and elsewhere, including such classics as "Joaquín Murrieta and Jacinto Treviño," but perhaps the most memorable is "El corrido de Gregorio Cortez," immortalized by Américo Paredes in his book *With His Pistol in His Hand,* which served as the basis for the film *The Ballad of Gregorio Cortez.* The corrido documents the odyssey of a Mexican Texan who fled for his life after he killed an Anglo sheriff in self-defense, because of a linguistic misunderstanding over some stolen horses.

The hero corrido was most prevalent during the early period of Anglo-Mexican contact. This period spans the years from about 1848 to the early 1900s—a period during which Mexicans entertained hopes, albeit diminishing with time, that they could still defeat the Anglos and drive them out of their territory. However, the hero corrido continued to enjoy prominence until the 1930s, when a new type emerged.

The new corridos, prevalent since the end of World War II, have been labeled victim corridos, and demonstrate sharp differences in subject matter from those of the earlier period. Foremost is the disappearance of the larger-than-life hero. In his place a new protagonist emerges, one who is usually portrayed as a helpless victim of Anglo oppression. This shift in the corrido of intercultural conflict from hero to victim is too fundamental to be considered a random event. In fact, it coincides with equally fundamental changes in Mexican-American society. It thus happens that the newer corridos appeared at the precise moment when Mexican Americans initiated a wholesale movement from rural to urban, from folk to modern, from a monocultural to a bicultural lifestyle, and from proletarian status to a more diversified social organization.

After World War II, in this climate of emergent political and economic diversification, new cultural directions and new modes of interpreting the Mexican-American experience were being charted. Fully conscious of their newfound power, the postwar Mexican Americans began to rethink their relationship with the dominant Anglo majority and to demand more economic and political equality (as well as acceptance). However, despite the tentative beginnings of an interethnic accommodation, the Anglos were not yet ready to accept the Mexicans as equal, and the intercultural friction persisted. This friction at times forced Mexican Americans to put aside growing internal class differences, as they closed ranks to fight racial discrimination. In this atmosphere of heightened political awareness, the corrido continued to play an important role. Chicanos [Mexican Americans],

"Gregorio Cortez" is the ideal example of the hero corrido. As a symbol of his people's hopes for deliverance, the hero achieves his revenge through the process of "status reversal," wherein the hero, who personifies the collective will, defeats or at least defies the American lawmen, who personify the dominant Anglos. Thus, through the exploits of the hero, the Mexican Americans of the Southwest symbolically invert the real world, assuming in vicarious fashion a dominant position over their oppressors and in this way achieving a sense of deliverance.

having developed more effectively organized political machinery to challenge Anglo supremacy, relied less on their corridos to uplift a battered cultural image and more to rally support for active political causes. A corrido is more likely to elicit an active response—outrage and group mobilization—if it depicts a helpless victim rather than a potent, larger-than-life hero. In a sense, the two types of corrido are antithetical—one reflecting pent-up frustration and powerlessness, the other active resistance.

Many victim corridos have been composed since the end of World War II. Typicallly, the Anglos openly abuse the basic rights of a Mexican, and the community responds vigorously to defend the victim(s). The corrido draws attention to the community's forceful actions in protesting Anglo injustice, and when the outcome permits, the corrido celebrates the community's victory. In any case, the Anglos are portrayed in a negative light, while the Mexicans are seen as a proud people fighting for their civil rights.

Both the hero and victim corridos of intercultural conflict have a long and auspicious history in the Mexican-American oral music tradition. As indicated, the former was prevalent at a time when conflict between Anglo and Mexican was rampant and undisguised. The hero corrido peaked in the early twentieth century, when the Mexican Americans reached the lowest point in their history of oppression in the United States. As they climbed out of their wretched state, during and after World War II, the victim corrido appeared and gained ascendancy. Both types of corrido have survived into the late twentieth century, but their presence in the musical repertory of Mexican Americans today is sporadic. They tend to surface only during moments of intercultural crisis—usually when the still-dominant Anglos commit a blatant act of discrimination.

MÚSICA NORTEÑA ✦

Of all the musical creations of the Latino community in the United States, música norteña (also known as the Mexican-Texan conjunto) is unquestionably one of the most culturally powerful. Anchored by the diatonic button accordion, this folk tradition had grown deep roots among the Mexicans living along the Texas-Mexico border by the early twentieth century. And, thanks to the commercialization introduced by the major

American recording labels in the 1920s, it eventually spread far beyond its origins in south Texas and northern Mexico.

How a music of such humble folk origins could develop into a powerful artistic expression with such widespread appeal is a provocative question. The answer lies in its beginnings along the Texas-Mexico border. The diatonic button accordion, which is the heart of música norteña, was evidently introduced into northeastern Mexico sometime in the middle of the nineteenth century—perhaps by German immigrants who settled in the Monterrey, Nuevo León, area of northeastern Mexico in the 1860s. Since the Mexican-Texans of this period maintained close cultural links with Mexican norteños (northerners), it is likely that the instrument quickly spread into south Texas. It is possible, however, that the accordion was introduced to the tejanos (Mexican-Texans) by way of the German, Czech, and Polish settlers who had migrated to south central Texas beginning in the 1840s. Since intense conflict, marked by overt discrimination against Mexicans, was the norm between tejanos and the latter groups, it is less likely that the interchange occurred on that front. In any case, the exact identity of the donor culture may never be known.

What we do know is that by the late nineteenth century the accordion, coupled with one or two other instruments—the *tambora de rancho* (ranch drum) and the *bajo sexto* (a twelve-string guitar)—had become the norm for music-and-dance celebrations in south Texas. The tambora was a primitive folk instrument fashioned out of native materials. It was usually played with wooden mallets, their tips covered with cotton wrapped in goatskin. The bajo sexto apparently originated in the Guanajuato-Michoacán area in Mexico; it is a twelve-string guitar tuned in double courses. How it migrated to and established itself in the border area is a mystery. But in its new locale it became an indispensable companion to the accordion, especially after 1930, when it and the accordion emerged as the core of the evolving ensemble.

The conjunto norteño, or conjunto, as it came to be known in Texas, thrived from early on. It soon became the preferred ensemble for the rural working-class folk who adopted it and eventually molded it into a genuine working-class expression. In its early days it relied on the salon music introduced from Europe in the eighteenth and nineteenth centuries and popularized first among the genteel city dwellers, then passed on to the masses later. The principal genres were the polka, the *redowa,* and the *schottishe,* although the mazurka was also current. Rounding out the repertoire was the *huapango*, culturally important because it was native to the Gulf Coast region of Tamaulipas and northern Vera Cruz, and thus represented a regional contribution. The huapango is more frequently associated with the music of the *huasteca* region of southern Tamaulipas, Mexico, where it has a ternary pulse built around a 3/4 meter. As performed by norteños, however, the huapango early on acquired a binary pulse built around the triplets of 6/8 meter.

Despite the presence everywhere of the accordion in the musical celebrations of the tejanos/norteños, the conjunto did not achieve dominance until the 1930s. Prior to this time it was still an improvised ensemble with little stylistic development and plenty of competition from other types of (also improvised) ensembles. In fact, the history of the Mexican-Texan conjunto can be divided into three distinct stages. The first, to the late 1920s, is the formative, when the ensemble was strictly improvisational and the accordion was still played either solo, with guitar or bajo sexto, or with the tambora de rancho. The technique used to play the accordion itself owed much to that of the Germans who had originally introduced the instrument to the Mexicans. This included the heavy use of the left-hand bass-chord buttons, a technique that lent the instrument a distinctive sound and articulation. As noted, this embryonic ensemble was common to Mexicans on both sides of the border.

The second stage begins in the mid-1930s, when the Mexican-Texan conjunto began to move beyond its counterpart across the border—gradually at first, radically after World War II. The sudden development of the conjunto during the second stage is undoubtedly linked to intervention of the large American recording labels, which began in earnest in the early 1930s. At this time RCA Victor (through its Bluebird subsidiary), Columbia, and Decca moved into the Southwest and began commercially exploiting the variety of music then flourishing in the region. But the rapid development of the conjunto cannot be explained simply in terms of its commercialization, which, in any case, was never as massive as that of general market American pop music. On the other hand, the ethnic/class dichotomy which came to dominate the political culture of Mexican-Texans after the 1930s was certainly a powerful catalyst.

Thus, by the mid-1930s, when accordionist Narciso Martínez began his commercial recording career, the first steps had been taken toward cementing the core of the modern conjunto—the accordion-bajo sexto combination. These two instruments would become inseparable after this time. Meanwhile, Martínez, who is acknowledged as the "father" of the modern conjunto, devised a new technique for the instrument, one that differed radically from the old Germanic style. He stopped using the left-hand bass-chord buttons, leaving the accompaniment to the bajo sexto, which was very capably played by his partner Santiago Almeida.

The resulting sound was dramatically novel—a clean, spare treble, and a staccato effect that contrasted sharply with the Germanic sound of earlier norteño accordionists. The Martínez style quickly took hold and became the standard that younger accordionists emulated, particularly those who established themselves after World War II.

The years immediately following the war ushered in the third stage in the conjunto's development. A younger group of musicians began charting a new direction for the rapidly evolving style. Foremost among these was accordionist Valerio Longoria, who was responsible for several innovations. Among these were two elements of the modern conjunto that Longoria introduced—the modern trap drums and the canción ranchera, the latter a working-class subtype of the Mexican *ranchera*, which dates from the 1930s. Obsessed with abandoned men and unfaithful women, the canción ranchera has always had special appeal for male patrons of conjunto music. Since it was often performed in the 2/4 meter of the traditional polka favored by Mexican-Texans, the ranchera quickly replaced the polka itself as the mainstay of the modern conjunto. Longoria's introduction of the drums and ranchera earned him a special leadership position in the unfolding style, and several younger conjunto musicians have cited his example as the source of their inspiration—Paulino Bernal and Oscar Hernández, to name two of the best.

Paulino Bernal is himself a major figure in the development of the modern ensemble. His conjunto is hailed as the greatest in the history of the tradition, an honor based on the craftsmanship and the number of innovations attributable to El Conjunto Bernal. The latter include the introduction of three-part vocals and the addition of the larger chromatic accordion. El Conjunto Bernal's greatest distinction, however, lies in its ability to take the traditional elements of the conjunto and raise them to a level of virtuosity that has not been matched to this day. Bernal had accomplished all of this by the early 1960s.

Meanwhile, after about 1960 the conjunto and the older norteño ensemble across the Rio Grande began to converge, as the norteños came under

Los Relámpagos was "discovered" by Paulino Bernal in 1964 while he was on a scouting trip to Reynosa, Tamaulipas, across the border from McAllen, Texas, in search of talent for a new recording label he had recently started.

the influence of their tejano counterparts. Especially responsible for this convergence was Los Relámpagos del Norte (The Northern Lightning Bolts), a group led by accordionist Ramón Ayala and bajo sexto player Cornelio Reyna. Ayala and Reyna were strongly influenced by El Conjunto Bernal.

Los Relámpagos began recording for Bernal's Bego label in 1965, and within two years had risen to unparalleled fame on both sides of the border. The group remained unchallenged until the mid-1970s, when Ayala and Reyna went their separate ways. Ayala shortly organized his own conjunto, Los Bravos del Norte (The Northern Brave Ones), and that group went on to dominate the norteño market for at least a decade.

Since the innovations of the 1960s, the conjunto has turned decidedly conservative, with both musicians and patrons choosing to preserve the elements of the style as these were worked out in the 1940s through the 1960s. Despite its conservatism, the tradition has expanded phenomenally, in the 1970s to 1990s spreading far beyond its original base along the Texas-Mexico border. In the last few years, the music has taken root in such far-flung places as Washington, D.C., California, and the Midwest, as well as the entire tier of northern Mexican border states and even in such places as Michoacán and Sinaloa. In its seemingly unstoppable expansion, conjunto music has always articulated a strong Mexicanized, working-class life-style, thus helping to preserve Mexican culture wherever it has taken root on American (and Mexican) soil.

The rapid rise and maturation of conjunto music is a remarkable phenomenon in itself, but more important from an anthropological perspective is its cultural significance, its strong "organic" connection to working-class Mexicans in the United States. Clearly, the music is anything but a casual item of entertainment among its supporters. In fact, as a musical expression the conjunto has become a symbolic emblem of Mexican working-class culture—those people employed in farm labor and other unskilled and semiskilled occupations found mostly in service industries. And, the conjunto's alliance with that class was cemented during its rapid evolution between the years 1936 and 1960.

Beyond this identification with the working class, in the years following World War II the conjunto became linked to the cultural strategies of Mexican Texans, in particular, as these proletarian workers faced continuing prejudice from a hostile Anglo population, as well as antagonism from a new class of upwardly mobile, acculturated Mexican Texans, who sought to put some distance between themselves and the more Mexican-ized common workers.

In the end, conjunto music came to symbolize the struggle of the workers to maintain a sense of social solidarity and cultural uniformity against the upwardly mobile Mexican Americans, who espoused a different musical ideal, in the form of the orquesta or big band, and who viewed conjunto music as the expression of a vulgar, unassimilatable class of people. This quality of conjunto—its strong endorsement by the common workers and repudiation by more affluent people—was particularly evident in its Mex-ican Texan home base, but it was carried over to new locales, such as Ari-zona, where it was derisively called *catachún* music, and California, where it was universally considered cantina "trash."

◆ ◆ ◆ ◆ ◆ ◆ ◆ ◆ ◆ ◆ ◆ ◆ THE MEXICAN-AMERICAN ORQUESTA

Three types of orquestas have been present in the Southwest at different periods in the last century. The earliest type is one that existed during the nineteenth century and the early part of the twentieth. This early ensem-ble, built primarily around the violin, was hardly an "orquesta." It was for the most part an improvised ensemble, one dependent on the availability of musicians and scarce instruments for composition.

The rudimentary nature of this early orquesta is linked to the marginaliza-tion of the Mexicans of the Southwest—their having been stripped of all political and economic stability by the Anglo-Americans who invaded the territory and eventually annexed it to the United States. Having become American citizens by default, the new Mexican Americans found them-selves at a decided disadvantage—as did all Mexican immigrants who came after them. The original settlers were gradually dispossessed of all their lands and forced into a state of subordination, setting a pattern that would apply to all those who migrated to the Southwest in the twentieth century. José Limón, the noted Mexican-American folklorist, has summa-rized developments in the Southwest following the American invasion:

> Between 1848 and 1890, an Anglo ranching society established
> itself among the native (also ranching) Mexican population, liv-
> ing with them in a rough equality. However, beginning in the

An orquesta típica *in Houston.*

1890s, a clear racial-cultural stratification and subordination began to emerge, as a new wave of Anglo-American entrepreneurs and farming interests established a political and economic hegemony over the native population as well as the thousands of Mexican immigrants entering the area after 1910.... With few exceptions, this total population...became the victim of class-racial exploitation and mistreatment.

Given their precarious social organization as a subordinate group in the new social order that was created in the Southwest, the resident Mexicans (now Mexican Americans) and all those who came afterward found it difficult to maintain any but the most rudimentary of musical traditions. To be sure, the norteños had never enjoyed the best of facilities for any kind of education, musical or otherwise. Throughout the Spanish colonial era and the period of Mexican independence, life in the north had been of a peasant, agrarian nature, with few of the amenities that Mexicans in more centralized and urban areas enjoyed. Despite their relative isolation, the norteños managed to keep up with musical developments in Mexico and, as early chroniclers have documented, were able to maintain reasonably equipped ensembles.

With the American invasion and the subsequent oppression of the native Mexicans, the opportunities for musical training all but disappeared, except in urban areas along the border, where the Mexicans preserved a degree of political and economic integration, even after the annexation of the Southwest by the United States. Thus, cities like Brownsville, Laredo, and El Paso managed to support modest resources for the training and equipping of musical groups. But in general, the American invasion reduced an orquesta tradition inherited from Greater Mexico to its bare and often improvised essentials—a violin or two plus guitar accompaniment, with other instruments added on an ad hoc basis.

The 1920s saw the emergence in the urban areas of better-organized orquestas, built, again, around the violin. This was the so-called *orquesta típica* (typical orchestra). The first típica was organized in Mexico City in 1880, and it was supposedly modeled after an earlier folk orquesta common in Mexican rural areas throughout the nineteenth century (also known as típica) and apparently similar in instrumentation to the folk orquestas of the Hispanic Southwest. The self-styled orquestas típicas of urban origin were clearly expressions of what is known as *costumbrismo*, a type of romantic nationalism in which the dominant groups find it appealing to imitate certain elements of the folk, or peasant classes. As such, these orquestas were given to wearing "typical" *charro* (cowboy) outfits similar to those worn by the Mexican mariachi, in an effort to capture in vicarious fashion some of the flavor of Mexican pastoral life.

In the United States, the first típica was probably organized in El Paso or Laredo sometime in the 1920s. These orquestas were strongly reminiscent of the modern mariachi, whose historical roots they may well share. The basic instrumentation of the orquesta típica consisted of violins, guitars, and psalteries, although in the Southwest other instruments were often added in ad hoc fashion. The size of the típica could vary from four or five musicians to as many as twenty.

Típicas were enlisted for almost any occasion, although they were ideally suited for patriotic-type celebrations, such as *cinco de mayo* (fifth of May, when the Mexican general Ignacio Zaragoza postponed the French invasion of Mexico by defeating General Laurencez at Puebla) and *dieciseis de septiembre* (sixteenth of September, Independence Day), two dates of special significance for Mexican people. The repertoire of orquestas típicas consisted of *aires nacionales*—tunes that over the years had acquired status as "national airs," such as "El Jarabe Tapatío" (The Jalisco Dance), "La

The early orquesta of the Hispanic Southwest enjoyed great prominence in the musical affairs of the Mexican communities across the territory—even in Texas, where the conjunto offered strong competition. Small orquestas were enlisted for all kinds of celebrations, which ran the gamut from private weddings and birthdays to public multievent celebrations known as funciones. *Again, almost without exception, these orquestas were of variable composition, although they seldom included more than the minimum instruments mentioned before—a violin or two with guitar accompaniment.*

Negra" (The Dark Beauty), "Pajarillo Barranqueño" (Little Bird of Barranca), and others. Típicas seem to have fallen out of favor among Mexican Americans during the Great Depression of the 1930s. They disappeared from the musical scene in the Southwest during World War II.

The 1930s saw the emergence of the third and most important type of orquesta, this one a version of the modern dance bands that swept through the urban landscapes of both Mexico and the United States during the 1920s and 1930s. The modern orquesta clearly represented a musico-cultural departure from earlier ensembles. In fact, it is tied to the fortunes of a new group of Mexican Americans who began to make an impact on Hispanic life in the United States during the 1930s and 1940s. Historian Mario García has aptly labeled this group The Mexican American Generation. This was the first generation of Americans of Mexican descent to aspire for inclusion in Anglo-American life. Consequently, it advocated the ideology of assimilation, an ideology based on the notion that Mexican Americans should detach themselves from their Mexican heritage and begin thinking like Americans. However, the persistent conflict with the Anglos and their continuing discrimination against Mexicans ultimately forced The Mexican American Generation to modify its ideology of assimilation and adopt a more biculturalist stance—to be both Mexican and American.

The modern orquesta played a prominent role in accommodating the Mexican American generation's biculturalist strategy. In the bimusical repertoire it adopted, the orquesta catered to the generation's bicultural nature. By performing music traditionally associated with Mexico and Latin America, it kept alive the Mexican Americans' ethnic roots; by performing music associated with American big bands, it satisfied The Mexican American Generation's desire to assimilate American culture. Thus, from Mexico and Latin America came the *danzón, bolero, guaracha, rumba,* and other dance genres; from the United States came the boogie, swing, fox-trot, and so on.

Very quickly, however, the Mexican-American orquesta began to experiment with various bimusical combinations—especially the orquestas in Texas, which, like the conjunto, assumed a leadership role in music developments in the Hispanic Southwest after World War II. As a result of their increasing exposure through commercial recordings (Texas had the biggest Hispanic recording companies), the most professional orquestas típicas became the models that others around the Southwest imitated. Co-

incident with this professionalization was the appearance and populariza-
tion of the public ballroom dance, which allowed the most successful
orquestas to rely exclusively on performance for full-time employment.

Thus, ever since the birth of the modern Mexican-American orquesta, the
most renowned names have come from Texas. There was, for example,
Beto Villa, from Falfurrias, Texas, sometimes called the "father" of the
Mexican-American orquesta. Acclaimed for a folksy, ranchero polka that
took the Southwest by storm, Villa deftly juxtaposed this "country" style
polka, which came to be known as Tex-Mex, against more sophisticated
genres drawn from Latin America and the United States—*danzones*,
guarachas, former, fox-trots, and swings.

Villa's influence on orquestas throughout the Hispanic Southwest was enormous during the 1940s and 1950s, and he inspired many imitators. A notable successor to the Tex-Mex tradition Villa inaugurated was Isidro López,
also from Texas. A singer-saxophonist, López deliberately emphasized the

Beto Villa y su Orquesta,

c. 1946.

ranchero mode of performance in an attempt to attract a larger share of the common workers, who were otherwise more faithful to the ever more powerful (and more ranchero) conjunto. López was thus the first orquesta leader to add the working-class *canción ranchera* to the orquesta repertoire. But he added his own touch to the ranchera, embellishing it with a blend of mariachi and Tex-Mex that López himself dubbed Texachi.

At least two other orquestas of note were active during the 1940s and 1950s—Balde González's, from Victoria, Texas, and Pedro Bugarín's, from Phoenix, Arizona. The former specialized in a smoother, more romantic delivery that appealed in particular to those upwardly mobile tejanos who were seen by working-class people as snobbish and who were derisively known as *jaitones* (from high tone). As such, Balde González, a pianist-singer, was best known for the smooth delivery of the romantic and sophisticated *bolero*, although he often turned as well to the American fox-trot, which he transformed by adding lyrics in Spanish. Bugarín pursued a more eclectic approach, one that included the full gamut of bimusical performance, from rancheras to fox-trots.

Alonzo y su Orquesta, a typical orchestra, c. 1950.

In the Los Angeles area, meanwhile, a number of orquestas operated during the maturational years of the Mexican-American *orquesta*—the 1940s and 1950s. Most of these took their cue from music developments in Latin America (including the Afro-Caribbean) and were less influenced by developments in the Tex-Mex field. One noteworthy exception was the orquesta that the legendary Lalo Guerrero fronted for a time. As Guerrero himself admitted, he "mixed it all up," combining Tex-Mex with boogie and Latin American, including salsa. But Guerrero was best known for his unique bimusical tunes, which fused music and linguistic elements from swing, rhumba, and *caló*, a folk dialect popular among working-class youth in the Southwest and elsewhere. Most of these tunes were written by Guerrero himself. Some achieved immortality through the movie *Zoot Suit*, produced in 1982 by the Chicano filmmaker and erstwhile activist Luis Valdez (for example, the tune "Marihuana Boogie").

But the most influential orquestas continued to originate in Texas. In the 1960s and 1970s, which may well have been the peak years for the Mexican-American *orquesta*, several groups emerged from the active tradition established in the Lone Star State. Foremost among these was Little Joe and the Latinaires, renamed Little Joe y la Familia in 1970. La Familia exploited the Tex-Mex ranchero sound fashioned by Isidro López to its utmost, fusing it to American jazz and rock *within the same musical piece* to achieve a unique bimusical sound that came to be known as La Onda Chicana (The Chicano Wave).

Little Joe first experimented with the fusion of Mexican ranchero and American jazz/rock in a hugely successful LP titled *Para la Gente* (For the People), released in 1972 by Little Joe's own company, Buena Suerte Records. On this album, Little Joe and his brother Johnny combined their voices duet-fashion to create a style of ranchera so appealing to Mexican Americans that La Familia was catapulted to the very top of La Onda Chicana. Backing Little Joe and Johnny was the usual complement of instruments found in the best-organized Mexican-American orquestas—two trumpets, two saxophones, a trombone, and a rhythm section of bass, electric guitar, drums, and keyboards.

The music selections on the landmark LP varied from the hard, brash sounds of traditional Tex-Mex rancheras, like "La Traicionera" (The Treacherous Woman), to the lush, big-band sounds of the Mexican fox-trot, as in "Viajera" (Traveler), to an interesting arrangement of an old folk song, "Las Nubes" (The Clouds). The last tune mentioned seemed to capture the cultural essence of La Onda Chicana and its obvious link to the cultural revivalism of the Chicano political and cultural movement that swept through the Mexican-American community in the late 1960s and early 1970s. Thanks, at least in part, to the nationalistic climate fostered by the Chicano movement, "Las Nubes" became a sort of anthem for Chicano music celebrations everywhere.

Many of the arrangements on the *Para la Gente* album were augmented with strings borrowed from the Dallas Symphony—a great novelty in itself—but most effective of all was the strategic interlacing of jazz riffs within the rancheras. The effects were stunning and captured the music sentiments of bicultural Mexican Americans everywhere. The impact of this trailblazing LP was so great that in the early 1990s, almost twenty years from the time it appeared, several of its tunes still formed part of the basic repertory of semiprofessional weekend dance orquestas still to be found in the Southwest.

As fashioned by Little Joe y la Familia, La Onda Chicana spread rapidly throughout the Southwest and beyond. Other orquestas followed La Familia's lead, as more and more efforts were directed at creating a synthesis of ranchera and jazz/rock. Many of these efforts were remarkable for their effect, with particularly successful results being achieved by the orquestas of Sunny and the Sunliners, Latin Breed, and Tortilla Factory, all from Texas.

By the mid-1980s, La Onda Chicana had receded from its watershed years, with the orquesta tradition generally suffering a noticeable decline. Not only did further innovation come to a stop, but the style suffered a retreat from its golden years of the 1960s and 1970s. The most notable sign of decline was the substitution, beginning in the early 1980s, of the horn section for synthesized keyboards. At first, these tried to imitate, synthetically, the sound of the trumpets, saxes, and trombone, but eventually the keyboards developed their own synthesized sound, one closer in spirit to the conjunto, and this became the norm after about 1985.

The reasons for the decline of the orquesta are not entirely clear, but they evidently have to do with the aging of the population that originally gave impetus to the orquesta tradition—the strongly bicultural Mexican American Generation and its immediate successors, the baby boomers born in the late 1940s and early 1950s. Except in Texas, where an entrenched tradition survived into the 1990s, Mexican Americans growing up in more recent years have been less attracted by the old-fashioned orquesta. The lack of support can be seen in the declining number of semiprofessional orquestas throughout the Southwest, as DJs and the smaller synthesizer-dependent groups have replaced the orquesta in most public and domestic celebrations.

The popularity of the Mexican-American orquesta, as well as its social power, is directly linked to the cultural economy of The Mexican Ameri-

Xavier Cugat and his orchestra.

can Generation and its immediate successors. From the outset, orquesta served as a link between the generation's ideology and its political economy. Unlike conjunto, which early on became a mirror for working-class life and the workers' resistance to the pressures of acculturation, orquesta was as culturally flexible as its clientele. In it early years, however, especially the 1940s and 1950s, the orquesta was rather tentative in its approach to bimusical performance—the mixing of American and Mexican styles. At a time when his clientele was still unaccustomed to its newfound prosperity and biculturalism, a Beto Villa could at best choose between one or the other: he could play a Tex-Mex polka or an American swing, but never the two simultaneously. In time, as the Mexican Americans adapted to their bicultural reality, orquesta performed a parallel synthesis—what we might call "compound bimusicality."

By the 1970s, this compound bimusicality had reached full expression in the orquestas' mastery of the art of musical code switching. Similar to the "compound bilingual," who code switches from one language to another within the same sentence, orquesta had learned to switch musical languages within the same musical sentence, that is, within the same musical piece. This is what Little Joe truly accomplished for the first time in his landmark album, *Para la Gente*. He succeeded in fusing two musical systems under one code of performance. This feat was repeated with equal success by many other orquestas in the succeeding years.

But the musical code switching of the Mexican-American orquesta was even more subtle than the linguistic code switching of its supporters, in that it took place on two distinct but overlapping planes. One switch occurred at the level of ethnicity, the other at the level of class. At the level of ethnicity, the switch was signified by the interlacing of jazz riffs within the flow of an otherwise Mexican ranchera. At the same time, this switch was mediated by parallel shifts occurring at another level of acoustic discrimination—class stylistics, or what Mexican-Texans used to distinguish between a *jaitón* (high-tone) versus a ranchero style. The former was a marker for alleged (or contrived) musical sophistication, but above all it was an index for "high class" snobbery. Ranchero, on the other hand, was a token for the simple, unpretentious life of the country and the barrio— a token The Mexican American Generation was reluctant to renounce.

Above all, in its bimusicality the Mexican-American orquesta represents the dialectical synthesis of two sets of opposed cultures—Mexican and American on the one hand, working and middle class on the other. This synthesis was masterfully articulated by the bimusical orquesta. The best were perfectly adept at this double code switching, as they moved effortlessly from ranchero to jaitón and from Mexican to American. At their very best, orquestas achieved a seamless stream of bimusical sound that found a fitting label—La Onda Chicana.

SALSA ◆

Salsa is Spanish for "sauce"—in this case a term that refers to the hot, spicy rhythms of Afro-Caribbean music. When people talk about salsa music, however, they are actually referring to a generic term that includes a number of distinct types of Afro-Caribbean music, although one in particular, the *son guaguancó*, has predominated since the 1960s. Whatever the origins of the term "salsa," the music has deep, even sacred, roots in its Afro-Caribbean context.

In a fine study of a religious musical ritual in the Dominican Republic called *salve*, Martha Ellen Davis informs us that the salve is a bimusical expression that, as usually performed, progresses from a purely Hispanic section (the *salve sagrada*) to a more intense, spontaneous, and Africanized section (the *salve secular*). The latter section incorporates many of the rhythms (and polyrhythms) of a generalized Afro-Caribbean music that we eventually distilled in the United States into what is now commonly known as salsa. Davis interprets the bicultural nature of the salve as the logical result of the syncretization of two radically different cultures in a historical relationship of domination/subordination—Hispanic and African.

What is most important about Davis's analysis of the salve is her conception of this ritual as a key symbol of Afro-Caribbean culture, specifically, its location at the center of the Afro-Dominicans' musical universe. As an expression of an Afro-Caribbean music that is rooted deep within the practice of everyday culture, the salve provides a powerful example of the essentially sacred origins of Afro-Caribbean music. This is a sacredness that Americans of Afro-Caribbean descent who subscribe to various offshoots of that music—including salsa—have been reluctant to give up.

Thus, in his 1974 study of the ritual aspects of Afro-Cuban music among Cubans and Puerto Ricans of New York City, Morton Marks argues that despite the commercialization of the music, strong elements of African Yoruba religion have survived in at least some of its development in urban areas such as New York City. In Cuba, these Yoruba elements were syncretized early on with Catholicism to create the Lucumí religious cults, while in New York, Yoruba religion survives in the Santería cults, which, again, combine in their worship deities from both Catholic and Yoruba religion. For Marks, moreover, the interplay of musical styles, as they unfold within a given song (like the salve, usually progressing from a Hispanic form of communication to an African one), is the centrally defining characteristic. Thus, in analyzing the songs "Alma con Alma" (Soul with Soul), by the great salsa singer Celia Cruz, and "El Santo en Nueva York" (The Saint in New York), by La Lupe, a Cuban vocalist, Marks proposes that "the process of `Africanization' underlies the performance, with the musical form proceeding from a strongly North American-influenced

Salsa as a Cultural Expression

As Jorge Duany wrote, "Salsa is neither a musical style nor a particular rhythm, but rather a hybrid genre." According to Duany, the word "salsa" was first used to refer to this hybrid genre in the 1960s, but it did not gain universal recognition until 1975, when it was used as the title for a popular movie.

dance band style, into an *emically* named Yoruba and Lucumí praise song style known as kasha."

The transformation described by Marks is, in fact, the hallmark of most salsa music since the 1960s. In piece after musical piece, particularly the vast majority that utilize the son guaguancó, the music begins with a standardized Hispanic section whose lyrics are divided into an "A" part, followed by a "B," then returning to the "A" part (ABA form). Meanwhile, the musical background, usually provided by brass instruments (trumpets and/or trombones) in obbligato mode, displays the strong influence of American jazz. Once this section is completed (often it is the shortest section of the tune), the *son montuno* section begins. It is in this section that the African style predominates, particularly through the call-and-response pattern, in which a solo and chorus keep alternating phrases.

Afro-Caribbean music, then, has dual roots, Hispanic and African, which in the United States have undergone further development with the infusion of jazz elements as articulated in the horn obbligatos. In its duality, the music richly displays the process of syncretization, although it has also maintained a dialectical relationship to its twin roots—a relationship that enables the participants in musical events to juxtapose one cultural domain against the other with dramatic effects. This is the point that both Marks and Davis are at pains to demonstrate. In the United States, meanwhile, Afro-Caribbean music has preserved much of this duality, despite the jazz accretions and heavy commercialization. Here, too, among initiates of Santería cults the music retains the ritual qualities and the dialectical movement between two cultures that are associated with sacred performances in the homeland.

Clearly, for people of Afro-Caribbean descent—Puerto Ricans, Cubans, Dominicans, and others—what is now called salsa has that kind of summarizing power. Salsa stands preeminently for their special sense of Afro-Hispanic "Caribbeanness." But salsa obviously has an audience that extends far beyond its core Caribbean setting. As a cultural symbol, it spreads out with diminishing influence toward audiences whose contact with the music's cultural roots is at best casual. Among these audiences the music's symbolic power is highly diluted or even nonexistent.

Dual origins of salsa recall that its antecedents are hybrid or syncretic expressions that draw from two cultures Hispanic and African. Modern salsa owes its greatest debt to the musical culture of Cuba, although Puerto

The Joe Cuba Sextet, one of the first groups to record salsa in English.

Rico and, to a lesser extent, the Dominican Republic are also contributing cultures. Two Puerto Rican musical genres, in particular, are legitimate antecedents of modern salsa—the *bomba* and the *plena*. The plena is more heavily influenced by European musical culture than the bomba.

Both the plena and the bomba were once integral elements in the life of Puerto Rican blacks. They are still performed on the island, though with decreasing frequency. In the United States, however, plena and bomba have undergone some transformation. Adopted (and adapted) by small salsa conjuntos (such as Julito Collazo and his Afro-Cuban Group), bomba and plena are reaching larger audiences, even as some of their elements are absorbed by salsa itself.

Cuba is the indisputable cradle of modern *salsa*, although in the United States the music is more intimately associated with Puerto Ricans. In Cuba, Africans established strong enclaves that carried on many of the musico-ritualistic traditions from the homeland, specifically those attached to the Lucumi cults mentioned earlier. Secularized and made popular commercially in the twentieth century, Afro-Cuban music attached to the Lu-cumi/Santería cults underwent further hybridization with Western musical forms. In its hybrid form, this music acquired strong stylistic features that came to appeal to millions of people outside the original cultural core.

It was out of this hybridization process that salsa emerged. However, salsa represents the end stage of this process. Earlier Afro-Cuban forms enjoyed their own moments of glory, as the pace of hybridization accelerated in the middle part of the twentieth century. In this, Cuba again took center stage. John Storm Roberts has described this hybridization as follows: "Taken as a whole, Cuban music presents a more equal balance of African and Spanish ingredients than that of any other Latin country except Brazil. Spanish folklore enriched the music of the countryside, of the city, and of the salon. At the same time—aided by an illicit slave trade that continued right through the nineteenth century—the pure African strain remained stronger in Cuba than anywhere else.... As a result, Western African melody and drumming...were brought cheek by jowl with country music based on Spanish ten-line *décima*."

It should come as no surprise that Cuba is the source of many of the musical genres that precede salsa—genres that in fact make up the tapestry of its sounds. Thus, important salsa antecedents such as the *dazón, rumba-guaguancó, charanga, mambo, guaracha, son, bolero,* and *cha cha cha* all originate in Cuba. The mambo and cha cha cha had an enormous impact in and of themselves, of course, but the two genres that most influenced modern salsa directly are the son and the rumba.

The rumba is actually a generic term for more specific Afro-Cuban genres—the *yambú, cumbia,* and guaguancó. Again, of these three, it is the guaguancó that is most closely identified with salsa. All, however, have common African characteristics—complex polyrhythms and alternating sections of solo voice and call-and-response. Originally, the rumba was played with African or Africanized instruments of the drum family—the *quinto, segundo,* and *tumba,* reinforced by *cáscara* (a pair of sticks struck against each other) and *claves* (a pair of smooth, cylindrical hardwood sticks struck against each other). Today the drum rhythms are executed on conga drums, but the clave effects remain essentially unchanged in modern salsa.

The son, meanwhile, describes more of a feeling than an actual musical form. It is, however, identifiable by the strong rhythmic patterns associated with it. Most notable among these is the anticipated bass, which is unique to Afro-Cuban music generally, and salsa in particular (Manuel 1985). The son emerged among Africans in the Cuban countryside and spread to the urban areas early in the twentieth century. It was in the latter areas that the son combined with European instruments to create its modern hybrid form. Earlier Africanized instruments were replaced by such European ones as the contrabass, trumpet, and guitar, although the basic percussion was necessarily retained—the bongos, claves, and the guitarlike *tres*. One of Cuba's greatest popular musicians, and the "father" of modern salsa, Arsenio Rodríguez, is credited with further upgrading the son ensemble in the 1930s. He did this by adding a second trumpet, conga drums, and, most important, a piano.

Rodríguez also anticipated some of the greatest modern *salseros* (salsa musicians) by moving away from the romantic themes of earlier *sones* and incorporating texts that addressed nationalist and social issues. Other important figures from the early period of Afro-Cuban music include Ernesto Lecuona, whose group, the Lecuona Cuban Boys, recorded for Columbia, and Arcano y sus Maravillas (Arcano and His Marvels), a charanga orchestra that was responsible for africanizing this erstwhile Europeanized ensemble.

The orquesta charanga is an interesting phenomenon in Afro-Cuban music history. Until the 1930s, this group espoused a genteel, Europeanized sound that appealed to middle-class whites. Its instrumentation consisted of lead flute and violins. Arcano moved to make his group conform more to an African style by adding percussion, such as the bongo and conga drums. Loza (1979) has suggested that Arcano y sus Maravillas actually led the way in the emergence of the phenomenally popular cha cha cha. The king of that genre, however, was La Orquesta Aragón (The Aragon Orchestra), a group popular from the 1940s through the 1960s, whose incomparable style of cha cha cha endeared the music to millions of Latinos across Latin America and the United States.

Meanwhile, several individuals who later went on to make their mark on modern salsa music actually played with charanga groups in the 1940s and 1950s. These included such well-known figures as Charlie Palmieri, Johnny Pacheco, and Ray Barreto. Along with a host of other salseros, these individuals brought a vitally evolving musical tradition to the United States, where both African- and European-oriented groups experienced a strong cross-fertilization with jazz—a fertilization that resulted in the final emergence of salsa.

Tito Puente.

Thus, by the late 1950s key performers, such as Tito Rodríguez, Tito Puente, and Machito, had laid the stylistic framework for the modern sound. In fact, when we listen to Tito Rodríguez's recordings from the late 1950s, we cannot but be impressed with how similar his rumbas and guaguancós are to latter-day salsa, even though the music was not recognized as such until the 1970s. Meanwhile, the style and instrumentation was further strengthened in the 1960s and 1970s by a host of great performers, which included such memorable names as Willie Colón, Eddie Palmieri, El Gran Combo (The Great Combo), as well as vocalists like Héctor Lavoe, Celia Cruz, and Rubén Blades. The last is particularly recognized for the poignant social themes that his lyrics often contained.

Born on July 16, 1948, in Panama City, Panama, Rubén Blades received all of his early education and his bachelor's degree there. In 1985 he was awarded a law degree from Harvard University. Despite beginning life in both Panama and the United States as a lawyer, Blades has become an outstanding singer and composer of salsa music, and a respected Hollywood

Eddie Palmieri.

actor. He has received four Grammy Awards and numerous gold records. His films include *The Last Fight* (1982), *Crossover Dreams* (1984), *Critical Condition* (1986), *The Milagro Beanfield War* (1986), *Fatal Beauty* (1987), and various made-for-television movies.

By the mid-1960s, the modern salsa sound had pretty much crystallized. And, its most basic genre remained the son/rumba/guaguancó complex, as it had been synthesized by Tito Rodríguez and others in the 1950s. Since the 1960s, this amalgamation of genres, which goes by the label "salsa," has served as the core for numerous explorations that have expanded the parameters of the music. Thus, as Jorge Duany wrote, "The main pattern for *salsa* music remains the *son montuno*, built on the alternation between soloist and chorus." Moreover, like the son, "[salsa's] characteristics are a call-and-response song structure; polyrhythmic organization with abundant use of syncopation; instrumental variety with extensive use of brass and percussion and strident orchestral arrangements...and, above all, a reliance on the sounds and themes of lower-class life in the Latin American *barrios* of U.S. and Caribbean cities."

All these elements had been worked out by Tito Rodríguez and other Afro-Caribbean performers by the late 1950s. Since that time, at its most basic level the music has remained faithful to those elements. And, as always, in its most intimate contexts the music still evokes strong feelings of African identification among its most devoted followers—some of whom belong to Santería cults. At the very least, the music provokes feelings of nationalist pride, a strong identity with the people whose culture it symbolizes. As salsa pianist Oscar Hernández observed, "There's a nationalistic sense of pride when people hear *salsa*. They say, "that's *our* music." It gives people a sense of pride in their Ricanness and Latinoness." And, at a more general level, salsa serves as a kind of pan-Latino link that unites many Hispanics under one musical banner.

LATIN JAZZ/ROCK ✦ ✦ ✦ ✦ ✦ ✦ ✦ ✦ ✦ ✦ ✦ ✦ ✦ ✦ ✦ ✦ ✦ ✦ ✦

Two important musical cousins of salsa are Latin jazz and Latin rock. The former is closely associated with the development of salsa music in the United States, although it represents a more self-conscious effort to link Afro-Caribbean with Afro-American music. One can argue, however, that Latin jazz possesses neither the cultural breadth nor depth of salsa, although it clearly represents some of the most experimental efforts in the whole field of Latino music. Outstanding among these efforts are those of Cuban *conguero* (conga player) and vocalist Chano Pozo, whose association with American jazz trumpetist Dizzy Gillespie produced such Latin jazz gems as "Algo Bueno" (Something Good), "Afro-Cuban Suite," and "Manteca" (Lard), the latter a piece that received high marks for its successful blend of Afro-Caribbean and Afro-American styles.

More recent standouts in the Latin jazz/rock movement include Chick Corea, who apprenticed with Afro-Cuban greats Mongo Santamaría and Willie Bobo. Meanwhile, Latin jazz's relative, Latin rock, has also had considerable impact on Latinos in the United States. Carlos Santana, the indisputable king of Latin rock since the 1960s, has continued to exploit a wide array of Afro-Cuban rhythms, fusing them to American rock to create a highly innovative style. Santana has inspired many imitators over the years, especially in California, where his music has had exceptional influence on young Chicanos.

Carlos Santana.

Again, it can be argued that Latin jazz and rock lack the cultural power of salsa, norteño, or orquesta. Fundamentally, they are creations of the commercial market, hence must be considered "superorganic" or "second-order" expressions, as opposed to salsa's organic, first-order links to the Afro-Caribbeans. Nonetheless, the contributions of the individuals mentioned, as well as those by such noted figures as José Feliciano, Cal Tjader, and others, cannot be underestimated. In sum, although offshoots of salsa, Latin jazz and rock lack the status of a strong symbol like that of *salsa*, which emanates from the deepest levels of Afro-Caribbean culture.

Neither Latin jazz nor rock can make that claim, of course; they are not "wired" into the core of any particular culture. For this, however, they should not be dismissed as transitory. Despite their cultural limitations, the degree of innovation in both Latin jazz and rock has been remarkable, and at times the popularity of Latin rock, especially, has had considerable impact on general market American music.

MÚSICA TROPICAL ◆

Música tropical has historically referred to any music with a "tropical" flavor, that is, any music identified with the tropics, usually the Afro-Caribbean rim. In the present instance, it is not an entirely accurate label, since the ensemble that represents this type of music—the grupo tropical/moderno—is not necessarily "tropical" in character. Aside from the fact that one of its musical mainstays is the *cumbia*, a dance originally from the tropics of Colombia, the grupo tropical/moderno need not feature any of the percussion instruments normally associated with tropical, that is, Afro-Caribbean, music. And, in fact, the *grupo tropical* is known today as much for its emphasis on another popular genre, *música moderna* (or *romántica*), as it is for the cumbia.

As it has evolved in recent years (the group was originally more "tropical" in that it featured instruments such as the conga drums and the *güiro,* or scrapergourd), the grupo tropical/moderno often features four instruments—keyboard (originally an electric organ, later synthesizer), electric guitar and bass, and trap drums. It originated in Mexico in the 1960s and then spread to the United States via the heavy Mexican immigration that has occurred during the last twenty-five years or so.

The grupo tropical's mainstay, the cumbia, was originally a Colombian folk dance that in the twentieth century became urbanized and diffused commercially throughout Latin America. Upon reaching Mexico in the mid-1960s, the cumbia was appropriated by the working-class masses at about the same time that the four-instrument ensemble was emerging as a favorite dance group among urban working-class Mexicans. This ensemble came to be associated with cumbia music (música tropical) in Mexico and the American Southwest. At about the same time, however, a slow-dance genre, influenced by American rhythm and blues, surged in popularity in Mexico—the *balada* (from the American pop "ballad," a lyrical love song). Popularized by such groups as Los Angeles Negros (The Black Angels), Los Terrícolas (The Earthlings), and others, the Mexican balada came to be known generally as "música romántica" (or "moderna"—the two terms are interchangeable), and in time most grupos tropicales/modernos began to alternate between the cumbia and the balada to fill out their repertories.

Besides Los Angeles Negros (who seldom performed the cumbia), the best-known exponents in the relatively short span of música tropical/moderna in Mexico and the United States have been Rigo Tovar (who is of Afro-Caribbean ancestry), Los Bukis (The Bukis), Los Sonics (The Sonics), Los Yonics, (The Ionics), and Los Temerarios (The Fearless). Besides their reliance on record sales for financial support, most of the commercially popular grupos tropicales/modernos also rely on personal appearances at large public dances. At these dances the cumbia reigns supreme, although, again, most groups depend to one extent or another on the balada, which, with its slow 4/4 or 6/8 meter, offers a contrastive alternative to the usually up-tempo, lighthearted spirit of the cumbia.

Almost nothing has been written about the Mexican grupo tropical/moderno, which for the past twenty-five years has been undisputed king among certain working-class segments of Mexican society. By musical standards, it is an unspectacular style, one that is dwarfed by both salsa and La Onda Chicana. But it exerts a powerful influence on the millions of Mexican proletarians who subscribe to it. In the United States, one has only to attend certain ballrooms in cities such as Los Angeles, San Jose, Phoenix, or El Paso to observe the enormous drawing power that groups such as Los Bukis, Los Yonics, and others command, especially among the undocumented and recently documented immigrants from Mexico.

Hispanics are a widely diverse group of people; yet they share one common characteristic: all of them, due to their Afro-Indo-Hispanic background, have experienced varying degrees of conflict with the dominant Anglo-European majority. The various Hispanic music forms have served to mediate this conflict, despite their differences in style and cultural function. It is the legacy of conflict and accommodation that channels Hispanic musical creation and the proliferation of culturally powerful traditions. As the various sectors of the Hispanic population continue to confront, accommodate, and otherwise amalgamate with the Euro-American majority, we may expect more musical experimentation and new traditions.

THE CONTEMPORARY MUSIC SCENE ♦ ♦ ♦ ♦ ♦ ♦ ♦ ♦ ♦ ♦ ♦ ♦ ♦ ♦

The early 90's saw Latin music in the United States enjoy a profound expansion period which included increased record sales, a steady growth of Spanish-language radio stations and newfound crossover success by several artists.

Top groups like Banda Machos, Banda Movil and Banda Vallarta Show regularly made impressive chart showings in Billboard and often headlined the biggest concert/dances in California and some parts along the Southwest. The success of banda is also reflected by the way that major labels have jumped on the bandwagon, either by signing and recording bandas or by generating an unusual amount of compilations of banda hits.

While the growing Hispanic population helped drive the market's expansion in general, a major force fueling these changes in particular is the nation's Hispanic youth, whose economic and political influence is being watched, studied and interpreted by major corporations, including Pepsi and Coca Cola, Budweiser and Miller Lite, Levi's jeans and Stetson hats, and any number of smaller, regional companies.

In all genres, from tropical/salsa to Tejano to Latin pop, new, young stars have entered the market with success. In tropical salsa, fresh faces like Rey Ruiz, Jerry Rivera, Marc Anthony and Los Fantasmas del Caribe have commanded top-draw status and record sales on their debut and followup albums.

In Tejano, Selena and Emilio Navaira led the pack from the top of Billboard's charts to stadium tours to multiple awards. In Latin pop, excitement was created by newcomers like the pop/dance/rap act the Barrio Boyzz, ballad singer Marcos Llunas and children's pop group Roxie y Los Frijolitos.

Whether the groups are producing fresh, original sounds or simply taking the old and rejuvenating it with a new urgent rhythms, the successful young acts in each genre have found the way to attract a new following.

New Rhythms

Banda music gained a new strong foothold, particularly in California, where KLAX-FM in Los Angeles became the number one radio station in the general market. Banda is a brass-heavy (akin to marching bands) take on polkas and cumbias. KLAX plays a heavy mix of banda and norteno music.

While it may seem Banda is new, it is not. Actually banda has been popular in the northern states of Mexico for more than 20 years. However the steady flow of Mexican immigrants from that area helped fuel the popularity of the music in Southwestern California. Again, it is the young banda artists that successfully blended the old horn-packed polka beats with a fresh sound and a modern, spiffy image to attract today's younger generation.

Vikki Carr (1940–)

Born on July 19, 1940, in El Paso, Texas, and baptized Florencia Bisenta de Casillas Martínez Cardona, under her stage name Vikki Carr has become one of the most successful Hispanic recording artists and international performers of popular music in history. Carr began her singing career in the Los Angeles area while still in high school. After touring with a band for a while, she signed her first recording contract with Liberty Records in 1961. Her first recording successes, however, were in Australia and England, and later in the United States. By 1967 Carr's international popularity was so great that she was invited to perform for Queen Elizabeth II at a command performance in London. The following year, she set a precedent for sold-out concerts in Germany, Spain, France, England, Australia, Japan, and Holland. In the United States, she became a favorite of the White House, performing repeatedly for each of the last four presidents.

To date, Carr has recorded forty-nine best-selling records, including fifteen gold albums. In 1985, she won a Grammy for her Spanish-language album *Simplemente Mujer*. For her Spanish-language records, she has won gold, platinum and diamond records. Her 1989 album *Esos Hombres* won gold records in Mexico, Chile, Puerto Rico, and the United States. Among her other awards are the *Los Angeles Times* 1970 Woman of the Year Award, the 1972 American Guild of Variety Artists' Entertainer of the Year Award, the 1984 Hispanic Woman of the Year Award, and the 1991 Girl Scouts of America Award. In 1971, Carr founded the Vikki Carr Scholarship Foundation to provide higher education scholarships to Mexican-American youths. Carr is also active in a number of other charities.

Grupos

Grupo is a Spanish word for group but the term is an overall description of bands, as opposed to, say, solo artists like Julio Iglesias, Vikki Carr or Jose Feliciano. And the styles of music covered by grupos also varies, from the pop ballads of Los Bukis or Los Temerarios, to the norteno/ranchera mix of Bronco or Los Tigres, to the Tejano polka/cumbia/ballad blend of La Mafia or Mazz.

According to Jesus Lopez, BMG Ariola managing director, grupos have overtaken the long dominant Latin pop music as well as teen pop and traditional rancheras, as the hottest selling genre in Mexico. BMG's top grupos include Bronco, Impacto De Montemorelos, Los Mier and Los Flamers.

The surge in grupo sales and concert attractions was particularly intense since 1990. "To me, grupos have always been popular through the years," says Ignacio "Nacho" Gomez, general manager for Musivisa in Mexico. "But it's only been in the last 18 months that there's been a sort of a 'boom' phase in grupos." In 1992 officials moved all their grupos from Melody to compile Musivisa's label roster, which included the aforementioned acts as well as the Campeche Show, Los Tigres, Grupo Lluvia and Industria del Amor.

Another major label that jumped into the fray was Sony Mexico. Houston's La Mafia was Sony's first signee. Later they signed Ramon Ayala and Los Rodarte. The success of La Mafia was particularly impressive, leading to record sales of their first U.S.-Mexico jointly promoted album "Estas Tocando Fuego."

The banda and grupo movements became so popular, they have each generated a variety of TV show and publications in both the U.S. and Mexico.

Tejano   Tejano music continued its explosive growth in the Southwest with top artists like Mazz, La Mafia, Selena and Emilio playing stadiums like San Antonio's Alamodome, Houston's Astrodome, Dallas' Texas Stadium as well as other major venues. In 1994, the Tejano Music Awards, which recognizes the best in Tex-Mex, moved in the Alamodome.

Since 1990, Tejano artists such as Mazz, La Sombra and La Mafia initiated major tours of Mexico and made regular appearances on national Mexican TV shows such as "Furia Musical" and "Siempre en Domingo."

In San Antonio, KXTN-FM remained the city's number one station with its all Tejano, bilingual format. Dallas got its first full-time Tejano station in KICK-FM 107.9 which went on air December 1, 1993. Houston, San Antonio, Corpus Christi, El Paso, Austin and Laredo are all cities now with two Tejano FM stations. Prior to 1990, none of the major markets had one station devoted to the genre. Since 1991, at least 75 stations from Brownsville to California, including Mexican border cities, have switched to full-time or part-time Tejano formats.

In record label action, the independent Manny Music was signed up for a multiyear distribution and promotion deal by WEA Latina. A new label, Arista/Texas open offices in Austin to sign up Texas talent from blues, jazz, country and folk to Tex-Mex. The first artist signed was San Antonio accordionist Flaco Jimenez. Mexico's DISA Records, one of the largest independents in that country, signed a distribution and promotion deal with Joey Records in San Antonio to promote Joey's Tejano artists in Mexico.

Across the Southwest, major nightclubs opened to spotlight Tejano music. New clubs include Dallas' Tejano Rodeo and Club Trends; Fort Worth had Tejano Rodeo and Zaps; San Antonio has Desperado's, Tejano Rose, T-Town and Bronco Bill's; Houston has Zaaz, Emilio's Country Club. Typically these clubs have capacities of 1,200 to 1,600 and feature live Tex-Mex acts two to four nights a week.

Tropical/Salsa

In the 1990s Puerto Rico continued to emerge as the dominant market in the New York-Miami-Puerto Rico triangle. The island, smaller in size than Connecticut with a population of 3.5 million, has 117 radio stations, most of which play salsa and merengue but with a top 40 format. Most of the top salsa artists such as Gilberto Santa Rosa, Luis Enrique, Juan Luis Guerra, Tito Rojas and others regularly sell more than 100,000 units on the island.

Recently several upstart Puerto Rican merengue artists broke into the market, including TTH's Zona Roja, WEA Latina's Olga Tanon, Sony's Grupo Wao, MP's Limite 21 and Fuera De Liga and Platano's Cana Brava. The activity on the island is attracting increased sponsorship at all levels—beer, liquor, and cigarette companies—and reportedly American distributors and retailers already on the island are looking to expand their presence.

Latin Pop

The vocal harmonies of the Barrio Boyzz and Las Triplets have found a strong, loyal following—enough to drive both groups to the top of the charts in 1993.

Jon Secada had a phenomenal success in 1991—92 with his pop singing style. But what was significant about Secada was that his smash debut album was recorded in with Spanish lyrics and also scored big on Billboard charts.

In 1993, that crossover success spurred another potential star in Selena, a Tejano star who was signed for a multi-year, English-language contract with SBK Records. More than a few people believe Selena has the talent and the moxie to score in the pop world. John Lannert, Latin Bureau Chief for Billboard, says the SBK deal will expand her following: "I think it's obvious that she will have a big Anglo following, a different type of following than she's had in the Tejano market. She will have an Anglo following from the pop urban side of the market. She will also have a lot of dance pop fans."

For 1993, the other big news in Latin pop was the launching of the MTV Latino network on October 1, 1993. Produced by MTV/Music Television in Miami, the Spanish-language channel is being seen in the United States and 20 other Latin countries.

The format features veejays and advertisers conducting business in Spanish with about 70 percent of the videos in English. According to officials, principal focus musically is on pop and rock, with banda, Tejano, salsa, merengue and other forms not featured—for the moment. As of December 1993 only Los Angeles, Miami and Tucson in the United States were contracting to receive the channel, although MTV officials hope to have all the U.S.'s major cities providing the service.

Retailing   America's major record retailers have not been immune to the Latin rage in the music business. A major reason why Latin music record sales have been steadily increasing is because more Latin music is being sold in general market retail stores such as Tower, Camelot, Sound Warehouse, and Sam Goody's. In the past, the large bulk of Latin product was sold through discounters like K-Mart, Target, Wal-Mart, as well as small mom-and-pop stores such as Casa Guadalupe in Laredo, Del Bravo's and Janie's in San Antonio, and Memo's Discoteca in Houston.

Also, the top Latin labels like EMI Latin, Sony and WEA began selling their product through their Anglo sales forces. Previously, the English-language and Spanish-language market sales staffs were separate. Today, for example, WEA's sales people fill out orders for general market artists such as Madonna and R.E.M. and also take orders for Spanish stars like Luis Miguel and Mana.

Like the general music market, the Latin field also saw a huge catalog of yesterday's heroes coming back in CD form. If not necessarily in single album formats, then in compilations of greatest hits in all genres, from Latin pop and salsa to Tejano, norteno and conjunto.

CDs

The results can be confusing to the average record buyer who sometimes sees up to three or four different greatest hits packages on different record labels by the same artist. This was sometimes so because veteran groups such as La Mafia, Little Joe, Willie Colon, and others recorded for various labels during their long careers. In addition, some labels were simply issuing compilations to generate sales, as in the general market.

Still to be determined in the 1990s is the effect of smaller, independent labels that do not have distribution contracts with the majors, such as Manny Music with WEA.

For example, although Emilio Navaira or Selena had only four or five studio albums since 1990, a check of available titles showed up to 30 records by EACH artist. These included not only the recompilations and assorted theme-albums, but also albums on which they have been featured as guest artists.

As the major record labels continued to streamline and commercialize the Latin industry, record sales grew. However, some groups and genres are still too regional because of demographics. Banda for example, remained hot in California but weak in Texas and Florida. Some say that is because most immigrants see California as a destination point for jobs while Texas cities like San Antonio, Houston and Dallas are way stations for better paying jobs up north in Chicago or Detroit. But if immigration from the northern, rural states of Mexico continues, it only bodes well for banda's future, especially in California.

The Future

Tejano made great strides in Mexico, California, Florida, New York and Chicago, but was still largely a powerhouse only in the Southwest. However, Tejano also benefited from its increasing tours of Mexico, both from the additional revenues in that country but also from the increasing base in the United States thanks to continued immigration of Mexico's citizens.

The impact of the North American Free Trade Agreement, in 1992, was still unclear for the entertainment industry. The only obvious benefits were simplified paperwork in customs and immigration for bordering crossings.

PROMINENT HISPANIC CLASSICAL MUSICIANS ◆ ◆ ◆ ◆ ◆ ◆ ◆ ◆

Gilda Cruz-Romo

Born in Guadalajara, Mexico, and educated there, Gilda Cruz-Romo graduated from the National Conservatory of Music in Mexico City in 1964 and embarked on her lifelong opera career as a soprano. From 1962 to 1967 she sang with the National Opera and the International Opera of Mexico, from 1966 to 1968 with the Dallas Civic Opera, and from 1969 to 1972 with the New York City Opera. Since 1970, she has been the leading soprano for the prestigious Metropolitan Opera Company of New York. As a professional opera singer, Cruz-Romo has sung in many countries and has won many awards, including first place in the Metropolitan Opera national auditions in 1970.

Suzanna Guzmán
(1955-)

Born in Los Angeles, California, On May 29, 1955, Guzmán is a 1980 graduate of California State University, Los Angeles, and the American Institute Music Theater in 1984. Although only at the beginning of her career, she has already sung as a soloist with the Los Angeles Philharmonic, the San Diego Opera, the Washington Opera, the Metropolitan Opera, and at Carnegie Hall and the Kennedy Center for the Performing Arts. Her awards include First Place, Metropolitan Opera National Council in 1985; First Place, International Competition, Center for Contemporary Opera in 1988; Western Region First Place, San Francisco Opera Center, 1985, and others. Guzmán has been an active performer for Hispanic schoolchildren in southern California and for the handicapped.

Tania J. León
(1943-)

Born on May 14, 1943, in Havana, Cuba, Tania León received degrees from the National Conservatory of Music in Havana, a B.S. in music education from New York University in 1973, and an M.A. degree in music composition from New York University in 1975. One year after arriving in the United States in 1968, she became the first music director of the Dance Theater of Harlem, and she has continued to be an important composer for the Dance Theater. León studied conducting under such teachers and coaches as Laszlo Halasz, Leonard Bernstein, and Seiji Ozawa.

She has maintained a busy schedule as a composer, recording artist, and as a guest conductor at most of the important symphonies throughout the United States and Puerto Rico, as well as in Paris, London, Spoleto, Berlin, and Munich. From 1977 to 1988, she was the director of the Family Concert Series for the Brooklyn Philharmonic Community. In 1985, León joined the faculty of Brooklyn College as an associate professor, teaching both composition and conducting. She has also served as music director for Broadway musicals, such as *The Wiz*.

León is just one of a handful of women to have made a successful career as a conductor. Her honors include the Dean Dixon Achievement Award in 1985, the ASCAP Composer's Award from 1987 to 1989, the National Council of Women Achievement Award in 1980, the 1991 Academy-Institute Award in Music of the American Academy and Institute of Arts and Letters, and many others.

Eduardo Mata (1942-)

Born in Mexico City on September 5, 1942, Eduardo Mata has dedicated his life to music and has become one of Mexico's most outstanding symphonic directors. Educated at the National Conservatory of Music from 1954 to 1963, and through private instruction, he began his conducting career in 1964 with the Guadalajara Symphony Orchestra. From 1966 to 1975, he was music director and conductor of the Orquesta Filarmónica of the National University in Mexico City. In 1975, he became the director of the National Symphony in Mexico City and also directed a number of international music festivals, including the 1976 Casals Festival in Mexico. Mata has been a guest conductor around the world and throughout the United States.

Since 1977, Mata has led the Dallas Symphony as music director, while also touring extensively and even continuing to serve as the principal conductor and musical advisor of the Phoenix Symphony (1974 to 1978) and the principal guest conductor of the Pittsburgh Symphony (since 1989). Mata was named conductor emeritus of the Dallas Symphony beginning with the 1993—94 season. Mata has also maintained a busy recording schedule that has resulted in top-quality albums of some of the world's leading orchestras under his direction. In Mexico he has been honored with the Golden Lyre Award (1974), the Elías Sourasky Prize in the Arts

Eduardo Mata conducting the Dallas Symphony Orchestra, 1976.

(1975), and the Mozart Medal conferred by the president of Mexico (1991). In the United States, he is the recipient of the White House Hispanic Heritage Award (1991).

Manuel Peña and Ramiro Burr

S*ports*

Hispanic participation and achievements in sports have been determined by Hispanic traditions of work, play, and ritual, both in the United States and in the greater Spanish-speaking world. As Hispanic customs in the United States and throughout Latin America have derived from the blending of various bloodlines and cultures—European, American Indian, and African—so too the types of sports practiced by Hispanics has evolved out of the rituals and traditions that can quite often be traced back to the peoples that encountered each other in the early sixteenth century when the Spaniards evangelized the Mesoamerican Indians and began importing slaves from Africa. In the United States, the descendants of this encounter also adopted Anglo-American traditions in sport and shared their own with the Anglo-Americans. The prime examples of this exchange are rodeo and baseball. Ranching and sport with horses and cattle were introduced to the Americas by the Spaniards. The Spanish customs mixed with some American Indian traditions and then were learned by Anglo-Americans and European immigrants.

HISPANICS AND SPORT ♦

Hispanic participation in professional sports in the United States has also depended on a number of factors other than customs and traditions. Various sports demand certain body types that seem to present relative advantages for success. The prime example, of course, is basketball, where tall players have proven to be more successful. Most Hispanics have descended from American Indians and Spaniards, both of whom are relatively short peoples compared to northern Europeans and many African peoples. As would be expected, there are very few Hispanics represented in professional basketball. The same is true of football, which also demands very large and strong bodies. Notwithstanding the general disadvantage of Hispanics as a whole, there have been great achievers, even in such contact sports as football, as the careers of Manny Fernández, Anthony Muñoz, and Tom Flores attest.

Another factor is education. College sports are quite often training grounds for the professional leagues. Hispanic dropout rates in high school are the highest in the country, and their admission to and graduation from college is the lowest compared with Anglo- and Afro-Americans. Hispanics thus have fewer opportunities to get involved in college sports, especially football and basketball, not to mention other more elite sports, such as tennis and golf. But, there are also "back doors" of entry to these sports, such as working as caddies and greens keepers, as the careers of Chi Chi Rodríguez and Lee Treviño exemplify.

Furthermore, various sports have traditionally been associated with certain social classes and have been restricted to members of these classes principally because of economic barriers, such as membership fees in private country clubs, the payment of fees for private lessons, the lack of public facilities, the high expense of specialized equipment, such as golf clubs and gear, and the high tuition of private schools where these sports are cultivated. Prime examples of these sports are polo, golf, lacrosse, and, before the construction of numerous tennis courts in public parks, tennis. On the other hand, boxing classes and sports facilites have traditionally been accessible to poor inner-city youths through boys clubs, police athletic leagues, and the military services. In addition, boxing has been a traditional avenue to economic success and fame for one immigrant and minority group after another and for poor inner-city youths in the United States. Hispanics have developed a long tradition of achievement in boxing, especially in the lighter-weight classes.

The wide world of sports holds relative advantages to being short, light-weight, and quick. Hispanics not only have excelled as bantamweights and lightweights in boxing, but also have earned an outstanding record as jockeys, quick-handed infielders in baseball, and star players in sports where speed and endurance are important, such as soccer. And soccer has also provided an opportunity for Hispanics to participate in professional football, which has recruited various Hispanic placekickers for the accuracy they have developed with their angled and powerful kicking.

But all of the aforementioned conditions are changing rapidly. American society is becoming more and more democratic and open. In the late 1940s, American baseball ceased to be segregated, then football also opened up. In the world of sports today, sports facilities are accessible to people from all social classes in public parks and schools, and universities are making more of an effort to recruit minorities. Universities are even recruiting and training from such countries as the Dominican Republic, Panama, and Puerto Rico players of Afro-Hispanic background for their basketball, football, and track teams.

♦ **BASEBALL**

Although many sportswriters in the United States have considered the presence of ballplayers from Latin America to be an "influx," as if baseball were a uniquely American sport being invaded by outsiders, the truth of the matter is that baseball in Spanish-speaking countries has not only had a parallel development to baseball in the United States, but it has been in-tertwined with American baseball almost from the beginning of the game itself. The professional Cuban Baseball League (Liga de Béisbol Profe-sional Cubana) was founded in 1878, just seven years after the National Baseball Association was founded in the United States. But, reportedly, Cuban baseball goes back to 1866, when sailors from an American ship in Matanzas harbor invited Cubans to play the game; they built a baseball di-amond together at Palmar del Junco and began playing while the ship re-mained in harbor. By 1874 Cuban teams had devloped and were playing each other regularly.

By 1891 seventy-five teams were active on the island. From that time on, Cuban baseball—and later, Mexican and Puerto Rican baseball—has served

The "national pastime" of baseball developed in the United States in the nineteenth century and was introduced then to Cuba and other nearby Hispanic countries by the last part of that century. As American teams needed warm wintering grounds and off-season play, the climates and facilities in Mexico and the Spanish-speaking Caribbean attracted American baseball players, thus exposing more and more Hispanics to the "all-American" sport.

baseball in the United States in various ways: as a training ground for the majors, formalized when the Cuban Sugar Kings were made a Triple A minor league team; as wintering and spring training grounds for the majors; and as permanent homes for players from the U.S. Negro Leagues, also providing a baseball team, the Havana Cubans, to the Negro Leagues. Since the early days of the National Baseball Association until Jackie Robinson broke the color line in 1947, about fifty Hispanic-American ballplayers played in the major leagues, some even becoming Hall of Famers and one achieving the position of manager. However, for the most part, these were Cuban players who were White or could pass for White. In fact, the acceptance of progressively darker-skinned Hispanics was used as a barometer by the Negro Leagues for the eventual acceptance of African Americans into the majors. The Hispanics that could not "pass" either played in the Negro Leagues or in Cuba, Mexico, or Venezuela. What is clear is that Cuba served as a free ground exempt from the segregation that dominated U.S. sports and provided playing fields where major-leaguers and players from the Negro Leagues and Latin America could play openly together.

As baseball continued its development in Mexico, pressure from fans and investors increased for expanding the U.S. major leagues to Mexico and for the creation of Mexico's own professional leagues. In 1946 the wealthy Pasquel family in Mexico founded a professional league and set about enticing major league and Negro League stars from the United States with salaries quite higher than were being offered in the United States. The whole Pasquel venture, which was seen by the U.S. media as "robbery" and a threat to the national pastime, even led to an official complaint by the U.S. State Department. Some twenty-three players jumped to Pasquel's league, but after continued financial problems the league ceased to exist in 1953. The northern teams of the league merged with the Arizona-Texas and Arizona-Mexico leagues from 1953 to 1957. The Mexican League began functioning again in 1955 and has continued to do so. The Mexican Central League has served since 1960—a year after the Cuban Revolution curtailed Triple A ball on the island—as a Class A minor league and was later joined by other Mexican leagues based on the earlier Pasquel circuit. Today the league has fourteen teams playing in two divisions, and both supply young ballplayers to the majors and receive former major-leaguers on their way out of baseball.

The Majors

The first Hispanic ballplayers in the United States played in the National Association and in the Negro League. Before 1947 the major league clubs that employed the most Hispanics were in Washington, Cincinnati,

*A baseball team of
Mexians and Anglos in
Los Angeles in the 1870s.*

Chicago, Cleveland, and Detroit. The New York Yankees did not employ Hispanics after 1918 and Pittsburgh did not employ any until 1943, when it hired one. The first Hispanic to join the majors was third baseman Esteban Bellán, a Black Cuban who was recruited from Fordham College by the Troy Haymakers in 1869 and actually took to the field in 1871—the year of the founding of the National Baseball Association—to spend three years in the majors. By the turn of the century, no Black Cubans were allowed in the majors, despite major leaguers observing their talents firsthand and suffering defeats from them. One such powerhouse was pitcher José Méndez. Méndez played with the Cuban Stars against the best of the Negro teams and won forty-four victories, with only two defeats on a tour of the United States in 1909. In Cuba, Méndez beat the Phillies and split two games against future Hall of Famers Christy Mathewson and John McGraw of the New York Giants. But light-skinned Cuban and Hispanic ballplayers soon began appearing more and more in American baseball, despite complaints that the racial puirity of the American sport was being contaminated. In 1911 the Cincinnati Reds had affidavits prepared to prove that their new Cuban players, Armando Marsans and Rafael Almeida, had only the purest Castilian blood flowing through their veins.

In 1912 Cuban Miguel González began playing for Boston as a catcher. González played for seventeen years on various teams and served fourteen seasons as a Cardinals coach, the first Hispanic to do so. But the greatest longevity by any Hispanic in major league baseball was attained by Adolfo Luque. A dark-skinned Cuban pitcher, Luque was jeered at and continuously faced racial epithets from fans from the time he took to the field for the Braves in 1914 until his retirement in 1935. Having played for the Braves, Cincinnati, Brooklyn, and the New York Giants, Luque pitched in two World Series, was credited with the decisive win in one of them and during his best year, 1923, led the league for Cincinnati in wins (27), earned run average (1.93), and shutouts (6).

The Washington Senators employed the greatest number of Hispanic ballplayers by far, beginning in 1911 and peaking from 1939 to 1947 with a total of nineteen players of Hispanic background. At Washington, as at other major league clubs, the Hispanics suffered not only racial attacks from fans and sportswriters, but also segregation in housing, uniforms, equipment, and travel conditions. Many of these conditions improved noticeably during the 1940s with the competition for ballplayers that was exerted by the Mexican League.

After the the color barrier was broken in 1947, things became much easier for Hispanic ballplayers of all colors and nationalities, and their representation in the major leagues quickly climbed. By the 1970s, a full 9 percent of the players were Hispanics. Due to the restrictions that came about after the Cuban Revolution—even baseball equipment was not to be had in Cuba due to the U.S. economic embargo—the flow of players from Cuba into the major leagues was curtailed. During the 1970s and 1980s Cubans no longer were the Hispanic nationality most represented. The lead passed to the Dominican Republic and Puerto Rico, with Venezuela and Mexico also making a strong showing. But by 1963 the Cuban National Team had begun to dominate amateur baseball and to cement its perennial championship of the Pan American Games. Although the caliber of play is equivalent to that of major league teams, the broken political relations between the United States and Cuba has made international professional play between the two countries impossible.

Major league baseball in the United States is and will continue to be a strong draw for Hispanic ballplayers, not only as an economic springboard with its lucrative salaries, but also because of the excellence and competitive nature of the game played here, made even more competitive by the quality Hispanic ballplayers have always contributed to the majors.

The Negro Leagues were a haven for Hispanic ballplayers whose skin color was a barrier to their admission to the major leagues in the United States. The Negro leagues and the leagues in Cuba, Mexico, Puerto Rico, and Venezuela were completely open to each other. Both Black and White players from the Hispanic world and from the United States played on the same teams and against each other freely in Cuba. In Latin America there were no color lines. By the 1920s not only were many Hispanics playing in the Negro Leagues, but many American Blacks had incorporated into their routine playing the winter season in Cuba, then later Puerto Rico, Mexico, and Venezuela. Among the Hispanic greats to play in the Negro Leagues were Cristóbal Torriente, Martín Dihigo, José Méndez, Orestes "Minnie" Miñoso, Alejandro Oms, Luis Tiant, Sr., and scores of others.

The Negro Leagues

As early as 1900, two of the five Black professional teams bore the name of Cuba: the Cuban Giants (with its home city shifting from year to year from New York to Hoboken, New Jersey, to Johnstown, Pennsylvania, and so on) and the Cuban X Giants of New York. (These teams should not be confused with one of the first black professional ball teams of the 1880s, which called itself the Cuban Giants, thinking that fans would be more attracted to the exotic Cubans than to ordinary American Blacks.) In the 1920s both the Eastern Colored League (NNL) and the Negro National League (NNL) had a Cuban Stars baseball team, one owned by Alex Pómpez, who at one point was vice president of the NNL, and the other by Agustín Molina. Cuban teams continued to be prominent during the heyday of the Negro leagues from the 1920s through the 1940s. There were also Hispanic players on teams throughout the Negro leagues, from the Indianapolis Clowns and Cleveland Buckeyes to the Memphis Red Sox and the New York Black Yankees. And, aside from the teams that identified themselves as Cuban, such as the New York Cubans and the Cuban Stars, there were others that had their rosters filled with Hispanics, such as the Indianapolis Clowns, which at one point was even managed by a Hispanic, Ramiro Ramírez. (In his long career from 1916 to 1948, Ramírez managed or played with most of the Cuban teams, plus the Baltimore Black Sox, the Bacharach Giants, and the Clowns.)

RODEO ✦

The Spaniards introduced cattle ranching to the New World, and with this industry the early settlers and soldiers also introduced the horse and its use for work and sport. Much of contemporary sports culture that depends upon horsemanship and cattle, such as equestrian contests, horse racing, bullfighting, and rodeo, is heavily indebted to the Spanish and Hispanic-American legacy. The evolution of rodeo as a sport goes back to the blending of Spanish and American Indian customs of animal handling and sport. A class of mestizo vaqueros developed in Mexico during the seventeenth, eighteenth, and nineteenth centuries on the large haciendas. These mestizo cowboys, called *charros,* eventually evolved their own subculture of unique customs, dress, music, and horsemanship, which in turn owed much to the Arab horsemen that had influenced Spanish culture during the seven hundred years of Moslem occupation of the peninsula. The charros, in fact, were the models for the development of the American cowboy, just as was Mexican ranching culture was essential in the development of that industry in the United States. During the late eighteenth and early nineteenth centuries, Anglo-American cowboys began working alongside Mexican cowboys on the same ranches in Texas and California.

The American cowboy was born when the United States expanded westward and encountered the Mexican cattle culture. Today's rodeo owes a great deal to the charrerías (contests) of the Mexican vaqueros, or cowboys.

The style of dress and horsemanship of the charro became more popularized even in the cities during the nineteenth century and was eventually adopted as the national costume. Their contests and games, charrería, became the Mexican national sport. The skillful games of the charros became games and shows on the large haciendas during the festive roundups in the nineteenth century, which drew guests from hundreds of miles around. The charros dressed in their finest outfits and displayed their skills in such contests as *correr el gallo* (running the rooster), horse racing, wild horse and bull riding, and roping horses or steers by their horns or back or front feet, bulldogging, and throwing bulls by their tails. Correr el gallo involved picking up something as small as a coin from the ground while riding a horse at full gallup. These fiestas were perhaps the most important forerunners of the modern American rodeo, and their events included almost all of those associated with today's rodeos. More important, these equestrian sports became part of the standard celebrations at fiestas and fairs among Mexicans and Anglos all along both sides of the border. Charrería, as a separate institution from rodeo, has continued to this day to be practiced by Mexicans in Mexico and throughout the American Southwest.

Luis Romero, left, with Ramón Ahumada. Ahumada, known as "El Charro Plateado" (the Silver Plated Cowboy), was elected to the Cowboy Hall of Fame.

During the early years of the twentieth century, local and state fairs and celebrations among Anglos in the West featured cowboy events in what they called "stampedes," "roundups," and "frontier days." These proliferated to the extent that professional contestants began to make a living traveling the circuit of these fairs. The events that became the heart of these contests were the traditional charro events of bronc riding, steer roping, and trick fancy roping. The first cowboy to win the World Chamionship of Trick and Fancy Roping in 1900 was Vicente Oropeza. Oropeza and many other charros and American cowboys continued to compete in both the United States and Mexico throughout the 1930s. By 1922, with the production by Tex Austin of the first World Championship Cowboy Contest in New York's Madison Square Garden, rodeo had officially become a sport, not just a show. Eight of the ten events featured in this new sport had long been a part of charrería. More important, the five standard events of contemporary professional rodeo all owe their roots to charrería: bareback bronc riding, saddle bronc riding, bull riding, steer wrestling, and calf roping.

OTHER SPORTS ♦

While baseball and rodeo are two sports that have been highly influenced by Hispanics in their evolution, other sports have benefited from the participation of outstanding Hispanic atheletes. First and foremost is boxing, which has a long history of Hispanic champions, especially in the lighter-weight classifications, where the speed and lighter body weight of many Cuban, Mexican, and Puerto Rican boxers has been used to advantage.

From the days of Sixto Escobar and Kid Chocolate to the present, boxing has also served for Hispanics, as it has for other immigrants and minorities, as a tempting avenue out of poverty. With more colleges and universities recruiting and graduating Hispanics, some of the other "money" sports, such as football and basketball, will also begin to incorporate more Hispanics in their ranks. Already, football stars such as Manny Fernández, Tom Flores, Anthony Muñoz, and Jim Plunkett have appeared on the scene, and there are many more to follow, especially from the universities of the Southwestern Conference. Finally, the mere fact that an island such as Puerto Rico, which extends only thirty-five by one hundred miles, has as many as ten professional-quality golf clubs has had its impact on that sport. Such golfers as Juan "Chi Chi" Rodríguez have become world-class competitors after beginning as caddies for tourists. And as more and more facilties, such as golf courses and tennis courts, become accessible in the United States through public parks or public schools, greater Hispanic participation and achievement will be recorded.

♦ ♦ ♦ ♦ ♦ ♦ ♦ ♦ ♦ ♦ ♦ ♦ ♦ PROMINENT HISPANIC ATHLETES

Luis Aparicio (1934–)

Baseball

Venezuelan Luis Aparicio was one of the greatest shortstops of all time. He still holds the records for games, double plays, and assists and the American League record for putouts. His 506 stolen bases also rank among the highest. Playing from 1956 to 1973, mostly with the White Sox, Aparicio began his career as Rookie of the Year and proceeded to maintain outstanding and inspired performance throughout his life as a ballplayer. Aparicio played on All-Star teams from 1958 to 1964 and then again from 1970 to 1972. He was the winner of the Gold Glove eleven times. In 1984 Luis Aparicio was inducted into the Hall of Fame.

Rod Carew is upended by Tommy Helms of Cincinnati after Helms was forced out at 2d base in the 4th inning of the 1968 All-Star Game.

Rod Carew (1945–)

Baseball

Born in the Panama Canal Zone, Carew moved with his mother to New York at age seventeen. He signed his first professional contract while he was still in high school in 1964, and when he made it into the majors in 1967 with the Minnesota Twins, he was named Rookie of the Year. From 1969 on, he had fifteen consecutive seasons batting over .300. Carew won seven American League batting championships. In his Most Valuable Player year he batted .388, fifty points better than the next-best average and the largest margin in major league history. His career batting average was .328, with 1,015 runs batted in and 92 home runs. In 1979 Carew forced a trade, in part because of racist comments regarding Black fans by Twins owner Calvin Griffith; he was traded to the Angels for four players. In 1977 Carew received more than 4 million All-Star votes, more than any other player ever. He would have played in eighteen consecutive All-Star games, but missed 1970 and 1979 because of injuries, and for the same reason was not chosen in 1982. Carew was one of the best base stealers, with 348 career stolen bases. In 1969 Carew tied the record with seven steals to home. He led the league three times in base hits and once in runs scored.

Rosemary Casals
(1948-)

Tennis

Born on September 16, 1948, in San Francisco, the daughter of Salvadoran immigrants, Rosemary Casals was brought up by her great-aunt and great-uncle. Casals began playing tennis at Golden Gate Park under the

Rosemary Casals and partner Dick Stockton after winning the Spalding World Mixed Doubles Tournament, 1976.

guidance of her adoptive father, Manuel Casals Y. Bordas, who has been her only coach to this date. Casals won her first championship at age thirteen and by age seventeen she was ranked eleventh by the United States Ladies Tennis Association (USLTA). At eighteen, her ranking was third in the nation. Casals and Billie Jean King were doubles champions five times from 1967 to 1973 at the All-England Championships at Wimbledon and twice at the USLTA championships at Forest Hills. The Casals-King team is the only doubles team to have won U.S. titles on grass, clay, indoor, and hard surfaces. Nine times, Casals was rated as number one in doubles by the USLTA, with teammates that included King, Chris Evert Lloyd, and Jo Anne Russell. Casals has also won mixed doubles championships, playing with Richard Stockton and Ilie Nastase.

Hugo M. Castelló (1914–)

Fencing

Born in La Plata, Argentina, on April 22, 1914, Hugo Castelló moved to the United States with his family at age eight and received his public education in New York City. He earned his bachelor of arts degree at Washington Square College in 1937 and his law degree from Georgetown University in 1941. Castelló became one of the nation's most outstanding fencers and fencing instructors and coaches. He was nationally ranked among the top four senior fencers from 1935 to 1936, the years that he was National Intercollegiate Foil Champion, and he was a member of the U.S. Olympic team in 1936. Castelló served as adjunct associate professor and head fencing coach at New York University from 1946 to 1975. Castelló is among a select group of coaches who have won at least ten National Collegiate team championships. Only five other NCAA coaches in all sports have won ten national team titles. Castelló was also director and head coach of the United States' first Olympic fencing training camp in 1962. He has also served as chief of mission and coach at the Pan American Games (1963) in Sao Paulo and at World Championships in Cuba (1969), Minsk (1970), and Madrid (1972). Castelló is a member of the Helms Sports Hall of Fame, the New York University Sports Hall of Fame, and the PSAL Hall of Fame.

Orlando Cepeda (1937–)

Baseball

Orlando Cepeda was born in Ponce, Puerto Rico, on September 17, 1937. After growing up playing sandlot baseball and later organized team play in New York City, Cepeda was discovered by talent scout Alex Pómpez and began as a major league outfielder with the San Francisco Giants in 1958, when he was named Rookie of the Year. Hitting his stride in 1961, Cepeda led the league in home runs. Cepeda remained on the team until May 1966, when he was transferred to the St. Louis Cardinals after having missed almost a whole season because of a leg injury. He stayed with the Cardinals until 1968. Before his retirement, he also played for the Braves, the A's, the Red Sox, and the Royals. He made a remarkable comeback with the Cardinals, winning the National League's Most Valuable Player Award, leading the league in runs batted in 1967 and making the All-Star team in that year, as well. Orlando Cepeda played on World Series teams in 1962 and 1967. In all, Cepeda played 2,124 games, with a lifetime batting average of .279. He hit 379 home runs and had 1,364 runs batted in. Cepeda had nine .300 seasons and eight seasons with twenty-five or more home runs.

Roberto Clemente (1934–1972)

Baseball

Roberto Walker Clemente is celebrated for being a heroic figure both on and off the baseball diamond. One of the all-time greats of baseball, he died in a tragic plane crash in an effort to deliver relief supplies to the victims of an earthquake in Nicaragua. Born on August 18, 1934, Clemente rose from an impoverished background in Carolina, Puerto Rico, to become the star outfielder for the Pittsburgh Pirates from the years 1955 to 1972. He assisted the Pirates in winning two World Series in 1960 and 1971. Among Clemente's achievements as a player, he was four times the National League batting champion—1961, 1964, 1965, and 1967—and he was voted the league's most valuable player in 1966. He was awarded twelve Gold Gloves and set a major league record in leading the National League in assists five times. He served on fourteen all-star teams, and he was one of only sixteen players to have 3,000 or more hits during their career. Clemente was promising a great deal more before his untimely death. Clemente had accumulated 240 home runs and a lifetime batting average of .317. Upon his death the Baseball Hall of Fame waived its five-year waiting period after a player's retirement and immediately elected him to membership. For his generosity, leadership, outstanding athletic achievements, and heroism, Roberto Clemente is considered by Puerto Ricans to be a national hero to this day.

Dave Concepción (1948–)

Baseball

Venezuelan David Concepción was one of baseball's greatest shortstops, playing for the Cincinnati Reds from 1970 to 1988. In 1973 Concepción was named captain of the Reds, and in 1978 he became the first Cincinnati shortstop to bat .300 since 1913. In World Series play, Concepción hit better than .300 three times and better than .400 in the 1975 and 1979 league championships. His lifetime batting average is .267 for 2,488 games played. He made All-Star teams in 1973 and from 1975 to 1982. He was also winner of the Gold Glove each year from 1974 to 1977 and in

1979. In 1977, he was the winner of the Roberto Clemente Award as the top Latin American ballplayer in the major leagues.

Angel Cordero
(1942–)

Horse Racing

Angel Tomás Cordero, born in San Juan, Puerto Rico, on November 8, 1942, is one of the most winning jockeys of all time. By December 1986, he was fourth in the total number of races won and third in the amount of money won in purses: $109,958,510. Included among Cordero's important wins were the Kentucky Derby in 1974, 1976, and 1985; the Preakness Stakes in 1980 and 1984; and the Belmont Stakes in 1976. He was the leading rider at Saratoga for eleven years in a row. In 1982, he was named jockey of the year.

Martín Dihigo
(1905–1971)

Baseball

Born in Matanzas, Cuba, Martín Dihigo is one of the few baseball players named to the American Hall of Fame based on his career in the Negro leagues. In addition, he was named to the Halls of Fame of Cuba, Mexico, and Venezuela. He was perhaps the best all-around baseball player that ever existed, yet there are few statistics and records to document his outstanding achievements. Called the "Black Babe Ruth," he played as an outstanding pitcher and outfielder, but he also played *every* other position. He was an outstanding hitter, as well. Dihigo began his career in the Negro leagues in 1923 with Alex Pómpez's Cuban Stars when he was only fifteen years old. By 1926 he was considered one of the top pitchers in Black baseball. During his career he played ball in all of the countries that have named him to their Hall of Fame. In each of these countries he led the leagues in home runs, batting average, number of victories, and lowest earned run average (ERA). In 1929 he is reported as having batted .386 in the American Negro League; in 1938 he batted .387 in the Mexican League and pitched 18-2 with an ERA of 0.90. After the failure of the Negro National League—when baseball was desegregated—Dihigo played in Mexico during the 1950s. He was then too old for the U.S. major leagues. After the Cuban Revolution, Dihigo—who had spent much of dictator Fulgencio Batista's rule in exile—returned to Cuba to assist in organizing amateur baseball leagues and to teach the game.

Sixto Escobar
(1913–)

Boxing

Sixto Escobar, known as *El Gallito de Barceloneta* (The Barceloneta Fighting Cock), was the first Puerto Rican boxer to win a world championship when he knocked out Tony Marino on August 31, 1936, in the thirteenth round. Escobar was born in Barceloneta, Puerto Rico, on March 23, 1913, and only grew to fight at 118 pounds and five feet, four inches. Although born in Puerto Rico, Escobar spent most of his professional career in New York; he also fought in Canada, Cuba, Mexico, and Venezuela. Escobar fought as a professional boxer from 1931 to 1941, after which he joined the U.S. Army. He is one of the few boxers ever to have regained his lost throne, accomplishing this feat twice: in 1935 and 1938. Escobar fought sixty-four times and was never knocked out. He ended his hold on the championship in 1939, when he could no longer make the required weight of 118 pounds.

Manuel José Fernández (1946–)

Football

Born on July 3, 1946, in Oakland, California, "Manny" was educated at Chabot University and the University of Utah, and went on to become an outstanding defensive tackle on one of professional football's winningest teams, the Miami Dolphins under Don Shula. Fernández has achieved the highest distinction of any Hispanic in football: he was named to the All-Time Greatest Super Bowl All-Star team. During his career with the Miami Dolphins, from 1968 to 1977, Fernández was voted the Dolphins' Most Valuable Defensive Lineman six consecutive years, 1968 to 1973. He helped the Dolphins win two Super Bowls, 1972 and 1973, and become the only undefeated team in NFL history, in 1973.

Tony Fernández (1962–)

Baseball

Born on June 30, 1962, in San Pedro de Macoris, Dominican Republic, Tony Fernández has been a Toronto Blue Jays shortstop since 1983. He made the American League All-Star team in 1986, 1987, and 1989. He holds the major league baseball record for highest fielding percentage in 1989, and the American League record for the most games played at shortstop, 1986.

Thomas Raymond Flores (1937–)

Football

Born on March 21, 1937, in Fresno, California, Thomas Flores, the son of Mexican-American farm workers, has risen to become an outstanding professional coach and manager. In fact, he is ranked as one of the most successful coaches in the National Football League, named to head the Oakland Raiders in 1979. Flores worked in the fields through elementary and junior high school, managed to get his high school and college education (University of the Pacific, 1958), and was drafted by the Calgary Stampeders (Canada) in 1958. After that he played with the Redskins and in 1960 joined the Raiders. As a quarterback for the Raiders for six seasons, he completed 48.9 percent of his passes for 11,635 yards and 92 touchdowns. Flores finished his ten years as a professional player with the Kansas City Chiefs in 1969. From then on he worked as a coach and was named assistant to Coach John Madden of the Raiders in 1972. When Madden resigned after the 1978 season, Flores took his place. In his second year as coach, the Raiders won Super Bowl XV. After two more years, Flores led the Raiders to another Super Bowl victory. Flores is only one of two people in NFL history to have a Super Bowl ring as a player, assistant coach, and head coach. After eight seasons, Flores's record with the Raiders was 78-43 in the regular season and 8-3 in playoffs and Super Bowls. In 1989 Flores became the president and general manager of the Seattle Seahawks, the highest rank ever achieved by a Hispanic in professional sports in the United States.

Born on November 26, 1908, in Rodeo, California, Vernon Louis Gómez, also known as "Lefty" and "The Gay Castilian," probably referring to his Spanish ancestry (he was half-Irish, half-Spanish), was one of baseball's most successful pitchers, ranking third in regular season wins, with 189 for the New York Yankees. He also holds the record for the most wins without a loss in World Series play (6-0) and three wins against one loss in All-Star play. Gómez was active from 1930 to 1943, pitching 2,503 innings, winning 189 games to 102 losses, and earning an ERA of 3.34. He scored twenty wins or more in 1931, 1932, 1934, and 1937. Gómez is number thirteen on the all-time winning percentage list. In all, Gómez made All-Star teams every year from 1933 to 1939, and he is a member of the Hall of Fame. During winter seasons, he played ball in Cuba, where he served for a while as manager of the Cienfuegos team, and once he taught a class on pitching at the University of Havana.

**Lefty Gómez
(1908-1989)**

Baseball

Richard Alonzo "Pancho" González was born on May 9, 1928, in Los Angeles to Mexican immigrant parents. His father, Manuel, fitted furniture and painted movie sets, and his mother, Carmen, was an occasional seamstress. González was a self-taught tennis player, having begun at age twelve on the public courts of Los Angeles. He won his first tournament as an Edison Junior High School student; because of excessive absenteeism, González was not allowed to compete in tennis while in high school. González served in the U.S. Navy and competed in the U.S. singles championship upon his return in 1947. That same year he placed seventeenth in the nation. In 1948 González became U.S. singles champion at Forest Hills and played on the U.S. Davis Cup team. He won Forest Hills again in 1949. After having won the U.S. grass, clay, and indoor championships, González turned pro. From 1954 to 1962 he was world professional singles champion. In 1968 he coached the U.S. Davis Cup team, and he was named to the International Tennis Hall of Fame.

**Pancho González
(1928-)**

Tennis

Pancho González after winning the National Men's Indoor Tennis Championship, 1949.

Keith Hernández (1953–)

Baseball

Born on October 20, 1953, in San Francisco, Keith Hernández attended San Mateo College. He played with the St. Louis Cardinals from 1974 to 1983, and then with the New York Mets until 1989; since 1990 he has been with the Cleveland Indians. Hernández has been considered the best fielding first baseman of his time, having won eleven Gold Gloves and leading the league in double plays and lifetime assists. He played on National League All-Star teams in 1979, 1980, 1984, 1986, and 1987. Hernández assisted the Cardinals in achieving pennant and World Series victories, and, was Most Valuable Player in 1979 and an All-Star in 1979, 1980, 1984, 1986, and 1987. In 1983 he was released under suspicion of using drugs, which later was proved to be true. A reformed and repentant Hernández was active with the Mets until 1989. In 1987, he was named team captain.

Al López (1908–)

Baseball

Al López has been rated as the seventh-best catcher and the seventh-best manager of all time, and he was elected to the Hall of Fame in 1977. For many years he held the record for the most games caught in the major leagues (1,918) and for the most years (twelve) spent in the National

Keith Hernández watches his drive over the right field fence at Shea Stadium, 1989.

League, catching in one hundred games or more. He tied the record for the most games caught in the National League without a passed ball in 1941, with 114 games. López played for the Dodgers from 1930 to 1947, and later with the Braves, the Pirates, and the Indians. He was an outstanding manager for the Indians from 1951 to 1956 and for the White Sox from 1957 to 1965 and 1968 to 1969. His record as a manager was 1,422-1,026 for a winning percentage of .581, the ninth all-time highest.

Nancy Marie López was born to Mexican-American parents in Torrance, California, on January 6, 1957, was raised in Roswell, New Mexico, and rose to become one of the youngest women golfers to experience professional success. She learned golf from her father, and by age eleven was already beating him. She won the New Mexico Women's Open when she was only twelve. In high school, López was the only female member of the golf team, and as an eighteen-year-old senior, she placed second in the U.S. Women's Open. After high school, she attended Tulsa University on a golf scholarship, but dropped out to become a professional golfer. In 1978, during López's first full season as a pro, she won nine tournaments,

**Nancy López
(1957–)**

Golf

including the Ladies Professional Golf Association. She was named Rookie of the Year, Player of the Year, Golfer of the Year, and Female Athlete of the Year; she also won the Vare Trophy. Also in 1978 she set a new record for earnings by a rookie: $189,813. In 1983 she took a break from her career when she became the mother of Ashley Marie, her child with her husband, baseball star Ray Knight. Two months after having Ashley, López began touring again, and by 1987, she had won thirty-five tournaments and qualified to become the eleventh member of the Ladies Professional Golf Association Hall of Fame. López's most outstanding year was 1985, when she won five tournaments and finished in the top ten of twenty-one others; that year she also won the LPGA again.

Juan Marichal

(1937–)

Baseball

Juan "Naito" Marichal is the right-handed Dominican pitcher who was signed to the minor leagues at age nineteen and whose wide variety of pitches and motions took him to the Hall of Fame. Marichal started with the San Francisco Giants in 1962, and from 1962 to 1971 he averaged twenty wins per year. He led the National League in wins in 1963 with a record of 25-8 and in 1968 with 26-9, in shutouts in 1965 with ten and 1969 with and in ERA in 1969 (2.10). He pitched in eight All-Star games for a 2-0 record and an 0.50 ERA for eighteen innings. Marichal's total innings pitched were 3,509, for a record of 243-142 and an ERA of 2.89. He was an All-Star from 1962 to 1969 and again in 1971, and was inducted into the Hall of Fame in 1983.

Rachel Elizondo

McLish (1958–)

Body Building

Born in Harlingen, Texas, McLish studied health and physical education at Pan American University. McLish has been a national champion bodybuilder, a successful model and actress, and spokesperson for health and physical fitness. McLish was the U.S. Women's Bodybuilding Champion in 1980, Ms. Olympia in 1980 and 1982, and world champion in 1982.

José Méndez

(1888?–1928)

Baseball

Cuban José Méndez was an outstanding pitcher and infielder who, because of his African ancestry and dark skin, was never allowed to play in the majors. Instead, he played in the Negro National League and in Cuba, and thus many of his statistics are missing. Such witnesses as Hall of Famer John Henry Lloyd said that he never saw a pitcher superior to Méndez, and Giants Manager John McGraw said that Méndez would have been worth $50,000 in the majors, an unusually high figure back in those days. Méndez came to the United States in 1908 with the Cuban Stars. In 1909 he went 44-2 as a pitcher for the Stars. During the winters he played in Cuba, where he compiled a record of 62-17 by 1914. From 1912 to 1916 Méndez played for the All-Nations of Kansas City, a racially mixed barnstorming club. From 1920 to 1926 he served as a player manager for the Kansas City Monarchs and led them to three straight Negro National League pennants from 1923 to 1925. During his long career, he also played for the Los Angeles White Sox, the Chicago American Giants, and the Detroit Stars.

Born in Perico, Cuba, on November 29, 1922, Saturnino Orestes Arrieta Armas Miñoso, nicknamed "Minnie," had one of the most outstanding careers of any Hispanic ballplayer in the major leagues. He began his career in Cuba on the semiprofessional Club Ambrosia team in 1942, and played semiprofessional ball on the island until he took to the field as a third baseman with the New York Cubans of the Negro leagues from 1946 to 1948. In 1949 he made his major league debut with the Cleveland Indians, but was soon traded to San Diego, returned to the Indians in 1951, and that same year went to the Chicago White Sox. He spent the greater part of his career playing on one or the other of these two teams, and with St. Louis and Washington until 1964. In 1976 Miñoso made a return as a designated hitter for the Chicago White Sox; he thus became one of only six players to be active in four separate decades, and only two other players in major league history have played at an older age: Satchel Paige and Nick Altrock. After that he remained active as a player-manager in Mexico. He ended his career as a third-base coach for Chicago. Miñoso's lifetime batting average was 299, with 1023 runs batted in, 186 home runs, and 205 bases stolen.

**Orestes Miñoso
(1922–)**

Baseball

Born on August 27, 1961, in Barquisimeto, Venezuela, Amleto Andrés Monacelli is a college graduate who has become one of the most popular and successful members of the Professional Bowling Association tour. After becoming a professional in 1982, his earnings continually grew until, by 1991, he was winning $81,000 in prizes, and in 1989 even achieved a record $213,815. The list of tournaments he has won includes the Japan Cup (1987), the Showboat Invitational (1988), the Miller Challenge (1989), the Wichita Open (1989 and 1990), the Budweiser Touring Players Championship (1989), the Cambridge Mixed Doubles (1989 and 1990), the Columbus Professional Bowling Classic (1990), the Quaker State Open (1991), and the True Value Open (1991). Among his many awards are the Professional Bowlers Association Player of the Year in 1989 and 1990, and the Harry Smith Point Leader Award in 1989. In 1990, he won the Budweiser Kingpin Competition for the highest average for the year, and sportswriters named him Bowler of the Year. Monacelli is still a Venezuelan citizen; this is the first time that a foreigner has ever been

**Amleto Andrés
Monacelli (1961–)**

Bowling

named Bowler of the Year. In his professional career, Monacelli has rolled sixteen perfect games, seven of them during the 1989 season, which established a new record for perfect games in a year. Three of these were accomplished during one week, thus tying the record.

First-round draft choice Anthony Muñoz stretches at rookie camp, 1980.

Anthony Muñoz (1958-)

Football

Born on August 19, 1958, in Ontario, California, Muñoz is a graduate of the University of Southern California. He has played football with the Cincinnati Bengals since 1980, distinguishing himself as All-Pro offensive tackle eight times. He was selected for the Pro Bowl in 1982, 1983, and 1984. In 1988, he was chosen as the Miller Lite/NFL Lineman of the Year.

Tony Oliva (1940-)

Baseball

Pedro "Tony" Oliva, a native Cuban, has been the only player to win batting championships during his first two major league seasons. Throughout his career, Oliva was an outstanding hitter and outfielder; however, an injured knee shortened his career. He was active from 1962 to 1976 with the Minnesota Twins, winning Rookie of the Year in 1964 and the league batting title in 1964, 1965 and 1971. Oliva led the league in hits five times in his career. He made All-Star teams from 1964 to 1971, tying Joe DiMaggio's record of having been named an All-Star in each of his six first seasons, and won the Golden Glove in 1966 as the league's best defensive right fielder. Oliva's career batting average was .304, with 220 home runs and 947 runs batted in, for 1,676 games played. Because of his knee, which had been operated on seven times, Oliva served the last years of his career mostly as a designated hitter and pinch hitter. Since 1977, he has been coaching for the Minnesota Twins.

Alejandro Oms (1895–1946)

Baseball

Martín Dihigo considered Alejandro Oms to have been the best batter in Cuban baseball. Born to a poor family in Santa Clara, Cuba, in 1895, he had to work as a child in an iron foundry. He started playing organized baseball in 1910 as a center fielder. He played in the Negro National League on the Cuban Stars and the New York Cubans from 1921 to 1935, while still managing to put in outstanding seasons during the winter in Cuban professional ball. On the most famous Cuban team of all time, Santa Clara, Oms batted .436 in the 1922–23 season. In Cuba, Oms achieved a lifetime batting average of .352; his average in the United States is not known. He was batting champion on the island three times: in 1924–25 with .393, in 1928–29 with .432 and in 1929–30 with .380. In 1928, he established a Cuban record for most consecutive games with hits (30).

Vicente Oropeza

Rodeo

The most famous and influential Hispanic rodeo performer of all time, the Mexican native Vicente Oropeza called himself the "premier charro Mexicano of the world," and on his first appearance in the United States in July 1891. As a headliner and champion in both Mexico and the United States, he is credited with having introduced trick and fancy roping in the United States. In 1893 Oropeza became the star of "Buffalo Bill" Cody's "Mexicans from Old Mexico" feature in his Wild West Show. In 1900 Oropeza won the first World's Championship of Trick and Fancy Roping, which was a major contest up through the 1930s. One of the most famous American ropers of all time, Will Rogers, credited Oropeza for inspiring his career. Oropeza was selected as a member of the National Rodeo Hall of Fame for his contributions to what may be considered both a sport and an art.

Carlos Ortiz (1936–)

Boxing

Carlos Ortiz was the second Puerto Rican boxer—the first being Sixto Escobar—to win a world title. Born in Ponce, Puerto Rico, on September 9, 1936, Ortiz made his professional debut in 1955. He was undefeated that year and in 1956, 1957, and almost all of 1958, suffering his first defeat on December 31 in a fight with Kenny Lane in Miami Beach. He later beat Lane in a rematch to win the junior welterweight championship. After losing the junior welterweight championship to Duilio Loi, he turned lightweight in 1962, and on April 21 won the world championship in that division from Joe Brown. He successfully defended his crown various times until April 10, 1965, when he lost in Panama to Ismael Laguna. But he recovered the title on November 13 of the same year in San Juan, Puerto Rico. Again he successfully defended his crown until losing in the Dominican Republic to Carlos "Teo" Cruz on June 29, 1968.

Manuel Ortiz

(1916–1970)

Boxing

A native of El Centro, California, Mexican-American boxer Manuel Ortiz became the bantamweight champion on August 7, 1942, when he beat Lou Salica. Ortiz totaled 41 knock-outs in his career and never once suffered one himself in 117 bouts. Ortiz tied Henry Armstrong in defending his title twenty times (only two other fighters had defended more often), and even successfully defended it three times in 1946 after a tour of duty in the army. Ortiz finally lost the crown on January 8, 1947, to Harold Dade in San Francisco, but he took it back on March 11 that same year. He lost it again on May 31, 1950, to Vic Toweel in Johannesburg, South Africa.

James Plunkett

(1947–)

Football

James William "Jim" Plunkett was born in Santa Clara, California, the son of William and Carmen Blea Plunkett, who had met at a school for the blind in Albuquerque, New Mexico. His father managed a newsstand in San Jose, where Plunkett became an outstanding year-round athlete in high school. Later, at Stanford University he became starting quarterback as a sophomore. During his junior year he threw passes for 2,671 yards and 20 touchdowns. He was named to the Associated press's all-American second team, won the Voit Memorial Trophy as the PAC's outstanding player and was eighth in the Heisman Trophy selection. It was as a senior that he finally was awarded the Heisman Trophy, as well as many other awards. He became the first major college football player to surpass 7,000 yards on offense. In 1971, Plunkett was the first pick for the New England Patriots, and passed for 2,158 yards and 19 touchdowns; he was chosen as NFL Rookie of the Year. Plunkett was injured during the next few years and was traded to the San Francisco 49ers who later released him. In 1978 he was signed by the Oakland Raiders, and in 1980 he led the Raiders to the Super Bowl. He became Super Bowl MVP and was named the NFL 1980 Comeback Player of the Year. In 1983 Plunkett again led the Raiders to a Super Bowl victory. That year he recorded his best season, with 230 completions for 1,935 yards and 20 touchdowns. Now retired, Plunkett passed for a total of 25,882 yards, with 164 touchdowns during his career.

*Jim Plunkett maneuvers
around New York Giant
George Martin, 1986.*

In nine years as a professional boxer, Armando "Mando" Ramos only fought forty bouts, but that was enough for him two win two world titles as a lightweight. Born on November 15, 1948, in Los Angeles, the Mexican-American boxer won his first seventeen bouts, eleven by knockouts. On February 18, 1969, he won the lightweight championship from Carlos Cruz in Los Angeles. On February 19, 1972, Ramos won the World Boxing Congress lightweight championship over Pedro Carrasco. In 1973 he retired after suffering a knockout by Arturo Piñeda.

**Armando Ramos
(1948–)**

Boxing

Born on October 23, 1935, in Río Piedras, Puerto Rico, Rodríguez came from an extremely impoverished family and found his way into golf as a caddy on the links that served Puerto Rico's booming tourism. His is one of the most famous Hispanic "rags to riches through sports" tales, his career earnings having passed the $3 million mark, and because he contributes financially to charities, including the Chi Chi Rodríguez Youth Foundation in Clearwater, Florida. Included among the important tournaments that he has won are the Denver Open (1963), Lucky Strike Inter-

**Juan "Chi Chi"
Rodriguez (1935–)**

Golf

national Open (1964), Western Open (1964), Dorado Pro-Am (1965), Texas Open (1967), and Tallahassee Open (1979). As a member of the Senior PGA Tour, he has won numerous tournaments, including the Silver Pages Classic (1987), GTE Northwest Classic (1987), and Sunwest Senior Classic (1990).

Lauro Salas
(1927-)

Boxing

Lauro Salas's boyhood dream was to become a bullfighter, but he started boxing as a teenager in his native Monterrey, Mexico, for the money. He left home and moved to Los Angeles at age nineteen to become a professional boxer. There he won fourteen of his first seventeen pro bouts as a featherweight. In 1952 he won the lightweight championship over Jimmy Carter, but lost it back to him that same year at Chicago Stadium. Salas retired in 1961 after being knocked out by Sebastiao Nascimento and Bunny Grant.

Alberto Bauduy
Salazar (1958-)

Track and Field

Born in Havana, Cuba, one year before the triumph of the Cuban Revolution, future track marathoner Alberto Salazar moved to Manchester, Connecticut, with his refugee parents when he was only two years old. The family moved to Wayland, Massachusetts, where Salazar was named high school all-American twice as a two- and three-mile racer. In 1976 he entered the University of Oregon, where he was coached by Olympian Bill Dellinger. In 1978 he won the NCAA individual championship. He went on to become a three-time cross-country all-American and helped Oregon win the 1977 NCAA team title and finish second in 1978 and 1979. In 1979, he set a U.S. road record of 22:13 for five miles. In 1980 Salazar made the Olympic team, but that was the year that the United States boycotted the games in Moscow. That same year, however, Salazar won the New York Marathon with the record for the fastest first marathon in history, and the second-fastest time ever run by an American. The next year he won more championships, often by establishing new records, and once again he was victorious in the New York Marathon, setting a new world record of 2:08:13. In 1982 Salazar won the Boston and New York Marathons and various other events around the world; that year and in 1981 and 1983 he was selected the top U.S. road racer. Despite some setbacks and injuries, Salazar made the U.S. Olympic team for the second time in 1984, but finished only fifteenth in the games at Los Angeles. Salazar has set one world record and six U.S. records, the most of any U.S. runner since Steve Prefontaine.

Vicente Saldívar became the first undisputed Mexican featherweight world champion and the twelfth left-handed title holder in history with his win over Sugar Ramos on September 26, 1964. Born the son of a businessman in Mexico City on May 3, 1943, Saldívar turned professional in 1961. On his way to the world crown he knocked out twenty-five opponents, and he won thirty-six of his first thirty-nine pro bouts. Saldívar defended his title in eight straight bouts, winning five by knockout. He retired in October 1967, but made a comeback and regained the championship on May 9, 1970, from Johnny Famechon in a fifteen-round decision. Saldívar lost the title to Kuniaki Shibata by knockout in the thirteenth round on December 11, 1970.

Vicente Saldívar (1943–)

Boxing

"Kid Chocolate" was one of the most celebrated Hispanic boxers of all time. Born in Havana, Cuba, on October 28, 1910, his career became an example of the fate that befalls boxers who battle their way out of poverty into fame and temporary riches. After winning eighty-six amateur and twenty-one professional fights in Cuba, he made his New York debut in 1928 and fought over one hundred bouts in the United States over the next ten years. He became a true champion, supported his community, and was memorized on stage and screen. However, he was severely exploited by his managers and owners and ultimately was done in by poverty and alcoholism.

Eligio "Kid Chocolate" Sardiñas (1910–)

Boxing

Luis Clemente Tiant Vega, the Cuban pitcher, broke into professional baseball in the Mexican League in 1959. Although best known for his play with the Boston Red Sox, Tiant's major league career in the United States—from 1964 to 1982—included seasons with the Indians, the Twins, the Yankees, the Pirates, and the Angels. After making an outstanding start as a rookie for Cleveland with a 10-4 record and a 2.83 ERA, Tiant hit his stride in 1968 with a 1.60 ERA, nine shutouts, 5.3 hits per nine innings, striking out more than one batter per inning and finishing the season with a 21-9 record. On July 3 of that year, he struck out nineteen Twins in a ten-inning game, setting an American League record. In his previous start he had struck out thirteen Red Sox for a major league record. While suffering a series of problems, including a hairline fracture, Tiant was traded and released various times during the next few years, finally joining Boston in 1971 after a stint with the Red Sox's Louisville farm team. In 1972 he was named Comeback Player of the Year and he won the ERA title with a 1.91 and a season record of 15-6. The next two years he won twenty and twenty-two games and in 1974 led the league

Luis Tiant (1940–)

Baseball

with seven shutouts. Tiant helped the Sox to a pennant and the World Series championship that year. In 1976 Tiant won twenty games for the last time and went 21-12 for the season. Tiant was known for his masterful changes of speed and a wide variety of release points and deceptive pitching motions.

José Luis Torres

(1936–)

Boxing

The third Puerto Rican boxer to ever win a world championship was José Luis "Chegui" Torres, who won the medium heavyweight championship from Willie Pastrano on March 30, 1965, with a technical knockout in the ninth round at Madison Square Garden in New York. Without a rival in the middle heavyweight division, Torres took on Tom McNeely in the heavyweight class, winning in a ten-round decision. Torres defended his medium heavyweight crown and fought as a heavyweight successfully on a number occasions until December 16, 1966 when, weakened from an old pancreatic injury, he lost on points to the Nigerian Dick Tiger, whom he had beaten earlier in his career. Born into a large, poor family, in Ponce, Puerto Rico, Torres dropped out of high school and joined the army. There he learned to box well enough to win the Antilles, Caribbean, Second Army, All-Army and Interservice championships as a light middleweight. In 1956 he won the U.S. Olympic title, but lost on points at the games in Melbourne to the Hungarian Laszlo Papp. After the army, Torres moved to New York, where he fought as an amateur to win the National A.A.U. championship and then turned pro. During and after his professional boxing career, Torres also developed a career as a singer and musician and worked in public relations, real estate, and as a New York newspaper columnist—all without a high school education!

Lee Treviño

(1939–)

Golf

Lee Buck Treviño was born in Dallas, Texas, on December 1, 1939, into an impoverished Mexican-American family. Fatherless, he was raised by his mother, a cleaning woman, and his maternal grandfather, a gravedigger. Their four-room farmhouse was located at the back of the Glen Lakes Country Club fairways. As a boy Treviño studied the form of the golfers on the course from his own backyard. He dropped out of school in the seventh grade and made his way into what was then an exclusively Anglo rich man's sport by working as a greens keeper and as a caddy. He later joined the marines and played a great deal of golf while he was stationed in Okinawa.

In 1966 Treviño became a professional golfer and achieved his first major victory in 1968 at the U.S. Open, where he became the first player in history to shoot all four rounds of the event under par. In 1970 he was the

Lee Treviño.

leading money winner on the Professional Golf Association tour. In 1971 Treviño won the U.S. Open for a second time, won five tournaments between April and July, and also won the British Open in that year and again in 1972. For his achievements in 1971, Treviño was named PGA Player of the Year, Associated Press Athlete of the Year, and *Sports Illustrated* Sportsman of the Year. After that, he won the 1974 PGA again, among many other tournaments. In 1975 Treviño and two other golfers were struck by lightning during a tournament near Chicago. To this day he still suffers from back problems due to the accident; it seriously affected his game, even causing him to go winless in 1976 and 1978. In 1980, he made a comeback, winning the Texas Open and the Memphis Classic and earning $385,814 for the year. He was also awarded the Vardon Trophy for the fewest strokes per round (69.73 for 82 rounds), the lowest since Sam Snead in 1958. Treviño retired from the PGA tour in October 1985, with his thirty tour victories and total career earnings of over $3 million (third highest). Treviño has been elected to the Texas Sports, American Golf, and World Golf Halls of Fame.

Fernando Valenzuela (1960–)

Baseball

Fernando Valenzuela has been one of the youngest and most celebrated baseball players because of his sensational introduction to the major leagues as an outstanding pitcher during his first seasons with the Los Angeles Dodgers. During his rookie year in 1981, Valenzuela won not only Rookie of the Year but also *The Sporting News* Player of the Year, and he was the first rookie ever to win the Cy Young Award. He won his first ten major league outings and his eight shutouts tied the rookie record in a season that was shortened because of a players' strike. Valenzuela is considered to have had the best screwball of his time. He led the league in strikeouts in 1981 and in wins in 1986. He was selected for the All-Star team five times; in 1986 he tied Carl Hubbell's record of five straight strikeouts in an All-Star game. That was also the year that he won the Gold Glove.

Nicolás Kanellos

*I*ndex

A

Abreu, Virgilio 456
Acevedo, Mario 357, 358
Aceves, José 325, 327
Acosta, Iván 410, 480
Acosta, Raymond L. 235
Affirmative action 178
AFL (American Federation of Labor) 156
AFL-CIO 162, 186
African slaves 21
Aguiar-Vélez, Deborah 145
Aguila, Guz. *See* Guzmán Aguilera, Antonio 452
Aguilar, Robert P. 236
Aguirre, Gabriel Eloy 145
Aguirre, Michael J. 248
ahijado/a (godchild) 36
Alagarín, Miguel 404
Alamo, The 79
Alarcón, Arthur L. 236
Alarcón, Francisco 401
Albizu, Olga 332, 336
Aleandro, Norma 539
Alexander VI, Pope 54
Alfonso, Carlos 353
Algarín, Miguel 406, 413
Alianza Hispano Americana 107
Allen v. State Board of Elections 191
Almaraz, Carlos 339
Almendros, Néstor 540
Altar, home 17
Alurista (Alberto Urista) 389, 415
Alvarado, Trini 540

Álvarez, Everett, Jr. 220
American Federation of Labor (AFL) 156
Amy, Francisco 378
Anaya, Rudolfo 392, 415
Anaya, Toney 228
Angeles Negros, Los 593
Anthony, Marc 594
Aparicio, Luis 613
Aparicio, Manuel 465, 480
Apodaca, Jerry 228
Aragón, José 314
Aragón, José Rafael 315
Aranda, Guillermo 357, 358
Arawak 55
Arboleya, Carlos José 145
Arcano y sus Maravillas 587
Arce, Miguel 379
Archuleta, Diego 221
Argüelles, John 236
Armendáriz, Pedro 540
Armida 541
Arnaz, Desi 541
Arte Público Press 397
Artes Guadalupanos de Aztlán 370
ASCO (Distasteful) 360
Astol, Lalo 468
Astol, Leonardo García 483
Austin, Moses 78
Avalos, David 347
Avila, María Inocenta 376
Ayala, Ramón 572
Az.T.K 381
Aztec 64
Azuela, Mariano 380

B

Baca, Joseph Francis 237
Baca, Judy 340, 360
Baca-Barragán, Polly 228
Badillo, Herman 207
Balada 593
Bancroft, Hubert H. 376
Banda 594
Bañuelos, Romana Acosta 221
Barajas, Salvador 357, 358
Baralt, Luis 457
Barela, Casimiro 229
Barela, Patrocino 321
Barreto, Lefty 405
Barreto, Ray 587
Barrio Boyzz 594
Barrio de la Logan 356
Barro, Mary Helen 296
Batista 121
Battle of San Pascual 81
Bautista de Anza, Juan 75
Becerra, Xavier 195
Bedoya, Alfonso 541
Bellán, Esteban 607
Berbers 52
Beristáin, Leopoldo 452
Bernal, Paulino 571
Betances, Ramón Emeterio 377
Bilingual-bicultural movement 3
Birthrates of Hispanics 30
Blades, Rubén 541, 588
Blancarte, James E. 249
Blaz, Ben 207
Boabdil, King of Granada 54
Bobo, Willie 590
Bolaños Cacho, Miguel 380

Bonaparte, Napoleon 77
Bonilla, Henry 195
Borinquen 12, 354
Borras, Edelmiro 460
Botero, Fernando 333
Bowie, Jim 80
Boxing 612
Bracero Program 23, 107, 162, 163, 180
Bravos del Norte, Los 572
Bronco 595
Brotherhood of the Penitentes 12
Bugarín, Pedro 578
Bukis, Los 593, 595
Burciaga, Juan C. 237
Bush, George 176-178
Bustamante, Albert G. 207
Bustamante, Anastasio 79

C

Caballeros de Labor (Knights of Labor) 156
Caballeros de San Juan 116
Cabañas, Humberto 146
Cabeza de Baca, Fernando E. 222
Cabeza de Vaca, Fabiola 383
Cabranés, José A. 237
Cabrera Infante, Gabriel 410
Cabrera, Lydia 410
Caicedo, Harry 296
California Labor Relations Act 186
California Land Act of 1851 85
Campeche Show 596
Campos, Santiago E. 238
canción 562
Cannella, John M. 238
Cansino, Rita. See Hayworth, Rita 505
Capetillo, Luisa 388
Caraballo, Wilfredo 249
Cárdenas, Rogelio 368
Carew, Rod 613
Carib 55
Carillo de Fotch, Josefa 376
Carino v. University of Oklahoma 172
Carlos López Press 385
Caro, Brígido 380
Carpa Cubana 456
Carpa García 456

Carpentier, Alejo 410
Carr, Vikki 595
Carrero, Jaime 403, 404
Carrillo, Eduardo 450
Carrillo, Leo 506, 542
Carrión, Arturo Morales 222
Carter, Jimmy 174
Carter, Lynda Córdoba 297
Casa Editorial Lozano 379
Casals, Rosemary 614
Casas, Melesio 332, 333
Castañeda, Tomás 357, 358
Castellanos, Leonard 360
Castelló, Hugo M. 615
Castillo, Ana 397
Castillo, Leonel J. 222
Castillo, Mario 363
Castro, Fidel 25, 121
Catholic Bishop's Committee for the Spanish-Speaking 13
Catholicism 36
Cavazos, Lauro F. 223
Celtic-Iberian culture 50
Central American immigration 26
Central Valley cotton strike 157
Centro Asturiano 464
Centro Cultural de la Raza 356
Cepeda, Orlando 615
Cerezo, Carmen C. 238
Cervantes, Lorna Dee 400, 419
Cervantes, Pedro 326
CETA (Comprehensive Employment and Training Administration) 174
Chacón, Eusebio 375
Chacón, Felipe Maximiliano 376
Chambers, Henry K. 384
Charles V 67
Charrería 610
Charros 610
Chaves, José Francisco 208
Chávez, Angelico 383, 416
Chávez, César 159, 162, 185
Chávez, Denise 397, 398, 417
Chávez, Dennis 208
Chávez, Edward 325, 327
Chicago Mural Group 363
Chicano Literature 389
Chicano Park 356
Chichimecas 63

Chicote 381
Child care 42
Chinese Exclusion Act of 1882 22
Cienfuegos, Lucky 404
CIO (Congress of Industrial Organizations) 157
Cisneros, Henry G. 217
Cisneros, Sandra 397
City of Mobile v. Bolden 192
Civil Rights Act of 1964 178
Civil Rights Act of 1991 178
Clemente, Roberto 616
Cobo Souza, Manuel 411
Colón, Jesús 388, 404, 420
Colón, Miriam 481
Colón, Willie 588
Colón-Morales, Rafael 354
Columbus, Christopher 55, 58
Community Action Program (CAP) 171
Community Service Organization 185
Compadrazgo (godparenthood) 34
Compadres (co-parents) 36
Compañía Dramática Española 447, 458
Compañía Española de Angel Mollá 447
Compañía Española de la Familia Estrella 446
Compañía, La 472
Comprehensive Employment and Training Administration (CETA) 174
Concepción, Dave 616
Conesa, María 458
Confianza (trust) 34
Congreso de Artistas Chicanos en Aztlan 347, 361
Congreso Mexicanista, El 102
Congress of Industrial Organizations (CIO) 157
Congressional Hispanic Caucus 194
conjunto 562, 568
Cordero, Angel 617
Corea, Chick 590
Corona, Bert 187
Coronado Bridge 356
Coronado, Gil 219

Coronel, Antonio F. 446
Corpi, Lucha 397
corridista 563
corrido 377, 562
Cortés, Hernán 64
Cotton 157
Council of the Indies 67
Cristal, Linda 543
Crockett, Davey 80
crónica, la 380
Cronista 380
Cruz Azaceta, Luis 354
Cruz, Celia 583, 588
Cruz, Nicky 405
Cruz-Romo, Gilda 600
Cuadra, Angel 411
Cuba 55, 58
Cuba Sextet, The Joe 585
Cuban Baseball League 605
Cuban immigration 118
Cuban Revolutionary Party 92
Cuban-American Literature 409
Cuéllar, Gilbert, Jr. 146
Cuesta, José Enamorado 387, 461
Cugat, Xavier 581
Cuza Malé, Belkis 412

D

Dantés 376
Darrow, Henry 543
Dávila, Luis 397
De Armiño, Franca 387, 461
De Burgos, Julia 403
De Cárdenas, Isidra T. 381
De Cépedes, Carlos Manuel 90
De Córdoba, Pedro 543
De Córdova, Arturo (Arturo García) 543
De Espejo, Antonio 70
De Garcés, Pedro 75
De Guzmán, Nuño 66
De Hoyos, Angela 397
De la Garza, E. (Kika) 194, 195
De Lugo, Ron 197
De Mendoza, Antonio 67
De Moncaleano, Blanca 382
De Oñate, Juan 70
De Perea, Pedro 73
De Soto, Hernando 67

De Tolosa, Juan 68
De Zumárraga, Juan 67
DeAnda, James 239
Del Casal, Julián 409
Del Junco, Tirso 223
Del Pozo 459
Del Río, Dolores 544
Delgado, Abelardo 389, 422
Diamond Phillips, Lou 544
Díaz Guerra, Alirio 385
Díaz, Nelson 219
Díaz, Porfirio 22
Diaz-Balart, Lincoln 197
Dihigo, Martín 609, 617
Diversity among Hispanics 20
Domínguez, Cari M. 224
Dos Streetscapers, Los 360

E

East Los Angeles Community
    Union, The (TELACU) 159
Echaveste, Maria 219
Echeverría, José 409
Echo Par 360
Economic Opportunity Act of 1964
    (EOA) 171
Editorial Quinto Sol 390
Education 11, 30
EEOC. *See* Equal Employment Op-
    portunity Commission 172
Elizondo, Hector 544
"English Only" movement 46
Enrique, Luis 597
EOA (Economic Opportunity Act
    of 1964) 171
Equal Employment Opportunity
    Commission (EEOC) 172,
    178
Escajeda, Josefina 383
Escalante, Esteban 379
Escalante, Esteban V. 450
Escalona, Beatriz 481
Escobar, Marisol 333
Escobar, Sixto 612, 617
Esparza, Moctezuma 520, 545
Espinosa, Conrado 380
Espinosa, Paul 545
*Espinoza v. Farah Manufacturing
    Company* 172

Esteves, Sandra María 407
Estévez, Emilio 545
Estrada Courts 360
Executive Branch, Hispanics in 216

F

Fábregas, Virginia 448
Fair Employment Practices Commit-
    tee (FEPC) 158, 172
Fajardo Ortiz, Desiderio 378
Fantasmas del Caribe, Los 594
Farándula Panamericana, La 473
familia, la 34
Federal Theater Project 464
Félix, Charles 360
Feminism 39
Ferdinand, King of Aragon 54, 67
Fernández Camus, Emilio 411
Fernández Huerta, Dolores 188
Fernández, Emilio "El Indio" 511, 545
Fernández, Ferdinand Francis 239
Fernández, Manuel José 618
Fernández, Roberto 410, 411, 424
Fernández, Tony 618
Ferrer, José 482
Ferrer, Mel 546
Ferrer, Rafael 332, 336
Festival Latino 472
Figueroa, Gabriel 546
Figueroa, Sotero 377
Flamers, Los 596
Flores, Julio 376
Flores, Patrick 13
Flores, Thomas Raymond 618
Football 612
Ford, Gerald 181
Foreign Miners Tax of 1850 84
Fornés, María Irene 482
Four, Los 344, 360
Fowler, Raúl A. 411
Franciscan missionaries 71
Franciscans 10, 12
*Fraternidad Piadosa de Nuestro Padre
    Jesús Nazareno* 12
Free Trade Agreement 167
Fremont, John C. 81
Fuste, José Antonio 239
Fuster, Jaime B. 210
Futurismo 473

G

Gadsden Purchase 93
Gadsden Treaty 84
Gadsden, James 21
Gaitán, Fernando J., Jr. 239
Galarza, Ernesto 159, 187
Gallegos, José Manuel 210
García Pérez, Luis 378
García, Andy 547
García, Antonio 325, 328
García, Arturo See De Córdova,
    Arturo) 543
García, Daniel P. 250
García, David 525
García, Edward J. 239
García, Hipolita Frank 239
García, Lionel G. 425
García, Rupert 341, 345
Garduño, Gerónimo 370
Garza, Emilio M. 240
Garza, Reynaldo G. 192, 240
Garza, Ygnacio D. 230
Gaytán y Cantú 565
Geographic concentration of His-
    panics 29
Germanic culture 52
Gierbolini, Gilberto 241
Gillespie, Dizzy 590
Goizueta, Roberto C. 147
Gold rush 83
Golf 612
Gómez de Avellaneda, Gertrudis
    409
Gómez Farías, Valentín 79
Gómez, Lefty 619
Gonzales, Stephanie 229
González Amezcua, Chelo 326
González Marín, Francisco 377
González, Adalberto Elías 450, 483
González, Alberto M. 387
González, Alfredo 380
González, Balde 578
González, Celedonio 411, 426
González, Fredrick J. 147
González, Henry B. 194, 198
González, José 352
González, José Luis 403
González, Jovita 383
González, Miguel 608
González, Raymond Emmanuel 224

González, Richard "Pancho" 619
González, Rodolfo "Corky" 390
González, Xavier 326, 330
Government, Roman style of 52
Gran Chichimeca, El 68
Gran Combo, El 588
Great Depression 23
Great Society 178
Griffith, D.W. 498
Grito de Lares, El 92
Gronk 361
Grupo, El 407
Grupo Lluvia 596
Grupo Ras 479
Grupos 595
Grupos cumbieros 563
Grupos modernos 563
Grupos tropicales 563
Guerra, Juan Luis 597
Guerrero, Lalo 579
Guerrero, Vicente 78
Guillén, Nicolás 409
Gurulé, Jimmy 224
Gutiérrez de Lara, Lázaro 380
Gutiérrez, Ana Sol 230
Gutierrez, Luis 199
Guzmán Aguilera, Antonio 484
Guzmán, Gilberto 370
Guzmán, Suzanna 600

H

H-2 Program 162, 170
Hayworth, Rita 505, 547
Henríquez Ureña, Pedro 378, 385
Hermanos Bañuelos, Los 565
Hermanos Chavarría, Los 565
Hernández Cruz, Victor 406, 421
Hernandez, Adán 348
Hernández, Antonia 250
Hernández, Benigno Cárdenas 211
Hernández, Ester 342, 346
Hernández, Joseph Marion 190
Hernández, Keith 620
Hernández, Oscar 571
Hero corrido 567
Herrera Chávez, Margaret 326
Herrera, Miguel 317
Herron, Willie 361
Hidalgo y Costilla, Miguel 21, 77

Hidalgo, Edward 225
Hidalgo, Francisco 72
Hijuelos, Oscar 410, 412, 427
Hinojosa, Ricardo H. 241
Hinojosa, Rolando 391, 427
Hispanic Generation 109
Hispanic Identity 4
Hispanicization 19
Hispanidad 18
Houston, Sam 80
Huitzilopochtli 64
Hunter, Duncan 167
Hunter, Pancho 370

I

Iberian-Celtic culture 50
Immigration Act of 1990 28
Immigration and Nationality Act of
    1952 27, 162
Immigration and Naturalization Ser-
    vice (INS) 179
Immigration Law 27
Immigration Reform and Control
    Act of 1986 (IRCA) 162,
    181
Impacto de Montemorelos 596
Imprenta Bolaños Cacho Hnos 379
Indians 55
Indias, Las 57
Industria del Amor 596
Industrial Workers of the World
    (IWW) 157
Inés de la Cruz, Juana 39
INS. *See* Immigration and Natural-
    ization Service 179
INTAR 475
International Arts Relations 474
International Mine, Mill and Smelter
    Workers Union 159
IRCA (Immigration Reform and
    Control Act of 1986) 162,
    181
Isabella, Queen of Castile 54, 67
Isleños 5

J

Jackson, Andrew 24
Jaramillo, Cleofas 383

Jesuits 10, 75
Jimenez, Flaco 597
Jiménez, Luis 332, 333
Job Corps 171, 176
Job Training Partnership Act of
    1983 175
Johnson, Lyndon B. 171, 173, 178
Jones Act 25, 111
Jones v. City of Lubbock 193
Juliá, Raúl 548
Junta Patriótica Mexicana 447
Jurado, Katy 549

K

Kanellos, Nicolás 396
Kaskabel (Benjamín Padilla) 381
Knights of Labor 156

L

La Loca, Juana 67
La Plata, George 242
Labor Council of Latin American
    Advancement (LCLAA) 162
Laffitte, Héctor M. 241
Laguna santero 313
Lamas, Fernando 549
Language 5
Lara, Javier 385
Laredo Publishing Company 379
Lasansky, Mauricio 333
Latin American Conference,
    Methodist 15
Latin American immigration 26
Latin Breed 580
Latin pop 594
Laviera, Tato 404, 406, 429
Lavoe, Héctor 588
Laws of Burgos 66
LCLAA (Labor Council of Latin
    American Advancement)
    162
Lecuona, Ernesto 587
Legal Services Corporation 248
León, Tania J. 600
Lewis and Clark 77
Leyba, Albert 370
Leyba, Carlos 370
Leyba, Samuel 370

Lezama Lima, José 410
Librería Española 379
Liga de Béisbol Profesional Cubana
    605
Limón, José 573
Little Joe y la Familia 579
Llorens Torres, Luis 402
Llunas, Marcos 594
Lomas Garza, Carmen 341, 346
Long, Stephen 78
Longoria, Valerio 571
López del Castillo, Gerardo 446,
    484
López, Al 620
López, Carlos 326, 330
López, Félix A. 351
López, George 322
López, Gerald P. 250
López, Isidro 577
López, José Dolores 319
López, Nancy 621
López, Yolanda 343, 346
Lorenzana, Apolinaria 376
Lorenzo, Frank A. 148
Louisiana Territory 77
Loyal, C. 375
Lozano, Ignacio 379
Lozano, Rudolpho 242
Lucer White Lea, Aurora 383
Luján, Manuel, Jr. 225
LULAC 107
Lupe, La 583
Luque, Adolfo 608

M

Machismo 34
Machito 588
Madero, Francisco I. 98
Madrugadores, Los 565
Mafia, La 595
Malcriado, El (Daniel Venegas) 381
Manifest Destiny 77
MAPA. *See* Mexican American Po-
    litical Organization 187
Maqueo Castellanos, Esteban 380
Maquiavelo 385
Maquiladora Program 165
Mara, Adele 549
Margo 550

María de Hostos, Eugenio 377
Marichal, Juan 622
Mariel boat lift 25, 125
Marielitos 127
Marín, Richard "Cheech" 522, 550
Maris, Mona 550
Marqués del Valle de Oaxaca, El 66
Marqués, René 403, 473, 485
Márquez, Alfredo C. 242
Marriage 37
Martí, José 92, 377, 409
Martin, Chris-Pin 551
Martínez, César 348
Martínez, Frank 387
Martínez, Matthew G. 199
Martínez, Narciso 570
Martínez, Robert 226
Martínez, Velia 467
Martínez, Vilma S. 191, 251
Mata, Eduardo 601
Matas, Julio 485
Mateos, Manuel 380
Maya 62
Mazz 595
McLish, Rachel Elizondo 622
Mechicano Art Center 360
Medellín, Octavio 325, 330
Medina, Harold R., Sr. 242
Mena, María Cristina 384
Méndez, José 607, 609, 622
Méndez, Miguel 391
Méndez-Longoria, Miguel Angel
    251
Mendoza, Lydia 565
Mendoza, Vicente 364
Menendez, Robert 200
Mesa-Baines, Amalia 343, 346
Mestizo 21
Mestre, Ricardo 520
Methodists 15
Mexican American Generation, The
    576
Mexican American Legal Defense
    and Educational Fund
    (MALDEF) 191, 248
Mexican American Political Organi-
    zation (MAPA) 187
Mexican American Youth Confer-
    ence 187

Mexican Farm Labor Supply Program 163
Mexican Immigration 93
Mexican Labor Agreement 163
Mexican League (baseball) 606
Mexican Liberal Party 376
Mexican Revolution 22, 98
Mexican War 93
Mexico 55, 60
México de afuera 379
Mexico Lindo 100
Mier, Los 596
Mier y Terán, Manuel 79
Migrant Legal Action Program 248
Migrant worker 167
Milán, Ed 148
Mining 69
Miñoso, Orestes "Minnie" 609, 623
Missions 9, 303
Moctezuma II 64
Mohr, Nicholasa 407, 430
Molina, Gloria 231
Molleno 314
Monacelli, Amleto Andrés 623
Montalbán, Ricardo 522, 551
Montalván, E. 376
Montañez-Ortiz, Rafael see Ortiz, Ralph 332
Montes Huidobro, Matías 410, 486
Montez, María 551
Montoya, Joseph M. 211
Montoya, Malaquías 345
Montoya, Nestor 212
Moors 53
Mora, Francisco Luis 325, 331
Mora, Pat 398
Moraga, Cherríe 431
Morales, Alejandro 432
Morales, Esai 524
Morales, Sylvia 552
Moreno, Antonio 552
Moreno, Federico A., Sr. 243
Moreno, Rita 487, 553
Morton, Carlos 391, 487
Movimiento Artístico Chicano 363
Moya del Pino, José 326, 331
Muñoz Marín, Luis 115
Muñoz Rivera, Luis 386
Muñoz, Anthony 624
Muñoz-Rivera, Luis 115

Música norteña 562, 568
Música romántica 593
Música tropical 563, 592
Muslims 53
Mutual aid societies 156
Mutualistas 156

N

Nadal de Santa Coloma, Juan 387, 487
NAFTA (North American Free Trade Agreement) 167
Náñez, Alfredo 15
Nario, José 364
National Agricultural Workers Union 159
National Congress of Spanish-Speaking People 187
National Farm Labor Union 159, 188
National Farm Workers Association 159
National Immigration Law Center 248
Nava, Julián 226
Navaira, Emilio 594
Navarro, Gabriel 379, 450, 488
Negro Leagues 606, 609
Neri, Manuel 332, 334
New Federalism 173
Newman, Philip 243
Newspapers, literature published in 374, 377
Niggli, Josephina 383, 433
Nixon, Richard M. 173
Noriega, Manuel 457, 489
North American Free Trade Agreement (NAFTA) 167
Norton, Barry 553
Novarro, Ramón 553
Novello, Antonia C. 226
Nuestra Señora de la Purísima Concepción de Acuña 310
Nuevo Círculo Dramático, El 473
Nuevo Teatro Pobre de las Américas, El 474
Núñez, Orlando 411
Nuyorican Literature 401
Nuyorican Poets' Café 406

O

O'Farrill, Alberto 385, 460, 489
O'Neill, Gonzalo 386, 461, 489
Oaxaca 66
Obledo, Mario G. 251
Ochoa y Acuña, Anastacio 377
Ochoa, Víctor 347, 357, 358
Odin, Jean Marie 12
Office of Economic Opportunity (OEO) 171
Oliva, Tony 624
Olivas, Michael A. 252
Olmos, Edward James 519, 554
Oms, Alejandro 609, 625
Onda Chicana, La 579
Onís Treaty 24
Operation Boot Strap 115
Operation Bootstrap 162
Operation Wetback 23, 180
Oropeza, Vicente 611, 625
orquesta 562, 573
Orquesta Aragón, La 587
Orquesta tejana 562
Ortega, José Benito 317
Ortega, Katherine D. 226
Ortega, Robert, Jr. 149
Ortiz Cofer, Judith 409, 420
Ortiz, Carlos 625
Ortiz, Francis V., Jr. 227
Ortiz, Manuel 626
Ortiz, Ralph 332, 336
Ortiz, Solomon P. 200
Osuna de Marrón, Felipa 376
Otero, Jack 219
Otero, Mariano S. 212
Otero, Miguel A., Sr. 213
Otero, Miguel Angel 376

P

Pacheco, Johnny 587
Pacheco, Romualdo 214
Pachón, Harry P. 190
Padilla, Benjamín 381
Padilla, Heberto 410
Padrinos (godparents) 36
Palés Matos, Luis 402
Palés, Vicente 386
Palmieri, Charlie 587

Palmieri, Eddie 588
Palomino, Ernesto 332, 334
Paredes, Américo 382
parentesco (familism) 34
Pastor, Ed Lopez 194, 200
Patlán, Raymond 363, 364
Patterson v. McLean Credit Union 177
Pecan shellers' strike 157
Pellón, Pedro C. de 447
Penitentes, Brotherhood of the 12
Pentecostalism 15
Peña, Elizabeth 555
Peña, Federico 219
Perea, Francisco 215
Perea, Pedro 215
Pérez de Villagrá, Gaspar 374
Pérez et al. v. Federal Bureau of Investigation 173
Pérez, Eulalia 376
Pérez, Minerva 297
Pérez, Severo 525
Pérez-Giménez, Juan M. 244
Perfecto de Cos, Martín 79
Phillip, Prince of Austria 67
Phos Press 385
Pieras, Jaime, Jr. 244
Pietri, Pedro 405, 434
Pike, Zebulon 77
Piñero, Miguel 404, 406, 490
Pious Fraternity of Our Father Jesús the Nazarene 12
Pimín, Eusebio 454, 491
Plan de San Luis Potosí 98
Plunkett, James 626
Poesía del presidio político 411
Ponce de Leon, Juan 24, 67
Ponce de León, Michael 332, 335
Popé 71
Porter, Edwin S. 498
Portillo Trambley, Estela 395, 437
Pottinger, J. Stanley 191
Pozo, Chano 590
Prado, Edward C. 244
Premio Quinto Sol (Fifth Sun Award) 391
Presbyterians 15
Prida, Dolores 491
Pro Arte Gratelli 479
Protectionism 27

Protestantism 14
Public Art Workshop 363
Public Service Employment 175
Pueblo uprising 71
Puente, Ramón 380
Puente, Tito 588
Puerto Rican Immigration 114
Puerto Rican Legal Defense and Education Fund 248
Puerto Rican Traveling Theater 475
Puerto Rico 55, 60

Q

Quesada, Eugenio 332, 335
Quevedo, Abraham 358
Quill Pen Santero 314
Quinceañera 17
Quinn, Anthony 555

R

Ramírez, Ramiro 609
Ramírez, Raul Anthony 244
Ramírez, Sara Estela 376
Ramón, Domingo 72
Ramona Gardens 360
Ramos, Armando 627
Ramos, Francisco 15
Raya, Marcos 352
Reagan, Ronald 159, 175, 177, 179
Real, Manuel L. 244
Reclamation Act of 1902 22
Reconquest 53, 54
Refugee Act of 1980 29
Reid, Marita 492
Relámpagos del Norte, Los 572
Religion 9, 52
Renaldo, Duncan 555
Requena, Manuel 231
Respeto (respect) 35
Revista política 451
Reyna, Cornelio 572
Reynoso, Cruz 245
Ricardo Alonso, Luis 411
Richardson, Bill 194, 201
Riley, Dorothy Comstock 246
Rincón de Gautier, Felisa 39

Rio Grande Conference, Methodist 15
Rios, Alberto 400
Ríos, Herminio 390
Rivera, Geraldo 297
Rivera, Jerry 594
Rivera, Juan C. 460
Rivera, Tomás 391
Rivero Collado, Andrés 411
Roche Rabell, Arnaldo 354
Rodeo 610
Rodrigo, Rosita 460
Rodríguez de Tió, Lola 377, 386
Rodríguez, Antonio 460
Rodríguez, Arsenio 587
Rodríguez, John 150
Rodríguez, Joseph H. 246
Rodríguez, Juan "Chi Chi" 627
Rodríguez, Oscar 150
Rodríguez, Patricia 344, 346
Rodríguez, Paul 298
Rodríguez, Pedro 368
Rodríguez, Peter 332, 335
Rodríguez, Roberto 473
Rodríguez, Tito 588
Rojas, Tito 597
Roland, Gilbert 556
Román, Arturo 358
Romano, Octavio 390
Romero, César 504, 556
Romero, Frank 344
Romero, Leo M. 252
Romero-Barcelo, Carlos 202
Ros-Lehtinen, Ileana 201
Rosete, Guillermo 358
Rovirá, Luis D. 246
Roxie y Los Frijolitos 594
Roybal, Edward R. 216
Roybal-Allard, Lucille 202
Ruiz de Burton, Pilar 375
Ruiz, Rey 594

S

Saavedra, Louis E. 232
Salas, Lauro 628
Salazar, Alberto Bauduy 628
Salazar, Manuel M. 375
Saldívar, Vicente 629
Salinas, Porfirio 326

Salsa 562, 582

"Salt of the earth" strike 159

Samurai 385

San José y San Miguel de Aguayo Mission 305

San Juan Capistrano Mission 304

San Xavier del Bac Mission 305

Sánchez Boudy, José 410

Sánchez Luján, Gilbert 345

Sánchez, Luis Rafael 403

Sánchez, Ricardo 389, 434

Sánchez, Theodora 324

Santa Anna, Antonio López de 79

Santa Rosa, Gilberto 597

Santamaría, Mongo 590

Santana, Carlos 590

Santeiro, Luis 298

Santeros 313

Santiago, Eduardo G. 151

Saralegui, Cristina 299

Sardiñas, Eligio "Kid Chocolate" 629

Scott, Winfield 81

Seasonal agricultural workers 181

Secada, Jon 598

Seguín, Erasmo 78

Selena 594

Sephardic (Judeo-) Spanish 5

Sephardic Jews 374

Serra, Junípero 75

Serrano, José E. 202

Seven Cities of Cíbola 68

Seven Laws, The 79

Seven Years' War 77

Sheen, Martin 557

Siete Leyes, Las 79

Silva, Rufino 332

Silva, Trinidad 524

Siqueiros, Alfaro 368

Slavery 86

Slidell, John 80

Smits, Jimmy 557

Solano, Gustavo 492

Solís Seger, Manuela 157

Sonics, Los 593

Sosa, Lionel 152

Soto, Gary 399, 435

Soto, Jorge 355

Soto, Pedro Juan 403

Spain 63

Spanish American Printing 379

Spanish American Publishing Company 385

Spanish Colonial Arts Society 319

Spanish language 51

Spanish language: Sephardic Spanish 5

Spanish-American War 24

Spanish-language newspapers 374

SPARC (Social and Public Art Resource Center) 360

Suárez, Robert 299

Suárez, Virgil 410, 412

Suárez, Xavier L. 233

Sunny and the Sunliners 580

T

Taino Indians 56

Taller Boricua (Puerto Rican Workshop) 355

Tapia, Luis 351

Taylor, Zachary 80

Teatro Alarcón 446

Teatro Americano 447

Teatro Arena 473

Teatro Bellas Artes 479

Teatro Campesino, El 468

Teatro Campoamor 459

Teatro Capitol 449

Teatro Cervantes 447, 459

Teatro Cuatro 474

Teatro de la Esperanza, El 470

Teatro de la Gente, El 470

Teatro de la Merced 446

Teatro Desengaño del Pueblo 471

Teatro Guazabara 474

Teatro Hidalgo 449

Teatro Hispano 459

Teatro Intimo, El 468

Teatro Jurutungo 474

Teatro La Danza 479

Teatro Las Máscaras 479

Teatro México 449

Teatro Miami 479

Teatro Nacional 449

Teatro Orilla 474

Teatro Principal 449

Teatro Recreo 447

Teatro Repertorio Español 475

Teatro Urbano 470

Teatro Zendejas 449

Tejano 594

Tejeda, Frank 203

TELACU (The East Los Angeles Community Union) 159

Temerarios, Los 593

TENAZ 471

Tennayuca, Emma 157

Tenochtitlán 64

Terrícolas, Los 593

Teurbe Tolón, Miguel 377

Texachi 578

Texas American Conference, Methodist 15

Texas rebellion 80, 93

The Colonial Period 374

Thomas, Piri 405, 436

Tiant, Luis 629

Tiant, Luis, Sr. 609

Tigres, Los 595

Tirado, Romualdo 454, 493

Title VII of the Civil Rights Act of 1964 172

Tlaxcala 64

Toltec 63

Toltecas en Aztlán 347, 357

Torero, Mario 361

Torres, Art 230

Torres, Ernest C. 247

Torres, Esteban E. 204

Torres, Gerald 252

Torres, José Luis 630

Torres, Omar 494

Torres, Roberto Hernán 383

Torres, Salvador Roberto 347, 356, 358

Torres, Teodoro 379

Torriente, Cristóbal 609

Torruella, Juan R. 247

Tortilla Factory 580

Tovar, Rigo 593

Travis, Colonel 79

Treaty of Guadalupe Hidalgo 11, 21, 81

Treaty of Paris 25, 93

Trejo, Ernesto 400

Treviño, Jesse 349

Treviño, Jesús 525

Treviño, Jesús Salvador 558

Treviño, Lee 630
Treviño, Rudy 349
Tropical/salsa 594
Trúan, George 350
Truchas Master 315
Trujillo-Herrera, Rafael 468, 494
Truman, Harry S 158
Turn Verein Hall 446

U

Ulibarrí, Sabine 438
Ulica, Jorge 381
Underwood, Robert A. 204
Undocumented workers 180
Unión libre (free union) 37
Unión Martí-Maceo 466
Union Theater 446
United Auto Workers 159
United Farm Workers 186
United Farmworkers of America 159
United Farmworkers Organizing Committee 186
U.S. Farm Placement Service 162

V

Valdez, Abelardo López 253
Valdez, Luis 390, 468, 495, 533
Valdez, Raúl 366
Valenzuela, Fernando 632
Valladares, Armando 411

Vandals 52
Vando, Erasmo 387
Vaqueros (cowboys) 610
Vásquez de Coronado, Francisco 67
Vazquez, Martha A. 247
Vega, Bernardo 388
Vega, Ed 405, 439
Vela, Filemón B. 247
Velásquez de Cuéllar, Diego 58
Velásquez v. City of Abilene 192
Velazquez, Nydia M. 205
Vélez, Lupe 505, 558
Venegas, Daniel 379, 440
Veracruz 64
Vespucci, Amerigo 57
Victim corridos 567
Vigil-Piñón, Evangelina 397
Villa, Beto 577
Villalpando, Catalina Vásquez 227
Villareal, José 220
Villarini, Pedro 332, 338
Villarreal, Andrea 381
Villarreal, Teresa 381
Villaseñor, Victor 401, 441
Villegas de Magnón, Leonor 382
Viola Novelty Company 379
Viramontes, Helena María 397
Visigoths 52
Volunteers in Service to America (VISTA) 171
Voting Rights Act Amendments of 1982 192

Voting Rights Act of 1975 191
Voting Rights Act of 1965 190

W

Walsh, Raoul 558
War on Poverty 171
Wards Cove Packing Co. v. Antonio 177
Warren Otero, Nina 383
Watts Kearny, Stephen 81
Welch, Raquel 505, 559
Western Federation of Miners 157
Whitehill, Clifford Lane 153
Whitt Company 379
Women's Issues 38, 39, 183
Work statistics 30

Y

Yonics, Los 593
Yoruba elements in music 583
Youth 44

Z

Zapata, Carmen 496
Zapotec 62
Zoot suit riots 389
Zuñiga, Daphne 559

*P*hotography Credits

Photographs and illustrations appearing in *The Hispanic Almanac: From Columbus to Corporate America* were received from the following sources:

307, 308, 311, 312; Jose Delores Lopez, courtesy of Jacinto Quirarte: **p. 320**; Courtesy of Eduardo Chavez: **p. 328**; Painting by Octavio Medellin, courtesy of Jacinto Quirarte: **p. 329**; Rafael Ortiz, courtesy of Jacinto Quirarte: **p. 337**; Courtesy of Jacinto Quirarte: **p. 340**; Painting by Carmen Lomas Garza, courtesy of Jacinto Quirarte: **p. 342**; Painting by Cesar Martinez, courtesy of Jacinto Quirarte: **p. 348**; Painting by Jessie Trevino, courtesy of Jacinto: **p. 350**; Painting by Marcos Raya, courtesy of Jacinto Quirarte: **p. 353**; Diagram by Jacinto Quirarte: **pp. 362, 367, 368 (top), 369, 370 (top), 371**; Photograph by Jose Gonzalez, courtesy of Jacinto Quirarte: **p. 364**; Courtesy of Miguel Antonio Collection, Special Collections, General Library, University of New Mexico, **p. 375, 376**; Photograph by Cynthia Farah: **p. 383**; The Jesus Colon Papers, Centro de Estudio Puertorriquenes, Binigno Giboyeaux for the Estate of Jesus Colon and the Communist Party of the United States of America: **p. 388**; Photograph by George McInnis, courtesy of Arte Publico Press: **pp. 396 (top), 419, 429**; Center for Puerto Rican Studies, Hunter College, CUNY: **p. 404**; Theatre of the Thirties Collection, Special Collections and Archives, George Mason University, Fairfax, VA: **pp. 463, 465**; Photograph by Delores Prida, courtesy of Arte Publico Press: **p. 473**; Photograph by Jonathan Snow, courtesy of Arte Publico Press: **p. 475**; The Granger Collection, New York: **p. 482**; Archive Photos: **pp. 504, 518, 544 (top)**; Archive Photos/Fotos International: **p. 547 (middle)**; Springer/Bettmann Film Archive: **p. 556**; Archive Photos/Darlene Hammond: **p. 557 (top)**; Courtesy of The Huntington Library, San Marino, CA: **pp. 563, 607**; Courtesy of Houston Metropolitan Research Center, Houston Public Library: **pp. 574, 578**; Courtesy of Chris Strachwitz: **p. 577**; Arizona Historical Society: **p. 611**; Archive Photos/Express Newspapers: **p. 621 (bottom)**.